VISUAL QUICK

CSS, DHTML, & AJAX

FOURTH EDITION

Jason Cranford Teague

Peachpit Press

Visual QuickStart Guide
CSS, DHTML, & Ajax, Fourth Edition
Jason Cranford Teague

Peachpit Press

1249 Eighth Street
Berkeley, CA 94710
510/524-2178
800/283-9444
510/524-2221 (fax)

Find us on the Web at peachpit.com

To report errors, please send a note to errata@peachpit.com

Peachpit Press is a division of Pearson Education

Editor: Jill Lodwig
Production Editor: Myrna Vladic
Technical Editor: Kimberly J. Blessing
Compositors: Rick Gordon, Emerald Valley Graphics; Debbie Roberti. Espresso Graphics
Indexer: James Minkin
Cover design: Peachpit Press

Notice of Rights

Notice of Liability

Trademarks

ISBN 0-321-44325-X

9 8 7 6 5 4 3 2 1

Printed and bound in the United States of America

Dedication

For Jocelyn and Dashiel,
the two most dynamic forces in my life.

Special Thanks to:

Tara, my soul mate and best critic.

Nancy, who got this project off to a great start.

Jill, who dotted my i's and made sure that everything made sense.

Kimberly, who held my feet to the fire on every line of code and made this book more standards-compliant.

Myrna and **Debbie** and **Rick**, who put the book together with great patience and made it look pretty.

Dad, **Nancy**, and **Mom** who made me who I am.

Uncle Johnny, for his unwavering support.

Pat and **Red**, my two biggest fans.

Thomas, who was always there when I needed help.

Heather, who gave me a chance when I needed it most.

Judy, Boyd, Dr. G and teachers everywhere who care. Keep up the good work.

Charles Dodgson (aka Lewis Carroll), for writing *Alice's Adventures in Wonderland*.

John Tenniel, for his incredible illustrations of *Alice's Adventures in Wonderland*.

Douglas Adams, **Neil Gaiman**, and **Carl Sagan** whose writings inspire me every day.

The Dresden Dolls, BBC 6 Music, The Craig Charles Funk Show, Goldfrapp, The The, Siouxsie and the Banshees, Absentee, The Nails, Cake Metric, Client, Delerium, Dennis Leary, Shakespeare's Sister, Type-O Negative, Jonathan Coulton, Cracker, Danielle Dax, Nine Inch Nails, 8mm, KMFDM, Nizlopi, the Pogues, Ramones, New Model Army, Cocteau Twins, the Sisters of Mercy, the Smiths, Mojo Nixon, Bauhaus, Lady Tron, David Bowie, T. R ex, Bad Religion, Fischerspooner, This Mortal Coil, Rancid, Monty Python, Al Franken, the Dead Milkmen, New Order, Regina Spektor, The Sex Pistols, Dead Can Dance, Slice of Sci-Fi, and **ZBS Studios** (for *Ruby*) whose noise helped keep me from going insane while writing this book.

TABLE OF CONTENTS

Introduction   **xi**

PART 1:   **CASCADING STYLE SHEETS**   **1**

Chapter 1:   **Understanding CSS**   **3**

What Is a Style? 5
What Are Cascading Style Sheets?.............. 6
Versions of CSS............................... 8
Types of CSS Rules 10
CSS and Markup Languages 13
Kinds of Tags................................. 18
Setting Your DTD 19

Chapter 2:   **CSS Basics**   **23**

Adding Styles to an HTML Tag: Inline 24
Adding Styles to a Web Page: Embedded........ 26
Adding Styles to a Web Site: External........... 29
(Re)Defining HTML Tags 36
Defining Classes for Any Tag................... 38
Defining ID Selectors to Identify an Object 41
Defining Selectors to Have the Same Styles 44
Making a Declaration !important............... 46
Defining Selectors Based on Context 48
Defining Selectors Based on Tag Attributes..... 53
Working with Pseudo-Classes 56
Working with Pseudo-Elements 67
Setting Styles for Print and Other Media........ 73
Adding Comments to CSS 80
Inheriting Properties from a Parent............. 81
Determining the Cascade Order............... 83
Using Conditional Comments to Fix CSS
     in Internet Explorer 86
Style Sheet Strategies 89

Chapter 3: Font Properties   **91**

Understanding Typography on the Web 92
Setting the Font-Family 96
Setting the Font Size 101
Making Text Italic 104
Setting Bold, Bolder, Boldest 106
Creating Small Caps 108
Setting Multiple Font Values 110

Chapter 4: Text Properties   **113**

Adjusting Text Spacing 114
Setting Text Case 120
Adding a Text Drop Shadow 122
Aligning Text Horizontally 124
Aligning Text Vertically 126
Indenting Paragraphs 129
Controlling White Space 131
Decorating Text 133
Setting Text Direction 136

Chapter 5: Color and Background Properties   **139**

Choosing Your Color Palette 140
Setting Text and Foreground Color 145
Setting a Background Color 147
Setting a Background Image 150
Setting Multiple Background Values.......... 154

Chapter 6: Box Properties   **159**

Understanding an Element's Box 160
Setting How an Element is Displayed......... 164
Setting an Element's Margins 171
Setting an Element's Border................... 174
Setting an Element's Outline 181
Setting an Element's Padding 184
Setting the Width and Height of
     an Element 187

Chapter 7: Visual Formatting Properties   **195**

Understanding the Window and
     Document 196
Setting the Positioning Type 198
Setting an Element's Position 204
Stacking Objects (3D Positioning)............ 209
Floating Elements in the Window............. 212
Clearing a Floated Element 215

**Chapter 8: Visual Effect and User
              Interface Properties   219**
Setting the Visibility of an Element. 220
Setting an Element's Visible Area (Clipping) . . . 222
Setting Where the Overflow Content Goes 224
Setting an Element's Opacity. 226
Changing the Mouse Pointer's Appearance 228
Changing the Scrollbar's Appearance
       (IE Windows Only). 231

Chapter 9: Table Properties   233
Setting the Table Layout 234
Setting the Space Between Table Cells 236
Collapsing Borders Between Table Cells. 238
Dealing with Empty Table Cells 240
Setting the Position of a Table Caption 242

**Chapter 10: Generated Content and
               List Properties   245**
Adding Content Using CSS 246
Teaching the Browser to Count 249
Specifying the Quote Style 252
Setting the Bullet Style. 254
Creating Your Own Bullets. 256
Setting Bullet Positions 258
Setting Multiple List Styles 260
Displaying an Element as a List 262

PART 2:   DYNAMIC HTML   265

Chapter 11: Understanding DHTML   267
What Is Dynamic HTML?. 268
The History of DHTML. 271
Why Should I Use DHTML?. 273
Flash vs. DHTML. 276
Should I Use DHTML or Flash? 279

Chapter 12: DHTML Basics   283
DOM: The Road Map to Your Web Page 284
Setting Up an Object 288
Understanding Events 290
Using Event Handlers. 292
Getting an Element. 294
Passing Events to a Function. 298
Binding Events to Objects 300
Using Feature Sensing 302

TABLE OF CONTENTS

Chapter 13: Learning About the Environment   305

Detecting the Operating System 306
Detecting the Browser's Name 308
Finding the Page's Location and Title 310
Determining the Number of Colors
    (Bit Depth) 312
Determining the Screen Dimensions 314
Determining the Browser Window's
    Dimensions 316
Determining the Page's Visible Dimensions 318

Chapter 14: Learning About an Object   321

Detecting Which Object Was Clicked 322
Determining an Object's Properties 324
Detecting an Object's Position 327
Finding an Object's Style Property Values 332
Finding an Object's 3D Position 334
Finding an Object's Visible Area 336

Chapter 15: Learning About an Event   341

Detecting Which Event Type Fired 342
Detecting Which Key Was Pressed 344
Detecting Which Modifier Key Was Pressed . . . 346
Detecting Which Mouse Button Was Clicked . . . 348
Detecting Where the Mouse Was Clicked 351

Chapter 16: Basic Dynamic Techniques   353

Changing CSS Property Values 354
Making Objects Appear and Disappear 356
Moving Objects from Point to Point 361
Moving Objects by a Certain Amount 363
Moving Objects in 3D 365
Changing an Object's Visible Area 368
Changing an Object's Content 370
Controlling Objects Between Frames 372

Chapter 17: Advanced Dynamic Techniques   375

Making a Function Run Again 376
Animating an Object 379
Using Input from a Form Field 384
Following the Mouse Pointer 386
Making an Object Draggable 389
Opening a New Browser Window 392
Moving the Browser Window 396
Changing the Browser Window's Size 398
Scrolling the Browser Window 400

TABLE OF CONTENTS

Chapter 18: Dynamic CSS   **403**
Finding a Style Property's Value 404
Adding or Changing a Style Declaration 406
Changing Classes 410
Disabling or Enabling a Style Sheet 412

PART 3: AJAX   **415**

Chapter 19: Understanding Ajax   **417**
What Is Ajax? 418
How Ajax Works 422
Why Should I Use Ajax? 425
What Is Web 2.0? 428

Chapter 20: Ajax Basics   **433**
Understanding Server Requests 434
Fetching Data 436
Fetching a Response 439
Filtering the Data 443
Utilizing the AjaxBasics.js Library 447

PART 4: USING CSS, DHTML, AND AJAX   **451**

Chapter 21: Layout   **453**
Structuring Your Page 454
Creating Multicolumn Layouts 460
Styling Headers 463
Styling Links and Navigation 465
Styling Copy and Content 467
Styling Tables 469
Styling Forms 471
Styling Frames 477

Chapter 22: Content   **481**
Importing External Content 482
Dynamically Controlling Form Data 486
Adding Pop-Up Layers 490
Dynamic Type Ahead 495

Chapter 23: **Navigation** **501**

Creating Navigation Buttons with
    CSS Sprites 502
Creating Drop-Down Menus 505
Creating Collapsible Menus 510
Creating a Tab Menu 513
Creating Sliding Menus 519
Creating a Remote Control. 523

Chapter 24: **Controls** **527**

Providing Page Controls 528
Creating Scroll Bars for a Layer. 533
Adding Style Controls 538
Putting Together a Photo Album 542

Index **547**

INTRODUCTION

Once upon a time creating Web pages was no more difficult than using a word processor. You learned a few HTML tags, created a few graphics, and presto: Web page. Now, with streaming video, JavaScript, ASP, JSP, PHP, Shockwave, Flash, and Java, the design of Web pages may seem overwhelming to anyone who doesn't want to become a computer programmer.

Enter Cascading Style Sheets (CSS), Dynamic HTML (DHTML), Asynchronous JavaScript and XML (Ajax) technologies that give you the ability to take static HTML and create an interactive webbed environment.

With CSS, you can create virtually any layout you can imagine, not only adding visual interest to your content, but also creating a more compelling design.

With DHTML, you don't have to rely on plug-ins that the visitor might not have or complicated programming languages (except maybe a little JavaScript).

With Ajax (the new kid on the block), you can go even further than DHTML can take you, by being able to easily fetch fresh data from the server without ever having to reload the entire Web page, which creates a far better experience for site visitors.

That's what this book is about: How to create attractive Web layouts and interactive Web pages as simply as possible. This book will not turn you into the ultimate Web-design guru overnight, but it will give you the foundations you need to realize your own Web-design vision.

If you are learning Web design and do not know CSS, DHTML, or Ajax, this is where you need to begin. Welcome!

What is this book about?

In the years since Netscape Navigator and Microsoft Internet Explorer began supporting CSS, DHTML, and Ajax, the Web itself has changed significantly. The browser wars, the dot-com explosion (and subsequent crash), and the Web's enormous growth in popularity have led to a shakedown of the technologies that are regularly used to create Web sites. CSS and DHTML remain the standards that are used to create some of the best Web sites around, while Ajax is quickly becoming the technology of choice for providing the best user interaction.

In this book, I'll show you the best ways to implement CSS, DHTML, and Ajax so that the broadest spectrum of the Web-surfing population can view your Web sites. To help organize the information, I have split this book into four parts:

- **Part 1 (CSS)** details how to use CSS to control the appearance of the content on Web pages. I'll show you some best-practices for controlling the various aspects of how your Web page is displayed.

- **Part 2 (DHTML)** shows you how to use the Document Object Model (DOM) with CSS and JavaScript to create basic dynamic functions. I'll show you how to use the DOM to run dynamic functions in most browsers, with as little redundant code as possible.

Additional Support

This book's support Web site (webbed-environments.com/css_dhtml_ajax) includes quick references online for all of the code presented in the book and information in the first three parts of the book, as well as a list of the browser-safe fonts, tools and resources for Web developers.

+ **Part 3 (Ajax)** introduces you to Ajax basics, teaching you how to dynamically retrieve data from the server without having to load a new Web page. Ajax concepts have been around for a while, but they have only recently matured to the point where designers are regularly using them to design their pages.

+ **Part 4 (Using CSS, DHTML, and Ajax)** is where you can find some of the most common practical applications of the techniques presented in the first three parts of the book. You will learn the best practices for Web layout, content presentation, navigation, and creating controls that put the visitor in charge.

Who is this book for?

If the title of this book caught your eye, you're probably already well acquainted with the ins and outs of the Internet's most popular offshoot, the World Wide Web (or perhaps you're just a severely confused arachnophile). To understand this book, you need to be familiar with HTML (Hypertext Markup Language). You don't have to be an expert, but you should know the difference between a `<p>` element and a `<br/>` tag. In addition, several chapters call for more than a passing knowledge of JavaScript. For the Ajax section, you can work with the basics without knowing how to program server code, but I will be referring to some PHP code used to process data on the server.

That said, the more knowledge of HTML, JavaScript, and PHP you bring to this book, the more you'll get out of it.

Everyone Is a Web Designer

Forget about your 15 minutes of fame: In the future, *everyone* will be a Web designer. As the Web continues to expand, a growing number of people are choosing this medium to get their messages— whatever they may be—to the rest of the world. Whether they are movie buffs extolling the virtues of *The Third Man* or multinational corporations extolling the virtues of their companies, everyone regards the Web as one of the best ways to spread the word.

The fact is, just as everyone who uses a word processor is at some level a typographer, as the Web grows in popularity, everyone who uses it to do more than passively view pages will need to know how to design for the Web.

Knowing how to design for the Web isn't always about designing complete Web sites. Many, if not more people these days are using HTML to create simple Web pages for auction sites, such as eBay, their own photo albums, or their own Web logs (blogs). So whether you are planning to redesign your corporate Web site or place your kid's graduation pictures online, learning CSS, DHTML, and Ajax is your next step into the larger world of Web design.

Why Standards (Still) Matter

The prime meridian and Greenwich Mean Time are standards that allow us to determine our position on earth with pinpoint accuracy. These standards can be applied anywhere, at any time, and by anybody; they are universally accessible and understood because everybody has agreed to do it that way. They allow ships to ply the seven seas without bumping into land (usually) and airplanes to fly in friendly skies without bumping into each other (most of the time). And they have opened the world to travel, not necessarily because they are a superior way of doing things, but simply because everyone has agreed to do things the same way. Sounds like a pretty good idea, doesn't it?

The idea of a standard was the principle behind the creation of the World Wide Web: Information should be able to be transmitted to any computer anywhere in the world and displayed pretty much the way the author intended it to look. In the beginning, only one form of HTML existed, and everyone on the Web used it. This situation didn't present any real problem, because almost everyone used Mosaic, the first popular graphics-based browser, and Mosaic stuck to this standard like glue. That, as they say, was then.

Then along came Netscape Navigator, and the first HTML extensions were born. These extensions worked only in Netscape, however, and anyone who didn't use that browser was out of luck. Although the Netscape extensions defied the standards of the World Wide Web Consortium (W3C), most of them—or at least some version of them—eventually became part of those very standards. According to some people, the Web has gone downhill ever since.

Figure i.1 The Web
Standards Project:
Keeping the Web
friendly for all comers.

The Web is a very public form of discourse, the likes of which has not existed since people lived in villages and sat around the campfire telling stories every night. The problem is that without standards, not everyone in the global village can make it to the Web campfire. You can use as many bleeding-edge techniques as you like. You can include Flash, JavaScript, VBScript, QuickTime video, layers, or data binding, but if only a fraction of browsers can see your work, you're keeping a lot of fellow villagers out in the cold.

In coding for this book, I spent a good 35–45 percent of the time trying to get the code to run as smoothly as possible in Internet Explorer 6+, Firefox 1+ (and related Mozilla browsers), Opera 7+, and Safari 1.5+. This situation holds true for most of my Web projects; much of the coding time is spent on cross-browser inconsistencies. If the browsers stuck to the standards, this time would be reduced to almost none.

Your safest bet as a designer, then, is to know the standards of the Web, try to use them as much as possible, and demand that the browser manufacturers use them as well. The Web Standards Project (web-standards.org) is a watchdog group working to make sure that browser manufacturers stick to the standards they helped create (**Figure i.1**). If you want a better Web, get involved.

WHY STANDARDS (STILL) MATTER

Values and Units Used in This Book

Throughout this book, you'll need to enter different values to define different properties. These values come in various forms, depending on the need of the property. Some values are straightforward—a number is a number—but others have special units associated with them.

Values in chevrons (<   >) represent one type of value (**Table i.1**). Words that appear in code font are literal values and should be typed exactly as shown.

Length values

Length values come in two varieties:

* **Relative lengths**, which vary depending on the computer being used (**Table i.2**).

* **Absolute values**, which remain constant regardless of the hardware and software being used (**Table i.3**).

I generally recommend using pixel sizes to describe font sizes for the greatest stability between operating systems and browsers.

Table i.1

Value Types		
VALUE TYPE	WHAT IT IS	EXAMPLE
<number>	A number	1, 2, 3
<length>	A measurement of distance	1in or size
<color>	A chromatic expression	red
<percentage>	A proportion	35%
<URL>	The absolute or relative path to a file on the Web	http://www.mySite.net/bob/graphics/image1.gif

Table i.2

Relative Length Values			
UNIT	NAME	WHAT IT IS	EXAMPLE
em	Em	Relative to width of the letter M for the font	3em
ex	x-height	Relative to height of the lowercase x of that font	5ex
px	Pixel	Relative to the monitor's resolution	125px

*Internet Explorer treats pixels as an absolute value rather than a relative one.

Table i.3

Absolute Length Values			
UNIT	NAME	WHAT IT IS	EXAMPLE
pt	Point	72pt = 1inch	12pt
pc	Picas	1 pc = 12 pt	3pc
mm	Millimeters	1mm = .24pc	25mm
cm	Centimeters	1cm = 10mm	5.1cm
in	Inches	1in = 2.54cm	8.25ini

Table i.4

Color Values		
FORMAT	WHAT IT IS	EXAMPLE
#RRGGBB	Red, green, and blue hex-code value of a color (00-99,AA-FF)	#CC33FF or #C3F
rgb(R#,G#,B#)	Red, green, and blue numeric-values of a color (0–255)	rgb(204,51,255)
rgb(R%,G%,B%)	Red, green, and blue percentage values of a color (0–100%)	rgb(81%,18%,100%)
<name>	The name of the color	Purple

Color values

You can describe color on the screen in a variety of ways (**Table i.4**), but most of these descriptions are just different ways of telling the computer how much red, green, and blue are in a particular color.

Percentages

Many of the properties in this book can have a percentage as their value. The behavior of this percentage value depends on the property being used.

URLs

A Uniform Resource Locator (URL) is the unique address of something on the Web. This resource could be an HTML document, a graphic, a CSS file, a JavaScript file, a sound or video file, a CGI script, or any of a variety of other file types. URLs can be local, simply describing the location of the resource relative to the current document; or global, describing the absolute location of the resource on the Web and beginning with http://.

In addition, throughout the book, I use links in the code examples. I use the number sign (#) as a placeholder in links that can be directed to any URL you want:

```
<a href="#">...</a>
```

The number sign is shorthand that links to the top of the current page. Replace these with your own URLs as desired.

Browser-Safe Colors

Certain colors always display properly on any monitor. These colors are called browser-safe colors. You'll find them fairly easy to remember because their values stay consistent. In hexadecimal values, you can use any combination of 00, 33, 66, 99, CC, and FF. In numeric values, use 0, 51, 102, 153, 204, or 255. In percentages, use 0, 20, 40, 60, 80, or 100.

Reading This Book

For the most part, the text, tables, figures, code, and examples should be self-explanatory. But you need to know a few things to understand this book.

CSS value tables

In Part 1, each section that explains a CSS property includes a table for quick reference with the different values the property can use, as well as the browsers and CSS levels with which those values are compatible (**Figure i.2**). The Compatibility column displays the first browser version that supported the value type. **Table i.5** lists the browser abbreviations used in this book. Keep in mind, though, that even if the value is available in a particular version of the browser, it may not be available for all operating systems. The support Web site (webbedenvironments.com) has tables that show in which operating systems values work and whether there are any problems.

Table i.5

Browser Abbreviations	
ABBREVIATION	BROWSER
IE6	Internet Explorer 6
IE7	Internet Explorer 7
FF1*	Firefox 1
FF1.5*	Firefox 1.5
FF2*	Firefox 2
O7	Opera 7
O8	Opera 8
O9	Opera 9
S1	Safari 1
S1.5	Safari 1.5
S2	Safari 2

* Includes other Mozilla based browsers: Camino and Flock

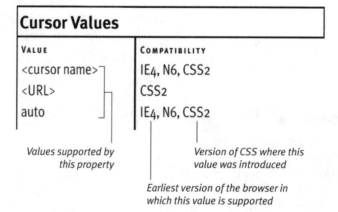

Figure i.2 The property tables in Part 1 of this book show you the values available with a property, the earliest browser version in which the value is available, and with which version of CSS the value was introduced.

The code

For clarity and precision, this book uses several layout techniques to help you see the difference between the text of the book and the code.

Code looks like this:

```
<style>

p { font-size: 12pt; }

</style>
```

All code in this book is presented in lower-case (see the sidebar "Uppercase or Lowercase Tags" in Chapter 1). In addition, quotes in the code always appear as straight quotes (" or '), not curly quotes (" or '). There is a good reason for this distinction: Curly quotes (also called *smart quotes*) will cause the code to fail.

When you type a line of code, the computer can run the line as long as needed, but in this book, lines of code have to be broken to make them fit on the page. When that happens, you'll see a gray arrow → , indicating that the line of code is continued from above, like this:

```
.title { font: bold 28pt/26pt times,
→ serif; color: #FFF; background-
→ color: #000; background-image:
→ url(bg_ title.gif); }
```

Production: please add arrows above.

I often begin a numbered step with a `line of code in red` from the main code block. This is intended as a reference to help you pinpoint where that step applies in the larger code block that accompanies the task. This code will then be highlighted in red in the code listing to help you more easily identify it.

HTML or XHTML?

The Web is currently undergoing a metamorphosis behind the scenes, as the markup language used to create Web pages migrates from HTML to XHTML. Although very similar in their syntax, XHTML is much less lenient with errors.

For this book, I use XHTML as the markup language. For more details, see "CSS and Markup Languages" in Chapter 1.

What Tools Do You Need for This Book?

The great thing about CSS and DHTML is that, like HTML, they don't require any special or expensive software. Their code is just text, and you can edit it with a program such as TextEdit (Mac OS) or NotePad (Windows).

The support Web site (webbedenvironments.com/css_dhtml_ajax) includes a list of extremely helpful (and mostly free or cheap) utilities and tools that I recommend to anyone who creates Web sites.

In addition, a couple of programs make life with DHTML and CSS much easier by automating many of the tedious and repetitive tasks associated with Web design. I recommend using Adobe GoLive or Dreamweaver.

Supported Browsers

All of the code in this book has been carefully tested in Microsoft Internet Explorer 6+, Firefox 1.5+ (and other Mozilla Browsers), Opera 7+, and Apple Safari 1.5+. These browsers make up a good 99 percent of the browsers being used to surf the Web. All code should work in these browsers unless otherwise noted in the text. If you experience any problems with the code, please check this book'sWeb site (webbedenvironments.com/css_dhtml_ajax) first for any updates, and then write me at dynamic@webbedenvironments.com.

Figure i.3 The support Web site for *CSS, DHTML, & Ajax: Visual QuickStart Guide*, open 24 hours a day.

Figure i.4 The Code Browser lets you quickly flip through the code examples in the book to test them out.

Using the Web Site for This Book

I hope you'll be using a lot of the code from this book in your Web pages, and you are free to use any code in this book without having to ask my permission (although a mention for the book is always appreciated). However, watch out—retyping information can lead to errors. Some books include a fancy-shmancy CD-ROM containing all the code from the book, and you can pull it off that disk. But guess who pays for that CD? You do. And CDs aren't cheap.

But if you bought this book, you already have access to the largest resource of knowledge that ever existed: the Web. And that's exactly where you can find the code from this book.

My support site for this Visual QuickStart Guide is at:

webbedenvironments.com/css_dhtml_ajax

This site includes all the code you see in the book (**Figure i.3**) as well as quick-reference charts. You can download the code and any important updates and corrections from this site. You can also view all of the various code examples from this book within an easy-to-use Code Browser (**Figure i.4**).

If you've got questions, I've got answers. You can contact me at:

vqs-dynamic@webbedenvironments.com

Part 1
Cascading
Style Sheets

Chapter 1: Understanding CSS 3

Chapter 2: CSS Basics 23

Chapter 3: Font Properties 91

Chapter 4: Text Properties 113

Chapter 5: Color and Background
Properties 139

Chapter 6: Box Properties 159

Chapter 7: Visual Formatting
Properties 195

Chapter 8: Visual Effect and User
Interface Properties 219

Chapter 9: Table Properties 233

Chapter 10: Generated Content,
Automatic Numbering,
and List Properties 245

1

Understanding CSS

Let's face it: HTML is not exactly a designer's dream come true. It is imprecise, unpredictable, and not terribly versatile when it comes to presenting the diverse kinds of content that Web designers have come to demand.

Then again, HTML was never intended to deliver high-concept graphic content and multimedia. In fact, it was never really intended to be anything more than a glorified universal word processing language delivered over the Internet—and a pretty limited one at that.

HTML is a markup language that was created to allow authors to define the structure of a document for distribution on a network such as the Web. That is, rather than being designed to set the styles of what is being displayed, it is intended only to show how the page should be organized.

Over time, new tags and technologies have been added to HTML that allow greater control of both the structure and appearance of documents—things such as tables, frames, justification controls, and JavaScript—but what Web designers can't do with fast-loading HTML, they have had to hack together using slow-loading graphics.

It's not a very elegant system.

continues on next page

However, rather than just adding more and more tags to HTML, the W3C (see the sidebar "What is the World Wide Web Consortium?" later in this chapter) introduced Cascading Style Sheets (CSS) to fill the design void of straight HTML (**Figure 1.1**).

Now, you're probably thinking, "Oh, great—just when I learn HTML, they go and change everything." But never fear: CSS is as easy to use as HTML. In fact, in many ways it's easier, because rather than introducing more HTML tags to learn, it works directly with existing HTML tags to tell them how to behave.

Take the humble bold tag, ..., for example. In HTML, it does one thing and one thing only: It makes text "stronger," usually by making it thicker. However, using CSS you can "redefine" the bold tag so that it not only makes text thicker, but also displays text in all caps and in a particular font to really add emphasis. You could even make the bold tag *not* make text bold.

This chapter presents some of the concepts and principles behind CSS for those who are new to the technology. However, for those eager beavers among you, you may want to skip to Chapter 2 to learn the basics of creating style sheets or to Chapters 3 through 10 to learn all of the many styles you can include in your design arsenal.

Figure 1.1 Say it loud and say it proud with the CSS button (http://www.w3.org/Style/CSS/Buttons/).

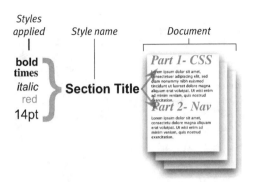

Figure 1.2 Styles being applied to section titles in a word-processing page.

What Is a Style?

Most word processors today include a way to make changes to text not just word by word, but throughout an entire document using *styles*.

Styles collect all the different properties, such as font family, size, and color, that you want to apply to similar types of text— titles, headers, captions, and so on—and give these groups of properties a common name. Suppose you want all the section titles in your document to be bold, Times font, italic, red, and 14-point. You could assign all those attributes to a style called Section Title (**Figure 1.2**).

Whenever you type a section title, all you have to do is use the Section Title style, and all those attributes are applied to the text in one fell swoop—no fuss, no mess. Even better, if you decide later that you really want all those titles to be 18 point instead of 14 point, you just change the definition of Section Title. The word processor then automatically changes the appearance of all the text marked with that style throughout the document.

What Are Cascading Style Sheets?

CSS brings to the Web the same "one-stop shopping" convenience for setting styles that's available in most word processors. You can set the CSS in one central location to affect the appearance of a particular HTML tag on a single Web page or across an entire Web site.

Although CSS works with HTML, it is not HTML. Rather, CSS is a separate code that enhances the abilities of HTML by allowing you to redefine the way that existing tags display their content.

For example, the heading level 1 tag container, <h1>...</h1>, allows you to apply styles to a section of HTML text, turning it into a heading. But the exact display of the heading is determined by the viewer's browser. You cannot control how it will be styled in your layout. Using CSS, however, you (the designer) can change the nature of the heading tag so that it will be displayed in the style you want—for example, bold, Times font, italic, red, and 14 points (**Figure 1.3**). As with word processor styles, you can later choose to change the definition of the <h1> tag (for example, make the text 18 points) and all heading level 1 elements on the affected Web page will automatically be restyled.

Table 1.1 shows some of the things you can do with CSS and where to find more information.

How does CSS work?

When a visitor loads one of your Web pages, either by typing the address into a browser or by clicking a link, the server (the computer that stores the Web page) sends the HTML file to the visitor's computer along with any files linked to or embedded in the HTML file, such as images or movies. The CSS code, or *style sheet*, can be either embedded directly in the HTML file or linked to it. Regardless

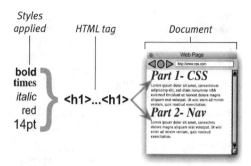

Figure 1.3 Styles being applied to an HTML tag.

Table 1.1

CSS Property Categories		
CATEGORY	WHAT YOU CONTROL	FOR MORE INFO
Font	Letter form, size, boldface, italic	Chapter 3
Text	Kerning, leading, alignment, case	Chapter 4
Color & background	Text color, color or image behind the page or behind a single element on the page	Chapter 5
Box	Margins, padding, borders, width, height	Chapter 6
Visual formatting	Exact placement in the browser window, text wrap	Chapter 7
Visual effect	Visibility, visible area, opacity	Chapter 8
User interface	Mouse pointer, scroll bars	Chapter 8
Table	Table borders, margins, captions	Chapter 9
Generated content, automatic numbering, and list	Bullets, numbered lists, indentation, quotes	Chapter 10

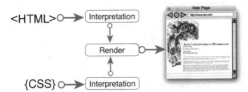

Figure 1.4 The code used to create the Web page is downloaded, interpreted, and then rendered by the browser to create the final display.

Figure 1.5 An HTML page using CSS to add an image in the background, position the content down and to the right, and format the text.

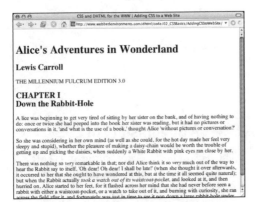

Figure 1.6 The same code displayed without the benefit of CSS. The page still displays, but without the formatting in Figure 1.5.

of where it's located, the visitor's browser will interpret this code by using its particular *rendering engine* to apply the CSS to the HTML, and then display the page in the browser window (**Figure 1.4**).

The interpretation and application of the style sheet by the browser's rendering engine is where our headaches begin. The W3C has gone to great lengths to specify how browser manufacturers should render the code, but bugs, omissions, and misinterpretations still creep in, meaning that no two browsers will render a Web page exactly the same. For the most part, these differences will go unnoticed by the user, but occasionally these differences are glaring and require you to do some extra work to get the page to look right in the broadest spectrum of browsers.

✔ Tips

- The power of CSS comes from its ability to mix and match different rules from different sources to tailor your Web pages' layout to your exact needs. In some ways, it resembles computer programming—which is not too surprising, because a lot of this stuff was created by programmers rather than designers. But once you get the hang of it, CSS will become as natural as putting together a sentence.

- Sometimes a Web browser will render HTML content before the style sheet is applied to it, so you may see a "naked" or unstyled page flash briefly on the screen.

- There is always the possibility that your Web page will be displayed *without* the CSS code, either because of an error or because the device being used does not accommodate CSS (such as a mobile phone browser, for instance). You should always consider how your page will look without the style sheet, and make sure that structurally it makes sense (**Figure 1.5** and **Figure 1.6**).

Versions of CSS

CSS has evolved over the past several years under the guidance of the W3C (**Figure 1.7**) into its current form. Most modern browsers (Microsoft Internet Explorer 7, Mozilla Firefox 2, Apple Safari 2, Opera 9) support CSS Level 2 (which includes CSS Level 1 and CSS-Positioning). However, after years of development, CSS Level 3 still remains a work in progress. The following are some details about each of the versions:

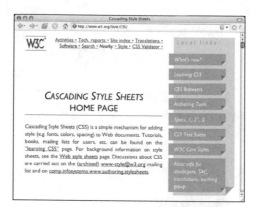

Figure 1.7 The W3C's CSS home page (www.w3.org/Style/CSS/). Although it can get a tad technical, this is the source of all CSS knowledge.

◆ **CSS Level 1 (CSS1).** The W3C released the first CSS recommendation in 1996, and revised it in 1999. This early version included core capabilities, such as the ability to format text, set fonts, and set margins. Netscape Navigator 4 and Microsoft Internet Explorer 3 and 4 support CSS Level 1—almost.

◆ **CSS Positioning (CSS-P).** Web designers needed a way to position elements on the screen precisely. CSS1 had already been released, and browser support for CSS Level 2 was still off in the distance, so the W3C released a stopgap solution: CSS Positioning. This working draft was a proposal that the various browser makers could debate for a while before it became official. Netscape and Microsoft jumped on these proposals, however, and included the preliminary ideas in their version 4 browsers. Do both Netscape and Internet Explorer support CSS-P? Sort of. Although most of the basic features are supported in both of the "name-brand" browsers, several features were left out.

◆ **CSS Level 2 (CSS2).** This version of CSS came out in 1998 and is the most widely adopted by browser makers. Level 2 includes all the attributes of the previous two versions, plus an increased emphasis on international accessibility and the capability to specify media-specific CSS.

A Brief History of CSS

The lack of design capabilities in HTML was apparent to many, especially to two men named Håkon Wium Lie and Bert Bos. They drafted the first Cascading Style Sheets (CSS) specification, released by the World Wide Web Consortium (W3C) in 1996, to fill this void.

If you want to read more about the saga of CSS, check out w3.org/Style/LieBos2e/history/

Microsoft Internet Explorer 5 and later, Opera 3.5 and later, Apple Safari 1 and later, and Mozilla Firefox 1 and later generally support Level 2.

The W3C has released updated drafts as CSS Level 2 Revision 1 (2.1). CSS 2.1 has corrected some errors, clarified a few issues, and included specifications for some features that have already been implemented in some browsers.

- **CSS Level 3 (CSS3).** Work on CSS3 began in 2000, not long after CSS2 was made official. While it is still under development, work on the specification has been divided into various topics, or modules. So, while it may be some time before all of CSS3 is completed, some modules will be ready before others. However, as is the case with previous versions of CSS, once each module is developed, it most likely will take several years for browsers to support it. Considering there was a six-year lapse between versions of Internet Explorer 6 and 7, CSS3 most likely won't be ready for prime time anytime soon.

See the sidebar "The Future of CSS? Level 3" for more details. Although this specification is still under development, some browsers (most notably Apple Safari and Mozilla Firefox) have started integrating some of its features, most notably opacity.

✔ Tip

- While the differences between the CSS versions may be interesting, it isn't necessary for you to be aware of them when using styles on the Web. What you do need to know is which styles are supported by the browsers you're designing for.

The Future of CSS? Level 3.

Never content to rest on its laurels, the W3C is hard at work on another rendition of Cascading Style Sheets: CSS Level 3 (w3.org/Style/CSS/current-work). Many of the problems that CSS2 doesn't adequately address will be resolved in this upcoming version.

Although the standard is still under construction (and has been for several years), many of the additions to CSS3 sound very exciting. Here are some highlights:

- **Columns.** The most exciting new feature proposed for CSS3 is the ability to create flexible columns for layout. CSS is complicated when used to replace tables for multiple-column layout. Ideally, CSS3 will take care of this problem.

- **Web fonts.** Although CSS2 theoretically provides downloadable-font capability, it's still too hard to use. The W3C wants to make fonts more Web-friendly in CSS3.

- **Color profiles.** One common problem with graphics is that they may be darker or lighter, depending on the computer being used. CSS3 will allow authors to include color descriptions to offset this problem.

- **User interface.** CSS3 will add more pointers, form states, and ways to use visitor-dictated color schemes.

- **Behaviors.** The most intriguing new capability uses CSS to dictate not only visual styles, but also the behavior of objects. This would provide further dynamic controls through CSS.

Types of CSS Rules

The best thing about Cascading Style Sheets is that they are amazingly simple to set up. They don't require plug-ins or fancy software—just text files with rules. A CSS rule specifies the HTML to which a style definition applies, and then defines the style, or how the selected HTML should behave in the browser window.

You can set up rules to tell a specific HTML tag how to display its content, or you can create generic rules and then apply them to tags at your discretion.

The three most common *selectors*, or ways to select the HTML to which a style applies, are:

- **HTML selector.** The HTML element's name is used as a selector to redefine the associated HTML tag. For example, the selector for the <h1> tag is h1. The HTML selector is used in a CSS rule to redefine how the tag displays (see "(re)Defining an HTML Tag" in Chapter 2). Example:

  `h1 { font: bold 12pt times; }`

- **Class selector.** A *class* is a "free agent" that can be applied to any HTML tag. You can name the class almost anything (see this book's support Web site, webbedenvironments.com/css_dhtml_ajax, for details on name limitations). Because it can be applied to multiple HTML tags, a class is the most versatile type of selector (see "Defining Classes for Any Tag" in Chapter 2). Example:

  `.myClass { font: bold 12pt times; }`

- **ID selector.** Much like classes, *IDs* can be applied to any HTML tag, but only once on a given page to a particular HTML tag, to create an object for use with a JavaScript function (see "Defining ID Selectors to Identify an Object" in Chapter 2). Example:

  `#myObject1 { position: absolute;`
  `→ top: '10px; }`

Tags or Selectors: What's the Big Difference?

An HTML element name is the text part of an HTML tag—the part that tells the browser what type of tag it is. So when you define an HTML selector in CSS using the element name, you are, in fact, redefining the HTML tag. Although the two components, tag and selector, seem to be identical, they aren't: If you used the full HTML tag—brackets and all—in a CSS rule, the tag would not work. So it's important to keep these two ideas separate.

Uppercase or Lowercase Tags?

HTML tags are not case-sensitive. That is, the browser does not care whether the element and attribute names (the text) in the tags are uppercase or lowercase. Most people prefer to use uppercase for tags, because this makes them stand out from the surrounding content.

I counted myself in that camp until the release of the XHTML standard. One important characteristic of XHTML is that it is case-sensitive, and all element and attribute names must be in lowercase. Therefore, to prepare for the next evolutionary step of HTML, I have started using lowercase selectors in all my HTML tags.

The parts of a CSS rule

All CSS rules consist of a *selector* and a *declaration block*. The declaration block, which is surrounded by curly braces, is made up of *declarations*, which are pairs of *properties* and *values* separated by a semicolon (;):

◆ **Selectors** start each rule, appearing before the left curly brace. The selector can be an HTML tag selector, a class, an ID, or a combination of these.

◆ **Properties** identify the style that is being defined. There are several dozen properties, each responsible for an aspect of the page content's behavior and appearance.

continues on next page

What Is the World Wide Web Consortium?

The World Wide Web Consortium (w3.org) is an organization that sets many of the standards that browser manufacturers eventually use to create their products.

Created in 1994, the W3C's mission is "to lead the Web to its full potential" by developing common protocols that promote its evolution and ensure its interoperability.

The W3C comprises more than 400 member organizations around the world. These organizations include vendors of technology products and services, content providers, corporate users, research laboratories, standards bodies, and governments.

According to its Web site, the W3C has three goals:

◆ **Web for Everyone.** To make the Web accessible to all people by promoting technologies that take into account the vast differences in culture, education, ability, material resources, and physical limitations of users on all continents.

◆ **Web on Everything.** To allow all devices easy access to the Web. Although most access is still through desktop or laptop computers, an increasing array of devices can access the Web.

◆ **Knowledge Base.** To develop an environment that permits each user to make the best use of the resources available on the Web.

◆ **Trust and Confidence.** To guide the Web's development with careful consideration for the novel legal, commercial, and social issues raised by this technology.

For more about the W3C and its mission, check out http://w3.org/Consortium/Points/

TYPES OF CSS RULES

- **Values** are assigned to a property to define its nature. A value can be a keyword such as "yes" or "no," a number, or a percentage. The type of value used depends solely on the property to which it is assigned.

Figure 1.8 illustrates the general syntax of a rule.

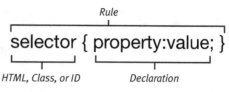

Rule

selector { property:value; }

HTML, Class, or ID   *Declaration*

Figure 1.8 The basic syntax of a CSS rule.

Where to put CSS rules

You can set up rules in three places:

- **In an HTML tag** within the body of your document, to affect a single tag in the document. This type of rule is often referred to as an *inline* rule (see "Adding Styles to an HTML Tag: Inline" in Chapter 2).

- **In the head of a document**, to affect a single Web page. This type of rule is called an *embedded* rule (see "Adding Styles to a Web Page: Embedded" in Chapter 2).

- **In an external document** that is then linked or imported into your HTML document(s), to affect an entire Web site. This type of rule is called an *external* rule (see "Adding Styles to a Web Site: External" in Chapter 2).

The position of a rule in relationship to the document and other CSS rules determines the scope of the rule's effect on the document (see "Determining the Cascade Order" in Chapter 2).

✔ Tips

- You don't have to include a semicolon with the last definition in a list, but experience shows that adding this semicolon can prevent headaches later. If you later decide to add a new definition to the rule and forget to put in the required semicolon before the addition, you may cause the rule to fail completely—not just that one definition, but all the definitions in the rule will fail to be used.

- When writing a rule with an HTML selector, don't confuse the element name of an HTML tag with its attribute names. In the following tag, for example, img is the element name and would be used as the selector, while src is an attribute name:

  <img src="picture.gif">

- Although Netscape Navigator 4 and later and Microsoft Internet Explorer 3 and later support CSS, none of these browsers supports all the CSS capabilities, and the support varies depending on the browser version. See this book's support Web site (webbedenvironments.com/css_dhtml_ajax) to help you determine whether a particular property of CSS is supported by the browser you are designing for.

CSS and Markup Languages

CSS is not HTML; it simply means that HTML now relies on the capabilities of CSS.

The W3C's thinking is this: Style sheets should be used to "relieve HTML of the responsibilities of presentation."

Translation: Don't bug us with requests for more HTML tags to do layout. Use style sheets instead.

That's probably a good idea. It means that anybody can use HTML tags, whether she is Jo Web Designer or not. But ol' Jo can use CSS to reassign standard HTML tags to do whatever she wants them to do, for more professional results.

In addition, this means that CSS can be used with other markup languages—such as XML (Extensible Markup Language), XHTML (Extensible Hypertext Markup Language), and even other Web technologies such as SVG (Scalable Vector Graphics) and Adobe Flash—just as easily as it can be used with HTML.

This book will focus on the use of CSS with the latest standards in Web markup languages (XHTML 1.0), but virtually all of this information can equally be applied to these other markup languages.

Converting HTML to XHTML

So what is the difference between HTML and XHTML? XHTML is far more restrictive than HTML: It will not allow you to bend the rules. However, because XHTML shares the same tags as HTML, it's fairly easy to convert if you keep the following points in mind:

- **No overlapping tags.** Most browsers don't care whether HTML tags are properly nested, so the following code works just fine:

  ```
  <p>Bad <b>Nesting</p></b>
  ```

  That is not the case in XHTML. You must use the correct syntax:

  ```
  <p>Good <b>Nesting</b></p>
  ```

- **Tags and attributes have to be lowercase.** XML is case-sensitive, so `<li>` and `<LI>` are different tags. Keep all your tags and attributes in lowercase, and you'll be fine.

- **Always use an end tag.** Often, Web designers simply slam in a `<p>` tag to separate paragraphs. With XHTML, however, you have to use this format:

  ```
  <p>Your text</p>
  ```

- **Use a space and slash in empty tags.** The preceding rule doesn't make much sense for `<br>` or `<hr>` tags, which have no closing tag. Instead, include a space and then a slash in the tag to make it self-closing:

  ```
  <br />
  ```

- **Don't nest links.** In XHTML, the following doesn't work:

  ```
  <a href="this.html">This <a href="that.html">That</a></a>
  ```

  But why would you want to do that in the first place?

- **Use id and name together.** If you're identifying an element on the screen, such as a layer, use both the id and name attributes, except in radio buttons:

  ```
  <div id="object1" name="object"1">object</div>
  ```

- **Place attribute values in quotes.** If a tag contains attributes, the values have to be in quotes. The following example is wrong:

  ```
  <img src=myImage.gif />
  ```

  Use this syntax instead:

  ```
  <img src="myImage.gif" />
  ```

- **Encode the ampersand in URLs or other attribute values.** The ampersand (&) has to be coded as &. The following example is wrong:

  ```
  <img src="bill&ted.gif" />
  ```

  Use this syntax instead:

  ```
  <img src="bill%26ted.gif" />
  ```

- **Don't use HTML comments in script or style containers.** One trick I show you in this book is to place HTML comment tags immediately after `<style>` or `<script>` tags to hide the code from older browsers. For XHTML, do not do this. The following example is wrong:

  ```
  <style> <!-- p { font: times; } //--> </style>
  ```

  Use this syntax instead:

  ```
  <style> p { font: times; } </style>
  ```

Figure 1.9 The W3C's HTML home page (www.w3.org/MarkUp/). You can find information about both HTML and XHTML here.

HTML

The latest version of the Hypertext Markup Language, HTML 4.01, was released in December 1999 by the W3C (w3.org/TR/html4/). HTML 4.01 includes the style-sheet methodology (previously maintained as a separate standard) as part of the HTML specification (**Figure 1.9**).

XML and XSL

Like HTML, the Extensible Markup Language—XML, for short (w3.org/XML/)—is an offshoot of SGML (see the sidebar "Where Did Markup Languages Come From?"). Unlike HTML, however, XML gives Web designers the ability to define not only the structure of the page, but also the types of information being presented. XML produces a Web page that works like a database and is convenient to search and manipulate, which is why XML is being touted as the greatest thing to happen to the Internet since HTML.

With XML, you can "teach" the browser how to tell the difference between the real name, the alias, and the person's organization. You can also tell the browser how each of these elements should be displayed.

XSL, which stands for Extensible Stylesheet Language (w3.org/Style/XSL/), is used to convert XML documents into other kinds of documents, such as HTML for display on the Web. This is especially useful for content destined for both screen and print, since it makes it easy to design for both.

XHTML

XML and XSL may hold many promises for Web designers, but how do you get Web designers to switch from HTML, with which they are comfortable, to the more complex XML?

continues on next page

Where Did Markup Languages Come From?

The Standard Generalized Markup Language (SGML) is the grandfather of most markup languages used for both print and the Internet. SGML is the international standard used to define the structure and appearance of documents. Different SGMLs have been created for a variety of document types and for different specialties, such as physics, accounting, and chemistry. HTML is the Web's version of SGML.

CSS AND MARKUP LANGUAGES

The answer: XHTML.

XHTML (w3.org/TR/xhtml1/) is a hybrid of the HTML 4.01 standard and XML. Many people hope that XHTML will begin a relatively painless transition from HTML to XML.

XHTML uses the XML Document Type Definitions (DTD)—collections of declarations that tell the browser how to treat the structure, elements, and attributes of the tags that it finds in a document. XHTML uses all the same tags as HTML with the upshot that, although XHTML Web pages can use the strength of XML, the code will still work even if the browser does not understand XML.

If the standards are so similar, why change? The W3C offers two good reasons:

- The *X* in *XHTML* stands for *extensible*, which means it's much easier to add new capabilities to XHTML than to HTML. The behavior of tags is defined in a DTD rather than by the individual browser, so XHTML is more modular. Therefore, the capabilities of XHTML can be enhanced for future browsers or other Web-enabled devices without sacrificing backward compatibility.

- A lot of Web traffic these days comes from "alternative" platforms, such as TV sets, handheld devices, and telephones. If you think it's hard to code HTML for a few different browsers, imagine coding for dozens of devices. A standard language is needed. In addition, because these devices generally have a smaller bandwidth, the code needs to be as compact as possible—something for which XHTML is perfect.

If Web designers begin using XHTML now, they can reap the benefits of XML without giving up the HTML skills they worked so long to develop. In fact, if you know HTML, you already know all the XHTML tags. The main thing you will have to learn is how these tags can (and cannot) be used. XHTML is a good deal stricter than HTML in terms of what it allows you to do, but these restrictions lead to cleaner, faster, easier-to-understand HTML code.

SVG

The Scalable Vector Graphics format—SVG, for short—is a method of creating vector graphics on the Web (w3.org/Graphics/SVG/). Like Flash, rather than plotting each point in the graphic, SVG describes two points and then plots the path between them as a straight line or curve.

Although still lagging far behind Flash in browser penetration, several browsers have included native support for SVG. Mozilla Firefox 1.5, Opera 8 and later, and Apple Safari will include it soon. Of course, the holdout is Microsoft's Internet Explorer, which apparently will not be supporting SVG anytime this decade, except through the use of a plug-in provided by Adobe (adobe.com/svg/).

Unlike Flash, which uses an editor to create its files and hides much of the code used to create the graphics, SVG uses a variation of XML to create its vector graphics. More important from a DHTML standpoint, SVG graphics can be scripted with the Document Object Model (for more information on the DOM, see Chapter 12), and can include all the DHTML capabilities described in this book.

Flash

Flash MX 2004 introduced general support for CSS, allowing designers to use the same style sheet for the presentation of both Web pages created using a markup language and proprietary Flash vector code.

✔ Tips

- XHTML and CSS are the future of Web design. Although browser manufacturers have been slow to adapt these standards, the W3C has made sure that XHTML will always be backward-compatible using Quirks mode. See the section, "Setting Your DTD," later in this chapter, for more details.

- Many of the design-related HTML tags (for example, <font>), if not already abandoned by the new HTML standard, are slated to be made obsolete in favor of CSS. The W3C calls this situation "deprecation." Although the tags still work, they are on the way out.

Kinds of Tags

Not all CSS definitions can be applied to all HTML or XHTML tags. Whether a particular CSS property can be applied (or not) depends on the nature of the tag. For the most part, it's fairly obvious if the property can be applied.

For example, you wouldn't expect the text-indent property, which indents the first line of a paragraph, to apply to an inline tag such as <b>, and it can't be. If you do find you need some help in this area, see this book's companion Web site (webbedenvironments.com/css_dhtml_ajax) for a list of the properties that can be used with a particular kind of HTML or XHTML tag.

HTML and XHTML tags can generally be sorted into three categories:

◆ **Block-level tags** place a line break before and after the element. **Table 1.2** lists the block-level tag selectors that CSS can use.

◆ **Inline tags** have no line breaks associated with the element. **Table 1.3** lists the inline-tag selectors that CSS can use.

✔ Tips

■ Some coders just slap the <p> tag into their code to start a new paragraph tag without its closing </p>. The closing tag *must* be included if you want to define paragraphs using CSS.

■ Although the break tag (<br>) does not have a closing tag, you can add styles to it. However, remember that in XHTML, the break tag becomes
 (with a space between the br and the /) so that it is self-closing.

Table 1.2

Selectors for Block-Level Tags

SELECTOR	HTML USE
blockquote	Quote style
br	Line break
center	Center text
dd	Definition description
div	Division
dl	Definition list
dt	Definition term
h1–6	Heading levels 1–6
li	List item
object	Object embedding
ol	Ordered list
p	Paragraph
pre	Preformatted text
table	Table
td	Table data
th	Table head
tr	Table row
ul	Unordered list

Table 1.3

Selectors for Inline Tags

SELECTOR	HTML USE
a	Anchored link
b	Bold
big	Bigger text
cite	Short citation
code	Code font
dfn	Defined term
em	Emphasis
font	Font appearance
i	Italic
img	Image embedding
span	Localized style formatting
strike	Strikethrough
strong	Strong emphasis
sub	Subscript
sup	Superscript
tt	Teletype font
u	Underlined text
input	Form input object
select	Form select input area
textarea	Form text input area

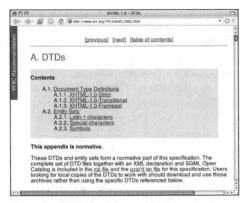

Figure 1.10 A Web browser displaying the XHTML 1.0 DTDs provided by the World Wide Web Consortium (www.w3.org/TR/xhtml1/dtds.html).

Code 1.1 The doctype tag (which references the DTD file created by the World Wide Web Consortium) is placed at the top of the code.

```
<!DOCTYPE html PUBLIC "-//W3C//DTD XHTML 1.0
→ Strict//EN" "http://www.w3.org/TR/html1/
→ DTD/xhtml1-strict.dtd">
<html xmlns="http://www.w3.org/1999/xhtml">
    <head>
        <title>HTML Strict Doctype</title>
    </head>
    <body>
        This document is XHTML 1.0
        → Strict.<br />
    </body>
</html>
```

Setting Your DTD

A document type definition, sometimes called a *doctype* or just *DTD*, is a text document that contains the rules for how a particular markup language works. Although anyone can create a DTD, Web designers use one of the ones created (and hosted) by the World Wide Web Consortium (**Figure 1.10**). When the page loads, the browser determines which DTD it uses, and then attempts to render the page based on that doctype.

You can place a document type declaration at the beginning of your code that includes a reference to the DTD for the markup language your Web page uses (**Code 1.1**). However, only in the most recent browser versions (Firefox 2, Internet Explorer 7, Safari, and Opera 9) will the doctype have any effect on how the content is displayed. If the doctype is left unspecified, the browser will display the page in *Quirks mode*, which will behave like a legacy browser. If a recognizable doctype is included, the browser will switch to *Strict* or *Standards mode*, which follows the specified standard.

continues on next page

There are three DTDs you need to worry about, which can be specified using the doctype tags in either HTML or XHTML (**Table 1.4**):

- **Strict.** Assumes that *all* styles will be handled by CSS. Thus no formatting tags are allowed.

- **Transitional.** Allows you to use a mixture of CSS and legacy HTML formatting to design your page. Sometimes called *loose*.

- **Frameset.** Used with HTML documents used to create framesets.

If you are working with or converting an older HTML site, you might have to resort back to transitional DTD. However, all your new work should use the strict DTD and XHTML. Although this means you will have to be a bit more careful when you code, it takes care of a lot of browser inconsistencies.

Quirks and Standards mode

Early implementations of CSS in browsers such as Microsoft Internet Explorer 4 and Netscape Navigator 4 were full of bugs, non-standard behaviors, and even some misinterpretations of the W3C standards. To make pages that looked right with the widest array of browsers, Web designers had to accommodate these CSS quirks. However, as manufacturers have developed new browser versions, they have tried to come closer to the standards without breaking older designs. As a result, most browsers have two or three layout modes:

- **Quirks mode.** Used by the browser if it detects that the page is not standards-compliant. This basically renders the page as if it were in one of these older browsers.

Table 1.4

Doctypes	
NAME	**CODE**

HTML Transitional	`<!DOCTYPE HTML PUBLIC "-`
	`→ //W3C//DTD HTML 4.01`
	`→ Transitional//EN"`
	`→ "http://www.w3.org/TR/`
	`→ html4/loose.dtd">`

HTML Strict	`<!DOCTYPE HTML PUBLIC "-`
	`→ //W3C//DTD HTML 4.01//EN"`
	`→ "http://www.w3.org/TR/`
	`→ html4/strict.dtd">`

HTML Frameset	`<!DOCTYPE HTML PUBLIC "-`
	`→ //W3C//DTD HTML 4.01`
	`→ Frameset//EN"`
	`→ "http://www.w3.org/TR/`
	`→ html4/frameset.dtd">`

XHTML Transitional	`<!DOCTYPE html PUBLIC "-`
	`→ //W3C//DTD XHTML 1.0`
	`→ Transitional//EN"`
	`→ "http://www.w3.org/TR/`
	`→ xhtml1/DTD/xhtml1-`
	`→ transitional.dtd">`

XHTML Strict	`<!DOCTYPE html PUBLIC "-`
	`→ //W3C//DTD XHTML 1.0`
	`→ Strict//EN"`
	`→ "http://www.w3.org/TR/`
	`→ xhtml1/DTD/xhtml1-`
	`→ strict.dtd">`

XHTML Frameset	`<!DOCTYPE html PUBLIC "-`
	`→ //W3C//DTD XHTML 1.0`
	`→ Frameset//EN"`
	`→ "http://www.w3.org/TR/`
	`→ xhtml1/DTD/xhtml1-`
	`→ frameset.dtd">`

◆ **Standards mode.** Uses the standards as defined by the particular browser. These may not be W3C standards, but they may be as close as the browser will get to the standards.

◆ **Almost Standards mode.** Firefox, Safari, and Opera (7.5 and later) have a third mode that uses all of the CSS 2 standards, except for table cell vertical sizing.

Choosing a doctype

Not including the doctype in your Web page means that newer browsers may not recognize all of the code you are using. Which doctype should you put at the top of your Web page? It depends on how you are coding it:

◆ **No Doctype.** Older Web pages containing a "tag soup" or using quirks from older browsers. If you do not use a doctype modern browsers are forced into into Quirks mode—a bad idea if you are creating new Web pages because it leaves the interpretation of the code soley at the discretion of the browsers, which can translate into a lot of inconsistencies in the display.

◆ **XHTML Transitional.** Web pages that use some deprecated HTML markup, but can still be validated as XHTML 1.0 Transitional. This puts modern browsers into standards or almost standards mode.

◆ **XHTML Strict.** Web pages that are strictly XHTML and CSS compliant. This doctype validates as XHTML 1.0 Strict and works with the CSS2 box layout model. It switches most modern browsers into Standards mode. If at all possible, this is your best choice.

◆ **XHTML Frameset.** Any Web pages that create a frameset must use this doctype.

✔ Tips

■ Earlier browsers that do not recognize DTDs will render the page based on their own definitions, which by default is Quirks mode.

■ *Do not* include an XML version definition and encoding value above the XHTML DTD:

```
<?xml version="1.0" encoding=
→ "iso-8859-1"?>
```

This causes Internet Explorer to use Quirks mode and will render standards-based content poorly. It will also disrupt dynamic content that uses JavaScript, PHP, ASP, or JSP.

Who Owns CSS?

On January 12, 1999, Microsoft Corp. (microsoft.com) was granted U.S. Patent #5,860,073. This particular patent, titled "Style sheets for publishing system(s)," covers "the use of style sheets in an electronic publishing system." Sound familiar?

The inventors listed in this patent claim to have developed a system whereby "text, or other media such as graphics, is poured into the display region," at which time style sheets—defined as "a collection of formatting information, such as fonts and tabs"—are applied. This patent seems to overlap concepts laid out in the W3C's specifications for CSS and the Extensible Stylesheet Language (XSL), which have been in development since at least 1994.

A brief analysis of the patent shows that it has two major flaws, which the W3C and the Web Standards Project (webstandards.org) have already been quick to point out:

◆ "The existence of prior art," referring to the fact that style sheets were proposed with the first Web browsers coming out of CERN laboratories in 1994. In fact, style sheets have been around since the 1960s, when they were used for print publications. At best, Microsoft is a Johnny-come-lately to the concept.

◆ The W3C's own licensing ensures that the standards developed under its banner are universally available and royalty-free. Because the W3C first developed the concept of style sheets, its license should hold precedence.

Microsoft had representatives on the committees that created these standards, and its own patent refers to documents produced by the W3C regarding CSS, so it seems highly improbable that this patent would stand up to much scrutiny.

George Olsen of the Web Standards Project questions whether the patent should have been granted in the first place, "because [there] are a number of prior examples of similar technology, including the original proposal for CSS," he says. Also, it is assumed that any organization—Microsoft included—with representatives in the W3C will detail any current or pending patents that might affect the W3C standards under consideration, which this patent certainly did. Yet the W3C first heard of the patent on February 4, 1999, when information about the patent was made publicly available. For its part, the W3C presents the claim on its Web site, but attempts to stay neutral as to its validity (w3.org/Style/CSS/Disclosures)

So what does this mean to you? Probably not much. The W3C has published CSS as an open standard, and the genie is already out of the bottle.

2

CSS Basics

Figure 2.1 Here's an HTML page displayed without the benefit of CSS. The page still displays, but without the formatting of Figure 2.2.

Figure 2.2 An HTML page using CSS to add an image in the background, position the content down and to the right, and format the text.

CSS lets you control your document's appearance—fonts, text, colors, backgrounds, sizes, borders, spacing, positioning, visual effects, tables, and lists. However, the real advantage of using CSS instead of HTML is that by changing a few lines of code, you can change the appearance of every page on your Web site.

With savvy use of CSS, you can take a plain page of text (**Figure 2.1**) and add visual design and interaction that turns it into a webbed environment (**Figure 2.2**).

In this chapter, you'll learn the basics of how to apply styles to HTML tags, Web pages, and entire sites. You'll also learn the following:

◆ Ways to define different selectors for different purposes

◆ How to use pseudo-classes and pseudo-elements to control different parts or aspects of an element

◆ How to create styles for more than just the computer screen

◆ Ways to exploit real-world strategies for getting the best results for your designs

Adding Styles to an HTML Tag: Inline

Although CSS means never having to set the appearance of each tag individually, you still have the freedom to set styles within individual tags, referred to as an *inline* style (**Figure 2.3**). This is especially useful if you've set styles for the page in the head or in an external style sheet, and you need to override them on a case-by-case basis.

In this example (**Figure 2.4**), the styles have been added directly to several HTML tags, including the h1 tag used for the book title.

To set the style properties of individual HTML tags:

1. `<h1 style=`

    Type `style=` in the HTML tag you want to apply styles to (**Code 2.1**).

2. `"font:small-caps bold italic 2.5em`
    `→ Georgia, 'Times New Roman',`
    `→ times, serif; color: red; "`

    In quotes, type your style declaration(s) as `property: value`, using a semicolon (`;`) and separating individual declarations. Make sure to close the declaration list with quotation marks.

3. `> Alice's Adventures in Wonderland'`
    `→ </h1>`

    After closing the tag, add the content to be styled. Then close the tag pair with the corresponding end tag.

✔ Tips

■ If you are adding styles to a non-closing tag, such as an image tag, and you're using XHTML, you will need to make the tag *self closing*. So, rather than:

`<img src="myImage.png">`

You would use:

`<img src="myImage.png" />`

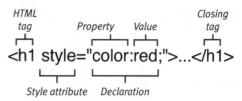

Figure 2.3 The general syntax for defining styles directly in an HTML tag.

Figure 2.4 The styles have been placed directly into the tags.

Code 2.1 Each tag receives instructions on how the content within it should behave, by means of the style attribute.

```
<!DOCTYPE html PUBLIC "-//W3C//DTD XHTML 1.0
→ Strict//EN" "http://www.w3.org/TR/xhtml1/
→ DTD/xhtml1-strict.dtd">
<html xmlns="http://www.w3.org/1999/xhtml">
<head>
<meta http-equiv="Content-Type"
→ content="text/html; charset=utf-8" />
<title>CSS, DHTML &amp; Ajax | Adding CSS
→ to an HTML Tag</title>
</head>
<body style="font-size: 1em; font-family:
→ Georgia, 'Times New Roman', Times, serif;
→ color: #000000;margin: 8px; background:
→ white url(alice23.gif) no-repeat;">
<div style="position: relative; top:190px;
→ left:165px; width:480px;">
<div>
<h1 style="font:small-caps bold italic 2.5em
→ Georgia, 'Times New Roman', Times, serif;
→ color: red;">Alice's Adventures in
→ Wonderland</h1>
     <p style="margin: 8px 0px; font: bold
     → 1em Arial, Helvetica, sans-serif;">
     → Lewis Carroll</p>
     <h2 style="color:#999;">Chapter I<br />
        <span style="display: block;
        → margin-bottom: 8px; font-size:
        → smaller; color:black;">Down the
        → Rabbit-Hole</span></h2>
</div>
<div style="line-height: 1.5">
     <p><span style="font: 300%/100% serif;
     → color: #999999;">A</span>lice was
     → beginning to get very tired of
     → sitting by her sister on the
     → bank…'</p>
</div></div>
</body></html>
```

- Although you do not gain the benefit of the universal style changes, using CSS in individual HTML tags is nevertheless very useful when you want to override universally defined styles. (See "Determining the Cascade Order" later in this chapter.)

- I've also shown how you can define the <body> tag in this example, but be careful—this can lead to more problems than it's worth (see "Inheriting Properties from a Parent" later in this chapter). In addition, many earlier browsers, including Microsoft Internet Explorer 5.5, balk at some properties being added to the <body> tag, especially the positioning properties discussed in Chapter 7.

- So as not to confuse the browser, it is best to use double quotation marks ("…") around the declaration list, and single quotation marks ('…') around any values in the declaration list, such as font names with spaces.

- Make sure that if you are copying and pasting code from an application such as Microsoft Word into a Web editing application such as Adobe Dreamweaver that you convert all smart quotes ("…") to straight quotes ("…").

- One common mistake is to confuse the equal sign (=) with the colon (:). Remember that although the style attribute in the tag uses an equal sign, CSS declarations always use a colon.

- You can also apply common styles to an entire Web page (see the following section) or to multiple Web pages (see "Adding Styles to a Web Site" later in this chapter).

- Font names made up of more than two words are placed in single quotes ('Font Name') when used with a style.

Adding Styles to a Web Page: Embedded

The main use for CSS is to define style rules for an entire document (Web page). To do this, you can *embed* your style rules in the head of the document within a style element (**Figure 2.5**).

While the results of adding styles in this manner can look identical to adding the styles directly to an HTML tag (shown in the previous section), placing styles in a common location lets you easily change all the styles in a document (**Figure 2.6**). For example, you can define the style for h1 tags in the head of your document and it will apply to all h1 tags in that document.

To set the style for tags in an HTML document:

1. `<style type="text/css"`
   → `media="all">...</style>`

   Type the opening `style` tag in the head of your document (**Code 2.2**). Define the `type` attribute as `"text/css"`, which defines the styles that follow as being not just any style, but CSS. Also define the `media` type, using a value of `all`, which will apply the style sheet to the page, regardless of the type of machine used to out put it. Then close the `style` tag.

continues on page 28

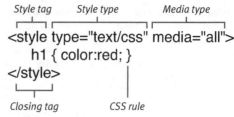

Figure 2.5 The general syntax of a CSS style placed in the head of an HTML document.

Figure 2.6 Although this figure is a doppelganger of Figure 2.4, the CSS used to create it is located in the head of the document rather than in each individual tag.

Code 2.2 Although the result of this code (Figure 2.2) may look identical to the preceding example (Figure 2.1), the style rules are collected in the head of the document, where they affect all tags within the HTML document.

```
a<!DOCTYPE html PUBLIC "-//W3C//DTD XHTML 1.0 Strict//EN" "http://www.w3.org/TR/xhtml1/DTD/
→ xhtml1-strict.dtd">
<html xmlns="http://www.w3.org/1999/xhtml">
<head>
<meta http-equiv="Content-Type" content="text/html; charset=utf-8" />
<title>CSS, DHTML &amp; Ajax | Adding CSS to a Web Page</title>
<style type="text/css" media="all">
body {
    font-size: 1em;
    font-family: Georgia, 'Times New Roman', times, serif;
    color: #000000;
    margin: 8px;
    background: white url(alice23.gif) no-repeat; }
h1 {
font: small-caps bold italic 2.5em Georgia, 'Times New Roman', times, serif;
color: red; }
h2 {
    color:#999; }
#content {
    position: relative;
    top: 190px;
    left: 165px;
    width: 480px; }
#content #copy {
    line-height: 1.5; }
p.authorName {
    margin: 8px 0px;
    font: bold 1em Arial, Helvetica, sans-serif; }
h2 .chapterName {
    display: block;
    margin-bottom: 8px;
    font-size: smaller;
    color:black; }
p.dropCap:first-letter {
    font: 300%/100% serif;
    color: #999999;}
</style>
</head>
<body>
<div id="content">
<div>
    <h1>Alice's Adventures in Wonderland</h1>
    <p class="authorName">Lewis Carroll</p>
    <h2>Chapter I<br />
        <span class="chapterName">Down the Rabbit-Hole</span></h2>
</div>
<div id="copy">
    <p class="dropCap">Alice was beginning to get very tired of sitting by her sister on the
    → bank…</p>
</div></div>
</body></html>
```

2. `h1 {…}`

In the `style` container from Step 1, start a new rule by typing the selector you want to add styles to, followed by opening and closing curly brackets ({}). The selector can be any of the following:

▲ **An HTML selector**, such as `h1` (see "(re)Defining an HTML Tag")

▲ **A class selector**, such as `.authorName` (see "Defining Classes for Any Tag")

▲ **An ID selector**, such as `#content` (see "Defining ID Selectors to Identify an Object")

3. `font:small-caps bold italic 2.5em`
→ `Georgia, 'Times New Roman', times,`
→ `serif; color: red;`

In the brackets of your rule, type the declaration(s) to be assigned to this rule—formatted as `property: value`—using a semicolon (;) and separating individual declarations in the list. To make the rule more easily decipherable, you can also add one or more line breaks, spaces, or tabs after a declaration without interfering with the code.

4. Repeat Steps 2 and 3 for all the selectors you want to define. To make the selectors easier to decipher, you can also add one or more line breaks, spaces, or tabs between rules without interfering with the code.

✔ Tips

■ If you're writing HTML, you don't have to include `type="text/css"`, because the browser should be able to determine the type of style being used. I always put it there, however, to allow browsers that do not support a particular type of style sheet to avoid the code. It also clarifies the type being used. However, if you are using XHTML (which I recommend), the type attribute is required.

■ You do not have to define the `media` type, but browsers will default to the `all` value if left unassigned. See "Setting Styles for Print and Other Media" later in this chapter to learn how to specify different style sheets for different media types such as print and handheld.

■ You can hide your CSS from non-CSS capable browsers by placing the HTML comment tags `<!--…-->` around all rules within the `style` tags. Otherwise, these browsers may display the text, which is not very attractive.

Adding Styles to a Web Site: External

A major benefit of CSS is that you can create a style sheet once to use either on a single Web page or throughout an entire Web site. You can apply this *external* style sheet to one or a hundred HTML documents, without having to retype the information.

Establishing an external CSS file is a two-step process. First, you must set up the rules in a text file; then you need to link or import this file into an HTML document, using either the <link> tag or the @import rule (**Figure 2.7**).

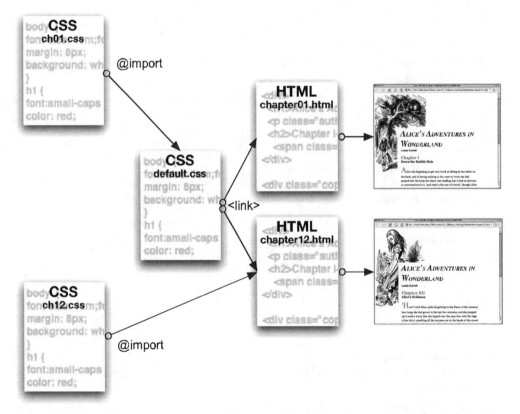

Figure 2.7 External CSS files can be not only used in multiple HTML files, but also imported into (but not linked to) another external CSS file.

Creating an external style sheet

The first step in using an external style sheet globally on a Web site is to create the text file that holds all of the CSS code. However, unlike adding embedded styles, you do *not* use `<style>` tags in an external CSS file. This would prevent it from working in most browsers.

In this example, I set up three CSS files: `default.css`, `ch01.css`, and `ch12.css`.

To set up an external CSS file:

1. `default.css`

Create a new file, using word processing or other software that allows you to save the document as a text file. Notepad or SimpleText will do (**Code 2.3**). You can set up as many different CSS files as you want for your site, such as `ch01.css` and `ch12.css` (**Code 2.4** and **Code 2.5**), and even link or import multiple style sheets to a single Web page.

2. `@import{ch01.css}`

You can start any external style sheet by importing other external style sheets. However, if included, the import rule must be placed before all other CSS code. See "Importing a style sheet" later in this section for more details.

3. `h1 {…}`

Add CSS rules to the page by typing the selector to which you want to add styles, followed by opening and closing curly brackets ({}). The selector can be any of the following:

▲ **An HTML selector**, such as `h1` (see "(re)Defining an HTML Tag")

▲ **A class selector**, such as `.authorName` (see "Defining Classes for Any Tag")

▲ **An ID selector**, such as `#content` (see "Defining ID Selectors to Identify an Object")

Code 2.3 `default.css`: This external CSS contains declarations that will be used to create the layout in Code 2.6 and Code 2.7. It begins, though, by importing the external style sheet ch01.html (Code 2.4).

```
/* Default CSS used in all Chapters */

@import url(ch01.css);

body {
    font-size: 1em;
    font-family: Georgia, 'Times New
    → Roman', times, serif;
    color: #000000;
    margin: 8px; }
h1 {
font:small-caps bold italic 2.5em Georgia,
→ 'Times New Roman', times, serif;
color: red; }
h2 {
    color:#999; }
#content {
    position: relative;
    top:   190px;
    left: 165px;
    width: 480px; }
#content #copy {
    line-height: 1.5; }
p.authorName {
    margin: 8px 0px;
    font: bold 1em Arial, Helvetica,
    → sans-serif; }
h2 .chapterName {
    display: block;
    margin-bottom: 8px;
    font-size: smaller;
    color:black; }
p.dropCap:first-letter {
    font: 300%/100% serif;
    color: #999999;}
```

Code 2.4 ch01.html: The majority of the styles applied to this HTML document are linked from the external CSS file called default.css, shown in Code 2.3. This code replaces the background image from Chapter 1.

```
/* Styles used in Chapter 1 */

body { background: white url(alice23.gif)
→ no-repeat; }
```

Code 2.5 ch12.css: This code ads a background image from Chapter 12.

```
/* Styles used in Chapter 12 */

body { background: white url(alice40.gif)
→ no-repeat; }
```

✔ Tips

■ Although the external CSS file can have any name you want, it's a good idea to use a name that will remind you of what these styles are for. The name "navigation.css," for example, probably is a more helpful name than "657nm87gp.css."

■ A CSS file should not contain any HTML tags (especially not the <style> tag) or other content, with the exception of CSS comments and imported styles.

■ You do not have to use the .css extension with CSS files. You could just call this file "default," and it would work just as well. Adding the extension, however, can prevent confusion.

Notice that you do not use the <style> tag here. Using that tag in this document will prevent the CSS from being applied to your Web page.

4. font:small-caps bold italic 2.5em → Georgia, 'Times New Roman', times, → serif; color: red;

In the brackets of your rule, type the declaration(s) to be assigned to this rule—formatted as property: value—using a semicolon (;) and separating individual declarations in the list. You can also add one or more line breaks, spaces, or tabs after a declaration without interfering with the code to make it more readable.

5. Repeat Steps 3 and 4 for all the selectors you want to define. You can also add one or more line breaks, spaces, or tabs between rules without interfering with the code to make it more readable.

6. Name and save this document.

In this example, I named the file default.css. The extension .css is not required, and files will work without it, but this has become the informal convention for identifying CSS files.

7. You now need to connect this file to your Web page(s) using one of the two methods presented in the remaining part of this section of the book:

▲ **Link.** Use the <link> tag to connect external CSS files to an HTML file.

▲ **Import.** Use @import to connect external CSS files to an HTML file.

Linking to a style sheet

External style sheet files can be used with any HTML file through the `<link>` tag. Linking a CSS file affects the document in the same way as if the styles had been typed directly in the head of the document.

Figure 2.8 shows the general syntax for linking style sheets, while **Figure 2.9** shows the results of linking to style sheet `default.css` (Code 2.3) from `chapter01.html` (**Code 2.6**).

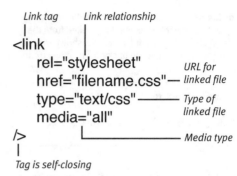

Figure 2.8 The general syntax for linking to an external style sheet.

Figure 2.9 While this page may look exactly the same as Figures 2.4 and 2.6, the CSS used to create it is mostly located in external files that have been linked to it.

Code 2.6 `chapter01.html`: This file links to an external style sheet `default.css` (Code 2.3).

```
<!DOCTYPE html PUBLIC "-//W3C//DTD XHTML 1.0
→ Strict//EN" "http://www.w3.org/TR/xhtml1/
→ DTD/xhtml1-strict.dtd">
<html xmlns="http://www.w3.org/1999/xhtml">
<head>
<meta http-equiv="Content-Type"
→ content="text/html; charset=utf-8" />
<title>CSS, DHTML &amp; Ajax | Adding CSS
→ to a Web Site</title>
<link rel="style sheet" href="default.css"
→ type="text/css" media="all" />
</head>
<body>
<div id="content">
<div>
      <h1>Alice's Adventures in Wonderland</h1>
      <p class="authorName">Lewis Carroll</p>
      <h2>Chapter I<br />
         <span class="chapterName">Down the
         → Rabbit-Hole</span></h2>
</div>
<div id="copy">
      <p class="dropCap">Alice was beginning
      → to get very tired of sitting by her
      → sister on the bank…</p>
</div></div>
</body></html>
```

To link to an external CSS file:

1. `<link`
Within the <head>…</head> of your HTML document, open your <link> tag and then type a space.

2. `rel="style sheet"`
Tell the browser that this will be a link to a style sheet.

3. `href="default.css"`
Specify the location, either global or local, of the CSS file to be used, where *default.css* is the full path and name (including extension) of your CSS document.

4. `type="text/css"`
Specify the type of information that is being linked—in this case a text file containing CSS.

5. `media="all"`
Specify the media type to which this style sheet should be applied. For more details, see "Setting Styles for Print and Other Media" later in this chapter.

6. `/>`
Close the `link` tag using a space, slash, and chevron (/>).

7. Repeat Steps 1 through 6 to add as many style sheets to the page as you want.

8. You can embed additional CSS rules in the head either before or after the links if needed (see the previous section, "Adding Styles to a Web Page").

Importing a style sheet

Another way to bring external style sheets into a document is to use the @import rule. The advantage of importing is that it can be used not only to put an external CSS file in an HTML document file, but also to import one external CSS file into another.

Figure 2.10 shows the general syntax for the @import rule, and **Figure 2.11** shows the result of importing the default.css (Code 2.3) and ch12.css (Code 2.5) style sheets into the chapter12.html HTML file (**Code 2.7**).

@import rule   URL for external file

Figure 2.10 The general syntax for importing an external style sheet.

Figure 2.11 The same CSS files were used to create this page that were used for Figure 2.9. This time, however, the files have been imported and a different background image has been defined for the body.

Code 2.7 chapter12.html: This file imports the external style sheets default.css (Code 2.3) and ch12.css (Code 2.5).

```
<!DOCTYPE html PUBLIC "-//W3C//DTD XHTML 1.0
→ Strict//EN" "http://www.w3.org/TR/xhtml1/
→ DTD/xhtml1-strict.dtd">
<html xmlns="http://www.w3.org/1999/xhtml">
<head>
<meta http-equiv="Content-Type"
→ content="text/html; charset=utf-8" />
<title>CSS, DHTML &amp; Ajax | Adding CSS
→ to a Web Site</title>
<style type="text/css" media="all">
@import url(default.css);
@import url(ch12.css);
</style>
</head>
<body>
<div id="content">

<div>
    <h1>Alice's Adventures in Wonderland</h1>
    <p class="authorName">Lewis Carroll</p>
    <h2>Chapter XII<br />
        <span class="chapterName">Alice's
→ Evidence</span></h2>
</div>
<div id="copy">
<p class="dropCap">'Here!' cried Alice,
→ quite forgetting in the flurry of the
→ moment how large she had grown in the
→ last few minutes…</p>
</div></div>
</body></html>
```

To import an external CSS file:

1. `<style type="text/css" media="all">…</style>`
   Within the head of your HTML document, add a style tag.

2. `@import url(default.css);`
   In the style tag, before any other CSS code you want to include, type `@import()` and include the URL of the CSS document to be imported between the parentheses. The URL can be global, in which case it would start with `http://`, or it could be a local path, pointing to another file on the same domain.

3. `@import url(ch12.css);`
   Repeat Step 2 for as many external CSS documents as you want to import.

4. You can include additional CSS rules here, if needed (see the previous section, "Adding Styles to a Web Page").

✔ Tip

- You can also place `@import` directly in another external style sheet. This will import the CSS code from one style sheet into the other so that when the second style sheet is linked or imported into an HTML file, the styles from the first style sheet are also included.

(Re)Defining HTML Tags

All HTML tags have styles associated with them. Take the italics tag, for example: Its inherent style declaration is `font-style: italic`.

Figure 2.12 shows the general syntax for adding a complete CSS rule using an HTML selector.

By adding new declarations to `i`, the HTML selector, you can change its appearance to be anything you want. For example, you could have all italicized text be bold, or even set `font-style: none`, preventing the italics tag from italicizing text.

In this example (**Figure 2.13**), I've set the style of several different HTML selectors, including the italics tag, paragraph tag, image tag, and even the body. Notice though, that I do not have to add any additional code in the HTML in order for these styles to work.

To define an HTML selector:

1. `i {…}`

Start with the HTML selector whose properties you want to define. Add a curly bracket ({) to open your rule (**Code 2.8**). Make sure you always close your declaration list with a curly bracket (}). If you forget this, it will ruin your day!

CSS rules can be defined within the `style` tags in the head of your document (see "Adding Styles to a Web Page" earlier in this chapter) or in an external CSS file that is then imported or linked to the HTML document (see "Adding Styles to a Web Site" earlier in this chapter).

2. `font-weight: bold;`

Within the brackets, type the style declaration(s) to be assigned to this HTML tag—formatted as `property: value`—using a semicolon (;) and separating

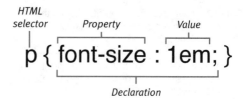

Figure 2.12 The general syntax used to define the styles for an HTML tag.

Figure 2.13 Several HTML tags have been styled, including the <p> tag, which makes the text in paragraphs red; the <i> tag, which makes italics bold; and the <img> tag, which adds a red border around all images.

Code 2.8 HTML tags can be directly styled, allowing you to directly manipulate any tag on the screen without ever adding anything directly to the HTML in the <body> tag.

```
<!DOCTYPE html PUBLIC "-//W3C//DTD XHTML 1.0
→ Strict//EN" "http://www.w3.org/TR/xhtml1/
→ DTD/xhtml1-strict.dtd">
<html xmlns="http://www.w3.org/1999/xhtml">
<head>
<meta http-equiv="Content-Type"
→ content="text/html; charset=utf-8" />
<title>CSS, DHTML &amp; Ajax | (re)Defining
→ HTML Tags</title>
<style type="text/css" media="all">
body {
    font: 1.2em Georgia, 'Times New Roman',
    → times, serif;
    color: #000000;
background-color: #fff;
    margin: 8px; }
p {
    font-size: 1em;
    color: #f00;
    line-height: 150%; }
i {
    font-weight: bold }
img {
    padding: 6px;
    border: 3px solid #f00;
    margin: 0px 0px 8px 8px;
    float: right; }
</style>
</head>
<body>
<div id="content">
<div id="header">
    <h1>Alice's Adventures in Wonderland</h1>
    <p class="authorName">Lewis Carroll</p>
    <h2>Chapter II<br />
        <span class="chapterName">The Pool
        of Tears</span>
    </h2>
</div>
<div id="copy">
<img src="alice07a.gif" height="236"
→ width="200" alt="Alice" />
<p><i>'Curiouser and curiouser!'</i> cried
→ Alice…</p>
</div></div>
</body></html>
```

individual declarations in the list. You can also add one or more line breaks, spaces, or tabs after a declaration without interfering with the code to make it more readable.

Add as many declarations as you want, but the properties have to work with the HTML tag in question. For example, you cannot use the `text-indent` property (which only works on block elements) to define the `bold` tag (which is an inline element). Refer to this book's Web site (webbedenvironments.com/css_dhtml_ajax) for a listing of which properties can be used with which kind of tag types.

✔ Tips

■ The syntax is slightly different for redefining an individual HTML tag inline within a document (see "Adding Styles to an HTML Tag" earlier in this chapter).

■ Redefining a tag does not override that tag's preexisting properties. Thus, the bold tag (`b`) still makes text bold no matter what other styles are added to it, unless you override it using that property's CSS equivalents; for example, set `font-weight:normal` for the bold tag (see "Inheriting Properties from a Parent" later in this chapter).

■ Although the `body` tag can also be redefined, it acts like a block-level tag (see "Kinds of Tags" in Chapter 1). Internet Explorer for Windows does not accept positioning controls in the `body` tag.

(RE)DEFINING HTML TAGS

Defining Classes for Any Tag

Using a class selector gives you the ability to set up an independent style that you can then apply to any HTML tag.

Unlike an HTML selector, which automatically targets a specific tag, a class is given a unique name that is then specified using the style attribute in the HTML tag or tags you want to use it in.

Figures 2.14 and **2.15** show the general syntax of a CSS class rule. In this example (**Figure 2.16**), two classes have been set up to define how the chapter name (.chapterName) and the author name (.authorName) should be styled, although the .authorName class can only be applied to the paragraph tag.

To define a class selector:

1. .chapterName {…}

Type a period (.) and a class name; then open and close your declaration block with curly brackets ({}) (**Code 2.9**).

CSS rules can be defined within the style tags in the head of your document (see "Adding Styles to a Web Page" earlier in this chapter) or in an external CSS file that is then imported or linked to the HTML document (see "Adding Styles to a Web Site" earlier in this chapter).

The class name can be anything you choose, with the following caveats:

▲ Use only letters and numbers. Hyphens and underscores can be used, but with caution. Some earlier browsers (notably Netscape 4) reject them.

continues on page 40

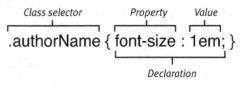

Figure 2.14 The general syntax of a CSS rule using a class selector.

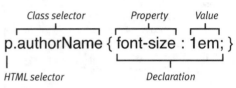

Figure 2.15 The general syntax of a dependent class selector rule.

Figure 2.16 Classes are used to style the chapter name, the name of the author, and to create the drop box embedded in the first paragraph with an image and caption.

Code 2.9 A class style can be set up to be applied to any HTML tag, as with copy, or only to specific HTML tags.

```
<!DOCTYPE html PUBLIC "-//W3C//DTD XHTML 1.0 Strict//EN" "http://www.w3.org/TR/xhtml1/DTD/
→ xhtml1-strict.dtd">
<html xmlns="http://www.w3.org/1999/xhtml">
<head>
<meta http-equiv="Content-Type" content="text/html; charset=utf-8" />
<title>CSS, DHTML &amp; Ajax | Defining Class Selectors to Create Your Own Tags</title>
<style type="text/css" media="all">
body {
     font: 1.2em Georgia, 'Times New Roman', times, serif;
     color: #000000;
background-color: #fff;
     margin: 8px; }
.chapterName {
     font-size: smaller;
     display: block;
     margin-bottom: 8px;
     color:red; }
     p.authorName {
     font-size: 1em;
     font-family: Arial, Helvetica, sans-serif;
     font-weight: bold;
     margin: 8px 0px;
     color: red; }
.dropBox {
     width: 208px;
     font: bold smaller Arial, Helvetica, sans-serif;
     padding: 6px;
     border: 3px solid #f00;
     margin: 0px 0px 8px 8px;
     float: right; }
</style>
</head>
<body>
<div id="content">
<div id="header">
     <h1>Alice's Adventures in Wonderland</h1>
     <p class="authorName">Lewis Carroll</p>
     <h2>Chapter III<br />
        <span class="chapterName">A Caucus-Race and a Long Tale </span>
     </h2>
</div>
<div id="copy">
<div class="dropBox">
<img src="alice09a.gif" height="236" width="200" alt="Alice" />
'Of course,' the Dodo replied very gravely. 'What else have you got in your pocket?' he went on,
→ turning to Alice.
</div>
<p>They were indeed a queer-looking party that assembled on the bank…</p>
</div></div>
</body></html>
```

▲ The first character cannot be a number.

▲ Don't use spaces.

chapterName is an independent class, so you can use it with any HTML tag you want, with one stipulation: The properties set for the class must work with the type of tag you use it on.

2. `font-size: smaller;`

Within the brackets, type your declaration(s) to be assigned to this class—formatted as `property: value`—using a semicolon (`;`) and separating individual declarations in the list. You can also add one or more line breaks, spaces, or tabs after a declaration without interfering with the code to make it more readable.

3. `p.authorName {…}`

You can also create dependent classes, which tie the declarations of the class to a particular HTML tag.

authorName is a dependent class and will only be applied to paragraph tags using `class="authorName"`.

In the same document, you can create different versions of the dependent class (using the same name) for different tags and also have an independent class (applied to all tags with the class), as shown in Step 1.

4. `<p class="authorName">…</p>`

Add the class attribute with the class name and its value to the tags to which you want to apply the class. Notice that when you defined the class in the CSS, it began with a period (`.`). However, you do not use the period when referencing the class name in an HTML tag.

✔ Tips

■ You can mix a class with ID and/or inline rules within an HTML tag (see "Adding Styles to an HTML Tag," earlier in this chapter, and the following section, "Defining ID Selectors to Identify an Object").

■ Because they have no preexisting properties, you can use div and span tags to create your own HTML tags by adding classes. However, use these sparingly, since once they are associated, you are locked into using those specific classes with those specific locations.

■ A class name cannot be a JavaScript reserved word. Refer to this book's Web site (webbedenvironments.com/css_dhtml_ajax) for the list.

40

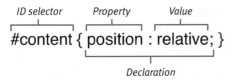

Figure 2.17 The general syntax for an ID selector rule.

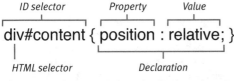

Figure 2.18 The general syntax for the dependent ID selector rule.

Figure 2.19 Each of the IDs used to create a discreet object on the page has a red box around it, which gets darker the further the box is nested.

Defining ID Selectors to Identify an Object

Like the class selector, the ID selector can be used to create unique styles that are independent of any particular HTML tag. Thus, they can be assigned to any HTML tag. **Figures 2.17** and **2.18** show the general syntax of ID selector rules.

IDs are used in HTML for layout to help establish the structure of your page, identifying unique elements in the code.

IDs are also the cornerstone of dynamic HTML (DHTML), in that they allow JavaScript functions to identify a unique object on the screen. This means that unlike a class, an ID can be used only once on a page to define a single element as an object. This object then can be manipulated using JavaScript.

In this example (**Figure 2.19**), I've set up several IDs to structure the page into several different components—content, header, copy, and drop box—each surrounded with a red border.

Elements or Objects?

There is often a lot of confusion over the terms *element* and *object* when discussing Web pages. Simply stated, an element is created by open and close markup tags. For example, <p>...</p> and all of the content between these two tags (even other tags) form an element. Any tags within the element are referred to as *child* elements, and the surrounding tags are the *parent* element.

An object, on the other hand, is created when an element is given a unique ID that allows the browser to access that element's properties.

See "Understanding an Element's Box" in Chapter 6 for more details on elements and "DOM: The Road Map to Your Web Page" in Chapter 12, for more details on objects.

To define an ID selector:

1. `#content {...}`

ID rules always start with a number sign (#) and then the name of the ID (**Code 2.10**). The name can be a word or any set of letters or numbers you choose, with the following caveats:

▲ Use only letters and numbers. Hyphens and underscores can be used, but with caution. Some earlier browsers (notably Netscape 4) reject them.

▲ The first character cannot be a number.

▲ Don't use spaces.

CSS rules can be defined within the `style` tags in the head of your document (see "Adding Styles to a Web Page" earlier in this chapter) or in an external CSS file that is then imported or linked to the HTML document (see "Adding Styles to a Web Site" earlier in this chapter).

2. `position:relative;`

Within the curly brackets, type your style declaration(s) to be assigned to this ID—formatted as `property: value`—using a semicolon (;) and separating individual declarations in the list. You can also add one or more line breaks, spaces, or tabs after a declaration without interfering with the code to make it more readable.

3. `div#copy {...}`

You can also create dependent IDs, which use the declarations of the ID only when applied to a particular HTML tag. `copy` is a dependent ID and will only be used if it is applied to the `div` tag.

In the same document, you can create different versions of the ID (using the same name) for different tags. However, including multiple instances of the same ID in the same HTML document is not recommended, since this will interfere with the DOM.

Code 2.10 Although ID selectors are seemingly similar to Class selectors, you generally should not use a single ID selector more than once per page to help create the structure of your content.

```
<!DOCTYPE html PUBLIC "-//W3C//DTD XHTML 1.0
→ Strict//EN" "http://www.w3.org/TR/xhtml1/
→ DTD/xhtml1-strict.dtd">
<html xmlns="http://www.w3.org/1999/xhtml">
<head>
<meta http-equiv="Content-Type"
→ content="text/html; charset=utf-8" />
<title>CSS, DHTML &amp; Ajax | Defining
→ ID's to Identify and Object</title>
<style type="text/css" media="screen">
body {
     font: 1.2em Georgia, 'Times New Roman',
     → times, serif;
     color: #000000;
     background-color: #fff;
     margin: 8px; }
#content {
     position: relative;
     top: 20px;
     left: 165px;
     width: 480px;
     padding: 4px;
     border: 3px solid #fcc; }
#header {
     margin: 4px;
     border: 3px solid #f99; }
div#copy {
     margin: 4px;
     border: 3px solid #f66;
     line-height: 1.5; }
#dropBox {
     width: 208px;
     font: bold smaller Arial, Helvetica,
     → sans-serif;
     padding: 4px;
     margin: 4px;
     border: 3px solid #f33;
     float: right; }
</style>
</head>
```

code continues on next page

Code 2.10 *continued*

```
<body>
<div id="content">
<div id="header">
    <h1>Alice's Adventures in
    → Wonderland</h1>
    <p class="authorName">Lewis Carroll</p>
    <h2>Chapter IV<br />
        <span class="chapterName">The Rabbit
        → Sends in a Little Bill</span>
    </h2>
</div>
<div id="copy">
<div id="dropBox">
<img src="alice12a.gif" height="236"
→ width="200" alt="Alice" />
She suddenly spread out her hand, and made
→ a snatch in the air.
</div>
<p>It was the White Rabbit, trotting slowly
→ back again, and looking anxiously about
→ as it went, as if it had lost
→ something...</p>
</div></div>
</body></html>
```

4. `<div id="content">...</a>`

An ID will not work until it is applied to an individual HTML tag within a document. Add the id attribute to the HTML tag of your choice, with the name of the ID as its value.

Notice, though, that although the number sign (#) is used to define an ID selector, it is *not* included for referencing the ID in the HTML tag.

✔ Tips

- Notice that although **dropBox** was a class in the previous section, I'm using it as an ID in this example and both seem to have about the same effect. Again, the main purpose of IDs will be for defining discrete objects on the page.

- While there is no rule against using the same name for both a class and ID, I would try to avoid this, since it will inevitably lead to confusion.

- You can mix an ID with a class and/or inline rules within an HTML tag (see "Adding Styles to an HTML Tag" and the previous section, "Defining Classes for Any Tag").

- Although I showed you in this section how to set up a style rule for an ID, you don't *have* to set up a style rule to add an ID to a tag and use it as an object with DHTML.

- The difference between IDs and classes will become apparent after you've learned more about using CSS positioning and after you've used IDs to create CSS layers. IDs are used to give each element on the screen a unique name and identity. This is why an ID is used only once, for one element in a document, to make it an object that can be manipulated with JavaScript.

DEFINING ID SELECTORS TO IDENTIFY AN OBJECT

Defining Selectors to Have the Same Styles

If you want two or more selectors to have the same declarations, just put the selectors in a list separated by commas. The general syntax for a selector grouping is shown in **Figure 2.20**.

You can define common attributes in the declaration block and then add rules for each selector individually, if you like, to refine them.

In this example (**Figure 2.21**), the heading level 1, level 2, and paragraph tags are grouped to give them the same basic styles. The heading level 2 tag is then further refined for its specific purposes.

To group selectors:

1. `h1,h2,p {...}`

   Type the list of selectors (HTML, class, or ID), separated by commas (**Code 2.11**). You can also add one or more line breaks, spaces, or tabs after a comma without interfering with the code to make it more readable.

   These selectors all receive the same declarations. CSS rules can be defined within the `style` tags in the head of your document (see "Adding Styles to a Web Page" earlier in this chapter) or in an external CSS file that is then imported or linked to the HTML document (see "Adding Styles to a Web Site" earlier in this chapter).

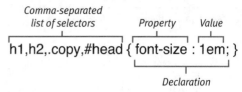

Figure 2.20 The general syntax for a list of selectors, all receiving the same declaration block.

Figure 2.21 The headers and paragraphs have the same styles set with the level-2 heading modified.

Code 2.11 the <h1>, <h2> and <p> tags will all receive the same styles.

```
<!DOCTYPE html PUBLIC "-//W3C//DTD XHTML 1.0
→ Strict//EN" "http://www.w3.org/TR/xhtml1/
→ DTD/xhtml1-strict.dtd">
<html xmlns="http://www.w3.org/1999/xhtml">
<head>
<meta http-equiv="Content-Type"
→ content="text/html; charset=utf-8" />
<title>CSS, DHTML &amp; Ajax | Defining
→ Tags with the Same Rules</title>
<style type="text/css" media="screen">
body {
      background-color: #fff;
      color: #000000;
      margin: 8px; }
h1,h2,p {
font: 1.5em Georgia, 'Times New Roman',
→ times, serif;
margin: 8px 0px;
color: #999; }
h2 {
color: red;
margin-top: 25px; }
```

code continues on next page

Code 2.11 *continued*

```
h1,h2,.authorName {
    font-variant: small-caps; }

p,#dropBox {
    font-size: 1em;
    margin: 12px 0px;
    line-height: 125%;
    color: #666; }
#dropBox {
    width: 300px;
    font: bold smaller Arial, Helvetica,
    → sans-serif;
    padding: 6px;
    border: 3px solid #999;
    margin: 0px 0px 8px 8px;
    float: right; }
</style>
</head>
<body>
<div id="content">
<div id="header">
    <h1>Alice's Adventures in
    → Wonderland</h1>
    <p class="authorName">Lewis Carroll</p>
    <h2>Chapter VII<br />
        <span class="chapterName">A Mad
        → Tea-Party </span>
    </h2>
</div>
<div id="copy">
<div id="dropBox">
<img src="alice25.gif" height="219"
→ width="288" alt="Alice" />'Do you mean
→ that you think you can find out the answer
to it?' said the March Hare.</div>
<p>There was a table set out under a tree
→ in front of the house, and the March Hare
→ and the Hatter were having tea at it…</p>
</div></div>
</body></html>
```

2. font: 1.5em Georgia, 'Times New
→ Roman', times, serif; margin:
→ 8px 0px; color: #999;

Within the curly brackets, type your style declaration(s) to be assigned to all of the listed selectors—formatted as property: value—using a semicolon (;) and separating individual declarations in the list. You can also add one or more line breaks, spaces, or tabs after a declaration without interfering with the code to make it more readable.

3. h2 {…}

You can then add or change declarations for each selector individually to tailor it to your needs. If you are overriding a declaration set in the group rule, make sure this rule comes after the group rule in your CSS (see "Determining the Cascade Order" later in this chapter).

✔ Tips

- IDs and/or classes can also be defined in the list:

  h1,h2,.authorName {…}

  or

  p,#dropBox {…}

- Grouping selectors like this can save a lot of time and repetition. But be careful—by changing the value of any of the properties in the combined declaration, you change that value for every selector in the list.

- Grouping selectors together does not directly affect their cascade order, but rather it is treated as if each one had this rule assigned to it in the order the selectors are listed.

Making a Declaration !important

The !important declaration can be added to a property-value declaration to give it the maximum weight when determining the cascade order. This ensures a declaration is applied regardless of what other rules are in play (see "Determining the Cascade Order" later in this chapter).

Figure 2.22 shows the basic syntax for using !important.

In this example (**Figure 2.23**), declarations made for the paragraph tag would normally be overridden by declarations in the .authorName class when that class is applied to the <p> tag, since its declarations come later in the code. However, if declarations for the <p> tag are made important, they will always be used, as is the case with the color red in this example.

To force a declaration to be used always:

1. p {…}

Create a CSS rule with a selector and curly brackets (**Code 2.12**). You can use an HTML, class, or ID selector. CSS rules can be defined within the style tags in the head of your document (see "Adding Styles to a Web Page" earlier in this chapter) or in an external CSS file that is then imported or linked to the HTML document (see "Adding Styles to a Web Site" earlier in this chapter).

2. color: red !important;

Type a style declaration, a space, !important, and a semicolon (;) to close the declaration.

Selector   *Important*

p { font-size : 1em !important; }

Declaration

Figure 2.22 The general syntax for making a declaration important.

Figure 2.23 Despite the fact that the .authorName class comes after the <p> tag rule, because the color declaration for paragraphs has been designated as important, it overrules the color declaration in the .authorName class.

Code 2.12 Add !important to a style declaration if you want to guarantee that it is the style applied, regardless of the cascade order.

```
<!DOCTYPE html PUBLIC "-//W3C//DTD XHTML 1.0
→ Strict//EN" "http://www.w3.org/TR/xhtml1/
→ DTD/xhtml1-strict.dtd">
<html xmlns="http://www.w3.org/1999/xhtml">
<head>
<meta http-equiv="Content-Type"
→ content="text/html; charset=utf-8" />
<title>CSS, DHTML &amp; Ajax | Making a
→ Definition !important</title>
<style type="text/css" media="screen">
body {
    font: 1.2em Georgia, 'Times New Roman',
    → times, serif;
    color: #000000;
    background-color: #fff;
    margin: 8px; }
p {
    color: red !important;
    font-family: Georgia, 'Times New
    → Roman', times, serif;
    font-size: 1em; }
p.authorName {
    color: black;
    font-family: arial, helvetica, geneva,
    sans-serif;
    font-size: 1.5em; }
</style>
</head>
<body>
<div id="content">
<div id="header">
    <h1>Alice's Adventures in
    → Wonderland</h1>
    <p class="authorName">Lewis Carroll</p>
    <h2>Chapter V<br />
        <span class="chapterName">Advice
        → from a Caterpillar</span>
    </h2>
</div>
<div id="copy">
    <p>The Caterpillar and Alice looked at
    → each other for some time in silence:
    → at last the Caterpillar took the
    → hookah out of its mouth, and
    → addressed her in a languid, sleepy
    → voice.</p>
</div></div>
</body></html>
```

3. `font-size: 1em;`

Add any other declarations you desire for this rule, making them !important, or not, as you desire.

4. `p.authorName{…}`

Add any other rules you want, designating their declarations !important as needed.

✔ Tips

- Setting a shorthand property to !important (for example background) is the same as setting each individual sub-property (for example background-color) to be !important.

- One common mistake is to locate !important *after* the semicolon in the declaration. This causes the browser to ignore the declaration and, possibly, the whole rule.

- If you are debugging your style sheet and can't get a particular style to work, try adding !important to it. If it still doesn't work, then most likely the problem is a typo rather than another style overriding it.

- Many browsers allow users to define their own style sheets for use by the browser. Most browsers follow the CSS 2.1 specification in which a user-defined style sheet overrides an author-defined style sheet.

Defining Selectors Based on Context

When a tag is surrounded by another tag, one inside another, we say that the tags are *nested*. In a nested set, the outer tag is called the *parent*, and the inner tag is the *child*. The child tag and any children of that tag are the parents' *descendants* (for more details see "Inheriting Properties from a Parent" later in this chapter). Two tags in the same parent are *siblings*, and two tags immediately next to each other are *adjacent siblings*.

So far, we have discussed ways to specify the styles of an individual element, regardless of where it is in the page. However, CSS also lets you specify the style of an element depending on its context. Using *contextual selectors*, you can specify styles based on where tags are in relationship to other tags, classes, or IDs on the page (**Table 2.1**). There are several contexts for which CSS allows us to style:

- **Descendant selectors** let you specify the style of a selector based on its position in the HTML code in relation to other selectors. Due to limitations in earlier versions of Microsoft Internet Explorer, this is currently the only reliable way to set contextual styles.

- **Child selectors** let you specify the style of elements that are the children (i.e. ,direct descendants) of another selector.

- **Adjacent sibling selectors** let you specify the style of a selector that immediately follows and shares the same parent as another selector.

- **Universal selectors** let you use a wildcard selector in place of an HTML selector.

Table 2.1

Contextual Selectors

Format	Description	Compatibility
a b c	Descendant	IE4, FF1, O3.5, S1, CSS1
a>b	Child	IE5* FF1, O3.5, S1, CSS1
a+b	Adjacent	IE7, FF1, O5, S1, CSS2
*	Universal	IE7, FF1, O4, S1, CSS2

*Mac only. IE7/Windows

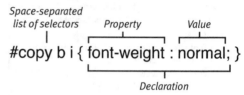

Figure 2.24 The general syntax for a contextual descendant selector.

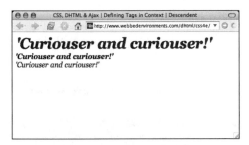

Figure 2.25 When the selector order is right, the text in the final selector's element is large and red.

Code 2.13 `<i>` tags that are nested within a`<b>` tag nested within the copy ID will receive the style.

```
<!DOCTYPE html PUBLIC "-//W3C//DTD XHTML 1.0
→ Strict//EN" "http://www.w3.org/TR/xhtml1/
→ DTD/xhtml1-strict.dtd">
<html xmlns="http://www.w3.org/1999/xhtml">
<head>
<meta http-equiv="Content-Type"
→ content="text/html; charset=utf-8" />
<title>CSS, DHTML &amp; Ajax | Defining Tags
→ in Context | Descendent</title>
<style type="text/css" media="all">
body {
    font: 1.2em Georgia, 'Times New Roman',
    → times, serif;
    background-color: #fff;
    color: #000000;
    margin: 8px; }
#copy b i {
    color: red;
    font-size: 2em;
    display: block; }
</style>
</head>
<body>
<div id="copy"><b><i>'Curiouser and
→ curiouser!'</i></b></div>
<div>
<b><i>'Curiouser and curiouser!'</i></b><br />
<i>'Curiouser and curiouser!'</i>
</div>
</body></html>
```

Descendant selectors

As discussed in "Inheriting Properties from a Parent" earlier in this chapter, descendants are the elements nested within an element, including the direct descendants (children).

We can style individual descendant elements depending on their parent selector or selectors in a space separated list. The last selector will receive the style if (and only if) it is the descendant of the preceding selectors. For example, if we wanted to prevent the italics tag from being bold if it is within the bold tag of text in the copy section of a page, we can specify that, as shown in **Figure 2.24**.

In this example (**Figure 2.25**), if the italics tag occurs and the parent is a bold tag with the ID copy, then the text will be larger, red, and a block-level element.

To define descendant selectors:

1. `#copy b i {…}`

   Type the HTML selector of the parent tag, followed by a space. You can type as many HTML selectors as you want for as many different parents as the nested tag will have, but the last selector in the list is the one that receives all the styles in the rule. You can specify exactly how a tag is styled based on where it is nested in the code and who its parents are (**Code 2.13**).

2. `<div id="copy"><b><i>…</i></b></div>`

   The style will be applied if, and only if, the final selector occurs as a descendant nested somewhere within the previous selectors.

continues on next page

✔ Tips

- Like grouped selectors, contextual selectors can include class selectors (dependent or independent) and/or ID selectors in the list, as well as HTML selectors.

- It is important to understand that descendant contextual selector styling is an incredibly powerful tool in Web design. When we examine layout techniques later in the book (Chapter 21), you'll discover that using contextual selectors lets you move HTML code around in your page and have it automatically restyled.

Child selectors

If you want to style only a parent's child elements (*not* a "grandchild" descendant), you must specify the parent selector and child selector separated by a chevron (>).

Figure 2.26 shows the general syntax of child contextual selectors.

In this example (**Figure 2.27**), only if the italics tag is within a bold element but not within another element will the text in the <i> tag be larger, red, and a block-level element.

To define child selectors:

1. b>i {…}

   Type the selector for the parent element (HTML, class or ID), followed by a chevron (>) and the child selector (HTML, class or ID) to which you want to apply the styles (**Code 2.14**).

2. <b><i>…</i></b>

   If, and only if, the second selector is an immediate child element nested in the element will the styles from Step 1 be applied. Placing the tag within any other HTML tags will disrupt the pattern.

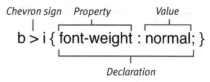

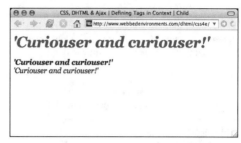

Figure 2.26 The syntax for child contextual selectors.

Figure 2.27 The second selector is the child of the first, so the text in the second element is large and red.

Code 2.14 <i> tags that are the direct child of a <b> tag are styled as red, large, and a block element.

```
<!DOCTYPE html PUBLIC "-//W3C//DTD XHTML 1.0
→ Strict//EN" "http://www.w3.org/TR/xhtml1/
→ DTD/xhtml1-strict.dtd">
<html xmlns="http://www.w3.org/1999/xhtml">
<head>
<meta http-equiv="Content-Type"
→ content="text/html; charset=utf-8" />
<title>CSS, DHTML &amp; Ajax | Defining
→ Tags in Context | Child</title>
<style type="text/css" media="all">
body {
     font: 1.2em Georgia, 'Times New Roman',
     → times, serif;
     background-color: #fff;
     color: #000000;
     margin: 8px; }
b>i {
     color: red;
     font-size: 2em;
     display: block; }
</style>
</head>
<body>
<div>
<b><i>'Curiouser and curiouser!'</i></b><br />
<b><span class="odd"><i>'Curiouser and
→ curiouser!'</i></span></b><br />
<i>'Curiouser and curiouser!'</i>
</div>
</body></html>
```

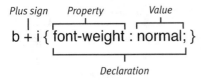

Figure 2.28 The general syntax for adjacent sibling contextual selectors.

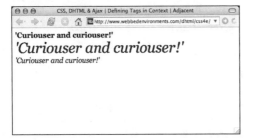

Figure 2.29 When the second tag is placed immediately after the first, the text is large and red in the second element.

Code 2.15 When an <i> tag occurs directly after a<b> tag, the style is applied.

```
<!DOCTYPE html PUBLIC "-//W3C//DTD XHTML 1.0
→ Strict//EN" "http://www.w3.org/TR/xhtml1/
→ DTD/xhtml1-strict.dtd">
<html xmlns="http://www.w3.org/1999/xhtml">
<head>
<meta http-equiv="Content-Type"
→ content="text/html; charset=utf-8" />
<title>CSS, DHTML &amp; Ajax | Defining Tags
→ in Context | Adjacent</title>
<style type="text/css" media="all">
body {
    font: 1.2em Georgia, 'Times New Roman',
    → times, serif;
    background-color: #fff;
    color: #000000;
    margin: 8px; }
b + i {
    color: red;
    font-size: 2em;
    display: block; }
</style>
</head>
<body>
<div>
<b>'Curiouser and curiouser!' </b>
<i>'Curiouser and curiouser!' </i>
<i>'Curiouser and curiouser!' </i>
</div>
</body></html>
```

Adjacent sibling selectors

Known as the adjacent sibling selector, this grouping lets you define a style for the first occurrence of a tag that appears immediately after another tag.

Figure 2.28 shows the general syntax of adjacent sibling contextual selectors.

In this example (**Figure 2.29**), the first italics tag that occurs immediately after a bold tag will be a block-level element that is larger and red.

To define adjacent sibling selectors:

1. b + i {…}

Type the selector for the first element (HTML, class or ID), a plus sign (+), and then the selector (HTML, class or ID) for the adjacent element to which you want the style applied (**Code 2.15**).

2. <b>…</b><i>…</i>

The styles will be applied to the second selector if, and only if, the second selector occurs immediately after first selector. Placing any tag between them (even a break tag) will disrupt the pattern.

DEFINING SELECTORS BASED ON CONTEXT

The universal selector

The universal selector is a wild card character that works as a stand-in to represent that any HTML type selector can appear in that position in a contextual list.

The general syntax for using a universal selector is given in **Figure 2.30**. Keep in mind, though, that the universal selector can be used in place of any HTML selector in any configuration, not just in the descendant selector shown in this section.

In this example (**Figure 2.31**), a universal selector is used in a descendant selector, meaning that any italics tag which has a "grandparent" one level above that uses the #copy ID will be a block-level element that is larger and red, regardless of which HTML tags are in between. However, if the #copy ID is more or less than one level up, the styles are not applied.

To use the universal selector:

1. #copy * i {…}

   Type a selector in one of the formats explained above (descendant, child, or adjacent sibling), substituting an asterisk (*) for any of the HTML selectors that you do not want to exactly define (**Code 2.16**). This selector is then a wildcard that can be any HTML tag.

2. <div id="copy"><b><i>…</i></b></div>

   HTML that is structured using the format provided in Step 1 will be assigned the style, allowing for any HTML tag to take the place of the asterisk.

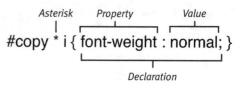

Figure 2.30 The general syntax for a universal selector.

Figure 2.31 Regardless of the tag or tags between them, when the italics tag is the descendant of the copy ID, the text is large and red.

Code 2.16 Any <i> tag nested in *any* tag nested within the copy ID will receive the style.

```
<!DOCTYPE html PUBLIC "-//W3C//DTD XHTML 1.0
→ Strict//EN" "http://www.w3.org/TR/xhtml1/
→ DTD/xhtml1-strict.dtd">
<html xmlns="http://www.w3.org/1999/xhtml">
<head>
<meta http-equiv="Content-Type"
→ content="text/html; charset=utf-8" />
<title>CSS, DHTML &amp; Ajax | Defining Tags
→ in Context | Universal</title>
<style type="text/css" media="all">
body {
     font: 1.2em Georgia, 'Times New Roman',
     → times, serif;
     background-color: #fff;
     color: #000000;
     margin: 8px; }
#copy * i {
     color: red;
     font-size: 2em;
     display: block; }
</style>
</head>
<body>
<div id="copy"><b><i>'Curiouser and
→ curiouser!'</i></b></div>
<div id="copy"><span class="odd">
→ <i>'Curiouser and curiouser!'</i>
→ </span></div>
<div id="copy"><i>'Curiouser and curiouser!'
→ </i></div>
</body></html>
```

Table 2.2

Attribute Selectors		
FORMAT	DESCRIPTION	COMPATIBILITY
[attr]	Attribute	IE7, FF1.5, O5, S2, CSS2
[attr="value"]	Exact value	IE7, FF1.5, O5, S2, CSS2
[attr~="value"]	Value in space-separated list	IE7, FF1.5, O5, S2, CSS2
[attr|="value"]	Begins with value in hyphen-separated list	IE7, FF1.5, O5, S2, CSS2

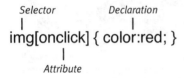

Figure 2.32 The general syntax for an attribute selector.

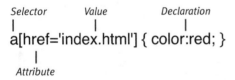

Figure 2.33 The general syntax for an exact value attribute selector.

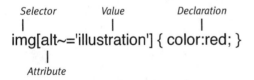

Figure 2.34 The general syntax for a value in a space-separated list-attribute selector.

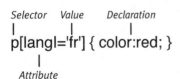

Figure 2.35 The general syntax for a value at the beginning of a hyphen-separated list-attribute selector.

Defining Selectors Based on Tag Attributes

Although style attributes should all be handled by CSS, many HTML tags still have attributes that define how they behave. For example, the image tag (img) always includes the src attribute to define the source for the image file to be loaded.

Styles can be assigned to an HTML element based on an attribute or an attribute value, allowing you to set styles if the attribute has been set, is or is not a specific value, or contains a specific value (**Table 2.2**).

The syntax for the different attribute selectors is shown in **Figures 2.32**, **2.33**, **2.34**, and **2.35**.

continues on next page

In this example (**Figure 2.36**), I've done the following:

◆ Set up a list of navigation links

◆ Set the style of the navigation link that has the URL "index.html" to be a good deal larger than the rest

◆ Set images with the `onclick` event handler to have a thick, red border

◆ Set styles for the images with an `alt` tag that contains the word "Illustration" in it.

Figure 2.36 The link for "Cover" is styled to make it more prominent; the text in French is black; the image labeled as an "illustration" has a red double-line border and the image with an `onclick` event handler has a thick solid red border.

To set styles based on an element's attributes:

1. `img[onclick] {…}`

To set styles based on the existence of an attribute, type the selector you want to style (HTML, class, or ID), an opening square bracket, the name of the attribute you want to check for, and the closing square bracket (**Code 2.17**).

This will assign the styles you declare only if the tag has this attribute assigned to it, regardless of the value.

2. `a[href='index.html'] {…}`

To set styles based on an attribute's exact value, type the selector you want to style (HTML, class, or ID), an opening square bracket, the name of the attribute you want to check for, an equal sign (=), the value you are testing for in quotes ('…'), and the closing square bracket.

This will assign the styles you declare only if the tag has this attribute assigned to it with the exact assigned value.

Code 2.17 There are several ways to define styles based on the attributes defined within an HTML tag.

```
<!DOCTYPE html PUBLIC "-//W3C//DTD XHTML 1.0
→ Strict//EN" "http://www.w3.org/TR/
→ xhtml1/DTD/xhtml1-strict.dtd">
<html xmlns="http://www.w3.org/1999/xhtml">
<head>
<meta http-equiv="Content-Type"
→ content="text/html; charset=utf-8" />
<title>CSS, DHTML &amp; Ajax | Defining Tags
→ in Context | Universal</title>
<style type="text/css" media="all">
body {
    font: 1.2em Georgia, 'Times New Roman',
    → times, serif;
    background-color: #fff;
    color: #000000;
    margin: 8px; }
a {
    color: red; }
img[onclick] {
    float: left;
    border: 4px red solid; }
a[href='index.html'] {
    font-size: 3em;
    color: black;
    text-decoration: none; }
img[alt~='Illustration'] {
    float: left;
    border: 6px red double; }
p[lang|="fr"] {
    color: black; }
p[lang|="en"] {
    color: #999; }
</style>
</head>
<body>
<div><a href="index.html">Cover</a> |
<a href="#">Table of Content</a> |
<a href="#">Photo Gallery</a> |
<a href="#">Credits</a>
<p lang="en-US">In US English: The color of
→ the leaves</p>
<p lang="en-UK">In UK English: The colour of
→ the leaves</p>
<p lang="fr">In French: La couleur des
→ feuilles</p>
</div>
<div>
<img src="aliceInLeaves.jpg"
onclick="photocredits('jason')" alt="Photo-
→ of-Alice" width="363" height="484" />
<img src="alice15a.gif" alt="Illustration of
→ Alice" width="363" height="480" />
</div>
</body></html>
```

3. img[alt~='Illustration'] {…}

To set styles based on an attribute's value that is within a list of space separated values (for example, a particular word in a sentence), type the selector you want to style (HTML, class, or ID), an opening square bracket, the name of the attribute you want to check for, a tilde (~), an equal sign (=), the value you are testing for in quotes ('…'), and the closing square bracket.

This will assign the styles you declare only if the tag has this attribute assigned to it with a value that contains the value as part of a list separated by spaces. Generally, this means that it is a word in a sentence. Partial words do not count. So, for example, testing for 'Ill' in this example will not work.

4. p[lang|='en'] {…}

To set styles based on an attribute's value being the first in a list separated by hyphens, type the selector you want to style (HTML, class, or ID), an opening square bracket, the name of the attribute you want to check for, a bar (|), an equal sign (=), the value you are testing for in quotes ('…'), and the closing square bracket.

This will assign the styles you declare only if the tag has this attribute assigned to it with a value that contains the value at the beginning of list separated by hyphens. Generally, this is used for styling languages as an alternative to using the language pseudo-class.

DEFINING SELECTORS BASED ON TAG ATTRIBUTES

Working with Pseudo-Classes

Many HTML elements have special states or uses associated with them that can be styled independently. One prime example of this is the link tag (`<a>`), which has not only its normal state, but also a visited state, in which the visitor has already been to the page represented by the link.

A *pseudo-class* (**Table 2.3**) is a predefined state or use of an element that can be styled independently of the default state of the element.

Picking Link Styles

Most browsers default to blue for unvisited links and either red or purple for visited ones. The problem with using two different colors for visited and unvisited links is that visitors may not remember which color is for which type of link. The colors you choose need to distinguish links from other text on the screen and to distinguish among the different states (link, visited, hover, and active), without dominating the screen and becoming distracting.

I recommend using a color for unvisited links that contrasts with both the page's background color and the text color. Then, for visited links, use a darker or lighter version of the same color that contrasts with the background but is dimmer than the unvisited-link color. Brighter unfollowed links will then stand out dramatically from dimmer followed links.

For example, if I were designing a page with a white background and black text, I might use bright red for my links (#ff0000) and pale red (#ff6666) for visited links. The brighter version stands out; the paler version is less distinctive, but still obviously a link.

Table 2.3

Pseud-Classes

PSEUDO-CLASS	DESCRIPTION	COMPATIBILITY
:active	Element being clicked	IE4*, FF1, O3.5, S1, CSS1
:first-child	Element that is the first child of another element	IE5/7, FF1, O7, S1, CSS1
:focus	Element that has screen focus	IE5*, FF1, O7, S1, CSS2
:hover	Element with mouse cursor over it	IE4*, FF1, O3.5, S1, CSS2
:lang()	Element with language code defined	FF1.5, O8.5, S1.5, CSS2
:link	Element that has not been visited	IE4, FF1, O3.5, S1, CSS1
:visited	Element that has been visited	IE4, FF1, O3.5, S1, CSS1

* Only available for link tags until IE7

Figure 2.37 Both :link pseudo classes are set so that unfollowed links are bold and bright red, while followed links are a duller, paler red.

Styling link pseudo-classes

Most browsers allow you to specify link colors for different states (a link, a visited link, and an active link) in the <body> tag of the document. With CSS, you can define not only color, but also any other CSS properties that you want the links to have.

Although a link is a tag (<a>), its individual states are not. To set properties for these states, you have to use the pseudo-classes associated with each state that a link can have:

◆ :link lets you declare the appearance of hypertext links that have not yet been selected.

◆ :visited lets you set the appearance of links that the visitor selected previously—that is, the URL of the href attribute in the tag is part of the browser's history.

In this example (**Figure 2.37**), I've set up styles for the general <a> tag style and separate styles for the link (unvisited) and visited link states. For ideas on what styles to use with links, check out the sidebar "Picking Link Styles."

Text Decoration: to Underline or Not

Underlining has been the standard way of indicating a hypertext link on the Web since its inception. The problem with underlining links is that if you have many links on a page, it becomes an impenetrable mass of lines, and the text is difficult to read. Furthermore, if visitors have underlining turned off, they cannot see links on the page, especially if both link and text colors are the same.

CSS allows you to turn off underlining for links, overriding the visitor's preference. I recommend this practice and prefer to rely on clear color choices to highlight hypertext links. You can use underlining with the :hover state, so when visitors place the mouse over a link, they see a clear visual change.

To set contrasting link appearances:

1. *a* {...}

Although not required, it's best to first define the general anchor style (**Code 2.18**). This differs from setting the :link pseudo-class in that these styles are applied to all of the link pseudo classes. So you want to declare any styles that will remain constant or are only changed in one of the states.

2. a:link {...}

Type the selector (HTML, class, or ID) of the element you want to style, followed by a colon (:), and then link. You can override styles set for the anchor tag, but this rule should always come before the :visited pseudo-class.

3. a:visited {...}

Type the selector (HTML, class, or ID) of the element you want to style, followed by a colon (:), and then visited.

✔ Tips

■ You can also apply the dynamic pseudo-classes :hover, :active , and :focus. See the next section for more information. However, it occurs to me that there should be one more pseudo-class that the W3C has not addressed (see the sidebar "The Missing Link (Pseudo-Class").

■ The link styles should be inherited by the different states (see "Inheriting Properties from a Parent" later in this chapter). The font you set for the :link appearance, for example, should be inherited by the :active, :visited, and :hover states. But some inconsistencies exist among browsers. That's why I recommend always putting common styles in the anchor tag rule.

Code 2.18 If the Web page for a link has not been visited, the :link pseudo-class styles are used. If visited, then the :visited pseudo-class styles are used.

```
<!DOCTYPE html PUBLIC "-//W3C//DTD XHTML 1.0
→ Strict//EN" "http://www.w3.org/TR/xhtml1/
→ DTD/xhtml1-strict.dtd">
<html xmlns="http://www.w3.org/1999/xhtml">
<head>
<meta http-equiv="Content-Type"
→ content="text/html; charset=utf-8" />
<title>CSS, DHTML &amp; Ajax | Working with
→ Pseudo-classes | Link</title>
<style type="text/css" media="screen">
body {
     font-size: 1.2em;
     font-family: Georgia, "Times New
     → Roman", times, serif;
     color: #000000;
     background-color: #fff;
     margin: 8px; }
#navigation {
     width: 240px;
     margin: 0px 8px 8px 0px;
     border: 3px solid #ccc;
     float: left; }
a {
     display: block;
     font-size: larger;
     padding: 2px 4px;
     text-decoration: none;
     border-bottom: 1px solid #ccc;
     font: small Arial, Helvetica,
     → sans-serif; }
a:link {
     color: #f00;
     font-weight: bold; }
     a:visited {
     color: #c99; }
.dropBox {
     width: 228px;
     border: 3px solid #999;
     margin: 0px 0px 8px 8px;
     float: right; }
</style>
</head>
<body>
<div id="navigation">
<p>Flip To Chapter</p>
<a href="#">A Mad Tea-Party</a>
<a href="#">The Queen's Croquet-Ground</a>
```

code continues on next page

Code 2.18 *continued*

```
<a href="index.html">The Mock Turtle's
→ Story</a>
<a href="#">The Lobster Quadrille</a>
<a href="index.html">Who Stole The Tarts? </a>
<a href="#">Alice's Evidence</a>
<a href="index.html">&lArr; Previous </a>
</div>
<div id="header">
<h1>Alice's Adventures in Wonderland</h1>
<p class="author">Lewis Carroll</p>
<form action="#" method="get" id="FormName">
    Search Book:
    <input class="formText" type="text"
    → name="searchTerm" size="24" />
    <input class="formButton" type="submit"
    → name="findSearchTerm" value="Find" />
</form>
<br />
<h2>CHAPTER IX
    <span class="chapterTitle"> The Mock
    → Turtle's Story </span></h2>
</div>
<div id="copy">
<div class="dropBox">
<img src="alice34a.gif" height="258"
→ width="220" alt="" />So they went up
→ to the Mock Turtle, who looked at them
→ with large eyes full of tears, but said
→ nothing.</div>
<p>'You can't think how glad I am to see
→ you again, you dear old thing!…</p>
</div>
</body></html>
```

- The Web is a hypertext medium, so it is important that users be able to distinguish among text, links, and visited links. Because you can't count on users having their Underline Links option turned on, it's a good idea to set the link appearance for every document.

- If you use too many colors, your visitors may not be able to tell which words are links and which are not.

- I set the link styles for the entire page in this example, but because the links are located only in the navigation, I should probably set them contextually so that those styles are only applied to the navigation links. Otherwise all of the links on the page would force a line break. To do that, I would simply have used:

  #navigation a {…}

  #navigation a:link {…}

  #navigation a:visited {…}

  Then those styles would be applied only to links in the navigation layer.

- By associating a class name with the link style, you can set multiple link colors for showing different kinds of links.

The Missing Link (Pseudo-Class)

It seems to me that one link pseudo-class is absent from the available pseudo-classes: :current. A :current pseudo class—if it existed, which it does *not*—could be used to set the style of a link if it was the same as the page currently being displayed. That is, you could set a special style for the menu link of the currently displayed page. This would allow you to easily set a style for the currently selected option in menus.

Until that day arrives, however, we'll have to make do with coding these menu links manually or using a system like the one shown in "Styling Links and Navigation" in Chapter 21.

Styling dynamic pseudo-classes

Once loaded, Web pages are far from static. Users usually start interacting with the page right away, moving their cursors across the screen and clicking hither and yon. The dynamic pseudo-classes allow you to style elements as the user interacts with them, providing visual feedback:

◆ :hover lets you set the appearance of the element when the cursor is hovering over it.

◆ :active sets the style of the element while it is being clicked or selected.

◆ :focus is used for elements that can receive focus, like form text fields.

Although dynamic pseudo-classes can be used to apply styles to any HTML element in theory, earlier versions of Internet Explorer only recognize them when associated with the anchor element. However, using them with other elements will not stop the page from working in Internet Explorer 6 and earlier, but they should only be relied on to enhance the user experience and not relate critical information.

In this example (**Figures 2.38**, **2.39**, **2.40**, and **2.41**), the :hover and :active pseudo-classes have been applied to a form input button (using the class name .formButton) to create styles when users hover their cursors over the button (Figure 2.39) and click it (Figure 2.40). In addition, the form text input box has the :focus pseudo-class applied to style the box when the user clicks it (Figure 2.41).

Figure 2.38 The page when it first loads, before any dynamic styles are applied.

Figure 2.39 The style for a form button when viewers hover their cursors over it (this is the :hover pseudo-class).

Figure 2.40 The style for a form button that has just been clicked (the :active pseudo-class).

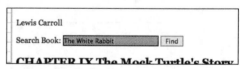

Figure 2.41 The style for a form field that has been clicked (:focus pseudo-class).

Code 2.19 Dynamic styles depend on interaction from the visitor. When they move the mouse cursor over an element, the :hover pseudo-class style is used. Clicking an element activates the :active styles, while clicking in a form field activates the :focus pseudo-class.

```
<!DOCTYPE html PUBLIC "-//W3C//DTD XHTML 1.0
→ Strict//EN" "http://www.w3.org/TR/xhtml1/
→ DTD/xhtml1-strict.dtd">
<html xmlns="http://www.w3.org/1999/xhtml">
<head>
<meta http-equiv="Content-Type"
→ content="text/html; charset=utf-8" />
<title>CSS, DHTML &amp; Ajax | Working with
→ Pseudo-classes | Dynamic</title>
<style type="text/css" media="screen">
body {
     font-size: 1em;
     font-family: Georgia, "Times New
     → Roman", times, serif;
     color: #000000;
     background-color: #fff;
     margin: 8px; }
#navigation {
     width: 240px;
     margin: 0px 8px 8px 0px;
     border: 3px solid #ccc;
     float: left;
     font: small Arial, Helvetica, sans-serif }
a {
     color: #ff0000;
     padding: 2px 4px;
     text-decoration: none;
     border-bottom: 1px dotted #999;
     display: block;
     border-bottom: 1px solid #ccc; }
input.formButton {
     border: 2px solid #999;
     background-color: #eee; }
input.formButton:hover {
     border: 2px solid red;
     color: #fdd;
     background-color: red; }
input.formButton:active {
     color: red;
     border: 2px solid red;
     background-color: #fdd; }
input.formText {
     border: 2px solid #999;
     background-color: #fff; }
input.formText:focus {
     border: 2px solid red;
     background-color: #fcc; }
```
code continues on next page

To define a dynamic pseudo-class:

1. input.formButton {…}

Although optional, it's generally a good idea to set the default, non-dynamic style for the element(s) you are about to apply dynamic styles to (**Code 2.19**).

2. input.formButton:hover

Type the selector (HTML, class, or ID), a colon (:), and then hover.

As soon as the mouse pointer enters the element's box (see Chapter 6), the style change will occur.

3. input.formButton:active {…}

Type the selector (HTML, class, or ID), a colon (:), and then active.

As soon as the mouse clicks within the element's box (see Chapter 6), the style change will occur and then revert to either the hover or default style when released.

4. input.formText:focus {…}

Type the selector (HTML, class, or ID), a colon (:), and then focus.

As soon as the element receives focus (is clicked in or tabbed to), the style change will occur and revert to the hover or default style when the element looses focus (called *blur*).

continues on next page

✔ Tips

■ The dynamic pseudo-classes are often associated with the link tag (<a>), allowing users to see when they are hovering over a link or clicking it. For more details on setting link styles, see Chapter 21.

■ The order in which you define your link and dynamic pseudo-classes makes a difference for some earlier browsers. For example, placing the :hover pseudo-class before the :visited pseudo-class keeps :hover from working after a link has been visited. For best results, define your styles in this order: link, visited, hover, focus, and active.

■ You may want to set :focus if you're setting :hover. Why? Hover is applied only to non-keyboard (mouse) interactions with the element. For visitors that cannot or prefer not to use a mouse and instead use only a keyboard to navigate a Web page,:focus will apply.

■ I recommend using caution when changing some attributes for :hover. Changing things such as typeface, font size, and weight may make the text grow larger than the space reserved for it in the layout, forcing the whole page to refresh, which can really annoy viewers.

Code 2.19 *continued*

```
.dropBox {
    width: 228px;
    border: 3px solid #999;
    margin: 0px 0px 8px 8px;
    float: right; }
</style>
</head>
<body>
<div id="navigation">
<p>Flip To Chapter</p>
<a href="#">A Mad Tea-Party</a>
<a href="#">The Queen's Croquet-Ground</a>
<a href="../Copy of LinkStyle/index.html">
→ The Mock Turtle's Story</a>
<a href="#">The Lobster Quadrille</a>
<a href="#">Who Stole The Tarts? </a>
<a href="#">Alice's Evidence</a>
<a href="#">&lArr; Previous </a>
</div>
<div id="header">
<h1>Alice's Adventures in Wonderland</h1>
<p class="author">Lewis Carroll</p>
<form action="#" method="get" id="FormName">
    Search Book:
    <input class="formText" type="text"
    → name="searchTerm" size="24" />
    <input class="formButton" type="submit"
    → name="findSearchTerm" value="Find" />
</form>
<h2>CHAPTER IX
    <span class="chapterTitle"> The Mock
    → Turtle's Story </span></h2>
</div>
<div id="copy">
<div class="dropBox">
<img src="alice34a.gif" height="258"
→ width="220" alt="" />So they went up
→ to the Mock Turtle, who looked at them
→ with large eyes full of tears, but said
→ nothing.</div>
<p>'You can't think how glad I am to see
→ you again, you dear old thing!…</p>
</div>
</body></html>
```

Figure 2.42 Because the paragraph is the first child immediately after its parent, it is styled big and red so that it stands out.

Code 2.20 If the <p> tag is the very first child element of another element, then styles will be applied to it.

```
<!DOCTYPE html PUBLIC "-//W3C//DTD XHTML 1.0
→ Strict//EN" "http://www.w3.org/TR/xhtml1/
→ DTD/xhtml1-strict.dtd">
<html xmlns="http://www.w3.org/1999/xhtml">
<head>
<meta http-equiv="Content-Type"
→ content="text/html; charset=utf-8" />
<title>CSS, DHTML &amp; Ajax | Working with
→ Pseudo-classes | First-Child</title>
<style type="text/css" media="screen">
body {
    font-size: 1em;
    font-family: Georgia, "Times New
    → Roman", times, serif;
    color: #000000;
    background-colr: #fff;
    margin: 8px; }
#navigation {
    width: 240px;
    margin: 0px 8px 8px 0px;
    border: 3px solid #ccc;
    float: left;
    font: small Arial, Helvetica, sans-serif }
a {
    color: #ff0000;
    padding: 2px 4px;
    text-decoration: none;
    display: block;
    border-bottom: 1px solid #ccc; }
```
                        code continues on next page

First child pseudo-class

Designers often want to apply a style to an element that is the first element to appear within another element, i.e., a parent's first child.

The `:first-child` pseudo-class lets you specify how to style a particular element when it is the first descendant immediately after its parent.

For example, you might want to style the first paragraph tag of any parent element in a particular way. In **Figure 2.42**, for instance, the text "Flip to a Chapter" is made more prominent.

To style the first-child of an element:

1. `p:first-child {…}`

   Type the selector (HTML, class, or ID) of the element you want to style, a colon (`:`), and then `first-child` (**Code 2.20**).

2. `<div id="navigation"><p>…</p></div>`

   Set up your HTML with the selector from Step 1 by placing it immediately after its parent tag where you want that style applied. Then if, and only if, the element is the first child element after its parent, it will receive the style.

Code 2.20 *continued*

```
p:first-child {
    color: red;
    font-weight: bold;
    font-size: 1.2em; }
.dropBox {
    width: 228px;
    border: 3px solid #999;
    margin: 0px 0px 8px 8px;
    float: right; }
</style>
</head>
<body>
<div id="navigation">
<p>Flip To Chapter</p>
<a href="#">A Mad Tea-Party</a>
<a href="#">The Queen's Croquet-Ground</a>
<a href="index.html">The Mock Turtle's Story</a>
<a href="#">The Lobster Quadrille</a>
<a href="#">Who Stole The Tarts? </a>
<a href="#">Alice's Evidence</a>
<a href="#">&lArr; Previous </a>
</div>
<div id="header">
<h1>Alice's Adventures in Wonderland</h1>
<p class="author">Lewis Carroll</p>
<form action="#" method="get" id="FormName">
    Search Book:
    <input class="formText" type="text" name="searchTerm" size="24" />
    <input class="formButton" type="submit" name="findSearchTerm" value="Find" />
</form>
<h2>CHAPTER IX
    <span class="chapterTitle"> The Mock Turtle's Story </span></h2>
</div>
<div id="copy">
<p>'You can't think how glad I am to see you again, you dear old thing!…</p>
<div class="dropBox">
<img src="alice34a.gif" height="258" width="220" alt="" />So they went up to the Mock Turtle, who
→ looked at them with large eyes full of tears, but said nothing.</div></div>
</body></html>
```

Figure 2.43 The text in the paragraphs that is labeled as being in French is bright red while English text is a lighter red. (Sorry about the French translation.)

Code 2.21 If the language attribute of a paragraph is set to French (fr), then it will be red. English (en) will be a paler shade of red.

```
<!DOCTYPE html PUBLIC "-//W3C//DTD XHTML 1.0
→ Strict//EN" "http://www.w3.org/TR/xhtml1/
→ DTD/xhtml1-strict.dtd">
<html xmlns="http://www.w3.org/1999/xhtml">
<head>
<meta http-equiv="Content-Type"
→ content="text/html; charset=iso-8859-1" />
<title>CSS, DHTML &amp; Ajax | Working with
→ Pseudo-classes | Language</title>
<style type="text/css" media="screen">
body {
    font-size: 1em;
    font-family: Georgia, "Times New
    → Roman", times, serif;
    color: #000000;
    background-color: fff;
    margin: 8px; }
#navigation {
    width: 240px;
    margin: 0px 8px 8px 0px;
    border: 3px solid #ccc;
    float: left;
    font: small Arial, Helvetica,
    → sans-serif; }
a {
    padding: 2px 4px;
    text-decoration: none;
    display: block;
    border-bottom: 1px solid #ccc; }
```

code continues on next page

Styling for a particular language

The World Wide Web is just that, all around the world, which means that anyone, virtually anywhere, can see your pages. This also means that Web pages are being created in any number of different languages.

The :lang() pseudo-class lets you specify styles that are dependent upon the language the Web page specifies it is using.

This next example highlights in red any text that is French (**Figure 2.43**).

To set a style for a particular language:

1. `p:lang(fr) {…}`

   Type the selector (HTML, class, or ID) of the element you want to style, a colon (:), lang, and the letter code for the language you are defining within parentheses (**Code 2.21**).

2. `<p lang="fr">…</p>`

   Set up your tag in the HTML with the language attributes as needed. If the indicated selector has its language attribute equal to the same value you indicated in parentheses in Step 1, the style will be applied.

✔ Tips

■ You can actually use any string as the language letter code, as long as it matches the value in the HTML. However, the W3C recommends using the codes from RFC 3066 or its successor. For a list of the current codes, check out: evertype.com/standards/iso639/iana-lang-assignments.html

Code 2.21 *continued*

```
p:lang(fr) {
     color:#f00; }
p:lang(en) {
     color:#f99; }
.dropBox {
     width: 228px;
     border: 3px solid #999;
     margin: 0px 0px 8px 8px;
     float: right; }
</style>
</head>
<body>
<div id="navigation">
<p>Flip To Chapter</p>
<a href="#">A Mad Tea-Party</a>
<a href="#">The Queen's Croquet-Ground</a>
<a href="index.html">The Mock Turtle's Story</a>
<a href="#">The Lobster Quadrille</a>
<a href="#">Who Stole The Tarts? </a>
<a href="#">Alice's Evidence</a>
<a href="#">&lArr; Previous </a>
</div>
<div id="header">
<h1>Alice's Adventures in Wonderland</h1>
<p class="author">Lewis Carroll</p>
<form action="#" method="get" id="FormName">
     Search Book:
     <input class="formText" type="text" name="searchTerm" size="24" />
     <input class="formButton" type="submit" name="findSearchTerm" value="Find" />
</form>
<h2>CHAPTER IX
     <span class="chapterTitle"> The Mock Turtle's Story </span></h2>
</div>
<div id="copy">
<div class="dropBox">
<img src="alice34a.gif" height="258" width="220" alt="" />So they went up to the Mock Turtle,
→ who looked at them with large eyes full of tears, but said nothing.</div>
<p lang="en">'You can't think how glad I am to see you again, you dear old thing!…</p>
<p lang="fr">Alice était très heureuse de la trouver dans un trempe si plaisant, et pensé à
→ elle-même que peut-être c'était seulement le poivre qui avait fait son si sauvage quand elles
→ se sont réunies dans la cuisine.</p>
</div>
</body></html>
```

Figure 2.44 The drop cap is applied to the first letter of the paragraph, making it large, a different font, red, and floating next to the paragraph.

Working with Pseudo-Elements

A *pseudo-element* is a specific, unique part of an element—such as the first letter or first line of a paragraph—the appearance of which can be controlled independent of the rest of the element. For a list of other pseudo-elements, see **Table 2.4**.

Styling the first letter of an element

You can access the first letter of any block of text directly using the :first-letter pseudo-element.

In this example (**Figure 2.44**), the first letter of paragraphs given the dropCap class will be made much larger, bolder, red, and will float to the left of the rest of the text in the paragraph.

continues on next page

Table 2.4

Pseudo-Elements		
PSEUDO-ELEMENT	DESCRIPTION	COMPATIBILITY
:first-letter	First letter in element	IE5*, FF1, O3.5, S1, CSS1
:first-line	First line of text in element	IE5*, FF1, O3.5, S1, CSS1
:after	Space immediately before element	FF1, O5, S1, CSS2
:before	Space immediately after element	FF1, O5, S1, CSS2
* IE5.5 for Windows		

WORKING WITH PSEUDO-ELEMENTS

To set a drop cap:

1. p {…}

Although not required, it's generally a good idea to set the default style of the selector for which you will be styling the :first-letter pseudo-element (**Code 2.22**).

2. p.dropCap:first-letter {…}

Type the selector (HTML, class, or ID) of which you want to style the first letter, a colon (:), and then first-letter.

In this example, we are using a dependent class, so we will need to set the class in the relevant tag (see "Defining Classes for Any Tag" earlier in this chapter).

3. <p class="dropCap">…</p>

Add the class attribute to the relevant HTML tag. Although you do not have to use a class, generally, you will want to be able to selectively style the first letter of elements rather than styling them all universally.

✔ Tips

■ Drop-cap-style letters are a time-honored way of starting a new section or chapter of lengthy text by making the first letter of a paragraph larger than subsequent letters, and moving the first several lines of text over to accommodate the larger letter. Medieval monks used drop caps with illuminated manuscripts—now you can use them on the Web.

■ To avoid odd positioning, it's a good idea to clear floating in the paragraph immediately after the paragraph with the drop cap in it. To do this, add clear:left to the paragraph, either as an inline style or as part of a class or ID.

Code 2.22 The first letter of paragraphs given the .dropCap class will stand off from the rest of the paragraph.

```
<!DOCTYPE html PUBLIC "-//W3C//DTD XHTML 1.0
→ Strict//EN" "http://www.w3.org/TR/xhtml1/
→ DTD/xhtml1-strict.dtd">
<html xmlns="http://www.w3.org/1999/xhtml">
<head>
<meta http-equiv="Content-Type"
→ content="text/html; charset=utf-8" />
<title>CSS, DHTML &amp; Ajax | Styling the
→ First-letter of an Element</title>
<style type="text/css" media="all">
body {
    font-size: 1.2em;
    font-family: Georgia, "Times New
    → Roman", times, serif;
    color: #000000;
    background-color: #fff;
    margin: 8px; }
#navigation {
    width: 240px;
    margin: 0px 8px 8px 0px;
    border: 3px solid #ccc;
    float: left;
    font: small Arial, Helvetica,
    → sans-serif; }
p {
    line-height: 150%; }
    p.dropCap:first-letter {
    font: bold 700% 'party let', 'comic
    → sans MS', fantasy;
    margin-right: 12px;
    color: red;
    float: left; }
.dropBox {
    width: 228px;
    padding: 6px;
    border: 3px solid #999;
    margin: 0px 0px 8px 8px;
    float: right; }
</style>
</head>
<body>
<div id="header">
<h1>Alice's Adventures in Wonderland</h1>
<p class="author">Lewis Carroll</p>
<h2>CHAPTER IX
    <span class="chapterTitle">The Lobster
    → Quadrille</span></h2>
</div>
```

code continues on next page

Code 2.22 *continued*

```
<div id="copy">
<p class="dropCap">The Mock Turtle sighed
→ deeply, and drew the back of one flapper
→ across his eyes…</p>
<div class="dropBox">
<img src="alice36a.gif" height="258"
→ width="220" alt="" />
'Change lobster's again!' yelled the
→ Gryphon at the top of its voice.
</div>
<p>'You may not have lived much under the
→ sea--' ('I haven't,' said Alice)…'</p>
</div>
</body></html>
```

Figure 2.45 The first line of text in the paragraph is larger, italicized, and red.

Figure 2.46 Even when the text is narrower, only the first line is styled.

- Earlier versions of Internet Explorer render floating letters with their baselines flush with the rest of the text (that is, the bottoms of letters on the same line). Therefore, the letter styled with `dropCap` does not actually drop down.

- Although I set the drop cap up as a class, in theory, you could actually just assign this to the paragraph tag, but then *all* paragraphs in the document would have a drop cap, which is not usually desirable.

- A better alternative than using a class to create the drop cap would be to use the first-child selector (see the previous section) to tell paragraph tags to use the drop-cap style only if immediately preceded by a heading level 3 <h3> tag:

  `p:first-child p:first-letter {…}`

  Thus, only the first paragraph after a header would receive the drop cap. But, alas, earlier versions of Internet Explorer for Windows do not support first-child selectors.

Styling the first line of an element

Like the first letter of an element, the first line of any block of text can be isolated for style treatment using the `:first-line` pseudo-element.

In the example (**Figures 2.45** and **2.46**), the first line of paragraphs that have been assigned the `.firstPage` class become much larger, bolder, and redder and than rest of the text in the paragraph.

continues on next page

To style the first line of text:

1. p {…}

Although not required, it's generally a good idea to set the default style for the selector for which you will be styling the :first-line pseudo-element (**Code 2.23**).

2. p.firstPage:first-line {…}

Type the selector (HTML, class, or ID) for which you want to style the first letter, a colon (:), and then first-line. In this example, we are using a dependent class, so we will need to set the class in the relevant tag (see "Defining Classes for Any Tag" earlier in this chapter).

3. <p class="firstPage">…</p>

Add the class attribute to the relevant HTML tag. Although you do not have to use a class, generally, you will want to be able to selectively style the first line of a single element rather than styling all of the same element types universally.

Code 2.23 The first line of text in a paragraph that receives the .firstGraph class will stand off from the rest of the text, providing an easy visual clue for where to start reading.

```
<!DOCTYPE html PUBLIC "-//W3C//DTD XHTML 1.0
→ Strict//EN" "http://www.w3.org/TR/xhtml1/
→ DTD/xhtml1-strict.dtd">
<html xmlns="http://www.w3.org/1999/xhtml">
<head>
<meta http-equiv="Content-Type"
→ content="text/html; charset=utf-8" />
<title>CSS, DHTML &amp; Ajax | Styling the
→ First-line of an Element</title>
<style type="text/css" media="all">
body {
    font-size: 1em;
    font-family: Georgia, "Times New
    → Roman", times, serif;
    color: #000000;
    background-color: #fff;
    margin: 8px; }
```

Code 2.23 *continued*

```
#navigation {
    width: 240px;
    margin: 0px 8px 8px 0px;
    border: 3px solid #ccc;
    float: left;
    font: small Arial, Helvetica,
    → sans-serif }
p {
    line-height: 150%; }
    p.firstGraph:first-line {
    font-style: italic;
    font-weight: bold;
    font-size: 150%;
    color: red; }
.dropBox {
    width: 228px;
    padding: 6px;
    border: 3px solid #999;
    margin: 0px 0px 8px 8px;
    float: right; }
</style>
</head>
<body>
<div id="header">
<h1>Alice's Adventures in Wonderland</h1>
<p class="author">Lewis Carroll</p>
<h2>CHAPTER IX
    <span class="chapterTitle">The Lobster
    → Quadrille</span></h2>
</div>
<div id="copy">
<p class="firstGraph">The Mock Turtle
→ sighed deeply, and drew the back of one
→ flapper across his eyes…</p>
<div class="dropBox">
<img src="alice36a.gif" height="258"
→ width="220" alt="" />
'Change lobster's again!' yelled the
→ Gryphon at the top of its voice.
</div>
<p>'You may not have lived much under the
→ sea--' ('I haven't,' said Alice)-- 'and
→ perhaps you were never even introduced
→ to a lobster…'</p>
</div>
</body></html>
```

Figure 2.47 CSS generates content that is placed before and after the chapter title when displayed in the Web browser, but it never appears in the HTML code.

Setting content before and after an element

The :before and :after pseudo-elements can be used to generate content that appears above or below a particular selector. Generally, though, these pseudo-classes are used with the content property (see "Adding Content Using CSS" in Chapter 10). The pseudo-elements let you add and style repetitive content to the page consistently.

In this simple example (**Figure 2.47**), I've simply added a little red text before and after the second level headings. Notice, though that it does not appear in the HTML code, only in the CSS.

To set content before and after an element:

1. h2 {…}

   Although not required, it's generally a good idea to set the default style of the selector for which you will be styling the :before and :after pseudo-elements (see **Code 2.24** on the next page).

2. h2:before {…}

   Type the selector (HTML, class, or ID) you want to add content before, a colon (:), and then the keyword before. Next you will need to declare the content property and define what generated content goes before the element and how it should be styled.

3. h2:after {…}

   Type the selector (HTML, class, or ID) you want to add content after, a colon (:), and then the keyword after. Next you will need to declare the content property and define what generated content goes after the element and how it should be styled.

continues on next page

Code 2.24 Content can be added before and/or after an element.

```
<!DOCTYPE html PUBLIC "-//W3C//DTD XHTML 1.0 Strict//EN" "http://www.w3.org/TR/xhtml1/DTD/
→ xhtml1-strict.dtd">
<html xmlns="http://www.w3.org/1999/xhtml">
<head>
<meta http-equiv="Content-Type" content="text/html; charset=utf-8" />
<title>CSS, DHTML &amp; Ajax | Setting the Style Before and After an Element</title>
<style type="text/css" media="all">
body {
    font-size: 1.2em;
    font-family: Georgia, "Times New Roman", times, serif;
    color: #000000;
    background-color: #fff;
    margin: 8px; }
#navigation {
    width: 240px;
    margin: 0px 8px 8px 0px;
    border: 3px solid #ccc;
    float: left;
    font: small Arial, Helvetica, sans-serif }
h2 {
    color: #966; }
    h2:before {
    content: 'This is before…';
    color: red; }
    h2:after {
    content: '…and this is after';
    color: red; }
.dropBox {
    width: 228px;
    padding: 6px;
    border: 3px solid #999;
    margin: 0px 0px 8px 8px;
    float: right; }
</style>
</head>
<body>
<div id="header">
<h1>Alice's Adventures in Wonderland</h1>
<p class="author">Lewis Carroll</p>
<h2>CHAPTER IX
    <span class="chapterTitle">The Lobster Quadrille</span></h2>
</div>
<div id="copy">
<div class="dropBox">
<img src="alice36a.gif" height="258" width="220" alt="" />
'Change lobster's again!' yelled the Gryphon at the top of its voice.
</div>
<p class="dropCap">The Mock Turtle sighed deeply…</p>
</div>
</body></html>
```

Table 2.5

Media Values	
VALUE	INTENDED FOR
screen	Computer displays
tty	Teletypes, computer terminals, and older portable devices
tv	Television displays
projection	Projectors
handheld	Portable phones and PDAs
print	Paper
braille	Braille tactile readers
speech	Speech synthesizers
all	All devices

Figure 2.48 What the screen displays is completely different than...

Figure 2.49 ...what the printer prints.

Setting Styles for Print and Other Media

When most people think of Web pages, they think of them displayed on a screen. But sooner or later, most people want to print at least some Web pages. What looks good on the screen, however, does not always look good when printed. Even more so, what looks good on a typical computer monitor may not even show up on a handheld Web-enabled device like a mobile phone or PDA. However, most designers only consider the computer monitor when they are creating their masterpieces.

CSS lets us tell the browser to use different style sheets depending on the media on which your HTML is being rendered (**Table 2.5**). However, unless you are creating pages specifically for one of the media, your primary concern will be for screen, print, and possibly handheld devices.

The sidebar "Looking Good in Print (on the Web)" offers some suggestions for creating Web pages that print as cleanly as possible, but the most important trick is to set up a separate style sheet for your medium and then use the media attribute in the link or style tags to apply it.

In this example (**Figures 2.48** and **2.49**), I've created two external style sheets, and then placed two link tags in the head of my HTML document, using the media attribute to define which should be used for screen and which should be used for print.

Looking Good in Print (on the Web)

I have never seen a paperless office and would be quite surprised if I ever did. But the big promise that came along with the computer was the elimination of paper from our lives—no more filing cabinets, clutter, or dead trees, just an entropy-free utopia in which electrons were constantly recycled and reused, just like in *Star Trek*.

But something tells me that we'll have the technology to fly between the most distant stars before we eliminate paper from our lives.

With the advent of laser and inkjet printers, we seem to be buried under mounds of perfectly printed paper. Even the Web seems to increase the amount of paper we use. If a Web page is longer than a couple of scrolls, most people print it.

But the Web was created to display information on the screen, not on paper. Web graphics look blocky when printed, and straight HTML lacks much in the way of layout controls. That said, you can take steps to improve the appearance of printed Web pages. Looking good in print on the Web may take a little extra effort, but your audience will thank you in the long run.

Here are eight simple things you can do to improve the appearance of your Web page when it gets printed:

- **Define your media.** CSS allows you to define different style sheets to be used depending on the way the page is displayed—usually on a screen or on paper.

- **Use page breaks before headers** to keep them with their text.

- **Separate content from navigation.** Try to keep the main content—the part your audience is interested in reading—in a separate area of the design from the site navigation. You can then use CSS to tell the navigation not to display for the print version.

- **Avoid using transparent colors in graphics.** This is especially true if the graphic is on a background color or a graphic other than white. The transparent area of a GIF image usually prints as white regardless of the color behind it in the window. This situation is not a problem if the graphic is on a white background to begin with, but the result is messy if the graphic is supposed to be on a dark background.

- **Avoid using text in graphics.** The irony of printing stuff off the Web is that text in graphics, which look smooth in the window, look blocky when printed, but regular HTML text, which may look blocky on the screen, prints smoothly on any decent printer. Try to stick with HTML text as much as possible.

- **Avoid dark colored backgrounds and light colored text.** Generally you want to keep white as your background color for most of the printed page, and black or dark gray for the text.

- **Do not rely on color to convey your message when printed.** Although color printers are quite common these days, many people are still printing on black-and-white printers or printing in black and white on color printers to save money.

To specify a style sheet for a particular medium:

1. Create two external style sheets: one optimized for use on a computer screen and the other tailored for the printed page (see "Adding Styles to a Web Site" earlier in this chapter).

   In this example, the screen version (**Code 2.25**) has white text on a black background—which, although it looks cool on the screen, would not only look messy if printed, but also eat through the toner cartridge. The print version (**Code 2.26**) reverses this with black text on a white (paper) background.

   continues on next page

Code 2.25 screen.css: This defines how the HTML page in Code 2.27 should be displayed on the screen.

```css
Body {
    color: white;
    font-family: arial, helvetica, geneva,
    → sans-serif;
    background: black url(alice23.gif)
    → no-repeat;
    word-spacing: 1px;
    position: relative;
    top: 200px;
    left: 165px;
    width: 480px; }
h1,h2 {
    font:small-caps bold italic 2.5em
    → 'minion web', Georgia, 'Times New
    → Roman', Times, serif; }
h2 {
    font-style: normal;
    font-variant: normal;
    font-size: 1.5em;
    color: #999; }
p.authorName {
    margin: 8px 0px;
    font: bold 1em Arial, Helvetica,
    → sans-serif;
    color: #999; }
h2 .chapterName {
    display: block;
    margin-bottom: 8px;
    font-size: smaller;
    color:#fff; }
p.dropCap:first-letter {
    font: 300%/100% serif;
    color: #999999; }
```

Code 2.26 print.css: This defines how the HTML page in Code 2.27 should be displayed when printed.

```css
Body {
    color: black;
    font-size: 10pt;
    line-height: 12pt;
    font-family: "Book Antiqua", "Times
    → New Roman", Georgia, Times, serif;
    background: white no-repeat;
    text-align: justify;
    position: relative;
    top: 10px;
    left: 40px;
    width: 575px; }
h1,h2 {
    color: black;
    font: italic small-caps bold 2.5em
    → "minion web Georgia", "Times New
    → Roman", Times, serif; }
h2 {
    color: black;
    font-style: normal;
    font-variant: normal;
    font-size: 1.5em; }
p.authorName {
    margin: 8px 0px;
    font: bold 1em Arial, Helvetica,
    → sans-serif; }
h2 .chapterName {
    display: block;
    margin-bottom: 8px;
    font-size: smaller;
    color:black; }
p.dropCap:first-letter {
    font: 300%/100% serif;
    color: #999999; }
```

SETTING STYLES FOR PRINT AND OTHER MEDIA

2. `<link href= "print.css" rel="style`
`→ sheet" media="print">`

In the head of your HTML document
(**Code 2.27**, type a `<link>` tag that references the print version of the CSS and
define media as print.

3. `<link href= "screen.css" rel="style`
`→ sheet" media="screen">`

Immediately after the `<link>` tag that references the printer version of the CSS,
add another `<link>` tag that references
the screen version of the CSS, and define
media as screen.

✔ Tips

■ Although several media types are available—including aural, Braille, projection,
and handheld—most common Web
browsers only support screen, projection,
and print.

■ Handhelds are increasingly becoming a
factor in Web design, and you may want
to consider style sheets tailored for this
growing medium. If you structure your
page correctly, though, it shouldn't be
difficult to tailor it for smaller screens.
That said, many popular handhelds
aren't designed to use the "handheld"
media type, and will still try to use the
"screen" media type.

```
<!DOCTYPE html PUBLIC "-//W3C//DTD XHTML 1.0
→ Strict//EN" "http://www.w3.org/TR/xhtml1/
→ DTD/xhtml1-strict.dtd">
<html xmlns="http://www.w3.org/1999/xhtml">
<head>
<meta http-equiv="Content-Type"
→ content="text/html; charset=utf-8" />
<title>CSS, DHTML &amp; Ajax | Setting the
→ CSS for the Output Medium</title>
<link href="print.css" rel="style sheet"
→ type="text/css" media="print" />
<link href="screen.css" rel="style sheet"
→ type="text/css" media="screen" />
</head>
<body>
<div id="content">
<div>
    <h1>Alice's Adventures in
    → Wonderland</h1>
    <p class="authorName">Lewis Carroll</p>
    <h2>Chapter I<br />
        <span class="chapterName">Down the
        → Rabbit-Hole</span></h2>
</div>
<div id="copy">
    <p class="dropCap">Alice was beginning
    → to get very tired of sitting by her
    → sister on the bank…</p>
</div></div>
</body></html>
```

Code 2.27 index.html: The HTML code links to two
different CSS files: One is to be used if the file is
output to the screen; the other is to be used if the file
is output to a printer.

Table 2.6

Page-Break-Before and Page-Break-After Values	
VALUE	COMPATIBILITY
auto	IE4, FF1, S1, O305, CSS2
always	IE4, FF1, S1, O5, CSS2
avoid	FF1, O3.5, CSS2
left	IE4, O3.5, CSS2
right	IE4, O3.5, CSS2
inherit	FF1, O4, CSS2

Figure 2.50 The screen presents a single scrollable page...

Figure 2.51 ...but the pages are split when printing.

Setting page breaks for printing

One problem you'll encounter when trying to print a Web site is that pages break wherever they happen to break. A Web page may actually contain several printed pages. So the header for a section might appear at the bottom of a page and its text at the top of the next page (**Table 2.6**).

If you want to force a page break when printing a Web page, use the following code to define an HTML tag (see "Adding Styles to an HTML Tag" earlier in this chapter).

In this example (**Figure 2.50**), the Web page has a new chapter starting in the middle of the screen. When this page is printed, this header might appear anywhere on the page. By adding a page break in the <h2> tag, however, you can force the chapter title to appear at the top of a new page when printed (**Figure 2.51**).

To define a page break for printing:

1. `style type="…"`

This CSS property works only if it is included in the `style` attribute of an HTML tag (**Code 2.28**).

2. `page-break-before:`

Within the quotes, type the `page-break-before` or `page-break-after` property name, followed by a colon (`:`), in the CSS declaration list.

3. `always;`

Type one of the following values to designate how you want page breaks to be handled:

- ▲ `always`, forces a page break before (or after) the element
- ▲ `auto`, allows the browser to place the page breaks

✔ Tip

- ■ If you are really concerned about how your page looks when it is printed, see the "Preventing Widows and Orphans" sidebar.

Preventing Widows and Orphans

Two unattractive problems can occur when printing Web pages:

- ◆ **Widows** occur when the last line from the end of a paragraph appears alone at the top of a page.
- ◆ **Orphans** occur when the first line of the beginning of a paragraph appears alone at the bottom of a page.

CSS allows you to specify how many lines of text must appear in a paragraph at the top (widow) or bottom (orphan) of a page before a page break is allowed, using the `widows` and `orphans` properties:

```
p {
widows:5;
orphans:10;
}
```

The above code forces at least five lines of text to appear at the top of a page in a paragraph and at least 10 lines of text to appear at the bottom of a page. Otherwise, the text for the paragraph is forced onto a new page so that it will fit.

Code 2.28 Page breaks have to be set directly in the HTML tags using inline styles.

```
<!DOCTYPE html PUBLIC "-//W3C//DTD XHTML 1.0 Strict//EN" "http://www.w3.org/TR/xhtml1/DTD/
→ xhtml1-strict.dtd">
<html xmlns="http://www.w3.org/1999/xhtml">
<head>
<meta http-equiv="Content-Type" content="text/html; charset=utf-8" />
<title>CSS, DHTML &amp; Ajax | Setting Page Breaks for Printing</title>
<style type="text/css" media="all">
body {
    font-size: 1em;
    font-family: Georgia, 'Times New Roman', times, serif;
    color: #000000;
    background-color: #fff;
    margin: 1in; }
h1 {
    font:small-caps bold italic 2.5em Georgia, 'Times New Roman', times, serif;
    color: red; }
h2 {
    color:#999;
    margin-top: 1in; }
#content {
    position: relative;
    background-color: white; }
#content #copy {
    line-height: 1.5; }
p.authorName {
    margin: 8px 0px;
    font: bold 1em Arial, Helvetica, sans-serif; }
h2 .chapterName {
    display: block;
    margin-bottom: 8px;
    font-size: smaller;
    color:black; }
p.dropCap:first-letter {
    font: 300%/100% serif;
    color: #999999; }
</style>
</head>
<body>
<div id="content">
<div>
    <h1>Alice's Adventures in Wonderland</h1>
    <p class="authorName">Lewis Carroll</p>
    <h2>Chapter I<br />
        <span class="chapterName">Down the Rabbit-Hole</span></h2>
</div>
<div id="copy">
    <p class="dropCap">Alice was beginning to get very tired of sitting by her sister on the bank…</p>
</div>
<div>
    <h2 style="page-break-before: always;">Chapter II<br />
        <span class="chapterName">The Pool of Tears</span></h2>
</div>
<div id="copy">
    <p class="dropCap">'Curiouser and curiouser!' cried Alice…
</p>
</div></div>
</body></html>
```

Adding Comments to CSS

Like any other part of an HTML document, style sheets can have comments. A comment does not affect code; comments only add notes or give guidance to anyone viewing your code. You can include comments in the style element in the head of an HTML document or in an external CSS file, as shown in **Code 2.29**.

To include comments in a style sheet:

1. /*

To open a comment area in a style sheet, type a slash (/) and an asterisk (*).

2. selector= HTML tags

Type your comments. You can use any letters or numbers, symbols, and even line breaks (by pressing the Return or Enter key).

3. */

Close your comment by typing an asterisk (*) and a slash (/).

✔ Tip

■ You cannot nest comments.

Code 2.29 You can use comments to add useful notes to a page without interfering with the code.

```
<!DOCTYPE html PUBLIC "-//W3C//DTD XHTML 1.0
→ Strict//EN" "http://www.w3.org/TR/xhtml1/
→ DTD/xhtml1-strict.dtd">
<html xmlns="http://www.w3.org/1999/xhtml">
<head>
<meta http-equiv="Content-Type"
→ content="text/html; charset=utf-8" />
<title>CSS, DHTML &amp; Ajax | CSS
→ Comments</title>
<style media="screen" type="text/css">
/* Sets the general apperance of code tags */
code
{
font-family: monaco,courier,monospace;
font-size: 10pt;
line-height: 12pt;
margin-left: 2em; }
/*
While this sets the apperance of special
→ cases for code
selector= HTML tags
rule= the CSS Rule that defines the apperance
comment= Comments in the CSS
*/
code.selector { color: #009900;}
code.rule { color: #990099;}
code.comment { color: #cc0000;}
</style>
</head>
<body>
<code class="comment">/* While this sets the
→ apperance of special cases for code<br />
selector= HTML tags<br />
rule= the CSS Rule that defines the
→ apperance<br />
comment= Comments in the CSS */<br />
</code><br />
<code class="selector">code.selector
→ { </code> <code class="rule">
→ color: #009900;</code>
→ <code class="selector">}</code><br />
<code class="selector">code.rule { </code>
→ <code class="rule">color: #990099;</code>
→ <code class="selector">}</code><br />
<code class="selector">code.comment {</code>
→ <code class="rule">color: #cc0000;</code>
→ <code class="selector">}</code>
</body></html>
```

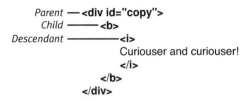

Figure 2.52 Parent, children, and descendants in HTML-structured code.

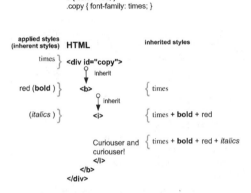

Figure 2.53 The final results of the styles being applied and inherited is bold, red, and italicized text in Times font.

Inheriting Properties from a Parent

No, this is not the *Visual QuickStart Guide to Real Estate*. Every HTML tag that can be controlled with CSS has a *parent*—a container tag that surrounds it. Those nested *child* tags are the parent to tags nested within them, and these are in turn its child tags, and *descendant* tags to its parents (**Figure 2.52**).

Child and descendant HTML tags generally assume the styles of their parents, whether the style is inherent (as with the bold tag) or applied using CSS. This is called *inheritance of styles*.

For example, if you set an ID called copy and give it a font-family value of Times, all of its descendants will inherit the Times font style. If you set a bold tag to red with CSS, then all of its descendants are going to inherit both the applied red and the inherent bold style (**Figure 2.53**).

In some cases, a style property is not inherited from its parent—obvious properties such as margins, width, and borders. You will probably have no trouble figuring out which properties are inherited and which are not. For example, if you set a padding of 4 pixels for the paragraph tag, you would not expect bold tags within the paragraph to also add a padding of 4 pixels around them.

If you have any doubts, though, check this book's Web site (webbedenvironments.com/css_html_ajax) for a list of all the properties, as well as whether or not they are inherited.

If you did want to force an element to inherit a property of its parent, many CSS properties include the inherit value. So, in the example above, if you did want to force all the bold tags in a paragraph to take on the 4px padding, you could set their padding value to inherit.

Managing existing or inherited property values

By defining the styles for a selector, you do not cause it to lose any of its inherited or inherent attributes, unless you specifically override those styles. All those properties are displayed, unless the specific existing properties that make up its appearance are changed.

For example (**Figure 2.54**), you could set the following for the bold tag to not display as bold when it is within a paragraph (**Code 2.30**).

In addition to simply overriding the relevant property with another value, many CSS properties have values that allow you to override inheritance:

- inherit: forces a property that would normally not be inherited to be inherited, or overrides other applied style values and inherits the parent's value

- none: forces a border, image, or other visual elements not to appear

- normal: forces no style to be applied.

- auto: allows the browser to determine how the element should be displayed based on context

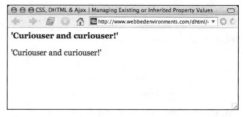

Figure 2.54 Despite being in the bold tag, the second line of text has had the inherent bold style overridden by another value.

Code 2.30 When the bold tag is in a paragraph, it will not be bold.

```
<!DOCTYPE html PUBLIC "-//W3C//DTD XHTML 1.0
→ Strict//EN" "http://www.w3.org/TR/xhtml1/
→ DTD/xhtml1-strict.dtd">
<html xmlns="http://www.w3.org/1999/xhtml">
<head>
<meta http-equiv="Content-Type"
→ content="text/html; charset=utf-8" />
<title>CSS, DHTML &amp; Ajax | Managing
→ Existing or Inherited Property
→ Values</title>
<style type="text/css" media="screen">
body {
    font: 1.2em Georgia, 'Times New Roman',
    → times, serif;
    color: #000000;
    background-color: #fff;
    margin: 8px; }
p b { font-weight: normal; }
</style>
</head>
<body>
<div>
<b>'Curiouser and curiouser!'</b>
<p><b>'Curiouser and curiouser!'</b></p>
</div>
</body></html>
```

Figure 2.55 Despite having the color set to blue and lime in previous style declarations, the final inline style wins out and the text is red.

Code 2.31 default.css: The external style sheet sets the <h2> tag to be blue.

```
h2 { color: blue; }
```

Code 2.32 index.html: The embedded style sheet sets the <h2> tag to lime, while the inline style sets the <h2> tag to red.

```
<!DOCTYPE html PUBLIC "-//W3C//DTD XHTML 1.0
Strict//EN"
"http://www.w3.org/TR/xhtml1/DTD/xhtml1-
strict.dtd">
<html xmlns="http://www.w3.org/1999/xhtml">
<head>
<meta http-equiv="Content-Type"
content="text/html; charset=utf-8" />
<title>CSS, DHTML &amp; Ajax | Determining
Cascade Order</title>
<link href="default.css" rel="style sheet"
type="text/css" media="screen" />
<style type="text/css" media="screen">
body {
     font: 1.2em Georgia, 'Times New Roman',
times, serif;
     color: #000000;
     background-color: #fff;
     margin: 8px; }
h2 {
color: lime; }
</style>
</head>
<body>
<div id="content">
```

Determining the Cascade Order

Within a single Web page, style sheets may be linked, imported, or embedded. Styles may also be declared inline, in the HTML.

In addition, many browsers allow visitors to have their own style sheets, which they can use to override yours. It's guaranteed, of course, that style sheets from two or more sources being used simultaneously will have conflicting declarations. Who comes out on top?

The cascade order refers to the way styles begin at the top of the page and, as they cascade down, collect and replace each other as they are inherited. The general rule of thumb is that the last style defined in order is the one that is used.

For example (**Figure 2.55**), you might define the color of the heading level 3 tag to be blue in an external style sheet (**Code 2.31** and **Code 2.32**), replace that declaration with the color lime in an embedded style, and then finally trump them all with an inline style that sets the color to red.

continues on next page

Code 2.32 *continued*

```
<div id="header">
     <h1>Alice's Adventures in Wonderland</h1>
     <p class="authorName">Lewis Carroll</p>
     <h2 style="color:red">Chapter VI<br />
          <span class="chapterName">Pig and
          → Pepper</span>
     </h2>
</div>
<div id="copy">
     <p>For a minute or two she stood
          → looking at the house, and wondering
          → what to do next, when suddenly a
          → footman in livery came running out
          → of the wood...</p>
</div></div>
</body></html>
```

However, there will be times when two or more styles will come into conflict. Use the steps below to determine which style will come out on top and be applied to a given element.

To determine the cascade-order value for an element:

1. Collect all styles that will be applied to the element.

   Find all of the inherent, applied, and inherited styles that will be applied to the element for the target media type (see the previous section).

2. Sort by origin, method, importance, and selector.

   Use the chart in **Figure 2.56** to determine the importance of a rule, based on who added it (origin), where it came from (method), and the type (selector).

   Including !important with a declaration gives it top billing when being displayed (see "Making a Declaration !important" earlier in this chapter).

   Many browsers let users define their own style sheets for use by the browser. If both the page author and the visitor have included !important in their declarations, the user's declaration wins.

   In theory, an author's style sheets override a visitor's style sheets, unless the visitor uses the !important value. In practice, however, most browsers favor a user's style sheet when determining which declarations are used for a tag.

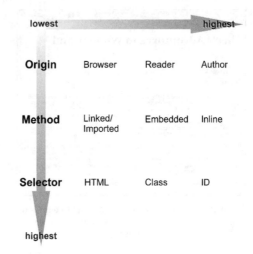

Figure 2.56 This chart shows the relevant importance of where particular rules come from when determining their cascade order.

DETERMINING THE CASCADE ORDER

3. Is the selector more specific?

The more contextually specific a rule is, the higher its cascade priority. So the more HTML, class, and ID selectors a particular rule has, the more important it is. In determining this priority, ID selectors count as 100, classes count as 10, and HTML selectors are worth only 1. Thus,

```
#copy p b { color: red; }
```

would be worth 102, while just

```
b { color : lime; }
```

would only be worth 1. So if these two declarations were in conflict, the first would have higher specificity and the color would be red.

This priority setting may seem a bit silly at first, but it allows context-sensitive and ID rules to carry more weight, ensuring that they will be used.

4. Last one in the pool wins.

If the conflicting declarations being applied to an element are equal at this point, then CSS gives priority to the last rule listed, in order. This is especially useful if you include an inline declaration to override style settings listed in the head.

Using Conditional Comments to Fix CSS in Internet Explorer

Even with the introduction of Microsoft Internet Explorer 7 in 2006, the most popular Web browser brand has a lot of shortcomings when it comes to Cascading Style Sheets. Most of these will become obvious as you look at the compatibility charts in Chapters 2 through 10, but generally will not detract from your designs. However, some of the problems, such as the box-model issue discussed in Chapter 6, are far more pervasive and harder to ignore.

Sometimes called the *IE factor*, these limitations are the bane of Web designers who not only want to stay standards-compliant but also refuse to ignore a large portion of the Web public who use Mozilla Firefox, Apple Safari, Opera, and other browsers.

For years Web designers struggled with these issues, developing a number of hacks to address them. However, there was always a simple solution, and it has been built into Internet Explorer since version 5.0: *conditional comments*.

Internet Explorer (and *only* Internet Explorer) has the ability to interpret conditional statements that are ignored by other browsers but allow you to insert links to style sheets that can tailor your CSS for that browser, even down to individual versions.

In this example (**Figures 2.57** and **2.58**), a default style sheet is loaded and used by all browsers (even Internet Explorer), which will hide the layer called IEMessage. However, Internet Explorer will also use a style sheet that will display the ID layer IEMessage, which displays a message inviting Microsoft Internet Explorer users to download the most recent version of their browser.

Figure 2.57 In Firefox, no message is displayed.

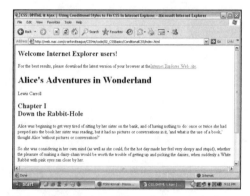

Figure 2.58 In Internet Explorer (any version), the message is displayed.

Code 2.33 default.css: This style sheet will be used in all browsers.

```
/* Default CSS used in all browsers */

body {
    font-size: 1em;
    font-family: Georgia, 'Times New
    → Roman', times, serif;
    color: #000000;
    margin: 8px;
    background: white url(alice23.gif)
    → no-repeat; }
h1 {
    font:small-caps bold italic 2.5em
    → Georgia, 'Times New Roman',
    → times, serif; }
h2 {
    color:#999; }
#content {
    position: relative;
    top: 190px;
    left: 165px;
    width: 480px; }
#content #copy {
    line-height: 1.5; }
#IEMessage {
    display: none; }
p.authorName {
    margin: 8px 0px;
    font: bold 1em Arial, Helvetica,
    → sans-serif; }
h2 .chapterName {
    display: block;
    margin-bottom: 8px;
    font-size: smaller;
    color:black; }
p.dropCap:first-letter {
    font: 300%/100% serif;
    color: #999999; }
```

Code 2.34 ie.css: These styles are used only if the visitor is using Internet Explorer.

```
/* Styles used for Internet Explorer */

#IEMessage {
    display: block;
    margin: 8px;
    border: 2px dotted red;
    padding: 4px;
    width: 480px; }
#IEMessage h2 {
    color:#f00; }
```

To set up styles using conditional comments:

1. Set up separate external style sheets for your default styles and save as default.css (**Code 2.33**). For your styles used only in Internet Explorer, save as ie.css (**Code 2.34**), as explained earlier in this chapter in "Adding CSS to a Web Site."

2. `<link rel="style sheet"`
   `→ href="default.css" type="text/css"`
   `→ media="all" />`

   Begin by linking to or importing your default style sheet for this page, and any other style sheets used to create this page index.html (**Code 2.35**). To ensure the cascade order works for this trick, all other CSS must come first.

3. `<!--[if IE]>`

   Within an HTML comment, use an if statement within square brackets and specify which version of Internet Explorer the linked CSS file should be used with. Using just IE will cause the CSS to be used in any version of Internet Explorer. Adding a space and then a number after that will specify the version number. For example, IE 6 allows CSS to be used only in Internet Explorer version 6. Use a closing chevron (>) at the end of the line.

continues on next page

4. `<link rel="style sheet" href="ie.css"`
`→ type="text/css" media="all" />`

Add the link to your external style sheet that has been specifically set up for the version(s) of Internet Explorer you specified in Step 2. In addition to linking, you can also embed CSS directly into this area, as discussed earlier in this chapter in "Adding Styles to a Web Page."

5. `<![endif]-->`

Close your conditional comment with an `endif` in square brackets, and then close the HTML comment.

✔ Tip

■ In this example, I used the conditional styles to turn a layer on and off, depending on whether the browser is Internet Explorer. You could also tailor messages for different versions by adding the version number:

`<!--[if IE 7]>…<![endif]-->`
`<!--[if IE 6]>…<![endif]-->`
`<!--[if IE 5.5]>…<![endif]-->`
`<!--[if IE 5.0]>…<![endif]-->`
`<!--[if IE 4.0]>…<![endif]-->`

For more details on conditional statements in Internet Explorer, check out msdn.microsoft.com/workshop/author/dhtml/overview/ccomment_ovw.asp

Code 2.35 index.html: The page links to default.css (Code 2.33) and then will link to ie.css (Code 2.34) only if the browser in which it is displayed is some version of Internet Explorer.

```
<!DOCTYPE html PUBLIC "-//W3C//DTD XHTML 1.0
→ Strict//EN" "http://www.w3.org/TR/xhtml1/
→ DTD/xhtml1-strict.dtd">
<html xmlns="http://www.w3.org/1999/xhtml">
<head>
<meta http-equiv="Content-Type"
→ content="text/html; charset=utf-8" />
<title>CSS, DHTML &amp; Ajax | Using
→ Conditional Styles to Fix CSS In Internet
→ Explorer</title>

<link rel="style sheet" href="default.css"
→ type="text/css" media="all" />

<!--[if IE]>
<link rel="style sheet" href="ie.css"
→ type="text/css" media="all" />
<![endif]-->

</head>
<body>
<div id="content">

<div id="IEMessage">
    <h2>Welcome Internet Explorer users!</h2>
    <p>For the best results, please
    → download the latest version
    → of your browser at the
    → <a href="http://www.microsoft.com/
    → windows/ie/default.mspx">Internet
    → Explorer Web site</a>.</p>
</div>

<div>
    <h1>Alice's Adventures in Wonderland</h1>
</div></div>
</body></html>
```

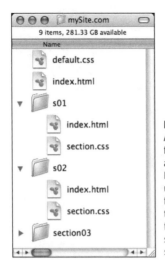

Figure 2.59
A typical tiered file structure that allows different HTML pages to use a global CSS file and then tailors the styles for the particular section with a sectional CSS file.

Style Sheet Strategies

Here are some useful tips for constructing a site using CSS:

◆ Wherever possible, place your styles in external style sheets (see "Adding Styles to a Web Site" earlier in this chapter).

◆ The power of CSS is that you can place your styles in one common location and change an entire Web site from one place (**Figure 2.59**). In the file structure example, notice that both sections use a file called section.css and not ones called s01.css and s02.css. This allows us to move HTML files between sections without needing to change the URLs used to link or import the documents.

◆ At the top level of your Web site, define a default default.css style sheet that can be applied to your entire Web site.

Generally speaking, you'll want certain characteristics to be ubiquitous throughout your Web site. You may want all your level 1 headings to be a certain size and font, for example (**Figure 2.60**).

continues on next page

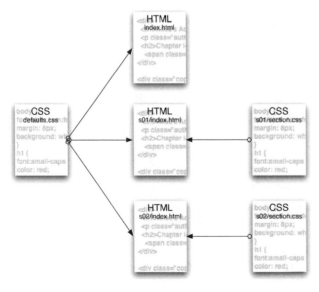

Figure 2.60 This diagram shows how the different HTML files will be linked to the associated CSS files. default.css is linked to all three files, while each section's individual section.css is linked to refine the page's layout.

STYLE SHEET STRATEGIES

◆ Refine styles at sublevels with a `section.css` style sheet. By doing this, you can change each section or add to the global style sheet. For example, you've already set the size and font for your `<h1>` tags in the global style sheet, but each section's headers are color-coded. This is your chance to set the color for each section individually.

◆ Use different .css files for distinctive uses. Placing all your CSS in one file can lead to larger files and longer download times if you use a lot of CSS. Instead, consider splitting your CSS into several files and importing them as needed for each page.

◆ Avoid using styles in tags unless you have a compelling reason.

◆ Again, the great thing about CSS is that you can apply styles to multiple tags and change those styles throughout a Web site on a whim. If you define the style directly in the tag, you lose this ability.

FONT
PROPERTIES

Typography is one of your most powerful tools for presenting organized, clean-looking documents. It's also the best tool for presenting chaotic, grungy-looking documents.

The fonts you use go a long way toward getting your message across in just the way you want—whether that message is classical, grunge, or anything in between. Boldface, italic, and other typographic effects help designers guide a visitor's eye around the page.

CSS gives you the ability to control the appearance of fonts, also known as *letterforms*, in your Web pages. But with CSS, you can set more than just the font family, boldface and italic attributes, and the limited font sizes available with HTML tags. CSS allows you to go a step further and set generic font families, various levels of boldness, different types of italic, and any font size, using a variety of measurements, including point, pixel, and pica.

Understanding Typography on the Web

A *type family* (commonly referred to in Web design as a *font family*) is a category of type-faces (*fonts*) that have similar characteristics. Each individual character within a font is referred to as a *glyph*. The text that you type in your HTML document acts, for the most part, like the text in a word processor. The advantages of HTML text are that it is easy to edit if changes are required, and it can adjust to the width of the screen on which it is being viewed. In addition, content is often stored within databases, and then out put as HTML text.

However, HTML text has some severe limita-tions for design purposes. By and large, most of the textual control is left up to the visitor's browser, and you can't do things like run text vertically rather than horizontally. Even more stifling is the fact that you are limited to the fonts that are available on the visitor's machine (see "Using Browser-Safe Fonts" later in this chapter). So if you have a specific font on your machine that you want to use, but the people viewing your site don't have that font on their machines, you're out of luck.

CSS gives designers greater control of many common typographic features (such as line and word spacing), but even with CSS, HTML text is severely limited, particularly in the special-effects department. This is why many designers turn to text in graphics or vector graphics to get the look they want.

Specifying the character set

If you are using XHTML instead of HTML, which—if you haven't caught on by now—is what I heartily recommend, then you will need to specify the character set in use by your page. A character set is simply a list or *repertoire* of characters with a unique code or name.

Table 3.1

Generic Font Families	
NAME	EXAMPLE
Serif	Times New Roman
Sans-serif	Helvetica and Arial
Monospace	Courier New
Cursive	Brush Script MT
Fantasy	Papyrus

You specify the character set in the head of your HTML page using a meta tag. The most popular international character set is the UTF-8 (8-bit Unicode Transformation Format) character set:

```
<meta http-equiv="Content-Type"
→ content="text/html; charset=
→ utf-8" />
```

Alternatively, if you are only writing in English, another common character set is the ISO 8859-1 character set:

```
<meta http-equiv="Content-Type"
→ content="text/html; charset=
→ ISO-8859-1" />
```

Both UTF-8 and ISO 8859-1 work about the same for English, but UTF-8 supports other alphabets.

If you specify a character in your HTML that doesn't exist in the specified character set, the browser generally will display an error marker in place of the character.

Generic font families

CSS defines five generic font families into which most fonts can be categorized (**Table 3.1**).

◆ **Serif.** A *serif* is the small ornamentation at the end of a letter that gives it a distinguishing quality. Serifs are holdovers from the days of stonecutting and pen strokes. Serifs often improve legibility by making individual letters stand out from their neighbors.

Serif fonts are generally best suited for the display of larger text on screen or for smaller printed text. They are not so good for smaller text on a screen, because the serifs often obscure the letter. Serif fonts often portray a more conservative feel.

continues on next page

UNDERSTANDING TYPOGRAPHY ON THE WEB

- **Sans-serif.** As you might guess, *sans-serif* fonts are those fonts without serifs. Although the characters are less distinctive, sans-serif fonts work better for smaller text on a screen. Sans-serif fonts often portray a more modern feel.

- **Monospace.** Although *monospace* fonts can have serifs or not, their distinguishing feature is that each letter occupies the same amount of space. The lowercase letter *l*, for example, is much thinner than the uppercase letter *M*. In non-monospace fonts, the letter *l* occupies less space than the *M*, but a monospace font adds extra space around the *l* so that it occupies the same amount of space as the *M*.

  Monospace fonts work best for text that has to be exactly (but not necessarily quickly) read, such as programming code, in which typos can spell disaster. Although easier to scan, monospace fonts can become monotonous for reading large amounts of text. Monospace fonts often give technical or typewritten feel to text.

- **Cursive.** *Cursive* fonts attempt to mimic cursive or calligraphic handwriting, usually in a highly stylized manner with the letters generally appearing partially or completely connected.

  Cursive fonts are best reserved for decoration and large headlines; they are not very good for reading large chunks of text. Cursive fonts give an energetic and expressive feel to text.

- **Fantasy.** Decorative fonts that don't fit into any of the preceding categories are referred to as *fantasy* fonts. These fonts usually are extremely ornamental but are still letters, so exclude dingbats or picture fonts, illustrations, or icons.

Graphic and Vector Text

Unlike HTML text, graphic text is a graphic (GIF, PNG, or JPEG) that just happens to have text in it. This means that you can do anything you want in terms of how the text looks and use any font you want, regardless of whether site visitors have that font on their machines.

You also have all the limitations that go along with using graphics, such as larger file sizes (larger graphics mean slower download times) and the difficulty of editing text. Graphics also take up a set amount of screen space and may be cut off if the visitor's screen is not large enough, do not re-flow to take up more space, and often do not print clearly.

Vector text combines the best of both worlds. Like HTML text, it is easy to edit and can position itself dynamically, depending on the screen size. But like graphic text, vector text allows you to apply special effects easily (on a slightly more limited scale), and you can use any font that you want.

Unfortunately, most browsers in use today do not natively support vector text (i.e., it isn't built in).

Currently, the only (mostly) universal way to get vector text into a Web site is to use Macromedia's Flash plug-in. Although a plug-in, most browsers come with it pre-installed.

The Scalable Vector Graphics (SVG) format, which is now a W3C standard, may also one day be a viable option, but is currently only natively supported in recent versions of Firefox and Opera, with implementation coming soon in Safari. Of course, this only makes up at most 15 percent of the Web-viewing public.

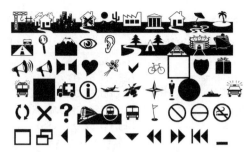

Figure 3.1 The dingbats for A-Z, a-z, and 0-9.

Figure 3.2 A few character entities. These are generally nonstandard typographic characters, math, and science symbols, as well as non-English characters.

Like cursive fonts, fantasy fonts are best reserved for decoration. You should choose fantasy fonts carefully to reinforce the look and feel of your Web site, since each fantasy font has its own particular personality.

Dingbats

Although it does not have an official CSS designation, there is another important category of fonts to consider. *Dingbats*, also called *symbol* or *picture* fonts, do not represent numbers or letters, but are instead a collection of icons or pictograms each corresponding to a letter on the keyboard. The most common example of this font type is Webdings, which is installed on most computers. Webdings is a collection of common international symbols (**Figure 3.1**). Although these glyphs can be used in place of a graphic version of the icon, there is no guarantee that the font will be installed.

Character entities

A more reliable alternative to dingbat fonts are HTML *character entities*. These are a collection of specialized glyphs that, instead of being represented by a single letter, are represented by code that begins with an ampersand (&) and ends with a semicolon (;). For example, the ampersand is represented in the code as:

    &

For many characters (such as the ampersand itself), this is the only way to have them display consistently across browsers and operating systems. **Figure 3.2** illustrates some common character entities.

Setting the Font-Family

The font-family property lets you determine the visual effect of your message by choosing the font for displaying your text (**Table 3.2**). The font you use to display your text can make a powerful difference in how readers perceive your message (**Figure 3.3**). Some fonts are easier to read on the screen; others look better when printed.

In this example (**Figure 3.4**), the level 1 header has been assigned the mono font family using Courier New (for Windows) and Courier as an alternative (for Macs).

To define the font family in a rule:

1. font-family:

   Type the property name font-family, followed by a colon (**Code 3.1**).

2. "Courier New"

   Type the name of the font you want to use.

3. , Courier, "Andale Mono"

   If you want, you can type a list of alternative fonts separated by commas. These fonts will be used (in the order specified) if the previous font in the list is not available on the visitor's computer.

4. , monospace;

   After the last comma, type the name of the generic font family for the particular style of font you're using. Table 3.2 lists generic values for font families. Although including this value is optional, doing so is a good idea.

Table 3.2

Font-Family Values	
VALUE	COMPATIBILITY
‹family-name›	IE3, FF1, S1, O3.5, CSS1
serif	IE3, FF1, S1, O3.5, CSS1
sans-serif	IE4/3, FF1, S1, O3.5, CSS1
cursive	IE4, FF1, S1, O3.5, CSS1
fantasy	IE4,FF1, S1, O3.5, CSS1
monospace	IE4,FF1, S1, O3.5, CSS1

Times
Arial
Courier
Brush Script
Papyrus

Figure 3.3 A few common fonts (maybe a little too common!) in 18pt type.

Figure 3.4 The font for the title, author, and chapter name, and text of the page have all been set, thus overriding the default font set in the body tag.

Code 3.1 You can specify as many fonts in your definition as you want. Separate names with a comma, and place quotes around font names that contain more than one word.

```
<!DOCTYPE html PUBLIC "-//W3C//DTD XHTML 1.0
→ Strict//EN" "http://www.w3.org/TR/xhtml1/
→ DTD/xhtml1-strict.dtd">
<html xmlns="http://www.w3.org/1999/xhtml">
<head>
<meta http-equiv="Content-Type" content=
→ "text/html; charset=UTF-8" />
<title>CSS, DHTML &amp; Ajax | Setting the
→ Font</title>
<style type="text/css" media="all">
body {
     font-size: 1.2em;
     font-family: Georgia, "Times New
     → Roman", times, serif; }
h1 {
     font-family: "Courier New", Courier,
     → "Andale Mono", monospace; }
h2 {
     font-family: Cracked, Impact, fantasy; }
p.copy {
     font-family: Arial, Helvetica,
     → sans-serif; }
.author {
     font-family: Zapfino, "Comic Sans MS",
     → cursive; }
</style>
</head>
<body>
<div id="header">
     <h1>Alice's Adventures in Wonderland</h1>
     <p class="author">Lewis Carroll</p>
     <h2>CHAPTER I<br />
     Down the Rabbit-Hole</h2>
</div>
<p>Alice was beginning to get very tired
→ of sitting by her sister on the bank,
→ and of having nothing to do…</p>
<p class="copy">So she was considering in
→ her own mind (as well as she could, for
→ the hot day made her feel very sleepy
→ and stupid)…</p>
<p>There was nothing so <i>very</i>
→ remarkable in that; nor did Alice think
→ it so <i>very</i> much out of the way to
→ hear the Rabbit say to itself, 'Oh dear!
→ Oh dear! I shall be late!'…</p>
</body></html>
```

✔ Tips

■ When you provide a list of fonts, the browser tries to use the first font listed. If that one isn't available to the browser, it works through the list until it encounters a font that is installed on the visitor's computer. If there are no matches, the browser displays the text in the visitor's default font. The advantage of specifying a generic font is that the browser tries to display the text in the same style of font, even if the specific ones you list are not available.

■ Your best strategy for listing fonts is to choose the first one from either the Mac or Windows System Fonts list (see the next section), the second one from the other list, and the final one from the generic font-family values.

■ Fonts that contain a space in their names must be enclosed in quotation marks (example: "Times New Roman").

■ Theoretically you can download a particular font to the visitor's computer and then specify the font by using the family-name property. However, in practice, this is at best impossible to pull off. See the sidebar "Downloadable Fonts" for details.

Using browser-safe fonts

Look around the Web, and what do you see? Two fonts: Arial and Times. Virtually every site whose designers made an effort to control the display of text uses either Times or Arial (or its Mac equivalent, Helvetica). This situation came about for one simple reason: Virtually every computer has these two fonts or some variant of them.

I am sick of them.

Don't get me wrong—these are great fonts, easy to read at many sizes. But as I said earlier, typography adds a language to text that goes far beyond the written word.

Web-based typography is mired in using Times for serif fonts and Helvetica/Arial for sans-serif fonts. This arrangement mutes the power of typography, and all Web pages begin to look the same.

What are the alternatives to the "terrible two"? That depends on the computer the person visiting your site is using. Mac and Windows computers have certain standard fonts that should always be installed. In addition, Internet Explorer (which comes installed on most computers these days) installs several additional fonts.

Of course, there's no guarantee that these fonts will be installed, but because they came with the operating system and unless they have been removed, they are just as likely to be available as Times, Helvetica, or Arial.

I have compiled lists of browser-safe fonts that should be available on each of the different platforms:

◆ Apple Macintosh (**Table 3.3**)

◆ Microsoft Windows (**Table 3.4**)

◆ Microsoft Core Fonts (**Table 3.5**) are installed with Internet Explorer for both Windows and Mac

Using CSS vs. the Font Tag

Other than CSS, the most common way to set a typeface is by using the <font> tag, as follows:

```
<font face="arial,helvetica">
→ Blah, 'blah, blah</font>
```

But the <font> tag is on the way out. The most recent versions of the HTML specification from the W3C does not include this tag, noting that fonts should be handled by CSS.

There are two basic problems with the <font> tag:

◆ You have to add this tag every time you set a font, which can significantly increase file size.

◆ If you need to change the font attributes, you have to change the value in every tag.

CSS solves both of these problems by allowing you to redefine how existing tags treat the text they contain, rather than adding more tags, and by allowing you to control these behaviors from a single line in the code.

Table 3.3

Mac System Fonts		Mac System Fonts (continued)	
FONT NAME	**STYLES**	**FONT NAME**	**STYLES**
Academy Engraved LET*		InaiMatha*	
American Typewriter	bold	Jazz LET*	
Andale Mono		Lucida Grande	bold
Apple Chancery		Marker Felt	
Apple Symbols		Mona Lisa Solid ITC TT*	
Arial	bold, italic, bold italic	Monaco	
Arial Black		Optima	bold, italic, bold italic
Arial Narrow	bold, italic, bold italic	Palatino	bold, italic, bold italic
Arial Rounded MT Bold		Papyrus	
Bank Gothic*	bold	Party LET*	
Baskerville	bold, italic, bold italic	PortagoITC TT*	
Big Caslon		Princetown LET*	
Blackmoor LET*		Santa Fe LET*	
BlairMdITC TT-Medium*		Savoye LET*	
Bodoni Ornaments ITC TT*		SchoolHouse Cursive B*	
Bodoni SvtyTwo ITC TT-Book*	bold, italic	SchoolHouse Printed A*	
Bodoni SvtyTwo SC ITC TT-Book*	bold, italic	Skia	
Bodoni SvtyTwo OS ITC TT-Book*	bold, italic	Snell Roundhand*	bold
Bordeaux Roman Bold LET*		Stone Sans ITC TT*	
Bradley Hand ITC TT*	bold	Stone Sans Sem ITC TT*	italic
Brush Script MT		Symbol	
Chalkboard*	bold	Synchro LET*	
Cochin*	bold, italic, bold italic	Times	bold, italic, bold italic
Comic Sans MS	bold	Times New Roman	bold, italic, bold italic
Copperplate	bold	Trebuchet MS	bold, italic, bold italic
Courier	bold	Type Embellishments One LET*	
Courier New	bold, italic, bold italic	Verdana	
Didot	bold, italic	Warnock Pro*	bold, italic, bold italic
Futura	bold	Warnock Pro Caption*	bold, italic, bold italic
Geneva		Warnock Pro Display*	bold, italic, bold italic
Georgia	bold, italic, bold italic	Warnock Pro Subhead*	bold, italic, bold italic
Gill Sans	bold, italic, bold italic		
Handwriting	Dakota		
Helvetica	bold		
Helvetica Neue	bold, italic, bold italic		
Helvetica Neue Black Condensed			
Helvetica Neue Bold Condensed			
Helvetica Neue Light	italic		
Helvetica Neue UltraLight	italic	Verdana	bold, italic, bold italic
Herculanum		Webdings	
Hoefler Text	bold, italic, bold italic	Zapf Dingbats	
Hoefler Text Ornaments		Zapfino	
Impact		*** = as of OS 10.4**	

As you can see, there are certainly more than two choices. This book's Web site (webbedenvironments.com/css_dhtml_ajax) also lists these fonts, and includes examples of what they should look like and which similar-looking fonts can be used as replacements.

✔ Tips

■ For more details on Mac fonts, see developer.apple.com/textfonts/.

■ For more details on Windows fonts, see microsoft.com/typography/fonts/.

■ Although these fonts have been listed for Web development, they can be used for any type of document (a presentation, a word-processor document, or whatever) that is being transferred between computer platforms.

Table 3.4

Microsoft Core Fonts

FONT NAME	STYLES
Andale Mono*	
Arial	bold, italic, bold italic
Arial Black	
Comic Sans MS	bold
Courier New	
Georgia	bold, bold italic, italic
Impact	
Times New Roman	bold, italic, bold italic
Trebuchet MS	bold, bold italic, italic
Verdana	bold, bold italic, italic
Webdings	

*Previously named Monotype.com

Table 3.5

Windows System Fonts

FONT NAME	STYLES
Arial	bold, italic, bold italic
Arial Black	
Calibri*	bold, italic, bold italic
Cambria*	bold, italic, bold italic
Candara*	bold, italic, bold italic
Comic Sans MS	bold
Consolas*	bold, italic, bold italic
Constantia*	bold, italic, bold italic
Corbel*	bold, italic, bold italic
Courier New	bold, bold italic, italic
Franklin Gothic Medium	italic
Georgia	bold, bold italic, italic
Impact	
Lucida Console	
Lucida Sans Unicode	
Palatino Linotype	bold, bold italic, italic
Symbol	
Tahoma	bold
Times New Roman	bold, bold italic, italic
Trebuchet MS	bold, bold italic, italic
Verdana	bold, bold italic, italic
Webdings	
Wingdings	

* = as of **Windows Vista**

Table 3.6

Font-Size Values	
VALUE	COMPATIBILITY
‹length›	IE3, FF1, S1, O3.5, CSS1
‹percentage›	IE3, FF1, S1, O3.5, CSS1
smaller	IE4, FF1, S1, O3.5, CSS1
larger	IE4, FF1, S1, O3.5, CSS1
xx-small	IE3, FF1, S1, O3.5, CSS1
x-small	IE3, FF1, S1, O3.5, CSS1
small	IE3, FF1, S1, O3.5, CSS1
medium	IE3, FF1, S1, O3.5, CSS1
large	IE3, FF1, S1, O3.5, CSS1
x-large	IE3, FF1, S1, O3.5, CSS1
xx-large	IE3, FF1, S1, O3.5, CSS1

8pt   12pt   16pt   20pt

.7pc   1pc   1.25pc   1.5pc

3mm   4mm   5mm   6mm

.7em   1em   1.25em   1.5em

1.5ex   2ex   2.5ex   3ex

10px   14px   18px   24px

Figure 3.5 A few font sizes in different units.

Setting the Font Size

With CSS, you can specify the size of the text on the screen using several notations or methods, including the traditional print based point-size notation, percentage, absolute size, and even a size relative to the surrounding text (**Table 3.6**). **Figure 3.5** shows text in different size units.

Fonts can either be set as absolute sizes, which defines the size based against a standard length measurement, or relative sizes, which are in relation to defaults set for the browser. Generally, relative sizes are preferred, since this gives users the power to display the text at whatever size is most comfortable for them.

Choosing Font Size Value Type for Screen or Print

Although they give you more exact control, absolute value types (such as point) are unreliable for the screen and can limit how the end user displays your work.

The *point* (abbreviated *pt*) is one way of referring to a font's absolute size. A 12-point font is a fairly average size for use in printed materials and is comfortable for most readers. The size of a point, however, varies slightly on the screen between operating systems, so a font set to 12 points in Windows appears larger than the same font set to 12 points on a Mac. Although an acceptable choice in CSS for print media (see "Setting Styles for Print and Other Media" in Chapter 2) point sizes are a poor choice for screen display.

I recommend sticking with relative value types (especially em) for screen and absolute value types for print.

In this example (**Figure 3.6**), I define the default size of text on the page to 1.2em and then set other font sizes on the page relative to that font-size.

To define the font size in a rule:

1. font-size:

Type the property name font-size, followed by a colon (**Code 3.2**).

2. 48px;

Type a value for the font size, which could be any of the following options:

▲ A relative or absolute length unit (often, the font size in pixels or em). See "Values and Units Used in This Book" in the Introduction for more detail.

▲ An absolute size keyword, relative to the default page size: xx-small, x-small, small, medium, large, x-large, and xx-large.

▲ A relative size keyword of smaller or larger, to describe the font size in relation to its parent element.

▲ A percentage, representing how much larger (values over 100%) or smaller (values less than 100%) the text is relative to the size of its parent element.

The value you use will depend on your need; however, it is generally recommended to set relative font sizes to allow visitors final control of how large they are displayed.

Figure 3.6 The size of the font helps determine its legibility and the emphasis it receives on the page. Titles usually are larger than copy, but some text needs a little more attention.

Code 3.2 The font size has been defined for the body—slightly larger than normal—and then sizes have been set relative to that font size for other elements.

```
<!DOCTYPE html PUBLIC "-//W3C//DTD XHTML
→ 1.0 Strict//EN" "http://www.w3.org/TR/
→ xhtml1/DTD/xhtml1-strict.dtd">
<html xmlns="http://www.w3.org/1999/xhtml">
<head>
<meta http-equiv="Content-Type"
→ content="text/html; charset=UTF-8" />
<title>CSS, DHTML &amp; Ajax | Setting the
→ Font Size</title>
<style type="text/css" media="all">
body {
    font-size: 1.2em;
    font-family: Georgia, "Times New
    → Roman", times, serif; }
h1 {
    font-size: 48px; }
h2 {
    font-size: larger; }
p.copy {
    font-size: small; }
.author {
    font-size: 156%; }
</style>
</head>
<body>
<div id="header">
    <h1>Alice's Adventures in Wonderland</h1>
    <p class="author">Lewis Carroll</p>
    <h2>CHAPTER II<br />
    The Pool of Tears</h2>
</div>
<p>'Curiouser and curiouser!' cried Alice
→ (she was so much surprised, that for the
→ moment she quite forgot how to speak good
→ English); 'now I'm opening out like the
→ largest telescope that ever was! Good-
→ bye, feet!'…</p>
<p class="copy">And she went on planning to
→ herself how she would manage it…</p>
<blockquote><p>
ALICE'S RIGHT FOOT, ESQ.<br />
HEARTHRUG,<br />
NEAR THE FENDER,<br />
(WITH ALICE'S LOVE).
</p></blockquote>
<p class="copy">Oh dear, what nonsense I'm
→ talking!'</p>
<p class="copy">Just then her head struck
→ against the roof of the hall: in fact she
→ was now more than nine feet high…</p>
</body></html>
```

✔ Tips

■ You may notice that I have set a size of 1.2em for text throughout this book. This is slightly larger than you might normally want the text on your pages to be (generally 1em or smaller), but works well for getting the text large enough so that you can see it in the figures.

■ Avoid defining screen media font sizes with points or other absolute font-sizes, since these tend to render inconsistently across platforms. However, they're fine to use for print style sheets. See the sidebar "Choosing Font Size Value Type for Screen or Print" for more detail.

■ Your best strategy for setting font sizes is to set a relative length size for the <body> tag (such as 1em), and then use absolute font sizes (such as small) or relative font sizes (such as larger) to adjust the size, based on the body size. This ensures the most consistent and versatile page viewing, regardless of the actual media being used (computer screen, printed page, handheld, etc.).

■ The term *copy* is used as a noun in the publishing world to refer to the main text of an article or book. Many Web designers will often create a class called .copy to format the main text on the page, generally used with the paragraph tag.

■ Notice in this section's example that paragraphs that are not assigned the copy class appear in the body default font-size.

Making Text Italic

Two kinds of styled text that are often confused are *italic* and *oblique*. An italic font is a special version of a particular font, redesigned with more pronounced serifs and usually a slight slant to the right. An oblique font, on the other hand, is simply a font that is slanted to the right by the computer.

Using the `font-style` element (**Table 3.7**), you can define a font as italic, oblique, or normal. When a font is set to italic but does not have an explicit italic version, the font defaults to oblique (**Figure 3.7**).

In this example (**Figure 3.8**), the h1 and h2 tags use the same serif font, but h1 is italic and h2 is oblique. Notice however, that they look the same. In reality, most browsers do not differentiate between the two values, generally using the italic version of the font for both if it is available.

To set font-style in an HTML tag:

1. `font-style:`

   Type the property name `font-style` (**Code 3.3**), followed by a colon (`:`).

2. `italic;`

   Type a value for the `font-style`. Your options are:

   ▲ `italic`, which displays the type in an italic version of the font

   ▲ `oblique`, which slants the text to the right

   ▲ `normal`, which overrides any other styles set

Table 3.7

Font-Style Values	
VALUE	COMPATIBILITY
normal	IE3, FF1, S1, O3.5, CSS1
italic	IE3, FF1, S1, O3.5, CSS1
oblique	IE4, N6, S1, O3.5, CSS1

normal *italic oblique*

Figure 3.7 Italic or oblique? To really tell the difference, take a careful look at the letter "i" in both words.

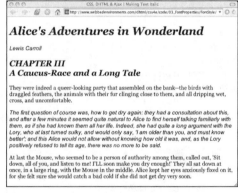

Figure 3.8 Book titles and quotes are generally italicized to set them off. Notice that serif fonts are truly italic, while sans-serif fonts are oblique, regardless of whether you set italic or oblique.

Code 3.3 The level 1 heading is italicized, while the level 2 heading is oblique. However, notice that they still look the same.

```
<!DOCTYPE html PUBLIC "-//W3C//DTD XHTML 1.0
→ Strict//EN" "http://www.w3.org/TR/
→ xhtml1/DTD/xhtml1-strict.dtd">
<html xmlns="http://www.w3.org/1999/xhtml">
<head>
<meta http-equiv="Content-Type"
→ content="text/html; charset=UTF-8" />
<title>CSS, DHTML &amp; Ajax | Making Text
→ Italic</title>
<style type="text/css" media="all">
body {
    font-size: 1.2em;
    font-family: Georgia, "Times New
→ Roman", times, serif;
    font-style: normal; }
h1 {
    font-style: italic; }
h2 {
    font-style: oblique; }
p.copy {
    font-family: arial,helvetica,serif;
    font-style: italic; }
.author {
    font-family: arial,helvetica,serif;
    font-style: oblique; }
</style>
</head>
<body>
<div id="header">
    <h1>Alice's Adventures in Wonderland</h1>
    <p class="author">Lewis Carroll</p>
    <h2>CHAPTER III<br />
    A Caucus-Race and a Long Tale</h2>
</div>
<p>They were indeed a queer-looking party
→ that assembled on the bank--the birds
→ with draggled feathers, the animals with
→ their fur clinging close to them, and all
→ dripping wet, cross, and uncomfortable.</p>
<p class="copy">The first question of course
→ was, how to get dry again: they had a
→ consultation about this, and after a few
→ minutes it seemed quite natural to Alice
→ to find herself talking familiarly with
→ them...</p>
<p>At last the Mouse, who seemed to be a
→ person of authority among them, called
→ out...</p>
</body></html>
```

✔ Tips

- Many browsers do not differentiate between italic and oblique, but will simply treat all serif fonts as italic, even when they are set to oblique. For example, with the class obliqueText, the Times New Roman font is still rendered as italic, even though it is set for oblique.

- Many Web designers underline words to draw visual attention to them. I recommend using italic or oblique text instead. Underlining often causes the page to look cluttered. More important, underlined text might be confused with hypertext links.

- Italicized text generally fits into a more compact space than does non-italic text (called *roman* in traditional typesetting terms) and could be used to save screen space. But be careful—at small point sizes, italic can be difficult to read on the screen.

Setting Bold, Bolder, Boldest

CSS provides several options that allow you to set different levels of boldness for text. Many fonts have various weights associated with them; these weights have the effect of making the text look more or less bold (**Table 3.8**). CSS can take advantage of this feature (**Figure 3.9**).

In this example (**Figure 3.10**), the h1 tag is set to be bolder (which it would normally be), but the h2 tag is set to be lighter, which has the effect of using the normal font. In reality, most fonts only support normal and bold, so relative values have an absolute effect. Notice also, though, that we can turn bold off in the middle of a paragraph of text by using normal or lighter to a child tag.

To define bold text in a CSS rule:

1. `font-weight:`

   Type the property name `font-weight` (**Code 3.4**), followed by a colon (`:`).

2. `bold;`

   Type the value for the `font-weight` property, using one of the following options:

   ▲ `bold`, which sets the font to boldface

   ▲ `bolder` or `lighter`, which sets the font's weight to be bolder or lighter relative to its parent element's weight

   ▲ A value from `100` to `900`, in increments of 100, which increases the weight, based on alternative versions of the font that are available

   ▲ `normal`, which overrides other weight specifications

✔ Tip

■ Use `font-weight` to add emphasis to text, but use it sparingly. If everything is bold, nothing stands out.

Table 3.8

Font-Weight Values	
VALUE	COMPATIBILITY
normal	IE3, FF1, S1, O3.5, CSS1
bold	IE3, FF1, S1, O3.5, CSS1
lighter	IE4, S1, O3.5, CSS1
bolder	IE4, S1, O3.5, CSS1
100-900*	IE4, FF1, S1, O3.5, CSS1

* Depending on available font weights

normal   **bold**

Figure 3.9 The difference between normal and bold text is evident here.

Figure 3.10 All the text has been set to bold except italicized words, which are a normal weight.

Font-Weight Numbers

Most fonts do not have nine weights, so if you specify a `font-weight` value that is not available, another weight is used, based on the following system:

◆ 100 to 300 use the next-lighter weight, if available, or the next-darker

◆ 400 and 500 may be used interchangeably

◆ 600 to 900 use the next-darker weight, if available, or the next-lighter

Code 3.4 The copy class is used to make boldface text. Italics within a paragraph with the copy class assigned have been set to non-bold.

```
<!DOCTYPE html PUBLIC "-//W3C//DTD XHTML 1.0 Strict//EN" "http://www.w3.org/TR/xhtml1/DTD/xhtml1-
→ strict.dtd">
<html xmlns="http://www.w3.org/1999/xhtml">
<head>
<meta http-equiv="Content-Type" content="text/html; charset=UTF-8" />
<title>CSS, DHTML &amp; Ajax | Setting Bold, Bolder, Boldest</title>
<style type="text/css" media="all">
body {
     font-size: 1.2em;
     font-family: Georgia, "Times New Roman", times, serif;
     font-weight: normal;
}
h1 {
     font-weight: bold;
}
h2 {
     font-weight: lighter;
}
p.copy {
     font-weight: bold;
}
p.copy em {
     font-weight: normal;
     }
.author {
     font-weight: bold;
}
</style>
</head>
<body>
<div id="header">
     <h1>Alice's Adventures in Wonderland</h1>
     <p class="author">Lewis Carroll</p>
     <h2>CHAPTER IV<br />
     The Rabbit Sends in a Little Bill</h2>
</div>
<p class="copy">It was the White Rabbit, trotting slowly back again, and looking anxiously about as
→ it went, as if it had lost something; and she heard it muttering to itself <em>'The Duchess! The
→ Duchess! Oh my dear paws! Oh my fur and whiskers! She'll get me executed, as sure as ferrets are
→ ferrets! Where CAN I have dropped them, I wonder?'</em> Alice guessed in a moment that it was
→ looking for the fan and the pair of white kid gloves, and she very good-naturedly began hunting
→ about for them, but they were nowhere to be seen--everything seemed to have changed since her
→ swim in the pool, and the great hall, with the glass table and the little door, had vanished
→ completely.</p>
</body>
</html>
```

SETTING BOLD, BOLDER, BOLDEST

Creating Small Caps

Small caps (sometimes referred to as *mini-caps*) are useful for emphasizing titles (**Table 3.9**). With small caps, lowercase letters are converted to uppercase, but in a slightly smaller size than regular uppercase letters (**Figure 3.11**).

In this example (**Figure 3.12**), small caps are applied to the entire header area, but this is overridden for the author's name.

To make a rule for small caps:

1. `font-variant:`

   Type the property name `font-variant` (**Code 3.5**), followed by a colon (:).

2. `small-caps;`

   Type the value of the `font-variant` property, using one of the following options:

   ▲ `small-caps`, which sets lowercase letters as smaller versions of true uppercase letters

   ▲ `normal`, which overrides other font-variant values that might be inherited

Table 3.9

Font-Variant Values	
VALUE	COMPATIBILITY
normal	IE4, FF1, S1, O3.5, CSS1
small-caps	IE4, FF1, S1, O3.5, CSS1

Normal   SMALLCAPS

Figure 3.11 All the letters are capitals, but the first letter is larger than the rest.

Figure 3.12 Using small caps for the title is an elegant way to set it off from the rest of the text.

Code 3.5 The header ID is set to be displayed in small caps, but the author class will override that.

```
<!DOCTYPE html PUBLIC "-//W3C//DTD XHTML 1.0
→ Strict//EN"
"http://www.w3.org/TR/xhtml1/DTD/xhtml1-
→ strict.dtd">
<html xmlns="http://www.w3.org/1999/xhtml">
<head>
<meta http-equiv="Content-Type"
content="text/html; charset=UTF-8" />
<title>CSS, DHTML &amp; Ajax | Creating
→ Small Caps</title>
<style type="text/css" media="all">
body {
    font-size: 1.2em;
    font-family: Georgia, "Times New
    → Roman", times, serif;
}
#header {
    font-variant: small-caps;
}
.author {
    font-variant: normal;
}
</style>
</head>
<body>
<div id="header">
    <h1>Alice's Adventures in Wonderland</h1>
    <p class="author">Lewis Carroll</p>
    <h2>CHAPTER V<br />
    Advice from a Caterpillar</h2>
</div>
<p> The Caterpillar and Alice looked at each
→ other for some time in silence: at last
→ the Caterpillar took the hookah out of
→ its mouth, and addressed her in a languid,
→ sleepy voice.</p>
</body>
</html>
```

✔ Tip

- Small caps are best reserved for titles or other special text; they are hard to read at smaller sizes.

Setting Multiple Font Values

Although you can set font properties independently, it is often useful, not to mention more concise, to put all font elements in a single declaration (**Table 3.10**). To do this, you use the shorthand font property.

This example (**Figure 3.13**) shows a level 1 heading tag being defined, along with a class called copy that will be applied to paragraphs of text. In addition, the author's name is defined with the shorthand font style (see the sidebar "Mimicking the Visitor's Styles").

To define several font attributes simultaneously in a rule:

1. font:

   Type the property name font (**Code 3.6**), followed by a colon (:). Then type the values in same order that they are typed in the remaining steps of this exercise.

2. italic

   Type a font-style value, followed by a space (see "Making Text Italic" earlier in this chapter).

3. small-caps

   Type a font-variant value, followed by a space (see the previous section, "Creating Small Caps").

4. bold

   Type a font-weight value, followed by a space (see "Setting Bold, Bolder, Boldest" earlier in this chapter).

5. xx-large

   Type a font-size value (see "Setting the Font Size" earlier in this chapter).

Table 3.10

Font Values	
VALUE	COMPATIBILITY
‹font-style›	IE3, FF1, S1, O3.5, CSS1
‹font-variant›	IE4, FF1, S1, O3.5, CSS1
‹font-weight›	IE3, FF1, S1, O3.5, CSS1
‹font-size›	IE3, FF1, S1, O3.5, CSS1
‹line-height›	IE3, FF1, S1, O3.5, CSS1
‹font-family›	IE3, FF1, S1, O3.5, CSS1
visitor styles	IE4/5.5, S2, O6, CSS2

Figure 3.13 You can set all the font properties (and the line height discussed in Chapter 4) in a single definition and even instruct the page to use styles defined by the visitor's computer.

Code 3.6 The h1 tag explicitly sets all of the font properties, while the author sets a user style value to mimic the caption style.

```
<!DOCTYPE html PUBLIC "-//W3C//DTD XHTML 1.0
→ Strict//EN" "http://www.w3.org/TR/
→ xhtml1/DTD/xhtml1-strict.dtd">
<html xmlns="http://www.w3.org/1999/xhtml">
<head>
<meta http-equiv="Content-Type"
content="text/html; charset=UTF-8" />
<title>CSS, DHTML &amp; Ajax | Setting
→ Multiple Font Values</title>
<style type="text/css" media="all">
body {
    font: normal normal normal 1.2em/1.3em
    → Arial, Helvetica, Geneva, sans-serif;
}
h1 {
    font: bold italic small-caps xx-
    → large/110% "Minion Web", Georgia,
    → "Times New Roman", Times, serif;
}
h2 {
    font: x-large Cracked, Impact, fantasy;
}
.author {
    font: icon;
}
p.copy {
    font: .9em/1.8em "Times New Roman",
    → times, serif ;
}
</style>
</head>
<body>
<div id="header">
    <h1>Alice's Adventures in Wonderland</h1>
    <p class="author">Lewis Carroll</p>
    <h2>CHAPTER I<br />
    Down the Rabbit-Hole</h2>
</div>
<p class="copy">Alice was beginning to get
→ very tired of sitting by her sister on
→ the bank…</p>
<p class="copy">There was nothing so
→ <i>very</i> remarkable in that; nor did
→ Alice think it so <i>very</i> much out of
→ the way to hear the Rabbit say to itself,
→ 'Oh dear! Oh dear! I shall be late!'…</p>
</body>
</html>
```

6. /110%

Type a forward slash (/), a line-height value, and a space (see "Adjusting Text Spacing" in Chapter 4).

7. 'minion web', Georgia, 'Times New → Roman', Times, serif;

Type a font-family value and closing semicolon (refer to "Setting the Font" earlier in this chapter).

✔ Tips

■ If you don't want to set a particular value in the list, just leave it out. The browser will use its default value instead.

■ If you need to override a value set by the font shorthand property, it's generally best to use the full property (such as font-style, font-varient, font-weight, and font-family).

■ The font shorthand property is a real time-saver, and I try to use it as often as possible. WYSIWYG programs such as GoLive and Dreamweaver, however, tend to default to using the individual properties.

Mimicking the Visitor's Styles

Wouldn't it be nice if you could match your visitor's system font styles? You can do this by simply declaring the font style to be one of the following keywords (for example, `font: icon;`):

- `caption`: the font style being used by controls, such as buttons

- `icon`: the font style being used to label icons

- `menu`: the font style being used in drop-down menus and menu lists

- `message-box`: the font style being used in dialog boxes

- `small-caption`: the font style being used for labeling small controls

- `status-bar`: the font style being used in the window's status bar

Downloadable Fonts

The Holy Grail of Web-based typography is downloadable fonts. Imagine if, rather than having to rely on the limited list of browser-safe fonts or having to create graphics just to get the typeface you want to use, you could send the font to the visitor's computer automatically.

Actually, the CSS Level 2 standard allows for downloadable fonts, so why don't we see downloaded fonts all over the Web? There are several impediments to simple font delivery:

- Many fonts are not free. There is some concern among font creators that they will not be compensated if their fonts are distributed over the Web. This assumes that users can download and reuse fonts without having to pay for them.

- Windows and Mac fonts are incompatible. You would have to include versions for both platforms.

- Font files can be quite large and, thus, take a while to download.

Netscape and Microsoft introduced schemes to overcome these problems and allow font downloading for Web pages. The problem is that you can't simply queue a font like a graphic and have it download. Instead, you have to process the font for the Web.

Unfortunately, Netscape and Microsoft came up with incompatible—not to mention difficult—systems for creating downloadable fonts.

For Internet Explorer, you have to convert your fonts to .eot format, using a program called WEFT (microsoft.com/typography/web/embedding/). This program, however, is Windows-only software.

For Netscape, you have to purchase software from Bitstream to convert your fonts to TrueDoc format (truedoc.com). According to Bitstream, this format works in both Netscape and Internet Explorer, but is extremely buggy.

On the distant horizon, CSS3 promises to sort out the font download problems. But, as I discussed in Chapter 1, that may be a long time in coming.

SETTING MULTIPLE FONT VALUES

TEXT
PROPERTIES

Text is everywhere around us. Text can be used for everything from listing the ingredients in breakfast cereal to writing an ode to a Grecian urn. It is the best system yet that humans have devised for relating complex thoughts.

Many people think of text as being simply a way of recording spoken words, but typography adds a language to text that goes far beyond the written word.

Typography affects how text appears by controlling not only the shapes and sizes of the letters being used (the font), but also the spaces between letters, words, lines, and paragraphs. On the Web, typography has taken up the challenges of displaying text on a computer screen to a wider audience.

Unfortunately, many of the challenges of typography on the Web have come about as a result of a need to circumvent the limitations of the medium.

In this chapter, I'll show you ways to present text using CSS to open up the screen and improve legibility, as well as to draw interest.

Adjusting Text Spacing

One feature of CSS that HTML styles have no parallel for is the ability to easily adjust the space between text, including the space between individual letters (kerning), words, and lines of text in a paragraph (leading). Of course, you could resort to non-breaking spaces and the line break tag to get a similar effect with straight HTML, but these are kludges that are difficult to implement, control, and change. With CSS, you have exact control over all of these elements and you can change them as desired.

Adjusting the space between letters

Tracking refers to the amount of space between letters in a word, which in CSS is controlled with the `letter-spacing` property (**Table 4.1**). More space between letters often improves the readability of the text. On the other hand, too much space can hamper reading by making individual words appear less distinct on the page.

In this example (**Figure 4.1**), space has been removed in the level 1 heading (the book title) to create a cramped effect. The author name and chapter number have been spaced out; however, the spacing was overridden in the actual chapter title ("Down the Rabbit Hole"), so it appears normal.

To define tracking:

1. `letter-spacing:`

   Type the `letter-spacing` property name, followed by a colon (:) in the CSS definition list (**Code 4.1**).

Table 4.1

Letter-Spacing Values	
VALUE	COMPATIBILITY
normal	IE4, FF1, S1, O3.5, CSS1
<length>	IE4, FF1, S1, O3.5, CSS1

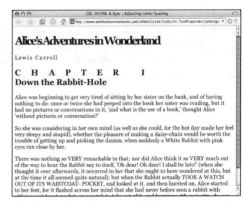

Figure 4.1 The titles have had their spacing altered for effect, while the main copy has been spaced out to look less crowded.

Tracking or Kerning?

While *tracking* refers to the spacing between letters in a word, *kerning* refers to the spacing between individual letter pairs in a proportional font. Is this splitting hairs? There is actually a distinction.

Tracking is applied to a word to equally space all of the letters, while kerning is applied between each letter to give each space the same visual appearance. However, using tracking may mean that some letters are spaced (absolutely speaking) more than others. Although you could use CSS letter spacing to set the space between each letter manually, generally text kerning is accomplished using specialized layout software because it's very hard to do just by eye-balling the letters.

Code 4.1 You can use letter spacing to create a visual effect by spacing out or crowding characters, using a positive or negative value, respectively.

```
<!DOCTYPE html PUBLIC "-//W3C//DTD XHTML 1.0
→ Strict//EN" "http://www.w3.org/TR/xhtml1/
→ DTD/xhtml1-strict.dtd">
<html xmlns="http://www.w3.org/1999/xhtml">
<head>
<meta http-equiv="Content-Type"
→ content="text/html; charset=UTF-8" />
<title>CSS, DHTML &amp; Ajax | Adjusting
→ Letter Spacing</title>
<style type="text/css">
<!--
body {
    font-size: 1.2em;
    font-family: Georgia, "Times New
    → Roman", times, serif;
    letter-spacing: normal;
}
h1 {
    letter-spacing: -5px;
}
h2 {
    letter-spacing: 1.25em;
}
.author {
    letter-spacing: 3px;
}
.chapterTitle {
    letter-spacing: normal;
}
-->
</style>
</head>
<body>
<div id="header">
    <h1>Alice's Adventures in Wonderland</h1>
    <p class="author">Lewis Carroll</p>
    <h2>CHAPTER I<br />
        <span class="chapterTitle">Down the
        → Rabbit-Hole</span></h2>
</div>
<p class="copy">Alice was beginning to get
→ very tired of sitting by her sister on
→ the bank...</p>
<p class="copy">So she was considering in
→ her own mind...</p>
<p class="copy">There was nothing so VERY
→ remarkable in that...<p>
</body>
</html>
```

2. -5px;

Type a value for the `letter-spacing` property, using either of these:

▲ A positive or negative **length value**, such as -5px, which sets the absolute space between letters. See "Values and Units Used in this Book" in the Introduction for more details.

▲ `normal`, which overrides inherited spacing attributes.

✔ Tip

■ A positive value for `letter-spacing` adds space between letters; a negative value closes the space. A value of 0 does not add or subtract space, but prevents justification of the text (see "Aligning Text Horizontally" later in this chapter).

ADJUSTING TEXT SPACING

115

Adjusting space between words

Just like adjusting tracking, adjusting word spacing can both help and hinder legibility. Adding a little space between words on the screen using the word-spacing property (**Table 4.2**) can help make your text easier to read, but too much space interrupts the path of the reader's eye across the screen and, therefore, interferes with reading.

In this example (**Figure 4.2**), the words in the level 1 heading overlap, while the words in the chapter title class are extremely spaced out. The copy (body text) is slightly spaced out, which has the overall effect of lightening the page by creating more white space.

To define word spacing:

1. word-spacing:

   Type the word-spacing property name, followed by a colon (:) in the CSS definition list (**Code 4.2**).

2. -1em;

   Set the value for word-spacing, using either of the following:

   ▲ A positive or negative **length value**, representing the amount of space between words (-1em, for example). See "Values and Units Used in this Book" in the Introduction for more details.

   ▲ normal, which overrides inherited values.

✔ Tip

■ A positive value for word spacing adds space between words, and a negative value closes the space. A value of 0 neither adds nor subtracts space, but prevents justification (see "Aligning Text Horizontally" later in this chapter).

Table 4.2

Word-Spacing Values	
VALUE	COMPATIBILITY
normal	IE4*, FF1, S1, O3.5, CSS1
‹length›	IE4*, FF1, S1, O3.5, CSS1
*IE 6 in Windows	

Figure 4.2 The space between the words has been changed for effect in the titles and slightly increased to lighten the copy.

Code 4.2 You can adjust the spacing between words either for effect or to lighten your page.

```
<!DOCTYPE html PUBLIC "-//W3C//DTD XHTML 1.0 Strict//EN" "http://www.w3.org/TR/xhtml1/DTD/xhtml1-
→ strict.dtd">
<html xmlns="http://www.w3.org/1999/xhtml">
<head>
<meta http-equiv="Content-Type" content="text/html; charset=UTF-8" />
<title>CSS, DHTML &amp; Ajax | Adjusting Word Spacing</title>
<style type="text/css">
<!--
body {
    font-size: 1.2em;
    font-family: Georgia, "Times New Roman", times, serif;
    word-spacing: normal;
}
h1 {
    word-spacing: -1em;
}
h2 {
    word-spacing: normal;
}
.chapterTitle {
    word-spacing: 36px;
}
p.copy {
    word-spacing: 2px;
}
-->
</style>
</head>
<body>
<div id="header">
    <h1>Alice's Adventures in Wonderland</h1>
    <p class="author">Lewis Carroll</p>
    <h2>CHAPTER II<br />
    <span class="chapterTitle">The Pool of Tears</span></h2>
</div>
<p class="copy">'Curiouser and curiouser!' cried Alice (she was so much surprised, that for the
→ moment she quite forgot how to speak good English)…</p>
<p class="copy">And she went on planning to herself how she would manage it…!</p>
<p> ALICE'S RIGHT FOOT, ESQ.</p>
<p> HEARTHRUG,</p>
<p> NEAR THE FENDER,</p>
<p> (WITH ALICE'S LOVE).</p>
<p class="copy">Oh dear, what nonsense I'm talking!'</p>
<p class="copy">Just then her head struck against the roof of the hall…</p>
</body>
</html>
```

117

Adjusting space between lines of text

Anybody who has ever typed a term paper knows that these papers usually have to be double-spaced to make reading easier and allow space for comments on the page. Space between lines *(leading)* also can be increased for a dramatic effect by creating areas of negative space between the text. The line-height property (**Table 4.3**) adds space between the baselines (the bottoms of most letters) of lines of text.

In this example (**Figure 4.3**), the copy has been double-spaced, and the citation text has its line height set slightly above the font size. In addition, the leading for the level 1 and 2 headings have been reduced below the font size to squeeze the lines together.

To define leading:

1. line-height:

   Type the line-height property name, followed by a colon (:), in the CSS definition list (**Code 4.3**).

2. 2.0;

   Type the value for line-height, using one of the following options:

   ▲ A **number** to be multiplied by the font size to get the spacing value (2.0 for double spacing, for example). Although a simple value of 2 works, it will not validate properly, so always include the decimal.

   ▲ A **length value**, such as 24px. The space for each line of text is set to this size regardless of the designated font size. So if the font size is set to 12px and the line height is set to 24px, the text will be double-spaced. See "Values and Units Used in this Book" in the Introduction for more details.

Table 4.3

Line-Height Values	
VALUE	COMPATIBILITY
normal	IE3, FF1, S1, O3.5, CSS1
‹number›	IE4, FF1, S1, O3.5, CSS1
‹length›	IE3, FF1, S1, O3.5, CSS1
‹percentage›	IE3, FF1, S1, O3.5, CSS1

Figure 4.3 The line height in the titles has been tightened for effect and loosened in the copy to open it up.

Code 4.3 The `line-height` property adjusts the spacing between lines of text in a single paragraph, allowing you to compress or expand for effect or better readability.

```
<!DOCTYPE html PUBLIC "-//W3C//DTD XHTML 1.0
→ Strict//EN" "http://www.w3.org/TR/xhtml1/
→ DTD/xhtml1-strict.dtd">
<html xmlns="http://www.w3.org/1999/xhtml">
<head>
<meta http-equiv="Content-Type"
→ content="text/html; charset=UTF-8" />
<title>CSS, DHTML &amp; Ajax | Setting Line
→ Spacing</title>
<style type="text/css">
<!--
body {
    font-size: 1.2em;
    font-family: Georgia, "Times New Roman",
    → times, serif;
    line-height: 100%;
}
h1, h2 {
    line-height: 75%;
}
p.copy {
    line-height: 2.0;
}
p cite {
    font-size: 12px;
    line-height: 14px;
}
-->
</style>
</head>
<body>
<div id="header">
    <h1>Alice's Adventures in Wonderland</h1>
    <p class="author">Lewis Carroll</p>
    <h2>CHAPTER III<br />
        <span class="chapterTitle">A
        → Caucus-Race and a Long
        → Tale</span></h2>
</div>
<p class="copy">They were indeed a queer-
→ looking party that assembled on the
→ bank...<p>
<cite>The first question of course was, how
→ to get dry again: they had a consultation
→ about this...<cite>
<p class="copy">At last the Mouse, who
→ seemed to be a person of authority among
→ them, called out...</p>
</body>
</html>
```

▲ A **percentage**, which sets the line height proportionate to the font size being used for the text.

▲ `normal`, which overrides inherited spacing values.

✔ Tips

■ Adding space between lines of text enhances legibility—especially in large amounts of text. Generally, a line height of 1.5 to 2 times the font size is appropriate for most text.

■ To double-space text, set the `line-height` value as either 2 or 200%. Likewise, 3 or 300% results in triple-spaced text.

■ You can use a percentage value lower than 100% or length values smaller than the font size to smash text lines together. Although this effect may look neat in moderation, it probably won't ingratiate you with your readers if they can't actually read the text.

■ Line height can also be defined at the same time as the font-size using the `font` shorthand property (see "Setting Multiple Font Values" in Chapter 3).

ADJUSTING TEXT SPACING

119

Setting Text Case

When you're dealing with dynamically generated output, from a database for example, you can never be sure whether the text will appear in uppercase, lowercase, or a mixture. With the `text-transform` property (**Table 4.4**), you can control the ultimate case of the text no matter what it begins with.

In this example (**Figure 4.4**), the level 1 heading tag is forced into uppercase, the level 2 heading is forced into lower case, although the chapter title class overrides this—displaying the text as typed—and the author name is forced to capitalize, even though all of the letters are lowercase.

To define the text case:

1. `text-transform:`

   Type the `text-transform` property name, followed by a colon (`:`), in the CSS definition list (**Code 4.4**).

2. `uppercase;`

   Type one of the following values for `text-transform` to specify how you want the text to be treated:

   ▲ `capitalize` sets the first letter of each word in uppercase

   ▲ `uppercase` forces all letters to be uppercase

   ▲ `lowercase` forces all letters to be lowercase

   ▲ `none` overrides inherited text-case values and leaves the text as-is

Table 4.4

Text-Transform Values	
VALUE	COMPATIBILITY
capitalize	IE4, FF1, S1, O3.5, CSS1
uppercase	IE4, FF1, S1, O3.5, CSS1
lowercase	IE4, FF1, S1, O3.5, CSS1
none	IE4, FF1, S1, O3.5, CSS1

Figure 4.4 The text in the level 1 heading is in all caps (typical for book titles). The chapter number is forced into lowercase, and the chapter title ignores the lowercase.

Code 4.4 You can add the `text-transform` property to various tags to ensure that the text appears the way you want it to, regardless of how it appears in the HTML.

```
<!DOCTYPE html PUBLIC "-//W3C//DTD XHTML 1.0
→ Strict//EN" "http://www.w3.org/TR/xhtml1/
→ DTD/xhtml1-strict.dtd">
<html xmlns="http://www.w3.org/1999/xhtml">
<head>
<meta http-equiv="Content-Type"
→ content="text/html; charset=UTF-8" />
<title>CSS, DHTML &amp; Ajax | Setting Text
→ Case</title>
<style type="text/css" media="screen">
<!--
body {
    font-size: 1.2em;
    font-family: Georgia, "Times New
→ Roman", times, serif;
    text-transform: none;
}
h1 {
    text-transform: uppercase;
}
h2 {
    text-transform: lowercase;
}
.author {
    text-transform: capitalize;
}
.chapterTitle {
    text-transform: none;
}
-->
</style>
</head>
<body>
<div id="header">
    <h1>Alice's Adventures in
→ Wonderland</h1>
    <p class="author">lewis carroll</p>
    <h2>CHAPTER IV<br />
        <span class="chapterTitle">The
        → Rabbit Sends in a Little
        → Bill</span></h2>
</div>
<p>It was the White Rabbit, trotting slowly
→ back again, and looking anxiously about
→ as it went, as if it had lost
→ something…</p>
</body>
</html>
```

✔ Tips

■ You shouldn't rely on text-case. If you want specific text to be uppercase, you should type it as uppercase.

■ The `text-transform` property probably is best reserved for formatting text that is being created dynamically. If the names in a database are all uppercase, for example, you can use `text-transform` to make them more legible when displayed.

SETTING TEXT CASE

121

Adding a Text Drop Shadow

The drop shadow is a time-honored method for adding depth and texture to two-dimensional designs. Apple's Safari browser has included the `text-shadow` property, which is part of CSS3 (**Table 4.5**), allowing you to define the color, offset (x and y), and blur for a drop shadow behind any text. Although this will not work in any browser except Safari, it will not interfere with other browsers either.

In this example (**Figure 4.5**), the level 1 heading has a nice reddish glow behind it, while other text has different drop shadows to make them stand out.

To define the text shadow:

1. `text-shadow:`

   Type the `text-shadow` property name, followed by a colon (`:`), in the CSS definition list (**Code 4.5**).

2. `#f66`

   Type a space and then a color value for the shadow. See "Values and Units Used in this Book" in the Introduction for more detail on color values.

3. `10px 12px`

   Type a space and then two positive or negative length values separated by a space. The first value is the vertical distance to offset the shadow (positive is down; negative is up). The second value is the horizontal offset (positive is right; negative is left).

4. `6px;`

   Type a space and then a positive length value for the amount of blur to apply to the shadow.

Table 4.5

Text-Shadow Values	
VALUE	COMPATIBILITY
‹color›	S1.1, CSS3
‹x-offset›	S1.1, CSS3
‹y-offset›	S1.1, CSS3
‹blur›	S1.1, CSS3

Figure 4.5 The title has a reddish glow beneath it, while the author's name and chapter number have a drop shadow.

Code 4.5 The drop-shadow property allows you to set the x,y offset and the blur radius.

```
<!DOCTYPE html PUBLIC "-//W3C//DTD XHTML 1.0
→ Strict//EN" "http://www.w3.org/TR/xhtml1/
→ DTD/xhtml1-strict.dtd">
<html xmlns="http://www.w3.org/1999/xhtml">
<head>
<meta http-equiv="Content-Type"
→ content="text/html; charset=UTF-8" />
<title>CSS, DHTML &amp; Ajax | Adding a Text
→ Drop Shadow</title>
<style type="text/css" media="screen">
<!--
body {
     font-size: 1.2em;
     font-family: Georgia, "Times New
     → Roman", times, serif;
     text-shadow: none;
}
h1 {
     text-shadow:#f66 10px 12px 6px;
}
h2 {
     text-shadow:#999 3px 4px 2px;
}
.chapterTitle {
     text-shadow:none;
}
.author {
     text-shadow:#333 0px 2px 3px;
}
a:hover {
     text-shadow: #999 2px 2px 2px;
}
-->
</style>
</head>
<body>
<div id="header">
     <h1>Alice's Adventures in Wonderland</h1>
     <p class="author">Lewis Carroll</p>
     <h2>CHAPTER V<br />
        <span class="chapterTitle">Advice
        → from a Caterpillar</span></h2>
</div>
<p>The Caterpillar and Alice looked at each
     other for some time in silence: at last
     the Caterpillar took the hookah out of
     its mouth, and addressed her in a
     languid, sleepy voice.</p>
</body>
</html>
```

✔ Tips

- Keep in mind that although this is a "shadow" you can use any color for the shadow. Thus, if your text is on a dark background, you could use a light color to create a drop "glow" instead.

- Although this example uses several different shadow strengths, colors, and offsets, if you want to make the shadows look natural, their offsets should all be proportional to each other.

- The W3C is also suggesting the inclusion of a box-shadow property in CSS3 that works a lot like the text-shadow property, but would be applied to the elements box. This property is not implemented in any browser currently.

- Text shadows are great way to have links pop-off the page when used with the :hover pseudo class.

- The text-shadow property actually allows for multiple shadows on a single element. A comma separates each value list. However, Safari does not support this feature.

ADDING A TEXT DROP SHADOW

123

Aligning Text Horizontally

Traditionally, text is either aligned at its left margin or fully justified (often called *newspaper style*, in which text is aligned at both left and right margins). In addition, for emphasis or special effect, text can be centered on the screen or even right-justified. The `text-align` property (**Table 4.6**) gives you control of the text's alignment and justification.

In this example (**Figure 4.6**), the level 1 heading and author class have been centered, while the level 2 heading has been right justified, and the copy has been fully justified.

To define text alignment:

1. `text-align:`

   Type the `text-align` property name, followed by a colon (:), in the CSS definition list (**Code 4.6**).

2. `center;`

   Set one of the following alignment styles:

   ▲ `left` to align the text on the left margin

   ▲ `right` to align the text on the right margin

   ▲ `center` to center the text within its area

   ▲ `justify` to align the text on both the left and right sides

Table 4.6

Text-Align Values	
VALUE	COMPATIBILITY
left	IE3, FF1, S1, O3.5, CSS1
right	IE3, FF1, S1, O3.5, CSS1
center	IE3, FF1, S1, O3.5, CSS1
justify	IE4, FF1, S1, O3.5, CSS1

Figure 4.6 The book title and author name are centered, while the chapter number and title are right aligned.

Code 4.6 The h1 tag and author class will be centered, while the h2 tag is right justified, including the chapterTitle class.

```
<!DOCTYPE html PUBLIC "-//W3C//DTD XHTML 1.0
→ Strict//EN"
"http://www.w3.org/TR/xhtml1/DTD/xhtml1-
→ strict.dtd">
<html xmlns="http://www.w3.org/1999/xhtml">
<head>
<meta http-equiv="Content-Type"
→ content="text/html; charset=UTF-8" />
<title>CSS, DHTML &amp; Ajax | Aligning Text
→ Horizontally</title>
<style type="text/css" media="screen">
<!--
body {
    font-size: 1.2em;
    font-family: Georgia, "Times New Roman",
    → times, serif;
    text-align: left;
}
h1 {
    text-align: center;
}
h2 {
    text-align: right;
}
.chapterTitle{
    text-align: left;
}
.author {
    text-align: center;
}
p.copy {
    text-align: justify;
}
-->
</style>
</head>
<body>
<div id="header">
    <h1>Alice's Adventures in Wonderland</h1>
    <p class="author">Lewis Carroll</p>
    <h2>CHAPTER VI<br />
        <span class="chapterTitle">Pig and
        → Pepper</span></h2>
</div>
<p class="copy">For a minute or two she
→ stood looking at the house, and wondering
→ what to do next, when suddenly a footman
→ in livery came running out of the wood…</p>
</body>
</html>
```

✔ Tips

■ Notice in the example that although the chapterTitle class has been set to left justify, it cannot override the justification of its parent element. Text alignment only applies to block level elements.

■ Fully justifying text may produce some strange results on the screen because spaces between words must be added to make each line the same length. In addition, there is considerable debate about whether full justification helps or hinders readability.

Aligning Text Vertically

With the `vertical-align` property, you can specify the vertical position of one inline element relative to the elements around it, either above or below. This means that the `vertical-align` property (**Table 4.7**) can be used only with inline tags and table tags—tags without a break before or after them, such as the anchor (<a>), image (<img>), bold (<b>), italic (<i>), and table data (<td>) tags.

This example (**Figure 4.7**) shows how the different vertical-alignment types should look.

To define vertical alignment:

1. `vertical-align:`

   Type the `vertical-align` property name, followed by a colon (:), in the definition list (**Code 4.7**).

2. `super;`

   Type a value for the vertical alignment of the text. Choose one of the following options:

   ▲ `super`, which superscripts the text above the baseline.

   ▲ `sub`, which subscripts the text below the baseline.

Table 4.7

Vertical-Align Values	
VALUE	COMPATIBILITY
super	IE4, FF1, S1, O3.5, CSS1
sub	IE4, FF1, S1, O3.5, CSS1
baseline	IE4, FF1, S1, O3.5, CSS1
<length>	IE5*, FF1, S1, O3.5, CSS1
<percentage>	IE5**, FF1, S1, O3.5, CSS1
* IE5.5 in Windows	
** IE7 in Windows	

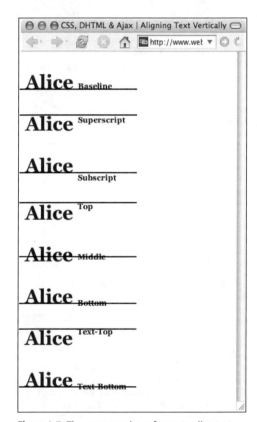

Figure 4.7 There are a variety of ways to align text relative to other text on the screen. The lines are shown as a guide for where the text is aligning.

Table 4.8

Setting an Element's Position Relative to the Parent Element

TYPE THIS	TO GET THE ELEMENT TO ALIGN LIKE THIS
top	Top to highest element in line
middle	Middle to middle of parent
bottom	Bottom to lowest element in line
text-top	Top to top of parent element's text
text-bottom	Bottom to bottom of parent element's text

Code 4.7 I've set up a class for each vertical alignment type.

```
<!DOCTYPE html PUBLIC "-//W3C//DTD XHTML 1.0
→ Strict//EN" "http://www.w3.org/TR/xhtml1/
→ DTD/xhtml1-strict.dtd">
<html xmlns="http://www.w3.org/1999/xhtml">
<head>
<meta http-equiv="Content-Type"
content="text/html; charset=UTF-8" />
<title>CSS, DHTML &amp; Ajax | Aligning Text
→ Vertically</title>
<style type="text/css" media="screen">
<!--
body {
    font-size: xx-large;
    font-family: Georgia, "Times New
    → Roman", times, serif;
    text-align: left; }
.superscript
    vertical-align: super;
    font-size: small; }
.baseline {
    vertical-align: baseline;
    font-size: small; }
.subscript {
    vertical-align: sub;
    font-size: small; }
.top {
    vertical-align: top;
    font-size: small; }
.middle {
    vertical-align: middle;
    font-size: small; }
.bottom {
    vertical-align: bottom;
    font-size: small; }
```

▲ baseline, which places the text on the baseline (its natural state).

▲ A **relative value** from **Table 4.8** that sets the element's alignment relative to its parent's alignment. To align the top of your text with the top of the parent element's text, for example, type text-top.

▲ A **percentage value**, which raises or lowers the element's baseline proportionate to the parent element's font size (25%, for example).

continues on next page

Code 4.7 *continued*

```
.texttop {
    vertical-align: text-top;
    font-size: small; }
.textbottom {
    vertical-align: text-bottom;
    font-size: small; }
.normal {
    font-weight: bold; }
-->
</style>
</head>
<body>
<p class="normal">Alice <span
→ class="baseline">Baseline</span></p>
<p class="normal">Alice <span
→ class="superscript">Superscript</span></p>
<p class="normal">Alice <span
→ class="subscript">Subscript</span></p>
<p class="normal">Alice <span
→ class="top">Top</span></p>
<p class="normal">Alice <span
→ class="middle">Middle</span></p>
<p class="normal">Alice <span
→ class="bottom">Bottom</span></p>
<p class="normal">Alice <span
→ class="texttop">Text-Top</span></p>
<p class="normal">Alice <span
→ class="textbottom">Text-Bottom</span></p>
</body></html>
```

ALIGNING TEXT VERTICALLY

127

✔ Tips

- Superscript and subscript are used for scientific notation. To express the Pythagorean theorem, for example, you would use superscripts:

$a^2 + b^2 = c^2$

A water molecule might be expressed with subscripts as follows:

$H_2 0$

However, keep in mind that neither sub- nor superscript will reduce the size of the text, so you may also want to include `font-size` in your definition for true scientific notation style (see "Setting the Font Size" in Chapter 3).

- Superscript is also great for footnotes in the text, which can then be hyperlinked to notes at the bottom of the current page or to another Web page.

- It's a good idea to reserve vertical alignment for relative positioning with another element or in a table data cell. For more exact positioning, use the position properties explained in Chapter 7.

ALIGNING TEXT VERTICALLY

Table 4.9

Text-Indent Values

Value	Compatibility
‹length›	IE3, FF1, S1, O3.5, CSS1
‹percentage›	IE3, FF1, S1, O3.5, CSS1

Figure 4.8 Paragraphs stand out better when they are indented, but the extra white space between them becomes redundant.

Indenting Paragraphs

Indenting the first word of a paragraph several spaces (traditionally, five) is the time-honored method of introducing a new paragraph.

On the Web, however, indented paragraphs haven't worked because most browsers compress multiple spaces into a single space. Instead, paragraphs have been separated by an extra line break.

With the `text-indent` property (**Table 4.9**), you can specify extra horizontal space at the beginning of the first line of text in a paragraph (**Figure 4.8**). You may want to collapse the paragraph margin, in addition, since that space is no longer needed to indicate a new paragraph.

continues on next page

To define text indentation:

1. `text-indent`:

Type the `text-indent` property name, followed by a colon (`:`), in the CSS definition list (**Code 4.8**).

2. `2em;`

Type a value for the indent, using either of these options:

▲ A **length value**, such as `2em`. This amount will create a nice, clear indent. See "Values and Units Used in this Book" in the Introduction for more details.

▲ A **percentage value**, which indents the text proportionate to the parent's (paragraph) width (`10%`, for example).

✔ Tips

■ If you are using indentation to indicate paragraphs, you can set the margin of a paragraph to `0` to override the `<p>` tag's natural tendency to add space between paragraphs.

■ Because indenting is more common in the print world than online, you may want to consider using indents only for the printer-friendly versions of your page.

Code 4.8 The code tells each paragraph using the copy class to indent 2em.

```
<!DOCTYPE html PUBLIC "-//W3C//DTD XHTML 1.0
→ Strict//EN" "http://www.w3.org/TR/xhtml1/
→ DTD/xhtml1-strict.dtd">
<html xmlns="http://www.w3.org/1999/xhtml">
<head>
<meta http-equiv="Content-Type"
→ content="text/html; charset=UTF-8" />
<title>CSS, DHTML &amp; Ajax | Indenting
→ Paragraphs</title>
<style type="text/css" media="screen">
<!--
body {
    font-size: 1.2em;
    font-family: Georgia, "Times New
    → Roman", times, serif;
}
p.copy {
    text-indent: 2em;
    margin: 0px; }
-->
</style>
</head>
<body>
<div id="header">
    <h1>Alice's Adventures in Wonderland</h1>
    <p class="author">Lewis Carroll</p>
    <h2>CHAPTER VII<br />
        <span class="chapterTitle">A Mad
        → Tea-Party</span></h2>
</div>
<p class="copy">There was a table set out
→ under a tree in front of the house, and
→ the March Hare and the Hatter were having
→ tea at it: a Dormouse was sitting between
→ them, fast asleep, and the other two were
→ using it as a cushion, resting their
→ elbows on it, and talking over its head.
→ 'Very uncomfortable for the Dormouse,'
→ thought Alice; 'only, as it's asleep, I
→ suppose it doesn't mind.'</p>
</body>
</html>
```

Table 4.10

White-Space Values	
VALUE	COMPATIBILITY
normal	IE5*, FF1, S1, O4, CSS1
pre	IE5*, FF1, S1, O4, CSS1
nowrap	IE5*, FF1, S1, O4, CSS1
* IE5.5 for Windows	

Controlling White Space

As I already mentioned, browsers in the past have collapsed multiple spaces into a single space unless the `<pre>` tag was used. CSS lets you allow or disallow the collapsing of spaces, as well as designate whether text can break at a space (similar to the `<nobr>` tag) using the `white-space` property (**Table 4.10**).

This example (**Figure 4.9**) shows a poem shaped like a curvy mouse tail. If the `white-space` property value is assigned `pre` for the `poem` class, all those spaces collapse (**Figure 4.10**). However, if assigned a value of `nowrap`, the spaces and line breaks are ignored, and the text will stretch as far to the right on the page as needed (**Figure 4.11**).

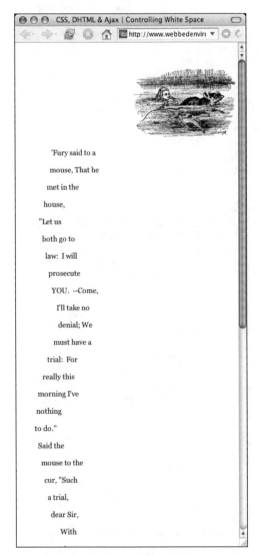

Figure 4.9 The `white-space` property keeps all spaces so the poem retains its distinctive mouse-tail-like shape rather than collapsing.

Figure 4.10 Without the `pre` value, the spaces collapse, as does the tail.

Figure 4.11 With the `no-wrap` value, the poem stretches vertically across the window, forcing a horizontal scroll to accommodate its width.

To define white space:

1. `white-space:`

Type the `white-space` property name, followed by a colon (:), in the CSS definition list (**Code 4.9**).

2. `pre;`

Type one of the following values to designate how you want spaces in text to be handled:

▲ `pre`, which preserves multiple spaces

▲ `nowrap`, which prevents line wrapping without a `<br />` tag

▲ `normal`, which allows the browser to determine how spaces are treated; this setting usually forces multiple spaces to collapse into a single space

✔ Tips

■ Do not confuse the `<nobr>` and `<pre>` tags with the `white-space` property values of `nowrap` and `pre`. Although they basically do the same thing, the HTML tags are being phased out (deprecated) or are not a part of the HTML specification and should not be used.

■ The text content of any tag that receives the `nowrap` value runs horizontally as far as it needs, regardless of the browser window's width. The user may be forced to scroll horizontally to read all the text, so this setting is usually frowned upon.

■ `nowrap` is great for preventing content from wrapping in table data cells.

Code 4.9 Adding `white-space: pre` to the paragraph tag means that all of the spaces will be displayed.

```
<!DOCTYPE html PUBLIC "-//W3C//DTD XHTML 1.0
→ Strict//EN" "http://www.w3.org/TR/xhtml1/
→ DTD/xhtml1-strict.dtd">
<html xmlns="http://www.w3.org/1999/xhtml">
<head>
<meta http-equiv="Content-Type"
→ content="text/html; charset=UTF-8" />
<title>CSS, DHTML &amp; Ajax | Controlling
→ White Space</title>
<style type="text/css" media="screen"><!--
body {
    font-size: 1.2em;
    font-family: Georgia, "Times New
    → Roman", times, serif;
    white-space: normal;
}
p.poem {
    white-space: pre;
}
-->
</style>
</head>
<body>
    <p class="poem"> <img src="alice08.gif"
    → width="200" height="131" alt="Alice"
/>
            'Fury said to a
         mouse, That he
       met in the
      house,
       "Let us
     both go to
      law:  I will
       prosecute
        YOU.  --Come,
       I'll take no
        denial; We
      must have a
      trial:  For
    really this
     morning I've
    nothing
    to do."
        </p>
    </body>
</html>
```

Table 4.11

Text-Decoration Values

VALUE	COMPATIBILITY
none	IE3, FF1, S1, O3.5, CSS1
underline	IE3, FF1, S1, O3.5, CSS1
overline	IE4, FF1, S1, O3.5, CSS1
line-through	IE3, FF1, S1, O3.5, CSS1
blink*	IE4, FF1 S1, O4, CSS1

*Although initially supported, many browsers have dropped support or allow blinking to be turned off.

Figure 4.12 There are a variety of ways to decorate your text, but the most useful is underlining.

Decorating Text

Using the `text-decoration` property (**Table 4.11**), you can adorn the text in one of four ways: underline, overline, line-through, or blink. Used to add emphasis, these decorations attract the reader's eye to important areas or passages on your Web page.

This example (**Figure 4.12**) is a mishmash of decorations, but it allows you to see what happens when you go crazy with all the possibilities.

To define text decorations:

1. `text-decoration:`

   Type the `text-decoration` property name, followed by a colon (`:`), in the CSS definition list (see **Code 4.10** on the next page).

2. `overline`

   Type a value for the `text-decoration` property. Choose one of the following:

   ▲ `underline`, which places a line below the text

   ▲ `overline`, which places a line above the text

   ▲ `line-through`, which places a line through the middle of the text (also called *strikethrough*)

   ▲ `blink`, which causes the text to blink on and off

   ▲ `none`, which overrides decorations set elsewhere

3. `underline;`

   You can also type a space and another `text-decoration` value (Table 4.11). As long as the first value is not `none`, you can use multiple text decorations by adding more values in a list separated by spaces, as follows:

   `overline underline blink`

Code 4.10 You can add multiple text decoration styles to the same text at once by combining decorations inherited from parent to child.

```
<!DOCTYPE html PUBLIC "-//W3C//DTD XHTML 1.0 Strict//EN" "http://www.w3.org/TR/xhtml1/DTD/xhtml1-
→ strict.dtd">
<html xmlns="http://www.w3.org/1999/xhtml">
<head>
<meta http-equiv="Content-Type" content="text/html; charset=UTF-8" />
<title>CSS, DHTML &amp; Ajax | Decorating Text</title>
<style type="text/css">
<!--
body {
    font-size: 1.2em;
    font-family: Georgia, "Times New Roman", times, serif;
    text-decoration: none;
}
h1 {
    text-decoration: overline underline;
}
h2 {
    text-decoration:underline;
}
p {
    text-decoration: underline;
}
p em {
    text-decoration: line-through;
}
.chapterTitle {
    text-decoration: none;
}
p.author {
    text-decoration: none;
}
-->
</style>
</head>
<body>
<div id="header">
    <h1>Alice's Adventures in Wonderland</h1>
    <p class="author">Lewis Carroll</p>
    <h2>CHAPTER VIII<br />
        <span class="chapterTitle">The Queen's Croquet-Ground</span></h2>
</div>
<p>A large rose-tree stood near the entrance of the garden: the roses growing on it were white,
→ but there were three gardeners at it, busily painting them red. <em>Alice thought this a very
→ curious thing,</em> and she went nearer to watch them, and just as she came up to them she heard
→ one of them say, 'Look out now, Five! Don't go splashing paint over me like that!'</p>
</body>
</html>
```

✔ Tips

- Notice in the example that although the `chapterTitle` class has its text decoration set to `none`, it is still underlined. Text decorations are applied across an entire text block element, rather than on a letter-by-letter basis. This means that a child element cannot override the text decoration set by its parent, unless the style is set to `none`.

- Although a child element can not override its parent's text decoration, child elements can have additional text decoration added to them. Notice in the example that the `emphasis` tag uses strikethrough, which is added to the underlining already supplied by the paragraph tag.

- Many visitors don't like blinking text, especially on Web pages where they spend a lot of time. In fact, many browsers allow the user to disable blinking or simply ignore it. Use this decoration sparingly.

- Striking through text is useful for text that you want to show as being deleted. For example, I've used strikethrough in online catalogs that include sale prices. I show the original price in strikethrough, with the sale price next to it.

- Underlining is often associated with hypertext links. See the sidebar "Underlining Links" for a better way to deal with link styles.

Underlining Links?

Setting `text-decoration: none;` in the `<a>` tag overrides the underline in hypertext links, even if the visitor's browser is set to underline links. In my experience, many visitors look for underlining to identify links. Although I don't like underlining for links—it clutters the page, and CSS offers many alternatives to identify links—I receive angry e-mails from visitors when I turn off underlining.

One alternative to using the `text-decoration` property for underlining is to use the `border-bottom` property with the link tag to provide faux-underlining. This gives you much better control over how the underline is presented, even allowing you to use different colors. For more detail, see "Styling Navigation and Links" in Chapter 21.

Setting Text Direction

Increasingly, the Web is being used to display text in non-Western languages. The direction of the text (left-to-right or right-to-left) can vary from language to language, so it may be necessary to override the browser's default display direction if you aren't using English (**Tables 4.12** and **4.13**).

In this example (**Figure 4.13**), the first block of text is set left-to-right, while the second paragraph runs right-to-left.

To set the direction text is displayed:

1. direction:

Type the direction property name, followed by a colon (:), in the CSS definition list (**Code 4.11**).

Table 4.12

Direction Values	
VALUE	COMPATIBILITY
rtl	IE5*, FF1, S1, CSS2
ltr	IE5*, FF1, S1, CSS2

*Windows version only. Not available in Mac.

Table 4.13

Unicode-Bidi Values	
VALUE	COMPATIBILITY
bidi-override	IE5*, FF1, CSS2
embed	IE5*, FF1, CSS2
normal	IE5*, FF1, CSS2

*Windows version only. Not available in Mac.

Figure 4.13 Although still using English characters, the second paragraph of text has had its direction reversed.

2. `rtl;`

Type a value for the direction, followed by a semicolon. Choose one of the following:

▲ `rtl`, which displays text right-to-left

▲ `ltr`, which displays text left-to-right (for Western languages)

3. `unicode-bidi:`

Type the `unicode-bidi` property name, followed by a colon (`:`), in the CSS definition list.

This property is used to define how the `direction` property is applied if there are multiple text directions being used in a single Web page.

continues on next page

Code 4.11 The class `rightToLeft` is created to force the text to display from right to left even if the browser uses left to right.

```
<!DOCTYPE html PUBLIC "-//W3C//DTD XHTML 1.0 Strict//EN" "http://www.w3.org/TR/xhtml1/DTD/xhtml1-
→ strict.dtd">
<html xmlns="http://www.w3.org/1999/xhtml">
<head>
<meta http-equiv="Content-Type" content="text/html; charset=UTF-8" />
<title>CSS, DHTML &amp; Ajax | Setting Text Direction</title>
<style type="text/css" media="screen">
<!--
body {
    font-size: 1.2em;
    font-family: Georgia, "Times New Roman", times, serif;
}
.leftToRight {
    direction: ltr;
    unicode-bidi: normal;
}
.rightToLeft {
    direction: rtl;
    unicode-bidi: bidi-override;
}
-->
</style>
</head>
<body>
<h2 class="leftToRight">Left to Right</h2>
<p class="leftToRight">Hardly knowing what she did, she picked up a little bit of stick, and held
→ it out to the puppy…</p>
<h2 class="rightToLeft">Right to Left</h2>
<p class="rightToLeft">Hardly knowing what she did, she picked up a little bit of stick, and held
→ it out to the puppy…</p>
</body></html>
```

4. `bidi-override;`

Type a value for the embedded bidirectional code. Choose one of the following:

▲ `bidi-override`, to override the currently set direction for text in the browser. This is needed to truly reverse the text.

▲ `embed`, to embed the bidirectional text within the current direction. This effectively justifies the text to the left (`ltr`) or right (`rtl`), although ending punctuation is shifted.

▲ `normal`, to use the browser's default for embedded bidirectional text.

✔ Tips

■ Keep in mind that this technique is effective only if the viewer's computer can display the text in the intended language.

■ The `unicode-bidi` property is not inherited by child elements and must be applied to each one separately.

COLOR AND BACKGROUND PROPERTIES

Color forms the cornerstone of all design, creating the first impression that most people will have of your site. Using bright, vibrant. jewel-tone colors makes a radically different statement than earth tones would make. Even if you choose *not* to use any colors, creating your design in black and white makes a statement. Beyond their visual language, colors can also guide the viewer's eye around the page, helping you to highlight important areas while downplaying others.

In this chapter, you will learn the primary methods designers use to add and control color, including the foreground color used for text and background colors. Keep in mind, however, that there are several other CSS properties in which you can specify color (see the sidebar "Other Ways to Add Color"). But before you learn how to code your colors, let's quickly explore how you can choose them.

Choosing Your Color Palette

There is a saying amongst graphic designers: "No color is better than bad color." If you are not careful, color can work against you by obscuring your message and confusing your visitor. The effective use of color in design takes a lot of practice to get it right.

Colors have powerful emotional meanings, which cannot always be predicted, especially when used in different combinations. **Table 5.1** presents some of the most common associations with different colors. Once you put two colors together, the meanings begin to interrelate, much like words in a sentence.

However, you want to make sure you don't just start slapping down colors on your page. If you do, they'll likely clash. The most important thing you can do to avoid this is to take time to plan. Begin by choosing the specific colors you will use and their exact RGB values, and then apply these colors consistently throughout your project.

You will need to consider the colors (including the colors in the background images)

Table 5.1

Color Associations	
COLOR	EMOTIONAL ASSOCIATIONS
Red	assertive, powerful, intense
Blue	consoling, fidelity, defense
Yellow	concern, rebirth, clarity
Green	wealth, fitness, food, nature
Brown	nature, maturity, wisdom
Orange	hospitality, exhilaration, vigor
Pink	vital, innocent, feminine
Purple	royalty, refinement, calm
Black	stark, stylish, somber
Gray	business-like, cool, detached
White	clean, pure, straightforward

Other Ways to Add Color

Although this chapter presents the primary methods for setting the colors in your design, several other CSS properties include color values as part of their intrinsic nature:

- **text-shadow Property** (Chapter 4). Although generally thought of as black or gray, CSS allows you to set the color of text shadows.

- **border Properties** (Chapter 6). An element's border colors can be set as part of any of the border properties, or directly in the border-color property.

- **outline Properties** (Chapter 6). Like the border property, the outline allows you to define a color around the edge of an element.

- **scrollbar Properties** (Chapter 8). Internet Explorer for Windows allows you to reach out of the Web page and specify the colors for the scroll bar used to control the page.

that you will be applying to the basic parts of your Web page (**Figure 5.1**). You do not have to choose a completely different color hue for each part, but you should define what the color would be for each component:

◆ **Page background.** Covering the entire visible area of the browser window, the background should generally provide the most contrast with the foreground text colors.

◆ **Content background.** Often you will use a different color for the background directly around the content of the page, allowing the page background color to absorb extra horizontal space in the browser window.

continues on next page

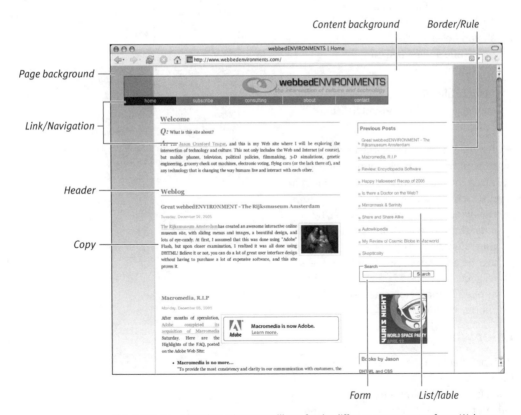

Figure 5.1 Consider what colors you will use for the different components of your Web page.

- **Border/Rule.** You may want to use contrasting colors around the borders of content areas, headers, navigation blocks, lists, and tables or use rules to separate different chunks of content. Choose a color that contrasts with the area the lines are meant to separate.

- **Header.** You may choose not to change the background color for section headers, but always make sure that the text color clearly contrasts with whatever background color you choose.

- **Copy.** Your copy (generally sentences or paragraphs of text) should have the highest contrast with the background to maximize legibility.

- **Link/Navigation.** You may choose different colors for your site navigation and for links in the copy, but these link colors should be easily discernable from other text while still contrasting the background.

- **List/Table.** You may choose different background colors behind lists and tables (or even alternating row colors).

- **Form.** You can specify the border, foreground, and background colors of many form elements to give them a more distinctive look for your site, apart from the default appearance. However, be careful not to customize them so much that the visitor does not know what they are. Be aware, too, that many browsers (especially on the Mac) will ignore styles applied to form elements, especially the submit buttons.

Color wheel basics

A color wheel is a disc or circle that shows the spectrum of color values, providing you a quick overview of all the possibilities, from red, orange, and yellow to green, blue, indigo,

Do Browser Safe Colors Matter?

The short answer: no.

The slightly longer answer: In the early days of Web design, many—if not most—of the computers in use had an incredibly limited color palette. Whereas almost all computer monitors today can display thousands to millions of different colors, in the 1990's a large segment of the Web-browsing world could only see as few as 256 colors and in extreme cases even fewer. The set of colors that both Mac and Windows computers could consistently display (a 211 color subset of the 256) was referred to as the *Browser Safe Color Palette*. These colors could always be relied on to properly and smoothly display in all computers.

For a long time, Web designers would restrict themselves to this extremely limited palette. In fact, you still see this palette widely used in many applications, including Photoshop and Dreamweaver. However, these limitations are becoming increasingly outdated, as virtually all computers today can use just about any colors you throw at them.

and violet, and back to red again. Some color wheels also allow you to view different brightnesses (dark to light) and saturations (full color tone to gray).

Unfortunately, because this book is produced in black and white (OK, it has is a little red, but that's hardly the whole spectrum), it doesn't really help to show a graphic of a color wheel. Most likely you're familiar with color wheels anyway, or if you're not, my description of one gives you a fairly good idea of what they look like. If not, check out the example on Wikipedia (http://en.wikipedia.org/wiki/Color_theory).

When you get down to it, though, color is a matter of preference. Colors that I swear look great together make my wife gag and usually result in my changing my outfit. To be safe, you can count on a single color (monochrome) or one of the color-combination schemes that follow as being (more or less) fail-safe:

- **Monochrome.** A single color with different brightnesses or saturations for contrast.

- **Complimentary.** Two colors from opposite sides of the color wheel (180 degrees), providing the highest contrast.

- **Triad.** Three colors and their tones, with one primary and two secondary colors that are at equal angles in the color wheel, 120 degrees to 180 degrees from the primary.

- **Tetrad.** Four colors that include one primary color, one secondary color (in direct contrast to the primary color), and two colors that are the same angle from the primary or secondary color, from 0 degrees to 90 degrees.

continues on next page

CHOOSING YOUR COLOR PALETTE

- **Analogic.** Three colors and their tones, with one primary color and two secondary colors that are the same angle from the primary color, from 0 degrees to 60 degrees.

All of the above color schemes allow you to choose the basic hues. You can then use different brightnesses and/or saturations of these colors to add additional colors to your palette.

Online color scheme tools

Not sure where to start planning your color scheme? Here are some excellent online tools you can use:

- **Build a palette.** The Visibone Webmaster's Color Laboratory (visibone.com/colorlab/) provides an excellent tool for comparing colors side by side in an interactive environment.

- **Color Wheel Selector.** Explore all of the different color wheel schemes using Wellstyled.com's Color Scheme 2 tool (wellstyled.com/tools/colorscheme2/index-en.html).

- **Duotones.** If you are trying to keep your design simple but want more than a monochromatic scheme, the Slayer Office Color Palette tool (slayeroffice.com/tools/color_palette/) lets you blend two colors together for a smooth duotone color palette.

- **Color palettes from photographs or other images.** If you are using graphics or photography with a particular color scheme in them, the Degrave.com Color Palette Generator (degraeve.com/color-palette/) will analyze the image and then produce a color palette based on the colors in the image.

Color and Accessibility

Beyond attractive and compelling design, another critical consideration with color is accessibility for people who are color-blind or have other vision impairments. The most important considerations are to provide enough contrast between foreground and background colors and to make sure that color is not critical for understanding information. For example, if you are using color for links, also set links off in some other way such as underlining or bold.

Of course, there are also several color combinations that you should avoid (blue/green being the most obvious) and some that are preferred:

- Red/blue

- Orange/blue

- Orange/purple

- Yellow/purple

For more details on color and accessibility, check out section 9 of the W3Cs white paper *CSS Techniques for Web Content Accessibility Guidelines*:

w3.org/TR/WCAG10-CSS-TECHS/#style-colors

Table 5.2

Color Value	
VALUE	COMPATIBILITY
‹color›	IE3, FF1, S1, O3.5, CSS1
inherit	IE3, FF1, S1, O3.5, CSS1

Figure 5.2 Choose your foreground colors carefully so that they contrast not only with the background color, but also with each other so that they guide the viewer's eye where you want it to go.

Setting Text and Foreground Color

The color property is used to set the foreground color of an element (**Table 5.2**). Although this property is primarily used to color text, you can also apply it as the foreground color for horizontal rules and form elements.

In this example (**Figure 5.2**), the header text is rendered in a variety of shades of red, the text is a dark gray, and the form button and the text that gets typed into the form field are red. The brighter red text is much more prominent than the lighter red and the gray text.

To define the foreground color:

1. color:

   Type the color property name, followed by a colon (:), in the CSS rule (**Code 5.1**).

   continues on next page

Code 5.1 The foreground color, primarily for text, can be set using the color name or RGB values.

```
<!DOCTYPE html PUBLIC "-//W3C//DTD XHTML 1.0 Strict//EN" "http://www.w3.org/TR/xhtml1/DTD/xhtml1-
→ strict.dtd">
<html xmlns="http://www.w3.org/1999/xhtml">
<head>
<meta http-equiv="Content-Type" content="text/html; charset=utf-8" />
<title>CSS, DHTML &amp; Ajax | Setting a Foreground Color</title>
<style type="text/css" media="screen">
<!--
body {
    font-size: 1.2em;
    font-family: Georgia, "Times New Roman", times, serif;
    color: #000000;
}
h1 {
    color: red;
}
h2 {
    color: #ff0000;
}
```

code continues on next page

SETTING TEXT AND FOREGROUND COLOR

2. `red;`

Now type a value for the color you want this element to be. This value can be the name of a color or an RGB value set using percentages, values from 0-255, or hexadecimal code (see "Values and Units Used in this Book" in the Introduction).

✔ Tips

■ Assigning a color to several nested elements can lead to unwanted color changes. The most obvious example of this kind of mistake happens when you set the color in the <body> tag. Older browsers tend to change the color of all elements in the body. Always consider which tag styles you redefine and how they might affect other tags on your Web page (see "Inheriting Properties from a Parent" in Chapter 2).

■ Notice that both the author and chapterTitle class use the same color of light red and both are set using a hexa-decimal RGB value. However, the author class uses the full hex number #ff9999, while the chapterTitle class uses the shorthand value #f99. When specifying hex RGB values in which both color value numbers are the same, you specify each value only once.

■ Be careful when choosing foreground text colors so that they contrast enough with the background color or image. The lower the contrast (i.e., the less dif-ference there is in the brightness of the foreground and background colors), the more your readers will have to strain their eyes when reading.

■ Color change is a great way to indicate when the visitor's cursor is hovering over a link. See "Working with Pseudo-Classes" in Chapter 2 for more details.

Code 5.1 *continued*

```
input {
     color: rgb(100%,0%,0%);
}
.chapterTitle {
     color: #ff9999;
}
.author {
     color: #f99;
}
.copy{
     color: rgb(102,102,102);
}
-->
</style>
</head>
<body>
<div id="header">
     <h1>Alice's Adventures in Wonderland</h1>
<form action="#" method="get"
→ id="FormName">
     Search Book:
     <input class="formText" type="text"
     → name="searchTerm" size="24" />
     <input class="formButton"
     → type="submit" name="findSearchTerm"
     → value="Find" />
</form>
     <p class="author">Lewis Carroll</p>
     <h2>CHAPTER I<br />
        <span class="chapterTitle">Down
        → the Rabbit-Hole</span></h2>
</div>
<p class="copy">Alice was beginning to
→ get very tired of sitting by her sister
→ on the bank, and of having nothing to
→ do: once or twice she had peeped into
→ the book her sister was reading, but it
→ had no pictures or conversations in it,
→ 'and what is the use of a book,' thought
→ Alice 'without pictures or
→ conversation?'</p>
</body>
</html>
```

Table 5.3

Background-Color Values	
VALUE	COMPATIBILITY
<color>	IE4, FF1, S1, O3.5, CSS1
transparent	IE4, FF1, S1, O3.5, CSS1

Figure 5.3 Background colors have been applied to various elements. A pink color has been set for the image of Alice. This color shows through where the GIF image has been made transparent.

Setting a Background Color

The ability to set the background color for an HTML page has been around almost since the first Web browsers. However, with CSS you can define the background color, not only for the entire page, but also for individual elements using the background-color property (**Table 5.3**).

In this example (**Figure 5.3**), the background color has been set behind various elements to make them stand out on the page. Notice that in addition to the headers and other text, you can use the background-color property to set the color of the input form field and the input button. Also notice that the pink background color is showing through the transparent areas in the GIF image of Alice.

continues on next page

To define the background color of an element:

1. `background-color:`

   Start your declaration by typing the background-color property name (**Code 5.2**), followed by a colon (:).

2. `#000;`

   Type a value for the color you want the background to be. This value can be the name of the color or an RGB value.

   Alternatively, you could type transparent, which allows the parent's background color to show through.

✔ Tips

- The default state for an element's background color is none, so the parent element's background will show through unless the background color or image for that particular child element is set.

- You can also set the background color using the background property, which is described later in this chapter.

- Most browsers (except Microsoft Internet Explorer 6 and earlier) let you set not only the background color for form fields, but also the :hover and :focus states, which gives you a handy way to show visitors which field they are currently working in.

Code 5.2 The background color for the page has been set to white. Other elements in the page can provide their own background color. Make sure you set the background color for the body tag, or the browser might set it for you.

```
<!DOCTYPE html PUBLIC "-//W3C//DTD XHTML 1.0
Strict//EN"
"http://www.w3.org/TR/xhtml1/DTD/xhtml1-
→ strict.dtd">
<html xmlns="http://www.w3.org/1999/xhtml">
<head>
<meta http-equiv="Content-Type"
content="text/html; charset=utf-8" />
<title>CSS, DHTML &amp; Ajax | Setting a
→ Background Color</title>
<style type="text/css" media="screen"><!--
body {
    font-size: 1.2em;
    font-family: Georgia, "Times New
    → Roman", times, serif;
    background-color: #fff;
    color: #000;
}
h1 {
    background-color: #000000;
    color: white;
    padding: 10px;
}
h2 {
    background-color: #ff9999;
    padding: 10px;
}
img {
    background-color: #ff9999;
    float: right;
}
input.formText {
    background-color: #fcc;
    color: red;
}
input.formButton {
    background-color: #fcc;
    color: red;
}
.chapterTitle {
    background-color: #ff3333;
    color: #ff9999;
}
.author {
    background-color: #f33;
    color: #f99;
}
```

code continues on next page

Code 5.2 *continued*

```
.copy {
    background-color: rgb(75%,75%,75%);
    padding: 10px;
}
--></style>
    </head>
    <body>
<div id="header">
    <h1>Alice's Adventures in
    ↪ Wonderland</h1>
<form action="#" method="get" id="FormName">
    Search Book:
    <input class="formText" type="text"
    ↪ name="searchTerm" size="24" />
    <input class="formButton" type="submit"
    ↪ name="findSearchTerm" value="Find" />
</form>
    <p class="author">Lewis Carroll</p>
    <h2>CHAPTER II<br />
        <span class="chapterTitle">The Pool
        ↪ of Tears</span></h2>
</div>
<p class="copy">
<img src="alice04a.gif" height="448"
↪ width="301" alt="Alice stretching"
↪ />'Curiouser and curiouser!' cried
↪ Alice (she was so much surprised, that
↪ for the moment she quite forgot how to
↪ speak good English); 'now I'm opening out
↪ like the largest telescope that ever was!
</p>
</body>
</html>
```

- Again, most browsers let you control the background color of the entire element with the `:hover` pseudo-class (guess which one is the holdout!). This kind of control is very useful for highlighting blocks of text in lists as the visitor rolls over them. Microsoft Internet Explorer 7 now supports the `:hover` pseudo-class on all elements.

- It can be confusing when both the input form field *and* the input buttons are the same color (as with the example in this section). So, rather than setting the color for the `input` selector, it's generally better to create classes that then get applied to individual form elements.

- If you are setting the color using a hex value couple (i.e., the color values for each color are the same number), you include only the first value. Thus, #000000 and #000 will both yield black.

Setting a Background Image

Beyond simply setting a background-image that tiles behind an element, CSS offers you great flexibility in the exact placement of the background behind the element using several different properties:

* **Repeat.** Whether the image tiles, only appears once, or repeats only horizontally or vertically.

* **Attachment.** Whether the image scrolls with the rest of the page or stays in one place.

* **Position.** Moves the image to the left and down (positive values) or to the right and up (negative values) from the top-left corner of the parent element.

In this example, a background image of a stretched Alice (**Figure 5.4** and **5.5**) is fixed to the top-left corner (**Figure 5.6**). In addition, the level 2 heading is given an extra flourish (**Figure 5.7**) with a background that repeats across the top and a background for form buttons (**Figure 5.8**) that creates a glossy plastic effect.

Figure 5.4 The background image (Alice) appears on the left side of the screen, and the text has been pushed over to the right.

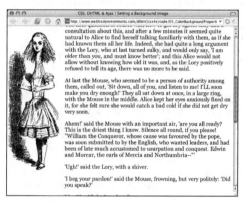

Figure 5.5 The actual image used in the background is relatively small, since we use the background color (white) to fill in the background behind the rest of the page.

Figure 5.7 The level 2 heading also uses a flourish background image to add an attractive rule above the chapter title.

Figure 5.8 The background image for form buttons. When repeated horizontally, it produces a glossy look.

Figure 5.6 Although the text has scrolled, the background image for the page (the telescoping Alice) stays in the same place.

Table 5.4

Background-Image Values	
VALUE	COMPATIBILITY
<url>	IE4, FF1, S1, O3.5, CSS1
none	IE4, FF1, S1, O3.5, CSS1

Code 5.3 This code sets backgrounds for the page, level 2 headings, and the form fields.

```
<!DOCTYPE html PUBLIC "-//W3C//DTD XHTML 1.0
→ Strict//EN" "http://www.w3.org/TR/xhtml1/
→ DTD/xhtml1-strict.dtd">
<html xmlns="http://www.w3.org/1999/xhtml">
<head>
<meta http-equiv="Content-Type"
→ content="text/html; charset=utf-8" />
<title>CSS, DHTML &amp; Ajax | Setting a
→ Background Image</title>
        <style type="text/css"
media="screen"><!--
body {
        font-size: 1.2em;
        font-family: Georgia, "Times New
        → Roman", times, serif;
        color: black;
        background-image: url(alice05.gif);
        background-color: white;
        background-repeat: no-repeat;
        background-attachment: fixed;
        background-position: -10px 10px;
        margin-left: 200px;
}
h2 {
        background-image: url(bg_flourish.png);
        background-repeat: repeat-x;
        background-attachment: scroll;
        background-position: -15px 0px;
        padding-top: 75px;
}
input {
        background-image: url(gell_red.png);
        background-repeat: repeat-x;
        background-attachment: scroll;
        color: white;
}
--></style>
</head>
```

To define a background image:

1. background-image: url(alice05.gif);

   Type the background-image property name, followed by a colon (:), url(), and a URL in the parenthesis for the location of the image file (GIF, JPEG, or PNG) that you want to use as the background. It can be either a complete Web address or a local filename (**Code 5.3**).

   Alternatively, you can type none instead of url() and a path to instruct the browser not to use a background image (**Table 5.4**).

   continues on next page

Code 5.3 *continued*

```
<body>
<div id="header">
        <h1>Alice's Adventures in Wonderland</h1>
<form action="#" method="get" id="FormName">
        Search Book:
        <input class="formText" type="text"
        → name="searchTerm" size="24" />
        <input class="formButton" type="submit"
        → name="findSearchTerm" value="Find" />
</form>
        <p class="author">Lewis Carroll</p>
        <h2>CHAPTER III<br />
            <span class="chapterTitle">A Caucus-
            → Race and a Long Tale</span></h2>
</div>
<p>They were indeed a queer-looking party
→ that assembled on the bank--the birds
→ with draggled feathers, the animals with
→ their fur clinging close to them, and all
→ dripping wet, cross, and uncomfortable.</p>
</body>
</html>
```

151

2. background-repeat: no-repeat;

Type the background-repeat property name, followed by a colon (:), and then define how you want your background to repeat by typing one of the following options (**Table 5.5**):

▲ repeat instructs the browser to tile the graphic throughout the background of the element horizontally and vertically. This is the default value if the property is left out.

▲ repeat-x instructs the browser to tile the background graphic only horizontally, so the graphic repeats in one straight horizontal line along the top of the element.

▲ repeat-y instructs the browser to tile the background graphic only vertically, so the graphic repeats in one straight vertical line along the left side of the element.

▲ no-repeat causes the background graphic to appear only once and not tile.

3. background-attachment: fixed;

Type the background-attachment property name, followed by a colon (:), and then define how you want the background to be treated when the page scrolls by typing one of the following options (**Table 5.6**):

▲ scroll instructs the background graphic to scroll with the element. This is the default value if the property is left out.

▲ fixed instructs the browser not to scroll the background content with the rest of the element. However, it will scroll with parent elements.

Table 5.5

Background-Repeat Values

VALUE	COMPATIBILITY
repeat	IE4, FF1, S1, O3.5, CSS1
repeat-x	IE4, FF1, S1, O3.5, CSS1
repeat-y	IE4, FF1, S1, O3.5, CSS1
no-repeat	IE4, FF1, S1, O3.5, CSS1

Table 5.6

Background-Attachment Values

VALUE	COMPATIBILITY
scroll	IE4, FF1, S1, O3.5, CSS1
fixed	IE4, FF1, S1, O3.5, CSS1

Table 5.7

Background-Position Values	
VALUE	COMPATIBILITY
‹length›	IE4, FF1, S1, O3.5, CSS1
‹percentage›	IE4, FF1, S1, O3.5, CSS1
top	IE4, FF1, S1, O3.5, CSS1
bottom	IE4, FF1, S1, O3.5, CSS1
left	IE4, FF1, S1, O3.5, CSS1
right	IE4, FF1, S1, O3.5, CSS1
center	IE4, FF1, S1, O3.5, CSS1

✔ Tips

■ A repeating background can sometimes be really annoying. It may repeat where it's not wanted, or you may want it to tile in only one direction. CSS gives you supreme control of how background graphics appear through the background-repeat property.

■ You can mix percentage and length values in the same background-position declaration, but you cannot mix length or percentages with plain-English keywords.

■ Any background space that does not have a background graphic will be filled with the background color, so I recommend always specifying a background color with a background image.

■ Background images can be a deceptively powerful tool for Web design, two of the most useful of which are CSS Sprites, discussed in Chapter 20.

4. background-position: -10px 10px;

Type the background-position property name, followed by a colon (:). Then type two values (x and y) separated by a space, to indicate where you want the background to appear in relation to the top-left corner of the element. Use one of the following values (**Table 5.7**):

▲ **Length values**, such as –10px. The values can be positive or negative. The first number tells the browser the distance the element should appear from the left edge of its parent; the second value specifies the position from the top edge of the parent. See "Values and Units Used in this Book" in the Introduction for more details.

▲ **Percentage values**, such as 25%. The first percentage indicates the horizontal position proportional to the parent element's size; the second value indicates the vertical position proportional to the parent element's size.

▲ **Keywords** in plain English: top, bottom, left, right, or center.

SETTING A BACKGROUND IMAGE

Setting Multiple Background Values

As discussed in the previous sections, CSS lets you define the background color and graphic for any individual element on the page, giving you much greater versatility when it comes to designing your Web pages.

The background shorthand property (**Table 5.8**) also allows you to define the background image and color for an entire page or single element by rolling these into a single quick and compressed declaration. From a coding standpoint, this method is better because it takes up less space, but requires that you remember what each of the values in the list is for.

In this example (**Figure 5.9**), the background image of the lizard popping out of the chimney has been placed in the top right corner of the page and will stay fixed even when the page scrolls (**Figure 5.10**). In addition, the level 2 heading has a textured area created using a background image (**Figure 5.11**) set to repeat vertically (**Code 5.4**).

Table 5.8

Background Values	
VALUE	COMPATIBILITY
‹background-color›	IE3, FF1, S1, O3.5, CSS1
‹background-image›	IE3, FF1, S1, O3.5, CSS1
‹background-repeat›	IE3, FF1, S1, O3.5, CSS1
‹background-attachment›	IE4, FF1, S1, O3.5, CSS1
‹background-position›	IE3, FF1, S1, O3.5, CSS1

Figure 5.9 The background image for the page (the lizard, bill) appears to the extreme right of the page.

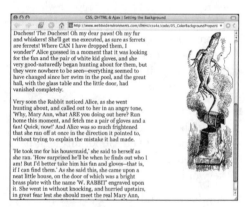

Figure 5.10 Although the text has scrolled down, the body's background (poor Bill the lizard) image stays frozen in place.

Figure 5.11 The chapter title heading has its own distinctive background that draws attention: a rough texture that repeats only on the left side and is flat gray in the rest.

Code 5.4 In this code, a background image is defined for the body of the page. This image is instructed not to repeat, to be fixed, and is positioned up and to the left using negative values. The h2 tag has also been defined with a rough background graphic that is repeated only across the left side of the element. Padding is included on the left for the heading so that the chapter title does not overlap the rough area.

```
<!DOCTYPE html PUBLIC "-//W3C//DTD XHTML 1.0 Strict//EN" "http://www.w3.org/TR/xhtml1/DTD/xhtml1-
→ strict.dtd">
<html xmlns="http://www.w3.org/1999/xhtml">
<head>
<meta http-equiv="Content-Type" content="text/html; charset=utf-8" />
<title>CSS, DHTML &amp; Ajax | Setting the Background</title>
<style type="text/css" media="screen"><!--
body {
    font-size: 1.2em;
    font-family: Georgia, "Times New Roman", times, serif;
    color: black;
    background: white url(alice13a.gif) no-repeat fixed right top;
    width: 60%;
}
h2 {
    color: white;
    background: #999999 url(background_rough.gif) repeat-y left top;
    padding: 35px;
}
input.formText {
    background: #fcc;
    color: red;
}
input.formButton {
    background: #333 url(gell_red.png) repeat-x scroll;
    color: white;
}
--></style>
    </head>
    <body>
        <div id="header">
        <h1>Alice's Adventures in Wonderland</h1>
<form action="#" method="get" id="FormName">
    Search Book:
    <input class="formText" type="text" name="searchTerm" size="24" />
    <input class="formButton" type="submit" name="findSearchTerm" value="Find" />
</form>
        <p class="author">Lewis Carroll</p>
        <h2>CHAPTER IV<br />
            <span class="chapterTitle">The Rabbit Sends in a Little Bill</span></h2>
    </div>
<p>It was the White Rabbit, trotting slowly back again, and looking anxiously about as it went, as
→ if it had lost something; and she heard it muttering to itself 'The Duchess! The Duchess! Oh my
→ dear paws! Oh my fur and whiskers! </p>
    </body>
</html>
```

To define the background:

1. background:

Start your declaration by typing the background property name, followed by a colon (:). Then define a background value.

2. white

Type a value for the color you want the background to be, followed by a space. This value can be the name of the color or an RGB value. See "Values and Units Used in this Book" in the Introduction for more details.

Alternatively, you could type transparent, which tells the browser to use the background color of elements behind this element.

3. url(alice05.gif)

Type url() with a URL for the location of the background image in the parenthesis (Table 5.4), followed by a space. This location is the image file (GIF, JPEG, or PNG) that you want to use as the background and is either a complete Web address or a local filename.

Alternatively, you can type none instead of a URL, which instructs the browser not to use a background image.

4. no-repeat

Type a value for how you want your background to repeat, followed by a space. Use one of the following options (Table 5.5):

▲ repeat instructs the browser to tile the graphic throughout the background of the element both horizontally and vertically.

▲ repeat-x instructs the browser to tile the background graphic only horizontally. In other words, the graphic repeats in one straight horizontal line along the top of the element.

SETTING MULTIPLE BACKGROUND VALUES

▲ `repeat-y` instructs the browser to tile the background graphic only vertically. In other words, the graphic repeats in one straight vertical line along the left side of the element.

▲ `no-repeat` causes the background graphic to appear only once and not tile.

5. `fixed`

Type a keyword for how you want the background attached—how it should be treated when the page scrolls—followed by a space. Use one of the following options (Table 5.6):

▲ `scroll` instructs the background graphic to scroll with the element.

▲ `fixed` instructs the browser not to scroll the background content with the rest of the element.

6. `right top;`

Type two values, separated by a space, to specify where you want the background positioned in relation to the top-left corner of the element. Use one of the following values (Table 5.7):

▲ A **length value**, such as `-10px`. The values can be positive or negative. The first number tells the browser the distance the element should appear from the left edge of its parent; the second value specifies the position from the top edge of the parent.

▲ A **percentage value**, such as `25%`. The first percentage indicates the horizontal position proportional to the parent element's size; the second value indicates the vertical position proportional to the parent element's size.

▲ A **position keyword**, such as `top`, `bottom`, `left`, `right`, or `center`.

continues on next page

SETTING MULTIPLE BACKGROUND VALUES

✔ Tips

■ The ability to place graphics behind any element on the screen is a very powerful tool for designing Web pages; it frees you from the constraints of having to create new graphics whenever text changes. You can combine the versatility of HTML text with graphics to create stunning effects.

■ The default state for an element's background is none, so the parent element's background image and/or color will show through unless the background color or background image for that particular child element is set.

■ A fixed background can be particularly effective if you're using a graphic background in your layout to help define the layout grid.

SETTING MULTIPLE BACKGROUND VALUES

Box Properties

In the physical world, atoms are the building blocks for all larger objects. Every type of atom, or *element*, has its own unique properties, but when bonded with other atoms, they create molecules—larger structures with properties different from the parts.

Likewise, HTML tags are the building blocks of your Web page. Each tag, or element, has its own unique capabilities. Tags can be combined to create a Web page that is greater than the sum of its parts.

Whether a tag is by itself or nested deep within other tags, it can be treated as a discrete element on the screen and controlled by CSS.

Web designers use the concept of the *box* as a metaphor to describe the various things that you can do to an HTML element in a window, whether it is a single tag or several nested tags. This box has several properties—including margins, borders, padding, width, and height—that can be influenced by CSS.

This chapter shows you how to control the box and its properties.

Understanding an Element's Box

The term *elements* refers to the various parts of an HTML document that are set off by HTML container tags.

The following is an HTML element:

```
<p>Alice</p>
```

This is another HTML element:

```
<div><p><b>Alice<img
→ src="alice11.gif"> </b></p></div>
```

The first example is an element made of a single tag. The second example is a collection of nested tags, and each of those nested tags is in turn an individual element. Remember that nested tags are referred to as the *children* of the tags within which they are nested; those tags in turn are referred to as the *parents* (see "Inheriting Properties from a Parent" in Chapter 2).

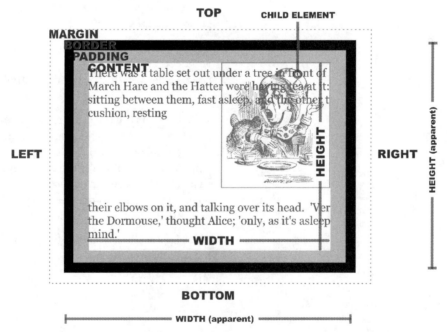

Figure 6.1 An element's box has a margin, a border, and padding on four sides around its central content. You can define the element's width and height or leave it to the browser's discretion.

Parts of the box

All HTML elements have four sides: top, bottom, left, and right (**Figure 6.1**). These four sides make up the element's box, to which CSS properties can be applied. Each side of the box has the following properties:

◆ **Content** and **Background** are at the center of the box. All other CSS properties (font, text, color, background, and lists) apply to this area. (Note: Background properties also apply to the padded area of an element's box.) The content includes all text, lists, forms, and images you care to use.

◆ **Child Elements** are elements contained within the parent element that are set off by their own HTML tags. Child elements also typically have their own box that can be controlled independent of the parent.

◆ **Width** and **height**, which are the dimensions of the content area. If you leave width and height undefined, these distances are determined by the browser (see "Setting the Width and Height of an Element" later in this chapter).

◆ **Margin**, which is the space between the border of the element and other elements in the window (see "Setting an Element's Margins" later in this chapter). If left unset, the margin is defined by the browser.

◆ **Border**, which is a rule (line) that surrounds the element. The border is invisible unless its color, width, and style—solid, dotted, dashed, and so on—are set (see "Setting an Element's Border" later in this chapter). If left unset, the border size is generally 0.

◆ **Padding**, which is the space between the border and the content of the element (see "Setting an Element's Padding" later in this chapter). Background colors and images will also fill this space. If left unset, the size of the padding is generally 0.

Limitations of the "box" model

So far it's fairly simple: All elements are rectangular "boxes" with a margin, border, padding, and content that has a width and height. But remember, this is Web design—it can never be that simple, right?

Right. The problems begin when you realize that not all browsers define boxes the same way.

According to the W3C definition of a box created using CSS, the width and height define the width and height of only the content area (the area where images and other objects are displayed). The *apparent* width and height, or the total width and height that the element takes up in the design, include the content area *plus* the padding and border sizes. So, the apparent width would be calculated in the following way:

```
width(content) + left padding +
→ right padding + left border +
→ right border = width(apparent)
```

Unfortunately, Microsoft Internet Explorer through version 5.5 defined width and height values as the apparent width and height (including padding and borders). This effectively subtracts the padding and border sizes to determine the content width and height:

```
width(apparent) - left padding -
→ right padding - left border -
→ right border = width(content)
```

So, given the following CSS:

```
#object1 {
    border: 5px solid #000;
    padding: 10px;
    width: 100px;
}
```

browsers using the W3C standard (Firefox, Safari, Opera) will set the content area to 100 pixels wide, but will have an apparent width of 130 pixels (**Figure 6.2**):

100 + 5 + 5 + 10 + 10 = 130

——— 130px ———

> There was a table set out under a tree in front of the house, and the March Hare and the Hatter were having tea at it: a Dormouse was sitting between them, fast asleep, and the other two were using it as a cushion, resting .

Figure 6.2 The box rendered by W3C-compliant browsers, including Safari, Firefox, and Opera, as well as Internet Explorer 6+ (if you're using Strict DTD), will be 130 pixels wide.

—100px—

There was a table set out under a tree in front of the house, and the March Hare and the Hatter were having tea at it: a Dormouse was sitting between them, fast asleep, and the other two were using it as a cushion, resting.

Figure 6.3 The same box rendered by Internet Explorer 5.5 and earlier and Internet Explorer 6+ using Transitional DTD will be 100 pixels wide.

Whereas Internet Explorer 5.5 and earlier will set a content area 70 pixels wide and an apparent width of 100 pixels (**Figure 6.3**):

70 + 5 + 5 +10 + 10 = 100

This is a problem, and it gets worse.

Recent versions of Internet Explorer (6 and later) fix this problem by following the W3C standards. However, remember our discussion about Quirks mode in Chapter 1 (see "Setting Your DTD")? If you are using the transitional DTD for your page, which is still very common, Internet Explorer 6 and later (including 7) revert to the "quirky" version of the box model.

So what's a good Web designer to do? You have several options:

◆ **Solution 1.** Do not use a border and or padding, or, if you do, do not expect pixel precision layout. Generally, this solution isn't practical, but for simple pages it might do the trick.

◆ **Solution 2.** Code for the Strict DTD only and hope that no one visits your site using Internet Explorer 5.5 and earlier. This approach has some obvious drawbacks, since there is still a sizable portion of the browsing public using these legacy browsers.

◆ **Solution 3.** Use one of the "hacks" (most likely the conditional comments) to code separate "equalizing" widths and/or heights for Internet Explorer. These techniques are discussed in the "Using Conditional Comments to Fix CSS in Internet Explorer" section of Chapter 2. This solution may require you to code twice for a lot of elements, but at least you ensure that your page will look right everywhere and every time.

✔ Tips

■ Element boxes can also wrap around other elements, embedding an element within another (see "Floating Elements in the Window" in Chapter 7).

■ The terms "apparent width" and "apparent height" are not official CSS terms, but I needed to be able to differentiate between width and height for content, and the total width and height that the element takes up in the design.

UNDERSTANDING AN ELEMENT'S BOX

Setting How an Element is Displayed

You may remember from Chapter 1 that all elements can be classified according to how they're displayed—inline or block (see "Kinds of Tags"). By default, every tag has a display style that defines how it will fit with other tags around it.

You can use the `display` property to define whether an element includes line breaks above and below (block), is included inline with other elements (inline), is treated as part of a list, or is displayed at all. **Table 6.1** shows the different values available for the `display` property:

- ◆ `list-item` places a list-item marker on the first line of text, as well as a break above and below. This code allows the item to be used as part of a list even if you're not specifically using a list element. Using list-item to create lists out of non-list elements is discussed in Chapter 10.

- ◆ `block` defines this tag as being a block-level box, placing a line break above and below the box. Setting this will automatically force the width of the box to the width of the parent element's box.

- ◆ `inline` defines this tag as being an inline box, suppressing line breaks immediately before and after the box.

- ◆ `table`, or any one of the other `table` values shown in Table 6.1, allows you to turn any tag into part of a data table. Unfortunately, these are not thoroughly implemented in Internet Explorer for Windows, and so may prove of limited use. Table values for the display property will be discussed in further detail in Chapter 9.

Table 6.1

Display Values	
VALUE	COMPATIBILITY
list-item	IE 5**, FF1, S1, O3.5, CSS1
block	IE4*, FF1, S1, O3.5, CSS1
inline	IE4*, FF1, S1, O3.5, CSS1
table	IE5***, FF1, S1, O4, CSS2
table-cell	IE5***, FF1, S1, O3.5, CSS2
table-footer-group	IE5**, FF1, S1, O3.5, CSS2
table-header-group	IE5, FF1, S1, O3.5, CSS2
table-row	IE5***, FF1, S1, O3.5, CSS2
table-row-group	IE5***, FF1, S1, O3.5, CSS2
none	IE4, FF1, S1, O3.5, CSS1
inherit	IE4, FF1, S1, O3.5, CSS1
* IE 5 for Windows	
** IE 6	
***Mac only, not available for Windows	

Figure 6.4 Block-level elements, like the paragraph, can be turned inline so that they run together without a break.

◆ inherit uses the display value set or implicit for the element's parent.

◆ none causes this element not to display in CSS browsers. It will look as though the content doesn't exist on the page.

To set an element to be placed inline:

1. display:

Start your declaration by typing the display property name, followed by a colon (:), in the CSS declaration block.

2. inline;

Type the inline value for how this element will be displayed, causing it to flow beside other elements before and after it. In this example (**Figure 6.4** and **Code 6.1**), several elements are set inline, most notably the paragraph tag within the copy ID, which overrides the p tag's natural inclination to have line breaks before and after.

continues on page 167

Code 6.1 Setting display to inline will remove line breaks above and/or below the element.

```
<!DOCTYPE html PUBLIC "-//W3C//DTD XHTML 1.0 Strict//EN" "http://www.w3.org/TR/xhtml1/DTD/
→ xhtml1-strict.dtd">
<html xmlns="http://www.w3.org/1999/xhtml">
<head>
<meta http-equiv="Content-Type" content="text/html; charset=utf-8" />
<title>CSS, DHTML &amp; Ajax | Setting How an Element is Displayed (or not) | Inline</title>
<style type="text/css" media="screen">
<!--
body {
    font-size: 1em;
    font-family: Georgia, "Times New Roman", times, serif;
    color: #000000;
    background-color: #fff;  }
h1, h2 {
    color: #999; }
```

code continues on next page

Code 6.1 *continued*

```
#navigation {
     background-color: #ccc;
     font: small Arial, Helvetica,
     → sans-serif; }
#navigation a {
     display: inline;
     color: red; }
#navigation a:hover {
     background-color: #fff; }
#copy p {
     display: inline; }
.chapterTitle {
     font-size: smaller;
     color:black; }
.dropBox {
     float: right;
     font: x-small Arial, Helvetica, sans-serif; }

-->
</style>
</head>
<body>
<div id="navigation"> Flip To Chapter:
<a href="#">Down the Rabbit-Hole </a>
<a href="#">The Pool of Tears </a>
<a href="#">A Caucus-Race and a Long Tale </a>
<a href="#">The Rabbit Sends in a Little Bill </a>
<a href="#">Advice from a Caterpillar </a>
<a href="#">Pig and Pepper </a>
<a href="#">NEXT &rArr; </a> </div>
<div id="header">
     <h1>Alice's Adventures in Wonderland</h1>
     <p class="author">Lewis Carroll</p>
     <form action="#" method="get" id="FormName">
     Search Book:
     <input class="formText" type="text" name="searchTerm" size="24" />
     <input class="formButton" type="submit" name="findSearchTerm" value="Find" />
     </form>
     <h2>CHAPTER I <span class="chapterTitle">Down the Rabbit-Hole</span> </h2>
</div>
<div id="copy">
     <div class="dropBox"> <img src="alice29.gif" height="236" width="200" alt="Alice in
     → Wonderland" /> Alice meets the Queen of Hearts.</div>
     <p>Alice was beginning to get very tired of sitting by her sister on the bank, and of having
     → nothing to do: once or twice she had peeped into the book her sister was reading, but it
     → had no pictures or conversations in it, 'and what is the use of a book,' thought Alice
     → 'without pictures or conversation?'</p>
</div>
</body></html>
```

Figure 6.5 Inline elements such as the menu links, the span tag, and images, can be turned into block elements that break, forcing content above and below onto another line.

To set an element to be placed as a block:

1. `display`:

   Start your declaration by typing the `display` property name, followed by a colon (:), in the CSS declaration block.

2. `block`;

   Type the `block` value for how this element will be displayed, rendering it separate from the elements before and after it.

   In this example (**Figure 6.5** and **Code 6.2**), the `img` tag for images is turned into a block-level element, forcing the text caption underneath it. Additionally, all links in the `navigation` box are forced to be block elements, creating a more readable list than when they were presented inline in the previous figure.

Code 6.2 Setting `display` to `block` forces line breaks above and below the element.

```
<!DOCTYPE html PUBLIC "-//W3C//DTD XHTML 1.0 Strict//EN" "http://www.w3.org/TR/xhtml1/DTD/
→ xhtml1-strict.dtd">
<html xmlns="http://www.w3.org/1999/xhtml">
<head>
<meta http-equiv="Content-Type" content="text/html; charset=utf-8" />
<title>CSS, DHTML &amp; Ajax | Setting How an Element is Displayed (or not) | Block</title>
        <style type="text/css" media="screen">
<!--
body {
    font-size: 1em;
    font-family: Georgia, "Times New Roman", times, serif;
    color: #000000;
    background-color: #fff; }
h1, h2 {
    color: #999; }
img {
    display: block; }
#navigation {
    background-color: #ccc;
    font: x-small Arial, Helvetica,
    → sans-serif;
    float: left; }
#navigation a {
    display: block;
    color: red; }
```

code continues on next page

Code 6.2 *continued*

```
#navigation a:hover {
     background-color: #fff; }
#copy p {
     display: block; }
.chapterTitle {
     display: block;
     font-size: smaller;
     color:black; }
.dropBox {
     float: right;
     font: x-small Arial, Helvetica, sans-serif; }
--></style>
     </head>
     <body>
<div id="navigation">
Flip To Chapter:
<a href="#">Down the Rabbit-Hole </a>
<a href="#">The Pool of Tears </a>
<a href="#">A Caucus-Race and a Long Tale </a>
<a href="#">The Rabbit Sends in a Little Bill </a>
<a href="#">Advice from a Caterpillar </a>
<a href="#">Pig and Pepper </a>
<a href="#">NEXT &rArr; </a>
</div>
<div id="header">
<h1>Alice's Adventures in Wonderland</h1>
<p class="author">Lewis Carroll</p>
<form action="#" method="get" id="FormName">
     Search Book:
     <input class="formText" type="text" name="searchTerm" size="24" />
     <input class="formButton" type="submit" name="findSearchTerm" value="Find" />
</form>
<h2>CHAPTER I
     <span class="chapterTitle">Down the Rabbit-Hole</span>
</h2>
</div>
<div id="copy">
<div class="dropBox">
<img src="alice29.gif" height="236" width="200" alt="Alice in Wonderland" />
Alice meets the Queen of Hearts.</div>
<p>Alice was beginning to get very tired of sitting by her sister on the bank, and of having
→ nothing to do: once or twice she had peeped into the book her sister was reading, but it had
→ no pictures or conversations in it, 'and what is the use of a book,' thought Alice 'without
→ pictures or conversation?'</p>
</div>
</body></html>
```

Figure 6.6 If you want to hide an element completely, you can use display:none. Notice that no space is reserved for the elements—it's as if they do not exist, even though they are still in the HTML code.

To set an element not to be displayed:

1. display:

Start your declaration by typing the display property name, followed by a colon (:), in the CSS declaration block.

2. none;

Type the none value to remove this element from the page. In this example (**Figure 6.6** and **Code 6.3**), the navigation, search, and figure have all been removed. While this doesn't look so interesting onscreen, it can be great for a print version of the page. Who needs navigation links, search forms, and low-resolution graphics on paper?

Code 6.3 Setting display to none will cause the element to disappear completely.

```
<!DOCTYPE html PUBLIC "-//W3C//DTD XHTML 1.0 Strict//EN" "http://www.w3.org/TR/xhtml1/DTD/
→ xhtml1-strict.dtd">
<html xmlns="http://www.w3.org/1999/xhtml">
<head>
<meta http-equiv="Content-Type" content="text/html; charset=utf-8" />
<title>CSS, DHTML &amp; Ajax | Setting How an Element is Displayed (or not) | None</title>
        <style type="text/css" media="screen">
<!--
body {
    font-size: 1em;
    font-family: Georgia, "Times New Roman", times, serif;
    color: #000000;
    background-color: #fff; }
h1, h2 {
    color: #999; }
form {
    display: none; }
#navigation {
    display: none; }
.chapterTitle {
    display: block;
    font-size: smaller;
    color:black; }
.dropBox {
    display: none;
    float: right;
    font: x-small Arial, Helvetica, sans-serif; }
--></style>
        </head>
        <body>
<div id="navigation">                                    code continues on next page
```

✔ Tips

■ Any elements that are assigned dis-play:none will simply be ignored by the browser. Be careful in using none, however-er. Although it is not an inherited attrib-ute, none turns off the display of the ele-ment as well as any children elements within it.

■ Another great use for none is to use it to create a print-specific style sheet that hides elements not needed on paper, such as navigation and form fields.

■ Although at first glance the none value may seem to be a description of its use-fulness, this will actually prove to be one of the most important CSS attributes we'll use with DHTML. By initially set-ting the display of an element to none, and then resetting the value using JavaScript, you can create several useful interface controls, such as drop-down menus, pop-up hypertext, and slide shows (see Chapter 24).

■ The display property should not be con-fused with the visibility property (see "Setting the Visibility of an Element" in Chapter 8). Unlike the visibility prop-erty, which leaves a space for the ele-ment, display:none; completely removes the element from the page, although the browser still loads its content.

■ Using JavaScript, you can create a simple collapsible menu by switching display between inline and none to make menu options appear and disap-pear (see "Creating Collapsible Menus" in Chapter 23).

SETTING HOW AN ELEMENT IS DISPLAYED

Code 6.3 *continued*

```
Flip To Chapter:
<a href="#">Down the Rabbit-Hole </a>
<a href="#">The Pool of Tears </a>
<a href="#">A Caucus-Race and a Long Tale </a>
<a href="#">The Rabbit Sends in a Little
→ Bill </a>
<a href="#">Advice from a Caterpillar </a>
<a href="#">Pig and Pepper </a>
<a href="#">NEXT &rArr; </a>
</div>
<div id="header">
<h1>Alice's Adventures in Wonderland</h1>
<p class="author">Lewis Carroll</p>
<form action="#" method="get" id="FormName">
    Search Book:
    <input class="formText" type="text"
    → name="searchTerm" size="24" />
    <input class="formButton" type="submit"
    → name="findSearchTerm" value="Find" />
</form>
<h2>CHAPTER I
    <span class="chapterTitle">Down the
    → Rabbit-Hole</span>
</h2>
</div>
<div id="copy">
<div class="dropBox">
<img src="alice29.gif" height="236"
→ width="200" alt="Alice in Wonderland" />
Alice meets the Queen of Hearts.</div>
<p>Alice was beginning to get very tired of
→ sitting by her sister on the bank, and
→ of having nothing to do: once or twice
→ she had peeped into the book her sister
→ was reading, but it had no pictures or
→ conversations in it, 'and what is the
→ use of a book,' thought Alice 'without
→ pictures or conversation?'</p>
</div>
</body></html>
```

Table 6.2

Margin Values

VALUE	COMPATIBILITY
‹length›	IE3, FF1, S1, O3.5, CSS1
‹percentage›	IE3, FF1, S1, O3.5, CSS1
auto	IE3, FF1, S1, O3.5, CSS1

Figure 6.7 Margins are used to add space between different elements, providing more white space and making the page easier on the eye.

Code 6.4 Set the margin on all four sides the same or each one individually.

```
<!DOCTYPE html PUBLIC "-//W3C//DTD XHTML 1.0
→ Strict//EN" "http://www.w3.org/TR/xhtml1/
→ DTD/xhtml1-strict.dtd">
<html xmlns="http://www.w3.org/1999/xhtml">
<head>
<meta http-equiv="Content-Type"
→ content="text/html; charset=utf-8" />
<title>CSS, DHTML &amp; Ajax | Setting an
→ Elements Margins</title>
        <style type="text/css"
            → media="screen">
<!--
body {
    font-size: 1em;
    font-family: Georgia, "Times New
    → Roman", times, serif;
    color: #000000;
    background-color: #fff;

    margin: 8px;
}
                        code continues on next page
```

Setting an Element's Margins

The margin shortcut property (**Table 6.2**) of an element allows you to set the space between that element and other elements in the window by specifying one to four values that correspond to all four sides together, the top/bottom and left/right sides as pairs, or all four sides independently.

In this example (**Figure 6.7**), margins have been added to accomplish two things: to set off the navigation block so that it isn't pressed against the header, and separate by 8 pixels the drop box from the copy it is floating in. In addition, a negative margin has been set for the ol tag to pull the numbered list to the left.

To define the margins of an element:

1. margin:

   Start your declaration by typing the margin shortcut property name, followed by a colon (:), in the declaration block (**Code 6.4**).

2. 0px 8px 8px 0px;

   Now type a value for the margin, which can be any of the following:

   ▲ A **length value**

   ▲ A **percentage**, which creates a margin proportional to the parent element's width

   ▲ **auto**, which returns control of the margins to the browser's discretion

   continues on Page 173

Code 6.4 *continued*

```
h1, h2 {
    color: #999;
    margin: 0em 0em .5em;
}

h2 {
    clear: both;
}

img {
    margin: 4px;
    display: block;
}

form {
    margin: 4px 0px;
}

#navigation {
    margin: 0px 8px 8px 0px;
    background-color: #ccc;
    float: left;
    font: small Arial, Helvetica,
    → sans-serif;
}

#navigation a {
    display: block;
    color: red;
}

#navigation a:hover {
    background-color: #fff;
}

#copy p {
    margin: 1em 5em;
}

.author {
    margin-top: 0cm;
    font: bold 1em Arial, Helvetica,
    → sans-serif;
    }

.chapterTitle {
    display: block;
    font-size: smaller;
    color:black;
}
.dropBox {
```

Code 6.4 *continued*

```
    margin-top: 0px;
    margin-right: 0px;
    margin-bottom: 8px;
    margin-left: 8px;
    float: right;
    font: xx-small Arial, Helvetica,
    → sans-serif;
}
--></style>
    </head>

    <body>
<div id="navigation">
Flip To Chapter:
<a href="#">Down the Rabbit-Hole </a>
<a href="#">The Pool of Tears </a>
<a href="#">A Caucus-Race and a Long Tale </a>
<a href="#">The Rabbit Sends in a Little
→ Bill </a>
<a href="#">Advice from a Caterpillar </a>
<a href="#">Pig and Pepper </a>
</div>
<div id="header">
<h1>Alice's Adventures in Wonderland</h1>
<p class="author">Lewis Carroll</p>
<form action="#" method="get" id="FormName">
    Search Book:
    <input class="formText" type="text"
    → name="searchTerm" size="24" />
    <input class="formButton" type="submit"
    → name="findSearchTerm" value="Find" />
</form>
<h2>CHAPTER II
    <span class="chapterTitle">The Pool of
    → Tears</span>
</h2>
</div>
<div id="copy">
<div class="dropBox">
<img src="alice07a.gif" height="236"
width="200" alt="Alice in Wonderland" />
Alice is drowning in a pool of her own making.
</div>
<p>'Curiouser and curiouser!' cried Alice
→ (she was so much surprised, that for the
→ moment she quite forgot how to speak good
→ English); 'now I'm opening out like the
→ largest telescope that ever was! </p>
</div>
</body>
</html>
```

Setting Negative Margins

Although you can use negative margins (for example, `margin:-5em;`) to create interesting effects for overlapping pieces of text, this method is frowned upon because various browsers present different results.

Overlapping text is better achieved with CSS positioning (see Chapter 7).

Be careful when setting negative margins around a hypertext link. If one element has margins that cause it to cover the link, the link will not work as expected.

You can enter between one to four values, separated by spaces, to define the margins as follows:

▲ **One value** sets the margin for all four sides.

▲ **Two values** set the top/bottom margins and left/right margins.

▲ **Three values** set the top margin, the left/right margins (the same), and the bottom margin.

▲ **Four values** set each individual margin, in this order: top, right, bottom, and left.

3. `margin-top: 5em;`

You can also set the margin for just one side of the box independently without having to worry about the other three margins. This is especially useful when used with an inline style to override margins set elsewhere. To do this, just specify the margin side you want to define (top, bottom, left, or right) and a legitimate margin value.

✔ Tips

■ You can also set margins for the <body> tag, in which case they define the distance at which elements nested in the body should appear from the top and left sides of the browser window. In theory, this would allow you to center the content of a page by setting the margins on both sides to auto. However, setting margins for the <body> tag tends to be buggy in Internet Explorer for Windows in version 5.5 and earlier and in version 6 if you are using Quirks mode.

■ When setting proportional margins, be aware that you might get very different results depending on the size of the user's window. What looks good at a resolution of 640 × 480 might be a mess at larger screen sizes.

■ The browser has a default margin it adds to the body of your page so that the content doesn't immediately begin at the edges of the screen. However, the default is not the same on all browsers, which can be a problem when you position your elements on the page (discussed in Chapter 7). So it's a good idea to set the margins in the body tag so that they remain consistent.

Setting an Element's Border

The border property allows you to set a *rule* (line) around your box on all four sides of any color and thickness, and you can select from a variety of line styles (**Table 6.3**). In addition, using additional border properties, you can set the borders on any of the four sides independently, giving you amazing design versatility.

In this example (**Figure 6.8**), borders have been set around the menu options; a simple red line border has overridden the form text field's 3D border; and the drop box has a festive multistyle, multicolor border.

To set the border:

1. border:

To set the border on all four sides, type the border property name, followed by a colon (:), in the CSS declaration block (**Code 6.5**).

continues on Page 176

Table 6.3

Border Values	
VALUE	COMPATIBILITY
‹border-width›	IE4, FF1, S1, O3.5, CSS1
‹border-style›	IE4, FF1, S1, O3.5, CSS1
‹border-color›	IE4, FF1, S1, O3.5, CSS1

Figure 6.8 A tacky harlequin-style multi-color, multi-style border has been added around the drop box.

Code 6.5 There are several border property types you can use to customize your design.

```
<!DOCTYPE html PUBLIC "-//W3C//DTD XHTML 1.0 Strict//EN" "http://www.w3.org/TR/xhtml1/DTD/
→ xhtml1-strict.dtd">
<html xmlns="http://www.w3.org/1999/xhtml">
<head>
<meta http-equiv="Content-Type" content="text/html; charset=utf-8" />
<title>CSS, DHTML &amp; Ajax | Setting an Element's Border</title>
        <style type="text/css" media="screen">
<!--
body {
    font-size: 1em;
    font-family: Georgia, "Times New Roman", times, serif;
    color: #000000;
    background-color: #fff;

    margin: 8px;
}
```
code continues on next page

Code 6.5 *continued*

```
h1, h2 {
    color: #999;
    margin: .5em 0em; }
h2 {
    clear: both; }
img {
    margin: 4px;
    display: block; }
form {
    margin: 4px 0px;  }
input.formText {
    border: 1px solid red;
    background-color: #fcc;  }
#navigation {
    margin-right: 8px;
    border: 3px solid #666;
    background-color: #ccc;
    float: left;
    font: small Arial, Helvetica,
    → sans-serif; }
input.formButton {
    border: 1px solid #fcc;
    background-color: #f00;
    color: white; }
#navigation a {
    border-top: 3px solid #fff;
    text-decoration: none;
    display: block;
    color: red; }
#navigation a:hover {
    border-top-width: 3px;
    border-top-style: solid;
    border-top-color: #999;
    color: red;
    background-color: #fff; }
#copy p {
    margin: 1em 5em; }
.author {
    margin-top: 0cm;
    font: bold 1em Arial, Helvetica,
    → sans-serif; }
.chapterTitle {
    display: block;
    font-size: smaller;
    color:black; }
.dropBox {
    border-style: solid dashed double ridge;
    border-width: 1px 2px 4px 8px ;
```

Code 6.5 *continued*

```
    border-color: red green blue purple;
    margin: 0px 0px 8px 8px;
    float: right;
    font: small Arial, Helvetica, sans-serif;
}
--></style>
    </head>
    <body>
<div id="navigation">
Flip To Chapter:
<a href="#">Down the Rabbit-Hole </a>
<a href="#">The Pool of Tears </a>
<a href="#">A Caucus-Race and a Long Tale </a>
<a href="#">The Rabbit Sends in a Little
→ Bill </a>
<a href="#">Advice from a Caterpillar </a>
<a href="#">Pig and Pepper </a>
<a href="#">NEXT &rArr; </a>
</div>
<div id="header">
<h1>Alice's Adventures in Wonderland</h1>
<p class="author">Lewis Carroll</p>
<form action="#" method="get" id="FormName">
    Search Book:
    <input class="formText" type="text"
    → name="searchTerm" size="24" />
    <input class="formButton" type="submit"
    → name="findSearchTerm" value="Find" />
</form>
<h2>CHAPTER III
    <span class="chapterTitle">A Caucus-
    → Race and a Long Tale</span>
</h2>
</div>
<div id="copy">
<div class="dropBox">
<img src="alice09a.gif" height="236"
→ width="200" alt="Alice in Wonderland" />
Alice makes some new friends?
</div>
<p>They were indeed a queer-looking party
→ that assembled on the bank--the birds
→ with draggled feathers, the animals with
→ their fur clinging close to them, and
→ all dripping wet, cross, and
→ uncomfortable.</p>
</div>
</body>
</html>
```

2. `1px`

Type a border-width value, followed by a space. This value can be one of the following (**Table 6.4**):

▲ A length value; a value of 0 prevents the border from appearing

▲ A relative-size keyword, such as thin, medium, or thick

▲ `inherit` will cause the element to use the same border styles as its parent element

3. `solid`

Type the name of the style you want to assign to your border. **Table 6.5** shows a complete list of available border styles.

Alternatively, you can type none, which prevents the border from appearing.

4. `red;`

Type a color value, which is the color you want the border to be (**Table 6.6**). This can be the name of the color or an RGB value.

5. `border-top: 3px solid #fff;`

You aren't stuck with having the same border on all four sides. You can set each side individually (top, bottom, left, and/or right). If those options aren't enough, check out the sidebar "Other Ways to Set a Border."

✔ Tips

■ Most browsers that do not support other border properties usually support the simple border property.

■ You do not have to include all the individual border attributes in your definition list, but if you don't, their defaults will be used.

Table 6.4

Border-Width Values

VALUE	COMPATIBILITY
‹length›	IE4, FF1, S1, O3.5, CSS1
thin	IE4, FF1, S1, O3.5, CSS1
medium	IE4, FF1, S1, O3.5, CSS1
thick	IE4, FF1, S1, O3.5, CSS1
inherit	IE4, FF1, S1, O3.5, CSS1

Table 6.5

Border-Style Values

VALUE	APPEARANCE	COMPATIBILITY
dotted		IE4*, FF1, S1, O3.5, CSS1
dashed		IE4*, FF1, S1, O3.5, CSS1
solid		IE4, FF1, S1, O3.5, CSS1
double		IE4, FF1, S1, O3.5, CSS1
groove		IE4, FF1, S1, O3.5, CSS1
ridge		IE4, FF1, S1, O3.5, CSS1
inset		IE4, FF1, S1, O3.5, CSS1
outset		IE4, FF1, S1, O3.5, CSS1
none		IE4, FF1, S1, O3.5, CSS1
inherit		IE4, FF1, S1, O3.5, CSS1

*IE 5.5 for Windows

Table 6.6

Border-Color Values

VALUE	COMPATIBILITY
‹color›	IE4, FF1, S1, O3.5, CSS1
transparent	IE4*, FF1, S1, O3.5, CSS1
inherit	IE4*, FF1, S1, O3.5, CSS1

* Mac Only

Table 6.7

-Moz-Border-Radius Values	
VALUE	COMPATIBILITY
<length>	FF1
<percentage>	FF1

Rounding border corners (Mozilla only)

If you're tired of square corners in your designs, but don't want to resort to graphics to create borders, Mozilla-based browsers (Netscape 6+, Firefox, and Camino) have a proprietary CSS property that allows you to set the corner radius for borders (**Table 6.7**). Although not implemented in Microsoft Internet Explorer, Apple Safari, or Opera, this Mozilla extension can be useful and does not interfere with how borders will appear in those other browsers.

continues on next page

Other Ways to Set a Border

CSS gives you the freedom to define aspects of the border's appearance one side at a time, as follows:

```
border-style: solid dashed double ridge;
border-width: 1px 2px 4px 8px ;
border-color: red green blue purple;
```

The values for these are shown in Tables 6.4 through 6.6.

As with margins, you can include one to four values for each of these properties to set each border side independently, as follows:

◆ **One value** sets the property for all four sides.

◆ **Two values** set the property for the top/bottom and left/right sides.

◆ **Three values** set the top property, the left/right properties (the same), and the bottom property.

◆ **Four values** set the property for each side individually, in this order: top, right, bottom, and left.

This method is especially useful for overriding the values set by the single border property.

Your final option for setting a border on a single side (as if you really needed another option!) is to set the individual properties for a specific side (top, bottom, left, right):

```
border-top-width: 3px;
border-top-style: solid;
border-top-color: #f00;
```

In this example (**Figure 6.9**), the borders of several elements have been rounded off, including the border of the form input text field. Each corner of the drop box has a different radius set.

To set rounded corners for Mozilla browsers:

1. `border: 1px solid red;`

   Set up the border or background for the element using any of the methods previously discussed (**Code 6.6**).

2. `-moz-border-radius:`

   After the border definition, type the `-moz-border-radius` property name, followed by a colon (:).

continues on Page 180

Figure 6.9 Mozilla-based browsers such as Firefox and Netscape are the only ones that show rounded corners. In this example, the menu, form text field, and drop box are rounded.

Code 6.6 After you set a border or background color for an element, you can set the border radius, and Mozilla browsers will show rounded corners.

```
<!DOCTYPE html PUBLIC "-//W3C//DTD XHTML 1.0
→ Strict//EN" "http://www.w3.org/TR/xhtml1/
→ DTD/xhtml1-strict.dtd">
<html xmlns="http://www.w3.org/1999/xhtml">
<head>
<meta http-equiv="Content-Type"
→ content="text/html; charset=utf-8" />
<title>CSS, DHTML &amp; Ajax | Setting an
→ Element's Border | Radius</title>
        <style type="text/css"
        → media="screen">
<!--
body {
    font-size: 1em;
    font-family: Georgia, "Times New
    → Roman", times, serif;
    color: #000000;
    background-color: #fff;

    margin: 8px;
}

h1, h2 {
    color: #999;
    margin: .5em 0em;
}
```

Code 6.6 *continued*

```
h2 {
    clear: both;
}

img {
    margin: 4px;
    display: block;
}

form {
    margin: 4px 0px;
}

input.formText {
    border: 1px solid red;
    -moz-border-radius: 5%;
    background-color: #fcc;
}

input.formButton {
    border: 1px solid #fcc;
    background-color: #f00;
    color: white;
}
```

code continues on next page

Code 6.6 *continued*

```
#navigation {
    -moz-border-radius: 5%;
    border: 3px solid #666;
    background-color: #ccc;
    float: left;
    font: small Arial, Helvetica,
    → sans-serif;
    margin-right: 8px;
}

#navigation a {
    border-top: 3px solid #fff;
    text-decoration: none;
    display: block;
    color: red;
}

#navigation a:hover {
    border-top-width: 3px;
    border-top-style: solid;
    border-top-color: #999;
    color: red;
    background-color: #fff;
}

#copy p {
    margin: 1em 5em;
}

.author {
    margin-top: 0cm;
    font: bold 1em Arial, Helvetica,
    → sans-serif;
    }

.chapterTitle {
    display: block;
    font-size: smaller;
    color:black;
}

.dropBox {
    border-style: solid dashed double ridge;
    border-width: 1px 2px 4px 8px ;
    border-color: red green blue purple;
    -moz-border-radius-topleft: 25px;
    -moz-border-radius-topright: 5px;
    -moz-border-radius-bottomleft: 20px;
    -moz-border-radius-bottomleft: 8px;
```

Code 6.6 *continued*

```
    margin: 0px 0px 8px 8px;
    float: right;
    font: small Arial, Helvetica,
    → sans-serif;
}
--></style>
</head>
<body>
<div id="navigation">
Flip To Chapter:
<a href="#">Down the Rabbit-Hole </a>
<a href="#">The Pool of Tears </a>
<a href="#">A Caucus-Race and a Long Tale
</a>
<a href="#">The Rabbit Sends in a Little
→ Bill </a>
<a href="#">Advice from a Caterpillar </a>
<a href="#">Pig and Pepper </a>
<a href="#">NEXT &rArr; </a>
</div>
<div id="header">
<h1>Alice's Adventures in Wonderland</h1>
<p class="author">Lewis Carroll</p>
<form action="#" method="get" id="FormName">
    Search Book:
    <input class="formText" type="text"
    → name="searchTerm" size="24" />
    <input class="formButton" type="submit"
    → name="findSearchTerm" value="Find" />
</form>
<h2>CHAPTER III
    <span class="chapterTitle">A Caucus-
    → Race and a Long Tale</span>
</h2>
</div>
<div id="copy">
<div class="dropBox">
<img src="alice09a.gif" height="236"
→ width="200" alt="Alice" />
Alice makes some new friends?
</div>
<p>They were indeed a queer-looking party
→ that assembled on the bank--the birds
→ with draggled feathers, the animals
→ with their fur clinging close to them,
→ and all dripping wet, cross, and
→ uncomfortable.</p>
</div>
</body>
</html>
```

3. 5%;

Type a `border-radius` value, followed by a semicolon. This value can be one of the following:

▲ A **length value**, which sets the radius of an imaginary circle at the corner, used to round it off. The larger the value, the rounder the edge.

▲ A **percentage** (`0%` to `50%`), which uses the size of the element to set the corner radius. Higher values produce rounder corners, with `50%` joining corners into a semi-circle.

You can include up to four values, separated by a space:

▲ **One value** sets all four-corner radii the same.

▲ **Two values** set the radius for the top-left/bottom-right and bottom-left/top-right corners.

▲ **Three values** set the corner radius for the top left, bottom left/top right (the same), and the bottom right corners.

▲ **Four values** set the radius for each corner individually, in this order: top left, top right, bottom right, and bottom left.

4. `-moz-border-radius-topleft: 25px;`

Each corner's border radius can also have all its values set independently (`topleft`, `topright`, `bottomleft`, `bottomright`) without having to specify the other corner radii. This method is especially useful for overriding the border values set by the single `-moz-border-radius` property.

✔ Tips

■ One problem with the way rounded corners are implemented is that the browser does not anti-alias them, so rather than smooth curves, we get blocky curves.

■ CSS3 includes the `border-radius` property (no "-moz"), but no browsers have implemented it, not even Firefox.

Table 6.8

Outline Values	
VALUE	COMPATIBILITY
‹border-width›	IE5*, FF1.5, S1.3, O7, CSS2.1
‹border-style›	IE5*, FF1.5, S1.3, O7, CSS2.1
‹border-color›	IE5*, FF1.5, S1.3, O7, CSS2.1
*Mac only, not available for Windows	

Figure 6.10 Unlike borders, outlines don't require additional space on the screen. Instead, they slide under surrounding elements in the background, making them very useful for highlighting pseudo-classes such as :hover and :focus.

Setting an Element's Outline

You may have noticed that I didn't mention the outline in the first section of this chapter when I detailed the parts of a box. This is because Internet Explorer doesn't support it. So although the outline is useful and will not interfere with Internet Explorer, you can't rely on using it to convey critical information to the viewer.

The outline (**Table 6.8**) surrounds the border and even uses the same values as the border, but unlike the border, it does not increase the apparent dimensions (width or height) of the box, and so does not actually take up any space on the screen. Instead, it will appear under any margin and out into the page under surrounding content.

An outline can be very useful for link-rollovers, allowing you to highlight them without displacing the surrounding content. Although outlines are not supported by Internet Explorer for Windows, they won't interfere with that browser if you decide to use them.

In this example (**Figure 6.10**), the links in the navigation have a red outline added when users hover their cursors over them. Unlike adding a border, this will not cause the surrounding links to shift around. In addition, outlines have been added to the form text field when it is in focus (or selected) and the form button when the user hovers over it. Although Internet Explorer does not support the outline property, it doesn't support the :focus pseudo-class at all or the :hover class for anything but links, so no harm done. Finally, I added a big outline around the drop box to show how the outline slides under surrounding content.

continues on next page

To set a box's outline:

1. `outline: 5px solid red;`

   The `outline` property looks identical to the border property: first width, then style, and then color separated by spaces (**Code 6.7**).

2. `outline-width: 50px;`
   `outline-style: solid;`
   `outline-color: #f00;`

   Also like the border property, `outline` can have each of its values defined individually, which is useful when you need to override one of them for an element without having to change the others.

✔ Tips

- Mozilla browsers originally used the `–moz-outline` property, but that has now been replaced.

- Unlike `border`, `outline` cannot be set independently for the sides.

Code 6.7 The outline goes around the border, but will not change the size of the element.

```
<!DOCTYPE html PUBLIC "-//W3C//DTD XHTML 1.0
→ Strict//EN" "http://www.w3.org/TR/xhtml1/
→ DTD/xhtml1-strict.dtd">
<html xmlns="http://www.w3.org/1999/xhtml">
<head>
<meta http-equiv="Content-Type"
content="text/html; charset=utf-8" />
<title>CSS, DHTML &amp; Ajax | Setting an
→ Elements Outline</title>
        <style type="text/css" media="screen">
<!--
body {
    font-size: 1em;
    font-family: Georgia, "Times New
    → Roman", times, serif;
    color: #000000;
    background-color: #fff;

    margin: 8px;
}

h1, h2 {
    color: #999;
    margin: .5em 0em;
}

h2 {
    clear: both;
}

img {
    margin: 4px;
    display: block;
}

form {
    margin: 4px 0px;
}

input.formText {
    border: 1px solid #666;
    background-color: #999;
}

input.formButton {
    border: 1px solid #999;
    background-color: #ccc;
    color: #333;
}
```

code continues on next page

Code 6.7 *continued*

```
input.formText:focus {
    outline: 5px solid red;
    background-color: #fcc;
}

input.formButton:hover {
    outline: 1px solid #f00;
    background-color: #f00;
    color: white;
}

#navigation {
    margin-right: 8px;
    border: 3px solid #666;
    background-color: #ccc;
    float: left;
    font: small Arial, Helvetica, sans-serif;
}

#navigation a {
    border-top: 3px solid #fff;
    text-decoration: none;
    display: block;
    color: red;
}

#navigation a:hover {
    outline: 3px solid #f00;
    color: red;
    background-color: #fff;
}

#copy p {
    margin: 1em 5em;
}

.author {
    margin-top: 0cm;
    font: bold 1em Arial, Helvetica,
    → sans-serif;
}

.chapterTitle {
    display: block;
    font-size: smaller;
    color:black;
}

.dropBox {
    outline-width: 50px;
    outline-style: solid;
    outline-color: #f00;
```

Code 6.7 *continued*

```
    border: 5px solid black;
    margin: 0px 0px 8px 8px;
    float: right;
    font: small Arial, Helvetica, sans-serif;
}
--></style>
    </head>

    <body>
<div id="navigation">
Flip To Chapter:
<a href="#">Down the Rabbit-Hole </a>
<a href="#">The Pool of Tears </a>
<a href="#">A Caucus-Race and a Long Tale </a>
<a href="#">The Rabbit Sends in a Little
→ Bill </a>
<a href="#">Advice from a Caterpillar </a>
<a href="#">Pig and Pepper </a>
<a href="#">NEXT &rArr; </a>
</div>
<div id="header">
<h1>Alice's Adventures in Wonderland</h1>
<p class="author">Lewis Carroll</p>
<form action="#" method="get" id="FormName">
    Search Book:
    <input class="formText" type="text"
    → name="searchTerm" size="24" />
    <input class="formButton" type="submit"
    → name="findSearchTerm" value="Find" />
</form>
<h2>CHAPTER III
    <span class="chapterTitle">A Caucus-
    → Race and a Long Tale</span>
</h2>
</div>
<div id="copy">
<div class="dropBox">
<img src="alice09a.gif" height="236"
→ width="200" alt="Alice" />
Alice makes some new friends?
</div>
<p>They were indeed a queer-looking party
→ that assembled on the bank--the birds
→ with draggled feathers, the animals
→ with their fur clinging close to them,
→ and all dripping wet, cross, and
→ uncomfortable.</p>
</div>
</body>
</html>
```

Setting an Element's Padding

At first glance, padding (**Table 6.9**) seems to have an effect identical to margins: It adds space around the element's content. The difference is that padding sets the space between the border of the element and its content, rather than between the element and the other elements in the window. Padding is especially useful if you're using borders and background colors and you don't want the content butting right up to the edges.

In this example (**Figure 6.11**), padding is set to help space the content away from the edge of its border, either defined by the border property or by the background. Rather than smashing up against the edge of the navigation box, the links now have a bit of breathing room, and so do the text in the form button and the figure caption in the drop box.

To set padding:

1. `padding:`
   Start your declaration by typing the `padding` property name, followed by a colon (**Code 6.8**).

2. `.5em 4em 1em 2em;`
   Next, type a value for the element's padding, which can be any of the following:

   ▲ **length values**, which creates padding of the exact size you specify

   ▲ A **percentage**, which creates padding proportional to the parent element's width

   ▲ `inherit` to use the parent's `padding` value

continues on Page 186

Table 6.9

Padding Values	
VALUE	COMPATIBILITY
‹length›	IE4, FF1, S1, O3.5, CSS1
‹percentage›	IE4, FF1, S1, O3.5, CSS1
inherit	FF1, S1, O7, CSS2

Figure 6.11 Like margins, padding can add white space to your design to open it up and make it easier to view.

Code 6.8 Setting padding allows you to space the content from the edge of the border of the element.

```
<!DOCTYPE html PUBLIC "-//W3C//DTD XHTML 1.0
→ Strict//EN" "http://www.w3.org/TR/xhtml1/
→ DTD/xhtml1-strict.dtd">
<html xmlns="http://www.w3.org/1999/xhtml">
<head>
<meta http-equiv="Content-Type"
content="text/html; charset=utf-8" />
<title>CSS, DHTML &amp; Ajax | Setting an
→ Element's Padding</title>
        <style type="text/css" media="screen">
<!--
body {
    font-size: 1em;
    font-family: Georgia, "Times New Roman",
    → times, serif;
    color: #000000;
    background-color: #fff;

    margin: 8px;
}

h1, h2 {
    color: #999;
    margin: .5em 0em;
}

h2 {
    clear: both;
}

img {
    margin: 4px;
    display: block;
}

form {
    padding: .5em 4em 1em 2em;
    margin: 4px 0px;
    border-bottom: 1px solid #f66;
}

input.formText {
    border: 1px solid #666;
    background-color: #999;
}

input.formButton {
    border: 1px solid #999;
    background-color: #ccc;
    color: #333;
}
```

Code 6.8 *continued*

```
#navigation {
    margin-right: 8px;
    border: 3px solid #666;
    background-color: #ccc;
    float: left;
    font: small Arial, Helvetica, sans-serif;
}

input.formText {
    border: 1px solid #999;
    background-color: #ccc;
}

input.formButton {
    padding-right: 16px;
    padding-left: 16px;
    border: 1px solid #f66;
    background-color: #f99;
    color: red;
}

#navigation a {
    padding: 2px 4px;
    border-top: 3px solid #fff;
    text-decoration: none;
    display: block;
    color: red;
}

#navigation a:hover {
    border-top: 3px solid #999;
    color: red;
    background-color: #fff;
}

#copy p {
    margin: 1em 5em;
}

.author {
    margin-top: 0cm;
    font: bold 1em Arial, Helvetica,
    → sans-serif;
}

.chapterTitle {
    display: block;
    font-size: smaller;
    color:black;
}
```

code continues on next page

To set each side's padding value separately, you can type from one to four values.

- ▲ **One value** sets the padding for all four sides.
- ▲ **Two values** set the padding for the top/bottom and left/right sides.
- ▲ **Three values** set the top padding, the padding for the left/right sides (the same), and the bottom padding.
- ▲ **Four values** set the padding for each side individually, in this order: top, right, bottom, and left.

3. `padding-right: 16px;`

   As with margins, padding can also be set independently on all four sides of the box (top, bottom, left, and right).

✔ Tips

- Padding and margins are easily confused because their results often look the same if no border or background is visible. Remember: Margins separate one element from other elements, but padding is the space between the border and the content of the element.

- Because of the limitations of the box model, discussed earlier in this chapter, be careful when setting padding. It will be rendered differently in Quirks mode of Internet Explorer versus other modern browsers.

- If there is no border around or background-color behind the element, setting the margin will have the same visual effect as padding, and you won't run into the issues surrounding box model measurements.

Code 6.8 *continued*

```css
.dropBox {
    padding: 6px;
    border: 3px solid #f66;
    margin: 0px 0px 8px 8px;
    float: right;
    font: small Arial, Helvetica, sans-serif;
}
--></style>
</head>
```

```html
<body>
<div id="navigation">
Flip To Chapter:
<a href="#">Down the Rabbit-Hole </a>
<a href="#">The Pool of Tears </a>
<a href="#">A Caucus-Race and a Long Tale </a>
<a href="#">The Rabbit Sends in a Little
→ Bill </a>
<a href="#">Advice from a Caterpillar </a>
<a href="#">Pig and Pepper </a>
<a href="#">NEXT &rArr; </a>
</div>
<div id="header">
<h1>Alice's Adventures in Wonderland</h1>
<p class="author">Lewis Carroll</p>
<form action="#" method="get" id="FormName">
    Search Book:
    <input class="formText" type="text"
    → name="searchTerm" size="24" />
    <input class="formButton" type="submit"
    → name="findSearchTerm" value="Find" />
</form>
<h2>CHAPTER IV
    <span class="chapterTitle">The Rabbit
    → Sends in a Little Bill</span>
</h2>
</div>
<div id="copy">
<div class="dropBox">
<img src="alice12a.gif" height="236"
→ width="200" alt="Alice" />
Alice makes some new friends?
</div>
<p>It was the White Rabbit, trotting slowly
→ back again, and looking anxiously about
→ as it went, as if it had lost
→ something…</p>
</div>
</body>
</html>
```

Table 6.10

Width and Height Values	
VALUE	COMPATIBILITY
‹length›	IE4, FF1, S1, O3.5, CSS1
‹percentage›	IE4, FF1, S1, O3.5, CSS1
auto	IE4, FF1, S1, O3.5, CSS1

Figure 6.12 Setting the width of an element lets you control the horizontal space your design will occupy. Height lets you control the vertical space, but needs a scroll-bar if there is more content than space.

Figure 6.13 The scroll bar only scrolls the content in the element.

Setting the Width and Height of an Element

The width and height of block-level elements can be specified using the `width` and `height` properties (**Table 6.10**).

Usually, the browser and default automatically set the width and height to 100 percent of the available width and whatever height is needed to display all the content. You can use CSS, however, to override both the `width` and `height` properties to your desire. Generally, you will be setting the width of an element more often than the height, unless you know the exact size of the content of the block.

In this example (**Figures 6.12** and **6.13**), the width and height of images on the page have been set using CSS, meaning that *all images* will be displayed using the exact same dimensions, regardless of what their natural dimensions are. In addition, the width of the navigation and form text field, as well as the width and height of the copy area, are set in CSS. However, there is too much content to display in the defined area, so I have used the `overflow` property (see "Setting Where the Overflow Content Goes" in Chapter 8) to allow the viewer to scroll the additional material.

continues on next page

To define the width of an element:

1. width:

   Type the width property name, followed by a colon (:), in the CSS declaration block (**Code 6.9**).

2. 700px;

   Type a value for the element's width, which can be any of the following:

   ▲ A **length value**

   ▲ A **percentage**, which sets the width proportional to the parent element's width

   ▲ auto, which uses the width calculated by the browser for the element— usually the maximum distance that the element can stretch to the right before hitting the edge of the window or the edge of a parent element

Code 6.9 Set the exact or relative width and height of an element to control your design.

```
<!DOCTYPE html PUBLIC "-//W3C//DTD XHTML 1.0
→ Strict//EN" "http://www.w3.org/TR/xhtml1/
→ DTD/xhtml1-strict.dtd">
<html xmlns="http://www.w3.org/1999/xhtml">
<head>
<meta http-equiv="Content-Type"
→ content="text/html; charset=utf-8" />
<title>CSS, DHTML &amp; Ajax | Setting the
→ Width and Height of an Element</title>
        <style type="text/css"
media="screen">
<!--
body {
    font-size: 1em;
    font-family: Georgia, "Times New
    → Roman", times, serif;
    color: #000000;
    background-color: #fff;
    margin: 8px;
    width: 756px;
}

h1, h2 {
    color: #999;
    margin: .5em 0em;
}

h2 {
    clear:both;
}

img {
    width: 100px;
    height: 200px;
    margin: 4px;
    display: inline;
}

form {
    padding: 1em 0em;
    margin: 4px 0px;
    border-bottom: 1px solid #666;
}

input.formText {
    width: 9cm;
    border: 1px solid #f66;
    background-color: #f99;
}
input.formButton {
    padding-right: 16px;
    padding-left: 16px;
```

code continues on next page

Code 6.9 *continued*

```
    border: 1px solid #999;
    background-color: #ccc;
    color: #333;
}

#navigation {
    margin-right: 8px;
    background-color: #ccc;
    float: left;
    font: small Arial, Helvetica, sans-serif;
}

#navigation a {
    padding: 2px 4px;
    border-top: 3px solid #fff;
    text-decoration: none;
    display: block;
    color: red;
}

#navigation a:hover {
    border-top: 3px solid #999;
    color: red;
    background-color: #fff;
}
#copy {
    width: 700px;
    height: 300px;
    overflow: auto;
    border: 3px solid red;
}

#copy p {
    margin: 1em 5em;
}

.author {
    margin-top: 0cm;
    font: bold 1em Arial, Helvetica,
    → sans-serif;
    }

.chapterTitle {
    display: block;
    font-size: smaller;
    color:black;
}

.dropBox {
    width: 236px;
    padding: 6px;
    border: 1px solid #f66;
    margin: 0px 0px 8px 8px;
```

Code 6.9 *continued*

```
    float: right;
    font: small Arial, Helvetica, sans-serif;
}
--></style>
    </head>

    <body>
<div id="navigation">
Flip To Chapter:
<a href="#">Down the Rabbit-Hole </a>
<a href="#">The Pool of Tears </a>
<a href="#">A Caucus-Race and a Long Tale </a>
<a href="#">The Rabbit Sends in a Little
→ Bill </a>
<a href="#">Advice from a Caterpillar </a>
<a href="#">Pig and Pepper </a>
<a href="#">NEXT &rArr; </a>
</div>
<div id="header">
<h1>Alice's Adventures in Wonderland</h1>
<p class="author">Lewis Carroll</p>
<form action="#" method="get" id="FormName">
    Search Book:
    <input class="formText" type="text"
    → name="searchTerm" size="24" />
    <input class="formButton" type="submit"
    → name="findSearchTerm" value="Find" />
</form>
<h2>CHAPTER V
    <span class="chapterTitle">Advice from
    → a Caterpillar</span>
</h2>
</div>
<div id="copy">
<div class="dropBox">
<img src="alice14a.gif" height="236"
→ width="200" alt="Alice" />
<img src="alice15a.gif" height="236"
→ width="200" alt="Alice" />
'One side will make you grow taller, and the
→ other side will make you grow shorter.'
</div>
<p>The Caterpillar and Alice looked at each
→ other for some time in silence: at last
→ the Caterpillar took the hookah out of
→ its mouth, and addressed her in a languid,
→ sleepy voice.</p>
</body>

</html>
```

To define the height of an element:

1. `height:`

Type the `height` property name, followed by a colon (:), in the CSS declaration block.

2. `300px;`

Type a value for the element's height, which can be any of the following:

▲ A **length value**

▲ A **percentage**, which sets the height proportional to the parent element's height

▲ `auto`, which uses a calculated height determined by the browser—however much space the element needs to display all the content.

3. `overflow: auto;`

If you set the height of an element where the content might be larger than the space provided, you will want to specify what happens to the overflow (extra content). For more details, see "Setting Where the Overflow Content Goes" in Chapter 8.

✔ Tips

■ You can resize an image (GIF, PNG, or JPEG) using the `width` and `height` properties, thus overriding the width and height set in the image tag. Doing this will more than likely create a severely distorted image, but that can sometimes be a pretty neat effect.

■ Use `width` and `height` to keep form fields and buttons a consistent size.

■ If you are setting the height of an element and forcing a scroll bar, be careful not to let that element be too close to the browser window's scroll bar, since this generally leads to confusion and an unpleasant experience for viewers.

Table 6.11

Max/Min-Width and Max/Min-Height Values

VALUE	COMPATIBILITY
‹length›	IE7, FF1, S1, O4, CSS2
‹percentage›	IE7, FF1, S1, O5, CSS2
auto	IE7, FF1, S1, O5, CSS2

Figure 6.14 At 1000 pixels wide, there is space for 344 pixels between the edge of the copy area and the right edge of the window.

Figure 6.15 Resizing the window to 800 pixels wide does not affect the copy area.

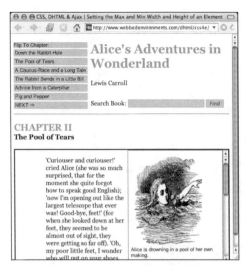

Figure 6.16 Resizing the window to 600 pixels wide compresses the copy area to accommodate, at least up to a point.

Figure 6.17 The copy area will not reduce its width below 500 pixels, as shown when the window's width is reduced to 450 pixels wide.

Setting maximum and minimum width and height

Although not implemented in Internet Explorer 6 or earlier, other modern browsers, including Firefox, Safari, Opera, and now Internet Explorer 7, have all implemented the CSS2 ability to set a minimum and maximum width and height for an element (**Table 6.11**). This can be unbelievably useful for creating flexible designs that will never stretch to unreasonable proportions on larger screens. The `max-height` and `min-height` properties work very much the same, but are dependent on the content being displayed, rather than the dimensions of the browser window.

In this example (**Figures 6.14**, **6.15**, **6.16** and **6.17**), the max/min width and height have been set for the copy layer (see **Code 6.10** on the next page). Although the area will resize its width with browser windows up to 700 pixels wide, it does not change the height for the window dimensions.

continues on next page

To set the maximum and minimum width:

1. `max-width: 756px;`
   `max-height: 300px;`

   Type the `max-width` and/or `max-height` property name, a colon (:), and an appropriate width or height value. The element will never grow wider than this value, regardless of the browser window width.

2. `min-width: 500px;`
   `min-height: 100px;`

   Type the `min-width` and/or `min-height` property name, a colon (:), and an appropriate width or height value. The element will never shrink to less than this value, regardless of the browser window width. However, min-height will not resize with the window.

✔ Tips

- Obviously, you don't have to include *both* the minimum and maximum values.

- If you set the width of the body tag to less than the max-width of an element, the max-width property is ignored, since the body never stretches wide enough.

- Generally, the max-height will act like the height attribute and the min-height is ignored since, unlike the max/min width, the element will not resize with the browser window.

Code 6.10 The `max-width`, `max-height`, `min-width`, and `min-height` properties can be used together to allow a flexible design that does not get out of control.

```
<!DOCTYPE html PUBLIC "-//W3C//DTD XHTML 1.0
→ Strict//EN" "http://www.w3.org/TR/xhtml1/
→ DTD/xhtml1-strict.dtd">
<html xmlns="http://www.w3.org/1999/xhtml">
<head>
<meta http-equiv="Content-Type"
→ content="text/html; charset=utf-8" />
<title>CSS, DHTML &amp; Ajax | Setting the
→ Max and Min Width and Height of an
→ Element</title>
        <style type="text/css"
        → media="screen">
<!--

body {
    font-size: 1em;
    font-family: Georgia, "Times New
    → Roman", times, serif;
    color: #000000;
        background-color: #fff;

    margin: 8px;
}

h1, h2 {
    color: #999;
}

h2 {
    clear: both;
}

img {
    display: block;
}

form {
    max-width: 756px;
    padding: 1em 0em;
    margin: 4px 0px;
    border-bottom: 1px solid #666;
}

input.formText {
    border: 1px solid #999;
    background-color: #ccc;
}

input.formButton {
    border: 1px solid #999;
    background-color: #ccc;
    color: #333;
}
```

code continues on next page

Code 6.10 *continued*

```css
#navigation {
    margin-right: 8px;
    background-color: #ccc;
    float: left;
    font: small Arial, Helvetica, sans-serif;
}

#navigation a {
    padding: 2px 4px;
    border-top: 3px solid #fff;
    text-decoration: none;
    display: block;
    color: red;
}

#navigation a:hover {
    border-top: 3px solid #999;
    color: red;
    background-color: #fff;
}

#navigation a {
    padding: 2px 4px;
    border-top: 3px solid #fff;
    text-decoration: none;
    display: block;
    color: red;
}

#copy {
    max-width: 756px;
    max-height: 300px;
    min-width: 500px;
    min-height: 100px;
    overflow: auto;
    border: 3px solid red;
}

#copy p {
    margin: 1em 5em;
}

.chapterTitle {
    display: block;
    font-size: smaller;
    color:black;
}

.dropBox {
    width: 236px;
    padding: 6px;
    border: 1px solid #f66;
    margin: 0px 0px 8px 8px;
```

Code 6.10 *continued*

```css
    float: right;
    font: small Arial, Helvetica, sans-serif;
}

--></style>
    </head>

    <body>
```
```html
<div id="navigation">
Flip To Chapter:
<a href="#">Down the Rabbit-Hole </a>
<a href="#">The Pool of Tears </a>
<a href="#">A Caucus-Race and a Long Tale </a>
<a href="#">The Rabbit Sends in a Little
→ Bill </a>
<a href="#">Advice from a Caterpillar </a>
<a href="#">Pig and Pepper </a>
<a href="#">NEXT &rArr; </a>
</div>
<div id="header">
<h1>Alice's Adventures in Wonderland</h1>
<p class="author">Lewis Carroll</p>
<form action="#" method="get" id="FormName">
    Search Book:
    <input class="formText" type="text"
    → name="searchTerm" size="24" />
    <input class="formButton" type="submit"
    → name="findSearchTerm" value="Find" />
</form>
<h2>CHAPTER II
    <span class="chapterTitle">The Pool of
    → Tears</span>
</h2>
</div>

<div id="copy">

<div class="dropBox">
<img src="alice07a.gif" height="236"
→ width="200" alt="Alice" />
Alice is drowning in a pool of her own
→ making.
</div>

<p>'Curiouser and curiouser!' cried Alice
→ (she was so much surprised, that for the
→ moment she quite forgot how to speak good
→ English); 'now I'm opening out like the
→ largest telescope that ever was! Good-
→ bye, feet!'…</p></div>
</body>
</html>
```

VISUAL FORMATTING PROPERTIES

7

One of the obstacles Web designers commonly face is getting a page to look the way they want it to without it taking forever to load. While it's true that graphics give you the flexibility to add text and layout exactly where you want them in your design, and tables enable you to position elements in the browser window or assemble graphics in jigsaw fashion, both graphics and tables take more time to render than straight HTML content. These elements can substantially slow the speed at which your page loads.

Using CSS to create Web layouts provides more accuracy than either graphics or tables, and the results are displayed much faster.

You've already learned how to use CSS to control margins and borders in your composition (Chapter 6). With CSS, you can also position elements in the window, either exactly (absolutely) or in relation to other elements (relatively). In addition, CSS also lets you "float" elements next to each other horizontally in the window, so that you can create columns and other robust layout formats.

This chapter introduces you to the different methods you can use to position HTML elements using CSS, including how to stack elements on top of one another and float elements next to each other.

Understanding the Window and Document

A Web page (also referred to as simply the *document*) is displayed within a browser window. Within the rectangular confines of the *viewport*, everything that you can present to the viewer is displayed. You can open multiple windows (each displaying its own documents in its own viewport), resize and position windows on the screen, and even break the window into smaller viewports called *frames*. Everything that you present, however, is displayed within a browser window as part of a document (**Figure 7.1**).

Figure 7.1 The browser window. The element on the gray background has been moved from its normal position to 125 pixels from the top and 12em from the left.

Like the elements contained within it (see "Understanding an Element's Box" in Chapter 6), the window has a width and height, as well as a top, bottom, left, and right. In fact, you can think of the browser window as being the ultimate element in your Web design—the parent of all other elements. Browser windows and the documents they contain have three distinct widths and heights and four different sides:

◆ **Browser width and height** refers to the dimensions of the entire window, including any browser controls and other interface items.

◆ **Viewport width and height** refers to the live *display area* of the browser window's viewport. The live dimensions, obviously, are always less than the full window dimensions. Generally, when I refer to "the window," I'm referring to the live window area.

- **Document width and height**, sometimes called the *rendered* width and height, refers to the overall dimensions of the entire Web page. If the document's width and/or height is larger than the live width and/or height, you'll see scrollbars that let you view the rest of the document.

- **Document origin** is the top left corner of the document. All absolutely positioned elements that have the body as their direct parent are positioned in relationship to this point.

- **Element positions (left, top, right, bottom)** are used to set exactly how an element is offset from the sides of the document, its parent element, or from its normal flow position.

- **Element origin** is the top-left corner of any element on the screen. The left- and top-element positions move the element from this corner. Bottom and right positions move the element from the bottom-right corner.

✔ Tips

- You'll learn how to use JavaScript to find all of these different dimensions in Chapter 13.

- *Normal flow* refers to where an element would appear in the Web page if no positioning is applied to it.

Setting the Positioning Type

When you set the style attributes of an HTML tag through CSS, you effectively single out any content within that tag's container as being a unique element in the window (see "Understanding an Element's Box" in Chapter 6). You can then manipulate this unique element through CSS positioning.

An element can have one of four position values—static, relative, absolute, or fixed (**Table 7.1**). The position type tells the browser how to treat the element when placing it in the document (**Figures 7.2 and 7.3** and **Code 7.1**).

Using static positioning

By default, elements are positioned as static in the document, unless you define them as being positioned absolutely, relatively, or fixed. Static elements, like the relatively positioned elements explained in the following section, flow into a document one after the next. Static positioning differs, however, in that a static element cannot be explicitly positioned or repositioned.

In the example shown in Figures 7.2 and 7.3, Object 1 is not positioned, so it simply appears in the top-left corner of the document since it is the first element in the normal flow of the HTML code. Notice that the static element is *not* at the very top-left corner of the document: It's offset by about 5 pixels top and left. This is because most browsers will add a margin to the body automatically.

Table 7.1

Position Values	
VALUE	COMPATIBILITY
static	IE4, FF1, S1, O4, CSS2
relative	IE4, FF1, S1, O4, CSS2
absolute	IE4, FF1, S1, O4, CSS2
fixed	IE5*, FF1, S1, O4, CSS2
inherit	IE5*, FF1, S1, O5, CSS2

*IE7 for Windows. Extremely buggy on the Mac.

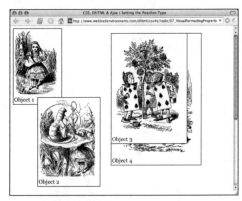

Figure 7.2 Elements being positioned in the window. Notice that both the absolute-positioned (Object 3) and fixed-positioned (Object 4) objects have the same top-left corner because they both have the same top and left values set.

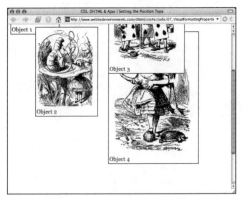

Figure 7.3 When the document is scrolled, all of the elements scroll with it, except for Object 4, which has a fixed position.

Code 7.1 The default position is static, but using relative, absolute or fixed, you can control the position of elements in the window.

```
<!DOCTYPE html PUBLIC "-//W3C//DTD XHTML 1.0
→ Strict//EN" "http://www.w3.org/TR/xhtml1/
→ DTD/xhtml1-strict.dtd">
<html xmlns="http://www.w3.org/1999/xhtml">
<head>
<meta http-equiv="Content-Type"
→ content="text/html; charset=utf-8" />
<title>CSS, DHTML &amp; Ajax | Setting the
→ Position Type</title>
        <style type="text/css"
        → media="screen">

body {
    font-size: 1.2em;
    font-family: Georgia, "Times New
    → Roman", times, serif;
    color: #000000;
    background-color: #fff;
    margin: 8px;
}

img {
    margin-bottom: 4px;
display: block;
}

.dropBox {
padding: 4px;
    background-color: #FFFFFF;
    border: 2px solid #f00;
}

#object1 {
    position: static;
    width: 158px;
}

#object2 {
    position: relative;
    top: -25px;
    left: 85px;
    width: 208px;
    z-index: 3;
}
```

Code 7.1 *continued*

```
#object3 {
    position: absolute;
    top: 25px;
    left: 350px;
    width: 258px;
    z-index: 2;
}

#object4 {
    position: fixed;
    top: 25px;
    left: 350px;
    width: 308px;
    z-index: 1;
}

</style>
    </head>

<body>

<div class="dropBox" id="object1">
<img src="alice22a.gif" height="220"
→ width="150" alt="Alice in Wonderland" />
Object 1</div>

<div class="dropBox" id="object2">
<img src="alice15a.gif" height="264"
→ width="200" alt="Alice in Wonderland" />
Object 2</div>

<div class="dropBox" id="object3">
<img src="alice28a.gif" height="336"
→ width="250" alt="Alice in Wonderland" />
Object 3</div>

<div class="dropBox" id="object4">
<img src="alice30a.gif" height="408"
→ width="300" alt="Alice in Wonderland" />
Object 4</div>

</body>
</html>
```

Using relative positioning

An element that is defined as being relatively positioned will be offset based on its position in the normal flow of the document. This technique is useful for controlling the way elements appear in relation to other elements in the window.

In the example shown in Figures 7.2 and 7.3, Object 2 would have appeared directly beneath Object 1 in the normal flow. However, Object 2 has been positioned relative to its position in the normal flow: It has been moved 85 pixels to the right and 25 pixels up, so that it overlaps Object 1.

Using absolute positioning

Absolute positioning takes an element out of the normal flow—separating it from the rest of the document. Elements that are defined in this way are placed at an exact point in the window by means of x and y coordinates. The top-left corner of the document or the element's parent is the origin (that is, coordinates `0,0`). Moving an element to a position farther to the right uses a positive x value; moving it farther down uses a positive y value.

Absolutely positioned elements take up no space within the parent element. So if you have an element like an image that is being absolutely positioned, it's width and height are *not* included as part of the width and height of the parent. Only static and relatively positioned content are included.

In the example shown in Figures 7.2 and 7.3, Object 3 is positioned 350 pixels from the left edge of the document (ignoring the document margin) and moved 258 pixels up and out of the document window.

Using fixed positioning

Fixing an element's position in the window works almost exactly like absolute positioning: The element's position is set to a specific point in the viewport, independent of all other content on the page. The big difference is that when the document scrolls in the viewport, fixed elements stay in their initial positions and do not scroll.

However, fixed positioning has not been widely used (or at least relied upon) because it is not implemented in Microsoft Internet Explorer 6 and earlier. The good news is that Internet Explorer 7 supports fixed positioning, which will be a boon for user interface design, allowing important elements such as navigation to stay in the same location on the screen without resorting to frames.

In the example shown in Figures 7.2 and 7.3, you cannot see all of Object 4 in the first figure because it occupies the exact same position as Object 3. However, as soon as the page is scrolled, the fixed element can be seen as the absolute element moves up and out of the viewport.

To set an element's position type:

1. `position:`

   Type the `position` property in a rule's declaration block or in the `style` attribute of an HTML tag, followed by a colon (Code 7.1).

2. `relative;`

   Type the position-type value, which can be one of the following:

   ▲ `static` flows the content normally; however, the position *cannot* be changed using the values set by the `top`, `left`, `right`, and `bottom` properties or by JavaScript. This is the default value.

continues on next page

▲ relative also flows the element normally, but allows the position to be set, relative to its normal position, using the values set on the top, left, right, and bottom properties.

▲ absolute places the element according to values set by the top, left, right, and bottom properties, independently of any other content in its parent. This will be the body of the document or the element within which it is nested.

▲ fixed places the element according to the values set by the top, left, right, and bottom properties, independently of any other content in its parent, just as with an absolutely positioned element. However, unlike an absolutely positioned element, when the window is scrolled, the fixed element stays where it is as the rest of the content scrolls.

▲ inherit uses the position type of the element's immediate parent. If no position is set, this will default to static (see the sidebar "Inheriting Position Types").

3. top: 70px;

Now that the position type has been set, as long as you didn't use static you can adjust or set the actual position of the element (see "Setting an Element's Position" later in this chapter). If you do not explicitly set a position, the element will default to auto, which is generally going to be its natural flow position.

Inheriting Position Types

inherit is another value for positioning. It simply tells the element to use the same positioning type as its parent, overriding the default static value. This can be tricky to use, though, since tying the child's position type to its parent can radically alter the layout if you change the parent's position type.

Is It Fixed? Not in IE on the Mac!

Although Internet Explorer 5 for the Mac supports fixed, a strange bug causes the link areas of a fixed element to scroll with the rest of the page. So while the graphic or text for a link stays in a fixed position, the invisible area that gets clicked moves.

However, since Internet Explorer for the Mac is rarely used, you probably should not let this stop you from using fixed positioning.

In addition to setting the position of an element, you may want to set the following for an element:

- ▲ **Stacking order**, discussed in "Stacking Objects (3D Positioning)" later in this chapter
- ▲ **Visibility**, discussed in "Setting the Visibility of an Element" in Chapter 8
- ▲ **Clipping**, discussed in "Setting the Visible Area of an Element (Clipping)" in Chapter 8

✔ Tips

- You can position elements within other positioned elements. For example, you can set the relative position of a child element that is within an absolutely positioned parent or set the absolute position of an element within an absolutely positioned parent.

- Remember that the browser adds a margin to the body of your Web page by default, but this is not a consistent value across all browsers. To correct this, you should always set your own margin in the body tag, which allows you to position elements consistently.

- Just a reminder: fixed does not work in Internet Explorer before version 7. Instead, the element will be treated as static, unless you use conditional CSS presented in Chapter 2 to provide additional CSS code tailored to that browser.

- Internet Explorer does not obey positioning on the <body> tag. If you need to position the entire body of a Web page, surround all the content with a <div> tag and apply positioning to that.

- After an element's position type has been set to anything other than static, you can use JavaScript or other scripting languages to move, change the clip, change the stacking order, hide, or display it (see Part 2 of this book, which discusses DHTML).

- The fixed position in Internet Explorer 5 for the Mac has a severe bug that makes it useless for creating fixed menus in the window (see the sidebar "Is It Fixed? Not in IE on the Mac!").

- Browsers that do not understand the fixed position type default to static for the position type.

Setting an Element's Position

In addition to the margins, which can be specified as part of the box properties (see "Setting an Element's Margins" in Chapter 6), a positioned element can have a top value, a left value, a bottom value, and a right value used to position the element from those four sides (**Table 7.2**).

Setting the position from the top and left

The top and left values are used to set the element's position from the top and left edges of its parent element for absolute and fixed positions or relative to its natural flow position for relative positioning (**Figures 7.4** and **7.5**).

To define the left and top positions:

1. position: absolute;

   To position an element using the left and top properties, you have to include the position property in the same rule or style attribute (**Code 7.2**).

2. left:

   Type the left property name, followed by a colon (:), in the CSS declaration block or in the style attribute of an HTML tag.

Table 7.2

Top and Left Values	
VALUE	COMPATIBILITY
‹length›	IE4, FF1, S1, O4, CSS2
‹percentage›	IE4, FF1, S1, O5, CSS2
auto	IE4, FF1, S1, O5, CSS2

Figure 7.4 The example without positioning.

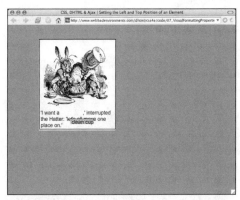

Figure 7.5 The object has been absolutely positioned from the top-left corner of the window and the words "clean cup" have been offset from the top and left of their normal position.

Code 7.2 After you set the position type (relative, absolute, or fixed), you can set the element's top and left distance from its origin (top/left corner).

```
<!DOCTYPE html PUBLIC "-//W3C//DTD XHTML 1.0
→ Strict//EN" "http://www.w3.org/TR/
→ xhtml1/DTD/xhtml1-strict.dtd">
<html xmlns="http://www.w3.org/1999/xhtml">
<head>
<meta http-equiv="Content-Type"
→ content="text/html; charset=utf-8" />
<title>CSS, DHTML &amp; Ajax | Setting the
→ Left and Top Position of an Element</title>
        <style type="text/css"
        → media="screen">
body {
    font-size: 1em;
    font-family: Georgia, "Times New
    → Roman", times, serif;
    color: #000000;
    background-color: #999;
    margin: 8px; }
img {
    margin-bottom: 4px;
    display: block; }
#object1 {
    position: absolute;
    top: 50px;
    left: 6em; }
.dropBox {
    padding: 4px;
    background-color: #fff;
    border: 2px solid #f00;
    width: 258px;
    font: large Arial, Helvetica,
    → sans-serif; }
.changeplace {
    position: relative;
    top: .81cm;
    left: 1cm;
    background-color: #ffcccc; }
</style>
</head>
<body>
<div id="object1" class="dropBox">
<img src="alice27.gif" height="225"
→ width="250" alt="Alice in Wonderland" />
'I want a<span class="changeplace"> clean
→ cup</span>,' interrupted the Hatter:
→ 'let's all move one place on.'
</div>
</body></html>
```

3. 12em;

Now type a value for how far from the left the element should appear. You can enter any of the following:

▲ A **length value** to define the distance of the element's left edge from the left edge of its parent or the window

▲ A **percentage value**, such as 55%, to set the left displacement relative to the parent element's width

▲ auto, which allows the browser to calculate the value if the position is set to absolute; otherwise, left will be 0

4. top:

Type the top property name, followed by a colon (:), in the CSS declaration block or in the style attribute of a tag.

continues on next page

5. 125px;

Type a value for how far from the top the element should appear. You can enter any of the following:

▲ A **length value** to define the distance of the element's top edge from the top edge of its parent or the window

▲ A **percentage value**, such as 55%, to set the top displacement relative to the window or parent element's height

▲ auto, which allows the browser to calculate the value if the position is set to absolute; otherwise, top will be 0

✔ Tips

■ You don't have to include both the top and left declarations, but if not included, they are treated as auto.

■ You can use negative values to move the content up and to the left instead of down and to the right.

■ Margins applied to a relatively positioned element are rendered in the natural flow of the document (i.e., they don't move with the positioned element). This means that setting the top and left margins may cause the positioned content to move outside its naturally defined box and overlap other content.

■ Child elements that are not absolutely positioned always move with their parent element.

Setting the position from the bottom and right

Although you can accomplish a lot by adjusting position from an element's top and left sides, it can be useful to position from the bottom and right sides as well (**Table 7.3**).

CSS Level 2 introduced the ability to set an element's position relative to the right and bottom edges of an element's parent (**Figure 7.6**).

Table 7.3

Bottom and Right Values	
VALUE	COMPATIBILITY
‹length›	IE5, FF1, S1, O4, CSS2
‹percentage›	IE5, FF1, S1, O4, CSS2
auto	IE5, FF1, S1.3, O4, CSS2

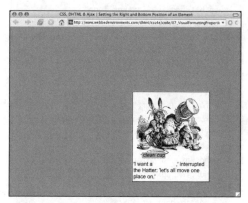

Figure 7.6 The element has been absolutely positioned from the bottom-right corner of the window, and the words "clean cup" have been offset from the bottom and right of their normal position.

Code 7.3 After you set the position type, you can set the element's right and bottom. The positions shift to the right and bottom edges of the element, however, so instead of the top-left corner, the origin will be the bottom-right corner of the window, the parent, or the element itself.

```
<!DOCTYPE html PUBLIC "-//W3C//DTD XHTML 1.0
→ Strict//EN" "http://www.w3.org/TR/xhtml1/
→ DTD/xhtml1-strict.dtd">
<html xmlns="http://www.w3.org/1999/xhtml">
<head>
<meta http-equiv="Content-Type"
→ content="text/html; charset=utf-8" />
<title>CSS, DHTML &amp; Ajax | Setting the
→ Right and Bottom Position of an
Element</title>
        <style type="text/css" media="screen">
body {
    font-size: 1em;
    font-family: Georgia, "Times New
    → Roman", times, serif;
    color: #000000;
    background-color: #999;
    margin: 8px; }
img {
    margin-bottom: 4px;
    display: block; }
.dropBox {
    padding: 4px;
    background-color: #fff;
    border: 2px solid #f00;
    width: 258px;
    font: large Arial, Helvetica, sans-serif; }
#object1 {
    position: absolute;
    bottom: 50px;
    right: 6em; }
.changeplace {
    position: relative;
    bottom: .81cm;
    right: 1cm;
    background-color: #ffcccc; }
</style>
</head>
<body>
<div id="object1" class="dropBox">
<img src="alice27.gif" height="225"
→ width="250" alt="Alice in Wonderland" />
'I want a<span class="changeplace"> clean
→ cup</span>,' interrupted the Hatter:
→ 'let's all move one place on.'
</div>
</body></html>
```

To define the right and bottom positions:

1. position: absolute;

   To position an element by using the right and bottom properties, you have to include the position property in the same rule (**Code 7.3**).

2. right:

   Type the right property name, followed by a colon (:).

3. 12em;

   Type a value to indicate how far from the right edge of the document the right edge of the element should appear. You can enter any of the following:

   ▲ A **length value** to define the distance of the element's right edge from the right edge of its parent or the window

   ▲ A **percentage value**, such as 55%, to set the right displacement relative to the parent element's width

   ▲ auto, which allows the browser to calculate the value if the position is set to absolute; otherwise, right will be 0

4. bottom:

   Type the bottom property name, followed by a colon (:).

   continues on next page

5. 125px;

Type in a value to specify how far from the bottom the bottom edge of the element should appear. You can enter any of the following (Table 7.3):

▲ A **length value** to define the distance of the element's bottom edge from the bottom edge of its parent or the window

▲ A **percentage value**, such as 55%, to set the bottom displacement relative to the window or parent element's height

▲ auto, which allows the browser to calculate the value if the position is set to absolute; otherwise, bottom will be 0

✔ Tips

■ You do not have to use both left and right positioning with the same element.

■ What happens if you set the top/left and bottom/right positions for the same element? The answer depends on the browser. Internet Explorer always defaults to the top and left positions. But most others will stretch elements that do not have a definitive width or height to accommodate the values that have been set.

■ What happens if the bottom position has been set, and the element is longer than the height of the page? Normally, the element would go off the bottom of the window, and you could access the rest of the content by using the scroll bar. If the bottom position of the element has been set, however, the element will be pushed up off the top of the window, and you cannot use the scroll bars to access it. So be careful when setting a bottom position for an element.

Table 7.4

Z-Index Values	
VALUE	COMPATIBILITY
<number>	IE4, FF1, S1, O3.5, CSS2
auto	IE4, FF1, S1, O3.5, CSS2

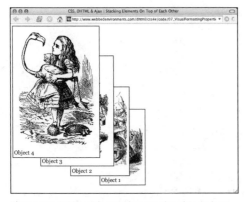

Figure 7.7 Without the z-index set, the objects keep the natural stacking order. Notice that Object 1 is now underneath everything else, because its natural z-index is 0.

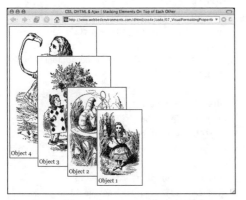

Figure 7.8 With the z-index set in the code, the stacking order is changed. Notice that although Object 1 should be on the bottom of the stack, its z-index has been set to 3, so it appears on top.

Stacking Objects (3D Positioning)

Although the screen is a two-dimensional area, elements that are positioned can be given a third dimension: a stacking order in relationship to one another.

Positioned elements are assigned stacking numbers automatically, starting with 0 and continuing incrementally with 1, 2, 3, and so on, in the order in which the elements appear in the HTML and relative to their parents and siblings. Elements with higher numbers appear above those with lower numbers. This system is called the *z-index* (**Table 7.4**). An element's z-index number is a value that shows its 3D relationship to other elements in the document or parent element.

If the content of elements overlap each other, the element with a higher number in the stacking order appears over the element that has a lower number.

You can override the natural order of the z-index (**Figures 7.7** and **7.8**) by setting a value for the z-index property.

continues on next page

STACKING OBJECTS (3D POSITIONING)

To define an element's z-index:

1. `position: absolute;`

To layer an element in the window, you have to define the `position` property (**Code 7.4**).

(See "Setting the Positioning Type" earlier in this chapter for more information.)

Code 7.4 In the code, positioned elements appear stacked on top of each other based on their order in the HTML code. Using the z-index property, you can override that natural stacking order to put whatever you want on top.

```
<!DOCTYPE html PUBLIC "-//W3C//DTD XHTML 1.0
→ Strict//EN" "http://www.w3.org/TR/xhtml1/
→ DTD/xhtml1-strict.dtd">
<html xmlns="http://www.w3.org/1999/xhtml">
<head>
<meta http-equiv="Content-Type"
→ content="text/html; charset=utf-8" />
<title>CSS, DHTML &amp; Ajax | Stacking
→ Elements On Top of Each Other</title>
        <style type="text/css"
        → media="screen">
body {
    font-size: 1.2em;
    font-family: Georgia, "Times New
    → Roman", times, serif;
    color: #000000;
    background-color: #fff;
    margin: 8px;
}

img {
    margin-bottom: 4px;
    display: block;
}

.dropBox {
    padding: 4px;
    background-color: #FFFFFF;
    border: 2px solid #f00;
}
#object1 {
    position: absolute;
    z-index: 3;
    top: 285px;
    left: 315px;
}
```

Code 7.4 *continued*

```
#object2 {
    position: absolute;
    z-index: 2;
    top: 210px;
    left: 210px;
}
#object3 {
    position: absolute;
    z-index: 1;
    top: 105px;
    left: 105px
}

#object4 {
    position: absolute;
    z-index: 0;
    top: 5px;
    left: 5px;
}

</style>
</head>
<body>

<div class="dropBox" id="object1">
<img src="alice22a.gif" height="220"
→ width="150" alt="Alice in Wonderland" />
Object 1</div>

<div class="dropBox" id="object2">
<img src="alice15a.gif" height="264"
→ width="200" alt="Alice in Wonderland" />
Object 2</div>

<div class="dropBox" id="object3">
<img src="alice28a.gif" height="336"
→ width="250" alt="Alice in Wonderland" />
Object 3</div>

<div class="dropBox" id="object4">
<img src="alice30a.gif" height="408"
→ width="300" alt="Alice in Wonderland" />
Object 4</div>

</body>
</html>
```

2. z-index:

Type the z-index property name, followed by a colon (:), in the same declaration block.

3. 3;

Now type a positive or negative number (no decimals allowed), or 0. This step sets the element's z-index in relation to its siblings, where 0 is on the same level.

Alternatively, type auto to allow the browser to determine the element's z-index order.

✔ Tips

■ Using a negative number for the z-index causes an element to be stacked that many levels below its parent instead of above.

■ You can change the stacking order of elements using JavaScript (see "Moving Objects in 3D" in Chapter 16).

Floating Elements in the Window

In addition to being able to exactly position elements within the document, CSS also allows you to set how an element interacts with other elements by *floating* it.

With HTML you can make text flow around a graphic using the `align` property. CSS takes this technique one step further by letting you flow text not only around graphics, but around any element. You accomplish this feat using the `float` property (**Table 7.5**).

In this example (**Figures 7.9** and **7.10**), the menu floats to the left so that the header flows around it on the right, while the drop-box floats to the right, with text floating around it to the left.

Table 7.5

Float Values	
VALUE	**COMPATIBILITY**
left	IE4, FF1, S1, O3.5, CSS1
right	IE4, FF1, S1, O3.5, CSS1
none	IE4, FF1, S1, O3.5, CSS1

Figure 7.9 Without floating, the menu stretches across the top of the page, and the drop box has text above and below it, but not beside.

Figure 7.10 The text in the page now wraps to the right of the menu and to the left of the drop-box. Notice, though that even the chapter title and copy text is floating for the first few lines around the menu. Check out the next section to learn how to clear that up.

Code 7.5 The float property allows either a block of text and/or a graphic to have the following elements wrap horizontally around it.

```
<!DOCTYPE html PUBLIC "-//W3C//DTD XHTML 1.0
→ Strict//EN" "http://www.w3.org/TR/xhtml1/
→ DTD/xhtml1-strict.dtd">
<html xmlns="http://www.w3.org/1999/xhtml">
<head>
<meta http-equiv="Content-Type"
→ content="text/html; charset=utf-8" />
<title>CSS, DHTML &amp; Ajax | Floating
→ Elements in the Window</title>
        <style type="text/css" media="screen">
h1, h2 {
    color: #999;
}
img {
    margin: 4px;
    display: block;
}
#navigation {
    float: left;
    margin: 0px 8px 16px 0px;
    background-color: #ccc;
    font: small Arial, Helvetica, sans-serif;
}
#navigation a {
    padding: 2px 4px;
    border-top: 3px solid #fff;
    text-decoration: none;
    display: block;
    color: red;
}
#navigation a:hover {
    border-top: 3px solid #999;
    color: red;
    background-color: #fff;
}
#copy {
    width: 700px;
    height: 300px;
    overflow: auto;
    border: 3px solid red;
}
.author {
    margin-top: 0cm;
    font: bold 1em Arial, Helvetica,
    → sans-serif;
}
```

code continues on next page

To float an element:

1. `float:`

   Start your definition by typing the `float` property name, followed by a colon (:).

   In this example (**Code 7.5**), I applied `float` to an image, which has the same effect as setting the `align` property in the <img> tag.

2. `right;`

   Next, type a keyword to tell the browser on which side of the screen the element should float. Choose one of the following:

   ▲ `right` aligns this element to the right, of other elements causing subsequent elements to wrap horizontally on the left of this element.

   ▲ `left` aligns this element to the left of other elements, causing subsequent elements to wrap horizontally on the right of this element.

   ▲ `none` overrides floating for this element.

continues on next page

FLOATING ELEMENTS IN THE WINDOW

✔ Tips

- Floating elements within other elements can often have odd consequences if both the child and parent are block elements. The child tends to ignore the height of the parent, which can have undesirable consequences (sounds like a child). The upshot is that the child element will appear to begin in the parent element, but then overlap the parent's border.

- You can use float with any tag, not just images, to cause text to float around it, so you can have text floating inside other text.

- In Chapter 21, I'll explain how to use the float property to set up separate columns to replace traditional table-based layout.

Code 7.5 *continued*

```
.chapterTitle {
    display: block;
    font-size: smaller;
    color:black;
}
.dropBox {
    float: right;
    width: 296px;
    padding: 6px;
    border: 1px solid #f66;
    margin: 0px 0px 8px 8px;
    font: small Arial, Helvetica, sans-serif;
}
</style>
</head>
<body>
<div id="navigation">
Flip To Chapter:
<a href="#">Down the Rabbit-Hole </a>
<a href="#">The Pool of Tears </a>
<a href="#">A Caucus-Race and a Long Tale </a>
<a href="#">The Rabbit Sends in a Little
→ Bill </a>
<a href="#">Advice from a Caterpillar </a>
<a href="#">Pig and Pepper </a>
<a href="#">NEXT &rArr; </a>
</div>
<div id="header">
<h1>Alice's Adventures in Wonderland</h1>
<p class="author">Lewis Carroll</p>
<h2>CHAPTER VII
    <span class="chapterTitle"> A Mad
    → Tea-Party</span>
</h2>
</div>
        <p>There was a table set out under a
        → tree in front of the house, and
        → the March Hare and the Hatter
        → were having tea at it...'</p>
<div class="dropBox">
        <img src="alice25.gif" height="219"
        → width="288" alt="Alice in
        → Wonderland" />
        A mad tea-party indeed!
</div>
        <p>The table was a large one, but
        → the three were all crowded together
        → at one corner of it...</p>
</body>
</html>
```

Table 7.6

Clear Values	
VALUE	COMPATIBILITY
left	IE4, FF1, S1, O3.5, CSS1
right	IE4, FF1, S1, O3.5, CSS1
both	IE4, FF1, S1, O3.5, CSS1
none	IE4, FF1, S1, O3.5, CSS1

Figure 7.11 The chapter title has been cleared to the left, so that it now sits underneath the menu (see Figure 7.10). In addition, the paragraph that begins "Have some wine…" is forced underneath the drop-box.

Clearing a Floated Element

Sometimes, you may find it necessary to override the float property to prevent elements that appear after a floating element from wrapping. Similar to the clear attribute of the HTML break tag, the CSS clear property allows you to specify whether you want to deny floating around the left, right, or both sides of the element (**Table 7.6**).

In this example (**Figure 7.11**), floating is set for the menu and the drop-box, but the level 2 heading uses clear to force itself below the menu. In addition, a class has been set up called .noFloat that will clear floating from any direction.

continues on next page

To stop text from floating:

1. `clear:`

Type the `clear` property name, followed by a colon (:), in the CSS rule to start your declaration (**Code 7.6**).

2. `right;`

Type the keyword for the side where you want to prevent floating. Choose one of the following:

▲ `left` to prevent wrapping on the left side of the element

▲ `right` to prevent wrapping on the right side of the element

▲ `both` to prevent wrapping on both sides of the element

▲ `none` to override a previously set `clear` property

3. `<p class="nofloat">…</p>`

One common usage of clear is to set up a CSS rule called something like `nofloat`, which can then be applied to any html tag.

✔ Tip

■ It's usually a good idea to set headers and titles to `clear:both`, so that they don't wrap around other objects.

Code 7.6 The `clear` property is used to stop the `float` property assigned to previous elements in the Web page. Here we not only apply it to the <h2> tag, but also set up a special .noFloat class that can be used anywhere.

```html
<!DOCTYPE html PUBLIC "-//W3C//DTD XHTML 1.0
→ Strict//EN" "http://www.w3.org/TR/xhtml1/
→ DTD/xhtml1-strict.dtd">
<html xmlns="http://www.w3.org/1999/xhtml">
<head>
<meta http-equiv="Content-Type"
→ content="text/html; charset=utf-8" />
<title>CSS, DHTML &amp; Ajax | Clearing
→ Floating</title>
<style type="text/css" media="screen">
h1, h2 {
    color: #999;
}

h2 {
    clear: left;
}

img {
    margin: 4px;
    display: block;
}

#navigation {
    float: left;
    margin: 0px 8px 16px 0px;
    background-color: #ccc;
    font: small Arial, Helvetica,
    → sans-serif;
}

#navigation a {
    padding: 2px 4px;
    border-top: 3px solid #fff;
    text-decoration: none;
    display: block;
    color: red;
}

#navigation a:hover {
    border-top: 3px solid #999;
    color: red;
    background-color: #fff;
}
```

code continues on next page

CLEARING A FLOATED ELEMENT

Code 7.6 *continued*

```
#copy {
    width: 700px;
    height: 300px;
    overflow: auto;
    border: 3px solid red;
}


.author {
    margin-top: 0cm;
    font: bold 1em Arial, Helvetica,
    → sans-serif;
}


.chapterTitle {
    display: block;
    font-size: smaller;
    color:black;
}


.dropBox {
    float: right;
    width: 296px;
    padding: 6px;
    border: 1px solid #f66;
    margin: 0px 0px 8px 8px;
    font: small Arial, Helvetica,
    → sans-serif;
}


.noFloat {
    clear: both;
}

</style>
</head>

<body>

<div id="navigation">
Flip To Chapter:
<a href="#">Down the Rabbit-Hole </a>
<a href="#">The Pool of Tears </a>
<a href="#">A Caucus-Race and a Long Tale </a>
<a href="#">The Rabbit Sends in a Little
→ Bill </a>
<a href="#">Advice from a Caterpillar </a>
<a href="#">Pig and Pepper </a>
<a href="#">NEXT &rArr; </a>
</div>
```

Code 7.6 *continued*

```
<div id="header">
<h1>Alice's Adventures in Wonderland</h1>
<p class="author">Lewis Carroll</p>
<h2>CHAPTER VII
    <span class="chapterTitle"> A Mad
    → Tea-Party</span>
</h2>
</div>
    <p>There was a table set out under a
    → tree in front of the house, and the
    → March Hare and the Hatter were having
    → tea at it…</p>
<div class="dropBox">
<img src="alice25.gif" height="219"
→ width="288" alt="Alice in Wonderland" />
A mad tea-party indeed!
</div>
    <p>The table was a large one, but the
    → three were all crowded together at
    → one corner of it: 'No room! No room!'
    → they cried out when they saw Alice
    → coming. 'There's <i>plenty</i> of
    → room!' said Alice indignantly, and
    → she sat down in a large arm-chair at
    → one end of the table.</p>
        <p class="noFloat">'Have some wine,'
        → the March Hare said in an
        → encouraging tone.</p>
</body>
</html>
```

VISUAL EFFECT AND USER INTERFACE PROPERTIES

Although the ability to show and hide elements or parts of elements is one of the cornerstones of dynamic HTML (DHTML), the ability to set the visibility of these elements is a feature of CSS.

Keep in mind, however, that until you learn to use JavaScript to change the visibility of an element (see Chapter 16), the visibility controls will not be of much use.

Setting the Visibility of an Element

The visibility property designates whether an element is visible when it is initially viewed in the window. If visibility is set to hidden (**Table 8.1**), the element is invisible but still takes up space in the document, and a big empty rectangle appears where the element should be.

In this example (**Figures 8.1** and **8.2**), the menu and the drop box have been hidden. But notice that unlike the example of display: none in Chapter 6 (Figure 6.6), the space does not collapse, and the elements leave empty space where they should be.

To set an element's visibility:

1. visibility:

Type the visibility property name, followed by a colon (:), in the element's CSS declaration block (**Code 8.1**).

2. hidden;

Now type one of the following keywords to specify how you want this element to be treated:

▲ hidden, which causes the element to be invisible when the document is initially rendered on the screen

▲ visible, which causes the element to be visible

▲ inherit, which causes the element to inherit the visibility of its parent element

✔ Tips

■ Though the properties seem similar, visibility differs radically from display (Chapter 6). When display is set to none, the element is scrubbed from the document, and no space is reserved for it, unlike visibility, which leaves the space

Table 8.1

Visibility Values	
VALUE	COMPATIBILITY
hidden	IE4, FF1, S1, O4, CSS2
visible	IE4, FF1, S1, O4, CSS2
inherit	FF1, S1, O3.5, CSS2

Figure 8.1 In this version, the menu and the drop box are visible.

Figure 8.2 In this version, the menu and drop box are hidden (but not forgotten).

Code 8.1 The `visibility` property is set for the navigation and drop-box to hide those objects.

```
<!DOCTYPE html PUBLIC "-//W3C//DTD XHTML 1.0
→ Strict//EN" "http://www.w3.org/TR/xhtml1/
→ DTD/xhtml1-strict.dtd">
<html xmlns="http://www.w3.org/1999/xhtml">
<head>
<meta http-equiv="Content-Type"
→ content="text/html; charset=utf-8" />
<title>CSS, DHTML &amp; Ajax | Setting the
→ Visibility of an Element</title>
<style type="text/css" media="screen">h1,
→ h2 { color: #999; }
img {
    margin: 4px;
    display: block; }
#navigation {
    visibility: hidden;
    margin: 0px 16px 8px 0px;
    background-color: #ccc;
    float: left;
    font: small Arial, Helvetica,
    → sans-serif; }
#navigation a {
    padding: 2px 4px;
    border-top: 3px solid #fff;
    text-decoration: none;
    display: block;
    color: red; }
.chapterTitle {
    display: block;
    font-size: smaller;
    color: black; }
#copy { clear: both; }
.dropBox {
    visibility: hidden;
    width: 358px;
    padding: 6px;
    border: 3px solid #f66;
    margin: 0px 0px 8px 8px;
    float: right;
    font: small Arial, Helvetica,
    → sans-serif; }
</style>
</head>
<body>
<div id="navigation">
Flip To Chapter:
<a href="#">Down the Rabbit-Hole </a>
<a href="#">The Pool of Tears </a>
<a href="#">A Caucus-Race and a Long Tale </a>
```

like the invisible man in his bandages. However, when an absolutely positioned element (see Chapter 7) has its visibility set to invisible, it leaves no noticeable trace on the screen.

- Generally, `display:none` is used for DHTML effects, such as drop-down menus and pop-up text, in which elements are hidden and shown. Since this will remove the element, it prevents the element from interfering with the layout of the page when not needed.

- I recommend using an ID if you want to define the visibility of a single element on the screen. This creates an object that you can change using JavaScript to make it visible.

Code 8.1 *continued*

```
<a href="#">The Rabbit Sends in a Little
→ Bill </a>
<a href="#">Advice from a Caterpillar </a>
<a href="#">Pig and Pepper </a>
<a href="#">NEXT &rArr; </a>
</div>
<div id="header">
<h1>Alice's Adventures in Wonderland</h1>
<b class="author">Lewis Carroll</b>
<h2>CHAPTER VI
    <span class="chapterTitle">Pig and
    → Pepper </span>
</h2>
</div>
<div id="copy">
<div class="dropBox">
<img src="alice24.gif" height="238"
→ width="350" alt="Alice in Wonderland" />
'Well!  I've often seen a cat without a
→ grin,' thought Alice; 'but a grin without
→ a cat!  It's the most curious thing I ever
→ saw in my life!'
</div></div>
</body></html>
```

Setting an Element's Visible Area (Clipping)

Unlike setting the width and the height of an element, which controls the element's dimensions (see Chapter 6), clipping an absolute or fixed position element designates how much of that element's content will be visible (**Table 8.2**). The part that is not designated as visible will still be there, but viewers won't be able to see it, and the browser will treat it as empty space.

In this example (**Figure 8.3**), the absolutely positioned drop box has been clipped so that only the cat's smiling face remains.

Table 8.2

Clip Values	
VALUE	COMPATIBILITY
rect (‹topLength› ‹rightLength› ‹bottomLength› ‹leftLength›)	IE5*, FF1, S1, O7, CSS2
auto	IE4*, FF1, S1, O7, CSS2
*IE5.5 for Windows	

Figure 8.3 The Cheshire Cat's face is all that appears from this image. The King, Queen, and Jack have all been clipped away.

Code 8.2 The clip region is defined for the dropBox class.

```
<!DOCTYPE html PUBLIC "-//W3C//DTD XHTML 1.0 Strict//EN" "http://www.w3.org/TR/xhtml1/DTD/
→ xhtml1-strict.dtd">
<html xmlns="http://www.w3.org/1999/xhtml">
<head>
<meta http-equiv="Content-Type" content="text/html; charset=utf-8" />
<title>CSS, DHTML &amp; Ajax | Setting the Visible Area of An Element (Clipping)</title>
<style type="text/css" media="screen">
img {
    display: block;
    margin: 4px; }
.dropBox {
    position: absolute;
    clip: rect(35px 350px 200px 50px);
    left: 10%;
    width: 377px;
    padding: 6px;
    border: 3px solid #f66;
    font: small Arial, Helvetica, sans-serif; }
</style>
</head>
<body>
<div class="dropBox">
    <img src="alice31.gif" height="480" width="379" alt="Alice in Wonderland" />The executioner's
    → argument was, that you couldn't cut off a head unless there was a body to cut it off
    → from.</div>
</body></html>
```

Left Clip
x=50px

Top clip
y=15px

Bottom clip
y=195px

Right clip
x=350px

Figure 8.4 The clipping region is defined by four values that detail how far from the origin the top, right, bottom, and left edges of the element's visible area should appear.

To define the clip area of an element:

1. `position: absolute;`

   Set the `position` property to `fixed` or `absolute` (**Code 8.2**). Although clipping should work with other position types, Internet Explorer only recognizes it if the position is set to fixed or absolute.

2. `clip:`

   Type the `clip` property name, followed by a colon (`:`).

3. `rect(15px 350px 195px 50px);`

   Type `rect` to define the shape of the clip as a rectangle, an opening parenthesis (`(`), four values separated by spaces, a closing parenthesis (`)`), and a semicolon (`;`).

   The numbers define the top, right, bottom, and left lengths of the clip area, respectively. All these values are distances from the element's origin (top-left corner), not from the indicated side (**Figure 8.4**).

   Each value can be either a length value or `auto`, which allows the browser to determine the clip size (usually, 100 percent).

✔ Tips

- The element's borders and padding, but not its margin, will be clipped along with the content of the element.

- Currently, clips can be only rectangular, but future versions of CSS promise to support other shapes.

- You can change the clipping using DHTML (see "Changing an Object's Visible Area" in Chapter 16).

Setting Where the Overflow Content Goes

When an element is clipped, or when the parent element's width and height are less than the area needed to display everything, some content is not displayed. The `overflow` property (**Table 8.3**) allows you to specify how this cropped content is treated.

In this example (**Figure 8.5** and **8.6**), the height of the menu is limited so that additional chapter links are accessible only by scrolling down that individual block. Additionally, the drop box has had its width and height limited, so some of the content lies well outside of its box.

To define the overflow control:

1. `width: 200px; height: 200px;`

   Type a width and/or height to which the element should be restricted (**Code 8.3**). You could also clip the element (see "Setting the Visible Area of an Element" earlier in this chapter).

2. `overflow:`

   Type the `overflow` property name, followed by a colon (`:`).

3. `auto;`

   Type in one of the following keywords to tell the browser how to treat overflow from the clip:

   ▲ `scroll`, which sets scroll bars around the visible area to allow the visitor to scroll through the element's content. When you set this value, space will be reserved for the scroll bars, even if they are not needed.

   ▲ `hidden`, which hides the overflow and prevents the scroll bars from appearing.

Table 8.3

Overflow Values	
VALUE	COMPATIBILITY
scroll	IE4, FF1, S1, O7, CSS2
hidden	IE4, FF1, S1, O4, CSS2
visible	IE4, FF1, S1, O5, CSS2
auto	IE4, FF1, S1, O7, CSS2

Figure 8.5 Viewers can use the scroll bars to access the overflow content of the menu and the drop-box element with the image of Alice and the Mock Turtle.

Figure 8.6 Scroll around to see the bottom of the menu and more of the picture.

Code 8.3 The overflow property is set for both the navigation object and .dropBox class.

```
<!DOCTYPE html PUBLIC "-//W3C//DTD XHTML
→ 1.0 Strict//EN" "http://www.w3.org/TR/
→ xhtml1/DTD/xhtml1-strict.dtd">
<html xmlns="http://www.w3.org/1999/xhtml">
<head>
<meta http-equiv="Content-Type"
→ content="text/html; charset=utf-8" />
<title>CSS, DHTML &amp; Ajax | Setting
→ Where the Over Flow Goes</title>
<style type="text/css" media="screen">
h1, h2 { color: #999; }
img {
    margin: 4px;
    display: block; }
#navigation {
    height: 75px;
    overflow: auto;
    margin: 0px 16px 8px 0px;
    background-color: #ccc;
    float: left;
    font: small Arial, Helvetica,
    → sans-serif; }
#navigation a {
    padding: 2px 4px;
    border-top: 3px solid #fff;
    text-decoration: none;
    display: block;
    color: red; }
#copy { clear: both; }
.chapterTitle {
    display: block;
    font-size: smaller;
    color:black; }
.dropBox {
    width: 200px;
    height: 300px;
    overflow: auto;
    padding: 6px;
    border: 3px solid #f66;
    margin: 0px 0px 8px 8px;
    float: right;
    font: small Arial, Helvetica,
    → sans-serif; }
</style>
</head>
<body>
<div id="navigation">
Flip To Chapter:
<a href="#">Down the Rabbit-Hole </a>
<a href="#">The Pool of Tears </a>
```

▲ visible, which forces the cropped part of the element to show up, essentially instructing the browser to ignore the cropping.

▲ auto, which allows the browser to decide whether scroll bars need to be displayed.

✔ Tips

■ If the overflow property is not set, or if it is set to auto, the browser will ignore the height property set for an element.

■ Generally, auto is preferred for overflow, since this will show the scroll bars only as needed and hide the scrollbar chrome when there is nothing to scroll.

■ The overflow property is also used to define how clipping overflow is treated.

Code 8.3 *continued*

```
<a href="#">A Caucus-Race and a Long Tale </a>
<a href="#">The Rabbit Sends in a Little
→ Bill </a>
<a href="#">Advice from a Caterpillar </a>
<a href="#">Pig and Pepper </a>
<a href="#">NEXT &rArr; </a>
</div>
<div id="header">
<h1>Alice's Adventures in Wonderland</h1>
<b class="author">Lewis Carroll</b>
<h2>CHAPTER IX
    <span class="chapterTitle">The Mock
    → Turtle's Story</span></h2>
</div>
<div id="copy">
    <div class="dropBox">
        <img src="alice35.gif" height="480"
        → width="401" alt="Alice in
        → Wonderland" />
        'Once,' said the Mock Turtle at
        → last, with a deep sigh, 'I was
        → a real Turtle.'</div>
</div>
</body></html>
```

Setting an Element's Opacity

One of the earliest CSS3 features to be implemented widely is the ability to set the opacity of an element, which lets you transform an element from opaque to transparent and anywhere in-between. However, different browsers implement opacity in different ways.

For example, rather than implement the W3C CSS syntax, Internet Explorer builds on its existing `filter` functionality, while other W3C-compliant browsers simply add the `opacity` property (**Table 8.4**). But because Internet Explorer ignores the other browser's code, you can place both declarations in the rule list for the element in question to control its opacity.

In this example (**Figure 8.7**), I'm using the same image stack as in Figures 7.7 and 7.8, but I've set different opacities so that the images underneath show through.

To set the opacity of an element:

1. `filter:`

   To control opacity of an element displayed in Internet Explorer for Windows, type the `filter` property name, followed by a colon (`:`), in the declaration block (**Code 8.4**).

2. `progid:DXImageTransform.Microsoft.`
   `BasicImage(opacity=0.75);`

   Add the `progid` code to define the filter and value being used. You do not want to change this code, except for the alpha value after `opacity`, which can range between `0.0` (completely transparent) and `1.0` (completely opaque). End the declaration with a semicolon (;).

3. `opacity:`

   To control the opacity of an element displayed in Mozilla-based browsers, add the `opacity` property name, followed by a colon (`:`), to the declaration block.

Table 8.4

Opacity Values	
VALUE	COMPATIBILITY
‹alphavalue›	FF1, S1.3,09, CSS2
inherit	FF1, S1.3,09, CSS2

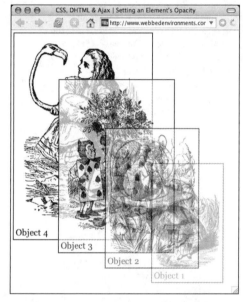

Figure 8.7 Object 1 is at 25 percent opacity (0.25), Object 2 is at 50 percent opacity (0.50), Object 3 is at 75 percent opacity (0.75), and object 4 is at 100 percent opacity (1.0).

Code 8.4 Using separate style declarations for Internet Explorer (filter) and CSS3 browsers (opacity), you can set the opacity of elements and be sure they'll appear the way you want them to in most browsers.

```
<!DOCTYPE html PUBLIC "-//W3C//DTD XHTML 1.0
→ Strict//EN" "http://www.w3.org/TR/xhtml1/
→ DTD/xhtml1-strict.dtd">
<html xmlns="http://www.w3.org/1999/xhtml">
<head>
<meta http-equiv="Content-Type"
→ content="text/html; charset=utf-8" />
<title>CSS, DHTML &amp; Ajax | Setting an
→ Element's Opacity</title>
<style type="text/css" media="screen">
img {
    margin-bottom: 4px;
    display: block; }
.dropBox {
    padding: 4px;
    background-color: #FFFFFF;
    border: 2px solid #f00; }
#object1 {
    filter:progid:DXImageTransform.
    → Microsoft.BasicImage(opacity=0.25);
    opacity: 0.25;
    position: absolute;
    z-index: 3;
    top: 285px;
    left: 315px; }
#object2 {
    filter:progid:DXImageTransform.
    → Microsoft.BasicImage(opacity=0.5);
    opacity: 0.5;
    position: absolute;
    z-index: 2;
    top: 210px;
    left: 210px; }
#object3 {
    filter:progid:DXImageTransform.
    → Microsoft.BasicImage(opacity=0.75);
    opacity: 0.75;
    position: absolute;
    z-index: 1;
    top: 105px;
    left: 105px; }
#object4 {
    filter:progid:DXImageTransform.
    → Microsoft.BasicImage(opacity=1);
    opacity: 1.0;
    position: absolute;
    z-index: 0;
    top: 5px;
    left: 5; }
</style>
</head>
```

4. 0.75;

Enter an alpha value for the opacity of the element, which can range between 0.0 (completely transparent) and 1.0 (completely opaque).

You could also use inherit, which will set the element's opacity to be the same as its parent. So if the parent has an opacity of 0.75, inherit will cause the child element to reduce its opacity 75 percent *in addition to* the 75 percent already set for the parent.

✔ Tips

- Opacity is applied to the entire element and to all of its children, with no way to override it in child elements. However, you can set the opacity of two sibling elements independently and then position one on top of the other.

- Opacity changes will *not* work in Internet Explorer for Macintosh, in earlier versions of Safari, or in earlier versions of Opera.

Code 8.4 *continued*

```
<body>
<div class="dropBox" id="object1">
<img src="alice22a.gif" height="220"
→ width="150" alt="Alice in Wonderland" />
Object 1</div>
<div class="dropBox" id="object2">
<img src="alice15a.gif" height="264"
→ width="200" alt="Alice in Wonderland" />
Object 2</div>
<div class="dropBox" id="object3">
<img src="alice28a.gif" height="336"
→ width="250" alt="Alice in Wonderland" />
Object 3</div>
<div class="dropBox" id="object4">
<img src="alice30a.gif" height="408"
→ width="300" alt="Alice in Wonderland" />
Object 4</div>
</body></html>
```

Changing the Mouse Pointer's Appearance

Normally, the mouse pointer's appearance is determined by the browser. The browser changes the mouse pointer's appearance according to the content over which the pointer currently happens to be resting.

If the pointer is over text, for example, the pointer becomes a text selector. Or if the browser is working and the visitor can't do anything, the pointer becomes a timer, letting visitors know they need to wait.

Sometimes, it's useful to override the browser's behavior and set the appearance of the pointer yourself, using the cursor property (**Table 8.5**).

In this example (**Figures 8.8**, **8.9**, and **8.10**), I've set up different pointer types that depend on the type of object or link over which the pointer is hovering.

Table 8.5

Cursor Values	
VALUE	COMPATIBILITY
‹cursor type name›	IE4, N6, S1, O7, CSS2
‹URL›	CSS2
auto	IE4, N6, S1, O7, CSS2
none	IE4, N6, S1, O7, CSS2

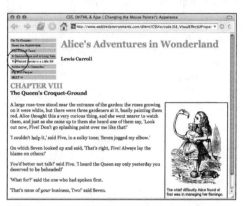

Figure 8.8 A right-pointing arrow is used for menu navigation.

Figure 8.10 When the mouse pointer is over an image, it changes to the crosshair cursor.

Figure 8.9 When the mouse pointer passes over the help link, a question mark displays.

Code 8.5 Because the link leads to a help screen, I've set the help class to change the cursor appearance to the help pointer. In addition, images will have a crosshair pointer, and the navigation will use a pointer that is generally used when selecting an area of an image.

```
<!DOCTYPE html PUBLIC "-//W3C//DTD XHTML 1.0
→ Strict//EN" "http://www.w3.org/TR/xhtml1/
→ DTD/xhtml1-strict.dtd">
<html xmlns="http://www.w3.org/1999/xhtml">
<head>
<meta http-equiv="Content-Type"
→ content="text/html; charset=utf-8" />
<title>CSS, DHTML &amp; Ajax | Changing the
→ Mouse Pointer's Apperance</title>
<style type="text/css" media="screen">
h1, h2 { color: #999; }
h2 { clear: both; }
img {
    cursor: crosshair;
    margin: 4px;
    display: block; }
a { color:red; }
#navigation {
    margin: 0px 16px 8px 0px;
    background-color: #ccc;
    float: left;
    font: x-small Arial, Helvetica,
    → sans-serif; }
#navigation a {
    padding: 2px 4px;
    border-top: 3px solid #fff;
    text-decoration: none;
    display: block;
    color: red; }
#navigation a:hover {
    cursor: e-resize;
    border-top: 3px solid #999;
    color: red;
    background-color: #fff; }
#copy { clear: both; }
.chapterTitle {
    display: block;
    font-size: smaller;
    color: black; }
.dropBox {
    width: 208px;
    padding: 6px;
    border: 3px solid #f66;
    margin: 0px 0px 8px 8px;
    float: right;
    font: small Arial, Helvetica,
    → sans-serif; }
```

To set the mouse pointer's appearance:

1. cursor:

   Type the cursor attribute, followed by a colon (:), in the CSS declaration block (**Code 8.5**).

   continues on next page

Code 8.5 *continued*

```
.help { cursor: help; }
</style>
</head>
<body>
<div id="navigation">
Flip To Chapter:
<a href="#">Down the Rabbit-Hole </a>
<a href="#">The Pool of Tears </a>
<a href="#">A Caucus-Race and a Long
→ Tale</a>
<a href="#">The Rabbit Sends in a Little
→ Bill</a>
<a href="#">Advice from a Caterpillar</a>
<a href="#">Pig and Pepper</a>
<a href="#">NEXT &rArr;</a>
</div>
<div id="header">
<h1>Alice's Adventures in Wonderland</h1>
<b class="author">Lewis Carroll</b>
<h2>CHAPTER VIII
<span class="chapterTitle">The Queen's
→ Croquet-Ground</span></h2>
</div>
<div class="copy">
    <div class="dropBox">
    <img src="alice30.gif" height="272"
    → width="200" alt="Alice in
    → Wonderland" />
    The chief difficulty Alice found at
    → first was in managing her
    → flamingo.</div>
    <p>A large rose-tree stood near the
    → entrance of the garden...</p>
    <p>'I couldn't <a class="help"
    → href="#">help</a> it,' said Five,
    → in a sulky tone; 'Seven jogged my
    → elbow.'</p>
</div>
</body></html>
```

2. `crosshair;`

Type one of the mouse-pointer names listed in **Table 8.6** to specify the pointer's appearance. Alternatively, type one of these other values for `cursor`.

▲ `auto` if you want the browser to decide which mouse pointer to use.

▲ `none` if you want the cursor to disappear altogether.

▲ `url` and the location of a graphic to use as a custom cursor; this can be either the complete Web address or the local file name of the image.

✔ Tips

■ In theory, you can use any Web graphic (GIF, PNG, or JPEG), as a custom cursor by specifying the URL for the image file. Unfortunately, this does not work in any browsers except Internet Explorer, which supports `.cur` or `.ani` file types for custom cursors.

■ Remember that the exact appearance of the cursor depends on the operating system and the Web browser being used.

■ Although it's fun to play around with switching the mouse pointers, I've tested this feature on my own Web site and have gotten several e-mails asking me to cut it out. Most Web users have learned to recognize what particular pointers are for and when they should appear. Breaking these conventions tends to confuse people.

Table 8.6

Cursor Types	
NAME	APPEARANCE (VARIES DEPENDING ON OS)
crosshair	✛
e-resize	�
hand*	🖑
help	▶?
move	🖐
ne-resize	↗
n-resize	↥
nw-resize	↖
pointer	🖑
progress	▶
se-resize	↘
s-resize	↧
sw-resize	↙
text	I
wait	⌚
w-resize	↤

* IE only; same as pointer

Table 8.7

Scrollbar Color properties	
PROPERTY	LOCATION
scrollbar-3dlight-color	Outer top and left sides of scroll face; used to create 3-D effect
scrollbar-arrow-color	Arrows in boxes
scrollbar-base-color properties set	Color used if no other
scrollbar-darkshadow-color	Outer bottom and right sides of scroll face; used to create 3-D effect
scrollbar-face-color	Flat areas in slider, except for track
scrollbar-highlight-color	Inner top and left sides of scroll face; used to create 3-D effect
scrollbar-shadow-color	Inner bottom and right sides of scroll face; used to create 3-D effect
scrollbar-track-color	Flat area that defines the scroller

Changing the Scrollbar's Appearance (IE Windows Only)

Microsoft Internet Explorer (versions 5.5 and later) for Windows allows you to set the color for all or part of the scrollbar (**Table 8.7**). These properties can be applied to the main scrollbar for the page or any scrollbar within the page, such as text-area scrollbars. They are not, however, a part of any W3C standard, so will not work in any browsers other than Internet Explorer. However, adding this code will not interfere with other browsers.

In this example (**Figure 8.11**), the scroll bars in the form text area and the main window have been altered from their default appearance.

continues on next page

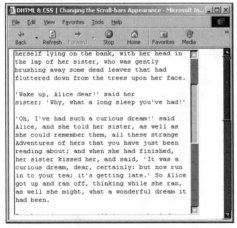

Figure 8.11 The main scrollbar for the page is red and the 3D appearance for the text-area scrollbar has been reversed.

To set a scrollbar's colors:

1. `scroll-base-color: red;`

   Type the `scroll-base-color` property name, followed by a colon (:), and then a color value and a semicolon (;). This will set the overall color scheme for the scrollbar (**Code 8.6**).

2. `scrollbar-3dlight-color: black;`

   Type one of the scrollbar color properties, followed by a colon (:), and then a color value and a semicolon (;). These are used to set the color of individual elements in the scrollbar. You do not have to use all of the scroll properties in a definition, but the browser will use default values for those left out.

✔ Tip

■ The "scroll-face" of the scroll bar includes the 3D beveled edges of the up/down arrows and scroller.

Code 8.6 You can control the color of each part of the scrollbar in Internet Explorer for Windows.

```
<!DOCTYPE html PUBLIC "-//W3C//DTD XHTML 1.0
→ Strict//EN" "http://www.w3.org/TR/xhtml1/
→ DTD/xhtml1-strict.dtd">
<html xmlns="http://www.w3.org/1999/xhtml">
<head>
<meta http-equiv="Content-Type"
→ content="text/html; charset=utf-8" />
<title>CSS, DHTML &amp; Ajax | Changing
→ the Scroll-bars Appearance</title>
<style type="text/css" media="screen">
body {
     scrollbar-base-color: red;
background-color: #fff; }
textarea {
     scrollbar-3dlight-color: black;
     scrollbar-arrow-color: white;
     scrollbar-darkshadow-color: white;
     scrollbar-face-color: #cccccc;
     scrollbar-highlight-color: black;
     scrollbar-shadow-color: white;
     scrollbar-track-color: gray;  }
</style>
</head>
<body class="bodyScroller">
<textarea style="float:left"
→ name="textareaName" rows="20" cols="45">
'Who cares for you?' said Alice, (she had
→ grown to her full size by this time.)
→ 'You're nothing but a pack of cards!'
</textarea><img src="alice42a.gif"
→ alt="Alice in Wonderland" height="480"
→ width="360" />
</body></html>
```

TABLE
PROPERTIES

Tables once ruled Web layout. Most designers relied on these structured elements to create the design grid for their pages. Because of CSS, using tables as the workhorse for design is increasingly becoming a thing of the past. However, tables are still the best way Web designers have for displaying tabular information.

All the CSS properties we've looked at so far can be applied to tables, with the table, caption, table header, table row, and table data tags all treated as boxes that can have borders, padding, width, and height applied to them.

In this chapter, we'll be exploring a few other useful CSS properties that will allow you to completely dispense with the tag properties often assigned to table tags.

Setting the Table Layout

Different browsers use different methods to calculate how a particular table should be displayed, with two primary `table-layout` (**Table 9.1**) methods favored:

- **Fixed** method bases its layout on the width of the table and the width of columns in the first row. This method is generally faster than automatic.

- **Automatic** uses the table column width along with the amount of content in the table data cell to calculate the final table data cell width. This will generally render more slowly than the fixed method, but it also produces more accurate results.

In this example (**Figure 9.1**), the same table code has had the fixed and automatic table-layout properties applied to it with obvious visual differences. Notice that although the word "Duchess" is cramped in the fixed version, there is plenty of space in the auto version.

Table 9.1

Table-Layout Values	
VALUE	**COMPATIBILITY**
fixed	IE5.5*, O5, S1.3, CSS2
auto	IE5.5*, O5, S1.3, CSS2
inherit	IE5.5*, O5, S1.3, CSS2
* For Windows only	

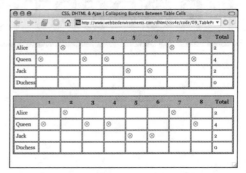

Figure 9.1 Notice the word "Duchess" in the top table, which uses the fixed table layout method, is more cramped than the bottom table, which uses auto. Fixed table layout sets the width of the column arbitrarily.

Code 9.1 The `table-layout` property lets you force the browser to use either the `fixed` or `auto` methods for rendering tables.

```
<!DOCTYPE html PUBLIC "-//W3C//DTD XHTML 1.0 Strict//EN" "http://www.w3.org/TR/xhtml1/DTD/
→ xhtml1-strict.dtd">
<html xmlns="http://www.w3.org/1999/xhtml">
<head>
<meta http-equiv="Content-Type" content="text/html; charset=utf-8" />
<title>CSS, DHTML &amp; Ajax |  Setting the Table Layout</title>
<style type="text/css" media="screen">
table {
    width: 680px;
    border: 2px solid red;
    background-color: #fcc; }
table.fixedWidth { table-layout: fixed; }
table.autoWidth { table-layout: auto;}
td {
    width: 50px;
    padding: 5px;
    border: 1px solid red;
    background-color: #fff; }
```

code continues on next page

Code 9.1 *continued*

```
th {
    width: 50px;
    padding: 5px; }
</style>
</head>
<body>
<table class="fixedWidth">
<caption>Results from the Queens Croquet
→ Tournament</caption>
<tr><th></th><th>1</th><th>2</th><th>3</th>
→ <th>4</th><th>5</th><th>6</th><th>7</th>
→ <th>8</th><th>Total</th>
</tr><tr>
<td>Alice</td>
...
</tr><tr>
<td>Queen</td>
...
</tr><tr>
<td>Jack</td>
...
</tr><tr>
<td>Duchess</td>
...
</tr></table>

<table class="autoWidth">
<caption>Results from the Queens Croquet
→ Tournament</caption>
<tr><th></th><th>1</th><th>2</th><th>3</th>
→ <th>4</th><th>5</th><th>6</th><th>7</th>
→ <th>8</th><th>Total</th>
</tr><tr>
<td>Alice</td>
...
</tr><tr>
<td>Queen</td>
...
</tr><tr>
<td>Jack</td>
...
</tr><tr>
<td>Duchess</td>
...
</tr></table>
</body></html>
```

To set the table layout method:

1. `table-layout:`

   Type the `table-layout` property name, followed by a colon (**Code 9.1**).

2. `fixed;`

   Type either of the following to specify which method you want used for laying out your table:

   ▲ `fixed`, which will use the first row to calculate the overall width of table data cells in that column of the table.

   ▲ `auto`, which will allow the browser to calculate the widths of table data cells based on their content and the overall width of the table.

✔ Tips

■ Internet Explorer 5 for the Mac has some strange bugs when rendering tables using CSS and padding. Backgrounds will not fill the padded area of a table cell and cells will overlap.

■ Internet Explorer for Windows will automatically ignore the border set in CSS for empty data cells, but will apply the background color.

Setting the Space Between Table Cells

Although they can use many of the box properties we discussed in chapter 6, table data cells (including table header cells) cannot use the margin property. Instead, CSS provides the border-spacing (**Table 9.2**) property, which provides the ability to set an equal amount of space between data cells' top, bottom, left, and right sides.

In this example (**Figure 9.2**), the table data cells have had an extra 8 pixels of space added around them to create a more open feeling to the table.

Table 9.2

Border-Spacing Values	
VALUE	COMPATIBILITY
‹length›	IE5.5*, FF1, O5, S1.3, CSS2
inherit	IE5.5*, FF1, O5, S1.3, CSS2
* For Windows only; buggy	

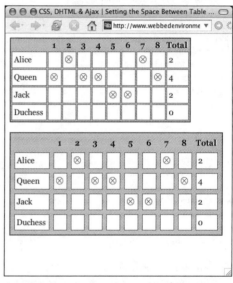

Figure 9.2 The top table shows the code without any extra spacing, while the bottom table has an extra 8 pixel spacing added around all 4 sides of each table data cell.

Code 9.2 The border-spacing property works like a margin around the table data cell.

```
<!DOCTYPE html PUBLIC "-//W3C//DTD XHTML 1.0
→ Strict//EN" "http://www.w3.org/TR/xhtml1/
→ DTD/xhtml1-strict.dtd">
<html xmlns="http://www.w3.org/1999/xhtml">
<head>
<meta http-equiv="Content-Type"
→ content="text/html; charset=utf-8" />
<title>CSS, DHTML &amp; Ajax | Setting the
→ Space Between Table Cells</title>
<style type="text/css" media="screen">
table {
    border: 2px solid red;
    background-color: #fcc; }
td {
    padding: 5px;
    border: 1px solid red;
    background-color: white; }
.spacey { border-spacing: 8px; }
</style>
</head>
<body>
<table class="spacey">
<caption>Results from the Queens Croquet
→ Tournament</caption>
<tr><th></th><th>1</th><th>2</th><th>3</th>
→ <th>4</th><th>5</th><th>6</th><th>7</th>
→ <th>8</th>
→ <th>Total</th>
</tr><tr>
<td>Alice</td>
...
</tr><tr>
<td>Queen</td>
...
</tr><tr>
<td>Jack</td>
...
</tr><tr>
<td>Duchess</td>
...
</tr></table>
</body></html>
```

To collapse the borders in a table:

1. border-spacing:

   Type the border-spacing property name, followed by a colon (**Code 9.2**).

2. 8px;

   Type a length value (such as 8px) to specify the distance each cell should be from another. See "Values and Units Used in this Book" in the Introduction for more details. Alternatively, use inherit to set the cell to use the same border spacing as its parent element.

Collapsing Borders Between Table Cells

Every table data cell defined by the `<td>` tag has four borders: top, right, bottom, and left. The `border-collapse` property (**Table 9.3**) allows you to set a table so that each table data cell will share its borders with an adjacent table data cell, rather than create a separate border for each.

In this example (**Figure 9.3**), the border between data cells has been collapsed into a single, thin red line.

To collapse the borders in a table:

1. `border-collapse`:

    Type the `border-collapse` property name, followed by a colon (**Code 9.3**).

2. `collapse`;

    Type either of the following to determine how you want the borders in the table to be treated:

    ▲ `collapse`, which will cause adjacent table data cells to share a common border; however, you won't be able to set `cell-spacing` if borders are collapsed.

    ▲ `separate`, which will cause each table data cell to maintain individual borders.

Table 9.3

Border-Collapse Values	
VALUE	COMPATIBILITY
collapse	IE5.5*, FF1, O5, S1.3, CSS2
separate	IE5.5*, FF1, O5, S1.3, CSS2
inherit	IE5.5*, FF1, O5, S1.3, CSS2
* For Windows only	

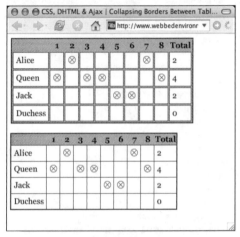

Figure 9.3 The top table shows the code without borders being collapsed, while the bottom table shows the same table with its borders collapsed.

Code 9.3 The border-collapse property lets you remove *all* space between the table data cells, giving each side a single border.

```
<!DOCTYPE html PUBLIC "-//W3C//DTD XHTML 1.0
→ Strict//EN" "http://www.w3.org/TR/xhtml1/
→ DTD/xhtml1-strict.dtd">
<html xmlns="http://www.w3.org/1999/xhtml">
<head>
<meta http-equiv="Content-Type"
→ content="text/html; charset=utf-8" />
<title>CSS, DHTML &amp; Ajax | Collapsing
→ Borders Between Table Cells</title>
<style type="text/css" media="screen">
table {
    border: 2px solid red;
    background-color: #fcc; }
td {
    padding: 5px;
    border: 1px solid red;
    background-color: white; }
.collapsus { border-collapse: collapse; }
</style>
</head>
<body>
<table class="collapsus">
<caption>Results from the Queens Croquet
→ Tournament</caption>
<tr><th></th><th>1</th><th>2</th><th>3</th>
→ <th>4</th><th>5</th><th>6</th><th>7</th>
→ <th>8</th><th>Total</th>
</tr><tr>
<td>Alice</td>
...
</tr><tr>
<td>Queen</td>
...
</tr><tr>
<td>Jack</td>
...
</tr><tr>
<td>Duchess</td>
...
</tr></table>
</body></html>
```

✔ Tips

- The final visual results can vary between different browsers, unless you set the border style using CSS.

- If the borders being collapsed do *not* share the same border thickness, the thicker border will be shown. If they have the same thickness, then the border for the data cell to the left will be used.

Dealing with Empty Table Cells

If a table data cell doesn't have any data (not even spaces or non-breaking spaces) it simply appears as a blank box, the default width and height of their columns and row. The `empty-cells` property **(Table 9.4)** allows us to define what happens to that data cell (most importantly its border) in these cases.

In this example (**Figure 9.4**), empty table data cells have been hidden so that their border and background color are not displayed, leaving an empty gap.

Table 9.4

Empty-Cells Values	
VALUE	COMPATIBILITY
show	FF1, O5, S1.3, CSS2
hide	FF1, O5, S1.3, CSS2
inherit	FF1, O5, S1.3, CSS2

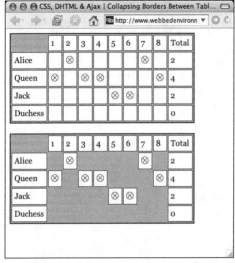

Figure 9.4 In the top table, the empty table data cells are shown, while in the bottom they are hidden so that the table's background color shows through.

Code 9.4 The empty-cells property lets you show (default) or hide empty table data cells. Hiding them allows the table background to show through instead.

```
<!DOCTYPE html PUBLIC "-//W3C//DTD XHTML 1.0
→ Strict//EN" "http://www.w3.org/TR/xhtml1/
→ DTD/xhtml1-strict.dtd">
<html xmlns="http://www.w3.org/1999/xhtml">
<head>
<meta http-equiv="Content-Type"
→ content="text/html; charset=utf-8" />
<title>CSS, DHTML &amp; Ajax | Dealing with
→ Empty Table Cells</title>
<style type="text/css" media="screen">
table {
    border: 2px solid #f00;
    background-color: #fcc; }
td {
    padding: 5px;
    border: 1px solid #f00;
    background-color: white; }
.hideEmpty { empty-cells: hide; }
</style>
</head>
<body>
<table class="hideEmpty">
<caption>Results from the Queens Croquet
→ Tournament</caption>
<tr><th></th><th>1</th><th>2</th><th>3</th>
→ <th>4</th><th>5</th><th>6</th><th>7</th>
→ <th>8</th><th>Total</th>
</tr><tr>
<td>Alice</td>
...
</tr><tr>
<td>Queen</td>
...
</tr><tr>
<td>Jack</td>
...
</tr><tr>
<td>Duchess</td>
...
</tr></table>

</body></html>
```

To hide empty table data cells:

1. empty-cells:

   Type the empty-cells property name, followed by a colon (**Code 9.4**).

2. hide;

   Type either of the following to specify how you want the borders in the table to be treated:

   ▲ show, which will force the empty data cell to display its background and border

   ▲ hide, which will leave a visual gap in place of the data cell

DEALING WITH EMPTY TABLE CELLS

Setting the Position of a Table Caption

The <caption> tag lets you embed identifying text in a table. You can set the align attribute in the caption tag to define where the caption should appear in relation to the table, but this is being deprecated in favor of the CSS caption-side property (**Table 9.5**), which does the same thing.

In this example (**Figure 9.5**), the caption is forced to the bottom of the table rather than its natural position at the top.

Table 9.5

Caption-Side Values	
VALUE	COMPATIBILITY
top	IE5.5*, FF1, O7, S1.3, CSS2
bottom	IE5.5*, FF1, O7, S1.3, CSS2
inherit	IE5.5*, FF1, O7, S1.3, CSS2
* For Windows only	

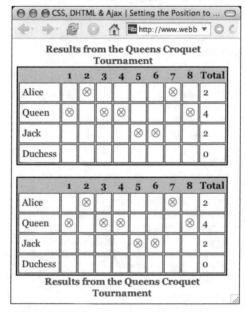

Figure 9.5 In the top table, the caption appears in its default location at the top, while in the second table, it has been moved to the bottom of the table.

Code 9.5 The caption-side property lets you specify whether the caption should appear above (top) or below (bottom) the table.

```
<!DOCTYPE html PUBLIC "-//W3C//DTD XHTML 1.0
→ Strict//EN" "http://www.w3.org/TR/xhtml1/
→ DTD/xhtml1-strict.dtd">
<html xmlns="http://www.w3.org/1999/xhtml">
<head>
<meta http-equiv="Content-Type"
content="text/html; charset=utf-8" />
<title>CSS, DHTML &amp; Ajax | Setting the
→ Position to a Table Caption</title>
<style type="text/css"media="screen">
table {
     border: 2px solid #000;
     background-color: #ccc; }
td {
     padding: 5px;
     border: 1px solid #000;
     background-color: white; }
caption {
     font-weight: bold;
     color: red; }
table.placeCaption { caption-side: bottom; }
</style>
</head>
<body>
<table class="placeCaption">
<caption>Results from the Queens Croquet
→ Tournament</caption>
<tr><th></th><th>1</th><th>2</th><th>3</th>
→ <th>4</th><th>5</th><th>6</th><th>7</th>
→ <th>8</th><th>Total</th>
</tr><tr>
<td>Alice</td>
...
</tr><tr>
<td>Queen</td>
...
</tr><tr>
<td>Jack</td>
...
</tr><tr>
<td>Duchess</td>
...
</tr></table>
</body></html>
```

To set the position of a caption in relation to its table:

1. caption-side:

   Type the caption-side property name, followed by a colon (**Code 9.5**).

2. bottom;

   Type a keyword indicating on which side of the table you want the caption to appear: top or bottom.

GENERATED CONTENT AND LIST PROPERTIES

Although for the most part, you want to place all of the content that is going to be displayed in your Web page directly into the HTML code, there are occasions where it is useful to have the content generated for you.

CSS provides several properties that let you specify content to be placed on the page (generated) for specific instances. For example, you might want all chapter titles to include the word "Chapter" before them.

One of the most common methods of generating content for the page is to use lists, in which items are automatically bulleted or numbered. CSS gives you many more choices, providing control over the type of marker used to denote the list items, which can be a bullet or an alphanumeric character. You can also create your own graphic bullets and make lists with hanging indents.

In this chapter, I'll show you not only how to whip your lists into shape using CSS but also how to automatically add content that is not placed directly in the HTML.

Adding Content Using CSS

For the purposes of search engine optimization, it is usually best to keep all of content of your page within the body tags, so that search engines can find it. However, there are times where you might have repetitive content that will not help your standing in a search index, or might even hinder it. To add content, you can use the content property (**Table 10.1**), which allows you to specify a text string, image or sound file URL, counter, quote, or even an attribute value that should be displayed on the page.

In this example (**Figure 10.1**), the word "Chapter" is inserted before the h2 tag; three copies of the flourish image (**Figure 10.2**) are inserted after the h2 tag; and the alt attribute text is displayed before the image as the caption.

To define generated content:

1. h2:before {…}

   Type a selector with the :before or :after pseudo-class (see "Defining Link and Dynamic Styles with Pseudo-classes" in Chapter 2), which defines where the content will be positioned in relation to the selector (**Code 10.1**).

2. content:

   In your declaration block, type the content property name, followed by a colon (:) and one of the values listed in Step 3.

continues on Page 248

Table 10.1

Content Values

VALUE	COMPATIBILITY
normal	FF1, S2, O4, CSS2
none	FF1, S2, O4, CSS2
⟨string⟩	FF1, S2, O4 CSS2
⟨url⟩	FF1, S2, O7, CSS2
⟨counter⟩	FF1, O4, CSS2
attr(⟨selector⟩)	O4, CSS2
open-quote	FF1, O4, CSS2
close-quote	FF1, O4, CSS2
no-open-quote	FF1, O4, CSS2
no-close-quote	FF1, O4, CSS2
inherit	FF1, S2, O4, CSS2

Figure 10.1 The word "Chapter" and the flourishes are inserted using CSS rather than being placed directly in the HTML, although visitors will not be able to tell the difference.

Figure 10.2 The image file bg_flourish.png.

Code 10.1 The content property is used to specify content that is inserted either before or after the selector.

```
<!DOCTYPE html PUBLIC "-//W3C//DTD XHTML 1.0
→ Strict//EN" "http://www.w3.org/TR/xhtml1/
→ DTD/xhtml1-strict.dtd">
<html xmlns="http://www.w3.org/1999/xhtml">
<head>
<meta http-equiv="Content-Type"
→ content="text/html; charset=utf-8" />
<title>CSS, DHTML &amp; Ajax | Adding
→ content With CSS</title>
<style type="text/css" media="screen">
h1, h2 {
    color: #999;
    margin: .5em 0em; }
h2 { clear: both; }
h2:before {
    content: 'Chapter '; }
h2:after {
    content: url(bg_flourish.png)
    → url(bg_flourish.png)
    → url(bg_flourish.png);
    display: block; }
img:after {
    content: attr(alt);
    display: block; }
#navigation {
    width: 240px;
    margin: 0px 8px 8px 0px;
    background-color: #ccc;
    float: left;
    font: small Arial, Helvetica,
    → sans-serif; }
#navigation a {
    padding: 2px 4px;
    border-top: 3px solid #fff;
    text-decoration: none;
    display: block;
    color: red; }
#navigation p {
    margin: 8px;
    font-weight: bold; }
.author {
    margin-top: 0cm;
    font: bold 1em Arial, Helvetica,
    → sans-serif }
.chapterTitle {
    display: block;
    margin-bottom: 8px;
    font-size: smaller;
    color:black; }
```

Code 10.1 *continued*

```
.dropBox {
    width: 228px;
    padding: 6px;
    border: 3px solid #999;
    margin: 0px 0px 8px 8px;
    float: right;
    font: small Arial, Helvetica,
    → sans-serif; }
</style>
</head>
<body>
<div id="navigation">
<p>Flip To Chapter</p>
<a href="#">A Mad Tea-Party</a>
<a href="#">The Queen's Croquet-Ground</a>
<a href="#">The Mock Turtle's Story</a>
<a href="#">The Lobster Quadrille</a>
<a href="#">Who Stole The Tarts? </a>
<a href="#">Alice's Evidence</a>
<a href="#">&larr; Previous </a>
</div>
<div id="header">
<h1>Alice's Adventures in Wonderland</h1>
<p class="author">Lewis Carroll</p>
<h2>VII
    <span class="chapterTitle">A Mad
    → Tea-Party</span></h2>
</div>
<div id="copy">
<div class="dropBox">
<img src="alice26a.gif" alt="The Hatter
→ opened his eyes very wide on hearing
→ this; but all he SAID was, 'Why is a
→ raven like a writing-desk?'" width="220"
→ height="246" />
</div>
<p>There was a table set out under a tree
→ in front of the house, and the March
→ Hare and the Hatter were having tea at
→ it...'</p>
</div>
</body></html>
```

3. `'Chapter ';`

Type one or more of the following values to define the content that is being added. Separate each value by a space:

- ▲ Type a string value within quotes (either single or double quotes), such as `'Chapter'`. Anything within the quotes will be displayed just as you typed it, even HTML code, although spaces are collapsed (i.e., more than two spaces are collapsed into a single space when displayed).

- ▲ `url()`, with an absolute or relative url within the parentheses pointing to an external file, such as an image or sound file. For example, `url(bg_flourish.png)` will load an image.

- ▲ `counter()`, with a counter name in parentheses. For example, `counter(chapterNum)` adds the counter number for the `chapterNum` counter. Counters are explained in the next section.

- ▲ `open-quote` or `close-quote` to add a quotation mark using the current quotation style (see the section "Specifying the Quote Style Later" later in this chapter).

- ▲ `no-open-quote` or `no-close-quote` to increase the level of quoting by one level.

- ▲ `attr()`, to display the value of the indicated attribute. For example, `attr(alt)` will display the value for the alt attribute.

- ▲ `inherit`, which will use whatever content is defined for the parent element.

- ▲ `normal` or `none`, which will not add any content or apply any other values.

✔ Tips

- ■ Since the `content` property is not supported in Internet Explorer (not even version 7), it is best not to rely on this property for critical information.

- ■ Information rendered using the `content` property will not be searchable by search-engine spiders, so never use it to insert information that defines what your page is about.

Table 10.2

Counter-Reset Values	
VALUE	COMPATIBILITY
<counterName>	FF1 , O4 CSS2
<num>	FF1 , O4, CSS2
none	FF1 , O4, CSS2
inherit	FF1 , O4, CSS2

Table 10.3

Counter-Increment Values	
VALUE	COMPATIBILITY
<counterName>	FF1 , O4 CSS2
<num>	FF1 , O4, CSS2
none	FF1 , O4, CSS2
inherit	FF1 , O4, CSS2

Figure 10.3 The chapter numbering starts at 7 instead of 1. (The counter is set to start at 6, but increments by 1 with each use.)

Teaching the Browser to Count

Browsers can create sequentially numbered lists automatically, starting at 1 and counting by ones. We will explore this concept in greater detail later in this chapter. However, what if you need to start numbering from 6 instead of 1? Or what if you need to create two sequential lists that are nested inside of each other?

CSS allows you to set up multiple counter lists to be used with the counter value of the content property (see the previous section). The counter-reset property (**Table 10.2**) is used to set the initial value for the count and the counter-increment property (**Table 10.3**) to increase the counter by a specific value.

In this example (**Figure 10.3**), the list that is used to create the table of contents begins at Chapter 6 and is increased by one every time the element is used.

continues on next page

To use a counter:

1. ol {…}

Set up a CSS rule for the selector that will be the parent element for your numbered list (**Code 10.2**). This can be the ol (ordered list) tag, but as you'll discover later in the chapter, you can turn any element into an item in a list, so you can use any parent container.

2. counter-reset: chapterNum 6;

Add the counter-reset property to your declaration block, a colon (:), and then the name of the counter identifier you are defining (this can be any name you want), a space, and then the number you want the list to start with.

3. li:before {…}

Type a selector with the :before or :after pseudo-class (see "Working with Pseudo-Classes" in Chapter 2), which defines where the number will be positioned in relation to the selector. Generally, this will be the li selector.

Code 10.2 The counter-reset and counter-increment properties are used with the counter() value for the content property to customize numbered lists.

```
<!DOCTYPE html PUBLIC "-//W3C//DTD XHTML 1.0
→ Strict//EN" "http://www.w3.org/TR/xhtml1/
→ DTD/xhtml1-strict.dtd">
<html xmlns="http://www.w3.org/1999/xhtml">
<head>
<meta http-equiv="Content-Type"
→ content="text/html; charset=utf-8" />
<title>CSS, DHTML &amp; Ajax | Teaching the
→ Browser to Count</title>
<style type="text/css" media="screen">
h1, h2 {
    color: #999;
    margin: .5em 0em; }
h2 { clear: both; }
#navigation {
    width: 240px;
    margin: 0px 8px 8px 0px;
    background-color: #ccc;
    float: left;
    font: small Arial, Helvetica,
    → sans-serif; }
ol { counter-reset: chapterNum 6; }
li {
    display: block;
    margin-left: -30px;
    padding-bottom: 4px; }
li:before {
    content: "Chapter " counter(chapterNum);
    counter-increment: chapterNum 1;
    font-weight: bold; }
#navigation a {
    padding: 2px 4px;
    border-top: 3px solid #fff;
    text-decoration: none;
    display: block;
    color: red; }
#navigation ol a:before {
    margin-left: 0px; }
#navigation p {
    margin: 8px;
    font-weight: bold; }
.author {
    margin-top: 0cm;
    font: bold 1em Arial, Helvetica,
    → sans-serif }
```

code continues on next page

Code 10.2 *continued*

```
.chapterTitle {
     margin-bottom: 8px;
     font-size: smaller;
     color:black; }
.dropBox {
     width: 228px;
     padding: 6px;
     border: 3px solid #999;
     margin: 0px 0px 8px 8px;
     float: right;
     font: small Arial, Helvetica,
     → sans-serif; }
</style>
</head>
<body>
<div id="navigation">
<p>Flip To Chapter</p>
<ol>
<li><a href="#">A Mad Tea-Party</a></li>
<li><a href="#">The Queen's Croquet-
→ Ground</a></li>
<li><a href="#">The Mock Turtle's
→ Story</a></li>
<li><a href="#">The Lobster
→ Quadrille</a></li>
<li><a href="#">Who Stole The Tarts?
→ </a></li>
<li><a href="#">Alice's Evidence</a></li>
</ol>
<a href="#">&larr; Previous </a>
</div>
<div id="header">
<h1>Alice's Adventures in Wonderland</h1>
<p class="author">Lewis Carroll</p>
<h2>Chapter VII
     <span class="chapterTitle">A Mad
     → Tea-Party</span></h2>
</div>
<div id="copy">
<div class="dropBox">
<img src="alice26a.gif" alt="The Mad Hatter
→ Speaks" width="220" height="246" />
The Hatter opened his eyes very wide on
→ hearing this; but all he SAID was, 'Why
→ is a raven like a writing-desk?' </div>
<p>There was a table set out under a tree in
→ front of the house, and the March Hare and
→ the Hatter were having tea at it...</p>
</div>
</body></html>
```

4. `content: "Chapter "`
`counter(chapterNum);`

As shown in the previous section, add the **content** property and the **counter()** value, with the name of the counter identifier in the parentheses. You can also add whatever other content you want with the number, such as the text "Chapter".

5. `counter-increment: chapterNum 1;`

Add the **counter-increment** property to the declaration block and include the name of the counter identifier, as well as a value for how much you want to increase the count for each instance. Generally this value will be 1.

✔ Tip

■ Because the **counter-reset** and **counter-increment** properties are not supported in Internet Explorer (not even version 7), it is best not to rely on these properties for critical information.

Specifying the Quote Style

Although most writers will simply use the keyboard to add quotation marks to their text, HTML includes the quotation tag: <q>...</q>. This tag places the browser default quotation marks around the indicated text. With CSS, you can define the exact characters to be used as quotation marks using the quotes property (**Table 10.4**). Although English uses either single ('...') or double ("...") quotation marks, this is by no means how all other languages do it.

In this example (**Figure 10.4**), the quotation marks are set to use « ...», which is standard for many other European languages, including French.

To define the bullet style:

1. quotes:

   In your declaration block, type the quotes property name, followed by a colon (:) and one of the values or value pairs listed below (**Code 10.3**).

2. '« ' ' »'

   Set the value of the open and closed quotation marks within standard English quotation marks.

3. '‹ ' ' ›';

After a space, you can add another grouping of quotation styles for the second level quotes.

✔ Tip

■ Because only Opera and Firefox currently support the quotes property, it is of limited use, especially since neither browser supports the :language pseudo-class, which would allow you to define the quotation marks to use with a particular language.

Table 10.4

Quotes Values	
VALUE	COMPATIBILITY
'<string>'	FF1 , O4 CSS2
none	FF1 , O4, CSS2
inherit	FF1 , O4, CSS2

Figure 10.4 Quotes appear in the French form (« »), rather than the English form (" ").

Code 10.3 The quotes property is used to specify what the quotation marks should look like.

```
<!DOCTYPE html PUBLIC "-//W3C//DTD XHTML 1.0
→ Strict//EN" "http://www.w3.org/TR/xhtml1/
→ DTD/xhtml1-strict.dtd">
<html xmlns="http://www.w3.org/1999/xhtml">
<head>
<meta http-equiv="Content-Type"
→ content="text/html; charset=utf-8" />
<title>CSS, DHTML &amp; Ajax | Specifying
→ the Quote Style</title>
<style type="text/css" media="screen">
h1, h2 {
     color: #999;
     margin: .5em 0em; }
h2 { clear: both; }
p q { quotes: '« ' ' »' '‹ ' ' ›'; }
#navigation {
     width: 240px;
     margin: 0px 8px 8px 0px;
     background-color: #ccc;
     float: left;
     font: small Arial, Helvetica, sans-serif; }
#navigation a {
     padding: 2px 4px;
     border-top: 3px solid #fff;
     text-decoration: none;
     display: block;
     color: red; }
#navigation ol a {
     display: list-item;
     list-style-type: decimal-leading-zero;
     list-style-position: inside;
     margin-left: -40px; }
#navigation p {
     margin: 8px;
     font-weight: bold; }
.author {
     margin-top: 0cm;
     font: bold 1em Arial, Helvetica,
       → sans-serif }
.chapterTitle {
     display: block;
     font-size: smaller;
     color:black; }
```

Code 10.3 *continued*

```
.dropBox {
     width: 228px;
     padding: 6px;
     border: 3px solid #999;
     margin: 0px 0px 8px 8px;
     float: right;
     font: small Arial, Helvetica,
       sans-serif; }
</style>
</head>
<body>
<div id="navigation">
<p>Flip To Chapter</p>
<a href="#">A Mad Tea-Party</a>
<a href="#">The Queen's Croquet-Ground</a>
<a href="#">The Mock Turtle's Story</a>
<a href="#">The Lobster Quadrille</a>
<a href="#">Who Stole The Tarts? </a>
<a href="#">Alice's Evidence</a>
<a href="#">&larr; Previous </a>
</div>
<div id="header">
<h1>Alice's Adventures in Wonderland</h1>
<p class="author">Lewis Carroll</p>
<h2>CHAPTER VIII
     <span class="chapterTitle">   The
       → Queen's Croquet-Ground </span></h2>
</div>
<div id="copy">
<div class="dropBox">
<img src="alice28a.gif" alt="# Cards
→ arguing" width="220" height="295" />
<q>Would you tell me,</q> said Alice, a little
→ timidly, <q>why you are painting those
→ roses?</q> </div>
<p>A large rose-tree stood near the entrance
→ of the garden:  the roses growing on it
→ were white, but there were three
→ gardeners at it, busily painting them
→ red.  Alice thought this a very curious
→ thing, and she went nearer to watch them,
→ and just as she came up to them she heard
→ one of them say, <q>Look out now, Five!
→ Don't go splashing paint over me like
→ that!</q> </p>
</div>
</body></html>
```

Setting the Bullet Style

The list-style-type property (**Table 10.5**) gives you control over the type of bullet to be used for list items—not just circles, discs, and squares, but also letters and numerals and dots. Oh, my!

In this example (**Figure 10.5**), I have added circle bullets in front of each chapter title link in the navigation. In addition, I've set the bullet to change to a solid disc when the user hovers over one of the links.

To define the bullet style:

1. list-style-type:

    Type the list-style-type property name, followed by a colon (**Code 10.4**).

2. circle;

    Type one of the bullet names listed in **Table 10.6**, or type none if you want no marker to appear.

✔ Tips

- Although we used the list item tag <li> in this example, you can turn any element into a list item by adding the CSS list properties along with the definition display: list-item.

- Earlier versions of Internet Explorer will not support the hover trick with bullets.

Table 10.5

List-Style-Type Values

VALUE	COMPATIBILITY
⟨bullet name⟩*	IE4, FF1, S1, O3.5, CSS1
none	IE4, FF1, S1, O3.5, CSS1
inherit	FF1, S1, O7, CSS1
* See Table 10.6	

Figure 10.5 In the chapter list, each item has a circle bullet. The chapter that the cursor is hovering over, though, has a solid disc.

Table 10.6

List-Style Bullets

NAME	APPEARANCE (VARIES DEPENDING ON SYSTEM)
disc	•
circle	o
square	■
decimal	1, 2, 3
decimal-leading-zero	01, 02, 03
upper-roman	I, II, III
lower-roman	i, ii, iii
upper-alpha	A, B, C
lower-alpha	a, b, c
lower-greek	α, β, χ

Code 10.4 The `list-style-type` property is used to choose between the different bullet and number styles for your list.

```
<!DOCTYPE html PUBLIC "-//W3C//DTD XHTML 1.0
→ Strict//EN" "http://www.w3.org/TR/xhtml1/
→ DTD/xhtml1-strict.dtd">
<html xmlns="http://www.w3.org/1999/xhtml">
<head>
<meta http-equiv="Content-Type"
→ content="text/html; charset=utf-8" />
<title>CSS, DHTML &amp; Ajax | Setting the
→ Bullet Style</title>
<style type="text/css" media="screen">
h1, h2 {
    color: #999;
    margin: .5em 0em; }
h2 { clear: both; }
li {
    list-style-type: circle;
    margin-left: -10px; }
li:hover {
    list-style-type: disc; }
#navigation {
    width: 200px;
    margin: 0px 8px 8px 0px;
    border: 3px solid #ccc;
    float: left;
    font: small Arial, Helvetica,
    → sans-serif; }
#navigation a {
    padding: 2px 4px;
    text-decoration: none;
    display: block;
    color: red; }
#navigation a {
    text-decoration: none;
    color: red; }
#navigation p {
    margin: 8px;
    font-weight: bold; }
.author {
    margin-top: 0cm;
    font: bold 1em Arial, Helvetica,
    → sans-serif }
.chapterTitle {
    display: block;
    font-size: smaller;
    color:black; }
```

Code 10.4 *continued*

```
.dropBox {
    width: 228px;
    padding: 6px;
    border: 3px solid #999;
    margin: 0px 0px 8px 8px;
    float: right;
    font: small Arial, Helvetica,
    → sans-serif; }
</style>
</head>
<body>
<div id="navigation">
<p>Flip To Chapter</p>
<ol>
<li><a href="#">A Mad Tea-Party</a></li>
<li><a href="#">The Queen's Croquet-
→ Ground</a></li>
<li><a href="#">The Mock Turtle's
→ Story</a></li>
<li><a href="#">The Lobster
→ Quadrille</a></li>
<li><a href="#">Who Stole The Tarts? </a></li>
<li><a href="#">Alice's Evidence</a></li>
</ol>
<a href="#">&larr; Previous </a>
</div>
<div id="header">
<h1>Alice's Adventures in Wonderland</h1>
<p class="author">Lewis Carroll</p>
<h2>CHAPTER IX
    <span class="chapterTitle"> The Mock
    → Turtle's Story </span></h2>
</div>
<div id="copy">
<div class="dropBox">
<img src="alice34a.gif" height="258"
→ width="220" alt="Alice" />So they went
→ up to the Mock Turtle, who looked at
→ them with large eyes full of tears, but
→ said nothing.</div>
<p>'You can't think how glad I am to see
→ you again, you dear old thing!' said
→ the Duchess, as she tucked her arm
→ affectionately into Alice's, and they
→ walked off together.</p>
</div>
</body></html>
```

Creating Your Own Bullets

You're not limited to the preset bullet styles built into the browser (see the previous section, "Setting the Bullet Style"). You can also use your own graphics as bullets, in GIF, JPEG, and PNG formats, with the list-style-image property (**Table 10.7**).

In this example (**Figure 10.6**), I've created a small arrow graphic (**Figure 10.7**) to be inserted as the bullet in front of the navigation links.

To define your own graphic bullet:

1. list-style-image:

   Type the list-style-image property name, followed by a colon (**Code 10.5**).

2. url(arrow_02.png);

   To include your own bullet, you have to tell the browser where your bullet graphic file is located. Type either the complete Web address or the local file name of the image. In this example, arrow_02.png is a local file.

   Alternatively, type none, which instructs the browser to override any inherited bullet images.

✔ Tips

- Graphic bullets are a great way to enhance the appearance of your page while minimizing download time.

- Keep in mind that the text being bulleted has to make space for the graphic you use. A taller graphic will force more space between individual bulleted items, and a wider graphic will force bulleted items farther to the right.

- As with the example in the previous section, we could change the graphic bullet to another graphic using the :hover pseudo-class. However, you will want to keep the two images the same size to avoid your design from jumping around unattractively.

Table 10.7

List-Style-Image Values

VALUE	COMPATIBILITY
<url>	IE4, FF1, S1, O3.5, CSS1
none	IE4, FF1, S1, O3.5, CSS1
inherit	FF1, S1, O4, CSS1

Figure 10.6 Rather than a boring old system bullet, I added this spiffy looking arrow that fades into the white background.

Figure 10.7 The image file arrow_02.png.

Code 10.5 The list-style-image property allows you to specify the URL for an image file to use as the bullet in your list.

```
<!DOCTYPE html PUBLIC "-//W3C//DTD XHTML 1.0
→ Strict//EN" "http://www.w3.org/TR/xhtml1/
→ DTD/xhtml1-strict.dtd">
<html xmlns="http://www.w3.org/1999/xhtml">
<head>
<meta http-equiv="Content-Type"
→ content="text/html; charset=utf-8" />
<title>CSS, DHTML &amp; Ajax | Creating
→ Your Own Bullet</title>
<style type="text/css" media="screen">
h1, h2 {
    color: #999;
    margin: .5em 0em; }
h2 { clear: both; }
li {
    list-style-image: url(arrow_02.png);
    list-style-type: square; }
#navigation {
    width: 200px;
    margin: 0px 8px 8px 0px;
    border: 3px solid #ccc;
    float: left;
    font: small Arial, Helvetica,
    → sans-serif; }
#navigation a {
    padding: 2px 4px;
    text-decoration: none;
    display: block;
    color: red; }
#navigation a {
    text-decoration: none;
    color: red; }
#navigation p {
    margin: 8px;
    font-weight: bold; }
.author {
    margin-top: 0cm;
    font: bold 1em Arial, Helvetica,
→ sans-serif }
.chapterTitle {
    display: block;
    font-size: smaller;
    color:black; }
```

Code 10.5 *continued*

```
.dropBox {
    width: 228px;
    padding: 6px;
    border: 3px solid #999;
    margin: 0px 0px 8px 8px;
    float: right;
    font: small Arial, Helvetica,
    → sans-serif; }
</style>
</head>
<body>
<div id="navigation">
<p>Flip To Chapter</p>
<ol>
<li><a href="#">A Mad Tea-Party</a></li>
<li><a href="#">The Queen's Croquet-
→ Ground</a></li>
<li><a href="#">The Mock Turtle's
→ Story</a></li>
<li><a href="#">The Lobster
→ Quadrille</a></li>
<li><a href="#">Who Stole The Tarts? </a></li>
<li><a href="#">Alice's Evidence</a></li>
</ol>
<a href="#">&larr; Previous </a>
</div>
<div id="header">
<h1>Alice's Adventures in Wonderland</h1>
<p class="author">Lewis Carroll</p>
<h2>CHAPTER IX
    <span class="chapterTitle"> The Mock
    → Turtle's Story </span></h2>
</div>
<div id="copy">
<div class="dropBox">
<img src="alice34a.gif" height="258"
→ width="220" alt="Alice" />So they went
→ up to the Mock Turtle, who looked at them
→ with large eyes full of tears, but said
→ nothing.</div>
<p>'You can't think how glad I am to see you
→ again, you dear old thing!'...</p>
</div>
</body></html>
```

Setting Bullet Positions

Often, the text of an item in a bulleted list is longer than one line. Using the `list-style-position` property (**Table 10.8**), you can specify the position of wrapping text in relation to the bullet. Wrapped text that is indented to start below the first letter of the first line of text is called a *hanging indent* (**Figure 10.8**).

In this example (**Figure 10.9**), I've set up a class called `.inside` that changes the bullet style position from the outside to the inside and applies it to the third link in the list.

To define the line position for wrapped text in a list item:

1. `list-style-position:`

   Type the `list-style-position` property name, followed by a colon (`:`) and one of the values presented in Step 2 (**Code 10.6**).

2. `inside;`

   Type either of the following to determine how you want the text to be indented:

   ▲ `inside`, which aligns subsequent lines of wrapped text with the bullet.

   ▲ `outside`, which aligns subsequent lines of wrapped text with the first letter in the first line of the text. Outside is the default style.

✔ Tip

■ Generally, bulleted lists that have a hanging indent (`outside` position) stand out much better than those without a hanging indent (`inside` position).

Table 10.8

List-Style-Position Values	
VALUE	COMPATIBILITY
inside	IE4, FF1, S1, O3.5, CSS1
outside	IE4, FF1, S1, O3.5, CSS1
inherit	FF1, S1, O4 CSS1

- **Outside**...Magnus es, domine, et laudabilis valde: magna virtus tua, et sapientiae tuae non est numerus. et laudare te vult homo.

- **Inside**...Magnus es, domine, et laudabilis valde: magna virtus tua, et sapientiae tuae non est numerus. et laudare te vult homo.

Figure 10.8 Outside is generally how bulleted lists are presented. You may want to override that by using Inside to save a little space on the page.

Figure 10.9 The third option in the navigation list shows how the Inside style affects an element in a list.

Code 10.6 The list-style-position property allows you to specify how lines of text flow under the bullet.

```
<!DOCTYPE html PUBLIC "-//W3C//DTD XHTML 1.0
→ Strict//EN" "http://www.w3.org/TR/xhtml1/
→ DTD/xhtml1-strict.dtd">
<html xmlns="http://www.w3.org/1999/xhtml">
<head>
<meta http-equiv="Content-Type"
→ content="text/html; charset=utf-8" />
<title>CSS, DHTML &amp; Ajax | Creating a
→ Hanging Indent</title>
<style type="text/css" media="screen">
h1, h2 {
    color: #999;
    margin: .5em 0em; }

h2 { clear: both; }
li {
    list-style-type: square;
    font-size: larger;
    margin-left: -10px; }
.inside { list-style-position: inside; }
#navigation {
    width: 200px;
    margin: 0px 8px 8px 0px;
    border: 3px solid #ccc;
    float: left;
    font: small Arial, Helvetica,
    → sans-serif; }
#navigation a {
    padding: 2px 4px;
    text-decoration: none;
    color: red; }
#navigation p {
    margin: 8px;
    font-weight: bold; }
.author {
    margin-top: 0cm;
    font: bold 1em Arial, Helvetica,
    → sans-serif }
.chapterTitle {
    display: block;
    font-size: smaller;
    color:black; }
```

Code 10.6 *continued*

```
.dropBox {
    width: 228px;
    padding: 6px;
    border: 3px solid #999;
    margin: 0px 0px 8px 8px;
    float: right;
    font: small Arial, Helvetica,
    → sans-serif; }
</style>
    </head>
    <body>
<div id="navigation">
<p>Flip To Chapter</p>
<ol>
<li><a href="#">A Mad Tea-Party</a></li>
<li><a href="#">The Queen's Croquet-
→ Ground</a></li>
<li class="inside"><a href="#">The Mock
→ Turtle's Story</a></li>
<li><a href="#">The Lobster
→ Quadrille</a></li>
<li><a href="#">Who Stole The Tarts? </a></li>
<li><a href="#">Alice's Evidence</a></li>
</ol>
<a href="#">&larr; Previous </a>
</div>
<div id="header">
<h1>Alice's Adventures in Wonderland</h1>
<p class="author">Lewis Carroll</p>
<h2>CHAPTER X<span class="chapterTitle">
→ The Lobster Quadrille </span></h2>
</div>
<div id="copy">
<div class="dropBox">
<img src="alice36a.gif" height="377"
→ width="220" alt="Alice" />
'Change lobster's again!' yelled the
→ Gryphon at the top of its voice.</div>
<p>The Mock Turtle sighed deeply...</p>
</div>
</body></html>
```

259

Setting Multiple List Styles

You can set all the list properties presented in the previous three sections in one line of code using the list-style shorthand property **(Table 10.9)**. This allows you to set the list-style-type, list-style-position, and line-style-image properties.

In this example **(Figure 10.10)**, I've set up the list to use the graphic arrow created earlier in this chapter with the square as a backup if the graphic doesn't load, in the inside position.

To define multiple list style attributes:

1. list-style:

   Type the list-style shorthand property name, followed by a colon **(Code 10.7)**.

2. url(arrow_02.png)

   Next, type a list-style-image value. To include your own bullet, you must first create the bullet graphic and then tell the browser where the graphic is located, using either the complete Web address or the local file name of the image. (See "Creating Your Own Bullets" earlier in this chapter for more information.)

3. square

   Type a list-style-type value from Table 10.5, followed by a space, or type none if you don't want a marker to appear.

4. outside;

   Type a list-style-position value from Table 10.8.

Table 10.9

List-Style Values	
VALUE	COMPATIBILITY
‹list-style-type›	IE4, FF1, S1, O3.5, CSS1
‹list-style-position›	IE4, FF1, S1, O3.5, CSS1
‹list-style-image›	IE4, FF1, S1, O3.5, CSS1

Figure 10.10 All three of the list style properties are set, via the list-style shorthand property, for the navigation list.

✔ Tips

- Although I used the list item <li> tag in this example, you can turn any element into a list item by adding the CSS list properties, along with the definition display:list-item.

- You do not need to include all of the values for this shorthand selector to work. Values omitted are set to the default. The following example works just fine:

  list-style: inside;

- If the visitor has turned off graphics in the browser, or if a graphical bullet does not load for some reason, the browser instead uses the list-style-type you defined in Step 3.

Code 10.7 The list-style property lets you set the type, image, and position all in one definition.

```
<!DOCTYPE html PUBLIC "-//W3C//DTD XHTML 1.0
→ Strict//EN" "http://www.w3.org/TR/xhtml1/
→ DTD/xhtml1-strict.dtd">
<html xmlns="http://www.w3.org/1999/xhtml">
<head>
<meta http-equiv="Content-Type"
→ content="text/html; charset=utf-8" />
<title>CSS, DHTML &amp; Ajax | Setting
→ Multiple list Properties</title>
<style type="text/css" media="screen">
h1, h2 {
    color: #999;
    margin: .5em 0em; }
h2 { clear: both; }
li { list-style: url(arrow_02.png) square
→ outside; }
#navigation {
    width: 200px;
    margin: 0px 8px 8px 0px;
    border: 3px solid #ccc;
    float: left;
    font: small Arial, Helvetica,
    → sans-serif; }
#navigation a {
    padding: 2px 4px;
    text-decoration: none;
    display: block;
    color: red; }
#navigation p {
    margin: 8px;
    font-weight: bold; }
.author {
    margin-top: 0cm;
    font: bold 1em Arial, Helvetica,
    → sans-serif }
.chapterTitle {
    display: block;
    font-size: smaller;
    color:black; }
.dropBox {
    width: 228px;
    padding: 6px;
    border: 3px solid #999;
    margin: 0px 0px 8px 8px;
    float: right;
    font: small Arial, Helvetica,
    → sans-serif; }
</style>
</head>
```

Code 10.7 *continued*

```
<body>
<div id="navigation">
<p>Flip To Chapter</p>
<ol>
<li><a href="#">A Mad Tea-Party</a></li>
<li><a href="#">The Queen's Croquet-
→ Ground</a></li>
<li><a href="#">The Mock Turtle's
→ Story</a></li>
<li><a href="#">The Lobster
→ Quadrille</a></li>
<li><a href="#">Who Stole The Tarts? </a></li>
<li><a href="#">Alice's Evidence</a></li>
</ol>
<a href="#">&larr; Previous </a>
</div>
<div id="header">
<h1>Alice's Adventures in Wonderland</h1>
<p class="author">Lewis Carroll</p>
<h2>CHAPTER XI<span class="chapterTitle">
→ Who Stole the Tarts? </span></h2>
</div>
<div id="copy">
<div class="dropBox">
<img src="alice37a.gif" height="298"
→ width="220" alt="Alice" />
'The Queen of Hearts, she made some tarts,
→        All on a summer day:      The Knave
→ of Hearts, he stole those tarts,
→ And took them quite away!'</div>
<p>The King and Queen of Hearts were seated
→ on their throne when they arrived...</p>
</div>
</body></html>
```

Displaying an Element as a List

The display element, discussed in Chapter 6, is used to specify how an element is displayed, allowing you to turn block items into inline items and visa-versa. One of the display values is list-item, which allows you to turn any element into a list item, basically assuming the properties of the list item (li) tag.

In this example (**Figure 10.11**), the chapter link tags in the navigation area are automatically numbered without having to place them in the li tag.

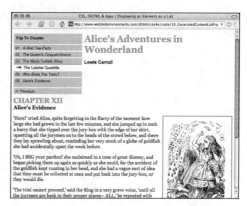

Figure 10.11 The menu links are turned into a numbered list. When visitors pass their cursors over a link, the bullet changes to the arrow graphic.

To set an element to be part of a list:

1. display:

   Start your declaration by typing the display property name, followed by a colon (:), in the CSS declaration block (**Code 10.8**).

2. list-item;

   Type the list-item property and value for how this element will be displayed, turning the element into a part of a list.

✔ Tips

■ Notice in the HTML code that the elements that are using the list-item display are nested in an ordered tag (<ol>...</ol>). If not used, the items will indent, but no number (ol) or bullet (ul) will appear next to them. Of course, it would be nice if **counter-reset** property worked here so that we could start the numbering at 6 instead of 1 (see earlier in this chapter), but it does not.

■ In the example in this section, I used the :hover pseudo element to change the bullet from a number to the arrow graphic. Although this is easily done now, earlier browsers tended to choke on this. As a result, most Web designers prefer to use a similar technique that utilizes the background-image property to add the graphic bullet (see "Creating Navigation Buttons with CSS Sprites" in Chapter 23).

Code 10.8 The list-item value used with the display property allows you to specify any item as being part of a list, effectively turning it into an li tag.

```
<!DOCTYPE html PUBLIC "-//W3C//DTD XHTML 1.0
→ Strict//EN" "http://www.w3.org/TR/xhtml1/
→ DTD/xhtml1-strict.dtd">
<html xmlns="http://www.w3.org/1999/xhtml">
<head>
<meta http-equiv="Content-Type"
→ content="text/html; charset=utf-8" />
<title>CSS, DHTML &amp; Ajax | Displaying
→ an Element as a List</title>
<style type="text/css" media="screen">
h1, h2 {
    color: #999;
    margin: .5em 0em; }

h2 { clear: both; }
#navigation {
    width: 240px;
    margin: 0px 8px 8px 0px;
    background-color: #ccc;
    float: left;
    font: small Arial, Helvetica,
    → sans-serif; }
#navigation a {
    padding: 2px 4px;
    border-top: 3px solid #fff;
    text-decoration: none;
    display: block;
    color: red; }
#navigation ol a {
    display: list-item;
    list-style-type: decimal-leading-zero;
    list-style-position: inside;
    margin-left: -40px; }
#navigation a:hover {
    border-top: 3px solid #999;
    color: red;
    background-color: #fff; }
#navigation ol a:hover {
    list-style-image: url(arrow_02.png); }
#navigation p {
    margin: 8px;
    font-weight: bold; }
.author {
    margin-top: 0cm;
    font: bold 1em Arial, Helvetica,
    → sans-serif; }
```

Code 10.8 *continued*

```
.chapterTitle {
    display: block;
    font-size: smaller;
    color:black; }
.dropBox {
    width: 228px;
    padding: 6px;
    border: 3px solid #999;
    margin: 0px 0px 8px 8px;
    float: right;
    font: small Arial, Helvetica,
    → sans-serif; }
</style>
</head>
<body>
<div id="navigation">
<p>Flip To Chapter</p>
<ol>
<a href="#">A Mad Tea-Party</a>
<a href="#">The Queen's Croquet-Ground</a>
<a href="#">The Mock Turtle's Story</a>
<a href="#">The Lobster Quadrille</a>
<a href="#">Who Stole The Tarts? </a>
<a href="#">Alice's Evidence</a>
</ol>
<a href="#">&larr; Previous </a>
</div>
<div id="header">
<h1>Alice's Adventures in Wonderland</h1>
<p class="author">Lewis Carroll</p>
<h2>CHAPTER XII
    <span class="chapterTitle"> Alice's
    → Evidence </span></h2>
</div>
<div id="copy">
<div class="dropBox">
<img src="alice42a.gif" height="293"
→ width="220" alt="Alice" />
'Who cares for you?' said Alice, (she had
→ grown to her full size by this time.)
→ 'You're nothing but a pack of
→ cards!'</div>
<p>'Here!' cried Alice, quite forgetting in
→ the flurry of the moment how large she
→ had grown in the last few minutes...</p>
</div>
</body></html>
```

Part 2
Dynamic
HTML

Chapter 11: Understanding DHTML 267

Chapter 12: DHTML Basics 283

Chapter 13: Learning About the
Environment 305

Chapter 14: Learning About an Object 321

Chapter 15: Learning About an Event 341

Chapter 16: Basic Dynamic Techniques 353

Chapter 17: Advanced Dynamic
Techniques 375

Chapter 18: Dynamic CSS 403

UNDERSTANDING DHTML

Figure 11.1 On the Panic Web site (panic.com), you can click an application icon to view details about the product or drag and drop the icon to download the application.

As powerful as Cascading Style Sheets are, they aren't really dynamic per se. They give you control of how a document looks when it's first put on the screen, but what about after that?

Web pages created with CSS can have their style properties changed on the fly (that is, dynamically) through a scripting language such as JavaScript.

In addition, dynamic HTML (DHTML) lets users directly interact with Web pages, so you can create far more sophisticated user interfaces than with simple HTML. For example, the Web site for Panic uses DHMTL, so users can quickly download the company's software (**Figure 11.1**). Clicking the application icon displays more information about the product, but dragging and dropping the same icon downloads the application. This kind of interface would not be possible without DHMTL.

This chapter discusses what makes DHTML dynamic and looks at how the technology compares to the other leading dynamic Web technology, Flash.

What Is Dynamic HTML?

I'll let you in on a little secret: There really isn't a DHTML language. At least, not in the way that there is an HTML language or a JavaScript language. HTML and JavaScript are specific, easily identified technologies for the Web. *Dynamic HTML*, on the other hand, is a marketing term coined by both Netscape and Microsoft to describe a set of technologies introduced in their version 4 Web browsers to enhance the interactive capabilities of those browsers (see "The History of DHTML" later in this chapter).

These interactive technologies were created or added in an attempt to overcome what were considered to be the chief limitations of Web pages designed with static HTML. Although the Web was great for delivering pages of text and graphics, they lacked the interactivity needed to create robust Web-based applications or deliver media beyond text. Those who were used to multimedia were left wanting more.

Adding DHTML to your Web site means that your pages can act and react to the user without continually returning to the Web server for more data. In programming terms, placing all of the code in the Web page is called *client-side code*. For you, it means not having to learn server-side programming to create interactive Web sites (see the sidebar "What DHTML *Should* Be").

DHTML is a combination of different standards-based Web technologies that, when used together, allow greater interactivity on your Web page (**Figure 11.2**).

What DHTML *Should* Be

Although there's no official or even standard definition of dynamic HTML, a few things are undeniably part of the DHTML mission:

◆ DHTML should use HTML or XHTML tags and scripting languages without requiring the use of plug-ins or any software other than the browser.

◆ DHTML, like HTML, should work (or at least have the potential to work) with all browsers and on all platforms.

◆ DHTML should enhance the interactivity and visual appeal of Web pages.

```
#obj1{...}      function doSomething(obj1)      document.obj1   <div id="obj1">...</div>
```

CSS ➕ JavaScript ➕ DOM ➕ XHTML 🟰 DHTML

Defines objects on the Web page | Changes objects on the Web page | Locates objects on the Web page | Creates objects on the Web page

Figure 11.2 The components of DHTML.

Cascading Style Sheets (CSS)

CSS allows you to define the style properties of any element on the page. Earlier browsers (such as Netscape Navigator 4 and Microsoft Internet Explorer 4) supported CSS Level 1 and CSS-P; most modern browsers support CSS Level 2.1. CSS is a standard defined by the World Wide Web Consortium (W3C). For more details on CSS, see Chapter 1.

Document Object Model (DOM)

The Document Object Model (DOM) describes how HTML and XML documents are represented using a tree-branching structure. The DOM allows you to treat individual elements on the page as objects, which can then be manipulated using JavaScript.

All DHTML-capable browsers have some version of the DOM that you can use to access the properties of any element-turned-object in the browser window. The problem is that the W3C did not standardize the DOM until 1998, and earlier browsers (Netscape Navigator 4 and Microsoft Internet Explorer 4) implemented their own conflicting DOMs. The good news is that the majority of modern browsers now support the W3C DOM, and legacy coding is becoming increasingly unnecessary, unless backward compatibility is required. For more details on the DOM, see Chapter 12.

JavaScript

The simple syntax of JavaScript lets you easily create code to control the behavior of Web page objects. Although browsers do not always agree on the exact implementation of JavaScript, they're close enough that you can work around the inconsistencies.

continues on next page

WHAT IS DYNAMIC HTML?

Unlike CSS and the DOM, JavaScript is *not* a standard set by the W3C. Instead, it has been standardized by the European Computer Manufacturers Association (ECMA) and is officially referred to as *ECMAScript* (**Figure 11.3**).

There were several versions of JavaScript in existence before ECMA started its standards initiative in 1996. Originally, JavaScript was incorporated into a beta release of Netscape Navigator 2.0. Microsoft implemented its own version, called *JScript*, in Internet Explorer 3.0. However, today, nearly all browsers support JavaScript 1.5 (its official designation is *ECMA-262 Edition 3*) as the JavaScript standard, so that's what we'll be using in this book.

JavaScript is far from frozen, though, and is still undergoing revisions. Mozilla, the rendering engine on which many browsers, including Firefox, are based, supports JavaScript 1.6.

Markup language

Markup languages are used by Web browsers to define how a Web page should be structured. This can take many forms. HTML (Hypertext Markup Language) is used to define the structure of a Web page, while XML (Extensible Markup Language) can define not only the structure but also the content of a page. In addition, there are several other specialized technologies such as SVG (Scalable Vector Graphics) and SMIL (Synchronized Multimedia Integration Language) used to add graphics and interactivity to the page. All of these languages can work with CSS, JavaScript, and the DOM to create dynamic Web pages.

XHTML (Extensible Hypertext Markup Language) is a hybrid of XML and HTML that is gradually replacing HTML in common use (see **Figure 11.4**). Although DHTML can be applied to a wide variety of markup languages, in this book we'll be coding using the XHTML standard.

Figure 11.3 ECMA International's ECMAScript Web page (ecma-international.org/publications/standards/Ecma-262.htm).

Figure 11.4 The W3C's HyperText Markup Language Web page (w3.org/MarkUp/).

The History of DHTML

When dynamic HTML was first being developed in the mid-1990s, Netscape and Microsoft had differing ideas about what technologies should be used to make HTML more dynamic.

Netscape-specific DHTML

Netscape brought several new technologies to the table, hoping to create more dynamic Web pages. Unfortunately, these technologies will never become standards because CSS does most of the same things and is endorsed by the W3C.

JavaScript Style Sheets (JSS) were introduced in Navigator 4 as Netscape's alternative to CSS. Like CSS, JSS lets you define how HTML tags display their content, but JSS uses JavaScript syntax. The only browser that supports JSS, however, is Navigator 4. Not even the latest versions of Netscape or Mozilla support this defunct technology.

In addition, Netscape offered HTML layers, which, like CSS positioning controls, let you control the position and visibility of elements on the screen. Again, however, only Navigator 4 supported layers, and Netscape abandoned this technology in favor of CSS positioning. I do not recommend using Netscape layers.

Although Mozilla, and by extension Firefox, inherited the mantle of Netscape browser development, it did not continue support for the Netscape-specific DHTML extensions.

Microsoft-specific DHTML

Much of the Microsoft-specific DHTML is based on proprietary Microsoft technologies, such as ActiveX. Because ActiveX is owned by Microsoft, it is unlikely that it will

continues on next page

THE HISTORY OF DHTML

ever be a cross-browser technology. In addition, legal actions have called the use of ActiveX controls into question and at the very least will make them more difficult to implement.

Microsoft also introduced dynamic visual filters (which use ActiveX controls) that let you add visual effects to graphics and text in your document. If you've ever worked with Photoshop filters, you'll most likely also understand how to work with visual filters. The problem is that these filters are not standard on all browsers, and aren't even supported in all versions of Internet Explorer.

I do not recommend using ActiveX or its visual filters except in the few cases where a similar effect can be achieved for other browsers using standard code, such as is the case with opacity (see "Setting an Element's Opacity" in Chapter 8).

Cross-browser DHTML

For years, the inconsistencies in supported technology between the two main browsers had Web developers who wanted to remain cross-browser compatible gnashing their teeth. Fortunately, the Netscape and Microsoft specifications for DHTML did overlap (**Figure 11.5**), and this area of overlap prevented DHTML from becoming just another proprietary technology.

Today, browsers implement CSS, DOM, and JavaScript standards, and the use of legacy browsers (such as Navigator 4) is diminishing, so DHTML can be used for a wide variety of applications. Although there are still browser inconsistencies, it is becoming easier to code for all browsers with minimal tweaking to accommodate the eccentricities of any particular browser.

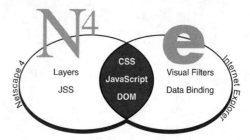

Figure 11.5 Where the two versions of dynamic HTML overlap is where you find cross-browser DHTML, including CSS, JavaScript, and the Document Object Model (DOM).

Why Should I Use DHTML?

Because you purchased this book, you've already made some commitment to using DHTML. But in case you haven't bought the book and are just flipping through and looking at the cool examples, let me try to make a balanced case for why you should use DHTML in your Web designs—and warn you about some of the troubles you may face.

DHTML advantages

Obviously, DHTML is not without its advantages or no one would use it. It has taken a few years, however, for the power of DHTML to be realized. Here are some advantages to using DHTML:

- **Supported by all browsers.** DHTML is supported in every major browser, including Opera, Safari, Internet Explorer, and Firefox. These browsers are used by most of the Web-browsing public.

- **Open standards.** Because DHTML uses standardized technologies that are open to any browser manufacturer, you can create your pages according to these standards and expect that, for the most part, they will display much the same on any major browser. Although there will be some inconsistencies in how the standards are implemented in each browser, the similarities outweigh the differences.

- **Change content on the fly.** One of DHTML's most obvious advantages is that you can make changes to the Web page content after it has loaded, without having to reload it. This is where the *dynamic* in DHTML comes from.

continues on next page

- **Small file sizes.** Like HTML, DHTML is created with text files, which are smaller than graphic files and generally render faster than alternatives such as Flash and Java.

- **No plug-ins required.** If a browser supports HTML, CSS, JavaScript, and the DOM (which all modern browsers do), it supports DHTML without the need for any additional plug-ins.

- **Easy to learn.** If you are already a Web designer, and you know HTML and JavaScript, you are halfway to knowing DHTML.

- **Fast development.** Many of the tricks that Web designers produced with graphics and JavaScript can be developed faster with DHTML.

- **Faster Web experience.** You can use DHTML to hide, show, and change content without having to load new pages. This capability speeds the performance of your site by requiring fewer calls to the server. In addition, since all DHTML code is text, it allows for fast downloads when compared to other interactive technologies such as Flash.

- **No Java programming required.** Although DHTML can do many of the same things and shares some of the same syntax as Java, you do not have to learn an entire programming language to use it. Although much of the power of DHTML is based on JavaScript, which is now a full-featured programming language, you do not have to have a degree in computer science to use the basics.

- **Can add even more interaction through Ajax.** As we'll explore in Part 3 of this book, DHTML and Ajax can make a powerful combination for creating responsive online applications.

DHTML disadvantages

It's not all smooth sailing with DHTML, however. To use DHTML, you need to understand its weaknesses as well as its strengths.

◆ **Browser and operating-system incompatibilities.** The implementation of CSS, JavaScript, and the DOM may vary slightly from browser to browser, and sometimes even between versions of the same browser on different operating systems. Although I've gone to great pains to present workaround solutions in this book, some browsers can do certain things that others simply cannot.

◆ **Picky, picky, picky.** JavaScript and CSS are notoriously finicky when it comes to syntax. Although most browsers will still display a page even if the HTML code isn't perfect, your entire page may fail to display if you have one too many brackets in a JavaScript function or forget a semicolon in a CSS definition list. In addition, if you're using XHTML instead of HTML, which is recommended, you won't be able to get away with the mistakes you could in HTML.

◆ **Handheld devices.** Most portable devices that can access the Internet, such as PDAs and mobile phones, have limited DHTML support or do not show up as having full support. These devices are increasingly becoming a factor in Web design, and at the very least, you will need to consider alternatives to DHTML visitors using these devices.

Flash vs. DHTML

Since their almost simultaneous release in the late 1990's, both Adobe Flash (formerly Macromedia Flash) and DHTML have seemed to be at odds, vying for Web designers' attention, as a way to add interactivity to Web sites.

Although DHTML adds interactivity to Web pages by using HTML, CSS, the DOM and JavaScript, Flash is a file format that can be integrated into and can interact with HTML pages but is itself a separate technology that is also delivered through Web browsers (see the sidebar "The History of Flash").

The rest of this book deals with how, where, and why you should use DHTML, but it's also important to understand the strengths and weaknesses of DHTML's chief dynamic competition so that you can better decide which technology to use.

Flash advantages

Flash has scored points with developers for several reasons, not the least of which is its consistency.

◆ **Consistent.** A Flash file will run more or less the same on a Mac using Internet Explorer 5.5 as it does on a Windows machine running Safari 2.1. Unlike HTML, JavaScript, and CSS, which are interpreted variously by the companies that make Web browsers, a single company develops Flash. Although there are a few diffences in how Flash is integrated with browsers, and occasionally there will be some bugs in beta or earlier releases, in general you only have to create a single Flash file for universal viewing.

> ### The History of Flash
>
> Macromedia acquired the vector animation program FutureSplash Animator in 1997. It added interactive and scripting capabilities, renamed the program Flash, and positioned it as a way to create dynamic graphic content for the Web. Up until then, graphics on the Web had been fairly lifeless; animated GIFs were the only substantial way to add motion to the browser window.
>
> Flash changed all that by letting Web designers control the appearance and behavior of Web content.
>
> Adobe bought Macromedia in 2005 and thus acquired Flash. Although it is clear that Adobe plans to continue the development of Flash, it is still unclear how this will change the nature of the program.
>
> It's important to remember that Flash is both a program (from Adobe) and a file format (which has the extension .swf, pronounced *swif*). When discussing "Flash" you may often find that you need to qualify whether you are talking about using the software or viewing its output.

- **Ubiquitous.** According to Macromedia, 95 percent of the Web-browsing public has some version of the Flash plug-in installed. Although this figure may be a tad optimistic, there is a good chance that the audience for your Web site will be able to view Flash content that you include in your Web site.

- **Attractive.** Flash gives designers a wide range of creative tools from which to choose. In addition, Flash Web sites win most of the design awards these days.

- **Small.** If they're created right, Flash files deliver a lot of dynamic bang for the buck.

Flash disadvantages

Things look good for Flash so far, but there is another side to the story:

- **Difficult to learn and create.** HTML, CSS, and JavaScript can be created with a basic text editor. But to create Flash files, you must purchase and learn to use Adobe Flash, which has a difficult learning curve.

- **Search Engine Optimization.** Although the exact alchemy used by search engines such as Google and Yahoo! to index the Web remains a mystery, we do know that they rely on the ability to find plain text. Obviously, since Flash code is not open for viewing, the text in a Flash file cannot be searched. Although there are methods to alleviate this, generally Flash pages will not appear as highly in search results.

continues on next page

FLASH VS. DHTML

- **Plug-in phobia.** Although the vast majority of users may have the Flash plug-in, they may not have the most current version; thus, they may not be able to run your cutting-edge Flash movie. To view your site, users may have to download the latest version. You could make a similar argument about browsers, but Web surfers traditionally resist downloading plug-ins. In addition, recent legal maneuvers by Eolas (a company that claims to have patented browser plug-ins) has cast doubt on the future of plug-in-based technology in Web browsers. Though this issue is far from settled, it may have a chilling effect on all plug-in technologies, including Flash.

- **Usability abuses.** Flash allows greater versatility with the interface design than straight HTML. But with great power comes great responsibility. Designers are more likely to flaunt standard Web interface conventions in Flash designs and this can lead to confusion for the user. See the sidebar "The Great Usability Debate" for more details.

- **Bloated downloads.** Although Flash movies can be very small, making them small takes skill and practice. Many enthusiastic designers forget that the people viewing their sites may have slow Internet connections, so downloading these large files can take a long time.

Should I Use DHTML or Flash?

Although I'm biased on this topic, I appreciate the simplicity that DHTML offers Web designers. Which technology you select, however, depends on a variety of factors (**Figure 11.6**). Ask yourself the following questions when determining which technology better satisfies your user interface needs:

- ◆ **What technology will my audience have?** Will they have DHTML-capable browsers? Will they have the current Flash plug-in installed? Do they have plug-in phobia? The first rule of design is "Know your audience."

continues on next page

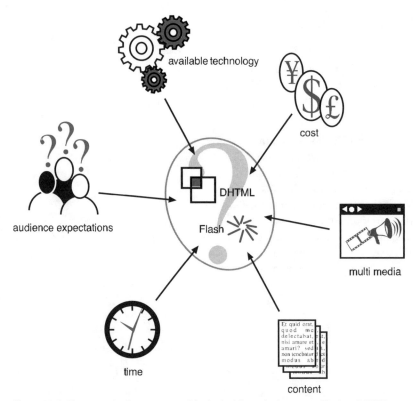

Figure 11.6 These are the factors to consider in deciding whether to use Flash or DHTML.

- **How much money do I have budgeted?**
  Unlike DHTML, which has no added
  costs over HTML, Flash requires that you
  purchase Flash-creation software. These
  programs can cost several hundred dol-
  lars, not to mention the cost of training.

- **Do I need to use sound, animation,
  or other media on my site?** Flash is
  often better than DHTML for creating
  and presenting multimedia content.
  However with the rise of Ajax (see Part 3
  of this book) the gap between them is
  closing quickly.

- **Am I presenting a lot of text?** HTML
  and DHTML are more versatile for presenting large amounts of text. Although
  Flash has made great strides in its print
  capability, it still can't hold a candle to
  HTML. In addition, text in Flash files is
  not crawlable by search engine spiders
  and tends to reduce the ranking of those
  pages in search engines.

- **How much development and mainte-
  nance time do I have?** Generally, DHTML
  is faster to create, but this depends on
  which technology you know better.

- **What are my audience's expectations?** If they want fireworks, Flash is
  the way to go. If they expect a straightforward site or do not like plug-ins,
  DHTML is the way to go. Again, though,
  with the development of Ajax systems,
  there is a lot of cool stuff you can do with
  DHTML to create interactive experiences
  that surpass those available with Flash.

The Great Usability Debate

Noted Web usability guru Jakob Nielsen takes a strong position against Flash on his Web site useit.com (**Figure 11.7**). In his essay "Flash: 99% Bad" (useit.com/alertbox/20001029.html), Nielsen comments that Flash designs have a tendency to break with established Web design conventions, which can lead to confusion for viewers.

Since he published this article in October of 2000, Macromedia and now Adobe have tried to work with Nielson to remedy the usability problems of Flash. Adobe currently hosts a Usability Topic Center Web site (**Figure 11.8**) to help Flash developers.

Despite the fact that this site includes an article titled "Flash 99% Good," by Kevin Airgrid, Nielson still listed Flash third in his list of Top 10 Design Mistakes of 2005, saying "I view it as a personal failure that Flash collected the bronze medal for annoyance."

Obviously if they were not appealing, Flash Web sites would have disappeared a long time ago. However, sites like The Favourite Website Awards present a different Flash site every day (**Figure 11.9**) and most entertainment Web sites include at least some Flash.

The debate continues.

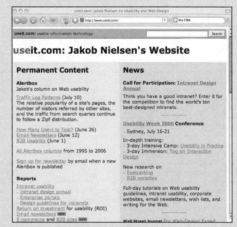

Figure 11.7 Jakob Nielson's useit.com.

Figure 11.9 The FWA: Favourite Website Awards (thefwa.com).

Figure 11.8 Adobe's Usability Topic Center (adobe.com/devnet/topics/usability.html).

DHTML BASICS

Figure 12.1 The Rijks Museum of Amsterdam uses some cool DHTML techniques integrated with a bit of Flash to create an interactive webbed environment (rijksmuseum.nl).

The ability to change a Web page dynamically with a scripting language is made possible by the Document Object Model (DOM), which makes any element on the page available to JavaScript. This powerful capability allows you to change not only virtually any attribute set for an element, but also any property that can be controlled with CSS (**Figure 12.1**).

Although the DOM didn't start out as a standard, the good news is that modern browsers now use the DOM standardized by the World Wide Web Consortium (W3C). You can think of a DOM as a map of your page, which locates every element, either through its HTML element name or more directly using an ID assigned to the element. Being able to address elements in this way gives you the ability to change the element or even add new elements to the page.

In this chapter, you'll learn how to use the W3C's standardized DOM, and how event handlers can be made to trigger actions with the DOM.

DOM: The Road Map to Your Web Page

When you write a letter to someone, you address the envelope, naming the country, city, street, number, and person for whom the letter is intended. If you put this process in JavaScript, it might look something like this:

```
usa.newyork.sesameST.123.ernie
```

Using this address, you can send a message to the intended recipient. The postal carrier simply uses the address you list and a road map to find the correct location. As long as there are no other Ernies at 123 Sesame Street in New York, you can feel safe that the addressee will receive your message.

If you need to send a message to someone else who happens to live at the same address as Ernie, however, all you have to do is change the name:

```
usa.newyork.sesameST.123.bert
```

Although the addresses are very similar, each is still unique.

The DOM allows you to find the "address," or *node*, of different elements on your Web page. You can then use JavaScript to send the object at a particular node a message telling the object what to do. The node can return messages about itself—what it is, where it is, and what it is up to.

The DOM describes a path beginning with the window itself and moving down through the various objects on the Web page. Each element represents a node within the document, which is defined by an HTML tag, creating a tree-like structure in which each node object is a leaf in the tree. For example, **Code 12.1** is broken down into nodes, as shown in **Figure 12.2**.

The following example is the path for the image called `alice1`:

```
window.document.images.alice1
```

Code 12.1 A simple Web page with its node structure broken down, as shown in Figure 12.2.

```
<!DOCTYPE html PUBLIC "-//W3C//DTD XHTML 1.0
→ Strict//EN" "http://www.w3.org/TR/xhtml1/
→ DTD/xhtml1-strict.dtd">
<html xmlns="http://www.w3.org/1999/xhtml">
<head>
<meta http-equiv="Content-Type"
→ content="text/html; charset=utf-8" />
<title>CSS, DHTML &amp; Ajax | Undestanding
→ DOM</title>
</head>
<body>
<form action="#" method="get">
<p><input type="text" size="24" /></p>
</form>
<div>
    <img src="alice28a.gif" id="alice1"
    → alt="Alice" />
    Your Message Here
</div>
</body></html>
```

This addresses an image object in the document in the current window called *alice1*.

If you needed to access an image called *alice2*, you would use this address instead:

```
window.document.images.alice2
```

You can use this path to make a JavaScript function send the object a message, such as what image it should be displaying (`src`) or what CSS styles it should use (`style`):

```
window.document.images.alice1.src =
"alice2.gif"
```

When you send a letter within the same country, you don't need to indicate the country in the address. The post office assumes it's going somewhere in the same country. The same is true of indicating which window you're referencing with your JavaScript. It's simply assumed to be the window that the code is in. So rather than starting your path with the `window` object, you begin the path with `document`:

```
document.images.alice1.src=
"alice2.gif"
```

continues on next page

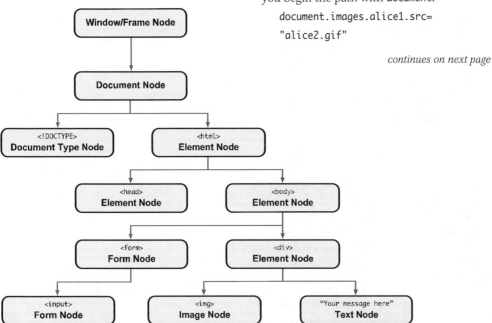

Figure 12.2 The Web page node for Code 12.1 begins at the top with the window, moving down to each individual element on the page.

Web pages created with CSS can have their properties changed while they are on the screen (that is, dynamically) through a scripting language and the DOM (**Table 12.1**). Because it's available almost universally, most people use JavaScript as their scripting language. CSS, however, can be affected by any scripting language that your browser can handle—VBScript in Internet Explorer, for example.

The W3C-standard DOM

The W3C defines the Document Object Model as:

"... a platform- and language-neutral interface that will allow programs and scripts to dynamically access and update the content, structure and style of documents. The document can be further processed and the results of that processing can be incorporated back into the presented page" (w3.org/DOM/#what).

Clear enough? Basically, this definition says that the DOM is not dependent on any specific operating system or programming language, and allows scripting languages to access and change your Web page.

Earlier versions of both Netscape Navigator and Microsoft Internet Explorer included their own DOMs, which didn't work the same way. This was like having two different systems for addressing letters in the same country. The letters from one mail carrier could not be sent to addresses defined by the other mail carrier. This meant that Web designers had to create two versions of their code, and then determine which browser it was being viewed in to deliver the right address.

The good news is that the W3C published a standardized DOM, to which all modern browsers adhere. Score one for standards!

Table 12.1

What DOM Allows	
CAPABILITY	COMPATIBILITY
Change the font and text properties of an element while it's on screen	IE4, FF1, S1, O3.5, DOM1
Change the z-index of elements	IE4, N4, S1, O3.5, DOM1
Hide or show elements on the screen	IE4, FF1, S1, O3.5, DOM1
Change the position of elements	IE4, FF1, S1, O3.5, DOM1
Animate elements on the screen	IE4, FF1, S1, O3.5, DOM1
Allow visitors to move objects on the screen	IE4, FF1, S1, O3.5, DOM1
Reclip the visible area of an element	IE5, FF1, S1, O3.5, DOM1
Change the content of a page after loading	IE5, FF1, S1, O3.5, DOM1

Table 12.2

DOM Versions		
BROWSER	VERSION	DOM
Netscape	4	Layer
	6+	W3C
Internet Explorer	4	All
	5+	All, W3C
Safari	1+	W3C
Opera	3.5+	W3C
Firefox	1+	W3C

We will be using only the W3C standard DOM in this book, but for more details on the earlier Netscape and Internet Explorer DOMs, see the sidebar "The History of the DOM."

The code presented in this chapter uses the W3C standardized DOM, which will *not* work in Internet Explorer 4 or Netscape Navigator 4 (**Table 12.2**).

The History of the DOM

The W3C realized that there would be a need to link scripting languages to objects on a Web page, so it diligently began working out the best method. Unfortunately, the browser manufacturers couldn't wait, and they introduced their own DOMs before the W3C could set the standard. Better late than never, the W3C released its standardized DOM late in 1998, which has been embraced by the browser-building community.

The Netscape Layer DOM

The Netscape Layer DOM lets you write scripts to control elements created with the <layer> tag and elements created with CSS positioning. This DOM lets you control the position, visibility, and clipping of the element. Changes made in these properties with either layers or CSS positioning occur immediately on the page.

The Layer DOM does not provide access to CSS properties other than the positioning controls. Thus, you cannot change the font, text, list, mouse, color, background, border, or margin of an object in Netscape 4 after the page has loaded unless you reload the page.

The Layer DOM does not work in Netscape 6 or later, and there was never a version 5 of Netscape. When Netscape started planning Netscape 6 (code-named Mozilla), it decided to start from scratch and attempt to make the browser as standards-compliant as possible. Unfortunately, and to the confusion of many Web designers, this meant abandoning any technologies that were never going to be standards, including the <layer> tag and the Layer DOM.

The Internet Explorer All DOM

The Internet Explorer All DOM allows you to write scripts that can access any element on the screen—at least, any element that Internet Explorer understands. These elements include CSS properties, which let you control the position and visibility of elements on the screen, as well as their appearance. Any changes made in these properties occur on the page immediately, and Internet Explorer redraws the page to comply.

Thus, any changes made in the font, text, list, mouse, color, background, border, margin, position, or visibility of an object are immediately discernible.

DOM: THE ROAD MAP TO YOUR WEB PAGE

Setting Up an Object

Simply stated, an *object* is an HTML element (see "Understanding an Element's Box" in Chapter 6) that can be uniquely identified in the Web page. The HTML element has a unique address in the browser window specified by the DOM.

Some objects are accessible by the DOM because of the type of element they are. For example, forms and images can be addressed by using their position in the form or image array for a page. However, this can be difficult to figure out, and it is often much easier to simply give the element a unique identity. Any element in the browser window—at least, any element enclosed within HTML tags—can be identified with an ID attribute to give it its own unique address and make it an object, rather than simply an element.

Identifying an HTML element as an object (**Figure 12.3**) allows you to change any of that element's attributes—at least, to the extent that the browser allows.

To set up an object:

1. #object1 {...}

   Add an ID selector rule to your CSS, and define the position as either absolute or relative (see "Defining ID Selectors to Identify an Object" in Chapter 2). You can also add any other definitions you desire, but you must include the position for this object to be a layer (**Code 12.2**).

2. <div id="object1">...</div>

   Apply the ID to an HTML tag—and it can now be identified and accessed using DOM. Notice in this example that not only is the image a part of the object, but the text within the <div> tag is a part of the object as well. All elements within the containing tag (the <div> tag, in this example) become a part of the object.

Figure 12.3 You can set up an object using the ID attribute that gives the element an easily recognizable and unique address.

Code 12.2 This code sets up a CSS layer, which is applied to a DIV tag with an ID.

```
<!DOCTYPE html PUBLIC "-//W3C//DTD XHTML 1.0
→ Strict//EN" "http://www.w3.org/TR/xhtml1/
→ DTD/xhtml1-strict.dtd">
<html xmlns="http://www.w3.org/1999/xhtml">
<head>
<meta http-equiv="Content-Type"
→ content="text/html; charset=utf-8" />
<title>CSS, DHTML &amp; Ajax | Creating An
→ Object</title>
<style type="text/css" media="screen">
body {
     font: 1em Georgia, "Times New Roman",
     → times, serif;
     color: #000;
     background-color: #ccc;
     margin: 8px; }
#object1 {
     padding: 4px;
     background-color: #fff;
     border: 2px solid #f00;
     position: absolute;
     z-index: 3;
     top: 100px;
     left: 150px;
     width: 210px;}
</style>
</head>
<body>
<div id="object1">
     <img src="alice04.gif" alt="alice"
     → height="298" width="200" />
     <h1>object 1</h1>
</div>
</body></html>
```

Should I Use a Name or ID?

To name objects on a page, you can use either the name attribute:

```
<img name="button1"
→ src="button_off.png" />
```

or the id attribute:

```
<img id="button1"
→ src="button_off.png" />
```

However, XHTML is phasing out the use of the name attribute and using id in its place. This is fine for newer browsers, but may cause problems in earlier browsers. The good news is that if you are using transitional XHTML, you can include both attributes, just in case.

CSS Layers

Often, objects using an ID are referred to as *layers*. These terms can lead to some confusion, however, because the term *layer* was actually coined to describe a similar technology in Netscape. Although any HTML tag can be turned into a CSS layer with the addition of the id attribute, Netscape Navigator 4 introduced a <layer> tag to achieve a similar result.

The term *layers* seems to be sticking to CSS objects, however, and Netscape layers have been forgotten since recent versions of Netscape (6+) and Mozilla do not support them.

To prevent confusion in this book, I will refer specifically to *Netscape layers* and refer to CSS layers simply as *layers*.

✔ Tips

- You don't actually have to set the object up as shown in Step 1 in order to create an object. All you need to do is add a unique ID to the tag as shown in Step 2.

- You can use a <div> tag for absolutely positioned objects or a <span> tag for relatively positioned objects.

- You may notice that IDs work a lot like the name attribute to identify the object on the page. However, name is being phased out. For more details, see the sidebar "Should I Use Name or ID?"

- A layer is an independent object on the page created using CSS that can be moved on top of other objects. For more details, see the sidebar "CSS Layers."

Understanding Events

In the world of JavaScript, *events* occur when something happens in the browser window, usually initiated by the visitor. One example is when the visitor moves the mouse pointer over a link; this action generates a mouseover event.

Events can also occur when the browser does something, such as loading a new document (load) or leaving a Web page (unload).

An *event handler*—which is the event name with the word *on* at the beginning (for example, onload)—allows you to define what should happen when a particular event is detected for a particular object (**Figure 12.4**).

Table 12.3 lists some of the more common event handlers that you'll be using and what elements they can be used with. To see all these events on a single page, visit webbedenvironments.com/dhtml/event-handlers/, a page I set up to demonstrate how the event handlers work (**Figure 12.5**).

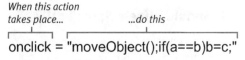

Figure 12.4 An event handler.

Figure 12.5 This Web page contains examples of all the events discussed in this chapter, so that you can see them in action.

Table 12.3

Event Handlers		
Event Handler	**When It Happens**	**Elements Affected**
onload	After an object is loaded	Documents and images
onunload	After the object is no longer loaded	Documents and images
onfocus	When an element is selected	Documents and forms
onblur	When an element is deselected	Documents and forms
onmouseover	When the mouse pointer passes over an area	Links and image map areas
onmouseout	When the mouse pointer passes out of an area	All
onclick	When an area is clicked in	All
onmousedown	While the mouse button is depressed	All
onmouseup	When the mouse button is released	All
onmousemove	As the mouse is moved	Document
onkeydown	While a keyboard key is down	Forms
onkeyup	When a keyboard key is released	Forms
onkeypress	When a keyboard key is down and immediately released	Forms
onresize	When the browser window or a frame is resized	Document
onmove*	When the browser window is moved	Document

***Not supported by IE4/5 or Netscape 6

■ Most changes made in an object's styles with the DOM should be triggered by an event handler. At times, in fact, the JavaScript *must* be triggered by an event to work. I've wasted many, many hours trying to figure out what was wrong with my JavaScript, only to find that I had simply forgotten to trigger the script from an event.

■ At first glance, onclick and onmouseup may seem to do the same thing. The click event, however, occurs only after the mouse button has been pressed and released. Both mousedown and mouseup break this action into two separate events, each of which can have a different action associated with it.

Events and the DOM

If you've used any type of scripting language in an HTML page, you've more than likely seen a DOM in action. The DOM works by targeting an element on the screen and providing the path a JavaScript function can use to address the element in response to an event triggered by an action in the browser window (**Figure 12.6**).

✔ Tips

■ Although the href acts like an onclick event handler, it isn't one, and DHTML code may not run if it's activated using href="javascript:"

■ The event handler can call JavaScript functions, or you can include JavaScript statements directly in the event handler.

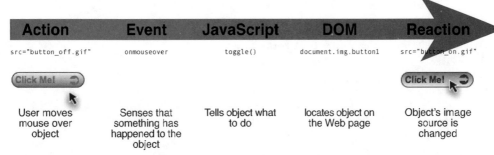

Figure 12.6 This example's process begins with the visitor's action (the mouseover) and ends with the browser's reaction (changing the graphic). In between, the browser senses the action (event), triggers a function, and uses DOM to change the image's source to a different graphic file.

Using Event Handlers

An event handler connects an action in the browser window to a JavaScript code, which in turn causes some reaction in the browser window.

Figure 12.7 Before the image is rolled over.

In this example, when the visitor rolls the mouse over (onmouseover) a button graphic (Figure 12.6), the original graphic is replaced by an activated button graphic (**Figures 12.7** and **12.8**).

Figure 12.8 After the image is rolled over.

To use an event handler:

1. `<a href="#"`

Start the tag to which you want to add an event handler. This typically will either be a link tag (`<a>`) or one of the form tags (**Code 12.3**).

2. `onmouseover=`

In the tag you started in Step 1, type a relevant event handler from Table 12.3, followed by an equal sign (=).

Code 12.3 When the visitor moves the mouse over the area of the link containing the image (b_off.gif), that image changes its source to a different graphic (b_on.gif).

```
<!DOCTYPE html PUBLIC "-//W3C//DTD XHTML 1.0 Strict//EN" "http://www.w3.org/TR/xhtml1/DTD/
→ xhtml1-strict.dtd">
<html xmlns="http://www.w3.org/1999/xhtml">
<head>
<meta http-equiv="Content-Type" content="text/html; charset=utf-8" />
<title>CSS, DHTML &amp; Ajax | Using Event Handlers</title>
</head>
<body>
<p>
    <a href="#"onmouseover="document.images.button01.src='b_on.png';"
    onmouseout="document.images.button01.src='b_off.png';">
    <img id="button01" src="b_off.png" alt="Alice" />
    </a>
</p>
</body></html>
```

3. `"document.images.button01.src=`
`→ 'b_on.png';"`

Type an opening quote ("), the JavaScript you want executed when the event occurs, and a close quote (").

The JavaScript can be anything you want, including function calls. If you want to run multiple lines of JavaScript off a single event handler, separate the statements with a semicolon (;), but do *not* use a hard return.

4. `onmouseout="document.images.`
`→ button01.src='b_off.png';"`

Add as many event handlers as you want to the HTML tag by repeating Steps 2 and 3.

5. `>`

Type a closing chevron (>) to close the tag you started in Step 1.

6. `<img src="button_off.png"`
`→ _id="button1" />`

Add an image, text, or other HTML content that you want to have that visually tells the visitor where to act in order to trigger the event.

7. `</a>`

Type the closing tag for the tag you started in Step 1.

✔ Tips

■ If you want a single event to perform multiple tasks, add each action inside the quotes, separating actions with a semicolon (;):

`onclick="action1; action2; action3;"`

■ You can not only use event handlers to run JavaScript functions, but also include JavaScript statements directly inside the quotes.

Getting an Element

The W3C's DOM, or standard DOM, lets you write scripts that can access any element on the screen. This allows you to make changes to any CSS property for an element, so you can control the position and visibility on the screen, as well as appearance. Any changes made in these properties are immediately reflected on the page.

So any changes made in the font, text, list, mouse, color, background, border, margin, position, or visibility of an object are discernible immediately.

Getting an element by its ID

Almost every time you access the DOM, it will be by using the getElementById() function, the general syntax for which is shown in **Figure 12.9**. This function, when given a string value for an ID attribute value, will locate that element, if it exists.

In this example (**Figure 12.10** and **Figure 12.11**), the getElementById() function is used to identify an element that is then moved slightly across the page by changing its top and left CSS properties.

To get an Element by its ID:

1. `function moveObject (objectID,`
   `→ newTop, newLeft) {…}`

   Add a function to your script (**Code 12.4**). In this example, we will be creating a simple script called moveObject() that will take the ID of an object (objectID) and move it to a new position on the screen (newTop and newLeft).

2. `var object =`

   Create a variable called object to store the address for the object.

Variable name   *Top level*   *ID name*

object = document.getElementByID(elementID)

Figure 12.9 The general syntax for using the getElementById() function, your guide for attaching JavaScript to elements on your Web page.

Figure 12.10 When the page first loads, the object is in one position until the visitor clicks it.

Figure 12.11 The object is moved from its original position, across the screen in response to the function that addresses the object using the getElementById() function.

Code 12.4 Using the getElementByID() function, you can find and manipulate the properties of any element that has an ID assigned to it on the page.

```
<!DOCTYPE html PUBLIC "-//W3C//DTD XHTML 1.0
→ Strict//EN" "http://www.w3.org/TR/xhtml1/
→ DTD/xhtml1-strict.dtd">
<html xmlns="http://www.w3.org/1999/xhtml">
<head>
<meta http-equiv="Content-Type"
→ content="text/html; charset=utf-8" />
<title>CSS, DHTML &amp; Ajax | Getting an
→ Element | By ID</title>
<script type="text/javascript">
function moveObject (objectID, newTop,
→ newLeft) {
    var object =
    → document.getElementById(objectID);
    object.style.top = newTop + 'px';
    object.style.left = newLeft + 'px';
}
</script>
<style type="text/css" media="screen">
body {
    font: 1em Georgia, "Times New Roman",
    → times, serif;
    color: #000;
    background-color: #ccc;
    margin: 8px; }
#object1 {
    padding: 4px;
    background-color: #fff;
    border: 2px solid #f00;
    position: absolute;
    z-index: 3;
    top: 100px;
    left: 150px;
    width: 210px; }
</style>
</head>
<body>
<div id="object1"
onclick="moveObject('object1', 50, 300);">
    <img src="alice04.gif" alt="alice"
    → height="298" width="200" />
    <h1>Click Me!</h1>
</div>
</body></html>
```

3. document.

Begin by identifying the object's location. If you're addressing an object on the same page, simply use document followed by a period. If you're addressing an object in a different window, begin with window, and then type the window's name and include a period after it. If you're addressing an object in a different frame, use top. or parent., followed by the frame's name and a period.

4. getElementById(objectID);

Add getElementById and then, in parentheses, add the ID of the object. The ID can either be the exact object ID in quotes ('object1') or a string variable that is storing the object ID name, as in this example.

If there is no element with that ID, then this function returns a value of null.

5. object.style.top = newTop + 'px';

To change an attribute of the object, use the object variable with a period after it and then the name of the attribute to be changed. If it's a CSS attribute (for example, top), you'll also need to include style. before the attribute name.

6. onclick="moveObject('object1',
→ 50, 300)"

In your HTML, create the object by giving an HTML tag the appropriate ID attribute and an event handler to trigger the function from Step 1.

✔ Tip

■ Notice that to assign a value to top or left, we had to add + 'px' to the code when assigning the values. To be DOM compliant, all style values must be assigned as strings because CSS requires units be specified with lengths. This is an easy way to turn the number into a string. If your DHTML code doesn't seem to be working, check to make sure that you translated all numeric values into strings.

Getting an element's attribute's value by its tag name

Although not as directly useful as the getElementById() method, the getElementsByTagName() method (**Figure 12.12**), when coupled with the getAttribute()method, lets you find the value of any attribute in any tag on the page without having to know its ID.

In this example (**Figure 12.13**), we will be using getElementsByTagName() and getAttribute() methods to find the ID values of <div> tags on the page, which is extremely useful if you are generating pages dynamically.

To get an element's attribute's value by its tag name:

1. `function findAttributeValue`
   → `(tagName, attributeName) {...}`

   Add a function to your script (**Code 12.5**). In this example, we will be creating a simple script called findAttributeValue() that will take a tag name and an attribute name and find the value of that attribute in that tag.

2. `var object =`

   Create a variable called object to store the array of objects for that particular element. There will be one object for every instance of the tag in the document, but remember, arrays always start with 0, so if there are six instances of the tag on the page, the array will run from 0 to 5.

3. `document.`

   Begin by identifying the object's location. If you're addressing an object on the same page, simply use document followed by a period. If you're addressing an object in a different window, start with window.,

Figure 12.12 The general syntax for using the getElementsByTagName() function.

Figure 12.13 When the visitor clicks the image, the ID for that object is displayed in an alert.

Code 12.5 Using the getElementsByTagName() function, you can find the value of any property of any tag on the page, including the IDs.

```
<!DOCTYPE html PUBLIC "-//W3C//DTD XHTML 1.0
→ Strict//EN" "http://www.w3.org/TR/xhtml1/
→ DTD/xhtml1-strict.dtd">
<html xmlns="http://www.w3.org/1999/xhtml">
<head>
<meta http-equiv="Content-Type"
→ content="text/html; charset=utf-8" />
<title>CSS, DHTML &amp; Ajax | Getting an
→ Element | By Tag Name</title>
<script type="text/javascript">
function findAttributeValue(tagName,
→ attributeName) {
    var object =
    → document.getElementsByTagName(tagName);
    for (var i = 0; i < object.length; i++) {
    alert(object[i].getAttribute
    → (attributeName));
}
}
</script>
<style type="text/css" media="screen">
body {
    font: 1em Georgia, "Times New Roman",
    → times, serif;
    color: #000;
    background-color: #ccc;
    margin: 8px; }
#object1 {
    padding: 4px;
    background-color: #fff;
    border: 2px solid #f00;
    position: absolute;
    z-index: 3;
    top: 100px;
    left: 150px;
    width: 210px; }
</style>
</head>
<body>
<div id="object1" onclick=
→ "findAttributeValue('div', 'id');">
    <img src="alice04.gif" alt="alice"
    → height="298" width="200" />
    <h1>Click Me!</h1>
</div>
</body></html>
```

followed by the window's name and a period after it. If you're addressing an object in a different frame, use top. or parent., followed by the frame's name and a period.

4. getElementsByTagName(tagName);

Add **getElementsByTagName** and the tag name in parentheses. This can either be the exact tab name in quotes ('div') or a string variable that is storing the tag name, as in this example.

If there are no tags with that tag name on the page, then this function returns a value of null.

5. for (var i = 0; i < object.length;
→ i++) {…}

Add a loop that starts at 0 and will loop for the same number of instances as there are of the tag in question (object.length). This allows you to look at each tag individually.

6. object[i].getAttribute(attributeName);

In the loop, now reference the object array using the i variable along with the **getAttributes()** function, feeding it the name of the attribute you are looking for.

In this example, each time an instance of the tag is found, an alert will appear, showing the value of the attribute for that instance. So, the more instances of the tag, the more alerts that will pop-up.

7. onclick="findAttributeValue
→ ('div', 'id');"

In your HTML, create the object by giving an HTML tag the appropriate ID attribute and an event handler to trigger the function from Step 1. Although the ID is not required here, it helps to see how the code works.

Passing Events to a Function

All events that take place in the browser window generate certain information about what occurred, where it occurred, and how it occurred. You can pass this information directly to a JavaScript function so that it can access the object without having to use the getElementByID method.

As seems true of all things in Web design, Internet Explorer has a different method for implementing event passing compared to all other browsers (see the sidebar "Alert! Results May Vary.") The good news is that the standard method and Internet Explorer method are easy to combine.

In this example (**Figure 2.14**), I've set up a simple function that registers the x-axis position where the visitor clicks the mouse pointer within object1. This information is passed to the function when the event occurs.

Figure 12.14 Clicking the page displays an alert showing the x-position where the visitor clicked the mouse pointer.

To pass an event to a JavaScript function:

1. `function passItOn() {…}`

In the variables being passed to the function, add an evt variable to record the event (**Code 12.6**).

2. `var evt = (evt) ? evt :`
`→ ((window.event) ? window.event :`
`→ null);`

Internet Explorer uses a slightly different syntax for tracking events. This line of code will bring the Internet Explorer version in line with the W3C standard for the evt variable. It is a conditional statement that determines whether the browser is using the evt or window.event method and assigns the correct value to the JavaScript variable evt, which can then be used in any browser to represent the event object.

Alert! Results May Vary

If you're using an alert to display the value of the object variable (for example, alert (object)), you'll see different values depending on which browser you're using. For example, Internet Explorer for Windows will actually show [object]. Rather than showing you the actual value, many browsers will display a variable that is then used to access the object in question. Don't worry, though: This variable contains the same information.

Code 12.6 The event variable passes information about the triggering event to the function, including where the mouse was when it was clicked.

```
<!DOCTYPE html PUBLIC "-//W3C//DTD XHTML 1.0
→ Strict//EN" "http://www.w3.org/TR/xhtml1/
→ DTD/xhtml1-strict.dtd">
<html xmlns="http://www.w3.org/1999/xhtml">
<head>
<meta http-equiv="Content-Type"
→ content="text/html; charset=utf-8" />
<title>CSS, DHTML &amp; Ajax | Passing
→ Events to a Function</title>
<script type="text/javascript">
function passItOn(evt) {
    evt = (evt) ? evt : ((window.event) ?
    → window.event : null);
    alert(evt.clientX);
}
</script>
<style type="text/css" media="screen">
body {
    font: 1em Georgia, "Times New Roman",
    → times, serif;
    color: #000;
    background-color: #ccc;
    margin: 8px; }
#object1 {
    padding: 4px;
    background-color: #fff;
    border: 2px solid #f00;
    position: absolute;
    z-index: 3;
    top: 100px;
    left: 150px;
    width: 210px; }
</style>
</head>
<body>
<div id="object1"
→ onclick="passItOn(event);">
    <img src="alice04.gif" alt="alice"
    → height="298" width="200" />
    <h1>Click Me!</h1>
</div>
</body></html>
```

3. `alert(evt.clientX);`

You can now use the evt variable to access information about the event. In this example, we're accessing the x-position where the visitor clicked the mouse during the event.

4. `onclick="passItOn(event);"`

Add one or more event handlers to an object to trigger the function. To include information about the triggering event, pass the variable **event** to the function. In this example, the event will fire when the user clicks the image.

✔ Tip

■ Although it may be tempting simply to use event passing in all circumstances to create DHTML, event passing has some shortcomings. For example, Internet Explorer doesn't always respond to events that happen in child elements of the tag containing the event handler. In addition, the object that is being changed is most often not the same object as the one originating the event. I primarily use the getElementByID method for the code in this book, except when event passing offers a particular advantage.

Binding Events to Objects

Event handlers are most often applied directly to the tag of the object when you want to detect the event. However, another useful technique is to bind an event to one or more objects. You can then use the evt variable to access the object without having to add JavaScript code directly in the HTML and make changes to the object without first having to know its ID.

In this example (**Figure 12.15**), one event has been bound to the entire page to display an alert message; the other is tied only to object1 and moves that object to wherever the visitor clicks.

To add a global event handler to a Web page:

1. `function initPage() {…}`

   Add the function initPage() to your JavaScript. This function prepares the global event handlers to be used, and then sets functions to be executed if those events are triggered (**Code 12.7**). Notice that when you call the function:

   `document.onclick = errorOn;`

   you don't include the parentheses with the function call. You can use any event handler listed in "Understanding Events" earlier in this chapter to set an event for any node in the document.

2. `function errorOn(evt) {…}`

   `function moveTo() {…}`

   Add to your JavaScript the functions that will be run when the events in the function from Step 1 are met.

Figure 12.15 Clicking the image causes it to move. Clicking anywhere on the window displays an alert, telling visitors not to click there.

Code 12.7 The function errorOn() is bound to the document by an onclick event handler, and the function moveTo() is bound only to object1 by an onclick event handler.

```
<!DOCTYPE html PUBLIC "-//W3C//DTD XHTML 1.0
→ Strict//EN" "http://www.w3.org/TR/xhtml1/
→ DTD/xhtml1-strict.dtd">
<html xmlns="http://www.w3.org/1999/xhtml">
<head>
<meta http-equiv="Content-Type"
→ content="text/html; charset=utf-8" />
<title>CSS, DHTML &amp; Ajax | Binding
→ Events to an Object</title>
<script type="text/javascript">
function initPage() {
    document.getElementById('object1').
    → onclick = moveObject;
    document.onclick = errorOn;
}
function errorOn(evt) {
    alert ('Please do not click here again!')
}
function moveObject (evt) {
    var evt = (evt) ? evt : ((window.event)
→ ? event : null);
    var object =
    → document.getElementById(this.id);
    var moveLeft=evt.clientX;
    var moveTop=evt.clientY;
    object.style.left = moveLeft + 'px';
    object.style.top = moveTop + 'px';
}
</script>
```

code continues on next page

Code 12.7 *continued*

```
<style type="text/css" media="screen">
body {
     font: 1em Georgia, "Times New Roman",
     → times, serif;
     color: #000;
     background-color: #ccc;
     margin: 8px; }
#object1 {
     padding: 4px;
     background-color: #fff;
     border: 2px solid #f00;
     position: absolute;
     z-index: 3;
     top: 100px;
     left: 150px;
     width: 210px; }
</style>
</head>
<body onload="initPage();" >
<div id="object1">
     <img src="alice04.gif" alt="alice"
     → height="298" width="200" />
     <h1>Click Me!</h1>
</div>
</body></html>
```

In this example, the functions errorOn() and moveObject() are both triggered when the onclick events are triggered in the browser window or on object1. For the moveObject() function, we're also passing the evt variable to it (see the previous section, "Passing Events to a Function"), allowing us to learn about the triggering event.

To address the event we want to change, we can then use

```
var object =
→ document.getElementById(this.id);
```

where this.id tells the function to use the ID of the triggering event. This will only work if the event has been bound to the object.

3. onload="initPage()"

Add an event handler in the <body> tag to trigger the function you created in Step 1, which will initialize the bound events for the page. If this step is left out, nothing will happen.

✔ Tip

- Notice that clicking the image will not only move the image, but also show the alert, because both events are called into play. However, clicking on any empty area of the screen will only trigger the errorOn() function.

Using Feature Sensing

The best way to determine whether the browser that is running your script has what it takes to do the job is to ask it. Finding out whether the browser has the feature(s) you need to use is a lot simpler than it sounds and requires only one additional line of code.

In most cases, feature sensing is a better alternative than browser sensing (see "Detecting the Browser's Name" in Chapter 13). If the current version of a browser cannot run your script, who's to say that another, more powerful version of the browser won't be released in the future that can run it? Feature sensing will let any able browser that can run the code run it.

In this example (**Figures 12.16** and **12.17**), I'm checking to see if the browser uses the `innerHeight` or `clientHeight` methods to find the height of the viewport in the browser window.

To sense whether a JavaScript feature is available:

1. `if (window.innerHeight) {…}`

    Within a `<script>` container, set up a conditional statement, as shown in **Code 12.8**. Within the parentheses of the `if` statement, place the JavaScript feature you need to use. In this example, you're checking to see whether the browser can handle the image object.

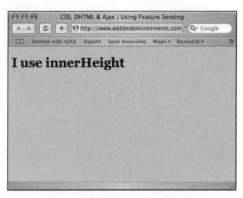

Figure 12.16 This browser, Safari uses the `innerHeight` method, as do all of the Mozilla-based browsers (Firefox, Netscape, and Camino).

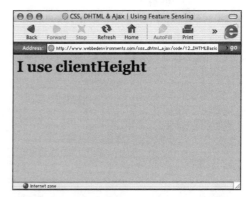

Figure 12.17 Internet Explorer uses the `clientHeight` method instead of `innerHeight`.

2. `document.writeln('<h1>I use`
`→ innerHeight</h1>');`

Within {} brackets, type the JavaScript code you want to execute if this feature is available on the browser. Keep in mind that to validate in XHTML, JavaScript code that writes out HTML code must be within HTML comments:

`<!--…//-->`

3. `else if (document.body.clientHeight)`
`→ { document.writeln('<h1>I use`
`→ clientHeight</h1>'); }`

You can include an `else` statement, specifying the code to be run, in the event that the JavaScript feature for which you're testing is not available.

Code 12.8 This code checks to see whether the `innerHeight` or `clientHeight` methods are used.

```
<!DOCTYPE html PUBLIC "-//W3C//DTD XHTML 1.0 Strict//EN" "http://www.w3.org/TR/xhtml1/DTD/
→ xhtml1-strict.dtd">
<html xmlns="http://www.w3.org/1999/xhtml">
<head>
<meta http-equiv="Content-Type" content="text/html; charset=utf-8" />
<title>CSS, DHTML &amp; Ajax | Using Feature Sensing</title>
<style type="text/css" media="screen">
body {
    font: 1em Georgia, "Times New Roman", times, serif;
    color: #000;
    background-color: #ccc;
    margin: 8px; }
</style>
</head>
<body>
<script type="text/javascript">
<!--
if (window.innerHeight) {
    document.writeln('<h1>I use innerHeight</h1>');
}
else if (document.body.clientHeight) {
    document.writeln('<h1>I use clientHeight</h1>');
}
else { return;}
// -->
</script>
</body></html>
```

LEARNING ABOUT THE ENVIRONMENT

13

"To change your world, you must first know yourself." I don't know whether this is an ancient proverb or whether I simply made it up, but it definitely applies to DHTML. Many of the functions you will be creating to add interactivity to your Web page rely on knowing where something is, how big it is, and what it is doing. So to change your Web page, the Web page must first know itself.

This chapter discusses the details of the environment in which an object is being displayed, such as the screen size and browser-window size. The two chapters after this will show you how to find out information about the object itself (Chapter 14) and events triggered by an object (Chapter 15).

Detecting the Operating System

The application-version object `navigator.platform` (**Figure 13.1**) identifies the operating system of the browser used to view the site, although it's embedded in a string of other information (**Figures 13.2 and 13.3**). This information can be very useful, especially if you need to overcome font-size inconsistencies, or other OS-related incompatibilities.

To detect the operating system being used:

1. `var isMac = 0;`

   Set up four variables (`isMac`, `isWin`, `isOtherOS`, `isUndetected`) in your JavaScript to record which OS the browser is using. Each of these variables is initially set to 0 (false) and will be reassigned to 1 (true) if the designated operating system is detected (**Code 13.1**).

2. `var agent = navigator.platform.`
   `→ toLowerCase();`

   Add the variable `agent`, which records the value of the `navigator.platform` object (the name of the operating system) and converts it to lowercase.

3. `if (agent.indexOf('mac') != -1)`
   `→ isMac = 1;`

   To reassign the variables from Step 1, check the name of the OS being used. This code looks for the word `mac` in the `agent string`, and changes `isMac` to 1 if it finds it.

Ask the browser...   ...for its OS

navigator.platform

Figure 13.1 The general syntax for the platform object.

Figure 13.2 The code is being run in Windows.

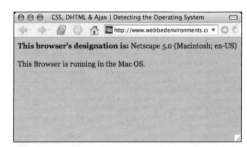

Figure 13.3 The same code is being run on a Mac.

Code 13.1 This code first writes the complete *appName* and *appVersion* on the page. It then uses that information to determine the operating system so that it can display the correct message.

```
<!DOCTYPE html PUBLIC "-//W3C//DTD XHTML 1.0
→ Strict//EN" "http://www.w3.org/TR/xhtml1/
→ DTD/xhtml1-strict.dtd">
<html xmlns="http://www.w3.org/1999/xhtml">
<head>
<meta http-equiv="Content-Type"
→ content="text/html; charset=UTF-8" />
<title>CSS, DHTML &amp; Ajax | Detecting the
→ Operating System</title>
</head>
<head>
</head>
<body onload="detectOS()">
<script type="text/javascript">
<!--
var isMac = 0;
var isWin = 0;
var isOtherOS = 0;
var isUndetected = 0;

var agent = navigator.platform.toLowerCase();
if (agent.indexOf('mac') != -1) isMac = 1;
else if (agent.indexOf('win') != -1) isWin = 1;
else if (
    agent.indexOf('unix') != -1 ||
    agent.indexOf('sunos') != -1 ||
    agent.indexOf('bsd') != -1 ||
    agent.indexOf('x11') != -1 ||
    agent.indexOf('linux') != -1) isOtherOS
    → = 1;
else ( isUndetected = 1 )

document.write('<b>This browser\'s
→ designation is:</b> ');
document.write(navigator.platform + '<br />');

if (isMac) { document.write('This Browser
→ is running in the Mac OS.'); }
else if (isWin) { document.write('This
→ Browser is running in the Microsoft
→ Windows OS.'); }
else if (isOtherOS) {
document.write('RESISTANCE IS FUTILE…YOU
→ WILL BE ASSIMULATED'); }
else { document.write('Sorry, I\'m not sure
→ what OS you are using.'); }
//-->
</script>
</body></html>
```

4. `else if (agent.indexOf('win') != -1)` `→ isWin = 1;`

To detect whether Windows is being used, the code simply looks for the word *win* in the *agent* string. If it's there, it sets *isWin* to 1.

5. `else if (…) isOtherOS = 1;`

To detect a specific operating system besides Macintosh and Windows, all you need to know is how the OS identifies itself in the *platform* object and then look for that string using the *indexOf* method.

6. `else ( isUndetected = 1 )`

Finally, you need to add a catch-all, in case some unknown (possibly future) operating system is being used.

7. `if (isMac) {…}`

Now you can use the variables you set up in Steps 1 and 2 for the OS that is being used. In this example, I simply have a message written out on the screen to tell viewers which OS they are using.

Detecting the Browser's Name

Although feature sensing is better for determining what a browser can and cannot do (see "Using Feature Sensing" in Chapter 12), sometimes you need to be able to tell your code what to do based on the type and version of browser in which the Web page is being viewed.

Initially, this information comes in a big chunk that lists in the navigator.userAgent object all the browsers and versions that the current browser is compatible with (**Figure 13.4**). Although having the exact name and version of the browser is useful, that information can be a bit bulky when it comes time to code. You can use this chunk to get the data you require and store it in variables for later use (**Figures 13.5** and **13.6**).

To determine the browser type and version:

1. var agent = navigator.userAgent.
   → toLowerCase();

   Add the variable agent that records the value of the navigator.userAgent object (the full list of compatible browsers) and converts it to lowercase (**Code 13.2**).

2. var isMoz = (agent.indexOf('mozilla')
   → != -1);

   Set up four variables (isMoz, isIE, isSafari, isOpera) that will be set to true if the browser designation shows up in the agent variable string.

   Keep in mind that a browser may show up as being compatible with other browsers as well. For example, Safari shows itself as being compatible with both Safari and Mozilla.

3. if (isMoz || isIE || isSafari ||
   → isOpera) {…}

   Check to see if a compatible browser was identified.

Ask the browser...   *...for its name(s)*

navigator.userAgent

Figure 13.4 The general syntax for the userAgent object.

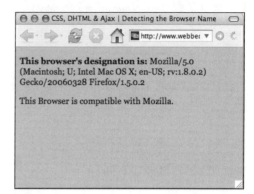

Figure 13.5 The code is being run in Firefox.

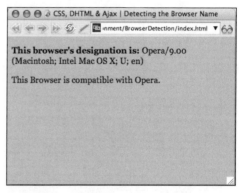

Figure 13.6 The code is being run in Opera.

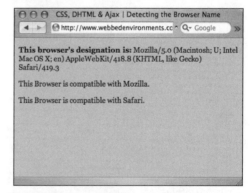

Figure 13.7 The code being run in Safari.

Code 13.2 This code first writes the complete userAgent on the page. It then uses that information to determine the browser name so that it can display the correct message(s).

```
<!DOCTYPE html PUBLIC "-//W3C//DTD XHTML 1.0
→ Strict//EN" "http://www.w3.org/TR/xhtml1/
→ DTD/xhtml1-strict.dtd">
<html xmlns="http://www.w3.org/1999/xhtml">
<head>
<meta http-equiv="Content-Type"
→ content="text/html; charset=UTF-8" />
<title>CSS, DHTML &amp; Ajax | Detecting
→ the Browser Name</title>
</head>
<body>
<script type="text/javascript">
<!--
var agent = navigator.userAgent.toLowerCase();

var isMoz = (agent.indexOf('mozilla') != -1);
var isIE = (agent.indexOf('msie') != -1);
var isSafari = (agent.indexOf('safari') != -1);
var isOpera = (agent.indexOf('opera') != -1);

document.write('<p><b>This browser\'s
→ designation is:</b> ');
document.write(navigator.userAgent + '</p>');

if (isMoz || isIE || isSafari || isOpera) {
    if (isMoz) { document.write('<p>This
    → Browser is compatible with
    → Mozilla.</p>'); }
    if (isIE) { document.write('<p>This
    → Browser is compatible with Internet
    → Explorer.</p>'); }
    if (isSafari) { document.write('<p>This
    → Browser is compatible with
    → Safari.</p>'); }
    if (isOpera) { document.write('<p>This
    → Browser is compatible with
    → Opera.</p>'); }

}
else document.write('<p>Sorry, I don\'t
→ recognize this browser.</p> ');
//-->
</script>
</body></html>
```

4. `if (isMoz) {…}`

   If a compatible browser was found, you can then add code specifically for that browser. In this case, I simply displayed a message stating which browser was found to be compatible.

5. `else document.write('<p>Sorry,`
   `→ I don\'t recognize this`
   `→ browser.</p> ');`

   If no compatible browser was found, then you can also add code to take care of that situation.

✔ Tips

- Some browsers, such as Safari, will show up as being compatible with other browsers (**Figure 13.7**), so you may need to take that into account when coding.

- There are, of course, more than four browsers. Many Web designers used to use browser detection to tailor their work for one browser over others, but this technique is quickly going out of use (see the sidebar "Feature Sensing or Browser Sensing?").

Feature Sensing or Browser Sensing?

Browser sensing, also known as browser detection, is often used instead of feature sensing to determine whether a DHTML function should be run in a particular browser. Using browser sensing, however, means that you have to know exactly what code will or will not run in the browsers you are including or excluding.

Using browser sensing to determine DHTML compatibility can cause problems, especially when newer browser versions either add new abilities or fix bugs that previously prevented code from working. I recommend using feature sensing if at all possible.

Finding the Page's Location and Title

The URL (Uniform Resource Locator) of a Web page is its unique address on the Web. The title is the designation you give that page between the <title> tags in the head of your document. You can easily display these two useful bits of information on the originating Web page using self.location and document.title objects (**Figures 13.8** and **13.9**).

In this example (**Figure 13.10**), the title for the page is used as the text for a hyperlink to the page.

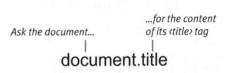

Figure 13.8 The general syntax for the location object.

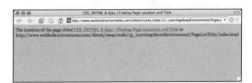

Figure 13.9 The general syntax for the title object.

Figure 13.10 The linked title and page URL are displayed.

URI or URL?

Notice that I call the variable that stores the page's location pageURI instead of pageURL. "URL" stands for Uniform Resource Locator, whereas "URI" stands for Uniform Resource Identifier. What's the difference? Not much, really, but for some reason the World Wide Web Consortium decided that the more commonly used URL was too specific a term and decided to switch to URI instead.

Does this really change your life? No.

Should you start using URI instead of URL when referring to a Web page's address? Only if you want to confuse your friends and impress your enemies.

Code 13.3 The variables pageTitle and pageURI are defined and then displayed on the page. The URI is also used to create a link back to this page when the user clicks the title.

```
<!DOCTYPE html PUBLIC "-//W3C//DTD XHTML 1.0
→ Strict//EN" "http://www.w3.org/TR/xhtml1/
→ DTD/xhtml1-strict.dtd">
<html xmlns="http://www.w3.org/1999/xhtml">
<head>
<meta http-equiv="Content-Type"
→ content="text/html; charset=utf-8" />
<title>CSS, DHTML &amp; Ajax | Finding Page
→ Location and Title</title>
<style type="text/css" media="screen">
body {
        font: 1em Georgia, "Times New Roman",
        → times, serif;
        color: #000;
        background-color: #ccc;
        margin: 8px;
}
</style>
</head>
<body>
<script type="text/javascript">
<!--
var pageURI = self.location;

var pageTitle = document.title;

document.writeln('The location of the page
→ titled <i><a href="' + pageURI + '">' +
→ pageTitle + '</a></i> is: <br>');
document.writeln(pageURI);
// -->
</script>
</body>
</html>
```

To find the page's location and title:

1. var pageURI = self.location;

Add the variable pageURI to your JavaScript, and assign to it the value self.location. This value is the address of your Web page (**Code 13.3**).

2. var pageTitle = document.title;

Add the variable pageTitle to your JavaScript, and assign to it the value document.title. This value is the title of your document—that is, whatever you place between the <title> and </title> tags on the page.

You can now use these variables for a variety of purposes. The simplest is to write them out on the page, as Code 13.3 does. In addition, I used the page's location to set up the title as a link back to this page.

✔ Tips

■ When creating a printer-friendly version of the page, adding the URL for the original link at the bottom of the page is a great way of ensuring that the reader can find the original source.

■ For more information about the difference between a URI and a URL, check out the sidebar "URI or URL?"

Determining the Number of Colors (Bit Depth)

Once upon a time, color was one of the biggest nightmares a Web designer could face. Not all computers are created equal, especially when it comes to color. On your high-end professional machine, you design a brilliant Web page with bold colors, deep drop shadows, anti-aliased text, and 3D buttons. But on the machine across the hall, it looks like a grainy color photo that's been left out in the sun too long (**Figure 13.11** and **13.12**).

The problem was that some computers displayed millions of colors, while others displayed only a few thousand or *(gasp)* a few hundred or less. Although few of these older machines are still in use, there's an increasing number of portable devices such as PDAs and mobile phones that do have color restrictions. So knowing the number of colors the person viewing your site (**Figure 13.13**) can actually see might be useful (**Figures 13.14** and **13.15**).

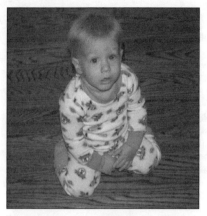

Figure 13.11 An image in all its 32-bit glory.

Figure 13.12 The same image in ho-hum 8-bit grayscale. Notice how much rougher the transitions are between areas of color than in the 32-bit version above.

Ask the screen...   ...for the number
                            of available colors

screen.colorDepth

Figure 13.13 The general syntax for the colorDepth object.

Table 13.1

Pixel-Depth Values	
COLOR-BIT DEPTH	NUMBER OF COLORS
4	16
8	256
16	65,536
32	16.7 million

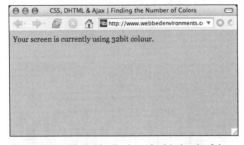

Figure 13.14 The code displays the bit depth of the monitor—in this case, 32-bit.

Figure 13.15 The code displays the bit depth of the monitor—in this case, 8-bit.

To detect the number of colors:

◆ `screen.colorDepth`

The number of colors that the visitor's screen can currently display is in the screen's color-depth object (**Code 13.4**). Using this code will return a color-bit depth value as shown in **Table 13.1**.

Code 13.4 The function numColors() returns one of the values in Table 13.1, depending on the number of colors available on the computer that is being used.

```
<!DOCTYPE html PUBLIC "-//W3C//DTD XHTML 1.0
→ Strict//EN" "http://www.w3.org/TR/xhtml1/
→ DTD/xhtml1-strict.dtd">
<html xmlns="http://www.w3.org/1999/xhtml">
<head>
<meta http-equiv="Content-Type"
→ content="text/html; charset=utf-8" />
<title>CSS, DHTML &amp; Ajax | Finding the
→ Number of Colors</title>
<style type="text/css" media="screen">
body {
     font: 1em Georgia, "Times New Roman",
     → times, serif;
     color: #000;
     background-color: #ccc;
     margin: 8px;
}
</style>
     </head>

     <body>
<script language="JavaScript"
→ type="text/javascript">
function numColors() {
     return (screen.colorDepth);
}
document.write('Your screen is currently
→ using ' + numColors() + 'bit color.');
</script>
     </body>

</html>
```

Determining the Screen Dimensions

The screen—that glowing, slightly rounded panel you stare at all day—is where all the windows that make up your Web site reside. You can try making Web sites with Morse code or punch cards, but trust me on this one: The computer monitor is currently the best medium for displaying Web sites.

One of the frustrations of Web design, however, is never knowing the size of the area in which your design will be placed or how much space is actually available. To find out how much space you're working with, you can use the screen.width and screen.height objects (**Figure 13.16**) to find the total dimensions of the screen, and the screen.availWidth, and screen.availHeight (**Figure 13.17**) objects to find the actual available space on the screen, once menus and other interface elements are taken into account (**Figures 13.18** and **13.19**).

So why don't you just ask the screen how big it is (**Figure 13.20**)?

Ask the screen...   ...for the width/height

screen.width

Figure 13.16 The general syntax for the width and height objects.

Ask the screen...   ...for the available width/height

screen.availWidth

Figure 13.17 The general syntax for the availWidth and availHeight objects.

Figure 13.18 The live area of the Windows screen includes everything but the bottom menu bar. However, this bar may appear on any side of the screen at the user's discretion.

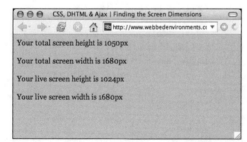

Figure 13.20 The code displays both the total and live dimensions of the screen for my computer.

Figure 13.19 The live area of the Mac OS X screen is everywhere but the top menu bar and approximately 6 pixels on the left and right sides. The Mac OS always displays a menu bar at the top of the screen.

Code 13.5 This code determines both the total and the live dimensions of the entire screen and assigns these values to variables, which it then uses to write the values in the browser window.

```
<!DOCTYPE html PUBLIC "-//W3C//DTD XHTML 1.0
→ Strict//EN" "http://www.w3.org/TR/xhtml1/
→ DTD/xhtml1-strict.dtd">
<html xmlns="http://www.w3.org/1999/xhtml">
<head>
<meta http-equiv="Content-Type"
→ content="text/html; charset=utf-8" />
<title>CSS, DHTML &amp; Ajax | Finding the
→ Screen Dimensions</title>
<style type="text/css" media="screen">
body {
    font: 1em Georgia, "Times New Roman",
    → times, serif;
    color: #000;
    background-color: #ccc;
    margin: 8px;
}
</style>
</head>
<body onresize="self.location.reload()">
<script type="text/javascript">
<!--
var screenHeight = screen.height;
var screenWidth = screen.width;

var liveScreenHeight = screen.availHeight;
var liveScreenWidth = screen.availWidth;

document.writeln('Your total screen height
→ is ' + screenHeight + 'px <br><br>');
document.writeln('Your total screen width
→ is ' + screenWidth + 'px <br><br>');
document.writeln('Your live screen height
→ is ' + liveScreenHeight + 'px <br><br>');
document.writeln('Your live screen width
→ is ' + liveScreenWidth + 'px <br><br>');
// -->
</script>
</body>
</html>
```

To find the screen's dimensions:

1. `screen.height;`

   Add the variables `screenHeight` and `screenWidth` to your JavaScript, and assign to them the values `screen.height` and `screen.width`, respectively. These variables will now record the *total* height and width of the screen, in pixels (**Code 13.5**).

2. `screen.availHeight;`

   Add the variables `liveScreenHeight` and `liveScreenWidth` to your JavaScript, and assign to them the values `screen.availHeight` and `screen.availWidth`, respectively.

   These variables will now record the *live* (available) height and width of the screen, in pixels. This differs from the total, in that it does not include any menu bars added by the OS—only the area in which windows can be displayed.

Determining the Browser Window's Dimensions

The browser window's current width and height can be determined. (Note: Internet Explorer does not support this JavaScript code.) This information is the total width and height of the browser window, including all the controls around the display area, and can be accessed using the `outerHeight` and `outerWidth` objects (**Figure 13.21**).

In this example (**Figure 13.22**), the browser windows dimensions are displayed when the page loads. Resizing the window and reloading the page will show the new dimensions (**Figure 13.23**).

To find the browser window's dimensions:

1. `window.outerHeight`

   Create a function that returns the value of the outer height of the window. This value is in pixels (**Code 13.6**).

2. `window.outerWidth`

   Create a function that returns the value of the outer width of the browser window. This value is in pixels.

✔ Tip

■ The live area of the browser window can be determined in both Internet Explorer as well as other browsers (see the following section, "Determining the Page's Visible Dimensions").

Ask the browser window...   ...for its width/height

window.outerWidth

Figure 13.21 The general syntax for the `outerWidth` and `outerHeight` objects.

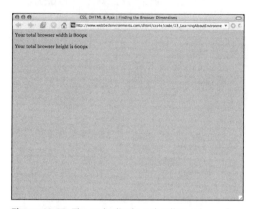

Figure 13.22 The code displays the dimensions of the browser window.

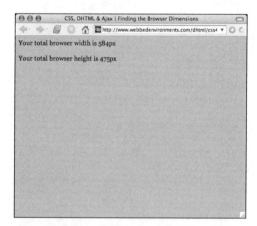

Figure 13.23 When the page is resized, the values will change.

Code 13.6 The functions findBrowserHeight() and findBrowserWidth() return the dimensions of the browser window in pixels. Another feature I added to this code is that when the page is resized, the values are recalculated by reloading the page.

```
<!DOCTYPE html PUBLIC "-//W3C//DTD XHTML 1.0 Strict//EN" "http://www.w3.org/TR/xhtml1/DTD/
→ xhtml1-strict.dtd">
<html xmlns="http://www.w3.org/1999/xhtml">
<head>
<meta http-equiv="Content-Type" content="text/html; charset=utf-8" />
<title>CSS, DHTML &amp; Ajax | Finding the Browser Dimensions</title>
<style type="text/css" media="screen">
body {
    font: 1em Georgia, "Times New Roman", times, serif;
    color: #000;
    background-color: #ccc;
    margin: 8px;
}
</style>
<script type="text/javascript">
function findBrowserHeight() {
    if (window.outerHeight != null)
        return window.outerHeight;
    return null;
}

function findBrowserWidth() {
    if (window.outerWidth != null)
        return window.outerWidth ;
    return null;
}
</script>
</head>
<body onresize="self.location.reload()">
<script type="text/javascript"><!--
browserHeight = findBrowserHeight() ;
browserWidth = findBrowserWidth();
if (browserWidth!= null) {
document.writeln('Your total browser width is ' + browserWidth + 'px <br><br>'); }
else {document.writeln ('The browser window\'s width can not be determined.'); }
if (browserHeight!= null) {
document.writeln('Your total browser height is ' + browserHeight + 'px <br><br>'); }
else {document.writeln ('The browser window\'s height can not be determined.<br><br>'); }
// -->
</script>
</body>
</html>
```

Determining the Page's Visible Dimensions

Knowing the size of the browser window is nice (see the previous section, "Determining the Browser Window's Dimensions"), but a much more useful ability is finding the dimensions of the live area in which your content will be displayed. This is the actual area you have in which to display your Web page, taking into account the current size of the window as well as all of the browser's chrome.

These dimensions are available in the clientHeight and clientWidth objects for Internet Explorer (**Figure 13.24**) and innerHeight and innerWidth for all other browsers (**Figure 13.25**).

In this example (**Figure 13.26**), when the page loads an alert displays the width and height of the display area of the window. If you resize the window, the alert will display again with the new values (**Figure 13.27**).

To find the dimensions of the live area:

1. function findLivePageHeight() {…}

   Add the function findLivePageHeight() to your JavaScript (**Code 13.7**). This function uses feature sensing to ensure that document.body.clientHeight can be used with the browser and then returns the browser's live display height.

2. function findLivePageWidth() {…}

   Add the function findLivePageWidth() to your JavaScript. This function uses feature sensing to ensure that document.body.clientWidth can be used with the browser and then returns the browser's live display width.

continues on Page 320

Ask the browser window...   ...for the display area's width/height

document.body.clientHeight

Figure 13.24 The general syntax for the clientWidth and clientHeight objects.

Ask the browser window...   ...for the display area's width/height

window.innerWidth

Figure 13.25 The general syntax for the innerWidth andinnerHeight objects.

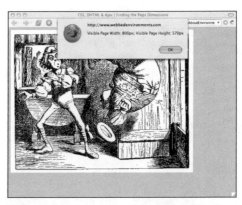

Figure 13.26 Loading the page triggers an alert that returns the dimensions of the browser window's live area.

Figure 13.27 Resizing the window will change the values in the alert.

Code 13.7 The functions findLivePageHeight() and findLivePageWidth() return the dimensions of the browser window's live area, in pixels.

```
<!DOCTYPE html PUBLIC "-//W3C//DTD XHTML 1.0 Strict//EN" "http://www.w3.org/TR/xhtml1/DTD/
→ xhtml1-strict.dtd">
<html xmlns="http://www.w3.org/1999/xhtml">
<head>
<meta http-equiv="Content-Type" content="text/html; charset=utf-8" />
<title>CSS, DHTML &amp; Ajax | Finding the Page Dimensions</title>
<style type="text/css" media="screen">
body {
    font: 1em Georgia, "Times New Roman", times, serif;
    color: #000;
    background-color: #ccc;
    margin: 8px;
}
</style>
<script type="text/javascript"><!--
function findLivePageHeight() {
    if (window.innerHeight) {
        return window.innerHeight;
        }
    if (document.body.clientHeight) {
        return document.body.clientHeight;
        }
    return (null);
}

function findLivePageWidth() {
    if (window.innerWidth)
        return window.innerWidth;
    if (document.body.clientWidth)
        return document.body.clientWidth;
    return (null);
}
function pageDim() {
    livePageHeight = findLivePageHeight();
    livePageWidth = findLivePageWidth();
    alert ('Visible Page Width: ' + livePageWidth + 'px; Visible Page Height: ' +
    → livePageHeight + 'px');
}
// -->
</script>
</head>
<body onresize="self.location.reload()" onload="pageDim()">
<div> <img src="alice17.gif" height="480" width="640" border="0" alt="alice" /> </div>
</body>
</html>
```

3. `function pageDim() {…}`

Add a function that calls the `findLivePageHeight()` and `findLivePageWidth()` functions. In this case, we're simply using the functions to display an alert for the current dimensions.

4. `onload="pageDim();"`

Add an event handler to trigger the `pageDim()` function from Step 3.

✔ Tips

■ One common use for determining the screen size is to help with creating a dynamic layout. However, more than often you may have a fixed width for your layout and allow extra screen space to simply remain blank. For more considerations on screen size and layout, see the sidebar "What Screen Size Should I Use for My Web Site?"

■ If you're creating a page with content layout dependent on the live page area, you may want to force the page to reload if the user resizes the browser, by placing the following code in the <body> tag:

`onresize="self.location.reload();"`

What Screen Size Should I Use for My Web Sites?

Although an 800 × 600–pixel screen size has become the design standard for most Web designers, 58 percent of Web users are now using screens as large as 1024 × 768 pixels (according to StatMarket, statmarket.com).

Keep in mind, however, that large screen sizes don't necessarily mean that the browser window will be open to that size. Significant content and design elements should be placed "above the fold" so that they're visible without vertical scrolling, and all important user-interface elements must be visible without horizontal scrolling within the 800 × 600 screen.

As with any design issue, it's important to keep your audience in mind. Always try to find out the average size of the monitor being used by the people likely to view your Web site. Although it's useful to know what the average Web browser is using, it could be that 100 percent of your audience falls in that 42 percent of viewers with smaller screen sizes.

LEARNING ABOUT AN OBJECT

In Chapter 12, we looked at how to turn an element defined by HTML tags into an object that can then be addressed by the Document Object Model. The DOM allows you to find out information about the object—such as its size, location, and whether it is visible—using JavaScript.

All the information gained about the environment in Chapter 13 was derived from asking the browser questions, such as its type and screen size. In this chapter, we will be looking at what information can be gained by querying objects in the browser window for information about themselves.

Detecting Which Object Was Clicked

In Chapter 12, I showed you how to use evt to find the object in which an event originated. Using the browser's DOM, though, you can also determine the ID of the object in which the event occurred. For Internet Explorer, this entails querying the srcElement object; for W3C-compliant browsers, it means using the target object (**Figures 14.1** and **14.2**).

In this example, (**Figure 14.3**), clicking any of the four objects will cause an alert to appear, displaying the ID value for the clicked element.

To determine the element in which the event occurred:

1. `function findObjectID(evt) {…}`

   Add the function findObjectID() to the JavaScript in the head of your document (**Code 14.1**). This script determines the CSS element on the screen in which the event occurred and then displays an alert telling you which one it was. To do this, we'll need to adapt the event equalizer to find the target (W3C browsers) or source element (Internet Explorer) of the event, which can then be used to find the object's ID:

   ```
   var objectID = (evt.target) ?
   → evt.target.id : ((evt.srcElement)
   → ? evt.srcElement.id : null);
   ```

2. `#object1 {…}`

   Set up your CSS rules, using whatever style properties you want. I set up four images (object1, object2, object3, and alice4), each with a unique ID.

3. `onclick="findObjectID(event);"`

   Add an event handler to trigger the function you created in Step 1, and pass to it the event object.

evt.srcElement.id

Figure 14.1 The general syntax for using an event object to find the triggering ID in Internet Explorer.

Ask the event object's...   ...target element...   what its ID is

evt.target.id

Figure 14.2 The general syntax for using an event object to find the triggering ID in W3C-compliant browsers.

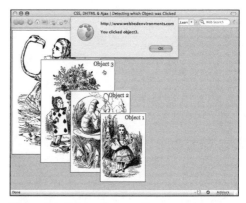

Figure 14.3 Pick an Alice, any Alice.

✔ Tip

■ Once the object ID has been found using the evt variable, you can use that information to address the object to find its properties, as explained in the next section, or make dynamic changes, as described in Chapters 16 through 18.

Code 14.1 The findObjectID() function will identify the object that triggered the event by using the evt object that is passed to it.

```
<!DOCTYPE html PUBLIC "-//W3C//DTD XHTML 1.0 Strict//EN" "http://www.w3.org/TR/xhtml1/DTD/
→ xhtml1-strict.dtd">
<html xmlns="http://www.w3.org/1999/xhtml">
<head>
<meta http-equiv="Content-Type" content="text/html; charset=UTF-8" />
<title>CSS, DHTML &amp; Ajax | Detecting which Object was Clicked</title>
<script type="text/javascript">
function findObjectID(evt) {
    var objectID = (evt.target) ? evt.target.id : ((evt.srcElement) ? evt.srcElement.id : null);
    if (objectID)    {
        alert('You clicked ' + objectID + '.');
    }
    return;
}
</script>
<style type="text/css" media="screen">
.dropBox {
    text-align: right;
    padding: 4px;
    background-color: #FFFFFF;
    border: 2px solid #f00;
    cursor: pointer; }
#object1 {
    position: absolute;
    z-index: 3;
    top: 285px; left: 315px;
    background: white url(alice22a.gif) no-repeat;
    height:220px; width:150px; }
#object2 {
    position: absolute;
    z-index: 2;
    top: 210px; left: 210px;
    background: white url(alice15a.gif) no-repeat;
    height:264px; width:200px; }
#object3 {
    position: absolute;
    z-index: 1;
    top: 105px; left: 105px;
    background: white url(alice28a.gif) no-repeat;
    height:336px; width:250px;}
#object4 {
    position: absolute;
    z-index: 0;
    top: 5px; left: 5px;
    background: white url(alice30a.gif) no-repeat;
    height:408px; width:300px; }
</style>
</head>
<body>
<div class="dropBox" id="object1" onclick="findObjectID(event)"> Object 1</div>
<div class="dropBox" id="object2" onclick="findObjectID(event)"> Object 2</div>
<div class="dropBox" id="object3" onclick="findObjectID(event)"> Object 3</div>
<div class="dropBox" id="object4" onclick="findObjectID(event)"> Object 4</div>
</body></html>
```

Determining an Object's Properties

The Document Object Model lets you connect scripts to the objects on your page, so it's possible to learn a wide range of information about that object.

The basic technique for finding this information is the same, regardless of the information you seek. **Figure 14.4** shows the basic structure for accessing the properties inherent in HTML elements. First begin by getting the object by its ID, which you do in the same way as you did with elements in Chapter 12 (see "Getting an Element" in Chapter 12). Then use one of the property keywords from **Table 14.1**.

As an example of how this works, let's look at finding the width and height of a given object.

All objects have a width and height that determine their dimensions (see "Understanding an Element's Box" in Chapter 6). For images, the width and height are an intrinsic part of the object. For most objects you'll be using the width and height styles to set their dimensions. However, to then find the width and height of an object using JavaScript, you'll use the offsetWidth and offsetHeight properties.

In this example (**Figure 14.5**), clicking any of the objects displays an alert showing that object's width and height.

Ask the element... ... *the value of one of its properties*

getElementById(objectID).offsetWidth

Figure 14.4 The general syntax for finding an element's HTML property value.

Table 14.1

DOM Element Properties

PROPERTY	DESCRIPTION
className	Gets/sets the class of an element
clientHeight*	Gets height of an element, including padding, and scrollbar
clientWidth*	Gets width of an element, including padding, and scrollbar
id	Gets/sets the ID of an element
innerHTML*	Gets/sets the mark-up and content in an element
lang	Gets language of an element
name	Gets/sets the name of an element
offsetHeight*	Gets height of element, including border, padding, and scrollbar
offsetLeft	Gets/sets position from left edge of parent
offsetParent	Gets first-positioned parent of element
offsetTop	Gets/sets position from top edge of parent
offsetWidth*	Gets width of element, including border, padding, and scrollbar
scrollHeight*	Gets total height of element discounting scroll
scrollLeft*	Gets number of pixels element is scrolled left
scrollTop*	Gets number of pixels element is scrolled upward
scrollWidth*	Gets total height of element discounting scroll
style	Gets a style value (e.g., style.width)
tabIndex	Gets/sets tab order of element

*Not currently part of the W3C DOM Specification, but in wide use.

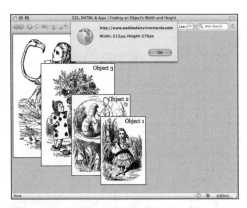

Figure 14.5 An alert appears, telling you the dimensions of the object. Keep in mind, though that this includes the padding and border, in addition to the width and height set in the CSS.

To find the width and height of an object:

1. function findWidth(objectID) {…}

Add the functions findWidth() and findHeight() to your JavaScript **(Code 14.2)**.

These functions use the ID of the object to be addressed—passed to it as the variable objectID—to locate the object. It then uses feature sensing to check that offsetWidth and offsetHeight work in the current browser and returns the object's width and height if they do.

continues on next page

Code 14.2 The functions findWidth() and FindHeight() return the dimensions of an individual object on the page.

```
<!DOCTYPE html PUBLIC "-//W3C//DTD XHTML 1.0 Strict//EN" "http://www.w3.org/TR/xhtml1/DTD/
→ xhtml1-strict.dtd">
<html xmlns="http://www.w3.org/1999/xhtml">
<head>
<meta http-equiv="Content-Type" content="text/html; charset=UTF-8" />
<title>CSS, DHTML &amp; Ajax | Determining An Object's Properties</title>
<script type="text/javascript">
function findWidth(objectID) {
    var object = document.getElementById(objectID);
    if (object.offsetWidth)
        return object.offsetWidth;
    return (null);
}
function findHeight(objectID) {
    var object = document.getElementById(objectID);
    if (object.offsetHeight)
        return object.offsetHeight;
    return (null);
}
function showDim(evt) {
    var objectID = (evt.target) ? evt.target.id : ((evt.srcElement) ? evt.srcElement.id : null);
    if (objectID) {
        widthObj = findWidth(objectID);
        heightObj = findHeight(objectID);
        alert('Width: ' + widthObj + 'px; Height: ' + heightObj + 'px' );
    }
    else return (null);
}
</script>
```

code continues on next page

2. `function showDim(evt) {…}`

Add a JavaScript function that uses the functions you created in Step 1. In this example, `showDim()` first finds the ID of the triggering object using the `evt` variable:

`var objectID = (evt.target) ?`
`→ evt.target.id : ((evt.srcElement)`
`→ ? evt.srcElement.id : null);`

It then passes this value to `findWidth()` and `findHeight()`, displaying the values they return in an alert.

3. `#object1 {…}`

Set up the CSS rules for your object(s) with the properties you need. You will use these to define the objects in your HTML code.

4. `onclick="showDim(event);"`

Add an event handler to trigger the function you created in Step 2, and pass to it the event.

Code 14.2 *continued*

```
<style type="text/css" media="screen">
.dropBox {
      position: absolute;
      text-align: right;
      padding: 4px;
      background-color: #FFFFFF;
      border: 2px solid #f00;
      cursor: pointer; }
#object1 {
      z-index: 3;
      top: 285px; left: 315px;
      background: white url(alice22a.gif)
      → no-repeat;
      height:220px; width:150px; }
#object2 {
      z-index: 2;
      top: 210px; left: 210px;
      background: white url(alice15a.gif)
      → no-repeat;
      height:264px; width:200px;}
#object3 {
      z-index: 1;
      top: 105px; left: 105px;
      background: white url(alice28a.gif)
      → no-repeat;
      height:336px; width:250px; }
#object4 {
      z-index: 0;
      top: 5px; left: 5px;
      background: white url(alice30a.gif)
      → no-repeat;
      height:408px; width:300px; }
</style>
</head>
<body>
<div class="dropBox" id="object1"
→ onclick="showDim(event)"> Object 1</div>
<div class="dropBox" id="object2"
→ onclick="showDim(event)"> Object 2</div>
<div class="dropBox" id="object3"
→ onclick="showDim(event)"> Object 3</div>
<div class="dropBox" id="object4"
→ onclick="showDim(event)"> Object 4</div>
</body></html>
```

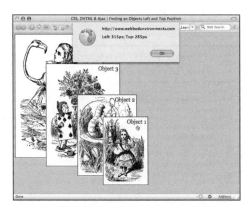

Figure 14.6 An alert appears, telling you the top and left positions of the object.

Detecting an Object's Position

In the previous section, I showed you how to find an object's properties, showing as an example how to find the object's width and height. Now let's apply that same process to locating the object's position.

You can use CSS to set the top, left, bottom, and/or right positions of objects (see "Setting an Element's Position" in Chapter 7). Then you can use JavaScript to detect those positions and change them to move the objects around.

One major use of DHTML is to make objects move around on the page (see "Moving Objects from Point to Point" in Chapter 16). But to make something move, you need to know where it is to begin with. Let's take a moment and look specifically at how to find the top/left position and the bottom/right position of an object.

Finding an object's top and left positions

To *set* the position of an object's top-left corner, you use the CSS `top` and `left` properties. You might, then, assume that you would also use these style properties in JavaScript to find what those values are. However, the browsers use the `offsetLeft` and `offsetTop` properties to find this information. Although not a part of the W3C DOM specification, these properties are universally available in all browsers.

In this example (**Figure 14.6**), clicking any of the objects makes an alert display showing that object's position from the top and left sides of its parent element—in this case, the body of the document.

continues on next page

To find the top and left positions of an object:

1. `function findLeft(objectID) {…}`

Add the functions `findLeft()` and `findTop()` to your JavaScript (**Code 14.3**). These functions use the ID of the object to be addressed—passed to them as the variable `objectID`—to identify the object. They then use feature sensing to determine whether the browser uses `offsetLeft` and `offsetTop` to return the left and top positions of the object in pixels.

2. `function showPosTL(evt) {…}`

Add a JavaScript function that uses the functions you created in Step 1. In this example, `showPosTL()` first finds the ID of the triggering object using the `evt` variable:

```
var objectID = (evt.target) ?
→ evt.target.id : ((evt.srcElement)
→ ? evt.srcElement.id : null);
```

It then passes this value to `findLeft()` and `findTop()`, displaying the values they return in an alert.

3. `#object1 {…}`

Set up the CSS rules for your object(s) with `left`, and `top` properties. You will use these to define objects in your HTML.

4. `onclick="showPos(event);"`

Add an event handler to trigger the function you created in Step 2, and pass to it the event.

✔ Tips

■ Microsoft Internet Explorer 4 also lets you use the `pixelLeft` and `pixelTop` properties to find the left and top position. However, since `offsetLeft` and `offsetTop` work in all other browsers, these are generally preferred.

Code 14.3 The functions `findLeft()` and `findTop()` detect the position of an individual object on the page.

```
<!DOCTYPE html PUBLIC "-//W3C//DTD XHTML 1.0
→ Strict//EN" "http://www.w3.org/TR/xhtml1/
→ DTD/xhtml1-strict.dtd">
<html xmlns="http://www.w3.org/1999/xhtml">
<head>
<meta http-equiv="Content-Type"
→ content="text/html; charset=UTF-8" />
<title>CSS, DHTML &amp; Ajax | Finding an
→ Objects Left and Top Position</title>
<script type="text/javascript">
function findLeft(objectID) {
    var object =
    → document.getElementById(objectID);
    if (object.offsetLeft)
        return object.offsetLeft;
    return (null);
}
function findTop(objectID) {
    var object =
    → document.getElementById(objectID);
    if (object.offsetTop)
        return object.offsetTop;
    return (null);
}
```

code continues on next page

■ Remember that unless you are using the Strict mode DTD, you will run into problems with discrepancies in how Internet Explorer and other browsers measure width and height and how they set the default page margin.

Code 14.3 *continued*

```
function showPosTL(evt) {
     var objectID = (evt.target) ? evt.target.id : ((evt.srcElement) ? evt.srcElement.id : null);
     if (objectID) {
        leftPos = findLeft(objectID);
        topPos = findTop(objectID);
        alert('Left: ' + leftPos + 'px; Top: ' + topPos + 'px' );
     }
     else return (null);
}
</script>
<style type="text/css" media="screen">
.dropBox {
     position: absolute;
     text-align: right;
     padding: 4px;
     background-color: #FFFFFF;
     border: 2px solid #f00;
     cursor: pointer; }
#object1 {
     z-index: 3;
     top: 285px; left: 315px;
     background: white url(alice22a.gif) no-repeat;
     height:220px; width:150px; }
#object2 {
     z-index: 2;
     top: 210px; left: 225px;
     background: white url(alice15a.gif) no-repeat;
     height:264px; width:200px; }
#object3 {
     z-index: 1;
     top: 105px; left: 115px;
     background: white url(alice28a.gif) no-repeat;
     height:336px; width:250px;}
#object4 {
     z-index: 0;
     top: 5px; left: 5px;
     background: white url(alice30a.gif) no-repeat;
     height:408px; width:300px; }
</style>
</head>
<body>
<div class="dropBox" id="object1" onclick="showPosTL(event)"> Object 1</div>
<div class="dropBox" id="object2" onclick="showPosTL(event)"> Object 2</div>
<div class="dropBox" id="object3" onclick="showPosTL(event)"> Object 3</div>
<div class="dropBox" id="object4" onclick="showPosTL(event)"> Object 4</div>
</body></html>
```

DETECTING AN OBJECT'S POSITION

Finding an object's bottom and right positions

Like the top and left positions, the bottom and right positions can be determined with DOM properties. However, you don't do this directly using a particular object. Instead, you find the left or top position of the object and the width or height of the object and add these values.

In this example (**Figure 14.7**), clicking any of the objects will cause a pop-up alert to appear, displaying the position of the bottom and right sides of the object.

To find the bottom and right positions of an object:

1. `function findRight(objectID) {…}`

   Add the functions `findRight()` and `findBottom()` to your JavaScript (**Code 14.4**).

   These functions use the ID of the object to be addressed—passed to them as the variable `objectID`—to find the object. They then use feature sensing to find the left position and width of the object, and add these to calculate the right position:

   `offsetLeft+offsetWidth`

   Then add the top position and height of the object to calculate the bottom position:

   `offsetTop+offsetHeight`

   See "Determining an Object's Properties" and "Finding an Object's Top and Left Positions" earlier in this chapter.

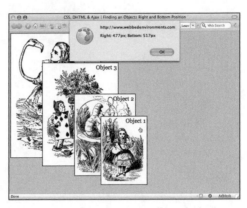

Figure 14.7 An alert pops up to tell you the bottom and right positions of the object.

Code 14.4 The functions `findRight()` and `findBottom()` calculate where the bottom and right sides o the object are on the page.

```
<!DOCTYPE html PUBLIC "-//W3C//DTD XHTML 1.0
→ Strict//EN" "http://www.w3.org/TR/xhtml1/
→ DTD/xhtml1-strict.dtd">
<html xmlns="http://www.w3.org/1999/xhtml">
<head>
<meta http-equiv="Content-Type"
→ content="text/html; charset=UTF-8" />
<title>CSS, DHTML &amp; Ajax | Finding an
→ Objects Right and Bottom Position</title>
<script type="text/javascript">
function findRight(objectID) {
    var object =
    → document.getElementById(objectID);
     if (object.offsetLeft) {
       return (object.offsetLeft +
       → object.offsetWidth);
    }
    return (null);
}
function findBottom(objectID) {
    var object =
    → document.getElementById(objectID);
    if (object.offsetTop) {
       return (object.offsetTop +
       → object.offsetHeight);
    }
    return (null);
}
function showPosBR(evt) {
    var objectID = (evt.target) ?
    → evt.target.id : ((evt.srcElement) ?
    → evt.srcElement.id : null);
```

code continues on next page

Code 14.4 *continued*

```
    if (objectID) {
        rightPos = findRight(objectID);
        bottomPos = findBottom(objectID);
        alert('Right: ' + rightPos + 'px;
        → Bottom: ' + bottomPos + 'px' );
    }
    else return (null);
}
</script>
<style type="text/css" media="screen">
.dropBox {
    position: absolute;
    text-align: right;
    padding: 4px;
    background-color: #FFFFFF;
    border: 2px solid #f00;
    cursor: pointer;}
#object1 {
    z-index: 3;
    top: 285px; left: 315px;
    background: white url(alice22a.gif)
    → no-repeat;
    height:220px; width:150px;}
#object2 {
    z-index: 2;
    top: 210px; left: 225px;
    background: white url(alice15a.gif)
    → no-repeat;
    height:264px; width:200px; }
#object3 {
    z-index: 1;
    top: 105px; left: 115px;
    background: white url(alice28a.gif)
    → no-repeat;
    height:336px; width:250px; }
#object4 {
    z-index: 0;
    top: 5px; left: 5px;
    background: white url(alice30a.gif)
    → no-repeat;
    height:408px; width:300px; }
</style>
</head>
<body>
<div class="dropBox" id="object1" onclick=
→ "showPosBR(event)"> Object 1</div>
<div class="dropBox" id="object2" onclick=
→ "showPosBR(event)"> Object 2</div>
<div class="dropBox" id="object3" onclick=
→ "showPosBR(event)"> Object 3</div>
<div class="dropBox" id="object4" onclick=
→ "showPosBR(event)"> Object 4</div>
</body></html>
```

2. `function showPosBR(objectID) {…}`

   Add a JavaScript function that uses the functions you created in Step 1. In this example, `showPosBR()` first finds the ID of the triggering object using the `evt` variable:

   ```
   var objectID = (evt.target) ?
   → evt.target.id : ((evt.srcElement)
   → ? evt.srcElement.id : null);
   ```

   It then passes this value to `findRight()` and `findBottom()`, displaying the values they return in an alert.

3. `#object1 {…}`

   Set up the CSS rules for your object(s) with `left` and `top` properties. You will use these to identify your objects in your HTML.

4. `onclick="showPosBR(event);"`

   Add an event handler to trigger the function you created in Step 2, and pass to it the event.

Finding an Object's Style Property Values

Part 1 of this book showed you how to set a variety of styles using CSS. Many of the properties set using CSS can be directly accessed using the DOM properties shown in Table 14.1. However, many of the style properties do not have direct DOM correlations, so we need to look at how to use the object ID to get at those values. **Figure 14.8** shows how to access those style values.

As an example of finding style property values, let's take a look at the visibility property.

All objects that have a position set also have a visibility state: hidden or visible (see Chapter 8). The default state is visible.

In this example (**Figure 14.9**), when the page first loads the visibility property is set for the object on the page. Clicking the visible object will cause an alert to appear showing you its visibility value.

To find the visibility of an object:

1. function initPage(objectID, state) {…}

   Add the initPage() function to your JavaScript (**Code 14.5**). This function sets the initial visibility of objects when the page first loads. Unfortunately, browsers cannot access the style that is initially set in the CSS; they're aware of the state only after it has been set dynamically. If you do not set this first, the value shows as null.

2. function findVisibility(objectID) {…}

   Add the function findVisibility() to your JavaScript. This function uses the ID of the object to be addressed—passed to it as the variable objectID—to find the object on the page. It then uses this ID to access the current visibility property

Ask the element's... ...style object... ...what its value is

getElementById(objectID).style.visibility

Figure 14.8 The general syntax for finding an element's CSS property value.

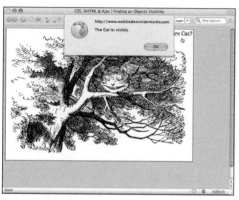

Figure 14.9 The Cheshire Cat is visible, but for how long?

Code 14.5 The function findVisibility() determines the current visibility state of an individual object in the window.

```
<!DOCTYPE html PUBLIC "-//W3C//DTD XHTML 1.0
→ Strict//EN" "http://www.w3.org/TR/xhtml1/
DTD/xhtml1-strict.dtd">
<html xmlns="http://www.w3.org/1999/xhtml">
<head>
<meta http-equiv="Content-Type"
→ content="text/html; charset=UTF-8" />
<title>CSS, DHTML &amp; Ajax | Finding an
→ Objects Visibility</title>
<script type="text/javascript">
function initPage(objectID, state) {
    var object =
    → document.getElementById(objectID);
    object.style.visibility = state;
}
function findVisibility(objectID) {
    var object =
    → document.getElementById(objectID);
    if (object.style.visibility)
        return object.style.visibility;
    return (null);
}
```

code continues on next page

Code 14.5 *continued*

```
function showVisibility(evt) {
    var objectID = (evt.target) ?
    → evt.target.id : ((evt.srcElement)
    → ? evt.srcElement.id : null);
    if (objectID) {
        var thisVis =
        → findVisibility(objectID);
        alert('The Cat is: ' + thisVis );
    }
    else return (null);
}
</script>
<style type="text/css" media="screen">
.dropBox {
    position: absolute;
    text-align: right;
    padding: 4px;
    background-color: #FFFFFF;
    border: 2px solid #f00;
    cursor: pointer; }
#object1 {
    z-index: 10;
    background: white url(alice24a.gif)
    → no-repeat;
    height:435px; width:640px; }
#object2 {
    z-index: 20;
    top: 100px; left: 160px;
    background: white url(alice31a.gif)
    → no-repeat;
    height:480px; width:379px; }
</style>
</head>
<body onload="initPage('object1','visible');
→ initPage('object2','hidden');">
<div class="dropBox" id="object1"
→ onclick="showVisibility(event)">
→ Where is the Cheshire Cat? </div>
<div class="dropBox" id="object2"
→ onclick="showVisibility(event)">
→ Where is the Cheshire Cat? </div>
</body>
</html>
```

value set for the object. Based on that value, the function returns either `visible` or `hidden`.

3. `function showVisibility(evt) {…}`

Create a JavaScript function `showVisibility()` that determines the ID of the initiating object from the `evt`:

`var objectID = (evt.target) ?`
`→ evt.target.id : ((evt.srcElement)`
`→ ? evt.srcElement.id : null);`

This function then passes that value to the function `findVisibility()` and displays the value that function returns.

4. `#object1 {…}`

Set up the CSS rules for your object. In your HTML, you will be using this ID to define a `<div>` tag as an object.

5. `onload="initPage('object1',`
`→ 'visible');"`

In the `<body>` tag, use the `initPage()` function to initialize the visibility of all the objects for which you need to know the initial visibility. It then displays those values in an alert.

6. `onclick="showVisibility(event);"`

Add an event handler to trigger the function you created in Step 3, and pass to it the event.

✔ Tips

■ You can also use JavaScript to change the visibility state, as explained in "Making Objects Appear and Disappear" in Chapter 16.

■ In Chapter 18, we'll explore ways to dynamically set CSS after the page has loaded.

■ An alternate (though no less complex) method for finding the visibility state of any object without first setting the value using JavaScript is presented in "Finding a Style Property's Value" in Chapter 18.

Finding an Object's 3D Position

The CSS property z-index lets you stack positioned elements in 3D (see "Stacking Objects" in Chapter 7). Using JavaScript, you can determine the z-index of individual objects on the screen using the style.zIndex property.

But there's a catch: Browsers can't easily see the z-index until it is set dynamically. To get around this little problem, you have to use JavaScript to set the z-index of each object when the page first loads.

In this example (**Figure 14.10**), clicking any of the objects will produce an alert displaying the z-index value for that element.

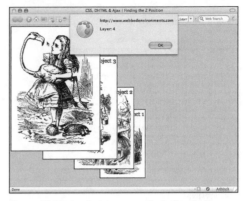

Figure 14.10 An alert appears, displaying the layer number of the object clicked.

Code 14.6 The function findLayer() determines the z-index of an individual object on the page after the layers are initialized using initPage().

```
<!DOCTYPE html PUBLIC "-//W3C//DTD XHTML 1.0 Strict//EN" "http://www.w3.org/TR/xhtml1/DTD/
→ xhtml1-strict.dtd">
<html xmlns="http://www.w3.org/1999/xhtml">
<head>
<meta http-equiv="Content-Type" content="text/html; charset=UTF-8" />
<title>CSS, DHTML &amp; Ajax | Finding the Z Position</title>
<script type="text/javascript">
function initPage() {
     for (i=1; i<=4; i++) {
          var object = document.getElementById('object' + i);
          object.style.zIndex = i;
     }
}
function findLayer(objectID) {
     var object = document.getElementById(objectID);
     if (object.style.zIndex)
          return object.style.zIndex;
     return (null);
}
function whichLayer(evt) {
     var objectID = (evt.target) ? evt.target.id : ((evt.srcElement) ? evt.srcElement.id : null);
     if (objectID) {
          layerNum = findLayer(objectID);
          alert('Layer: ' + layerNum );
     }
}
</script>                                                            code continues on next page
```

Code 14.6 *continued*

```
<style type="text/css" media="screen">
.dropBox {
     position: absolute;
     text-align: right;
     padding: 4px;
     background-color: #FFFFFF;
     border: 2px solid #f00;
     cursor: pointer; }
#object1 {
     z-index: 3;
     top: 285px; left: 315px;
     background: white url(alice22a.gif)
     → no-repeat;
     height:220px; width:150px; }
#object2 {
     z-index: 2;
     top: 210px; left: 225px;
     background: white url(alice15a.gif)
     → no-repeat;
     height:264px; width:200px; }
#object3 {
     z-index: 1;
     top: 105px;
     left: 115px;
     background: white url(alice28a.gif)
     → no-repeat;
     height:336px; width:250px; }
#object4 {
     z-index: 0;
     top: 5px; left: 5px;
     background: white url(alice30a.gif)
     → no-repeat;
     height:408px; width:300px;}
</style>
</head>
<body onload="initPage()">
<div class="dropBox" id="object1"
→ onclick="whichLayer(event)">
→ Object 1</div>
<div class="dropBox" id="object2"
→ onclick="whichLayer(event)">
→ Object 2</div>
<div class="dropBox" id="object3"
→ onclick="whichLayer(event)">
→ Object 3</div>
<div class="dropBox" id="object4"
→ onclick="whichLayer(event)">
→ Object 4</div>
</body></html>
```

To find the z-index of an object:

1. `function initPage() {…}`

Add the `initPage()` function to your JavaScript (**Code 14.6**). This function sets the initial z-index of objects when the page first loads.

2. `function findLayer(objectID) {…}`

Add the function `findLayer()` to your JavaScript. This function uses the ID of the object to be addressed—passed to it as the variable `objectID`—to find the object. The function then uses this ID to access the `z-index` property and returns that value.

3. `function whichLayer(evt) {…}`

Create a JavaScript function called `whichLayer()` that passes the ID value for the initiating object to the function `findLayer()`:

`var objectID = (evt.target) ?`
`→ evt.target.id : ((evt.srcElement)`
`→ ? evt.srcElement.id : null);`

The function then displays the returned values in an alert.

4. `#object1 {…}`

Set up the CSS rules for your objects with `position` and `z-index` properties.

5. `onload="initPage();"`

In the <body> tag, use the `initPage()` function to initialize the z-index of all the objects for which you need to know the initial z-index.

6. `onclick="whichLayer(event);"`

Add an event handler to trigger the function you created in Step 3, and pass to it the event.

✔ Tip

- An alternate (though no less complex) method for finding the z-index of any object without first setting the value using JavaScript is presented in "Finding a Style Property's Value" in Chapter 16.

Finding an Object's Visible Area

The width and height of an object tell you the maximum area of the element (see "Determining an Object's Properties" earlier in this chapter). When an object is clipped (see "Setting the Visible Area of an Element" in Chapter 8), the maximum area is cut down, and you can view only part of the object's total visible area.

Using JavaScript, you can find not only the width and height of the visible area, but also the top, left, bottom, and right borders of the clipping region. However, unlike other CSS values, the clip values are in an array.

In this example (**Figures 14.11** and **14.12**), the object has been clipped. Clicking one of the controls at the top will produce an alert showing the value for that clip dimension, either extracted from the array or calculated from array values.

To find the visible area and borders of an object:

1. `function setClip(objectID, clipTop,`
   `→ clipRight, clipBottom, clipLeft) {…}`

   Add the setClip() function to your JavaScript (**Code 14.7**). This function sets the initial clip region of objects when the page first loads, with values the same as those set in the CSS.

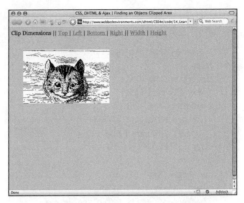

Figure 14.11 The clipped element, with controls above to find its clipping properties.

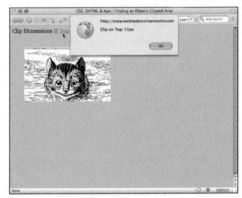

Figure 14.12 An alert appears, telling us the location of the top border of the clip region.

continues on Page 339

Code 14.7 The functions findClipTop(), findClipRight(),findClipBottom() , findClipLeft(), findClipWidth(), and findClipHeight() find the clip region and borders of an individual object in the window.

```
<!DOCTYPE html PUBLIC "-//W3C//DTD XHTML 1.0 Strict//EN" "http://www.w3.org/TR/xhtml1/DTD/
→ xhtml1-strict.dtd">
<html xmlns="http://www.w3.org/1999/xhtml">
<head>
<meta http-equiv="Content-Type" content="text/html; charset=UTF-8" />
<title>CSS, DHTML &amp; Ajax | Finding an Objects Clipped Area</title>
<script type="text/javascript">
function setClip(objectID, clipTop, clipRight, clipBottom, clipLeft) {
     var object = document.getElementById(objectID);
     object.style.clip = 'rect(' + clipTop + 'px ' + clipRight + 'px ' + clipBottom + 'px ' +
     → clipLeft +'px)';
}
function findClipTop(objectID) {
     var object = document.getElementById(objectID);
     if (object.style.clip !=null) {
        var clip = findClipArray(object.style.clip);
        return (clip[0]) ;
     }
     return (null);
}
function findClipRight(objectID) {
     var object = document.getElementById(objectID);
     if (object.style.clip !=null) {
        var clip = findClipArray(object.style.clip);
        return (clip[1]) ;
     }
     return (null);
}
function findClipBottom(objectID) {
     var object = document.getElementById(objectID);
     if (object.style.clip !=null) {
        var clip = findClipArray(object.style.clip);
        return (clip[2]) ;
     }
     return (null);
}
function findClipLeft(objectID) {
     var object = document.getElementById(objectID);
     if (object.style.clip !=null) {
        var clip = findClipArray(object.style.clip);
        return (clip[3]) ;
     }
     return (null);
}
function findClipWidth(objectID) {
     var object = document.getElementById(objectID);
     if (object.style.clip !=null) {
        var clip = findClipArray(object.style.clip);
        return (clip[1] - clip[3]) ;
     }
     return (null);
}
```

code continues on next page

Code 14.7 *continued*

```
function findClipHeight(objectID) {
    var object = document.getElementById(objectID);
    if (object.style.clip !=null) {
        var clip = findClipArray(object.style.clip);
        return (clip[2] - clip[0]) ;
    }
    return (null);
}
function findClipArray(clipStr) {
    var clip = new Array();
    var i;
    i = clipStr.indexOf('(');
    clip[0] = parseInt(clipStr.substring(i + 1, clipStr.length), 10);
    i = clipStr.indexOf(' ', i + 1);
    clip[1] = parseInt(clipStr.substring(i + 1, clipStr.length), 10);
    i = clipStr.indexOf(' ', i + 1);
    clip[2] = parseInt(clipStr.substring(i + 1 , clipStr.length), 10);
    i = clipStr.indexOf(' ', i + 1);
    clip[3] = parseInt(clipStr.substring(i + 1, clipStr.length), 10);
    return clip;
}
</script>
<style type="text/css" media="screen">
.dropBox {
    text-align: right;
    padding: 4px;
    background-color: #FFFFFF;
    border: 2px solid #f00;
    cursor: pointer;
}
#object1 {
    position: absolute;
    top: 60px;
    left: 0;
    overflow: hidden;
    clip: rect(15px 350px 195px 50px)
    }
</style>
</head>
<body onload="setClip('object1',15,350,195,50)">
Clip Dimensions ||
<a onclick="alert('Clip on Top: ' + findClipTop('object1') + 'px')" href="#">Top </a>|
<a onclick="alert('Clip on Left: ' + findClipLeft('object1') + 'px')" href="#">Left </a>|
<a onclick="alert('Clip on Bottom: ' + findClipBottom('object1') + 'px')" href="#">Bottom </a>|
<a onclick="alert('Clip on Right: ' + findClipRight('object1') + 'px')" href="#">Right </a>||
<a onclick="alert('Clip Width: ' + findClipWidth('object1') + 'px')" href="#">Width </a>|
<a onclick="alert('Clip Height: ' + findClipHeight('object1') + 'px')" href="#">Height </a>
<div class="dropBox"id="object1" > <img src="alice31.gif" height="480" width="379" border="0"
/></div>
</body></html>
```

2. `function findClipTop(objectID) {…}`

Add these functions to your JavaScript: `findClipTop()`, `findClipRight()`, `findClipBottom()`, and `findClipLeft()`.

All these functions do the same thing on different sides of the object. They use the ID of the object to be addressed—passed to the function as the variable `objectID`—to find the object on the Web page. They use the `findClipArray()` function to determine the clip array and then access that array by using 0, 1, 2, 3 for top, right, bottom, and left, respectively.

3. `function findClipWidth(objectID) {…}`

Add the functions `findClipWidth()` and `findClipHeight()` to your JavaScript.

These functions use the ID of the object to be addressed—passed to them as the variable `objectID`—to find the object. The functions then use the object to capture the visible area's height and width by subtracting the top from the bottom value for the height or the left from the right values for the width.

4. `function findClipArray(str) {…}`

Add the `findClipArray()` function to your JavaScript.

This function translates the string of characters used to store the four clipping sides into an array of numbers, with each number in the array corresponding to a clip dimension.

5. `#object1 {…}`

Set up the CSS rules for your objects with `position` and `visibility` properties. In your HTML you will define `<div>` tag, using this object as its ID.

continues on next page

FINDING AN OBJECT'S VISIBLE AREA

6. `onload="setClip(…);"`

In the `<body>` tag, use the `setClip()` function to initialize the clip area of all the object(s).

7. `onclick="alert(…);"`

Trigger the functions in Steps 3 and 4 from an event handler.

✔ Tips

- Mozilla browsers can also access the clipping values using the `clip.height`, `clip.width`, `clip.top`, `clip.left`, `clip.bottom`, and `clip.right` objects to directly access the values. However, since Microsoft Internet Explorer does not support this, the array method described here is preferred.

- Like other CSS visibility properties, browsers can't easily read the clipping values until they've been set dynamically. I'll show you a relatively easy workaround for this problem later—changing the clipping area (see "Changing an Object's Visible Area" in Chapter 16).

- An alternate (though no less complex) method for finding the clip area of any object without first setting it using JavaScript is presented in "Finding a Style Property's Value" in Chapter 18.

LEARNING ABOUT AN EVENT

In Chapter 12, we looked at how to use event handlers to trigger JavaScript functions. An event handler can be applied to various objects on the page to tell the object how to react when a particular action occurs. However, events also include information about how a particular event was generated, such as which event type occurred, what object generated the event, and (for keyboard and mouse events) which button was pressed.

In this chapter, you'll learn how to find the information generated by an event and how to process it.

Detecting Which Event Type Fired

Once an event is fired, the function it triggers doesn't inherently know how it was triggered. The `type` event property can tell you what event type was fired, allowing you to write a function that can respond differently depending on how the action was initiated (**Figure 15.1**).

In this example (**Figure 15.2**), clicking anywhere outside of the image will trigger the `click` event, but clicking the image will detect the `mousedown` event.

To find which event type fired:

1. `function initPage(objectID) {…}`

   Add the function `initPage()` to your code (**Code 15.1**). You can bind events to a single object, multiple objects, or the entire document (see "Binding Events to Objects" in Chapter 12).

2. `function findEventType(evt) {…}`

   Add the function `findEventType()` to your code.

   This code first uses the event equalizer discussed in Chapter 12 ("Passing Events to a Function") to allow Internet Explorer and W3C-compliant browsers to play together:

   `var evt = (evt) ? evt :`
   `→ ((window.event) ? window.event :`
   `→ null)`

   It then uses the `type` event property to identify the event that triggered the function.

   For this example, I simply added an alert to report the event type, but you could use `if` or `switch` statements to tailor the code for different event types.

Ask the event object...   ... what type of event just fired

event.type

Figure 15.1 The general syntax for detecting the event type.

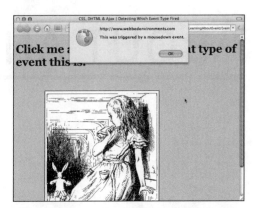

Figure 15.2 The event type that triggered the function (in this case, `mousedown`) is displayed in the alert message.

3. onload="initPage('object1');"

Add an onload event handler in the
<body> tag to trigger the initPage()
function created in Step 1. This sets
up the events for the page.

✔ Tip

■ Although this example uses event binding, you could also use it with an event
handler placed directly in an HTML tag.
But remember to pass the event variable
in the function call:

onclick="findEventType(event);"

Code 15.1 The type event property is used to identify the type of event that triggered the function.

```
<!DOCTYPE html PUBLIC "-//W3C//DTD XHTML 1.0 Strict//EN" "http://www.w3.org/TR/xhtml1/DTD/
→ xhtml1-strict.dtd">
<html xmlns="http://www.w3.org/1999/xhtml">
<head>
<meta http-equiv="Content-Type" content="text/html; charset=utf-8" />
<title>CSS, DHTML &amp; Ajax | Detecting Which Event Type Fired</title>
<script type="text/javascript">
function initPage(objectID) {
     var object = document.getElementById(objectID);
     object.onmousedown = findEventType;
     document.onclick= findEventType;
}
function findEventType(evt) {
     var evt = (evt) ? evt : ((window.event) ? window.event : null);
     if (evt.type)
         alert('This was triggered by a ' + evt.type + ' event.');
}
</script>
<style type="text/css" media="screen">
#object1 {
     position: relative;
     top: 50px;
     left: 100px;
     width: 392px;
     cursor: pointer;
     border: solid 2px #f00; }
</style>
</head>
<body onload="initPage('object1');">
<h1>Click me and I will tell you what type of event this is.</h1>
<div id="object1"><img src="alice06a.gif" height="480" width="392" alt="alice" /></div>
</body></html>
```

Detecting Which Key Was Pressed

Although the onkeydown, onkeyup, and onkeypress event handlers allow you to detect when a key is pressed, they don't tell you which key was actually pressed. To find that out, you'll need to use the charCode event property for Mozilla and Opera browsers or keyCode event property for Internet Explorer and Safari (**Figure 15.3** and **15.4**). Both of these return a numeric value for the key pressed. You can then use that code to determine the actual key pressed. A list of all the code numbers and their associated characters are provided on this book's Web site (webbedenvironments.com/css_dhtml_ajax).

In this example (**Figure 15.5**), pressing any key will report that key's code number. I've gone ahead and set up an array to hold the first three characters (A, B, and C) but you can add the rest by consulting the book's Web site.

To find which key was pressed:

1. `var keyChar = new Array();`
   `keyChar[65] = 'A';`

   If you need to be able to quickly translate the character code into the actual character, you will need to set up an array that associates the number (used as the array position) with the character (**Code 15.2**).

2. `function initPage() {...}`

   Add the function initPage() to your code and bind a keyDown event to an object.

   In this example, I wanted to detect whenever a key is pressed with the page loaded, so I used window.document. However, you could also bind the event to a form input field to detect key presses only there.

Ask the event object... ... the character code of the keyboard key

event.charCode

Figure 15.3 The general syntax for detecting the character code in Mozilla and Opera.

Ask the event object... ... the character code of the keyboard key

event.keyCode

Figure 15.4 The general syntax for detecting the character code in Internet Explorer and Safari.

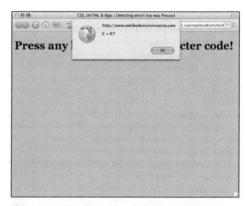

Figure 15.5 The numeric code for the key that the user pressed is displayed in an alert message.

Code 15.2 The event object's keyCode property is used to find the code for the key that the user pressed.

```
<!DOCTYPE html PUBLIC "-//W3C//DTD XHTML 1.0
→ Strict//EN" "http://www.w3.org/TR/xhtml1/
→ DTD/xhtml1-strict.dtd">
<html xmlns="http://www.w3.org/1999/xhtml">
<head>
<meta http-equiv="Content-Type"
→ content="text/html; charset=utf-8" />
<title>CSS, DHTML &amp; Ajax | Detecting
→ which Key was Pressed</title>
<script type="text/javascript">
var keyChar = new Array();
     keyChar[65] = 'A';
     keyChar[66] = 'B';
     keyChar[67] = 'C';
function initPage() {
     window.document.onkeydown=findKey;
}
function findKey(evt) {
     var evt = (evt) ? evt : ((window.event) ?
     → event : null);
     if (evt.type == 'keydown') {
        if (keyChar[evt.keyCode]) alert
        → (keyChar[evt.keyCode] + ' = ' +
        → evt.keyCode);
        else alert ('Character Code = ' +
        → evt.keyCode);
}}
</script>
</head>
<body onload="initPage();">
<h1>Press any key to find its character
→ code!</h1>
<br />
</body></html>
```

3. `function findKey(evt) {...}`

   Add the function `findKey()` to your code.

   This code first uses the event equalizer discussed in Chapter 12 ("Passing Events to a Function") to allow Internet Explorer and W3C-compliant browsers to play together:

   ```
   var evt = (evt) ? evt :
   → ((window.event) ? window.event :
   → null);
   ```

   It then uses either `evt.charCode` if the browser being used is Firefox (or any Mozilla-type browser) or `evt.keyCode` for Internet Explorer and (oddly) Safari to identify the key that was pressed by its numeric value (see this book's Web site for more information).

   For this example, I simply added an alert to report the character value if there is no entry for that code in the array.

4. `onload="initPage();"`

   Add an `onload` event handler in the `<body>` tag to trigger the `initPage()` function created in Step 1. This sets up the events for the page.

✔ Tip

- Although Safari works with both `keyCode` and `charCode`, the values delivered using `charCode` do not match the standard codes.

Should I Use onkeydown, onkeyup, or onkeypress?

Although the onkeypress and onkeyup event handlers also detect when a key is pressed, onkeydown gives more consistently reliable results between browsers for character detection.

Detecting Which Modifier Key Was Pressed

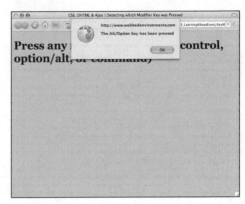

Unlike other keyboard keys, modifier keys (Shift, Control, Alt/Option, and Command) do not register with a numeric value in all browsers on all operating systems. Instead, these keys can be detected directly from the event, so you can tailor your code depending on which key was pressed. Each of these keys has its own unique event property: shiftKey, ctrlKey, altKey, and metaKey (for the Apple Command key).

Figure 15.6 The modifier key the user pressed is displayed in an alert message.

In this example (**Figure 15.6**), press any of the modifier keys (plus any character key on the Mac), and an alert will appear telling you which modifier key was pressed.

To find which modifier key has been pressed:

1. `function initPage() {…}`

   Add the function `initPage()` to your JavaScript and bind a `keydown` event to an object (**Code 15.3**).

   In this example, to detect whenever a key is pressed with the page loaded, I used `window.document`. However, you could also bind the event to a form input field to detect key presses there.

2. `function findModifierKey(evt) {…}`

   Add the function `findModifierKey()` to your JavaScript.

   This code first uses the event equalizer discussed in Chapter 12 ("Passing Events to a Function") to allow Internet Explorer and W3C-compliant browsers to play together:

   ```
   var evt = (evt) ? evt :
   → ((window.event) ? window.event :
   → null);
   ```

   It then evaluates the event for each modifier key object to see if it is true (if that was the key pressed).

For this example, I simply added an alert to report which modifier key was pressed, but you could use the if or switch statements to tailor the code for different modifier keys.

3. onload="initPage();"

Add an onload event handler in the <body> tag to trigger the initPage() function created in Step 1. This sets up the events for the page.

✔ Tips

■ Windows users should know that on the Mac, the Alt key is labeled Option, but both keys do the same thing.

■ The Mac will not detect the modifier key until pressed in combination with a character key.

■ On the Mac, the Control key can be used as a modifier key with the mouse button, in place of the Windows right-mouse click.

Code 15.3 The event object properties shiftKey, ctrlKey, altKey, and metaKey are used to test for which modifier key the user pressed.

```
<!DOCTYPE html PUBLIC "-//W3C//DTD XHTML 1.0 Strict//EN" "http://www.w3.org/TR/xhtml1/DTD/
→ xhtml1-strict.dtd">
<html xmlns="http://www.w3.org/1999/xhtml">
<head>
<meta http-equiv="Content-Type" content="text/html; charset=utf-8" />
<title>CSS, DHTML &amp; Ajax | Detecting which Modifier Key was Pressed</title>
<script type="text/javascript">
function initPage() {
    window.document.onkeydown=findModifierKey;
}
function findModifierKey(evt) {
    var evt = (evt) ? evt : ((window.event) ? window.event : null);
    if (evt) {
        if (evt.shiftKey) alert ('The Shift Key has been pressed');
        if (evt.ctrlKey) alert ('The Control Key has been pressed');
        if (evt.altKey) alert ('The Alt/Option Key has been pressed');
        if (evt.metaKey) alert ('The Command Key has been pressed');
}}
</script>
</head>
<body onload="initPage()">
<h1>Press any modifier key (shift, control, option/alt, or command)</h1>
</body></html>
```

Detecting Which Mouse Button Was Clicked

The computer mouse is an important device, not only for controlling a computer, but also for navigating Web pages. Web pages only interact with one mouse button (the left one, if there is more than one). The right button is used to trigger a contextual menu.

However, using DHTML, you can detect which mouse button is being clicked using the button event property (**Figure 15.7**) to get the button's value (**Table 15.1**) and tailor scripts accordingly.

In this example (**Figure 15.8**), clicking anywhere in the image will display an alert showing which mouse button was pressed.

To find which mouse button was clicked:

1. `var isIE = 0;`

   We need to do a quick browser check for Safari (which is designated KHTML) and Internet Explorer (**Code 15.4**).

2. `if(isIE) var buttonRosetta = new`
   `→ Array('None','Left','Right','',`
   `→ 'Middle');`

   Next, initialize an array to hold the button names. Using your browser detection from Step 1, assign the values to the array according to the browser, with each name in the array ordered according to its mouse button value (Table 15.1).

continues on Page 350

Ask the event object... ... which mouse button was pressed

event.button

Figure 15.7 The general syntax for detecting the mouse button pressed.

Table 15.1

Mouse Button Values

BUTTON	INTERNET EXPLORER*	FIREFOX**
None	0	null
Left	1	0
Middle	4	1
Right	2	2

*Includes Safari
**Includes all Mozilla browsers and Opera

Figure 15.8 The mouse button that the user clicked is displayed in the alert.

Code 15.4 The button event property is used to determine which mouse button was clicked to trigger the event.

```
<!DOCTYPE html PUBLIC "-//W3C//DTD XHTML 1.0 Strict//EN" "http://www.w3.org/TR/xhtml1/DTD/
→ xhtml1-strict.dtd">
<html xmlns="http://www.w3.org/1999/xhtml">
<head>
<meta http-equiv="Content-Type" content="text/html; charset=utf-8" />
<title>CSS, DHTML &amp; Ajax | Detecting Which Mouse Button was Clicked</title>
<script type="text/javascript">
var isIE = 0;
if ((navigator.appVersion.indexOf('KHTML') != -1)|| (navigator.appName.indexOf('Microsoft Internet
→ Explorer') != -1)) {isIE = 1;}
if(isIE) var buttonRosetta = new Array('None','Left','Right','','Middle');
else var buttonRosetta = new Array('Left','Middle','Right');

function initPage(objectID) {
    var object = document.getElementById(objectID);
    object.onmousedown = findMouseButton;
    document.onclick = findMouseButton;
}
function findMouseButton(evt) {
    evt = (evt) ? evt : ((window.event) ? window.event : null)
    if (typeof evt.button != 'undefined') {
        alert('Mouse Button Value = ' + buttonRosetta[evt.button])
}}
</script>
<style type="text/css" media="screen">
#object1 {
    position: relative;
    top: 50px;
    left: 100px;
    width: 392px;
    cursor: pointer;
    border: solid 2px #f00; }
</style>
</head>
<body onload="initPage('object1');">
<h1>Click me and I will tell you which mouse button you pressed.</h1>
<br />
<div id="object1"><img src="alice06a.gif" height="480" width="392" alt="alice" /></div>
</body></html>
```

3. `function initPage() {…}`

Add the function `initPage()` to your JavaScript and bind a `mousedown` event to an object.

In this example, I'm binding an element with a particular ID (`object1`) to an `onmousedown` handler, and the whole document to an `onclick` handler, to detect whenever a mouse button is pressed anywhere in the Web page. You can use one or the other depending on need.

4. `function findMouseButton(evt) {…}`

Add the function `findMouseButton()` to your JavaScript.

This code first uses the event equalizer discussed in Chapter 12 ("Passing Events to a Function") to allow Internet Explorer and W3C-compliant browsers to play together, and then evaluates the `button` event property to determine its value. Unfortunately, W3C-compliant browsers and Internet Explorer will report different values.

For this example, I simply added an alert to report the value of the mouse button pressed.

5. `onload="initPage('object1');"`

Add an `onload` event handler in the `<body>` tag to trigger the `initPage()` function created in Step 1. This sets up the events for the page.

✔ Tips

- Keep in mind that older Mac mice only have one button (treated as the left button), and Control-clicking with a Mac mouse is treated as a right-click. Also, some PC-compatible mice don't have a middle button, so clicking the scroll wheel acts as the middle button.

- Right- or Control-clicking normally brings up a contextual menu. If you use `onmouseup` or `onclick` as the event handler to detect a right-click event, it will be ignored, since the contextual menu trumps all other events.

Ask the event object... ... the X/Y coordinate of where in the window the mouse was clicked

event.clientX

Figure 15.9 The general syntax for detecting where the mouse was clicked in the browser window.

Ask the event object... ... the X/Y coordinate of where on the screen the mouse was clicked

event.screenX

Figure 15.10 The general syntax for detecting where the mouse button was clicked within the screen.

Figure 15.11 An alert tells you where you clicked in the browser window.

Figure 15.12 An alert tells you where you clicked within the entire screen area.

Detecting Where the Mouse Was Clicked

Remember, no matter where you go, there you are. And if you want to know where you are in the browser window, this is the script for you.

All mouse-generated events include information in the event object, specifying not only where the event occurred in the browser window using the clientX and clientY properties (**Figure 15.9**), but also where within the entire screen using screenX and screenY the event occurred (**Figure 15.10**).

In this example (**Figures 15.11** and **15.12**), clicking anywhere will produce an alert that displays the coordinates for where you clicked within the browser window and then an alert showing the coordinates for where you clicked on the screen.

continues on next page

To find the mouse pointer's position:

1. function initPage() {…}

Add the function initPage() to your JavaScript and bind a mouseDown event to an object (**Code 15.5**).

In this example, I'm including event binders for a particular element (object1) and to detect where the mouse cursor is pressed, although it shows you the position relative to the entire Web page. You can use one or the other, depending on your needs.

2. function findMouseLocation(evt) {…}

Add the function findMouseLocation() to your JavaScript. This code first uses the event equalizer discussed in Chapter 12 ("Passing Events to a Function") to allow Internet Explorer and W3C-compliant browsers to play together.

Use the clientX and clientY event properties to find the mouse's position in the browser window. Use the screenX and screenY event properties to find the mouse's position in the screen. For this example, I simply added an alert to report the mouse's position.

3. onload="initPage();"

Add an onload event handler in the <body> tag to trigger the initPage() function created in Step 1. This sets up the events for the page.

✔ Tips

- Although the mouse's y-position in the browser (clientY) is measured from the top of the browser window, its y-position in the screen (screenY) is measured from the bottom of the screen.

- The obvious application of this is to use the onmousemove event handler so that your JavaScript can track where the mouse is at any given moment.

Code 15.5 The event object properties clientX and clientY are used to find the mouse's place in the browser window. The event object properties screenX and screenY are used to determine the mouse's position within the entire screen.

```
<!DOCTYPE html PUBLIC "-//W3C//DTD XHTML 1.0
→ Strict//EN" "http://www.w3.org/TR/xhtml1/
→ DTD/xhtml1-strict.dtd">
<html xmlns="http://www.w3.org/1999/xhtml">
<head>
<meta http-equiv="Content-Type"
→ content="text/html; charset=utf-8" />
<title>CSS, DHTML &amp; Ajax | Detecting
→ Where the Mouse Clicked</title>
<script type="text/javascript">
function initPage(objectID) {
     var object =
     → document.getElementById(objectID);
     object.onmousedown = findMouseLocation;
     window.document.onclick =
     → findMouseLocation;
}
function findMouseLocation(evt) {
     var evt = (evt) ? evt : ((window.event) ?
     → window.event : null);
     alert ('Browser horizontal = ' +
     → evt.clientX + ', Browser vertical =
     → ' + evt.clientY);
     alert ('Screen horizontal = ' +
     → evt.screenX + ', Screen vertical =
     → ' + evt.screenY);
}
</script>
<style type="text/css" media="screen">
#object1 {
     position: relative;
     top: 50px;
     left: 100px;
     width: 392px;
     cursor: pointer;
     border: solid 2px #f00; }
</style>
</head>
<body onload="initPage('object1')">
<h1>Click me and I will tell you where you
→ clicked.</h1>
<div id="object1"><img src="alice06a.gif"
→ height="480" width="392" alt="alice"
/></div>
</body></html>
```

BASIC DYNAMIC TECHNIQUES

Almost all of DHTML is based on a few basic tricks that allow you to hide or show elements, move them around, and make other changes. For the most part, these techniques are based on the ability to change the CSS properties of an element with JavaScript using the `getElementbyId()` method to find it. However, you can also change the actual content between the tags of an object.

In this chapter, we'll look at simple examples of how to create functions that change the following:

◆ An element's visibility or display state to show and hide it

◆ An element's position either to a specific location or by a certain amount.

◆ An element's clipping region to show and hide parts of an element

◆ An element's content after the page is loaded

We'll also look at how to change an element's properties across different frames or windows.

These techniques are the building blocks from which you can create a wide variety of dynamic effects. Let's start with the most basic: changing any object's CSS properties.

Changing CSS Property Values

Although DHTML incorporates a lot of different techniques, the simplest and one of the most common tasks you will be performing is to make changes to CSS properties on the fly. CSS already includes several dynamic pseudo-classes (:hover, :active, and :focus) that let you make changes without using JavaScript, and these pseudo-classes are preferred whenever they can be used. However, JavaScript provides you with a much broader toolset for changing styles on the fly.

In this simple example (**Figures 16.1** and **16.2**), I've set up a function that takes as its input the ID of an element, the CSS property to be changed, and the new value to be assigned to the property.

To change an element's style properties:

1. `function changeStyle(objectID,`
   `→ CSSProp, newVal) {…}`

   Add the function `changeStyle()` to your JavaScript (**Code 16.1**).

   This function uses the ID of the object to be addressed—passed to it as the variable `objectID`—to find the element to be changed. It then uses that object address to change the style of the indicated property (`CSSProp`) to the new value (`newVal`).

   Notice that since we are using a variable in place of the actual property name, the variable `CSSProp` is placed in square brackets.

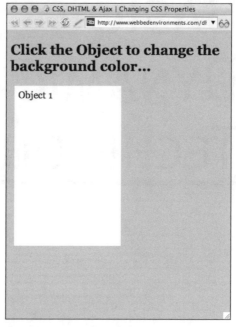

Figure 16.1 Before the object gets clicked, it is a perfectly innocent white box.

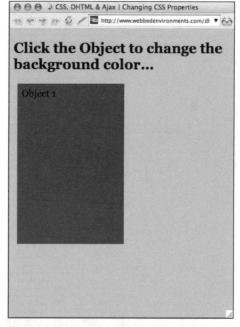

Figure 16.2 After clicking, though, the object's background-color CSS property changes to a vibrant red.

CHANGING CSS PROPERTY VALUES

Code 16.1 the function changeStyle() allows you to change the value of any CSS property.

```
<!DOCTYPE html PUBLIC "-//W3C//DTD XHTML 1.0
→ Strict//EN" "http://www.w3.org/TR/xhtml1/
→ DTD/xhtml1-strict.dtd">
<html xmlns="http://www.w3.org/1999/xhtml">
<head>
<meta http-equiv="Content-Type"
→ content="text/html; charset=utf-8" />
<title>CSS, DHTML &amp; Ajax | Changing CSS
→ Properties</title>
<script type="text/javascript">
function changeStyle(objectID,CSSProp,newVal) {
    var object = document.getElementById
    → (objectID);
    object.style[CSSProp] = newVal;
}
</script>
<style type="text/css" media="screen">
#object1 {
    background-color: #fff;
    width: 200px;
    height:300px;
    margin: 8px;
    padding: 8px;
}
</style>
</head>
<body>
<h2>Click the Object to change the background
→ color...</h2>
<div id="object1"
onclick="changeStyle('object1',
→ 'backgroundColor', 'red');">Object 1 </div>
</body></html>
```

2. `#object1{...}`

Add a CSS rule for the object. You can include the initial value of the CSS property you will be changing in the function from Step 1, but you don't have to.

3. `onclick="changeStyle('object1',` `→ 'backgroundColor', 'red');"`

Add an event handler to an element that triggers the function from Step 1, passing it the ID of the object being changed, the property name, and the new value.

✔ Tips

■ Notice in this section's example that the CSS property name background-color is written as backgroundColor in JavaScript. JavaScript doesn't like hyphens, so hyphenated CSS property names are written without them, but the first letter of subsequent words are capitalized.

■ Although CSS includes several dynamic pseudo-classes, they only work for the link tag in older versions of Microsoft Internet Explorer. Fortunately, Internet Explorer 7 corrects this.

■ In order to be read by JavaScript, CSS properties have to be set by JavaScript first, or the value will appear as null. There is a way around this, but requires a good deal of additional code. See "Finding a Style Property's Value" in Chapter 18 for more details.

Making Objects Appear and Disappear

One of the core features of any dynamic Web site is the ability to control the visibility of an element, allowing it to be shown or not shown at any given moment while the visitor is using the Web site. Whether an object is visible or hidden on the page can be changed using JavaScript, which offers two distinct methods for controlling an object's visibility:

◆ Using `visibility: hidden` will preserve the space needed to show the object even when it's hidden (like the Invisible Man, who still takes up space in his clothes showing his outline, even though you can't see him). When visibility is set back to `visible`, the object simply fills the space.

◆ Using `display: none` completely removes the object from display, leaving no space. If the object's display style is then changed to one of the other visible display styles (`block`, `inline`, and so on), the object will be placed back into the Web page, even if that means redrawing the page to accommodate the "new" object.

Changing the visibility style

The `visibility` property allows you to tell an object whether to appear (`visible`) or not (`hidden`) on the screen (see "Setting the Visibility of an Element" in Chapter 8). Using JavaScript, you can not only determine the current visibility state (see "Finding an Object's Style Property Values" in Chapter 14), but also change the state back and forth.

In this example (**Figures 16.3** and **16.4**), the Cheshire cat's visibility can either be turned on, off, or toggled back and forth, like a switch. Notice that although the image disappears, the text underneath does *not* move, because space is still reserved in the layout for the hidden element.

Figure 16.3 Before the link is clicked to change the visibility style, the cat is visible with the title underneath the image.

Figure 16.4 After the link is clicked, the Cheshire cat does its vanishing act, but the title underneath remains in the exact same position because the invisible object still takes up space.

Code 16.2 The setVisibility() and toggleVisibility() functions change the visibility state of the designated object in the browser window.

```
<!DOCTYPE html PUBLIC "-//W3C//DTD XHTML 1.0
→ Strict//EN" "http://www.w3.org/TR/xhtml1/
→ DTD/xhtml1-strict.dtd">
<html xmlns="http://www.w3.org/1999/xhtml">
<head>
<meta http-equiv="Content-Type"
→ content="text/html; charset=utf-8" />
<title>CSS, DHTML &amp; Ajax | Making
→ Objects Appear and Disappear | Changing
→ Visibility Style</title>
<script type="text/javascript">
function setVisibility(objectID, state) {
    var object =
    → document.getElementById(objectID);
    object.style.visibility = state;
}
function toggleVisibility(objectID) {
    var object =
    → document.getElementById(objectID);
    state = object.style.visibility;
    if (state == 'visible')
        object.style.visibility = 'hidden';
    else
        object.style.visibility = 'visible';
}
</script>
<style type="text/css" media="screen">
#cheshireCat {
    visibility: visible;
    margin: 8px;}
</style>
</head>
<body onload="setVisibility('cheshireCat',
→ 'visible');">
<div id="controls">
<a
    onclick="setVisibility('cheshireCat',
    → 'hidden'); return false;"
    href="#">Hide The Cat</a> |
<a
    onclick="setVisibility('cheshireCat',
    → 'visible'); return false;"
    href="#">Show the Cat</a> |
<a
onclick="toggleVisibility('cheshireCat');
→ return false;"
    href="#">Change the Cat's Visibility</a>
</div>
<div id="cheshireCat">
<img src="alice24.gif" height="283"
→ width="416" alt="The Cheshire Cat" />
</div>
<h1>The Cheshire Cat</h1>
</body></html>
```

To change the visibility state of an object:

1. function setVisibility(objectID,
   → state) {...}

   Add the function setVisibility() to your JavaScript (**Code 16.2**).

   This function uses the ID of the object to be addressed—passed to it as the variable objectID—to find the object to be changed. It can then use this ID to access the object's current visibility property value and change it to whatever state you specify when you trigger it from an event handler, as shown in Step 5.

2. function toggleVisibility(objectID) {...}

   Add the function toggleVisibility() to your JavaScript.

   This function uses the ID of the object to be addressed—passed to it as the variable objectID—to find the object. It then checks the current visibility state of the object and switches it to its opposite. If the value is null, it assumes that the element should be shown.

3. #cheshireCat {...}

   Set up the CSS rules for your object(s) with a visibility value.

4. onload="setVisibility('cheshireCat',
   → 'visible');"

   In the <body> tag, use the setVisibility() function to initialize the visibility of all the objects for which you need to know the initial visibility.

continues on next page

5. `onclick="setVisibility('cheshireCat',`
`→ 'hidden');"`

Add an event handler to an element to trigger the function you created in Step 1, and pass to it the ID for the object you want to address, as well as the visibility state you want it to have.

6. `onclick="toggleVisibility`
`→ ('cheshireCat');"`

Add an event handler to an element to trigger the function you created in Step 2, and pass to it the ID for the object you want to address. Repeat this step for each object you defined in Step 3.

7. `<div id="cheshireCat">…</div>`

Set up the object(s) that will have visibility changed.

Changing the display style

The `display` property lets you tell an object how it should be treated by the surrounding content, for example, as a block element, an inline element, or as if it weren't there at all (see "Setting How an Element Is Displayed" in Chapter 6). Using JavaScript, you can not only determine the current display state, but also change the state.

In this example (**Figures 16.5** and **16.6**), the Cheshire cat can be made to appear, disappear, or toggle back and forth between the two. However, the difference between this example and the previous example is that the image is completely removed from the page, as evidenced by the title moving up to fill what would be empty space.

To change the display state of an object:

1. `function setDisplay(objectID,`
`→ state) {…}`

Add the function `setdisplay()` to your JavaScript (**Code 16.3**).

Figure 16.5 Before the link is clicked to change the display state, the cat is visible with the title underneath the image.

Figure 16.6 After the link is clicked, the Cheshire cat does its vanishing act, but the title underneath moves up because the object is no longer there (unlike in Figure 16.4, where the title stays in the same place).

Code 16.3 The setDisplay() andtoggleDisplay() functions change the display style of the designated object in the browser window.

```
<!DOCTYPE html PUBLIC "-//W3C//DTD XHTML 1.0
→ Strict//EN" "http://www.w3.org/TR/xhtml1/
→ DTD/xhtml1-strict.dtd">
<html xmlns="http://www.w3.org/1999/xhtml">
<head>
<meta http-equiv="Content-Type"
→ content="text/html; charset=utf-8" />
<title>CSS, DHTML &amp; Ajax | Making Objects
→ Appear and Disappear | Changing Visibility
→ Style</title>
<script type="text/javascript">
function setDisplay(objectID, state) {
    var object =
    → document.getElementById(objectID);
object.style.display = state;
}

function toggleDisplay(objectID) {
    var object =
    → document.getElementById(objectID);
    state = object.style.display;
    if (state == 'none')
        object.style.display = 'block';
    else if (state != 'none')
        object.style.display = 'none';
}
</script>
<style type="text/css" media="screen">
#cheshireCat {
    display: block;
    margin: 8px;}
</style>
</head>
<body onload="setDisplay('cheshireCat',
→ 'block');">
<div id="controls">
<a
    onclick="setDisplay('cheshireCat',
    → 'none'); return false;"
    href="#">Remove The Cat</a> |
<a
    onclick="setDisplay('cheshireCat',
    → 'block'); return false;"
    href="#">Display the Cat</a> |
<a
    onclick="toggleDisplay('cheshireCat');
    → return false;"
    href="#">Change the Cat's Display State</a>
</div>
<div id="cheshireCat">
<img src="alice24.gif" height="283"
→ width="416" alt="The Cheshire Cat" />
</div>
<h1>The Cheshire Cat</h1>
</body></html>
```

This function uses the ID of the object to be addressed—passed to it as the variable objectID—to find the object to be changed. It then uses this ID to access the object's current display property and change it to whatever state you specify when you trigger it from an event handler, as shown in Step 5. To hide the object, you'll need to desinate none for the state.

2. function toggleDisplay(objectID) {…}

Add the function toggleDisplay() to your JavaScript.

This function uses the ID of the object to be addressed—passed to it as the variable objectID—to find the object. It then checks the current display state of the object and switches it to either none to hide the object or block to display it. If the value is null, then the object is set to none.

3. #cheshireCat {…}

Set up the CSS rules for your object(s) with a display value.

4. onload="setDisplay('cheshireCat',
→ 'block');"

In the <body> tag, use the setDisplay() function to initialize the visibility of all the objects for which you need to know the initial display value.

5. onclick="setDisplay('cheshireCat',
→ 'none');"

Add an event handler to an element to trigger the function you created in Step 1, and pass to it the ID for the object you want to address, as well as to the display state you want it to have. Add this code to each object.

continues on next page

MAKING OBJECTS APPEAR AND DISAPPEAR

6. `onclick="toggleDisplay`
`→ ('cheshireCat');"`

Add an event handler to an element to trigger the function you created in Step 2, and pass to it the ID for the object you want to address. Repeat this step for each object.

7. `<div id="cheshireCat">…</div>`

Set up your object(s).

✔ Tips

■ In both examples, we used a JavaScript function to initially set the values rather than relying on the CSS. We did this because JavaScript cannot directly access the value of a style until it has been set using JavaScript. For an alternative method, see "Finding a Style Property's Value" in Chapter 18.

■ Although these examples show the ID being passed directly to the function using an anchor element to trigger the event, you can also pass the event to the function (as shown in "Changing CSS Property Values" earlier in this chapter) if you trigger the function with an event handler directly from the object.

■ It may seem like a good idea to set the initial `visibility` of elements to `hidden` or their `display` to `none` using CSS so that you don't have to muck around with JavaScript to set the initial state of the object when the page loads. The problem, though, is that if the visitor has JavaScript turned off, then you run the risk of having the content not ever showing up. Instead, make sure you design pages to be displayed without JavaScript, and then use JavaScript to hide elements when the page loads.

Figure 16.7 The Mad Hatter is dashing for a fresh cup of tea.

Code 16.4 The moveObjectTo() function changes the position of the designated object in the browser window.

```
<!DOCTYPE html PUBLIC "-//W3C//DTD XHTML 1.0
→ Strict//EN" "http://www.w3.org/TR/xhtml1/
→ DTD/xhtml1-strict.dtd">
<html xmlns="http://www.w3.org/1999/xhtml">
<head>
<meta http-equiv="Content-Type"
→ content="text/html; charset=utf-8" />
<title>CSS, DHTML &amp; Ajax | Moving
→ Objects from Point to Point</title>
<script type="text/javascript">
function moveObjectTo(objectID, x, y) {
    var object =
    → document.getElementById(objectID);
        object.style.left = x +'px';
        object.style.top = y + 'px';
}
</script>
<style type="text/css" media="screen">
#madHatter {
    position: absolute;
    top: 40px;
    left: 30px;}
</style>
</head>
<body>
<div id="controls">
<a
    onmouseover="moveObjectTo('madHatter',
    → 200, 200); return false;"
```

Moving Objects from Point to Point

Using CSS, you can position an object on the screen (see "Setting an Element's Position" in Chapter 7); then you can use JavaScript to find the object's position (see "Detecting an Object's Position" in Chapter 14). But to make things really dynamic, you need to be able to move things around on the screen by changing the values for the object's position.

In this example (**Figure 16.7**), the Mad Hatter moves from his initial position to a new position in the Web page when visitors pass their mouse over the link.

To change the position of an object:

1. `function moveObjectTo(objectID,`
   `→ x, y) {…}`

   Add the function moveObjectTo() to your JavaScript (**Code 16.4**).

   This function uses the ID of the object to be addressed—passed to it as the variable objectID—to find the object on the Web page. It then uses the x and y values to reset the left and top positions of the object. Remember that to be valid CSS, you cannot simply assign the raw numeric values to the top and left styles, but must assign them length values. This is why we use +'px'.

continues on next page

Code 16.4 *continued*

```
    onmouseout="moveObjectTo('madHatter',
    → 30, 40); return false;"
    href="#">I want a fresh cup…
</a>
</div>
<div id="madHatter">
<img src="alice39.gif" height="163"
→ width="200" alt="The Mad Hatter" />
</div>
</body></html>
```

2. #madHatter {…}

Set up the CSS rules for your object(s) with initial values for position and top and left position coordinates.

3. onmouseover="moveObjectTo
→ ('madHatter', 200, 200);"

Add an event handler to an element to trigger the function you created in Step 1, and pass to it the ID for the object you want to address and the new coordinates for the object.

4. <div id="madHatter">…</div>

Set up your object(s).

✔ Tips

■ Although I set both top and left positions to move the object, you can use just one of these to have the object move vertically or horizontally.

■ You can use negative values to move the content up and to the left instead of down and to the right.

■ If an element's position is defined as relative, its margins remain unaffected by the top and left properties. This means that setting the top and left margins may cause the content to move outside its naturally defined box for that object and overlap other content.

Figure 16.8 The Mad Hatter is now staggering for a new cup of tea.

Moving Objects by a Certain Amount

Moving an object from one precise point to another (as shown in the previous section) is very useful, but to do this you have to know exactly where it is you want to move the object. Often, though, you simply want the object to move by a certain amount from its current location. To do this, you'll first need to find the location of the object and then add to that the amount by which you want to move it.

In this example (**Figure 16.8**), every time visitors hover over the link, the Mad Hatter staggers forward. Every time they move back off the link, the Mad Hatter staggers back some.

continues on next page

To change the position of an object by a certain amount:

1. `function moveObjectBy(objectID,`
   `→ deltaX, deltaY) {…}`

Add the function **moveObjectBy()** to your JavaScript (**Code 16.5**).

This function uses the ID of the object to be addressed—passed to it as the variable **objectID**—to find the object that's being moved on the Web page. The function then uses **offsetLeft** and **offsetTop** (see "Determining an Object's Position" in chapter 14) to find the current position of the object and adds the **deltaX** and **deltaY** values to move the object to its new position.

2. `#madHatter {…}`

Set up the IDs for your object(s) with values for position and top and left coordinates.

3. `onmouseover="moveObjectBy('madHatter',`
   `→ 75, 100);"`

Add an event handler to an element to trigger the function you created in Step 1, and to pass it the ID for the object you want to address and the number of pixels you want to move it from its current location. Positive numbers move the object down and to the right; negative move it up and to the left.

4. `<div id="madHatter">…</div>`

Set up your object(s).

Code 16.5 The moveObjectBy() function changes the position of the designated object in the browser window by a certain amount every time the mouse pointer rolls onto and then off the link.

```
<!DOCTYPE html PUBLIC "-//W3C//DTD XHTML 1.0
→ Strict//EN" "http://www.w3.org/TR/xhtml1/
→ DTD/xhtml1-strict.dtd">
<html xmlns="http://www.w3.org/1999/xhtml">
<head>
<meta http-equiv="Content-Type"
→ content="text/html; charset=utf-8" />
<title>CSS, DHTML &amp; Ajax | Moving Things
→ By a Certain Amount</title>
<script type="text/javascript">
function moveObjectBy(objectID,deltaX,deltaY) {
    var object =
    → document.getElementById(objectID);
    if (object.offsetLeft != null) {
        var plusLeft = object.offsetLeft;
        var plusTop = object.offsetTop;
        object.style.left = deltaX + plusLeft
        → + 'px';
        object.style.top = deltaY + plusTop
        → + 'px';
    }
}
</script>
<style type="text/css" media="screen">
#madHatter {
    position: absolute;
    top: 40px;
    left: 30px;}
</style>
</head>
<body>
<a
    onmouseover="moveObjectBy('madHatter',
    → 75, 100); return false;"
    onmouseout="moveObjectBy('madHatter',
    → -25, -55); return false;"
    href="#">I want a fresh cup…</a>
<div id="madHatter">
<img src="alice39.gif" height="163"
→ width="200" alt="The Mad Hatter" />
</div>
</body></html>
```

Figure 16.9 This is the stacking order when the page is first loaded.

Figure 16.10 The hapless servants to the queen now pop to the front.

Moving Objects in 3D

All positioned objects can be stacked (see "Stacking Objects" in Chapter 7), and you can use JavaScript to find the object's order in the z-index as well as to change that order.

In this example (**Figures 16.9** and **16.10**), clicking any of the objects will bring it to the front of the stack. Clicking another object will cause the last clicked to revert to its original position, and the new element to come to the front.

To set the 3D position of an object:

1. `var prevObjectID = null;`

   `var prevLayer = 0;`

   In your JavaScript (see **Code 16.6** on the next page), initialize two variables:

   ▲ `prevObjectID`, which stores the ID of the previously selected object

   ▲ `prevLayer`, which stores the z-index of the previously selected object

   continues on Page 367

Code 16.6 The swapLayer() function works in conjunction with the findLayer() and setLayer() functions to pop an object to the top of the stack.

```
<!DOCTYPE html PUBLIC "-//W3C//DTD XHTML 1.0
→ Strict//EN" "http://www.w3.org/TR/xhtml1/
→ DTD/xhtml1-strict.dtd">
<html xmlns="http://www.w3.org/1999/xhtml">
<head>
<meta http-equiv="Content-Type"
content="text/html; charset=utf-8" />
<title>CSS, DHTML &amp; Ajax | Moving
→ Objects in 3-D</title>
<script type="text/javascript">
var prevObjectID = null;
var prevLayer = 0;
function setLayer(objectID,layerNum) {
    var object =
    → document.getElementById(objectID);
    object.style.zIndex = layerNum;
}
function findLayer(objectID) {
    var object =
    → document.getElementById(objectID);
    if (object.style.zIndex != null)
        return object.style.zIndex;
    return (null);
}
function swapLayer(evt) {
    var objectID = (evt.target) ?
    → evt.target.id : ((evt.srcElement) ?
    → evt.srcElement.id : null);
    if (prevObjectID != null)
    → setLayer(prevObjectID,prevLayer);
    prevLayer = findLayer(objectID);
    prevObjectID = objectID;
    setLayer(objectID,1000);
}
</script>
<style type="text/css" media="screen">
.dropBox {
    position: absolute;
    text-align: right;
    padding: 4px;
    background-color: #FFFFFF;
    border: 2px solid #f00;
    cursor: pointer; }
```

Code 16.6 *continued*

```
#object1 {
    z-index: 3;
    top: 285px;
    left: 315px;
    background: white url(alice22a.gif)
    → no-repeat;
    height:220px;
    width:150px;}

#object2 {
    z-index: 2;
    top: 210px;
    left: 225px;
    background: white url(alice15a.gif)
    → no-repeat;
    height:264px;
    width:200px; }
#object3 {
    z-index: 1;
    top: 105px;
    left: 115px;
    background: white url(alice28a.gif)
    → no-repeat;
    height:336px;
    width:250px; }
#object4 {
    position: absolute;
    z-index: 0;
    top: 5px;
    left: 5px;
    background: white url(alice30a.gif)
    → no-repeat;
    height:408px;
    width:300px; }
</style>
</head>
<body>
<div class="dropBox" id="object1"
→ onclick="swapLayer(event);" >Object 1</div>
<div class="dropBox" id="object2"
→ onclick="swapLayer(event);">Object 2</div>
<div class="dropBox" id="object3"
→ onclick="swapLayer(event);">Object 3</div>
<div class="dropBox" id="object4"
→ onclick="swapLayer(event);">Object 4</div>
</body></html>
```

2. `function setLayer(objectID,`
`→ layerNum) {…}`

Add the function **setLayer()** to your JavaScript. This function reassigns the z-index of an object to the indicated layer number.

3. `function findLayer(objectID) {…}`

Add the function **findLayer()** to your JavaScript.

This function uses the ID of the object to be addressed—passed to it as the variable **objectID**—to find and return the current z-index of the layer.

4. `function swapLayer(evt) {…}`

Add the function **swapLayer()** to your JavaScript.

This function demotes the previously selected layer (if there is one) back to its previous z-index and then promotes the selected layer (as indicated by the **objectID**) to the top.

5. `#object1 {…}`

Set up the CSS rules for your object(s) with position and z-index values.

6. `id="object1"`

Set up your object(s).

7. `onclick="swapLayer(event);"`

Add to the element an event handler that triggers the **swapLayer()** function.

✔ Tip

■ Using a negative number for the z-index causes an element to be stacked that many levels below its parent instead of above.

Changing an Object's Visible Area

The clipping region of an object defines how much of that object is visible in the window (see "Setting the Visible Area of an Element" in Chapter 8). If it is left alone, the entire object is visible. But if you clip the object, you can have as much or as little of it visible as you want. You can then use JavaScript to determine the clipping region (see "Finding an Object's Visible Area" in Chapter 14). In addition, DHTML allows you to change the clipping region on the fly, allowing you to not just show and hide the entire object, but select parts of it.

In this example (**Figures 16.11** and **16.12**), the layer with the image is initially clipped such that part of the image is not shown. Passing their mouse over the link allows visitors to see the rest of the image, while passing out of the link hides parts of the image again.

To change the visible area of an object:

1. `function setClip(objectID, clipTop, clipRight, clipBottom, clipLeft) {…}`

   Add the function `setClip()` to your JavaScript (**Code 16.7**).

   This function uses the ID of the object to be addressed—passed to it as the variable `objectID`—to find the object that will be reclipped. The function then uses the clip style to set a new clipping region for the object:

   ```
   object.style.clip = 'rect(' +
   → clipTop + 'px ' + clipRight +
   → 'px ' + clipBottom + 'px ' +
   → clipLeft +'px)';
   ```

Figure 16.11 What is the Cheshire cat smiling about? Roll over the link and find out.

Figure 16.12 The Cheshire cat is smiling because the King can't order his executioner to chop off a head that has no body. This fact makes the Queen of Hearts very, very angry.

Code 16.7 The setClip() function redraws the boundaries of the clipping region set around an object.

```
<!DOCTYPE html PUBLIC "-//W3C//DTD XHTML 1.0
→ Strict//EN" "http://www.w3.org/TR/xhtml1/
→ DTD/xhtml1-strict.dtd">
<html xmlns="http://www.w3.org/1999/xhtml">
<head>
<meta http-equiv="Content-Type"
→ content="text/html; charset=utf-8" />
<title>CSS, DHTML &amp; Ajax | Finding an
→ Objects Visible Area</title>
<script type="text/javascript">
function setClip(objectID, clipTop,
→ clipRight, clipBottom, clipLeft) {
    var object =
    → document.getElementById(objectID);
    object.style.clip = 'rect(' + clipTop +
    → 'px ' + clipRight + 'px ' +
    → clipBottom + 'px ' + clipLeft +'px)';
}
</script>
<style type="text/css" media="screen">
#cheshireCat {
    position: absolute;
    top: 60px;
    left: 0;
    overflow: hidden;
    clip: rect(15px 350px 195px 50px)}
</style>
</head>
<body>
<div id="controls">
<a
    onmouseover="setClip('cheshireCat',
    → 35, 320, 400, 70); return false;"
    onmouseout="setClip('cheshireCat',
    → 15, 350, 195, 50); return false;"
    href="#">What is the Cheshire Cat
    → smiling about? </a>
</div>
<div id="cheshireCat">
    <img src="alice31.gif" height="480"
    → width="379" alt="Alice" />
</div>
</body></html>
```

2. `#cheshireCat {…}`

   Set up the CSS rule(s) for your object(s), with values for `clip` (the initial clipping region).

3. `onmouseover="setClip('cheshireCat',` → `35, 320, 400, 70);"`

   Include an event handler on an element to trigger the `setClip()` function. Remember that because this function will be using the DOM, it has to be triggered from an event and cannot be triggered from JavaScript in the `href` of the link.

4. `<div id="cheshireCat">…</div>`

   Set up your object(s) for which you want to change the clipping region.

✔ Tips

- The element's borders and padding will be clipped along with the content of the element, but its margin will not be.

- Currently, clips can only be rectangular, but future versions of CSS promise to support other shapes.

Changing an Object's Content

Another important method for making changes to a Web page without having to reload the page is to use the innerHTML property. This allows you to replace or add to the current content within an object, including text and HTML tags. Not only can you change content (for example, changing a layer's visibility), but you can also react to input from the user—for example, from a form field. This can be an amazingly powerful technique, which forms the basis of a lot of Ajax techniques for updating pages on the fly.

In this example (**Figures 16.13** and **16.14**), the name typed into a form field is printed on the page without the form actually ever being submitted to the server.

To change the content of an element:

1. function writeName() {…}

   Add the function writeName() to your JavaScript (**Code 16.8**).

   This function first looks in the form field yourName to get its content and assigns it to the variable userName, and then uses that variable, combined with other text and HTML tags, to change the content of the object named response by means of the innerHTML property:

   object.innerHTML = '…'

2. <input type="text" id="yourName"
   → size="30" />

   Add the input field that is queried by the function from Step 1.

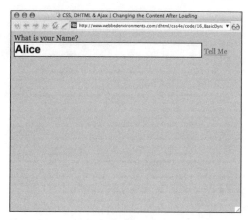

Figure 16.13 Initially the message is to enter your name.

Figure 16.14 After you enter text and click the link, the message is changed without reloading the page or changing the visibility of layers by changing the content of the element.

Code 16.8 The function writeName() is just one way to use innerHTML to change the content of a layer using input from a form field.

```
<!DOCTYPE html PUBLIC "-//W3C//DTD XHTML 1.0
→ Strict//EN" "http://www.w3.org/TR/xhtml1/
→ DTD/xhtml1-strict.dtd">
<html xmlns="http://www.w3.org/1999/xhtml">
<head>
<meta http-equiv="Content-Type"
→ content="text/html; charset=utf-8" />
<title>CSS, DHTML &amp; Ajax | Changing the
→ Content After Loading</title>
<script type="text/javascript">
<!--
function writeName(objectID) {
    var object =
    → document.getElementById(objectID);
    var userName =
    → document.getElementById
    → ('yourName').value;
    object.innerHTML = '<h1>Hello <i>' +
    → userName + '</i>!</h1><img
    → src="alice09a.gif" alt="Alice"
    → width="278" height="312" />'
}
// -->
</script>
<style type="text/css" media="screen">
h1 {
    color: red;
    font-size: 3em; }
input {font:bold 1.5em Arial, Helvetica,
→ sans-serif; border: 2px solid black;}
</style>
</head>
<body>
<div id="response">What is your Name?
<input type="text" id="yourName" size="30" />
<a
    onclick="writeName('response'); return
    → false;"
    href="#">Tell Me</a></div>
</body></html>
```

3. onclick="writeName();"

Add an event handler to trigger the writeName() function from Step 1. You could use any element you want, including a form button, but I chose to use a link.

For simplicity in this example, I left out the <form> tag, so we are not restricted to using the form button and having to override its default action.

4. <div id="response">…</div>

Set up the object whose content you'll be changing, making sure to give it a unique ID. You can enter the initial content for the object or simply leave it empty to fill in later.

✔ Tips

■ One shortcoming of this technique is that it is not a part of the W3C DOM specification, but was created by Microsoft for Internet Explorer 4+. The good news is that most browsers, such as Mozilla browsers (including Firefox), Opera, and Safari, are also supporting the method.

■ If you simply want to add to the current content in a layer without replacing it, you can just use += rather than = to assign the values. The new content is added after the current content of the layer.

Controlling Objects Between Frames

You can use JavaScript to control objects within one frame without much trouble. Controlling objects in another frame, however, is a little more complicated. To do this, rather than just passing the function the name of the object you want to change, you also have to pass the function the name of the frame the object is in.

In this example (**Figure 16.15**), a link in the bottom frame will cause the object in the top frame to move.

To control elements in other frames:

1. `index.html`

   Set up your frameset document, making sure to name the frames that will have dynamic content (**Figure 16.16**). Save this file as index.html (**Code 16.9**).

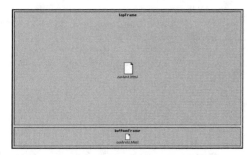

Figure 16.15 The Rabbit may be in a different frame, but the code will hunt him down and make him run.

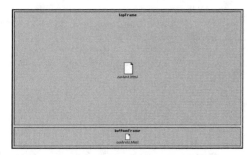

Figure 16.16 The frameset set up by index.html.

Code 16.9 In this example, I have set up a frame document (index.html) with frames named "topFrame" and "bottomFrame". The frames' sources are content.html and control.html, respectively. Notice that his uses the XHTML frameset DTD.

```
<!DOCTYPE html PUBLIC "-//W3C//DTD XHTML 1.0 Frameset//EN" "http://www.w3.org/TR/xhtml1/DTD/
→ xhtml1-frameset.dtd">
<html xmlns="http://www.w3.org/1999/xhtml">
<head>
<meta http-equiv="Content-Type" content="text/html; charset=utf-8" />
<title>DHTML &amp; CSS for the WWW | Dynamic Control Between Frames</title>
</head>
<frameset rows="*,50">
    <frame src="content.html" name="topFrame" scrolling="no" noresize="noresize" id="topFrame" />
    <frame src="controls.html" name="bottomFrame" scrolling="no" noresize="noresize"
    → id="bottomFrame" />
<noframes><body><p>Frames not supported.</p></body></noframes>
</frameset></html>
```

Code 16.10 The object whiteRabbit has been set up and can now be controlled from this frame or any other frame by adding the frame name to the path when finding the object.

```
<!DOCTYPE html PUBLIC "-//W3C//DTD XHTML 1.0
→ Strict//EN" "http://www.w3.org/TR/xhtml1/
→ DTD/xhtml1-strict.dtd">
<html xmlns="http://www.w3.org/1999/xhtml">
<head>
<meta http-equiv="Content-Type"
→ content="text/html; charset=utf-8" />
<title>CSS, DHTML &amp; Ajax | Content
→ Frame</title>
<style type="text/css" media="screen">
#whiteRabbit {
    position: absolute;
    top: 125px;
    left: 350px; }
</style>
</head>
<body>
<div id="whiteRabbit"> <img src="alice02.gif"
→ height="300" width="200" alt="" /> </div>
</body></html>
```

2. content.html

   Now set up an HTML document with the objects to be controlled from the other frame. Include positioned objects with IDs that can be controlled with JavaScript (**Code 16.10**). In this example, I've set up an object called whiteRabbit. Save this file as content.html.

3. controls.html

   Set up the HTML document that will control the element in the other frame. You have to change the function moveObject() (shown earlier in this chapter in "Moving Objects from Point to Point") to become moveObjectFrame() to use the variable frameName—which, along with the objectID variable is used to find the object (**Code 16.11**):

   var object = top[frameName].
   → document.getElementById(objectID);

continues on next page

Code 16.11 The code in controls.html uses a variation of the moveObject() function presented earlier in this chapter. The main difference is that the function is passed not only the ID of the object to be moved, but also the name of the frame the object is in.

```
<!DOCTYPE html PUBLIC "-//W3C//DTD XHTML 1.0 Strict//EN" "http://www.w3.org/TR/xhtml1/DTD/
→ xhtml1-strict.dtd">
<html xmlns="http://www.w3.org/1999/xhtml">
<head>
<meta http-equiv="Content-Type" content="text/html; charset=utf-8" />
<title>CSS, DHTML &amp; Ajax | Controls Frame</title>
<script type="text/javascript">
function moveObjectFrame(objectID, frameName, x, y){
    var object = top[frameName].document.getElementById(objectID);
    object.style.left = x + 'px';
    object.style.top = y + 'px';
}
</script>
</head>
<body>
<a href="#" onmouseover="moveObjectFrame('whiteRabbit', 'topFrame', 10, 10); return false;"
→ onmouseout="moveObjectFrame('whiteRabbit', 'topFrame', 350, 125); return false;" >Run Rabbit,
→ Run!</a>
</body></html>
```

CONTROLLING OBJECTS BETWEEN FRAMES

4. Save this file as *controls.html*.

Now, when you load the file index.html into a Web browser, the files content.html and controls.html are loaded into the frames. The bottom frame (`bottomFrame`) includes a link that controls the object `whiteRabbit` in the upper frame (`topFrame`).

✔ Tips

■ Notice that the frames use the `name` attribute rather than `id`. The `name` attribute is being phased out for most uses, but frames will still use it.

■ This example shows you how to move an object across frames, but you can use any of the other dynamic functions described in this book in your frames.

■ For all intents and purposes, another window is like another frame. If you have two windows open, you can use this technique to communicate between two windows, as long as they're named. In addition, this will work with iframes.

ADVANCED DYNAMIC TECHNIQUES

In Chapter 16, you learned about the basic building blocks for creating a dynamic Web site. These include relatively simple tasks, such as changing an object's position and visibility. Now, it is time to combine those techniques to not only change objects spatially, but also add a temporal element so that objects change over time. This process lets you animate objects and enables users to interact more extensively with the objects.

In this chapter we'll look at ways to do the following:

- Loop functions to continue running at specific intervals

- Make objects appear to move fluidly around the window

- Use form input to make dynamic changes

- Allow the visitor to move objects around on the page

- Create objects that appear to follow the mouse pointer around the screen

We'll also look at how to make changes to the browser window so that it is located exactly where you need it while you're working.

Making a Function Run Again

To create a DHTML function, you often need to have that function run repeatedly until, well, until you don't want it to run anymore. This repeated running of the function lets you animate objects or cause objects to wait for a particular event to happen in the browser window before continuing. To do this, we will be using the setTimeout() method, which lets you run a function after a specific delay. See the sidebar "Why setTimeout()" for more details.

In this example (**Figure 17.1**), I modified the toggleVisibility() function from Chapter 16, causing it to leap continuously until the visitor clicks the image to stop it.

Why setTimeout()?

One common question I get about running a function repeatedly with the setTimeout() function is, "Why not just call the function from within itself?" There are two reasons:

◆ Netscape Navigator 4 has a bug that causes the entire browser to crash when a function calls itself recursively. Although Netscape 4 does not need to be an ongoing concern, this can be very annoying if a user visits your site using this browser.

◆ setTimeout() makes it easy to control a pause between the function's looping back and running again. This can come in handy if you need the function to run more slowly than the computer would run it automatically.

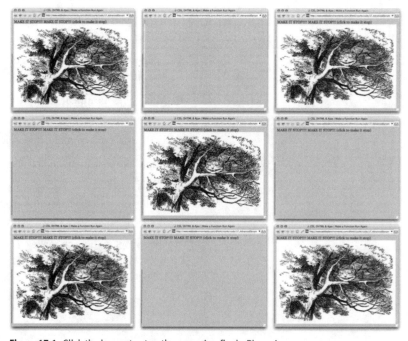

Figure 17.1 Click the image to stop the annoying flash. Please!

Code 17.1 The setUpAnnoyingFlash() function prepares the initial values of variables that are then run in the annoyingFlash() function.

```
<!DOCTYPE html PUBLIC "-//W3C//DTD XHTML 1.0
→ Strict//EN" "http://www.w3.org/TR/xhtml1/
→ DTD/xhtml1-strict.dtd">
<html xmlns="http://www.w3.org/1999/xhtml">
<head>
<meta http-equiv="Content-Type"
→ content="text/html; charset=utf-8" />
<title>CSS, DHTML &amp; Ajax | Make a
→ Function Run Again</title>
<script type="text/javascript">
var theDelay = 500;
var state = null;
var object = null;
var toRepeat = 0;
function setUpAnnoyingFlash(objectID,
→ onOffon) {
    if (onOffon == 1) {
        toRepeat = 1;
        object =
        → document.getElementById(objectID);
        object.style.visibility = 'visible';
        state = 'visible';
        annoyingFlash();
    }
    else toRepeat = 0;
}
function annoyingFlash() {
    if (toRepeat == 1) {
        if (state == 'hidden' )
        object.style.visibility = 'visible';
        else {
        if (state == 'visible')
        object.style.visibility = 'hidden';
        else object.style.visibility =
        → 'visible';
        }
        state = object.style.visibility;
        setTimeout ('annoyingFlash()',
        → theDelay);
    }
    else{
        object.style.visibility = 'visible';
        return;
}}
</script>
<style type="text/css" media="screen">
#cheshireCat {
    visibility: visible;
    position: relative; }
</style>
</head>
```

To call a function repeatedly:

1. `var theDelay = 500;`
   Initialize the global variables (**Code 17.1**):
   ▲ `theDelay` sets the amount of time in milliseconds between each running of the function. The value `1,000` milliseconds equates to a one-second delay, so `500` is half a second.
   ▲ `object` is used to record the ID of the object that is being changed and is initially set to `null`.
   ▲ `toRepeat` records whether the function should be repeating (1) or stopped (0).

2. `function setUpAnnoyingFlash(objectID,`
   `→ onOffon) {…}`
   Add a function that sets initial parameters for the repeating function, and then calls the function to start it.
   In this example, `setUpAnnoyingFlash()` first checks to see whether it's being told to start or stop the function it is controlling. If starting, it finds the object to be used, sets its initial state to visible, and triggers the function `annoyingFlash()`. Otherwise it stops the function by setting the variable `toRepeat` to 0.

continues on next page

Code 17.1 *continued*

```
<body onload="setUpAnnoyingFlash
→ ('cheshireCat', 1);">
<p>MAKE IT STOP!!!! MAKE IT STOP!!! (click
→ to make it stop)</p>
<div id="cheshireCat" onclick=
→ "setUpAnnoyingFlash('cheshireCat', 0);">
<img src="alice24.gif" height="435"
→ width="640" alt="Cheshire Cat" /></div>
</body></html>
```

3. `function annoyingFlash() {…}`

Add the function you want to repeat. In this example, `annoyingFlash()` is started by the `setUpAnnoyingFlash()` function in Step 2.

If `toStop` is 1, the visibility is toggled (`visible` if hidden, `hidden` if visible). The function then uses the `setTimeout()` method to call itself to run again after a delay:

```
setTimeout ('annoyingFlash()',
→ theDelay);
```

The `annoyingFlash()` function keeps running until `toStop` is 0, in which case the visibility is finally set to `visible`, and the function stops running.

4. `#cheshireCat {…}`

Set up the CSS rules for your object(s) with the relevant styles—in this example, the `visibility` state.

5. `onload="setUpAnnoyingFlash`
`→ ('cheshireCat', 1);"`

Add an event handler to the body element to trigger the function you created in Step 2, and pass to it the ID for the object. Indicate whether you want in this example to retain the annoying flash (1) or not (0).

6. `<div id="cheshireCat" onclick=`
`→ "setUpAnnoyingFlash('cheshireCat',`
`0)">…</div>`

Set up your object(s) as needed, based on the ID from Step 4, with an event handler to stop the repeating function.

✔ Tip

■ When you run this example code, notice that you can click the cat to stop the flashing only while the image is visible. That's because the event can only be triggered when the layer is visible.

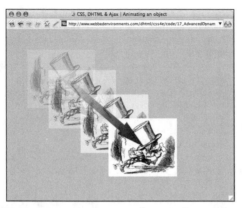

Figure 17.2 The Mad Hatter dashes across the screen.

Animating an Object

When most people think about dynamic techniques, they don't think of simply moving objects from one point to another (see "Moving Objects from Point to Point" in Chapter 16), but of making objects slide across the screen from one point to another or along a curved path.

Using a function that runs recursively (see the previous section, "Making a Function Run Again"), you can make any object that has been positioned (see "Setting an Element's Position" in Chapter 7) seem to glide from one point to another.

Animating an object in a straight line

For a straight line, the process of animation is relatively straightforward: Simply move the object incrementally horizontally and/or vertically step-by-step from its first position to its last position.

There is one small snag, though; if the horizontal and vertical distances the object has to move are not the same value, you'll need to adjust step movement to get a straight line. This is handled by calculating the slope of the angle between the two points, and using this value to adjust how far the object should be moved in a single step.

In this example (**Figure 17.2**), we set the initial starting point of our object, and then calculate each point along the path to its final position, moving it just a little bit with each step.

continues on next page

To animate an object in a straight line:

1. `var animateSpeed = 5;`

Initialize the following global variables (**Code 17.2**):

▲ `animateSpeed` sets the increment the object is moved with each step. The larger the number, the slower the object slides, but the choppier the animation looks.

▲ `object` records the object's ID.

▲ `fX` records the final left position of the object.

▲ `fY` records the final top position of the object.

▲ `cX` records the current left position of the object.

▲ `cY` records the current top position of the object.

▲ `dX` keeps track of the amount the object has moved to the left while being animated.

▲ `dY` keeps track of the amount the object has moved from the top while being animated.

▲ `stepX` records how far the object should move horizontally for each step in the animation.

▲ `stepY` records how far the object should move vertically for each step in the animation.

▲ `slope` records the ratio of x to y, for the slant of the object's path from the starting position to its final position. This is used to calculate the x and y step values so that the object goes in a straight line between the two points.

2. `function initAnimate(objectID, x,`
`→ y){...}`

Add the function `initAnimate()` to your JavaScript. This function uses the ID of the object to locate it on the screen, sets the final x, y position of the object

Code 17.2 The `startAnimate()` function finds the initial left and top positions of the object and then triggers the `animateObject()` function to start the animation.

```
<!DOCTYPE html PUBLIC "-//W3C//DTD XHTML 1.0
→ Strict//EN" "http://www.w3.org/TR/xhtml1/
→ DTD/xhtml1-strict.dtd">
<html xmlns="http://www.w3.org/1999/xhtml">
<head>
<meta http-equiv="Content-Type"
→ content="text/html; charset=utf-8" />
<title>CSS, DHTML &amp; Ajax | Animating an
→ object</title>
<script type="text/javascript">
<!--
var animateSpeed = 5;
var object = null;
var fX = null; var fY = null;
var cX = null; var cY = null;
var dX = null; var dY = null;
var stepX = null; var stepY = null;
var slope = null;
function initAnimate(objectID,x,y) {
     object =
     → document.getElementById(objectID);
     fX = x;
     fY = y;
     cX = object.offsetLeft;
     cY = object.offsetTop;
     dX = Math.abs(fX-cX);
     dY = Math.abs(fY-cY);
     if ((dX == 0) || (dY == 0)) slope = 0;
     else slope= dY/dX;
        if (dX>=dY) {
        if (cX<fX) stepX = animateSpeed;
        else if (cX>fX) stepX = -
        → animateSpeed;
        if (cY<fY) stepY =
        → animateSpeed*slope;
        else if (cY>fY) stepY = -
        → animateSpeed*slope;
        }
        else if (dX<dY) {
        if (cY<fY) stepY= animateSpeed;
        else if (cY>fY) stepY= -
        → animateSpeed;
        if (cX<fX) stepX =
        → animateSpeed/slope;
        else if (cX>fX) stepX = -
        → animateSpeed/slope;
        }
     animateObject()
}
```

code continues on next page

Code 17.2 *continued*

```
function animateObject() {
    if (( dX > 0 ) || (dY > 0)) {
        object.style.left = Math.round(cX) +
        → 'px';
        object.style.top = Math.round(cY) +
        → 'px';
        cX = cX + stepX;
        cY = cY + stepY;
        dX = dX - Math.abs(stepX);
        dY = dY - Math.abs(stepY);
        setTimeout ('animateObject()',0);
    }
else {
    object.style.left = fX + 'px';
    object.style.top = fY + 'px';
}
    return;
}
// -->
</script>
<style type="text/css" media="screen">
#madHatter {
    position: absolute;
    left: 10px;
    top: 10px; }
</style>
</head>
<body onload="initAnimate('madHatter', 300,
→ 250);">
<div id="madHatter"><img src="alice39.gif"
→ height="163" width="200" alt="Mad Hatter"
/></div>
</body></html>
```

(fX and fY), calculates the current x,y position of the object (cX and cY), calculates the slope of the animation path, and then uses that to calculate how far the object should move horizontally and vertically for each step in the animation. Finally, this function runs the animateObject() function.

The mathematics in this function may look a bit complex at first, but it's really straightforward addition and/or subtraction. To allow for the final position being above, below, to the left, or to the right of the initial position, we have to add several conditionals.

3. `function animateObject() {…}`

Add the function animateObject() to your JavaScript. This function checks to see if the object has moved past its final position. If not, it moves the object to its new position, calculates the next position it should be moved to by adding the step variables to the current position, recalculates the current position, and then runs the function again. If the object has moved to its final position, it is moved back slightly to compensate, and then the function ends.

4. `#madHatter {…}`

Set up the CSS rule for your animated object with values for position and top and left positions.

5. `onload="initAnimate('madHatter',`
`→ 200, 200);"`

Add an event handler to the body element to trigger the function you created in Step 2, passing the function the ID of the object you want to animate and the final x,y position to which you want that object to move.

6. `<div id="madHatter">…</div>`

Set up the object to be animated.

ANIMATING AN OBJECT

Animating an object in a circle

In many ways, a circular animation is easier to code than a straight line, because you don't need to keep track of the slope. Instead, simply feed the formula for the radius of the circle and the script takes it from there.

In this example (**Figure 17.3**), the cosine (Math.cos()) and sine (Math.sin()) methods are used to calculate the circumference with the given radius, creating a roughly circular path.

To animate an object in a circle:

1. animateSpeed = 10;

   Initialize the following global variables (**Code 17.3**):

   ▲ animateSpeed sets the amount of delay in the recursive running of the function. The larger the number, the slower the object slides, but the choppier the animation looks.

   ▲ object records the object's ID.

   ▲ cX records the current left position of the object.

   ▲ cY records the current top position of the object.

   ▲ fX records the final left position of the object.

   ▲ fY records the final top position of the object.

   ▲ next keeps track of the amount that the object has moved around the circular path.

   ▲ radius keeps track of the distance from the object to the center of the circle around which the object is being animated.

2. function initAnimateCircle(objectID,
   → theRadius) {…}

   Add the function initAnimateCircle() to your JavaScript.

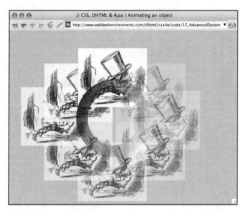

Figure 17.3 The Mad Hatter dashes around in a circle.

Code 17.3 The circular animation script calculates where the object should be displayed along the circumference of a circle, based on a radius that you initially feed it.

```
<!DOCTYPE html PUBLIC "-//W3C//DTD XHTML 1.0
→ Strict//EN" "http://www.w3.org/TR/xhtml1/
→ DTD/xhtml1-strict.dtd">
<html xmlns="http://www.w3.org/1999/xhtml">
<head>
<meta http-equiv="Content-Type"
→ content="text/html; charset=utf-8" />
<title>CSS, DHTML &amp; Ajax | Animating an
→ object</title>
<script type="text/javascript">
<!--
var animateSpeed = 10;
var object = null;
var cX = null;
var cY = null;
var fX = null;
var fY = null;
var next = null;
var radius = null;
function initAnimateCircle(objectID,
→ theRadius) {
    object = document.getElementBy
    → Id(objectID);
    radius = theRadius;
    cX = fX = object.offsetLeft;
    cY = fY = object.offsetTop;
    next=1;
    animateObjectCircle();
}
```
code continues on next page

Code 17.3 *continued*

```
function animateObjectCircle() {
    if (next < 72) {
        var nX = cX + (Math.cos(next *
        → (Math.PI/36)) * radius);
        var nY = cY + (Math.sin(next *
        → (Math.PI/36)) * radius);
        object.style.left = Math.round(nX) +
        → 'px';
        object.style.top = Math.round(nY) +
        → 'px';
        cX = nX;
        cY = nY;
        next++;
        setTimeout ('animateObjectCircle()',
        → animateSpeed);
    }
    else {
        object.style.left = fX + 'px';
        object.style.top = fY + 'px';
    }
    return;
}
// -->
</script>
<style type="text/css" media="screen">
#madHatter {
    position: absolute;
    left: 200px;
    top: 50px; }
</style>
</head>
<body onload="initAnimateCircle('madHatter',
→ 10);">
<div id="madHatter"><img src="alice39.gif"
→ height="163" width="200" alt="Mad Hatter"
/></div>
</body></html>
```

✔ **Tip**

■ The formula used to calculate the circumference of the circle could be replaced by any mathematical formulae to create a variety of curved paths.

This function uses the ID of the object to locate it on the screen, finds the current x,y position of the object (cX and cY), and also stores this as the object's final x,y position (fX and fY). Finally, this function runs the animateObjectCircle() function.

3. `function animateObjectCircle() {…}`

   Add the function animateObjectCircle() to your JavaScript.

   This function first checks to see if the object has made a full circle (in this example, 72 steps around the circumference). If not, the function calculates the next position of the object along the circumference of the circle:

   `var nX = cX + (Math.cos(next *`
   `→ (Math.PI/36)) * radius);`
   `var nY = cY + (Math.sin(next *`
   `→ (Math.PI/36)) * radius);`

   The function then moves the object, increases next by 1, and runs the function again. Once the function reaches 72, the object is reset to its initial (final) position. This ensures that the object is exactly positioned in case of any mathematical discrepancies that might offset it by a few pixels.

4. `#madHatter {…}`

   Set up the CSS rule for your animated object with values for position and top and left positions.

5. `onload="initAnimateCircle('madHatter',`
   `→ 10);"`

   Add an event handler to the body element to trigger the function you created in Step 2, passing the function of the ID of the object you want to animate and the radius of the circle around which you want to animate it.

6. `<div id="madHatter">…</div>`

   Set up the object to be animated.

Using Input from a Form Field

The most common way users interact with a Web page is with the mouse. But you can also use forms in which visitors enter information, which is then used to perform a specific action, without having to reload the page.

In Chapter 16, I showed you how to move objects from point to point, but you defined those points. Now it's the visitors' turn to define the movement, by allowing them to enter coordinates into form fields.

In this example (**Figure 17.4**), two form fields are presented to define the x,y position of the object on the page. After entering their desired coordinates, the visitor can click the form button, and the object will be moved.

To receive visitor input through a form:

1. function moveObjectTo(objectID,
→ formNum) {…}

Add moveObjectTo() to the JavaScript at the head of your document (**Code 17.4**).

This function is a modified version of the moveObjectTo() function from Chapter 16. The function reads the values from the indicated form (formNum) using the forms[] array and form field names (xVal and yVal):

x = document.forms[formNum].xVal.value;

It then uses those values for the object's new left and top position.

The form number is an array, with each <form> element given a unique number. The first form is form 0, while subsequent forms are 1, 2, 3, etc.

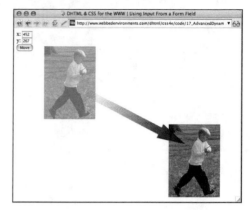

Figure 17.4 The visitor enters the new coordinates for the picture to dash to.

Code 17.4 To show how to read data from form fields, we adapted the moveObjectTo() function to read values from the input fields.

```
<!DOCTYPE html PUBLIC "-//W3C//DTD XHTML 1.0
→ Strict//EN" "http://www.w3.org/TR/xhtml1/
→ DTD/xhtml1-strict.dtd">
<html xmlns="http://www.w3.org/1999/xhtml">
<head>
<meta http-equiv="Content-Type"
→ content="text/html; charset=utf-8" />
<title>CSS, DHTML, &amp; Ajax | Using Input
→ From a Form Field</title>
<script type="text/javascript">
function moveObjectTo(objectID,formNum) {
    x = document.forms[formNum].xVal.value;
    y = document.forms[formNum].yVal.value;
    var object = document.getElementById
    → (objectID);
    object.style.left = x + 'px';
    object.style.top= y + 'px';
    return false;
}
</script>
<style type="text/css" media="screen">
#dash {
    visibility: visible;
    position: absolute;
    top: 36px;
    left: 137px;}
</style>
</head>
<body>
<div id="dash">
<img src="dash.jpg" height="203" width="150"
→ alt="Walking Boy" /></div>
<div id="controls">
<form name="newXY" id="newXY" action="#"
→ method="get">
    x:
    <input type="text" name="xVal" size="3" />
    <br />
    y:
    <input type="text" name="yVal" size="3" />
    <br />
    <input onclick="moveObjectTo('dash',0)"
    → type="button" value="Move" />
</form></div>
</body></html>
```

2. `#dash {…}`

Set up a CSS layer positioned with the top and left properties.

3. `<div id="dash">…</div>`

Set up the object you want to control with the form data.

4. `<form action="#" name="newXY" → id="newXY" method="get">…</form>`

Set up a simple form, and give it a name.

5. `<input type="text" name="xVal" → id="xVal" size="3">`

Add form fields that allow visitors to enter the x and y coordinates of the object's new position.

6. `onclick="moveObjectTo('dash', 0);"`

Add an event handler that triggers moveObjectTo(). Pass the function the ID of the object you want to move and the number of the form you created in Step 4. Remember, each form is automatically numbered by the Web page, with the first form on the page being 0. Clicking this button causes the element to move to the specified coordinates.

✔ **Tip**

■ This example is admittedly of limited use for most Web page applications. However, the technique described has broad applications, especially when we start looking at Ajax.

Following the Mouse Pointer

The mouse pointer is part of the user interface over which designers have limited control. Although you can control the pointer's appearance to a limited degree (see "Changing the Mouse Pointer's Appearance" in Chapter 8), you're stuck with the pointers provided by the browser.

By using a bit of DHTML, however, you can create a layer that follows the mouse on the screen. In browsers that let you set the pointer's appearance to none, you can thus replace the pointer with a graphic of your own.

In this example (**Figure 17.5**), the background color is set to black with black text on top. However, a white circular image below the text can be controlled with the mouse. The effect looks like a flashlight making the black text appear wherever it is in the window.

To create an object that follows the mouse pointer:

1. `function initPage() {...}`

   Add `initPage()` to the JavaScript (**Code 17.5**).

Figure 17.5 This technique can be used to create a flashlight effect.

Code 17.5 A global event handler lets you track the path of the mouse and move an object along with it using the followMe() function.

```
<!DOCTYPE html PUBLIC "-//W3C//DTD XHTML 1.0
→ Strict//EN" "http://www.w3.org/TR/xhtml1/
→ DTD/xhtml1-strict.dtd">
<html xmlns="http://www.w3.org/1999/xhtml">
<head>
<meta http-equiv="Content-Type"
→ content="text/html; charset=utf-8" />
<title>DHTML &amp; CSS for the WWW | Follow
→ the Mouse Pointer</title>
<script type="text/javascript">
function initPage() {
    document.onmousemove = followMe;
}
function followMe(evt) {
    var evt = (evt) ? evt : ((window.event)
    → ? window.event : null);
    var object = document.getElementById
    → ('spotLight');
        object.style.left = evt.clientX -
        → (object.offsetWidth/2) + 'px';
        object.style.top = evt.clientY -
        → (object.offsetHeight/2) + 'px';
        return;
}
</script>
<style type="text/css" media="screen">
body {
    margin: 8px;
    color: black;
    background-color: black;
    cursor: crosshair; }
#spotLight {
    position: absolute;
    width: 300px;
    height: 300px;
    background: url(spotLight.gif) black
    → no-repeat;
    z-index: 0;
    top: 20px;
    left: 20px; }
#content {
    font: bold 40px fantasy;
    position: absolute;
    z-index: 100;
    top: 100px;
    left: 100px; }
</style>
</head>
<body onload="initPage();">
<div id="spotLight"></div>
<div id="content">Are you afraid of the
→ dark?</div>
</body></html>
```

This function sets up an event handler that is bound to the entire page (see "Binding Events to Objects" in Chapter 12); whenever the mouse moves, the followMe() function executes.

2. function followMe(evt) {…}

Add followMe() to the JavaScript.

This function moves a specific object (in this example, spotLight), so the center of the object follows the mouse as it moves.

3. #spotLight {…}

Set up the CSS rule for the object you'll be controlling with the mouse's movement, making it absolutely positioned. The initial top and left positions don't matter, because they'll change as soon as the visitor moves the mouse pointer. However, you can use the background property to place whatever image you want to use,

4. onload="initPage();"

When the page loads, the default events need to be initialized, so place an onload event handler in the <body> tag to run the initPage function.

5. <div id="spotLight">…</div>

Set up the layer that will be moved by the mouse movement. Although this example places a background image in this layer, you can use HTML text, GIF animations, or anything else that can go in a CSS layer.

✔ Tips

■ Although you can place anything you want in the layer to be moved, larger objects take longer for the computer to draw and redraw, so their movement will appear slower and choppier than that of smaller items.

continues on next page

■ Notice that I set the `cursor` value to `crosshair`. Most browsers do not support `cursor:none`, and crosshair is generally the most inconspicuous cursor.

■ You can combine this technique with a variety of other techniques

for some stunning effects. You could use layers in different z-indexes (see "Stacking Objects in Chapter 7) to create a puzzle Web page (**Figure 17.6**). Or you can use a PNG graphic to create a crosshair target (**Figure 17.7**).

Figure 17.6 The screen is a mass of overlapping text, until you pass the cursor over the link.

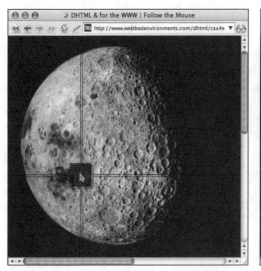

Figure 17.7 The crosshair moves over the intended target.

FOLLOWING THE MOUSE POINTER

Code 17.6 The three functions pickIt(), dragIt(), and dropIt() let the visitor move an object around on the screen.

```
<!DOCTYPE html PUBLIC "-//W3C//DTD XHTML 1.0
→ Strict//EN" "http://www.w3.org/TR/xhtml1/
→ DTD/xhtml1-strict.dtd">
<html xmlns="http://www.w3.org/1999/xhtml">
<head>
<meta http-equiv="Content-Type"
→ content="text/html; charset=utf-8" />
<title>CSS, DHTML &amp; Ajax | Drag and
→ Drop</title>
<script type="text/javascript">
var object = null;
var cX = 0;
var cY = 0;
function initPage () {
    document.onmousedown = pickIt;
    document.onmousemove = dragIt;
    document.onmouseup = dropIt;
}
function pickIt(evt) {
    var evt = (evt) ? evt : ((window.event)
→ ? window.event : null);
    var objectID = (evt.target) ?
→ evt.target.id : ((evt.srcElement) ?
→ evt.srcElement.id : null);
    if (objectID.indexOf('chip')!=-1)
→ object = document.getElementById
→ (objectID);
    if (object) {
```

code continues on next page

Making an Object Draggable

Another staple of GUIs is drag-and-drop: the ability to drag windows, files, and whatnot across the screen and drop them into a new element or location.

As an example of this technique, we'll create a poetry kit for a Web page (**Figure 17.8**). You may have one of these games on your refrigerator right now: Each word is on a magnetic chip, which can be moved around and combined with other chips to create phrases.

To set up object dragging:

1. `var object = null;`

   Initialize the following global variables (**Code 17.6**):

   ▲ object records the ID of the object being moved.

   ▲ cX records the current left position of the object.

   ▲ cY records the current top position of the object.

continues on next page

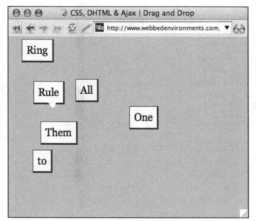
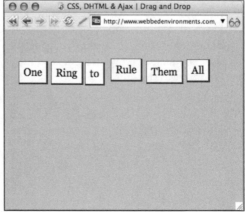

Figure 17.8 Can you figure out the word jumble?

2. `function initPage() {…}`

Add the `initPage()` function to the body element.

This function sets the event handlers to be automatically triggered for `mousedown`, `mousemove`, and `mouseup` events that occur anywhere on the page (see "Binding Events to Objects" in Chapter 12).

3. `function pickIt(evt) {…}`

Add `pickIt()` to the JavaScript.

This function—which is very much like the `findObject()` function (see "Detecting Which Object Was Clicked" in Chapter 14)—finds the ID of the object that the visitor clicked.

However, we don't want to move all of the objects on the screen; we only want to move one of them at a time. So, if the visitor clicked one of the objects that contain the word "chip" in its ID, the function sets the z-index of that object to 100, which should place it well above all other objects on the page. Otherwise, if a chip is not clicked, the function does nothing.

4. `function dragIt(evt) {…}`

Add the `dragIt()` function to your JavaScript.

This function will be triggered every time the visitor moves the mouse. The function doesn't do anything unless the visitor first clicks one of the chips, in which case the function moves the chip as the visitor moves the mouse.

Code 17.6 *continued*

```
                object.style.zIndex = 100;
                cX = evt.clientX - object.offsetLeft;
                cY = evt.clientY - object.offsetTop;
                return;
        }
        else {
                object = null;
                return;
        }
}}
function dragIt(evt) {
        evt = (evt) ? evt : ((window.event) ?
        → window.event : null);
        if (object) {
                object.style.left = evt.clientX - cX
                → + 'px';
                object.style.top = evt.clientY - cY
                → + 'px';
                return false;
        }
}}
function dropIt() {
if (object) {
                object.style.zIndex = 0;
                object = null;
                return false;
}
}
</script>
<style type="text/css">
.chip {
        position: absolute;
        padding: 8px;
        border: 1px solid #333;
        border-right: 3px solid #333;
        border-bottom: 3px solid #333;
        background-color: #fff;
        cursor: move;
        z-index: 0; }
#chip1 { top: 123px; left: 225px; }
#chip2 { top: 5px; left: 25px; }
#chip3 { top: 200px; left: 45px; }
#chip4 { top: 55px; left: 55px; }
#chip5 { top: 150px; left: 60px; }
#chip6 { top: 75px; left: 125px; }
</style>
</head>
<body onload="initPage();" >
<div id="chip1" class="chip">One</div>
<div id="chip2" class="chip">Ring</div>
<div id="chip3" class="chip">to</div>
<div id="chip4" class="chip">Rule</div>
<div id="chip5" class="chip">Them</div>
<div id="chip6" class="chip">All</div>
</body></html>
```

5. `function dropIt() {…}`

Add the `dropIt()` function to the JavaScript.

This function is triggered when the visitor releases the mouse button. It sets the object's z-index at `0` and then resets the variable `object` to `null`. This releases the object from being dragged, dropping it in its new position.

6. `.chip {…}`

Set up a class style rule to define the appearance of the movable objects on the screen. Make sure to define the chips as being absolutely positioned with a z-index of `0`.

7. `#chip1 {…}`

Set up a different ID selector CSS rule for each object on the screen. Give each object an initial top and left position.

8. `onload="initPage();"`

In the `<body>` tag, add an `onload` event handler to trigger `initPage()`.

9. `<div id="chip1" class="chip">…</div>`

Set up layers for as many objects as needed, each with its own unique ID that includes the word `chip`.

✔ Tips

■ Dragging and dropping has a variety of applications, including allowing you to create movable areas of content and navigation.

■ Drag-and-drop code can be very sensitive, so be careful when making changes, and test often to make sure you haven't inadvertently upset the script.

Opening a New Browser Window

An often-used interface trick on the Web is opening a new browser window. These pop-up windows are useful for a variety of purposes, including navigation controls, advertisements, and other content that supplements what's in the main window.

In this example (**Figure 17.9**), three function controls are provided:

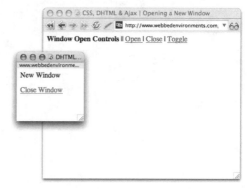

Figure 17.9 The screen with a pop-up window.

◆ **Open the window.** This function opens a new window and brings it to the front of the screen.

◆ **Close the window.** This function closes the window.

◆ **Toggle the window.** This function can both open and close the window. If the window is closed, the function opens a new window and brings it to the front of the screen. If the window is open, the function closes the window.

To open and close a new browser window:

1. `index.html`

Start a new file, and save it as something like `index.html` (**Code 17.7**).

This file will contain the controls that open and close the pop-up window. Steps 2 through 7 apply to this file.

2. `var newWindow = null;`

Initialize the variable `newWindow`. This variable will record the current state (open or closed) of the window. `null` means that the window is closed.

continues on Page 394

Code 17.7 index.html: the openWindow(), closeWindow(), and toggleWindow() functions open and close a pop-up window.

```
<!DOCTYPE html PUBLIC "-//W3C//DTD XHTML 1.0 Strict//EN" "http://www.w3.org/TR/xhtml1/DTD/
→ xhtml1-strict.dtd">
<html xmlns="http://www.w3.org/1999/xhtml">
<head>
<meta http-equiv="Content-Type" content="text/html; charset=utf-8" />
<title>CSS, DHTML &amp; Ajax | Opening a New Window</title>
<script type="text/javascript">
var newWindow = null;
function openWindow(contentURL,windowName,windowWidth,windowHeight) {
    widthHeight = 'height=' + windowHeight + ',width=' + windowWidth;
    newWindow = window.open(contentURL,windowName,widthHeight);
    newWindow.focus()
}
function closeWindow() {
    if (newWindow != null) {
    newWindow.close();
    newWindow = null;
    }
}
function toggleWindow(contentURL,windowName,windowWidth,windowHeight) {
    if (newWindow == null) {
        widthHeight = 'height=' + windowHeight + ',width=' + windowWidth;
        newWindow = window.open(contentURL,windowName,widthHeight);
        newWindow.focus()
    }
    else {
    newWindow.close();
        newWindow = null;
}}
</script>
</head>
<body onunload="closeWindow();" >
<div id="controls">
<b>Window Open Controls</b> ||
<a onclick=" openWindow(this.href,'myNewWindow', 150, 50); return false;"
href="newWindow.html">Open </a>|
<a onclick="closeWindow(); return false;" href="#">Close</a> |
<a onclick="toggleWindow(this.href,'myNewWindow',150,50); return false;"
href="newWindow.html">Toggle </a>
</div>
</body></html>
```

3.
```
function openWindow(contentURL,
→ windowName, windowWidth,
→ windowHeight) {…}
```

Add the function openWindow() to your JavaScript. This function opens a new window:

```
newWindow = window.open(contentURL,
→ windowName, widthHeight);
```

It uses the following variables:

▲ contentURL for the name of the HTML file to be placed in the new window

▲ windowName for the name of the new window

▲ windowWidth and windowHeight for the width and height of the new window

The new window is forced to the front of the screen by newWindow.focus().

4.
```
function closeWindow() {…}
```

Add the function closeWindow() to your JavaScript.

This function checks to see whether the pop-up window is, in fact, open. If so, the function tells the window to close (newWindow.close()) and sets the newWindow variable to null (closed).

5.
```
function toggleWindow(contentURL,
→ windowName, windowWidth,
→ windowHeight) {…}
```

Add the function toggleWindow() to your JavaScript.

This function combines the functions added in Steps 3 and 4 but allows the window to open only if newWindow is equal to null (closed); otherwise, it closes the window.

Modal Problems with Pop-Up Windows

Many site developers who use pop-up windows complain about what mode the window is in when it is being used.

Suppose that you use a pop-up window to allow a visitor to enter information in a form that is then used to update information in the main window. What happens if the visitor doesn't enter the information in the pop-up window, doesn't close the window, and returns to the main page? The system is waiting for information that may never come. The visitor might make other changes and return to the pop-up window, enter the information, and really mess up the system.

My advice is simple. If the pop-up window can cause trouble when left open, place the following code in the <body> tag of the document in the pop-up window:

```
onblur="self.close();"
```

This code forces the window to close whenever visitors leave it. They can always open it again from the main page but cannot return directly to this window.

Code 17.8 newWindow.html: This Web page, which will be used in the pop-up window, includes JavaScript that positions the window and a link to close the window using a local version of the closeWindow() function.

```
<!DOCTYPE html PUBLIC "-//W3C//DTD XHTML 1.0
→ Strict//EN" "http://www.w3.org/TR/xhtml1/
→ DTD/xhtml1-strict.dtd">
<html xmlns="http://www.w3.org/1999/xhtml">
<head>
<meta http-equiv="Content-Type"
→ content="text/html; charset=utf-8" />
<title>CSS, DHTML &amp; Ajax | Opening a New
→ Window</title>
<script type="text/javascript">
function closeWindow() {
    self.close();
}
</script>
</head>
<body onload="window.moveTo(100, 100);"
→ onunload="opener.newWindow = null;">
<p>New Window</p>
<p><a onclick="closeWindow(); return false;"
→ href="#">Close Window</a></p>
</body></html>
```

✔ Tips

■ Keep in mind that a lot of browsers now block pop-up windows unless they are triggered by visitor's click event.

■ Why not always use the toggle version of the open window functions? Generally, toggling the open state of the window is preferable, but sometimes it's useful to have the other two functions, in case you need to make sure the window is either open or closed.

■ I especially like using the closeWindow() function if I'm using a frame to create my Web site. I place the onunload event in the <frameset> . When the visitor leaves the site and the frame document unloads, the pop-up window also automatically disappears, preventing any model problems (see the sidebar "Modal Problems with Pop-up Windows").

6. onunload="closeWindow();"

Optionally, you can add an onunload event handler to the body element to force the new window to close when this page (the opening page) is left or closed. This event handler keeps the pop-up window from hanging around when the user moves on.

7. openWindow ('newWindow.html',
→ 'myNewWindow',150,50)

Add a function call to your HTML. This function call can be part of an event handler (as shown in Step 6).

8. newWindow.html

Start a new file, and save it as something like newWindow.html (**Code 17.8**). This file will be loaded into the pop-up window. You can add anything to this document that you would normally have in a Web page. Steps 9 through 12 apply to this file.

9. function closeWindow() {...}

Add the function closeWindow() to the JavaScript in this file. When triggered, this function closes the pop-up window.

10. onload="window.moveTo(100, 100);"

Add an onload event handler to the <body> tag to move the window to a particular position on the screen when it first opens (see the next section of this chapter).

11. onunload="opener.newWindow = null;"

In the <body> tag, include an onunload event handler that sets the variable newWindow in the opening window to null if this window is closed. This variable tells the opening window when the pop-up window closes.

12. closeWindow()

Set up a link to trigger closeWindow() so that visitors can close this window when they don't need it anymore.

Moving the Browser Window

When you create a user interface on the Web, it's often helpful to position the browser window on the visitor's computer screen, or to be able to have the browser window move by a certain amount. This is especially useful if your site will be opening multiple windows and you want to set an initial position so that the windows don't crowd one another (see the previous section). The moveTo and moveBy methods provide this control.

In this example (**Figure 17.10**), two controls are provided for functions that calculate a new position for the window, which is based on the available screen width and height (see "Determining the Screen Dimensions" in Chapter 13).

To set the position of a window on the screen:

1. `function moveWindowTo() {…}`

   Add the moveWindowTo() function to your page (**Code 17.9**).

   This uses the built-in JavaScript method moveTo, which tells the browser window to move its top-left corner to the calculated x,y (nX and nY) coordinates in relation to the top-left corner of the live screen area (**Figure 17.11**).

2. `function moveWindowBy() {…}`

   Add the moveWindowBy() function to your JavaScript. This uses the built-in JavaScript method moveBy, which moves the browser window by the calculated x,y amounts (dX and dX) indicated (**Figure 17.12**).

3. `onclick="moveWindowTo(0,0); return` → `false;"`

   Add controls to trigger the functions from Steps 1 and 2.

Figure 17.10 The initial position of the browser window on the screen.

Figure 17.11 After the window has been moved to 10 pixels from the left edge of the screen and 15 pixels from the top.

Figure 17.12 After the browser window has been moved an additional 10 pixels over and 15 pixels down.

✔ Tips

- These functions are best used to move a window when it first opens. You do so by placing the moveTo() or moveBy() code in an onload event handler in the <body> tag, as shown in the previous section.

- If you really want to have some fun with your visitor, use the animation script shown earlier in this chapter with the moveBy() function to have the window move around on the screen or even appear to vibrate.

- These functions will not work in Opera, and visitors can disable these functions in Mozilla browsers.

Code 17.9 The JavaScript functions moveWindowTo() andmoveWindowBy() move the entire browser window to a certain position on the screen or by a specific amount.

```
<!DOCTYPE html PUBLIC "-//W3C//DTD XHTML 1.0 Strict//EN" "http://www.w3.org/TR/xhtml1/DTD/
→ xhtml1-strict.dtd">
<html xmlns="http://www.w3.org/1999/xhtml">
<head>
<meta http-equiv="Content-Type" content="text/html; charset=utf-8" />
<title>CSS, DHTML &amp; Ajax | Moving the Browser Window</title>
<script type="text/javascript">
function moveWindowTo() {
    nX = Math.abs(screen.availWidth/10);
    nY = Math.abs(screen.availHeight/10);
    moveTo(nX,nY)
}
function moveWindowBy() {
    dX = Math.abs(screen.width/10);
    dY = Math.abs(screen.height/10);
    moveBy(dX,dY)
}
</script>
</head>
<body>
<div id="controls">
<b>Window Controls</b> ||
<a href="#" onclick= "moveWindowTo(0,0);return false;">Move To Top/Left </a>|
<a href="#" onclick= "moveWindowBy();return false;">Move By Amount</a>
</div>
<div id="object1">
<img src="alice42.gif" height="480" width="360" alt="Alice" />
</div>
</body></html>
```

Changing the Browser Window's Size

When you open a new window, you can set the initial size of that window (see the earlier section, "Opening a New Browser Window"). However, most modern browsers (with the important exceptions of Microsoft Internet Explorer and Opera) allow you to resize the window dynamically after the window is open.

In this example (**Figure 17.13**), controls are provided that allow the visitor to move the window, to resize the window to a specific size, to increase or decrease the size of the window, or to enlarge it to fill the entire screen.

To change a window's size:

1. function changeWindowSize
   → (windowWidth, windowHeight) {...}

   Add the function changeWindowSize() to your JavaScript (**Code 17.10**).

   This function first uses feature sensing to see whether it can determine the outer width of the browser window. If so, this browser is capable of resizing the window (see "Determining the Browser Window's Dimensions" in Chapter 13). Then the function uses the resizeTo method to change the size of the window to windowWidth and windowHeight (**Figure 17.14**).

2. function magnifyWindow(dWindowWidth,
   → dWindowHeight) {...}

   Add the function magnifyWindow() to your JavaScript. This function first uses feature sensing to see whether it can determine the outer width of the browser window. If so, the browser window can be resized. The function will then use the

Figure 17.13 The initial size of the browser window.

Figure 17.14 After the window has been resized to 300 × 300 pixels.

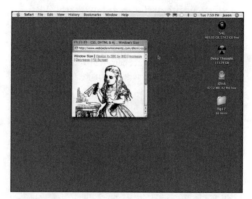

Figure 17.15 The window's size has been increased by 30 pixels in both dimensions.

Figure 17.16 The browser window fills the entire screen.

Code 17.10 The changeWindowSize(), magnifyWindow(), and fillScreen() functions control the browser window's size.

```
<!DOCTYPE html PUBLIC "-//W3C//DTD XHTML 1.0
→ Strict//EN" "http://www.w3.org/TR/xhtml1/
→ DTD/xhtml1-strict.dtd">
<html xmlns="http://www.w3.org/1999/xhtml">
<head>
<meta http-equiv="Content-Type"
→ content="text/html; charset=utf-8" />
<title>CSS, DHTML &amp; Ajax | Changing A
→ Window's Size</title>
<script type="text/javascript">
function changeWindowSize
→ (windowWidth,windowHeight) {
    if (window.outerWidth) {
        resizeTo(windowWidth,windowHeight);
}}
function magnifyWindow
→ (dWindowWidth,dWindowHeight) {
    if (window.outerWidth) {
        resizeBy(dWindowWidth,dWindowHeight);
}}
function fillScreen() {
    if (window.outerWidth) {
        windowWidth = screen.availWidth;
        windowHeight = screen.availHeight;
        resizeTo(windowWidth,windowHeight);
        moveTo(0,0);
}}
</script>
</head>
<body>
<div id="controls"> Window Size ||
```

JavaScript resizeBy method to add or subtract dWindowWidth and dWindowHeight to or from the window dimensions (**Figure 17.15**).

3. `function fillScreen() {…}`

Add the function fillScreen() to your JavaScript.

This function first uses feature sensing to see whether it can determine the outer width of the browser window. If so, the browser window can be resized. The function then finds the width and height of the live screen area, moves the top-left corner of the window to the top-left corner of the screen, and resizes the window to the size of the live area of the screen (**Figure 17.16**).

4. `onclick="changeWindowSize(300, 300); → return false;"`

Add calls to the functions from Steps 1, 2, and 3, passing to each function the appropriate parameters. This function call can be associated with an event handler.

Code 17.10 *continued*

```
<a href="#" onclick=
→ "changeWindowSize(300,300);return
→ false;">Resize to 300 by 300</a> |
<a href="#" onclick=
→ magnifyWindow(30,30);return
→ false;">Increase</a> |
<a href="#" onclick="magnifyWindow(-30,
→ -30)">Decrease</a> |
<a href="#" onclick="fillScreen()">Fill
→ Screen</a>
</div>
<div id="object1">
<img src="alice04.gif" height="448"
→ width="301" alt="Alice" />
</div>
</body></html>
```

Scrolling the Browser Window

Normally, most people think of scrolling the Web page as something that the visitor does using the built-in scroll bars on the right side or bottom of the window or frame. However, Web designers can use JavaScript to enable visitors to scroll around the page without having to interact with the window's built-in scroll controls.

In this example (**Figures 17.17**, **17.18**, and **17.19**), three objects are positioned far apart on the page. Each position has controls to scroll directly to the other positions.

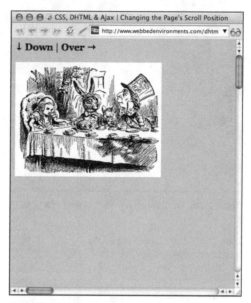

Figure 17.17 The links "Down" and "Over" scroll the page horizontally and vertically without using the scrollbars.

Figure 17.19 Clicking "Over" scrolls the Web page to the right, as indicated by the change in the scrollbar position.

Figure 17.18 Clicking "Down" scrolls the Web page down and back to the left.

Code 17.11 The scrollPage() function takes the coordinates fed to it and scrolls the page to that position.

```
<!DOCTYPE html PUBLIC "-//W3C//DTD XHTML 1.0
→ Strict//EN" "http://www.w3.org/TR/xhtml1/
→ DTD/xhtml1-strict.dtd">
<html xmlns="http://www.w3.org/1999/xhtml">
<head>
<meta http-equiv="Content-Type"
→ content="text/html; charset=utf-8" />
<title>CSS, DHTML &amp; Ajax | Changing the
→ Page's Scroll Position</title>
<script type="text/javascript">
function scrollPageTo(objectID) {
    var object = document.getElementById
    → (objectID);
    var nX =object.offsetLeft - 8;
    var nY = object.offsetTop - 8;
    if (document.body.scrollLeft) {
        document.body.scrollLeft = nX;
        document.body.scrollTop = nY;
        return;
    }
    else {
        scrollTo(nX, nY);
        return;
    }
}
</script>
<style type="text/css" media="screen">
a {
    text-decoration: none;
    font-weight: bold;
    color: red; }
#topPage {
    position: absolute;
    top: 8px;
    left: 8px;}
#overHere {
    position: absolute;
    top: 10px;
    left: 2000px;
    width: 1024px;}
#downHere {
    position: absolute;
    top: 2000px;
    left: 10px;
    height: 1024px;}
</style>
</head>
```

code continues on next page

To scroll a Web page:

1. `function scrollPageTo(objectID) {…}`

   Add the function `scrollPageTo()` to your JavaScript (**Code 17.11**).

   This function calculates the position to which the element is being scrolled (`object.offsetLeft` and `object.offsetTop`) and subtracts 8 pixels to give it a little space. It then uses the `scrollLeft` and `scrollRight` properties for Internet Explorer, or it uses the `scrollTo` method for other browsers to scroll the page to the specified object on the page.

2. `#overHere {…}`

   Set up the CSS rules for your object(s) with values for position and top and left positions.

   In this example, I've set up two objects: one positioned well below the top of the page and one positioned to the far-right side of the page. Now the `scrollPageTo()` function has somewhere to go.

3. `onclick="scrollPageTo('overHere');`
   `→ return false;"`

   Set up a link to trigger the `scrollPageTo()` function, and pass to the function the ID for the element to which you want to scroll.

   continues on next page

401

Code 17.11 *continued*

```
<body>
<div id="topPage">
<a href="#" onclick=scrollPageTo
→ ('downHere')">&darr; Down</a> |
<a href="#" onclick=scrollPageTo
→ ('overHere')">Over &rarr;</a>
<p><img src="alice25.gif" height="228"
→ width="300" alt="Tea Party" /></p>
</div>
<div id="downHere">
<a href="#" onclick=scrollPageTo
→ ('topPage')">&uarr; Back to Top</a> |
<a href="#" onclick=scrollPageTo
→ ('overHere')">Over &rarr;</a>
<p><img src="alice27.gif" height="180"
→ width="200" alt="Mad Hatter" /></p>
</div>
<div id="overHere">
<a href="#" onclick=scrollPageTo
→ ('downHere')">&darr; Down</a> |
<a href="#" onclick=scrollPageTo
→ ('topPage')">&larr; Back to Left</a>
<p><img src="alice26.gif" height="200"
→ width="179" alt="Picture 3" /></p>
<br />
</div>
</body></html>
```

✔ Tips

■ Although the example in this section still relies on the visitor to click something to cause the page to scroll, you could just as easily have used some other event handler to cause the page to scroll without the direct command of the visitor (by using onload, for example). Be careful when doing this, however. If the page suddenly starts jumping around, the effect can be confusing—not to mention unnerving— to the person viewing your Web page.

■ Netscape Navigator 4 (Windows) and Netscape 6 (all platforms) have an unfortunate "feature" that prevents this technique from working in a frame where the scrollbars have been hidden (scrolling="no"). Rather than simply making the scrollbars disappear, setting scrolling to no in these browsers will prevent the frame from scrolling at all— even with JavaScript.

■ To add a bit of flair to this script, you could add the animation functionality shown earlier in this chapter to have the page gradually scroll from point-to-point rather than just jumping around.

DYNAMIC CSS

In the previous chapters we've looked at ways to change specific CSS attributes for specific effects, such as showing and hiding objects and moving objects across the screen. However, you can make changes to *any* of the CSS properties available. As a result, you can dynamically control your CSS in the browser window by making changes to styles, with these changes becoming visible immediately—using dynamic CSS.

For many years, the full power of dynamic CSS techniques was stymied by the fact that very few of them worked in Netscape Navigator 4. However, now that Netscape 4 makes up less than 1 percent of the browser market, a whole new horizon of dynamic techniques is open to Web designers (unless, of course, you know that a significant portion of your likely audience is using Netscape 4).

In this chapter, you'll learn how to treat style sheets as objects to accomplish the following:

◆ Add and remove CSS declarations

◆ Change an object's class value, to change its appearance on the fly

◆ Enable or disable entire style sheets

However, let's first take a look at how to find CSS property values using JavaScript without first having to initialize them.

Finding a Style Property's Value

Although JavaScript can be used to determine the current value of a CSS property simply enough by using the DOM, it can do so only *after* the style property's value has been set using JavaScript. In other words, JavaScript cannot directly read the styles set in the style sheet. The workaround I've shown in previous examples in this book is simply to initialize the styles using JavaScript (see "Finding an Object's Style Property Values" in Chapter 14, for example).

There is a method that allows you to directly query the styles. However, because of cross-browser differences, the cure may end up being worse than the poison.

The biggest problem is that different browsers will often deliver the same values, but in completely different formats. For example, while Mozilla browsers will always return color in RGB units (regardless of the color units used to define the property in the style sheet), Internet Explorer and Opera will always return the color value as set in the style sheet (**Figures 18.1** and **18.2**).

Another distinct disadvantage of this method is that it will not work in Safari or earlier versions of Opera.

To find the value of a style property as set in a style sheet:

1. `function findStyleValue(objectID,`
   `→ styleProp, IEStyleProp) {…}`

   Add the function `findStyleValue()` to your Web page (**Code 18.1**).

   This script uses the `event` object passed to it to address the object and then uses feature sensing to use either the `currentStyle[]` array (for Internet Explorer and Opera 9+) or `getPropertyValue()` method (for Mozilla) to return the style value.

Figure 18.1 In Firefox, the font-size value is displayed as 16px, the calculated value from 1em.

Figure 18.2 In Opera, the value for the font size is reported exactly as it is entered in the style sheet.

Code 18.1 The function `findStyleValue()` can be used in Internet Explorer, Firefox, or Opera to directly query the property values set in a style sheet.

```
<!DOCTYPE html PUBLIC "-//W3C//DTD XHTML 1.0
→ Strict//EN" "http://www.w3.org/TR/xhtml1/
→ DTD/xhtml1-strict.dtd">
<html xmlns="http://www.w3.org/1999/xhtml">
<head>
<meta http-equiv="Content-Type"
→ content="text/html; charset=utf-8" />
<title>CSS, DHTML &amp; Ajax | Finding an
→ Object's Set Style Property Value</title>
<script type="text/javascript">
function findStyleValue(evt, styleProp,
→ IEStyleProp) {
    var objectID = (evt.target) ?
    → evt.target.id : ((evt.srcElement) ?
    → evt.srcElement.id : null);
    var object = document.getElementById
    → (objectID);
    if (object.currentStyle) return
    → object.currentStyle[IEStyleProp]
    else if (window.getComputedStyle) {
        compStyle = window.getComputedStyle
        → (object, '');
        return compStyle.getPropertyValue
        (styleProp);
}}
</script>
<style type="text/css" media="screen">
.dropBox {
    position: absolute;
    text-align: right;
    padding: 4px;
    background-color: #FFFFFF;
    border: 2px solid #f00;
    cursor: pointer; }
#object1 {
    z-index: 3;
    top: 285px;
    left: 315px;
    background: white url(alice22a.gif)
    → no-repeat;
    height:220px;
    width:150px;}
#object2 {
    z-index: 2;
    top: 210px;
    left: 225px;
    background: white url(alice15a.gif)
    → no-repeat;
    height:264px;
    width:200px;}
```

Notice that you're actually passing two different versions of the style property being queried. This is because Mozilla uses the standard CSS format for the style property, while Internet Explorer uses the style name in JavaScript notation.

2. `#object1 {…}`

Set up the object(s) you'll be querying as IDs in your CSS and then in your HTML.

3. `findStyleValue(event, 'font-size',`
`→ 'fontSize')`

Add a function call for `findStyleValue`, passing it the triggering event object as well as both forms of the CSS property name you are accessing.

Code 18.1 *continued*

```
#object3 {
    z-index: 1;
    top: 105px;
    left: 115px;
    background: white url(alice28a.gif)
    → no-repeat;
    height:336px;
    width:250px;}
#object4 {
    z-index: 0;
    top: 5px;
    left: 5px;
    background: white url(alice30a.gif)
    → no-repeat;
    height:408px;
    width:300px;}
</style>
</head>
<body>
<div class="dropBox" id="object1" onclick=
→ "alert(findStyleValue(event, 'font-size',
→ 'fontSize'));"> Object 1</div>
<div class="dropBox" id="object2" onclick=
→ "alert(findStyleValue(event, 'font-size',
→ 'fontSize'));"> Object 2</div>
<div class="dropBox" id="object3" onclick=
→ "alert(findStyleValue(event, 'font-size',
→ 'fontSize'));"> Object 3</div>
<div class="dropBox" id="object4" onclick=
→ "alert(findStyleValue(event, 'font-size',
→ 'fontSize'));"> Object 4</div>
</body></html>
```

Adding or Changing a Style Declaration

One powerful feature of dynamic HTML is the ability to change the styles that are applied to an object. CSS lets you set up rules; JavaScript lets you change those rules on the fly by adding new declarations, which (because of the cascade order) can replace previous declarations. You can change or add to any CSS property defined for any object on the screen.

In this example (**Figures 18.3** and **18.4**), controls are provided that allow the user to apply very large or very small text font sizes to the contents of the element with the ID copy.

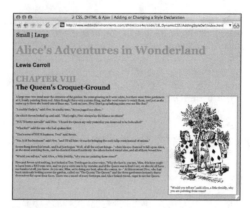

Figure 18.3 When the page loads, the default style for the page uses a very small font size.

Figure 18.4 After clicking the "Large" control at the top of the screen, the text is now much larger and easier to read.

To change the declarations in an object:

1. `function addStyleDef(objectID,`
   `→ styleName, newVal) {…}`

   Add the function addStyleDef() to your JavaScript (**Code 18.2**).

   This function addresses the object by its ID, and assigns the style styleName the new value newVal:

   `object.style[styleName] = newVal;`

Code 18.2 The addStyleDef() function changes or adds styles to the definition of a particular object in the browser window.

```
<!DOCTYPE html PUBLIC "-//W3C//DTD XHTML 1.0 Strict//EN" "http://www.w3.org/TR/xhtml1/DTD/
→ xhtml1-strict.dtd">
<html xmlns="http://www.w3.org/1999/xhtml">
<head>
<meta http-equiv="Content-Type" content="text/html; charset=utf-8" />
<title>CSS, DHTML &amp; Ajax | Adding or Changing a Style Declaration</title>
<script type="text/javascript">
function addStyleDef(objectID, styleName, newVal) {
    var object = document.getElementById(objectID);
    object.style[styleName] = newVal;
}
</script>
```

code continues on next page

Code 18.2 *continued*

```
<style type="text/css" media="screen">
h1, h2 {
     color: #999;
     margin: .5em 0em; }
#controls {
     cursor:pointer;
     color: red; }
#copy { font-size: .5em;}
.author {
     margin-top: 0cm;
     font: bold 1em Arial, Helvetica,
     → sans-serif; }
.chapterTitle {
     display: block;
     font-size: smaller;
     color:black; }
.dropBox {
     width: 228px;
     padding: 6px;
     border: 3px solid #999;
     background-color: #fff;
     margin: 0px 0px 8px 8px;
     float: right; }
</style>
</head>
<body>
<div id="controls">
<span onclick="addStyleDef('copy',
→ 'fontSize', '.5em');">Small</span> |
<span onclick="addStyleDef('copy',
→ 'fontSize', '2em');">Large</span>
</div>

<div id="header">
<h1>Alice's Adventures in Wonderland</h1>
<p class="author">Lewis Carroll</p>
<h2>CHAPTER VIII
     <span class="chapterTitle"> The Queen's
     → Croquet-Ground </span></h2>
</div>
<div id="copy">
<div class="dropBox">
<img src="alice28a.gif" alt="# Cards
→ arguing" width="220" height="295" />
"Would you tell me", said Alice, a little
→ timidly, why you are painting those roses?
</div>
<p>A large rose-tree stood near the entrance
→ of the garden…</p>
</div>
</body></html>
```

Because this new declaration is essentially added as an inline style, it will supersede any other rules applied to the element. However, it can be overridden by declarations set later in JavaScript code.

2. `#copy {…}`

Set up your CSS rule(s).

3. `<div id="copy">…</div>`

Set up the IDs for your object(s).

4. `onclick="addStyleDef('copy',`
   `→ 'fontSize', '.5em');"`

Add event handlers to trigger the function `addStyleDef()`. Pass the function the ID for the object you want to address, as well as the style property you want to change and its new value. Notice that the style name is using JavaScript notation (see the sidebar "JavaScript Naming Convention").

✔ Tips

- Notice that I've placed the event handler inside the `<div>` tag. Remember, event handlers don't have to appear only in `<link>` tags. For most browsers, events can be triggered from any object in the page.

- Style names that are composed of two or more words are linked with hyphens in CSS (`font-size`). To use them for dynamic CSS, you need to translate style names into the JavaScript naming style (`fontSize`).

Adding or changing styles in Internet Explorer

Although the method for changing styles presented in the previous section works in most modern browsers (Internet Explorer 4+, Netscape 6+, Safari, and Opera), Internet Explorer can also add or change styles by adding new rules to an existing style sheet. First, you must give the `<style>` element an ID that allows it to be addressed as an object. Then you can use JavaScript to access the style sheet using the DOM.

The advantage of using this technique over simply adding a style declaration is that you can quickly redefine several properties with a single function call.

In this example (**Figures 18.5** and **18.6**), the body tag has its background and foreground colors swapped back and forth from the controls at the top of the page.

To add a new rule to a Web page dynamically in Internet Explorer:

1. `function addStyleDefIE(selector,`
   `→ definition) {…}`

   Add the function `addStyleDefIE()` to your JavaScript (**Code 18.3**).

   This function adds the new rule to the style sheet that you identify in Step 2,

Figure 18.5 When the page loads, the default values are used to display the page (black text on a white background).

Figure 18.6 After the link is clicked, the new style rule is added to the `<body>` tag, turning the background red and the text white.

JavaScript Naming Convention

JavaScript has a very particular naming convention. Identifiers cannot include periods, hyphens, spaces, or any other separators, except for underscores (_). Instead, multiple words are expressed in the following manner:

All letters are lowercase except for the first letter of any words after the first word.

The CSS property `font-size`, for example, would be expressed as `fontSize`.

I recommend sticking to this naming convention for JavaScript function names and variables, as well as CSS class and ID names, just to make things easier.

Code 18.3 The addStyleDefIE() function adds a new CSS rule to the style sheet called myStyles.

```
<!DOCTYPE html PUBLIC "-//W3C//DTD XHTML 1.0
→ Strict//EN" "http://www.w3.org/TR/xhtml1/
→ DTD/xhtml1-strict.dtd">
<html xmlns="http://www.w3.org/1999/xhtml">
<head>
<meta http-equiv="Content-Type"
→ content="text/html; charset=utf-8" />
<title>CSS, DHTML &amp; Ajax | Adding or
→ Changing Styles in Internet Explorer</title>
<script type="text/javascript">
function addStyleDefIE(selector, definition) {
    document.styleSheets.MyStyles.addRule
    → (selector, definition);
}
</script>
<style type="text/css" id="MyStyles" >
h1, h2 {
    color: #999;
    margin: .5em 0em; }
#controls {
    cursor:pointer;
    color: red; }
.author {
    margin-top: 0cm;
    font: bold 1em Arial, Helvetica,
    → sans-serif;
    }
.chapterTitle {
    display: block;
    font-size: smaller; }
.dropBox {
    width: 228px;
    padding: 6px;
    border: 3px solid #999;
    background-color: #fff;
    margin: 0px 0px 8px 8px;
    float: right; }
</style>
</head>
<body>
<div id="controls">
<span
onclick="addStyleDefIE('body','background-
→ color:white; color: black;');">Style
→ 1</span> |
<span
onclick="addStyleDefIE('body','background-
→ color:black; color: white;');">Style
→ 2</span>
</div>
```

using the name of the selector for which you want to add a rule and the definition(s) you want to apply to that selector:
```
document.styleSheets.MyStyles.addRule
→ (selector, definition)
```

2. `id="MyStyles"`

Add a `<style>` element in the head of your document—even if you don't set any initial rules—and give it a unique ID that can be used by the function in Step 1 to address this style sheet.

3. `onclick="addStyleDefIE('body',`
   `'background-color:red; color:white;');"`

Add an event handler to trigger the `addStyleDefIE` function from Step 1. Pass to this function the selector for which you want to add a new rule and the definitions you want to assign for this new rule.

✔ Tip

■ To reiterate: this method will not work in any browser other than Internet Explorer.

Code 18.3 *continued*

```
<div id="header">
<h1>Alice's Adventures in Wonderland</h1>
<p class="author">Lewis Carroll</p>
<h2>CHAPTER VIII
    <span class="chapterTitle"> The Queen's
    → Croquet-Ground </span></h2>
</div>
<div id="copy">
<div class="dropBox">
<img src="alice28a.gif" alt="# Cards
→ arguing" width="220" height="295" />
"Would you tell me", said Alice, a little
→ timidly, why you are painting those roses?
</div>
<p>A large rose-tree stood near the entrance
→ of the garden…</p>
</div>
</body></html>
```

Changing Classes

Although being able to add or change an individual declaration is great (see the previous section, "Adding or Changing a Style Declaration"), doing this for more than one declaration at a time is time-consuming. Instead, you need the ability to change multiple declarations or an entire rule at once. You can accomplish this task simply by setting up multiple classes and then swapping the entire CSS class assigned to an object.

In this example (**Figures 18.7** and **18.8**), controls are provided to switch the #copy object between the style1 and style2 classes.

To change the CSS class of an object:

1. `function setClass(objectID,`
   `→ newClass) {…}`

   Add the function `setClass()` to your JavaScript (**Code 18.4**).

   This function uses the ID of the object to find its address, and then uses the address to change the CSS class being applied to this object to the new CSS class (`newClass`):

   `object.className = newClass;`

2. `#copy {…}`

   Set up the CSS rule for your object(s) with whatever styles you desire. These styles will not be affected by the change, but can be overridden if the attribute is changed in the `.style1` class.

Figure 18.7 When the page loads, it defaults to Style 1, which uses large, red, serif text on a white background.

Figure 18.8 After clicking the "Style 2" control, the text column narrows, and the text is black sans-serif on a gray background.

Code 18.4 The setClass() function assigns a different CSS class to a particular object in the browser window.

```
<!DOCTYPE html PUBLIC "-//W3C//DTD XHTML 1.0
→ Strict//EN" "http://www.w3.org/TR/xhtml1/
→ DTD/xhtml1-strict.dtd">
<html xmlns="http://www.w3.org/1999/xhtml">
<head>
<meta http-equiv="Content-Type"
→ content="text/html; charset=utf-8" />
<title>CSS, DHTML &amp; Ajax | Changing a
→ Class</title>
<script type="text/javascript">
function setClass(objectID, newClass) {
    var object = document.getElementById
    → (objectID);
    object.className = newClass;
}
</script>
<style type="text/css" media="screen">
h1, h2 {
    color: #999;
    margin: .5em 0em; }
#controls {
    cursor:pointer;
    color: red; }
.author {
    margin-top: 0cm;
    font: bold 1em Arial, Helvetica,
    → sans-serif; }
.chapterTitle {
    display: block;
    font-size: smaller; }
.dropBox {
    width: 228px;
    padding: 6px;
    border: 3px solid #999;
    background-color: #fff;
    margin: 0px 0px 8px 8px;
    float: right; }
.style1 {
    background-color: #fff;
    font-size: 1em;
    width: 600px;
    color: red;}
.style2 {
    background-color: #ccc;
    font-family: Arial, Helvetica,
    → sans-serif;
    font-size: .75em;
    width: 400px;}
</style>
</head>
```

3. `.style1 {…}`

Set up the class selector CSS rules that you'll be applying to your objects.

4. `onmouseover="setClass('copy',` `→ 'style1');"`

Add event handlers to trigger the function you created in Step 1, and pass it the ID for the object you want to address and the name of the class you want to apply to that object.

5. `<div id="copy" class="style1">…</div>`

Set up your HTML element(s).

Code 18.4 *continued*

```
body>
<div id="controls">
<span onclick="setClass('copy',
→ 'style1');">Style 1</span> |
<span onclick="setClass('copy',
→ 'style2');">Style 2</span>
</div>
<div id="header">
<h1>Alice's Adventures in Wonderland</h1>
<p class="author">Lewis Carroll</p>
<h2>CHAPTER XI<span class="chapterTitle">
→ Who Stole the Tarts? </span></h2>
</div>
<div id="copy" class="style1">
<div class="dropBox">
<img src="alice37a.gif" alt="" height="298"
→ width="220" />
'The Queen of Hearts, she made some tarts,
→ All on a summer day: The Knave of Hearts,
→ he stole those tarts, And took them quite
→ away!'
</div>
<p>The King and Queen of Hearts were seated
→ on their throne when they arrived…</p>
</div>
</body></html>
```

411

Disabling or Enabling a Style Sheet

Although being able to swap around classes is a quick way to change specific styles, your final alternative for dynamically changing CSS is to swap entire style sheets.

Sometimes, your visitors might want to see just the text without all those fancy styles. Their loss—but everyone has their own taste. Internet Explorer and Mozilla browsers let you turn style sheets on and off using JavaScript.

In this example (**Figures 18.9** and **18.10**), controls are provided that allows the visitor to choose between two distinct styles that are enabled by different style sheets.

To switch style sheets:

1. `function setStyle(objectID,`
   `→ disableState) {…}`

   Add the function `setStyle()` to your JavaScript (**Code 18.5**).

   This function lets you disable or enable any style element that has a specific ID using the disable state value of either true (disabled) or false (enabled):

   `object.disabled = disableState;`

2. `function toggleStyle(objectID) {…}`

   Add the function `toggleStyle()` to your code.

   This function first disables any previously enabled style sheets and then uses the object ID to address and enable the new style sheet by setting disabled to false:

   `object.disabled = false;`

Figure 18.9 When the page loads, the style1 style sheet is enabled and style2 is disabled. The text, however, is extremely light and hard to read.

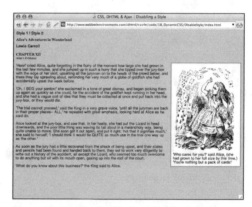

Figure 18.10 After the "Style 2" link is clicked, a higher contrast design is presented.

Code 18.5 The controls trigger the function toggleStyle(), which will disable one style sheet (disabled=true) while enabling another (disabled=false).

```
<!DOCTYPE html PUBLIC "-//W3C//DTD XHTML 1.0
→ Strict//EN" "http://www.w3.org/TR/xhtml1/
→ DTD/xhtml1-strict.dtd">
<html xmlns="http://www.w3.org/1999/xhtml">
<head>
<meta http-equiv="Content-Type"
→ content="text/html; charset=utf-8" />
<title>CSS, DHTML &amp; Ajax | Disabling a
→ Style Sheet</title>
<script type="text/javascript">
function setStyle(objectID, disableState) {
    var object =
    → document.getElementById(objectID);
    object.disabled=disableState;
    oldStyle = object;
}
function toggleStyle(objectID) {
    if (oldStyle) oldStyle.disabled=true;
    var object =
    → document.getElementById(objectID);
    object.disabled=false;
    oldStyle = object;
}
</script>
<style type="text/css" media="screen">
h1, h2 {
    color: #999;
    margin: .5em 0em; }
#controls {
    cursor:pointer;
    color: red; }
.author {
    margin-top: 0cm;
    font: bold 1em Arial, Helvetica,
    → sans-serif; }
.chapterTitle {
    display: block;
    font-size: smaller; }
.dropBox {
    width: 228px;
    padding: 6px;
    border: 3px solid #999;
    background-color: #fff;
    margin: 0px 0px 8px 8px;
    float: right; }
.copyHuge {
    background-color: #fff;
    font-size: 2em;
    width: 600px;
    color: red; }
```

Code 18.5 *continued*

```
.copyTiny {
    background-color: #ccc;
    font-size: .5em;
    width: 300px; }
</style>
<style type="text/css" id="style1">
h1 {
    color: #eeeeee;
    font: italic 3em fantasy; }
#copy { color: #999; }
</style>
<style type="text/css" id="style2">
h1,h2 {
    font-size: 1.75em;
    color: #000000;
    font: bold 1em "times new roman",
    → times, serif; }

#copy { color: #000; }
</style>
</head>
<body onload="setStyle('style2', 'true');">
<div id="controls">
<span onclick="toggleStyle('style1');">
→ Style 1</span> |
<span onclick="toggleStyle('style2');">
→ Style 2</span>
</div>
<div id="header">
<h1>Alice's Adventures in Wonderland</h1>
<p class="author">Lewis Carroll</p>
<h2>CHAPTER XII
    <span class="chapterTitle"> Alice's
    → Evidence </span></h2>
</div>
<div id="copy">
<div class="dropBox">
<img src="alice42a.gif" alt="" height="293"
→ width="220" />
'Who cares for you?' said Alice, (she had
→ grown to her full size by this time.)
→ 'You're nothing but a pack of
→ cards!'</div>
<p>'Here!' cried Alice, quite forgetting in
→ the flurry of the moment how large she
→ had grown in the last few minutes...</p>
</div>
</body></html>
```

3. `id="style1"`

Set up style sheets in the head of your document. Give each `style` element a unique ID.

In this example, I created two styles to toggle between: a style sheet called *style1* and another called *style2*.

4. `onload="setStyle('style2', 'true');"`

Add an `onload` event handler to the `body` element and disable any style sheets that you don't want to be initially used using the function from Step 1 and passing it the ID for the style sheet and the value `true`.

5. `onclick="toggleStyle('style1');"`

Set up an event handler that calls the `toggleStyle()` function to turn on or off the desired style sheet using the function from Step 2.

✔ Tips

- This technique doesn't work in Netscape 6.

- A distinct disadvantage of this method is that it is not supported in Safari and Opera browsers.

Part 3
Ajax

Chapter 19: Understanding Ajax 417

Chapter 20: Ajax Basics 433

UNDERSTANDING AJAX

Figure 19.1 Google Maps (maps.google.com) is one of the most popular (and commonly cited) uses of Ajax on the Web.

After a Web page loads, it becomes—to take a famous phrase out of context—"an island, entire of itself." No matter how much code is used to generate a Web page on the server, and no matter how many sources from which the data is pulled, after the Web page is displayed in the browser, it is cut off from the rest of the Web.

Web pages created with DHTML, for instance, can change the content displayed in the window on the fly, but all of that content has to be in the file when it's downloaded from the server, and new data requires that a new Web page be loaded.

Reloading an entire Web page full of content is overkill, though, when you need to change only a small portion of the content, such as updating a form select field based on input information, or when the content on the page needs to change fluidly without interruptions, such as when visitors are scrolling around on a map (**Figure 19.1**).

It's in these cases where Ajax comes to the rescue. This chapter introduces you to Ajax (Asynchronous JavaScript and XML), which allows you to make updates to a Web page's content from the server without having to reload the entire page.

What Is Ajax?

I have some bad news: There really isn't an Ajax. Like DHTML, Ajax is not a single technology created to fill the needs of the Web design community, but a collection of existing technologies that was given a cool sounding acronym to better categorize them.

You may remember me telling you in Part 2 of this book that there isn't a DHTML (see Chapter 11). Now, in this chapter, I'm telling you there isn't an Ajax. You're probably saying, "The Web sure seems to be based on a lot of non-existent technologies." But this is the glory of the Web. It evolves not just from recognized standards, but in a way that anyone can combine and mutate those standards to create unexpected results.

HTML, JavaScript, CSS, and the DOM are technologies that were created by standards bodies in response to a specific need. For example, there was need to create pages of content on the Internet that could easily link to each other, so Tim Berners-Lee defined HTML. There was a need to be able to script actions on those pages, so Netscape created JavaScript. The pages needed a better way to be styled, so the W3C developed CSS.

DHTML and Ajax, on the other hand, have evolved synergistically out of existing technologies without an exact purpose in mind. This development happened more or less organically within the Web development community over several years. The term used to describe these technologies was coined only after someone recognized a common thread maturing.

Other Famous Ajaxes

Ajax (the Web development technology) should never be confused with these other uses of the word Ajax:

- Ajax (a.k.a. Telamonian Ajax) was a warrior in the Trojan War, according to Homer's *Iliad*.

- Ajax cleanser is a popular bleach-based cleaning product introduced in 1947 by Colgate-Palmolive.

- Ajax is a town of 90,000 inhabitants located in Ontario, Canada.

- Ajax is the football club of Amsterdam, Netherlands.

Figure 19.2 The original article coining the term Ajax, written by Jesse James Garrett.

The story behind Ajax is that renowned Web designer and pundit Jesse James Garrett coined the term in 2005 while he was in the shower. Jesse needed a catchy idiom to describe the suite of technologies he was getting ready to propose using to a client (**Figure 19.2**). By the time he had toweled off, Ajax was born.

So, why "Ajax"? Here's the break down:

- **Asynchronous.** Actions and reactions don't have to happen at the same time. In other words, the user can do something while the browser is waiting to get information back from the server.

- **JavaScript.** It can be scripted to do stuff. Really this part of the acronym should have been DHTML, since Ajax also relies on XHTML, CSS, and the DOM. But then the acronym would have been *Adax*, which doesn't sound nearly as cool.

- **and.** A conjunction that keeps the acronym from being unpronounceable.

- **XML.** One of the data formats that can be used to create and transfer content between the server and the Web page. However, the format can be almost anything, including HTML/XHTML and server-side scripting languages, such as PHP, ASP, or JSP.

Developers have been steadily moving towards using this combination of technologies for several years. Many Web designers recognized the need to move beyond the Web page metaphor and think of a Web page as an application through which the Web site visitor interacted with data. Many solutions, mostly involving frames, have been tried, but none has ever proven completely satisfactory.

continues on next page

WHAT IS AJAX?

Ajax brings together a number of different Web technologies that, when used together, let designers take dynamic Web pages much further by enabling visitors to interact with the entire Web through a single Web page interface.

Let's take a closer look at what's involved (**Figure 19.3**).

Dynamic HTML (DHTML)

Ajax uses XHTML for content and CSS for presentation, as well as the Document Object Model and JavaScript for dynamic content display. For more details on DHTML, see Chapter 11.

XMLHttpRequest

All Ajax solutions require a method for passing data between the Web page in the client (the visitor's browser) and the files on the server used to create the Web page.

One early attempt to allow this type of back and forth communication between the client and the server was through *iframes*. Often invisible, these "windows to the server" could be used to pass data back and forth.

Although iframes are still used with some Ajax applications, many designers now use the XMLHttpRequest object, because it can be used in JavaScript to retrieve data from a Web server, whereas iFrames still require an entire page be fetched from the server.

The original XMLHttpRequest object—or a semblance thereof—was created by Microsoft to be used with Outlook as an ActiveX object. Called *XMLHTTP*, it has been part of the

What is an API?

An Application Programming Interface (API) can be thought of as a library of code that describes how particular data or functionality—generally provided by a third party such as an OS manufacturer or software developer—can be accessed without direct contact with the original source code.

For example, both Microsoft and Apple provide APIs that allow programmers to access and enable operating system functionality within their software. However the actual code used to create that functionality is never shown directly to the programmers, only the hooks they need in order to integrate it into their work.

For the Web, many Web sites provide APIs that will allow Web designers to integrate functionality into their Web sites. For example, Google offers an API that lets you place Google Maps functionality directly into your Web page, without having to know how to code the maps yourself (google.com/apis/maps/).

DHTML + XMLHttpRequest + Server Files = Ajax

Filters data for
display on the
page.

Transfers data
between the server
and the page.

Provides data that is
either static or
dynamically generated.

Figure 19.3 The components of Ajax.

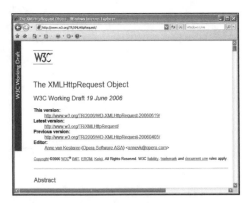

Figure 19.4 Information about the work by the W3C on the XMLHttpRequest object can be found at w3.org/TR/XMLHttpRequest/.

Windows version of Internet Explorer since version 5. Other browsers, including Firefox 1.0, Safari 1.2, and Opera 8.0, support compatible versions of the same type of request object, but with those browsers it is referred to as *XMLHttpRequest*.

The W3C published in mid-2006 a working draft that documents the common features between both XMLHTTP and XMLHttpRequest, which at some point will likely become a formal standard (**Figure 19.4**). There are a few minor differences between the two objects, but these differences are mitigated using JavaScript.

Server files

Although Ajax can retrieve any kind of file from the server (including a simple text or HTML file), much of the power of Ajax comes when it works with server-side scripting languages such as PHP, ASP, JSP, ColdFusion, SSI, server-side JavaScript, or SMX, or by using XML and XSL (see the sidebar "Server-Side Code Used in This Book").

A lot of common APIs (see the sidebar "What is an API?") are also available that let you add Ajax functionality to your Web site without having to create the server-side code yourself. We'll take a look at those in more detail in Chapter 20.

WHAT IS AJAX?

Server-Side Code Used in This Book

Although server-side scripting falls outside of the scope of this book, I've created a few code blocks in my examples in this book that use the open-source programming language PHP. However, much of Ajax's functionality comes from what these server-side files do with and to data, so if you are serious about doing more with Ajax, you will need to learn some server-side scripting language, and I recommend PHP.

For more details on PHP, check out Larry Ullman's *PHP for the World Wide Web: Visual QuickStart Guide* from Peachpit Press. This is the book that I used to learn about PHP.

How Ajax Works

Although it may not be a standardized technology or even a completely new idea, Ajax is quickly changing not only the way that Web designers think about visitors' experiences, but also the expectations of Web surfers themselves.

The reason for this is simple: Ajax allows for a more fluid and seamless interaction model over the "classic" Web-interaction model.

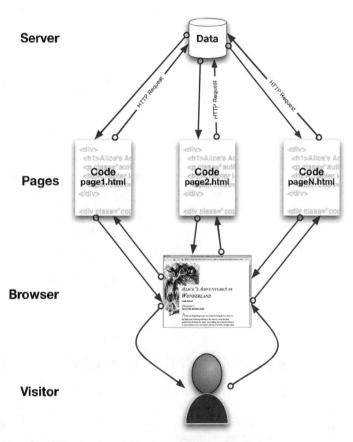

Figure 19.5 The classic model for delivering Web applications.

How the classic Web user experience works

Although you can use DHTML to make changes to the content being displayed on the screen, all of the data used to create the content (displayed or not) of a Web page must be contained within the code that was initially sent. If the user interacts with the page and new data is required to respond to what they have done, a new Web page must be sent from the server and loaded in the browser (**Figure 19.5**).

However, for making small changes to the content of a page or when the content of the page needs to change fluidly without interruption, this model is not only inconvenient, it leads to a deeply unsatisfying Web experience. As time passes, the visitor interacts with the page and then has to wait as data is transferred back and forth (**Figure 19.6**).

continues on next page

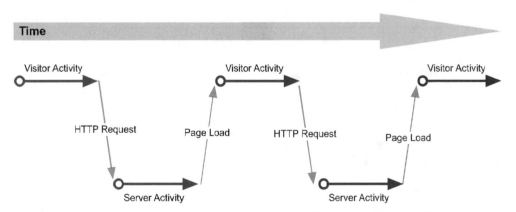

Figure 19.6 As time progresses, visitors' Web experiences are constantly interrupted as they wait for data to be sent back and forth, to and from, the server.

How the Ajax Web user experience works

Ajax changes the classic Web experience by allowing the browser to go back to the server incrementally to make changes to the content, turning the Web page into a filter that processes data coming from the server (**Figure 19.7**).

Instead of having to wait as data is sent to the server, the data is sent and received in the background while the visitor continues to work (**Figure 19.8**). That's the asynchronous part of Ajax. The Web page acts as filter for the data being sent from the server, generally using DHTML to add content to the page using the innerHTML method (see "Changing an Object's Content" in Chapter 16).

So not only do visitors not have to wait as small amounts of new data are processed and loaded, but the server also doesn't have to reprocess an entire Web page worth of data just to make small incremental changes.

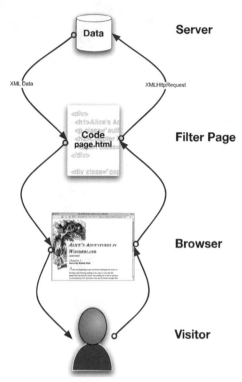

Figure 19.7 The Ajax model for delivering Web applications.

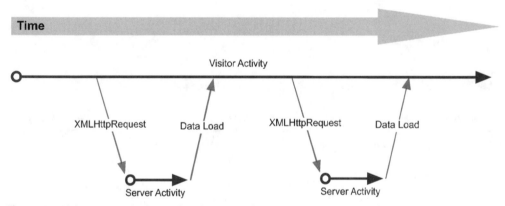

Figure 19.8 Visitors can continue to work as data is transferred between the page and the server.

Why Should I Use Ajax?

Ajax generally can be a benefit to at least some aspect of any Web site. By opening a quick conduit back to the data and functionality stored on the server, Ajax can improve the user experience of e-mail list submissions, message boards, online shopping, photo sharing, and much, much more. In fact, the use of Ajax is still so young, we are only beginning to see some of the possible applications.

Ajax advantages

Being able to turn static Web pages into an interactive environment has several advantages over classic Web interactions:

- **A unified and consistent interface.** By not requiring constant page reloads, the Web page interface is not always blinking or jumping around within the window.

- **A fluid user experience.** Rather than dealing with individual pages of information, the visitors can work with the page almost as if it were the interface to an application, one that has all the information of the Web behind it.

- **Improved usability.** By turning Web pages into Web-enabled applications, many of the paradigms associated with standard software can be implemented, leading to improved usability.

- **Optimal use of bandwidth.** Most of the time, Ajax allows for a speedier display of content, since smaller data chunks are needed to update the Web page.

- **Perceived speed increase.** Whether the data is delivered more quickly or not, users feel as if the experience is much faster because the system does not pause to reload pages.

continues on next page

WHY SHOULD I USE AJAX?

◆ **Content and functionality sharing.**
By sharing code, the Web itself will
become an open platform and Web sites
less insular. Functionality and content
created for one Web site can be easily
shared around the Web.

◆ **Heightened interactivity.** Because of
the real and perceived speed increases
mentioned above, Web visitors are more
likely to interact with the pages to make
small data changes that can be just as
quickly undone. For example, given a
page of DVDs to rate, Ajax allows the
user to quickly move through the list
making rating decisions; whereas the
classic Web experience requires that they
wait for a new page to load after every
change to save and display the changes,
making most visitors less inclined
to bother.

Ajax disadvantages

There is no such thing as a perfect technology, and using Ajax in your Web site
comes with its own set of worries. In fact,
many of Ajax's advantages can prove to
be a double-edged sword:

◆ **Unexpected or uncertain behaviors.**
Although usability might be improved by
making Web pages more application-like,
the reverse argument can be made that
they then become less Web-page-like,
breaking expected Web behaviors.

◆ **Response time delays.** Although Ajax
should speed things up, any network
problems or other speed bumps in getting the data to and from the server can
cause downtime. Since this effect can be
extremely unpredictable, it is hard to
create useful contingency plans.

- **Security concerns.** Although in their infancy, exploits of Ajax have already appeared on the Web, in which hackers have accessed the data being passed back and forth. Precautions can and should always be taken.

- **Accessibility limitations.** Because Ajax is such a new technology and relies on particular user interactions, Ajax-enabled Web sites often have a hard time meeting the WAI accessibility guidelines (w3.org/TR/WCAG10/) or adhering to the U.S. government's Section 508 Compliance Standards (section508.gov).

- **Search Engine Optimization.** Dynamically changing content *after* the initial page load currently means that Web page search engine "spiders" will not see all of the content you have available. This can lead to lower rankings for your Web pages when they have content relevant to a given search.

WHY SHOULD I USE AJAX?

What Is Web 2.0?

If you have been paying attention to any-thing Web-related in the last few years, then you have probably come across the term *Web 2.0*. Although some might dismiss it as another techno-babble buzzword, it is becoming increasingly pervasive with many companies building their strategies around the concept. At it's simplest, Web 2.0 embodies the belief that the World Wide Web is break-ing away from its origins and evolving into the next stage of human interaction with a computer and the global community.

The buzzword took on a life of its own, when in 2004 Tim O'Reilly hosted the first Web 2.0 Conference (**Figure 19.9**), where he and other Web and business pundits laid down the core Web 2.0 principals:

◆ **The Web as application delivery plat-form.** Rather than purchasing software to be run from your desktop, applications can be licensed and run over the Web.

◆ **The end of software versioning.** Rather than having discreet software ver-sions, applications are constantly being updated and improved.

◆ **Data as a driving force.** Information becomes the center of development.

◆ **Visitor contributions through an "Architecture of Participation."** Everyone is able to create and distribute content in an open community.

◆ **Ubiquitous content and service syn-dication.** Rather than isolated islands of information, the Web becomes a person-alized distribution network.

◆ **A "long tail" approach to content delivery.** Rather than a few creating con-tent for the masses, the masses create content for the few. For more details, see the sidebar "The 'Long Tail' of Content."

Figure 19.9 The Web 2.0 Conference (patent pending) is the center of the buzz.

The "Long Tail" of Content

Chris Anderson coined the phrase the *long tail* to describe a trend he was noticing on the Web in which goods and services that normally might be considered part of a niche market, such as a cult movie, songs by a fringe band, or an obscure weblog, end up being very popular in aggregate compared to other obviously popular goods and services.

For example, any one of thousands of cult movies available from Netflix might have extremely low rental rates compared to a typical "blockbuster" movie. But because the Web doesn't have limited shelf space available to house rentals like the local video rental store does, online rental companies like Netflix can afford to make "unpopular movies" available. If you add up the rental of all of these unpopular movies, you might be surprised to find that they can actually account for more sales than the blockbusters.

While this explanation is somewhat simplified—there's more to it than just the niche market—the big idea is that Web 2.0 can accommodate niche markets and specialized content and make it easily available to a wider audience.

For more details (and to find out where the term "long tail" comes from), there is no better place to start than with Anderson's original article (wired.com/wired/archive/12.10/tail.html).

Regardless of how the term came about, Web 2.0 appears to be sticking as a way to describe next generation Web applications. For it's part, Ajax also seems to be forming the technological cornerstone of Web 2.0, since it allows for a smoother online application user interface and data transfer. In fact, Ajax is becoming such an integral part of the fabric of the Web that it has it's own recognizable design style (see the sidebar "What Does Web 2.0 Look Like?").

Why Web 2.0 now?

A variety of different influences have made this a ripe time to think about new ways of dealing with the Web.

◆ Browser standards are becoming increasingly solid and predictable, allowing Web designers to create innovative Web pages they know will work for the majority of their users, with few caveats.

◆ High-speed Internet access is becoming increasingly ubiquitous, meaning that visitors have to wait less for more robust content.

◆ Better delivery systems for robust graphic, audio, and video content have evolved and matured in the last few years.

◆ As a social platform, the Web is becoming increasingly indispensable, especially among younger audiences.

◆ Familiarity and reliance on the Web is consistently growing, allowing content providers to rely on a steadily growing and increasingly Web-savvy audience.

continues on next page

WHAT IS WEB 2.0?

What Does Web 2.0 Look Like?

The term may be only a few years old, but it has already spawned a noticeable design trend amongst Web sites that claim to be a part of the Web 2.0 revolution (**Figure 19.10**). These sites tend to include:

◆ A lot of gradient or diagonal hatch-mark (or both) backgrounds

◆ Large colorful icons, with 3D effects such as reflections (called the *Wet Floor effect*) and drop shadows

◆ Large, bold header text

◆ Glossy 3D elements like what you see in Apple's OS X interface

◆ Lots of highlights and text call-outs that appear for no obvious reasons

For a wry look at the Web 2.0 design phenomena (and what it looks like), check out Hypocritical's "Web 2.0 interface design checklist" (hypocritical.com/blog/2005/12/web-20-interface-design-checklist.asp).

Figure 19.10 The home page for "The Web 2.0 Show" podcast is a good example of the Web 2.0 "look."

Web 2.0 is an attempt to capture this rising "upgrade" to the Web. However, it also emphasizes the increasingly participatory nature of the Web through the use of tags, blogs, comments, wikis, ranking, and the general free sharing of content using APIs, Ajax, and other open-source technologies that free Web sites from their "walled garden" mentality.

Ajax and Rich Internet Applications

Although there are a lot of technologies that allow the delivery of applications that feel like stand-alone software over the Web (such as Flash, Java, and ActiveX), Ajax is proving to be a driving force in many Web 2.0 Rich Internet Applications (RIA).

RIAs make use of Ajax to create robust user interfaces within the browser window to do everything that you might be able to do with a stand-alone application downloaded directly to your computer. We still have a long way to go before we see RIAs that truly rival their desktop counterparts, but this is a growing area of Web development. For a list of some of the more interesting RIAs already deployed, see **Table 19.1**.

WHAT IS WEB 2.0?

Table 19.1

Rich Internet Applications		
NAME	URL	DESCRIPTION
Google Maps	maps.google.com	World maps
24SevenOffice	24sevenoffice.com	Resource planning and customer relationship software
Flickr	flickr.com	Photo storage and cataloging software
FORScene	forbidden.co.uk/products/scene/	Video logging, editing, and reviewing tools

Ajax Basics

Despite appearances, setting up basic Ajax functionality is not that difficult. It involves three main parts: making the server call, having the server process the call, and then filtering the data that comes back. This can be as simple as grabbing a chunk of HTML code from the server to place on the current page, or as complex as submitting multiple variables to a database to update a 3D map of the earth. Let's start with the simple stuff.

In this chapter, you will learn how to do the following:

◆ Fetch content directly from the server and place it onto the current page

◆ Send data from the current page back to the server and get a response to place on the page

◆ Filter responses from the server for different situations

◆ Set up an external JavaScript library file to hold Ajax functions to be used across multiple Web pages

Let's get started with an overview of how Ajax code works by sending requests to the server.

Understanding Server Requests

Ajax functionality relies on the relatively straightforward ability to request data from the server. Every time you load a Web page, you are making a server request, so that's nothing new. However, the HTTP request is all or nothing: you have to load the complete and entire file used to render the Web page. You can overcome that somewhat using iframes, but, like many solutions to problems on the Web, iframes were never meant to be used this way.

It wasn't until Microsoft introduced the XMLHttpRequest object in Internet Explorer 5, which allowed JavaScript to make a server requests and to hold the information returned in a variable, that data could be transferred without having to reload the entire page, and without requiring the use of iframes.

These days, along with the DOM and JavaScript, server requests are used to dynamically change a page's content. The general Ajax function works something like this (**Figure 20.1**):

1. **Action**. An event happens in the browser window. For example, the user begins to type something into a form field.

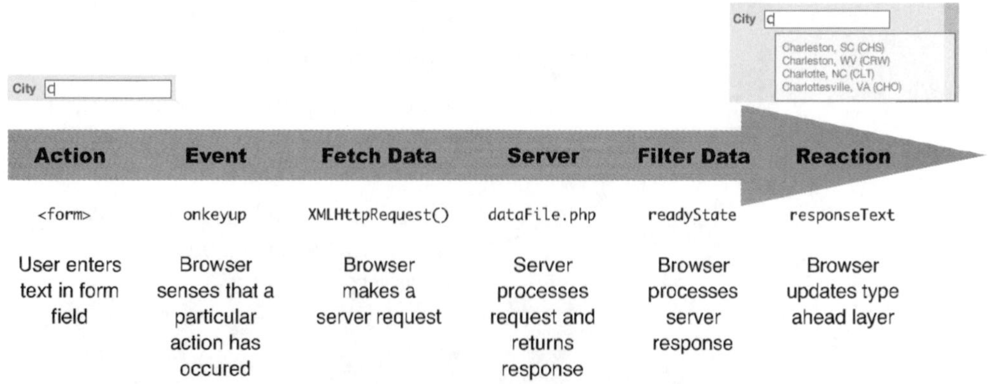

Action	Event	Fetch Data	Server	Filter Data	Reaction
<form>	onkeyup	XMLHttpRequest()	dataFile.php	readyState	responseText
User enters text in form field	Browser senses that a particular action has occured	Browser makes a server request	Server processes request and returns response	Browser processes server response	Browser updates type ahead layer

Figure 20.1 The general Ajax process flow, showing the dynamic type-ahead functionality discussed in Chapter 22.

Table 20.1

Ajax Properties	
PROPERTY	DESCRIPTION
onreadystatechange	Event handler triggered when the state of the request object changes
readyState	Status code for the current state of the server request object (see Table 20.3)
responseText	String value of the data from the server
responseXML	DOM-compatible XML document object of the data from the server
status	Status code of the HTTP response from the server
statusText	String value of the HTTP status message

Table 20.2

Ajax Methods	
METHOD	DESCRIPTION
abort()	Cancels the current HTTP request
getAllResponseHeaders()	String value of all HTTP headers
getResponseHeader(‹label›)	Value of specified HTTP header
open(‹method›,‹URL›, ‹asynchFlag›)	Initializes the XML HTTP request
send(‹content›)	Sends the request to the server and receives the response
setRequestHeader (‹label›,‹value›)	Sets an HTTP header and value to be sent

2. **Event**. The event handler for the object that initiated the action (for example, the form field) will trigger a function used to request data from the server (I generally call that function `fetchData()`).

3. **Fetch Data**. This is the server request, where a JavaScript object is created (I call mine `pageRequest`) that will be used to send and receive data from the server. You initialize this object as either `ActiveXObject("Microsoft.XMLHTTP")` for Internet Explorer or `XMLHttpRequest()` for all other browsers.

4. **Server Process**. The page on the server processes the request. I usually call this page `dataPage`, with the relevant extension (for example, `dataPage.php`). If you used the GET method to make the request, then the contents of the data page are simply returned to the `fetchData()` function. If you use POST, then data can be sent to that page and used to return specific content. For example, you might pass a numeric value that is then used to send back a specific word based on that value.

5. **Filter Data**. Once the data is passed back to the page, it can be passed on to a function used to interpret it and display it in the Web page. I usually call this function `filterData()`.

6. **Reaction**. Finally, the data is used by or placed onto the page, generally by using the `innerHTML` method to place it into a specific object.

Ajax properties and methods

Although the format outlined above takes care of the basic needs for fetching data off the server for use on a Web page, there are several JavaScript properties (**Table 20.1**) and methods (**Table 20.2**) that are commonly used to control Ajax functionality.

UNDERSTANDING SERVER REQUESTS

Fetching Data

At its most basic; Ajax can be used to retrieve a chunk of content from the server. It doesn't pass any information back to the server; it simply retrieves a file, which can then be used by the Web page. This content file can be in virtually any format, as long as when it is inserted into the page the browser can interpret it.

In this example (**Figure 20.2**), we'll simply fetch a small chunk of code (<h1>Hello World</h1>) when the visitor clicks the conspicuous control and then place that code onto the page (**Figure 20.3**).

To fetch data from the server:

1. dataPage.php

   Create your data page and save it as dataPage.php (**Code 20.1**).

   This file is used to hold the content that is going to be fetched by the Ajax function on our Web page.

   For this example, I used the PHP extension, but this is really nothing more than a text file since there is nothing but HTML code in it. This file could be an HTML, ASP, JSP or any other file format that a server can store.

2. index.html

   Create an HTML file and save it as index.html (**Code 20.2**). The rest of the steps in this example apply to this file.

3. function fetchData(url, objectID){…}

   Add the function fetchData() to a JavaScript block.

   This function will be used to grab whatever code is located at the URL specified by the variable url and place it in the object specified by objectID. Steps 4 through 8 apply to this function.

4. var pageRequest = false;

   Initialize the variable pageRequest and set it to false.

Figure 20.2 When the page loads, only the control is displayed.

Figure 20.3 Clicking the control causes the browser to fetch the code from the server and place it onto the page.

Code 20.1 dataPage.php: The data page is on the server and contains a simple line of HTML code that can be inserted into any Web page.

```
<h1>Hello World!</h1>
```

This variable is used as the conduit to exchange information between the Web page (index.html) and the data page (dataPage.php).

5. pageRequest = new XMLHttpRequest();

If the Web page is loaded in a browser that uses the XMLHttpRequest method for making requests, such as Mozilla, Safari, or Internet Explorer 7, add code to initialize the pageRequest variable as an XMLHttpRequest object.

continues on next page

Code 20.2 index.html: The fetchData() function requests a file from the server based on the URL passed to it and then displays that URL's content directly in the page.

```
<!DOCTYPE html PUBLIC "-//W3C//DTD XHTML 1.0 Strict//EN" "http://www.w3.org/TR/xhtml1/
→ DTD/xhtml1-strict.dtd">
<html xmlns="http://www.w3.org/1999/xhtml">
<head>
<meta http-equiv="Content-Type" content="text/html; charset=UTF-8" />
<title>CSS, DHTML &amp; Ajax | Fetching Data</title>
<style type="text/css" media="screen">
h1 { color: red; }
#control {
    color: red;
    background-color: #fcc;
    border: 1px solid red;
    padding: 4px; }
</style>
<script type="text/javascript">
function fetchData(url,objectID){
    var pageRequest = false;
    if (window.XMLHttpRequest)pageRequest = new XMLHttpRequest();
    else if (window.ActiveXObject) pageRequest = new ActiveXObject("Microsoft.XMLHTTP");
    else return false;
    pageRequest.onreadystatechange = function() {
        var object = document.getElementById(objectID);
        object.innerHTML = pageRequest.responseText;
    }
    pageRequest.open('GET',url,true);
    pageRequest.send(null);
}
</script>
</head>
<body>
<div id="control" onclick="fetchData('dataPage.php', 'message');"> Click Me! </div>
<div id="message"> </div>
</body>
</html>
```

6. `pageRequest = new`
`→ ActiveXObject("Microsoft.XMLHTTP");`

If the Web page is loaded in a browser that uses the `ActiveXObject` method for making requests, add code to initialize the `pageRequest` variable as an `ActiveXObject` object:

7. `pageRequest.onreadystatechange =`
`→ function() {…}`

Tell the function what to do when the status of the page request object changes as the data is fetched and loaded into the `pageRequest` object. In this example, we simply place content returned from the data page (`responseText`) into an object on our page:

`object.innerHTML =`
`→ pageRequest.responseText;`

8. `pageRequest.open('GET', url, true);`

Now we add the real action to our function. By initiating the `open()` method with the `pageRequest` object, we can get information from the file specified by the `url` variable, but no data is being sent:

`pageRequest.send(null);`

9. `onclick="fetchData('dataPage.php',`
`→ 'message');"`

Add an event handler to your HTML to trigger the `fetchData()` function.

In this example, I set up a simple `onclick` event handler so that the function is triggered when the visitor clicks the control, passing it the URL for the page where the data is located (`dataPage.php`), as well as the ID for the object that the results are to be placed into (`message`).

10. `<div id="message"> </div>`

Finally, set up the object that will contain the final results fetched using our Ajax function from Step 3.

Figure 20.4 The page loads with the controls.

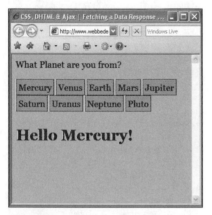

Figure 20.5 Depending on the planet you click, you will get a different message retrieved from the server.

Figure 20.6 Click a different planet (or former planet), and get a different message.

Fetching a Response

The real power of Ajax doesn't come from the code in your Web page, but in the support files that stay on the server. Retrieving chunks of data (described in the previous section) can be useful, but to create an Ajax Web page that truly interacts with the user, you need to be able to both *send* to the server as well as receive data back from it.

In this section, we'll continue building on the fetchData() function from the previous section by adding the capability to not only GET data from the server, but POST data to it as well.

In the next example (**Figure 20.4**), the visitor can click on their planet of origin. The planet's number is sent to the data page, which then returns a custom message for that planet (**Figures 20.5** and **20.6**).

Keep in mind that in all the examples in this book, I'm using PHP for my server side files. Not all Web servers are set up to handle PHP, so if you are not sure, then check with your server administrator. If you do not have PHP on your Web server, then these examples will not work.

continues on next page

FETCHING A RESPONSE

To fetch a data response from the server:

1. `dataPage.php`

Create your data page and save it as `dataPage.php` (**Code 20.3**).

In this example, I've used PHP to create a simple logical structure that will evaluate the value of the variable sent to the data page from the Web page through the `sendData` variable:

`$searchString = $_POST["sendData"];`

2. `index.html`

Create an HTML file and save it as index.html (**Code 20.4**). The rest of the steps in this example apply to this file.

3. `function fetchData`
`→ (url, dataToSend, objectID) {…}`

Add the function `fetchData()` to a JavaScript block.

This function is identical to the `fetchData()` function presented in the previous section, but adds the ability to send information to the data page as well as receive data back from it. Steps 4 through 8 apply to this function.

4. `if (dataToSend) {…}`

If data is being sent back to the server from the page (`dataToSend` is not `null`):

`var sendData = 'sendData=' +`
`→ dataToSend;`

Initialize the variable `sendData`, which stores a string with the `dataToSend` value assigned to the `sendData` variable. This string is passed along to the data page.

continues on Page 442

Code 20.3 `dataPage.php`: The data page contains a simple PHP example that takes the posted value out of the HTTP headers and then delivers back a message based on that value.

```php
<?php
if(isset($_POST["sendData"]))
{ $searchString = $_POST["sendData"];
    if ($searchString == 1) $dataResults =
    → sprintf("<h1>Hello Mercury!</h1>");
    else if ($searchString == 2)
    → $dataResults = sprintf("<h1>Hello
    → Venus!</h1>");
    else if ($searchString == 3)
    → $dataResults = sprintf("<h1>Hello
    → Earth!</h1>");
    else if ($searchString == 4)
    → $dataResults = sprintf("<h1>Hello
    → Mars!</h1>");
    else if ($searchString == 5)
    → $dataResults = sprintf("<h1>Hello
    → Jupiter!</h1>");
    else if ($searchString == 6)
    → $dataResults = sprintf("<h1>Hello
    → Saturn!</h1>");
    else if ($searchString == 7)
    → $dataResults = sprintf("<h1>Hello
    → Uranus!</h1>");
    else if ($searchString == 8)
    → $dataResults = sprintf("<h1>Hello
    → Neptune!</h1>");
    else if ($searchString == 9)
    → $dataResults = sprintf("<h2>Sorry
    → Pluto… You aren't a planet
    → anymore.</h2>");
    else $dataResults = sprintf("<p>You are
    → no longer in the solar system.</p>");
}
echo $dataResults;
?>
```

FETCHING A RESPONSE

Code 20.4 `index.html`: The `fetchData()` function passes a value to the data page on the server and then displays the results it returns.

```
<!DOCTYPE html PUBLIC "-//W3C//DTD XHTML 1.0
→ Strict//EN" "http://www.w3.org/TR/xhtml1/
→ DTD/xhtml1-strict.dtd">
<html xmlns="http://www.w3.org/1999/xhtml">
<head>
<meta http-equiv="Content-Type"
→ content="text/html; charset=UTF-8" />
<title>CSS, DHTML &amp; Ajax | Fetching a
→ Data Response</title>
<style type="text/css" media="screen">
h1 { color: red; }
#control {
    float: left;
    cursor: pointer;
    margin-right: 4px;
    color: red;
    background-color: #fcc;
    border: 1px solid red;
    padding: 4px; }
</style>
<script type="text/javascript">
function fetchData(url,dataToSend,objectID){
    var pageRequest = false
    if (window.XMLHttpRequest) pageRequest
→ = new XMLHttpRequest();
    else if (window.ActiveXObject)
→ pageRequest = new
ActiveXObject("Microsoft.XMLHTTP");
    else return false;
    pageRequest.onreadystatechange =
→ function() {
       var object =
→ document.getElementById(objectID);
       object.innerHTML =
→ pageRequest.responseText;
    }
    if (dataToSend) {
       var sendData = 'sendData=' +
→ dataToSend;
    pageRequest.open('POST',url,true);
    pageRequest.setRequestHeader('Content-
→ Type', 'application/x-www-form-
→ urlencoded');
    pageRequest.send(sendData);
    }
    else {
    pageRequest.open('GET',url,true);
    pageRequest.send(null);
}}
```

Code 20.4 *continued*

```
</script>
</head>
<body>
<p>What Planet are you from?</p>
<div id="control"
→ onclick="fetchData('dataPage.php',1,
→ 'message');"> Mercury </div>
<div id="control"
→ onclick="fetchData('dataPage.php',2,
→ 'message');"> Venus </div>
<div id="control"
→ onclick="fetchData('dataPage.php',3,
→ 'message');"> Earth </div>
<div id="control"
→ onclick="fetchData('dataPage.php',4,
→ 'message');"> Mars </div>
<div id="control"
→ onclick="fetchData('dataPage.php',5,
→ 'message');"> Jupiter </div>
<div id="control"
→ onclick="fetchData('dataPage.php',6,
→ 'message');"> Saturn </div>
<div id="control"
→ onclick="fetchData('dataPage.php',7,
→ 'message');"> Uranus </div>
<div id="control"
→ onclick="fetchData('dataPage.php',8,
→ 'message');"> Neptune </div>
<div id="control"
→ onclick="fetchData('dataPage.php',9,
→ 'message');"> Pluto </div>
<p> </p>
<div id="message"> </div>
</body>
</html>
```

5. `pageRequest.open('POST', url, true);`

Open a conduit to the data page, but rather than using `GET` you will be using the `POST` method to send data along with the request.

`pageRequest.setRequestHeader`
`→ ('Content-Type', 'application/`
`→ x-www-form-urlencoded');`

6. `pageRequest.send(sendData);`

Set the header that will be sent with the request. Send the data to the data page you set up in Step 1, using the `sendData` variable.

7. `else {...}`

If no data is being sent to the page, then we use the `GET` method as specified in Step 8 of the previous section ("Fetching Data").

8. `onclick = "fetchData('dataPage.php',`
`→ 3, 'message');"`

Add an event handler to your HTML to trigger the `fetchData()` function.

In this example, I set up a simple `onclick` event handler to trigger the function when the visitor clicks one of the controls. The event sends to the function the URL for the page where the data is located (`dataPage.php`), a value that will be sent to the data page and used to determine its response (if you want to simply fetch a data chunk, pass the value `null`), and the ID for the object to have the results placed into (`message`).

9. `<div id="message"> </div>`

Finally, set up the object that will contain the final results fetched using our Ajax function from Step 3.

Figure 20.7 The text has been fetched from the server after the page loads.

Filtering the Data

If you've ever written any computer code, then you have had errors. Things never work exactly the way you plan, so you need contingency plans. With Ajax, the risks for things going wrong increases, because you cannot predict the reliability of the connection between visitors' computers and the Web server where the data is coming from.

The code presented in the previous two sections assumes the data will arrive as planned. However, if it doesn't, the page simply waits obediently until the visitor gets bored and/or frustrated and then abandons the ship. You do not want that to happen.

Building off the `fetchData()` function from the previous section ("Fetching a Response"), in this section we'll add the ability to specify another function to be used to process and filter the messages and data coming from the server and display the current status and final data response on the Web page. If there is a problem retrieving the data from the server, the function will alert visitors that something went wrong, rather than leave them hanging.

In this example (**Figure 20.7**), when the page first loads, it immediately fetches a message from the server based on the value passed to the data page on the server.

To filter a data response from the server:

1. `dataPage.php`

   Create your data page and save it as `dataPage.php` (Code 20.3).

   In this example, I'm using the same data page as in the previous section ("Fetching a Response").

continues on next page

2. `index.html`

Create an HTML file and save it as index.html (**Code 20.5**). The rest of the steps in this section apply to this file.

3. `function fetchData`
`→ (url, dataToSend, objectID) {…}`

Add the function `fetchData()` to a JavaScript block.

This function is identical to the `fetchData()` function presented in the previous section, but specifies the function to be executed when the request state changes.

For this example, I've instructed the function to trigger the `filterData()` function every time the state of the `pageRequest` object changes, passing to the function the `pageRequest` object and the `objectID` variable:

`filterData(pageRequest, objectID);`

4. `function filterData(pageRequest,`
`→ objectID){…}`

Add the `filterData()` function to your JavaScript.

This function process the `pageRequest` object's current `readyState` value (**Table 20.3**) and acts accordingly. Steps 5 through 8 apply to this function.

5. `var object =`
`→ document.getElementById(objectID);`

Get the object that the data will eventually be placed into, based on the `objectID` variable.

6. `if (pageRequest.readyState == 0)`

Add conditionals to test for each of the possible ready states, and write a message into the HTML object.

For this example, I simply add a message specifying the current state:

`object.innerHTML += '<h3>Fetching`
`→ Data… </h3>';`

Table 20.3

ReadyState Values	
VALUE	DESCRIPTION
0	Uninitialized. The object has no data.
1	Loading. The object has data loading.
2	Loaded. The object has finished loading data.
3	Interactive. Data is still loading, but the object can be interacted with.
4	Complete. Data is fully loaded and ready for use.

continues on Page 446

Code 20.5 index.html: The fetchData() function passes a value to the data page on the server and then passes the request object (pageRequest) to the function filterData() every time there is a change in the readyState.

```html
<!DOCTYPE html PUBLIC "-//W3C//DTD XHTML 1.0 Strict//EN" "http://www.w3.org/TR/xhtml1/DTD/
→ xhtml1-strict.dtd">
<html xmlns="http://www.w3.org/1999/xhtml">
<head>
<meta http-equiv="Content-Type" content="text/html; charset=UTF-8" />
<title>CSS, DHTML &amp; Ajax | Filtering the Data</title>
<style type="text/css" media="screen">
h1 { color: red; }
h3 { color: #666; }
</style>

<script type="text/javascript">

function fetchData(url,dataToSend,objectID){
    var pageRequest = false
    if (window.XMLHttpRequest) pageRequest = new XMLHttpRequest();
    else if (window.ActiveXObject) pageRequest = new ActiveXObject("Microsoft.XMLHTTP");
    else return false;
    pageRequest.onreadystatechange = function() {
    filterData(pageRequest,objectID);
}
    if (dataToSend) {
        var sendData = 'sendData=' + dataToSend;
pageRequest.open('POST',url,true);
pageRequest.setRequestHeader('Content-Type', 'application/x-www-form-urlencoded');
    pageRequest.send(sendData);
    }
    else {
pageRequest.open('GET',url,true);
    pageRequest.send(null);
    }
}
function filterData(pageRequest,objectID){
    var object = document.getElementById(objectID);
    if (pageRequest.readyState == 0)
        object.innerHTML += '<h3>Fetching Data… </h3>';
    if (pageRequest.readyState == 1)
        object.innerHTML += '<h3>Loading Data… </h3>';
    if (pageRequest.readyState == 2)
        object.innerHTML += '<h3>Data Loaded… </h3>';
    if (pageRequest.readyState == 3)
        object.innerHTML += '<h3>Data Ready!</h3>';
    if (pageRequest.readyState == 4)
        {if (pageRequest.status==200) object.innerHTML += pageRequest.responseText ;
            else if (pageRequest.status == 404) object.innerHTML += 'Sorry, that information is not
            → currently available.';
        else object.innerHTML += 'Sorry, there seems to be some kind of problem.';
    }
}
</script>
</head>
<body onload="fetchData('dataPage.php',5,'message');">
<div id="message"> </div>
</body></html>
```

Notice that I used plus and equal signs (+=) to append each message to the object, rather than replace it. I did this because the messages would pass so quickly in this example you would never see anything but the final results. Generally, you will want to replace += with a simple equal sign (=).

7. `if (pageRequest.readyState == 4) {…}`

For the fourth `readyState` value (at which point the data is ready for display), we need to do a bit more than display the results in our message object.

To display the results (`responseText`), we need to check that the status of the request is "OK" (`status` equals `200`):

`pageRequest.status==200`

If the page is not found (`status` equals `404`), we need to alert the visitor that the data isn't available:

`pageRequest.status == 404`

If all else fails, we need to display a message in case some other problem occurs.

8. `onload = "fetchData('dataPage.php', → 5, 'message');"`

Add an event handler to your HTML to trigger the `fetchData()` function.

In this example, I set up an `onload` event handler in the body so that the function is triggered as soon as the page loads, passing it the URL for the page where my data is located (`dataPage.php`), the value being sent to the data page (in this case, hard coded as 5), and the ID for the object I want the results placed into (`message`).

9. `<div id="message"> </div>`

Finally, set up the object that will contain the final results fetched using our Ajax function from Step 3.

Figure 20.8 The text has been fetched from the server using the code in the `AjaxsBasics.js` library file.

✔ **Tip**

■ The filter function in this example is fairly simple in that all it does is display the data sent to it from the server. However, you can add whatever JavaScript code you desire in order to process the data before final output.

Code 20.6 `ajaxBasics.js`: This external JavaScript file contains the `fetchData()` function so that you do not have to add it directly to every page in the site.

```
// ajaxBasics.js: Include this file when
→ creating Ajax enabled functions.

function fetchData(url,dataToSend,objectID){
    var pageRequest = false
    if (window.XMLHttpRequest) pageRequest
→ = new XMLHttpRequest();
    else if (window.ActiveXObject)
→ pageRequest = new
→ ActiveXObject("Microsoft.XMLHTTP");
    else return false;
    pageRequest.onreadystatechange =
→ function() {
    filterData(pageRequest,objectID);
}

    if (dataToSend) {
        var sendData = 'sendData=' +
→ dataToSend;
    pageRequest.open('POST',url,true);
    pageRequest.setRequestHeader('Content-
→ Type', 'application/x-www-form-
→ urlencoded');
    pageRequest.send(sendData);
    }
    else {
        pageRequest.open('GET',url,true);
        pageRequest.send(null);    }
}

function filterData(pageRequest,objectID){
    var object =
→ document.getElementById(objectID);
    if (pageRequest.readyState == 4){
    if (pageRequest.status==200)
→ object.innerHTML =
→ pageRequest.responseText ;
    else if (pageRequest.status == 404)
→ object.innerHTML = 'Sorry, that
→ information is not currently
→ available.';
    else object.innerHTML = 'Sorry,
→ there seems to be some kind of
→ problem.';
    }
    else return;
}
```

Utilizing the AjaxBasics.js Library

For the most part, once you create the `fetchData()` Ajax function, you can leave it alone. This function will form the workhorse of your Ajax code, but it is also general enough to handle a variety of situations.

Building on the code from the previous sections in this chapter, we'll put together an external JavaScript file that can be included on any Web page that lets you access server pages. You can then create a control function to prepare the data before invoking the `fetchData()` function and a `filterData()` function tailored to the specific needs of the Web page in which it is included.

In this example (**Figure 20.8**), a message pulled from a page on the server is displayed.

To set up a globally available Ajax function library:

1. `ajaxBasics.js`

   Create a JavaScript file and save it as `ajaxBasics.js` (**Code 20.6**). This file will contain the final version of the `fetchData()` function presented in the previous section ("Filtering the Data").

2. `dataPage.php`

   Create your data page and save it as `dataPage.php` (Code 20.3).

   In this example, I'm using the same data page as in the "To fetch a data response from the server," earlier in this chapter.

   continues on next page

3. `index.html`

Create an HTML file and save it as index.html (**Code 20.7**). The rest of the steps in this section apply to this file.

4. `<script src="ajaxBasics.js"`
`→ type="text/javascript"></script>`

Call the `ajaxBasics.js` file from Step 1. This will reference the code without having to embed it on every Web page it needs to be used with.

5. `function prepData(requestedData) {...}`

Add the `prepData()` function to your JavaScript.

This is the control function that invokes the `fetchData()` function located in the external JavaScript file `ajaxBasics.js`. Although you could bypass this and pass the information directly to the `fetchData()` function, you will often want to process the raw data coming from a function before sending it to the data page.

In this example, I hardcoded the URL data page and the ID for the object where the response is displayed, so that all the triggering function has to include is the value to be sent to the data page.

6. `function filterData(pageRequest,`
`→ objectID){...}`

Add the `filterData()` function to your JavaScript.

This function is almost identical to the `filterData()` function presented in the previous section ("Filtering the Data"), but it removes the status updates for the state changes, which are generally not necessary except when you need to debug your code.

Code 20.7 `index.html`: The `prepData()` function triggers the `fetchData()` function.

```
<!DOCTYPE html PUBLIC "-//W3C//DTD XHTML 1.0
→ Strict//EN" "http://www.w3.org/TR/xhtml1/
→ DTD/xhtml1-strict.dtd">
<html xmlns="http://www.w3.org/1999/xhtml">
<head>
<meta http-equiv="Content-Type"
→ content="text/html; charset=UTF-8" />
<title>CSS, DHTML &amp; Ajax | Creating the
→ ajaxBasics.js Library</title>
<style type="text/css" media="screen">
h1 { color: red; }
</style>
<script src="ajaxBasics.js"
→ type="text/javascript"></script>
<script type="text/javascript">
function prepData(requestedData) {
    fetchData('dataPage.php',
    → requestedData, 'message');
}
</script>
</head>
<body onload="prepData(4);">
<div id="message"> </div>
</body></html>
```

Ajax APIs and Design Patterns

◆ **Ajax Patterns** (ajaxpatterns.org): A wiki devoted to Ajax design patterns. The site contains a collection of public articles on everything Ajax.

◆ **Yahoo! UI Library** (developer.yahoo.com/yui/): A set of utilities and controls that lets you write Web-based applications that take advantage of existing Yahoo! functionality.

◆ **Yahoo! Maps Web Services** (developer.yahoo.com/maps/ajax/): lets you embed dynamic maps directly into your Web page.

◆ **Google Search Ajax API** (code.google.com/apis/ajaxsearch/): lets you integrate dynamic Google search directly into any Web page.

7. `onload="prepData(4);">`

Add an event handler to your HTML to trigger the `prepData()` function.

In this example, I set up a simple `onload` event handler so that the function is triggered as soon as the page loads, passing it the value being sent to the data page (in this case, hardcoded as 4).

8. `<div id="message"> </div>`

Finally, set up the object that will contain the final results fetched using our Ajax function.

✔ Tip

■ The ajaxBasics.js file works as a simple Ajax design pattern that can be shared throughout a site. There are many different design patterns and existing Ajax-based and DHTML-based APIs that you can implement with only a basic knowledge of Ajax coding. See the sidebar "Ajax APIs and Design Patterns" for more details.

UTILIZING THE AJAXBASICS.JS LIBRARY

Part 4
Using CSS, DHTML, and Ajax

Chapter 21: Layout 453

Chapter 22: Content 481

Chapter 23: Navigation 501

Chapter 24: Controls 527

21

LAYOUT

Designers are still discovering the capabilities and limitations of layout with Cascading Style Sheets. Some designers who were initially captivated by the "gee-whiz" typographic abilities of CSS neglected its many layout strengths. In the rush to experiment with the dynamic aspects of CSS, many designers overlooked some of the nuts-and-bolts problems that CSS solves: It facilitates solid, compelling page layout on the Web without having to resort to tables.

In this chapter, you will learn about the following:

◆ Structuring your HTML code for more effective design

◆ Setting up a multicolumn layout grid

◆ Best practices for applying styles to headers, headers, navigation, links, and content

◆ Creating attractive and dynamic tables and forms

◆ Styling frames for better visual integration

Structuring Your Page

Before you start a painting, you first have to stretch the canvas. The canvas frame (usually a wooden rectangle) gives the limp cloth a taut structure. In the same vein, before you start applying your designs, you need to add structure to your HTML code to give your CSS, DHTML, and Ajax code something to hook into. This structure generally comes in the form of adding IDs and classes around particular blocks of content using either `<div>` or `<span>` tags.

In this first example (**Figure 21.1**), we will add structure to the HTML code to accommodate the design for the upcoming sections on multicolumn layouts, headers, navigation and links, and copy and content so that we can create our final layout (**Figure 21.2**).

Figure 21.1 The page created from Code 21.1 displayed without CSS.

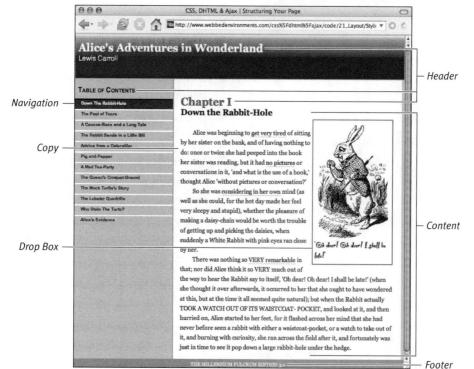

Figure 21.2 The same HTML code as shown in Figure 21.1 with the external CSS file default.css (Code 21.3) applied to it.

Code 21.1 Although already marked up with HTML tags, there are no "hooks" for CSS to use to create the type of layout we want.

```
<!DOCTYPE html PUBLIC "-//W3C//DTD XHTML 1.0
→ Strict//EN" "http://www.w3.org/TR/xhtml1/
→ DTD/xhtml1-strict.dtd">
<html xmlns="http://www.w3.org/1999/xhtml">
<head>
<meta http-equiv="Content-Type"
→ content="text/html; charset=utf-8" />
<title>CSS, DHTML &amp; Ajax | Structuring
→ Your Page</title>
</head>
<body>
<h1>Alice's Adventures in Wonderland</h1>
<p>Lewis Carroll</p>
<h3>Table of Contents</h3>
<ol>
     <li><a href="#">Down The Rabbit-
     → Hole</a></li>
     <li><a href="#">The Pool of Tears</a></li>
     <li><a href="#">A Caucus-Race and a
     → Long Tale</a></li>
     <li><a href="#">The Rabbit Sends in a
     → Little Bill</a></li>
     <li><a href="#">Advice from a
     → Caterpillar</a></li>
     <li><a href="#">Pig and Pepper</a></li>
     <li><a href="#">A Mad Tea-Party</a></li>
     <li><a href="#">The Queen's Croquet-
     → Ground</a></li>
     <li><a href="#">The Mock Turtle's
     → Story</a></li>
     <li><a href="#">The Lobster
     → Quadrille</a></li>
     <li><a href="#">Who Stole The
     → Tarts?</a></li>
     <li><a href="#">Alice's Evidence </a></li>
</ol>
<div>
<h2>Chapter I Down the Rabbit-Hole</h2>
<img src="alice02a.gif" alt="the White
→ Rabbit" height="270" width="180" />'Oh
→ dear! Oh dear! I shall be late!'
<p>Alice was beginning to <a href="#">get
→ very tired</a> of sitting by her sister
→ on the bank, and of having nothing to do:
→ once or twice she had peeped into the
→ book her sister was reading, but it had
→ <a href="#">no pictures</a> or
→ conversations in it, 'and what is the
→ use of a book,' thought Alice 'without
→ pictures or conversation?'</p>
<p>THE MILLENNIUM FULCRUM EDITION 3.0</p>
</div>
</body></html>
```

To structure your HTML markup for layout:

1. Initially the code is already structured by the HTML, but it may not be optimally structured for layout using CSS. Evaluate the code carefully and look for blocks of code that should be separated out so that you can structure the page logically.

   In the page for this example (**Code 21.1**), I see a need for a header, navigation, content, a pull-quote box (drop box), and footer. In addition, I'll want to individually style the author name and chapter title.

   continues on next page

2. `<div id="chapter01" class="page">`
`→ …</div>`

Surround your entire page (between the `<body>` tags) with a `<div>` element **(Code 21.2)**. Generally, you will want to provide the page a unique ID name, or at least the section of the site where the page is located (the ID is used later in this chapter to help us with styling the global navigation). Also add a class called **page** to the tag, which is often used to help control columns in the design.

In theory, the ID and class could go directly in the body tag, but I find this sometimes causes problems.

3. `<div id="header">…</div>`

Surround the content of the page that makes up the main header with a `<div>` element. The header will generally stretch across the top of the page, and may have title, sub-titles, global navigation, or other elements that will need to be at the top of every page in the Web site.

4. `<div id="navigation">…</div>`

If you have navigation that is not in the header, identify it with a `<div>` element. This is only a two-column example, so I'm assuming that this will be the content in the left column and I have assigned it the navigation ID. However, you can call this block anything you want or even introduce another `<div>` to be used as a third column.

You might also want to put search forms, e-mail sign-ups, link lists, or whatever you want into the header.

Code 21.2 This is the same basic code as Code 21.1 (and will display the same if no CSS is added), but the structural "hooks" have been added that will allow us to create the desired layout.

```
<!DOCTYPE html PUBLIC "-//W3C//DTD XHTML 1.0
→ Strict//EN" "http://www.w3.org/TR/xhtml1/
→ DTD/xhtml1-strict.dtd">
<html xmlns="http://www.w3.org/1999/xhtml">
<head>
<meta http-equiv="Content-Type"
→ content="text/html; charset=utf-8" />
<title>CSS, DHTML &amp; Ajax | Structuring
→ Your Page</title>
<link href="default.css" rel="stylesheet"
→ type="text/css" media="all" />
</head>
<body>
<div id="chapter01" class="page">
<div id="header">
<h1>Alice's Adventures in Wonderland</h1>
<span class="authorName">Lewis
→ Carroll</span> </div>
<div id="navigation">
<h3>Table of Contents</h3>
<ol>
<li><a id="ch01" href="#">Down The Rabbit-
→ Hole</a></li>
<li><a id="ch02" href="#">The Pool of
→ Tears</a></li>
<li><a id="ch03" href="#">A Caucus-Race and
→ a Long Tale</a></li>
<li><a id="ch04" href="#">The Rabbit Sends
→ in a Little Bill</a></li>
<li><a id="ch05" href="#">Advice from a
→ Caterpillar</a></li>
<li><a id="ch06" href="#">Pig and
→ Pepper</a></li>
<li><a id="ch07" href="#">A Mad Tea-
→ Party</a></li>
<li><a id="ch08" href="#">The Queen's
→ Croquet-Ground</a></li>
<li><a id="ch09" href="#">The Mock Turtle's
→ Story</a></li>
<li><a id="ch10" href="#">The Lobster
→ Quadrille</a></li>
<li><a id="ch11" href="#">Who Stole The
→ Tarts?</a></li>
<li><a id="ch12" href="#">Alice's Evidence
→ </a></li>
</ol>
</div>
<div id="content">
```

code continues on next page

Code 21.2 *continued*

```
<h2>Chapter I <span class="chapterTitle">
→ Down the Rabbit-Hole</span> </h2>
<div class="dropBox"> <img src="alice02a.gif"
→ alt="The White Rabbit" height="270"
→ width="180" />
<p>'Oh dear! Oh dear! I shall be late!'</p>
</div>
<div class="copy">
<p>Alice was beginning to <a href="#1">get
→ very tired</a> of sitting by her sister
→ on the bank,and of having nothing to do:
→ once or twice she had peeped into the
→ book her sister was reading, but it had
→ <a href="#2">no pictures</a> or
→ conversations in it, 'and what is the
→ use of a book,' thought Alice 'without
→ pictures or conversation?'</p>
</div></div>
<div id="footer">
<p>THE MILLENNIUM FULCRUM EDITION 3.0</p>
</div></div>
</body></html>
```

5. `<div id="content">…</div>`

   Add a `<div>` element around the primary content of your page. Generally, these are the articles, registration forms, photo galleries, or other content that the visitor came to the page looking for.

6. `<div class="copy">…</div>`

   Add a `<div>` element that will contain all of the copy (the text) of your content. Generally you will want to style the copy text in your content section independent of other content in the page.

7. `<div id="footer">…</div>`

   Add a `<div>` at the very bottom of your content for the footer. Even if you don't plan to use it to display content, it has to be included for the 2-column layout presented in the next section to work successfully.

8. `<div class="dropBox">…</div>`

   Add other `<div>` elements with class names as needed to set off specialized content types that may be reused throughout the page.

   For this page, I wanted to create a floating "drop box" that will contain images and text that other text on the page can wrap around.

9. `<span class="authorName">…</span>`

   Finally, add individual classes as needed to style particular elements, based on the type of content they contain. In general, try to avoid "classitis" as much as possible, since using large numbers of classes can severely limit you in future redesigns. The better tactic is to rely on contextual styling instead, which does not require you to add anything to the HTML code.

   For this example, I found I needed a class for the author name and a class for the chapter title.

continues on next page

STRUCTURING YOUR PAGE

10.
```
<link href="default.css"
→ rel="stylesheet" type="text/css"
→ media="all" />
```

Back in the head of your document, you can go ahead and add the links to any external style sheets or JavaScript you will be using with this page.

In this example, I've included a link to default.css (**Code 21.3**) that you will be creating in the next four sections of this chapter. This file will contain all of the code used to style the page.

✔ Tip

■ A major trend in Web design today is to separate the content, design, and functionality as much as possible to make changes to any one of these categories as easy as possible without affecting the others. This allows for what is called *progressive enhancement* (see the sidebar "What is Progressive Enhancement?").

Code 21.3 default.css: This is the final version of the CSS code that will be applied to the HTML in Code 21.2. The individual components are explained in Codes 21.4, 21.5, 21.6, and 21.7.

```
body {
    font-size: 1.2em;
    font-family: Georgia, "Times New
    → Roman", times, serif;
    color: #000000;
    background-color: #999;
    margin: 0px; }
/*** Multi-column ***/
.page {
    display: block;
    width: 100%;
    padding: 0px;
    background-color: #ccc; }
#header, #footer {
    clear: both;
    background-color: #999; }
#navigation {
    float: left;
    width: 30%;
    max-width: 250px;
```

Code 21.3 *continued*

```
    min-width: 100px;
    font: bold 12px "Helvetica Neue
    → Narrow", Arial, Helvetica,
    → sans-serif; }
#content {
    float: left;
    width: 65%;
    padding: 2%;
    max-width: 756px;
    min-width: 200px;
    border-left: 2px solid #999;
    background-color: #fff; }
.dropBox {
    float: right;
    padding: 4px;
    margin: 4px;
    background-color: white;
    border: 2px solid #666; }
.dropBox img {
    display: block; }
/*** Headers ***/
h1, h2, h3 {
    padding-bottom: 0px;
    margin-bottom: 0px; }
h1 {
    font-size: 28px; }
h2 {
    color: #666; }
h3 {
    margin-left: 8px;
    font: small-caps bold 18px "Helvetica
    → Neue Narrow", Arial, Helvetica,
    → sans-serif; }
#header {
    height: 100px;
    color: #fff;
    border: 1px solid RGB(255,204,204);
    border-bottom: 2px solid #999;
    background: #f99 url(header_01.png)
    → repeat-x;
    padding: 0px 8px; }
.authorName {
    font: 18px "Helvetica Neue", Arial,
    → Helvetica, sans-serif; }
h2 .chapterTitle {
    display: block;
    font-size: smaller;
    color: black; }
/*** Navigation and Links ***/
p a {
    color: #f33;
```

code continues on next page

Code 21.3 *continued*

```
      text-decoration: none;
      padding-bottom: 0px; }
p a:link {
      color: #f33;
      border-bottom: 2px dotted #fcc; }
p a:visited {
      color: #966;
      border-bottom: 2px dotted #fcc; }
p a:hover {
      color: #f00;
      border-bottom: 2px solid #f99; }
p a:active {
      color: #966;
      border-bottom: 2px double #f66; }
#navigation ol {
list-style-type: none;
margin: 0px;
padding: 0px; }
#navigation ol li {
margin: 0px;
margin-bottom: 0px;
padding-bottom: 0px; }
#navigation a {
      padding: 2px 2px 8px 16px;
      border-top: 3px solid #fff;
      text-decoration: none;
      display: block; }
#navigation a:link {
      color: red; }
#navigation a:visited {
      color: red; }
#navigation a:hover {
      background-color: #fff;
      border-top: 3px solid #666;
      color: red; }
#navigation a:active {
      background-color: red;
      border-top: 3px solid #fff;
      color: #fff; }
#chapter01 #ch01, #chapter02 #ch02,
→ #chapter03 #ch03, #chapter04 #ch04,
→ #chapter05 #ch05, #chapter06 #ch06,
→ #chapter07 #ch07 ,#chapter08 #ch08,
→ #chapter09 #ch09, #chapter10 #ch10,
→ #chapter11 #ch11, "Comic Sans MS",
→ Helvetica, Arial, sans-serif; }
#footer p {
      color: white;
      font-size: small;
      text-align: center;
      padding-top: 4px;
      border-top: 2px solid #999; }
```

What Is Progressive Enhancement?

Today, all Web design layout should be done with CSS. This lets you separate the content and structure created by the markup (whether it is in HTML, XHTML, or XML) from the styles (CSS) and functionality (JavaScript) used for presentation on a particular technology (like a Web browser). This Web design strategy is called *progressive enhancement*, which promotes the following principals:

◆ Basic content and functionality that is native to the particular medium should be accessible to all browsers.

◆ All content is contained in the markup if possible, which should have no styling.

◆ Enhanced styles, layout, and functionality are provided by external CSS or JavaScript files.

Following these principals takes some extra effort, especially at first. However, you will benefit in the long run from amazing power and flexibility with your Web site designs. Separating content, style, and functionality lets you completely redesign an entire Web site by simply supplying new CSS and JavaScript files.

Beyond the flexibility, following these principals increases accessibility and doesn't tie your content down to being used by any particular technology. The basic content can go to Braille readers or Web-enabled cell phones, while CSS-enhanced and JavaScript-enhanced versions can be used by computers.

For more details, check out Steve Champeon's seminal article on the topic from Webmonkey (webmonkey.com/03/21/index3a.html).

Creating Multicolumn Layouts

Although tables have dominated Web site design for years, Web designers increasingly recognize the power of creating layouts using pure CSS. Although CSS positioning—explained in Chapter 7—lets you precisely place elements on the page, it turns out that these controls are not well suited for dynamic multicolumn layouts. Instead, it's the float property that gives us the ability to create the most flexible designs. For more details, see the sidebar "Layout with CSS vs. Tables."

In this example (**Figure 21.3**), we will be adding styles to the default.css file that is being linked to our structured HTML code shown in Code 21.2. I'm using the float property to place the #navigation and #content layers next to each other, creating a simple two-column layout.

Figure 21.3 Columns have been set up for the navigation and content areas from Figure 21.1.

Layout with CSS vs. Tables

Before tables, Web layout consisted of wide pages of text stretching from the left side of the window to the right. Designers had no way to break up this single column of content. Yet most designers came from a print background, and they were used to breaking text into two or more columns.

Tables allowed designers to create a layout grid with multiple columns. Although tables were never meant to be the workhorse of Web layout, it was the only game in town until CSS.

Layout with CSS offers two main advantages over table-based layout. The first, although minor, is that CSS layouts will usually load faster than table-based layouts. More importantly, CSS layouts are extremely modular, allowing you to quickly reshuffle and rearrange layouts without having to rip apart the HTML code (like you have to do with tables).

Initially, Web designers tried to use absolute positioning to precisely place columns across the page. However, this did not deliver satisfactory results, because no content could be placed beneath the columns. So designers went back to the drawing board and found that the unassuming float property could be used to simply stack columns next to each other. However, this still has one drawback: the column heights are independent of each other. Unlike with tables, where the shortest column stretches down to the height of the tallest column, CSS columns end abruptly.

Code 21.4 default.css: Add this code to create the columns defined in the HTML of Code 21.2.

```
.page {
    display: block;
    width: 100%;
    padding: 0px;
    background-color: #ccc; }
#header, #footer {
    clear: both;
    background-color: #999; }
#navigation {
    float: left;
    width: 30%;
    max-width: 250px;
    min-width: 100px;
    font: bold 12px "Helvetica Neue
    → Narrow", Arial, Helvetica,
    → sans-serif; }
#content {
    float: left;
    width: 65%;
    padding: 2%;
    max-width: 756px;
    min-width: 200px;
    border-left: 2px solid #999;
    background-color: #fff; }
.dropBox {
    float: right;
    padding: 4px;
    margin: 4px;
    background-color: white;
    border: 2px solid #666;
    font-size: small; }
.dropBox img {
    display: block; }
```

To set up a multicolumn layout using CSS:

1. default.css

   Create an external CSS file called default.css (**Code 21.4**). We'll add to this file in this and the next three sections of this chapter ("Styling Headers," "Styling Links and Navigation," and "Styling Copy and Content") to create the full code shown in Code 21.3.

2. .page {...}

   Add the .page class to your CSS code Although this may not seem necessary, it prevents the columns from splitting apart if the browser window isn't wide enough. Most importantly, though, this class will control the width of the page.

   In this example, I set the width to 100%, so it will stretch the available width of the browser window. However, you could set this to an absolute width (such as 756px).

3. #header, #footer {...}

   Add ID selector rule(s) for the header and the footer that run across the top and bottom of the columns, setting whatever styles you want to include, but make sure to include clear: both. This ensures that the header and footer do not wrap to the left or right of the columns and also forces the surrounding container using the .page class to stretch the height of our design.

continues on next page

CREATING MULTICOLUMN LAYOUTS

4. `#navigation {…}`

Set up an ID selector rule for your left column. The only mandatory property is `float:left`. The selector rule makes all three columns stack next to each other horizontally, rather than appearing underneath one another. In addition, you will want to set the width of the column.

In this example, I'm using `width:30%` so that the column will have a width relative to the surrounding `.page` class. The advantage of using relative values for the column width is that now I can set the page width in the `.page` rule and never have to adjust the column widths individually. However, I did set a minimum and maximum width so that the column never gets too narrow or too wide.

5. `#content {…}`

Set up an ID selector rule for the right column, using `float: left`. Actually, a float value of left or right will work, but left keeps the right column and left column together to the left of the window.

In this example, I used `width:65%` and `padding:2%` to give the content a little breathing room.

6. `.dropBox {…}`

Although not technically a column, you can also float elements to create a box that has surrounding content (including text and images) wrap around it. This is often used to add images or pull-quotes in text.

In this example, I created the `.dropBox` class to add a box that contains an image and a quote to go with it. In addition, I used a contextual selector to force a return after the image so that the caption will appear beneath it.

✔ Tips

■ If you add the relative column widths together (30 percent + 65 percent +2 percent), you get 92 percent. Why not use the full 100 percent? I find that if you fill the entire width of your area (whether the width is set with relative or absolute values), your columns will break, stacking vertically rather than beside one another. Why? Browsers don't do math very well, especially when you mix absolute and relative units.

■ My general rule of thumb is to leave 1 to 5 pixels or 1 to 10 percent for a fudge factor between floated elements. However, you will need to test your design on multiple browsers at multiple window sizes to find the exact fudge factor for your individual design.

■ Although I used two columns here, you can add as many columns as you want for your design. Just add more `<div>` elements with the float property and adjust your column widths.

■ To see an example of the three-column layout, see the Web site for this book (webbedenvironments.com/css_dhtml _ajax). Other "tableless" Web sites I have designed include Yuri's Night (yuris-night.net) and webbedENVIRONMENTS (webbedenvironments.com).

■ If you design a great layout using CSS without tables, send me the URL (vqs-dynamic@webbedenvironments.com). I'd love to check it out.

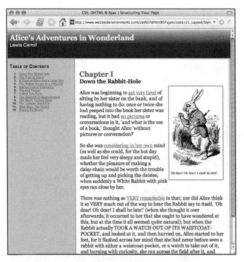

Figure 21.4 The site header now has a very Web 2.0 look, while the Table of Contents and chapter headers have more distinction.

Figure 21.5 The background graphic used to create the Web 2.0 effect for the site header.

Styling Headers

One hassle in Web design is headlines created from a graphic, which usually means creating a new graphic for every headline. Using the CSS background property, however, you can create as many different title graphics as you want—without having to create new graphics and without incurring the additional download time involved with using text in graphics.

In this example (**Figure 21.4**), we will be adding styles to the `default.css` file that is being linked to our structured HTML code shown in Code 21.2. I added styles to the first three heading levels (which are the only three we use in the code) and a graphic background to the main page header.

To create a headline with a graphic background:

1. `header_01.png`

   Create and save your background. Call the graphic something like `header_01.png` (**Figure 21.5**).

continues on next page

STYLING HEADERS

2. h1, h2, h3 {…}

In the default.css file, set all of the style properties you want your heading elements to have in common (**Code 21.5**). In this case, I've set no margin or padding on the bottom.

3. h1 {…}

Set all of the specific styles for each of the heading levels, generally colors and font sizes. You want the header to stand out from the rest of the content, without overwhelming it.

4. #header {…}

To create a compelling graphic header for your page, add a CSS rule for the #header element. Include the background property, and point to the graphic you created in Step 1 (see "Setting Multiple Background Values" in Chapter 5).

5. .authorName {…}

You can identify parts of a title for special treatment, as with the author's name in this example.

6. h2 .chapterTitle {…}

Another good trick is to use contextual selectors with a class to specify how the class should look if it is in the header (see "Defining Selectors Based on Context" in Chapter 2). This way, you could define separate styles for the .chapterTitle class in case it is *not* in a title (for example in a footer or in navigation).

Code 21.5 default.css: Add this code to style the headers defined in Code 21.2.

```
h1, h2, h3 {
     padding-bottom: 0px;
     margin-bottom: 0px; }
h1 {
     font-size: 28px; }
h2 {
     color: #666; }
h3 {
     margin-left: 8px;
     font: small-caps bold 18px "Helvetica
     → Neue Narrow", Arial, Helvetica,
     → sans-serif; }
#header {
     height: 100px;
     color: #fff;
     border: 1px solid RGB(255,204,204);
     border-bottom: 2px solid #999;
     background: #f99 url(header_01.png)
     → repeat-x;
     padding: 0px 8px; }
.authorName {
     font: 18px "Helvetica Neue", Arial,
     → Helvetica, sans-serif; }
h2 .chapterTitle {
     display: block;
     font-size: smaller;
     color: black; }
```

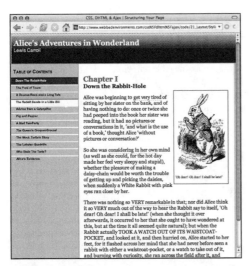

Figure 21.6 The navigation menu includes a rollover, while standard hypertext links in the page are given a light red, dotted underline when the page loads. The underline becomes a darker red line when the mouse cursor passes over it.

Code 21.6 default.css: Add this code to style the navigation defined in Code 21.2.

```
p a {
    color: #f33;
text-decoration: none;
    padding-bottom: 0px; }
p a:link {
    color: #f33;
    border-bottom: 2px dotted #fcc; }
p a:visited {
    color: #966;
    border-bottom: 2px dotted #fcc; }
p a:hover {
    color: #f00;
    border-bottom: 2px solid #f99; }
p a:active {
    color: #966;
    border-bottom: 2px double #f66; }
#navigation ol {
    list-style-type: none;
    margin: 0px;
    padding: 0px;
}
#navigation ol li {
    margin: 0px;
```

code continues on next page

Styling Links and Navigation

The Web is nothing without links. Many designers are content to rely on default browser styles being applied to their links, but not only is this boring, the defaults can often make all the links on your page look exactly the same whether they are global navigation or content links.

In this example (**Figure 21.6**), we will be adding styles to the default.css file (Code 21.3) that is being linked to our structured HTML code shown in Code 21.2 to give link styles for link tags in the content (in a paragraph) and in the navigation.

To style navigation and links:

1. p a {...}

In the default.css file, add a contextual selector rule for the anchor tag if it is within the paragraph tag, and then set the different link states: :link, :visited, :hover, and :active (**Code 21.6**). For more information on links and dynamic pseudo-classes, see "Working with Pseudo-Classes" in Chapter 2.

In this example, I've prevented links from using the underline by setting text-decoration: none. However, I'm using border-bottom: 2px dotted #f99 to reinstate a link "underline" that can control the style in all four link states, unlike a true underline style. This gives a much more dynamic and visually appealing look to the links.

continues on next page

2. #navigation ol {…}

Notice in Code 21.2 that the navigation links are set up in a list. This is to allow the links to appear in a list even if there is no CSS (remember progressive enhancements?). However, notice that I also set the margin and padding of #navigation ol to 0 so that the numbers don't display and the links are flush to the left.

3. #navigation a {…}

Set up the styles for your navigation links, and variations for all four link-states.

In this example, I've set the links to have a light white line above them and to then turn the background white when the visitor's mouse curses over them, creating a nice rollover effect.

4. #chapter01 #ch01 {…}

When I was setting up the structure of the HTML page earlier in this chapter, I mentioned that adding the surrounding <div> element around the entire page was going to come in handy later with our navigation. Here is where it helps: Because each link is identified and the page is identified, we can set a special style to be used only if the link is within a specific page with that page's unique ID. The upshot is that the global navigation will automatically highlight the page it is on without additional coding from us.

The downside is that you have to include this contextual selector grouping for every link in your global navigation.

✔ Tip

■ You may notice in the figure that the new underlining of the links in the content paragraphs looks a little cramped right now, butting up against the text in the line beneath. We'll take care of that in the next section when we style our content.

Code 2.16 *continued*

```
       margin-bottom: 0px;
       padding-bottom: 0px;
}
#navigation a {
       padding: 2px 2px 8px 16px;
       border-top: 3px solid #fff;
       text-decoration: none;
       display: block; }
#navigation a:link {
       color: red; }
#navigation a:visited {
       color: red; }
#navigation a:hover {
       background-color: #fff;
       border-top: 3px solid #666;
       color: red; }
#navigation a:active {
       background-color: red;
       border-top: 3px solid #fff;
       color: #fff; }
#chapter01 #ch01, #chapter02 #ch02,
→ #chapter03 #ch03, #chapter04 #ch04,
→ #chapter05 #ch05, #chapter06 #ch06,
→ #chapter07 #ch07, #chapter08 #ch08,
→ #chapter09 #ch09, #chapter10 #ch10,
→ #chapter11 #ch11, #chapter12 #ch12 {
       background-color: #333;
       color: #fff;
       border-top: 3px solid #000; }
```

Figure 21.7 Our final design, with the copy and other content on the page nicely styled.

Code 21.7 default.css: Add this code to style the content defined in Code 21.2.

```
#content .copy {
     margin-top: 24px; }
#content .copy p {
     font-size: smaller;
     line-height: 1.5;
     margin: 0px;
     text-indent: 2em; }
.dropBox p {
     margin: 0px;
     padding: 0px;
     width: 175px;
     font: x-large "Party Let", "Comic Sans
     → MS", Helvetica, Arial, sans-serif; }
#footer p {
     color: white;
     font-size: small;
     text-align: center;
     padding-top: 4px;
     border-top: 2px solid #999; }
```

Styling Copy and Content

The copy and content on your Web page is generally the reason a person will visit your page, and you should take great care to make it as attractive and easy to read as possible.

In our final example using the HTML shown in Code 21.2, we will be adding a few simple styles to clean up the layout of the content on the page and improve the readability of the text (**Figure 21.7**).

To add styles to copy and content:

1. `#content .copy { }`

   Add the `.copy` class selector to your `default.css` file (**Code 21.7**). You can set any global style you want applied to all text in that block, but I generally find it better to apply these styles directly to the `<p>` tag, as shown in Step 2.

   In this example, I use this rule to add some extra space between the text and the chapter title head.

   continues on next page

2. `#content .copy p {…}`

Add a contextual selector to style the <p> element if it is within a parent using the `.copy` class in the `#content` layer. This styles all the paragraphs of text that are part of the copy in the content area of the page.

In this example, I wanted to space out the lines of text to make it easier to read and to give some breathing room to the link underlines.

3. `#content .dropBox p {…}`

You can also style content defined by other <p> tags on the page independently, as with the paragraphs in the `.dropBox` class and the `#footer` layer.

In this example, I'm limiting the width of the caption—so that it won't force the drop box to be too wide—and giving it a fun and funky font face.

✔ Tip

- You could also set a general style for the <p> element and specify typographic controls there that could then be modified by the particular rules shown in this section. However, we already set the default font for the <body> tag and everything we would add to the <p> tag would be redundant to those styles. In general, you don't want to repeat style declarations that have already been applied earlier in the style sheet.

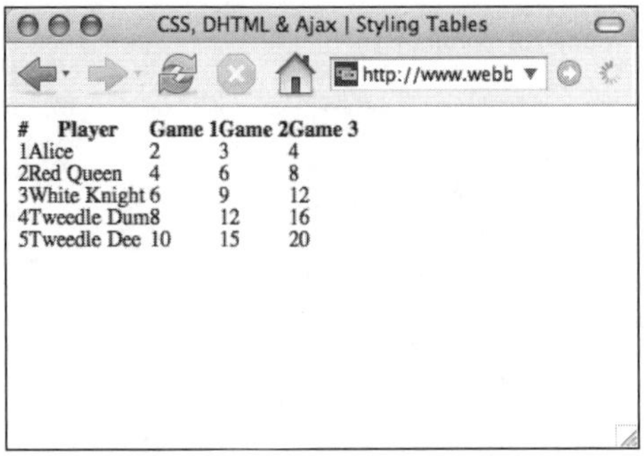

Figure 21.8 The ho-hum design with default table styles.

Figure 21.9 The exciting new table design—now with bonus row highlighting!

Styling Tables

We covered many of the specific styles that can only be applied to tables in Chapter 9. However, tables can benefit from many other CSS properties. You can set common attributes (such as vertical alignment) and change them in a single place without having to go to every <table>, <tr>, and <td> tag and change them individually. CSS can do many things to make table layout easier.

In this example (**Figures 21.8** and **21.9**), border, padding, text alignment, color, and background attributes are used to create a table that is more elegantly styled than the default. In addition, the :hover dynamic pseudo-class is used to highlight the table row being pointed at using the mouse.

To style a table's elements:

1. table {…}

   You can style the table either directly through a type selector or by applying classes or IDs (**Code 21.8**). In this example, font styles have been applied directly to all tables on the page, while an ID (#dataTable01) is used to control a particular table's width.

   continues on next page

Code 21.8 You can use CSS to style all of the different table elements and even use dynamic pseudo-classes (like :hover) to create an interactive interface for the data.

```
<!DOCTYPE html PUBLIC "-//W3C//DTD XHTML 1.0 Strict//EN" "http://www.w3.org/TR/xhtml1/DTD/
⇢ xhtml1-strict.dtd">
<html xmlns="http://www.w3.org/1999/xhtml">
<head>
<meta http-equiv="Content-Type" content="text/html; charset=utf-8" />
<title>CSS, DHTML &amp; Ajax | Styling Tables</title>
<style type="text/css" media="screen">
table {
     font: 1em helvetica, arial, sans-serif; }
#dataTable01 {
     width: 400px;
}
```

code continues on next page

2. `tr {…}`

In HTML, data cells are organized into rows using the <tr> element. Applying styles to it lets you create a style applied horizontally (styling columns is a lot trickier). You can also create specialized row styles using classes to alternate styles between rows.

In this example, I created `tr.oddRow` to give odd numbered rows a slightly darker background color. However, I did have to add the class to the HTML by hand.

3. `th {…}`

The table header cell is a special cell used to hold labels that identify the data in a particular column or row of the table. You should generally style these to contrast the table data rows.

4. `tr:hover {…}`

Beyond simple static style, you can also apply the `:hover` dynamic pseudo-class to table rows so that when the visitor rolls over the table, each row highlights independently. Keep in mind, though, that earlier versions of Internet Explorer (before version 7) will ignore this, so don't rely on it for critical information.

5. `td {…}`

Finally, you can apply styles directly to the individual table data cells defined by the <td> element. As with table rows (see Step 3), you can also create specialized classes and apply the `:hover` dynamic pseudo-class.

✔ Tips

- Without CSS, table borders are fairly boring, and must be set the same on all sides. With CSS, you can set the table borders on each side individually, greatly enhancing the design possibilities.

- CSS also lets you collapse the borders between table data cells (Chapter 9).

Code 2.8 *continued*

```
tr {
    color: #333;
    background: #eee; }
tr.oddRow {
    background: #ccc; }
tr:hover {
    color: #000;
    background: #f99;
    cursor: pointer; }
th {
    color: #fff;
    background-color: #000;
    text-align: left;
    padding: 5px;
    border-bottom: 1px solid #000; }
td {
    padding: 5px;
    border-bottom: 1px solid #000; }
</style>
</head>
<body>
<table id="dataTable01" summary="Scores
→ from the game" cellspacing="0"
→ cellpadding="0" border="0">
    <thead>
      <tr>
        <th scope="col">#</th>
        <th scope="col">Player</th>
        <th scope="col">Game 1</th>
        <th scope="col">Game 2</th>
        <th scope="col">Game 3</th>
      </tr>
    </thead>
    <tbody>
    <tr
class="evenRow"><td>1</td><td>Alice</td>
→ <td>2</td><td>3</td><td>4</td>
</tr>
<tr class="oddRow"><td>2</td><td>Red Queen
→ </td><td>4</td><td>6</td><td>8</td>
</tr>
<tr class="evenRow"><td>3</td><td>White
→ Knight</td><td>6</td><td>9</td><td>12</td>
</tr>
<tr class="oddRow"><td>4</td><td>Tweedle
→ Dum</td><td>8</td><td>12</td><td>16</td>
</tr>
<tr class="evenRow"><td>5</td><td>Tweedle
→ Dee</td><td>10</td><td>15</td><td>20</td>
</tr>
</tbody></table>
</body></html>
```

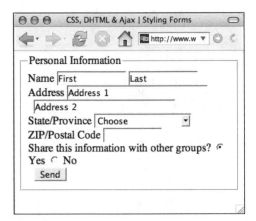

Figure 21.10 Would you want to fill out this form?

Legend   Label   Input (form field)   Fieldset

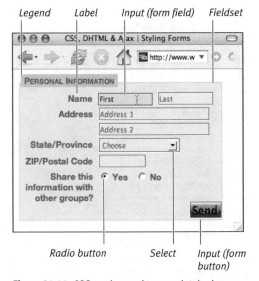

Radio button   Select   Input (form button)

Figure 21.11 CSS can be used to completely change the appearance of form elements from their standard look. But beware: Some users may get confused if you stray too far from the norm.

Styling Forms

Forms are an easy way for you to get information back from site visitors. However, many Web developers think that it's enough just to throw a few form fields into a table, and let them fall where they may in the Web page. They then expect the visitor to be willing to sift through this mess of roughly aligned text and 3D-beveled boxes to figure out what information is needed.

However, with only a little extra effort you can control the appearance of forms (text fields, select boxes, buttons, labels, etc.) using CSS, as well as greatly enhance their functionality with interactive styles, all without ever having to break out HTML tables.

In this example, I took a standard form for collecting personal information (**Figure 21.10**) and cleaned it up, making it easier to use (**Figure 21.11**).

continues on next page

To style form elements:

1. `fieldset {…}`

The fieldset is an optional border around a form that can be used in conjunction with a form legend to set the form or parts of the form off from the rest of the page (**Code 21.9**). With CSS, you can define the border and background that will go behind the form, as well as the general foreground colors and fonts to be used for the form text.

continues on Page 474

Code 21.9 Add styles directly to form tags, or use classes for the input tag (which can take many forms).

```
<!DOCTYPE html PUBLIC "-//W3C//DTD XHTML 1.0
→ Strict//EN" "http://www.w3.org/TR/xhtml1/
→ DTD/xhtml1-strict.dtd">
<html xmlns="http://www.w3.org/1999/xhtml">
<head>
<meta http-equiv="Content-Type"
→ content="text/html; charset=utf-8" />
<title>CSS, DHTML &amp; Ajax | Styling
→ Forms</title>
<script type="text/javascript">

function clearField(obj) {
    if (obj.defaultValue==obj.value)
    → obj.value = ''; }
</script>
<style type="text/css">
fieldset {
    font: 0.8em "Helvetica Neue",
helvetica, arial, sans-serif;
    color: #666;
    background-color: #efefef;
    padding: 2px;
    border: solid 1px #d3d3d3;
    width: 350px; }
legend {
    color: #666;
    font-weight: bold;
    font-variant: small-caps;
    background-color: #d3d3d3;
    padding: 2px 6px;
    margin-bottom: 8px; }
```

Code 21.9 *continued*

```
label {
    font-weight: bold;
    line-height: normal;
    text-align: right;
    margin-right: 10px;
    position: relative;
    display: block;
    float: left;
    width: 125px; }
label.fieldLabel {
    display: inline;
    float: none; }
input.formInputText {
    font-size: .8em;
    color: #666;
    background-color: #fee;
    padding: 2px;
    border: solid 1px #f66;
    margin-right: 5px;
    margin-bottom: 5px;
    height: 15px; }
input.formInputText:hover {
    background-color: #ccffff;
    border: solid 1px #006600;
    color: #000;
}
input.formInputText:focus {
    color: #000;
    background-color: #ffffff;
    border: solid 1px #006600; }
select.formSelect {
    font-size: .8em;
    color: #666;
    background-color: #fee;
    padding: 2px;
    border: solid 1px #f66;
    margin-right: 5px;
    margin-bottom: 5px;
    cursor: pointer; }
select.formSelect:hover {
    color: #333;
    background-color: #ccffff;
    border: solid 1px #006600; }
select.formSelect:focus {
    color: #000;
    background-color: #ffffff;
    border: solid 1px #006600; }
input.formInputButton {
    font-size: 1.2em;
    vertical-align: middle;
    font-weight: bolder;
    text-align: center;
    color: #300;
    background: #f99 url(bg_button.png)
    → repeat-x;
```

code continues on next page

Code 21.9 *continued*

```
    padding: 1px;
    border: solid 1px #f66;
    cursor: pointer;
    float: right; }
input.formInputButton:hover {
    background-image:
    → url(bg_button_hover.png);
}
input.formInputButton:active {
    background-image: url(bg_button.png); }
</style>
</head>
<body>
<form action="#" method="get" id="myForm">
    <fieldset>
    <legend>Personal Information</legend>
    <label for="firstName">Name</label>
    <input class="formInputText" type="text" name="firstName" id="firstName" value="First"
    → size="12" maxlength="16" tabindex="1" onfocus="clearField(this);" />
    <input class="formInputText" type="text" name="lastName" id="lastName" value="Last" size="12"
    → maxlength="16" tabindex="2" onfocus="clearField(this);"/>
    <br />
    <label for="address1">Address</label>
    <input class="formInputText" type="text" name="address1" id="address1" value="Address 1"
    → size="26" maxlength="24" tabindex="3"onfocus="clearField(this);"/>
    <br />
    <label> </label>
    <input class="formInputText" type="text" name="address2" id="address2" value="Address 2"
    → size="26" maxlength="24" tabindex="4"onfocus="clearField(this);"/>
    <br />
    <label for="state">State/Province</label>
    <select class="formSelect" name="state" id="state" size="1" tabindex="5">
        <option selected="selected">Choose</option>
        <option value="nc">North Carolina (NC)</option>
        <option value="va">Virginia (VA)</option>
    </select>
    <br />
    <label for="postalCode">ZIP/Postal Code</label>
    <input class="formInputText"type="text" name="postalCode" id="postalCode" size="10"
    → maxlength="10" tabindex="6"/>
    <br />
    <label>Share this information with other groups?</label>
    <input type="radio" name="share" id="shareYes" value="no" checked="checked" tabindex="7"/>
    <label class="fieldLabel" for="shareYes">Yes</label>
    <input type="radio" name="share" id="shareNo" value="yes" tabindex="8"/>
    <label class="fieldLabel" for="shareNo">No</label>
    <br />
    <div style="clear:both;">
        <label> </label>
        <input class="formInputButton" type="submit" name="submitButtonName" id="submitButtonName"
        → value="Send" tabindex="9"/>
    </div>
    </fieldset>
</form>
</body></html>
```

2. `legend {…}`

The legend is a label for the form that, by default, sits over the top-left corner of the border of the fieldset. The legend is a great way to add a description of the form that will stand out.

3. `label {…}`

The <label> tag is designed for use with form fields to identify which label goes with which form element. The advantage of the label tag is that you can directly associate a particular label with a particular form field element so that clicking the label is the same as clicking the form element itself. For example, when a label is associated with a checkbox field, you can click the associated label and the checkbox toggles states.

We need to style labels as block elements with a specific width and float them to the left. The width of the label will then cause the form fields associated with them to align flush on the right side, creating a very neat appearance that is easy to read—and with no tables in sight.

4. `label.fieldLabel {…}`

Add a class, associated with the label element, called something like `label.fieldLabel`. This will be used to override the general label style when we need a label that sits directly next to the form element with which it is associated (such as radio buttons).

5. `input.formInputText {…}`

The default appearance of text input fields is determined by the operating system, but generally they have a clunky 3D-beveled border that can be very unattractive. However, you can control the border, background, foreground color, and font for input fields. Generally, you will still want these to appear as boxes that contrast other content on the page.

One thing to keep in mind, though, is that some browsers (most notably Apple Safari) do not allow you to change the border of form elements.

6. `input.formInputText:hover {…}`

In addition to the default static state for the text field, add `:hover` and `:focus` pseudo-classes for the `formInputField` class. This will trigger a change of styles whenever the visitor's mouse curses over or tabs into a text field. In our example, the box turns blue.

7. `select.formSelect {…}`

This code is used to add styles to drop-down or multiselect form elements. Although I have set the border for this class, many browsers will ignore this or place it only around the existing border.

Again, we can add both `:hover` and `:focus` pseudo-classes to the selected element to increase its interaction with the user.

8. `input.formInputButton {…}`

Add a `formInputButton` class and `:hover` state so that you can set a style for what happens when the visitor hovers over the button.

In this example, I simply created a new background graphic by removing the gloss in the existing graphic, so it looks as if the button is pressed. You can then also set an `:active` state for the button so that the button reverts back to its normal state before the form is sent.

continues on next page

STYLING FORMS

9. `<form action="#" method="get"`
`→ id="myForm" name="myForm">…</form>`

Once you have set up your CSS rules, it's time to set up your form. Don't worry about making it look pretty in the HTML code (that's what CSS is for), but do use the `for` attribute with labels to associate them with a form field.

10. `function clearField(obj) {…}`

I'm also using a simple JavaScript function that erases any initial value in the form field when the user clicks in it. This allows me to pre-populate input fields with additional instructions or sample text that disappears when the form field receives focus.

✔ Tips

■ In theory, you could create styles based on element attribute values (see "Defining Selectors Based on Tag Attributes" in Chapter 2) to style the different versions of the `<input>` element, rather than using classes. But because this method works inconsistently across browsers, it cannot be relied upon to produce consistent results.

■ The Mac OS X browsers, Safari and Camino, will only apply font style changes made to `input`, `textarea`, or `select` form elements. All other styles, including background and border changes, are ignored.

■ Notice that in the example code I also included a version of the input form button using `:hover`. This will actually change the appearance of the form button when the user rolls over it. Unfortunately the rollover trick won't work in Internet Explorer for Windows, which only supports `:hover` with hypertext links.

■ Although styles will affect radio buttons and checkboxes, the result is generally not what the designer intended. Most browsers will simply apply the styles to the rectangular box around the button or box, leaving the central element unchanged. Generally, these types of input fields are best left alone.

■ There are actually several kinds of input elements that can be created with the `<input>` tag, each defined by a different type of attribute, and each with its own idiosyncrasies. It's generally not a good idea to set a universal style for the `<input>` tag, since these styles are applied to all the various kinds of inputs, including text, checkboxes, and radio buttons. Instead, create a class for each input type and apply the class directly to the input tags as needed.

Figure 21.12 A frameset with default frame borders. It's nice if you like that kind of thing.

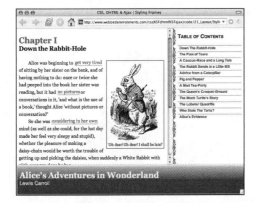

Figure 21.13 A frameset created with CSS, showing an ornate red border separating the frames.

Figure 21.14 The graphic used to create the border for the right frame. Remember, you can use anything you want for your borders. Go wild!

Styling Frames

One of the most frustrating aspects of using frames is the clunky-looking borders that standard HTML puts between them (**Figure 21.12**). When you use the background property, however, you can use any border design you dream up.

Although these borders can be placed only along the left side or top of an individual frame, they're still very useful for showing boundaries between frames, as shown in **Figure 21.13**.

To create a frame border:

1. border.gif

Create the frame-border graphic. For this example, I'm using an ornate design that I saved as "border.gif" (**Figure 21.14**). You can use anything you want for this graphic.

continues on next page

2. `index.html`

Create a frame document, and save it as "index.html," making sure that you turn off the default border (**Code 21.10**):

```
frameborder="no" framespacing="0"
→ border="0"
```

3. `right_frame.html`

Use the background property in the `<body>` tag of an HTML document (**Code 21.11** and **Code 21.12**) to place the border graphic from Step 1 in the background of the desired frame(s). Repeat this graphic either horizontally

```
(background: #f99 url(header_01.png)
repeat-x)
```

or vertically

```
(background: white url(border2.gif)
repeat-y)
```

for a full border (see "Setting Multiple Background Values" in Chapter 5).

continues on Page 480

Code 21.10 `index.html` : The frameset document.

```
<!DOCTYPE html PUBLIC "-//W3C//DTD XHTML 1.0 Frameset//EN" "http://www.w3.org/TR/xhtml1/DTD/
→ xhtml1-frameset.dtd">
<html xmlns="http://www.w3.org/1999/xhtml">
<head>
<meta http-equiv="Content-Type" content="text/html; charset=utf-8" />
<title>CSS, DHTML &amp; Ajax | Styling Frames</title>
</head>
<frameset rows="*,100">
<frameset cols="*,250">
    <frame src="center_frame.html" name="centerFrame" noresize="noresize" id="centerFrame" />
    <frame src="right_frame.html" name="rightFrame" noresize="noresize" id="rightFrame" />
    </frameset>
    <frame src="bottom_frame.html" name="bottomFrame" scrolling="no" noresize="noresize"
    → id="bottomFrame" />
</frameset>
<noframes></noframes>
</html>
```

Code 21.11 `right_frame.html`: A frame with a custom vertical border that has been set using the background property.

```
<!DOCTYPE html PUBLIC "-//W3C//DTD XHTML 1.0
→ Strict//EN" "http://www.w3.org/TR/xhtml1/
→ DTD/xhtml1-strict.dtd">
<html xmlns="http://www.w3.org/1999/xhtml">
<head>
<meta http-equiv="Content-Type"
→ content="text/html; charset=utf-8" />
<title>CSS, DHTML &amp; Ajax | Styling
→ Frmaes</title>
<style type="text/css" media="screen">
body {
    font-size: 1.2em;
    font-family: Georgia, "Times New
    → Roman", times, serif;
    color: #000000;
    background: white url(border2.gif)
    → repeat-y;
    margin-left: 20px;
}
h3 {
    font: small-caps bold 18px "Helvetica
    → Neue Narrow", Arial, Helvetica,
    → sans-serif; }
/*** Navigation ***/
#navigation {
    font: bold 12px "Helvetica Neue
    → Narrow", Arial, Helvetica, sans-
    → serif; }
#navigation ol {
    list-style-type: none;
    margin: 0px;
    padding: 0px; }
#navigation ol li {
    display: block;
    margin: 0px;
    margin-bottom: 0px;
    padding-bottom: 0px;
    margin-left: -40px; }
#navigation a {
    padding: 2px 4px;
    border-top: 3px solid #ccc;
    text-decoration: none;
    display: block; }
#navigation a:link { color: red; }
#navigation a:visited {
    color: red; }
#navigation a:hover {
    background-color: #ccc;
    border-top: 3px solid #666;
    color: red; }
```

Code 21.11 *continued*

```
#navigation a:active {
    background-color: red;
    border-top: 3px solid #fff;
    color: #fff; }
</style>
</head>
<body>
<div id="navigation">
<h3>Table of Contents</h3>
<ol>
    <li><a id="ch01" href="#">Down The
    → Rabbit-Hole</a></li>
    <li><a id="ch02" href="#">The Pool of
    → Tears</a></li>
    <li><a id="ch03" href="#">A Caucus-Race
    → and a Long Tale</a></li>
    <li><a id="ch04" href="#">The Rabbit
    → Sends in a Little Bill</a></li>
    <li><a id="ch05" href="#">Advice from a
    → Caterpillar</a></li>
    <li><a id="ch06" href="#">Pig and
    → Pepper</a></li>
    <li><a id="ch07" href="#">A Mad Tea-
    → Party</a></li>
    <li><a id="ch08" href="#">The Queen's
    → Croquet-Ground</a></li>
    <li><a id="ch09" href="#">The Mock
    → Turtle's Story</a></li>
    <li><a id="ch10" href="#">The Lobster
    → Quadrille</a></li>
    <li><a id="ch11" href="#">Who Stole
    → The Tarts?</a></li>
        <li><a id="ch12" href="#">Alice's
        → → Evidence </a></li>
</ol></div>
</body></html>
```

✔ Tips

- Remember that in addition to the border, you can give separate styles to each frame. Each frame is a different Web page and can, thus, include completely different styles, including backgrounds, colors, and fonts. However, it is a good idea to keep the frames visually similar so that they mesh well together.

- The design of the border can be anything you want, and it can be as thick or thin as you want. Just remember that the image repeats along whichever axis you specify.

- These borders have one big drawback compared with the default frame-border style: Neither you nor the visitor can use these borders to resize the frame.

Code 21.12 bottom_frame.html: A frame with a custom horizontal border set using the background property.

```
<!DOCTYPE html PUBLIC "-//W3C//DTD XHTML 1.0
→ Strict//EN" "http://www.w3.org/TR/xhtml1/
→ DTD/xhtml1-strict.dtd">
<html xmlns="http://www.w3.org/1999/xhtml">
<head>
<meta http-equiv="Content-Type"
→ content="text/html; charset=utf-8" />
<title>CSS, DHTML &amp; Ajax | Styling
→ Frames</title>
<style type="text/css" media="screen">
body {
    font-size: 1.2em;
    font-family: Georgia, "Times New
    → Roman", times, serif;
    color: #000000;
    margin: 0px;
    background: #f99 url(header_01.png)
    → repeat-x; }
h1 {
    font-size: 28px;
    padding-bottom: 0px;
    margin-bottom: 0px; }
#header {
    height: 100px;
    color: #fff;
    border: 1px solid RGB(255,204,204);
    padding: 0px 8px;
    vertical-align: middle; }
.authorName {
    font: 18px "Helvetica Neue", Arial,
    → Helvetica, sans-serif; }
</style>
</head>
<body>
<div id="header">
<h1>Alice's Adventures in Wonderland</h1>
<span class="authorName">Lewis
Carroll</span> </div>
</body></html>
```

CONTENT

The phrase "content is king" has long been a truism for the Web. A Web page lives or dies based not on how it looks, but on what's in it. If you don't have great content, you don't have a Web page. However, over the past several years, what Web designers have also come to discover is that it's not enough to pour static content into the page. The content has to be able to act and react to the whims of the visitor at a moment's notice.

Ajax is a technology that was developed primarily to allow Web designers to quickly change some or all of the content on a page without having to tediously reload the entire page.

This chapter explores some ways to quickly add and change content on the fly within a single HTML page.

Importing External Content

One of Ajax's primary capabilities is that it facilitates grabbing raw HTML or text from a file located on the server. So you can load the shell of your basic Web page and then pull in additional content as needed.

In this simple example (**Figure 22.1**), when the visitor clicks on an HTML link, the page pulls one of three blocks of HTML code from the server and places the new chunk of HTML code into the existing page (**Figure 22.2**).

To import external content using Ajax:

1. `externalContent.js`

   Create a new external JavaScript file and save it as `externalContent.js` (**Code 22.1**). Steps 2 and 3 apply to this file.

2. `function changePage(pageName,` `→ objectID) {…}`

   Add the function `changePage()` to your JavaScript.

   This function takes the URL for the page of content to be loaded and the ID of the object it is being placed into, and passes this info to the basic Ajax `fetchData()` function from Chapter 20 (see Code 20.6).

   The `fetchData()` function grabs from the server the contents of the file specified by `pageName`, and passes it to the `filterData()` function, along with the ID of the object the content should be placed into.

Figure 22.1 When the page first loads, it displays Chapter 1.

Figure 22.2 Using Ajax, the link fetches the content for Chapter 2 or Chapter 3 without ever reloading the page.

Code 22.1 `externalContent.js`: Functions used for importing external content using Ajax.

```
function changePage(pageName, objectID) {
fetchData(pageName,null,objectID);
}
function filterData(pageRequest, objectID){
    if (pageRequest.readyState == 4 &&
→ (pageRequest.status==200 ||
→ window.location.href.indexOf
→ ("http")==-1))
    document.getElementById
→ (objectID).innerHTML=
→ pageRequest.responseText;
}
```

Code 22.2 `externalContent.css`: Styles to be used with the external content.

```
#col-A {
    width: 240px;
    margin: 0px 8px 8px 0px;
    background-color: #ccc;
    float: left; }
#col-B {
    width: 490px;
    float: left;
    background-color: #fff;
    padding: 8px; }
```

Code 22.3 `external/chapter01.html`: A sample of external HTML code imported using Ajax.

```
<h2>CHAPTER I
<span class="chapterTitle">Down the
→ Rabbit-Hole</span>
</h2>
<div id="copy">
<div class="dropBox">
<img src="images/alice02a.gif" height="285"
→ width="190" alt="" />
Oh dear! I shall be late!</div>
<p>Alice was beginning to get very tired of
→ sitting by her sister on the bank…</p>
```

3. function filterData(pageRequest,
→ objectID){…}

Add the `filterData()` function to your JavaScript code. This function overrides the default version in the `ajaxBasics.js` file we will be adding to the code later.

After being processed, the data from the `fetchData()` function needs to be filtered and placed on the page. This function simply places the data received into the indicated object, as defined by `objectID`.

4. externalContent.css

Create a new external style sheet and save it as `externalContent.css` (**Code 22.2**). Step 5 applies to this file.

5. #col-A {…} #col-B {…}

Add ID selector rules to create two columns, one to hold the links used to trigger the `changePage()` function (A), and the other (B) to hold the results. In this example, I float them next to each other so that they appear side-by-side.

6. external/chapter01.html

Set up the external files that you will be importing into your main Web page using Ajax (**Code 22.3**). You only need to include the HTML code found between the `<body>` tags of a typical HTML page. You do not need to include the doctype or the `<html>` and `<head>` elements. In this example, I've placed all the external content into a common directory to keep things organized.

continues on next page

7. `index.html`

Start a new HTML file and save it as index.html (**Code 22.4**). Steps 8 through 14 apply to this file.

8. `src="ajaxBasics.js"`

Add a call to the `ajaxBasics.js` file created in Chapter 20 (Code 20.6). You will need to add a copy of this file to the directory or change the `src` value to the path where your `ajaxBasics.js` file is located.

9. `src="externalContent.js"`

Add a call to the `externalContent.js` file created in Step 1.

10. `href="externalContent.css"`

Add a link to the `externalContent.css` file from Step 4.

Code 22.4 `index.html`: The HTML "envelope" page that external content is imported into.

```
<!DOCTYPE html PUBLIC "-//W3C//DTD XHTML 1.0 Strict//EN" "http://www.w3.org/TR/xhtml1/DTD/
→ xhtml1-strict.dtd">
<html xmlns="http://www.w3.org/1999/xhtml">
<head>
<meta http-equiv="Content-Type" content="text/html; charset=utf-8" />
<title>CSS, DHTML &amp; Ajax | Importing External Content</title>
<script src="ajaxBasics.js" type="text/javascript"></script>
<script src="externalContent.js" type="text/javascript"></script>
<link href="externalContent.css" rel="stylesheet" type="text/css" media="screen" />
</head>
<body onload="changePage('chapter01.html', 'col-B');">
<div id="page">
    <div id="header">
    <h1>Alice's Adventures in Wonderland</h1>
    <p class="author">Lewis Carroll</p>
    </div>
<div id="col-A"> <a href="#" onclick="changePage('external/chapter01.html','col-B');">1 : Down The
→ Rabbit-Hole</a> <a href="#" onclick="changePage('external/chapter02.html','col-B');">2 : The
→ Pool of Tears </a> <a href="#" onclick="changePage('external/chapter03.html','col-B');">3 : A
→ Caucus-Race and a Long Tale </a> </div>
<div id="col-B"> </div>
</div>
</body></html>
```

11. `onload= "changePage('chapter01.html', → 'col-B');"`

    In the `<body>` tag, add an `onload` event handler to trigger the `changePage()` function from Step 2, which then passes the function the name of the first page to be displayed, as well as information about where it should be displayed.

12. `<div id="col-A">…</div>`

    Create column A by adding a `<div>` element and giving it the `col-A` ID.

13. `<a href="#" onclick="changePage → ('chapter01.html', 'col-B');">…</a>`

    In column A, add controls that trigger the `changePage()` function, passing it the URL of the content to be retrieved from the server and the ID for the object into which it should be placed.

14. `<div id="col-B"> </div>`

    Create column B by adding a `<div>` element and giving it the `col-B` ID. This identifies the area that the content being grabbed from the server should be inserted into.

✔ Tip

■ Of course, the example in this section brings up issues of search engine optimization. If the content is dynamically loaded by Ajax, then it will *not* get crawled by search engine spiders that ignore JavaScript. If you are worried about being found by search engines, never place important content in dynamically loaded files. Instead, code loaded in this way should include information that is changed on a daily basis or is open-ended, such as a map, where it is not feasible to load all of the data in a single server call.

Dynamically Controlling Form Data

When filling out a form online, the answer given to one question can often determine the data that needs to be provided for another question. For example, answering "yes" to a question on a form may require one set of options being provided, while answering "no" requires a different set of options be presented. Rather than trying to load all of the data for any situation, using Ajax we can simply go back to the server and load data contextual to the answers provided by the visitor.

In this example (**Figure 22.3**), when visitors select a country (**Figure 22.4**), the state/province list underneath is dynamically updated with data from the server, depending on whether they chose "United States" or "Canada" (**Figure 22.5**).

To create dynamically updated form data:

1. `dynamicForm.js`

   Start a new JavaScript file and save it as `dynamicForms.js` (**Code 22.5**). Steps 2 and 3 apply to this file.

2. `function chooseCountry(requestedData, → objectID) {...}`

   Add the function `chooseCountry()` to your JavaScript.

   When triggered from Step 10, this function uses the basic Ajax function `fetchData()`, passing it the value for the selected country (`requestedData`), the ID for where the returned data should be placed (`objectID`), and the page on the server that this data should be passed to (`dataPage.php`).

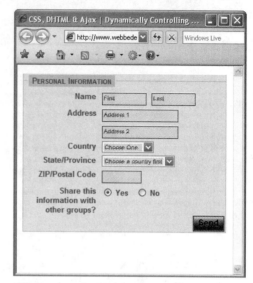

Figure 22.3 When the page first loads, the State/Province field is empty.

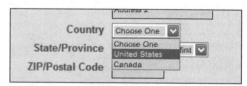

Figure 22.4 After selecting the country...

Figure 22.5 ...the State/Province drop-down menu has the correct data loaded into it.

Code 22.5 dynamicForms.js: Functions used for updating form data using Ajax.

```
function clearField(obj) {
    if (obj.defaultValue==obj.value)
    → obj.value = '';
}
function chooseCountry(requestedData,
→ objectID) {
    fetchData('dataPage.php',
    → requestedData,objectID);
}
function filterData(pageRequest, objectID){
    if (pageRequest.readyState == 4 &&
    → (pageRequest.status==200 ||
    → window.location.href.indexOf
    → ("http")==-1)) {
        var object = document.getElementById
        → (objectID);
        object.options.length = 0;
    if(pageRequest.responseText != '') {
    var arrSecondaryData =
    → pageRequest.responseText.split(',');
        for(i = 0; i <
        → arrSecondaryData.length; i++) {
        if(arrSecondaryData[i] != '')
    object.options[object.options.length] =
    → new Option(arrSecondaryData[i],
    → arrSecondaryData[i]);
}}}}
```

3. function filterData(pageRequest,
→ objectID){…}

Add the function filterData() to your JavaScript. This function replaces the default version of filterData() that will be imported in Step 7.

This version of the function takes a comma separated list, splits it into an array (secondaryData[]) and then places each item into it's own <option> element in the <select> element specified by objectID.

4. dataPage.php

Set up a page on your server that holds and processes the data you will be placing in your HTML page (**Code 22.6**).

In this example, I'm using a simple PHP file to create an array ($dataOptions[]) that uses a country name as its index to hold a list of states or provinces.

The script takes the value passed to it through the dataRequest variable in the XMLHttpRequest call, in order to determine which list of comma separated values to deliver back to the filter script in Step 3.

continues on next page

Code 22.6 dataPage.php: A server page using PHP that takes the data sent to it and delivers back the relevant list of U.S. states or Canadian provinces.

```
<?php
    $dataOptions = array();
    $dataOptions["United States"] = array("Alabama (AL)", "Alaska (AK)", "Arizona (AZ)", "Arkansas
    → (AR)", "California (CA)", "Colorado (CO)", "Connecticut (CT)");
    $dataOptions["Canada"] = array("Alberta (AB)", "British Columbia (BC)", "Manitoba (MB)", "New
    → Brunswick (NB)", "Nova Scotia (NS)", "Ontario (ON)", "Prince Edward Island (PE)", "Quebec (QC)");
    if(isset($_POST["dataRequest"]) && isset($dataOptions[$_POST["dataRequest"]]))
    { foreach($dataOptions[$_POST["dataRequest"]] as $secondaryOptions)
        {
            printf("%s,", $secondaryOptions);
    }}
?>
```

5. dynamicForms.css

Create an external style sheet that holds your styles for this page and save it as **dynamicForms.css**. I used styles similar to those I set up in "Styling Forms" in Chapter 21.

6. index.html

Set up an HTML file and save it as index.html (**Code 22.7**). Steps 7 through 12 apply to this file.

7. src="ajaxBasics.js"

Add a call to the ajaxBasics.js file created in Chapter 20 (Code 20.6). You

Code 22.7 index.html: The page with the dynamic form.

```
<!DOCTYPE html PUBLIC "-//W3C//DTD XHTML 1.0 Strict//EN" "http://www.w3.org/TR/xhtml1/DTD/
→ xhtml1-strict.dtd">
<html xmlns="http://www.w3.org/1999/xhtml">
<head>
<meta http-equiv="Content-Type" content="text/html; charset=utf-8" />
<title>CSS, DHTML &amp; Ajax | Dynamically Controlling Form Data</title>
<script src="ajaxBasics.js" type="text/javascript"></script>
<script src="dynamicForm.js" type="text/javascript"></script>
<link href="dynamicForm.css" rel="stylesheet" type="text/css" />
</head>
<body>
<form action="#" method="get" id="myForm">
    <fieldset>
    <legend>Personal Information</legend>
    <label for="state">Country</label>
    <select class="formSelect" name="country" id="country" size="1" tabindex="5" onchange=
    → "chooseCountry(this.options[this.selectedIndex].text, 'state');">
<option value="" selected="selected">Choose One</option>
<option>United States</option>
<option>Canada</option>
</select>
    <label for="state">State/Province</label>
    <select class="formSelect" name="state" id="state" size="1" tabindex="5">
    <option selected="selected">Choose a country first</option>
    </select>
    <div style="clear:both;">
    <label> </label>
    <input class="formInputButton" type="submit" name="submitButtonName" id="submitButtonName"
    → value="Send" tabindex="9"/>
</div></fieldset></form>
</body></html>
```

will need to add a copy of this file to the directory or change the src value to the path where your Ajax basics file is located. This file includes the fetchData() and filterData() functions.

8. `src="dynamicForm.js"`

Add a call to the dynamicForms.js file you set up in Step 1.

9. `href="dynamicForm.css"`

Add a link to the dynamicForms.css file you set up in Step 5.

10. `onchange="chooseCountry(this.options` → `[this.selectedIndex].text,` → `'state');"`

In the form on your page, add a <select> element with an ID value of country and an onchange event handler that triggers the function chooseCountry() from Step 2. Pass the function the currently selected value:

`this.options[this.selectedIndex].text`

and the ID of the <select> element you want the dynamically gathered options to be placed into, which in this example is state.

11. `<option>United States</option>`

In the <select> element from Step 10, set up <option> elements that have text and values corresponding to the values used in the `$dataOptions[]` array from Step 4.

12. `<select class="formSelect"` → `name="state" id="state" size="1"` → `tabindex="5">…</select>`

Add the select element into which the filterData() function will place the dynamic data, giving the element an ID that corresponds to the value passed to the function in Step 10 (such as "state").

Adding Pop-Up Layers

Hypertext is a great way to link the information on your page to information on other pages. But to access that information, visitors have to click a link, which opens a new document and replaces what they were reading with the new material. This setup can be highly distracting, not to mention confusing, when trying to return to the originating page.

Wouldn't it be better if that information—written or visual—simply appeared below the link when the visitor passes the mouse cursor over it? That arrangement would truly be hypertext.

In this example (**Figure 22.6**), each link on the page includes a pop-up hypertext that displays additional information relevant to the link and page (**Figures 22.7** and **22.8**).

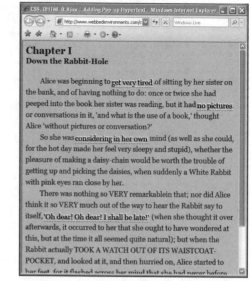

Figure 22.6 A normal-looking page of hypertext links.

Figure 22.8 It may even reveal an image.

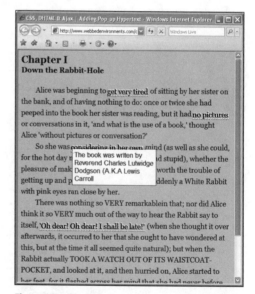

Figure 22.7 Placing your mouse over the link reveals more text.

To add pop-up layers:

1. `popUpHypertext.js`
   Start a new JavaScript file and save it as
   `popUpHypertext.js` (**Code 22.8**). Steps 2
   through 5 apply to this file.

2. `var objPopUp = null;`
   Initialize the variable `objPopUp`, which
   will keep track of which pop-up message
   is being displayed.

3. `function popUp(whichLink) {…}`
   Add the function `popUp()` to the JavaScript.
   This function identifies which object triggered the function (`whichLink`), triggers the
   `fetchData()` function to get the data that
   will be placed into the pop-up, and finally
   positions and displays the pop-up layer. At
   this point, there is no content (other than
   the default message "Loading") in the pop-
   up. The `filterData()` (Step 5) function will
   place the data into the pop-up.

continues on next page

Code 22.8 `popUpHypertext.js`: Functions used to create pop-ups with content imported using Ajax.

```
var objPopUp = null;
function popUp(whichLink) {
    fetchData('dataPage.php',whichLink,'popUpMessage');
    objPopTrig = document.getElementById(whichLink);
    objPopUp = document.getElementById('popUpMessage');
    objPopUp.innerHTML='<b>Loading</b>';
    xPos = objPopTrig.offsetLeft;
    yPos = (objPopTrig.offsetTop + objPopTrig.offsetHeight);
    if (xPos + objPopUp.offsetWidth > document.body.clientWidth) xPos = xPos - objPopUp.offsetWidth;
    if (yPos + objPopUp.offsetHeight > document.body.clientHeight) yPos = yPos - objPopUp.offsetHeight
    → - objPopTrig.offsetHeight;
    objPopUp.style.left = xPos + 'px';
    objPopUp.style.top = yPos + 'px';
    objPopUp.style.visibility = 'visible';
}
function popHide() {
    objPopUp.style.visibility = 'hidden';
    objPopUp = null;
}
function filterData(pageRequest ,objectID){
    if (pageRequest.readyState == 4 && (pageRequest.status==200 ||
    → window.location.href.indexOf("http")==-1))
        document.getElementById(objectID).innerHTML=pageRequest.responseText;}
```

4. `function popHide() {...}`

Add the function `popHide()` to the JavaScript. This function hides the pop-up object and sets the variable `objPopUp` back to null.

5. `function filterData(pageRequest, → objectID) {...}`

Add the function `filterData()` to the JavaScript, which will replace the default version of the function included in the `ajaxBasics.js` file you will be linking to in Step 9.

This function receives the data back from the Ajax request in the variable `pageRequest` and places it in the layer identified using the `objectID` variable.

6. `dataPage.php`

Set up a page on your server that holds and processes the data you will be using for your pop-up hypertext (**Code 22.9**).

In this example, I'm using a PHP file that checks the value of the variable `dataRequest` that's sent in the HTTP header and then returns a string (which can include HTML code) to the originating function.

7. `popUpHypertext.css`

Create a new external CSS file ad save it as popUpHypertext.css (**Code 22.10**). This file will include the styles you need for your pop-uphypertext layer. Make sure to include the class:

`.popUp {...}`

This class will be applied to all pop-up objects and sets their basic appearance.

Code 22.9 `dataPage.php`: A server page using PHP to find the right message for the triggering link.

```php
<?php
$needMessage = $_POST['dataRequest'];
if ($needMessage == "pop1") $dataResponse =
→ '<i>Alice\'s Adventures in Wonderland</i>
→ was published in 1865.';
if ($needMessage == "pop2") $dataResponse =
→ '<div class="dropBox"> <img src=
→ "alice02a.gif" alt="The White Rabbit"
→ height="270" width="180" /><p>John Tenniel
→ did the original illustrations</p></div>';
if ($needMessage == "pop3") $dataResponse =
→ 'The book was writen by Reverend Charles
→ Lutwidge Dodgson (A.K.A Lewis Carroll)';
if ($needMessage == "pop4") $dataResponse =
→ 'The sequal was called <i>Through the
→ Looking-Glass, and What Alice Found
→ There</i> and was published in 1871.
→ Tenniel did the illustrations for that
→ one as well.';
if ($dataResponse) echo ($dataResponse);
else echo ('Sorry! There was an error');
?>
```

Code 22.10 `popUpHypertext.css`: The style used to create a pop-up layer.

```css
.popUp {
      font-size: .9em;
      font-family: "Helvetica Neue",
Helvetica, Arial, sans-serif;
      background-color: #fff;
      visibility: hidden;
      margin: 0 10px;
      padding: 5px;
      position: absolute;
      width: 200px;
      opacity: .8;
      border: 1px solid black;}
```

8. `index.html`

Set up an HTML file and save it as `index.html` (**Code 22.11**). Steps 8 through 12 apply to this file.

9. `src="ajaxBasics.js"`

Add a call to the `ajaxBasics.js` file created in Chapter 20 (Code 20.6). You will need to add a copy of this file to the directory or change the `src` value to the path where your Ajax basics file is located. This file includes the `fetchData()` and `filterData()` functions.

10. `id="pop1"`

In a container element such as a `<div>`, add an ID to define the tooltip object. Remember that each object needs a unique ID. The container element can be anything you want that can use the `onmouseover` and `onmouseout` event handlers; however, the link tag (`<a>`) is most commonly used.

continues on next page

Code 22.11 `index.html`: The Web page with the links triggering the hypertext pop-ups.

```
<!DOCTYPE html PUBLIC "-//W3C//DTD XHTML 1.0 Strict//EN" "http://www.w3.org/TR/xhtml1/DTD/
→ xhtml1-strict.dtd">
<html xmlns="http://www.w3.org/1999/xhtml">
<head>
<meta http-equiv="Content-Type" content="text/html; charset=utf-8" />
<title>CSS, DHTML &amp; Ajax | Adding Pop-up Hypertext</title>
<script src="ajaxBasics.js" type="text/javascript"></script>
<script src="popUpHypertext.js" type="text/javascript"></script>
<link href="popUpHypertext.css" rel="stylesheet" type="text/css" />
</head>
<body>
<div id="chapter01" class="page">
    <div id="content">
    <h2>Chapter I <span class="chapterTitle">Down the Rabbit-Hole</span> </h2>
<div class="copy">
    <p>Alice was beginning to <a href="#1" id="pop1" onmouseover="popUp(this.id);"
    → onmouseout="popHide();">get very tired</a> of sitting by her sister on the bank, and of
    → having nothing to do: once or twice she had peeped into the book her sister was reading,
    → but it had <a href="#2" id="pop2" onmouseover="popUp(this.id);" onmouseout="popHide();">
    → no pictures </a> or conversations in it, 'and what is the use of a book,' thought Alice
    → 'without pictures or conversation?'</p>
</div></div></div>
<div id="popUpMessage" class="popUp"> Loading </div>
</body></html>
```

11. `onmouseover="popUp(this.id);"`

In the container you created in the last step, add an `onmouseover` event handler that triggers the `popUp()` function, passing it the ID for "this" object, which is also the ID for the pop-up message you want displayed.

12. `onmouseout="popHide();"`

After the `onmouseover` event handler, add an `onmouseout` event handler to trigger the `popHide()` function, which hides the pop-up object.

13. `<div id="popUpMessage"`
`→ class="popUp">…</div>`

Create an object with the class set to `popUp` and a unique ID, which will then be used by the `popUp()` function you created in Step 3.

✔ Tips

■ Notice that the links associated with the pop-up text go nowhere (actually, they link to the top of the page using #). You could, however, link to documents that elaborate on the concepts presented in the pop-up text or to anything else you want to use. Or you could use a simple function that returns no value, to have the links do nothing when clicked. You decide.

■ You can use pop-up text as tooltips that explain the purpose of a particular link in the navigation.

■ You can include pop-up text in an image map. This technique is nice if you have a large graphic with areas that need explanation.

Dynamic Type Ahead

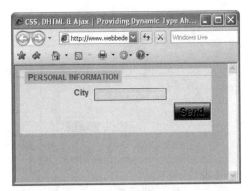

Figure 22.9 The form field, waiting for a city name to be entered.

Some people want the computer to read their minds. With a bit of Ajax and DHTML, we designers can make it appear as if the computer is doing just that, to a limited extent. Given a good database, as soon as visitors start typing information into a form field, the computer can begin to predict what they are looking for, and narrow it down further the more information they enter.

In this example (**Figure 22.9**), I'm using the common example of a form field used to submit a city name that a Web site visitor might be traveling to.

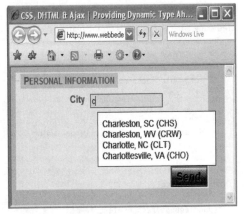

Figure 22.10 As the visitor types, the browser displays possible matches underneath.

In cases in which visitors may not know the exact spelling of the city's name, a *type ahead* input field can help by displaying a list of potential names based on the letters the visitor has typed into the form field (**Figure 22.10**). The more of the name that is entered, the more the possibilities narrow and the options drop out (**Figure 22.11**), until the visitor clicks the correct city name (**Figure 22.12**). In addition, depending on

continues on next page

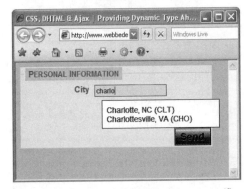

Figure 22.11 The possibilities become more specific as the visitor types in more letters.

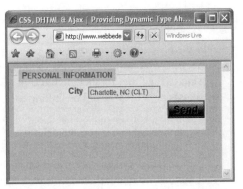

Figure 22.12 At any time, the visitor can click one of the options to have the form field populated automatically.

DYNAMIC TYPE AHEAD

how the database is set up, visitors can search based on airport codes or other criteria, such as a state abbreviation (**Figure 22.13**).

To add a dynamic type-ahead input field:

1. typeAhead.js

   Open a new external JavaScript file and save it as typeAhead.js (**Code 22.12**). Steps 2 through 5 apply to this file.

2. function typeAhead(objectPlace) {…}

   Add the function typeAhead() to your JavaScript.

   This function uses the ID for the input field to grab its current value (requestedValue). The function then passes that data and the name of the popup layer used to display the results ('results'), as well as the URL for the file on the server used to process the data (dataPage.php) to the Ajax basic function fetchData().

3. function setCity(cityNameVal) {…}

   Add the function setCity() to your JavaScript. This function will take a value passed to it in the cityNameVal variable and place that into the cityName form input field.

4. function filterData(pageRequest, → objectID){…}

   Add the function filterData() to your JavaScript, which will replace the default version of the function included in the ajaxBasics.js file you will be linking to in Step 9.

   This function takes the comma delimited list of city names delivered dynamically from dataPage.php, splits it up and turns each name into a link that calls the setCity() function, passing it the name of the city. It displays this list of links in the object specified by the variable objectID

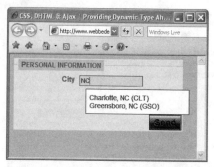

Figure 22.13 The type-ahead input field can be based on a variety of criteria. For example, visitors can type in a state abbreviation to see all the cities in the same state.

Code 22.12 typeAhead.js: Functions used for predicting what the visitor is typing using Ajax.

```
function typeAhead(objectPlace) {
    requestedData = objectPlace.value;
    fetchData('dataPage.php',
    → requestedData,'results');
}
function setCity(cityNameVal) {
    document.forms.myForm.cityName.value =
    → cityNameVal;
}
function filterData(pageRequest,objectID){
var objectResults =
→ document.getElementById(objectID);
if(pageRequest.responseText != '')
    {
    objectResults.style.display = 'block';
    objectResults.innerHTML = '';
    resultsList =
    → pageRequest.responseText.split(',');
    for(i = 0; i < resultsList.length; i++)
    {
if(resultsList[i] != "")
    objectResults.innerHTML += '<a href=
    → "javascript:setCity(\'' +
    → resultsList[i] + '\')"
    → onclick="popHide(\'' + objectID +
    → '\')">' + resultsList[i] + '</a>';
    }
} else {
    objectResults.style.display = 'none';
    }}
function popHide(objectID) {
    var objPopUp =
    → document.getElementById(objectID);
    objPopUp.style.display = 'none';}
```

5. `function popHide(objectID) {…}`

Add the function `popHide()` to your JavaScript. This function simply hides the layer in which the type-ahead list is being displayed.

6. `dataPage.php`

Set up a page on your server that holds and processes the data you will be placing in your HTML page (**Code 22.13**).

In this example, I'm using a PHP file to create an array (`$cityName[]`) that records a city name and state as the index and then a list of corresponding strings that are associated with the city (city name, state, and airport code).

continues on next page

Code 22.13 `dataPage.php`: A server page using PHP to store arrays of city names and possible matches.

```php
<?php

$cityName = array();
$cityResults = "";
$lastQuery = "";

$cityName["Charleston&sbquo; SC (CHS)"] = array("Charleston", "SC", "CHS");
$cityName["Charleston&sbquo; WV (CRW)"] = array("Charleston", "WV", "CRW");
$cityName["Charlotte&sbquo; NC (CLT)"] = array("Charlotte", "NC", "CLT");
$cityName["Charlottesville&sbquo; VA (CHO)"] = array("Charlottesville", "VA", "CHO");
$cityName["Greensboro&sbquo; NC (GSO)"] = array("Greensboro", "NC", "GSO");
if(isset($_POST["dataRequest"]))
{ $searchString = strtolower($_POST["dataRequest"]);
$searchStringLength = strlen($searchString);
        foreach($cityName as $query=>$keywords)
        { foreach($keywords as $word)
            { $subString = substr($word,0,$searchStringLength);
                if (strtolower($subString) == $searchString) {
                    if ($query != $lastQuery) {
    $cityResults .= sprintf("%s,",$query);
    $lastQuery = $query;
}}}}
        echo $cityResults;
}
?>
```

Chapter 22

The script takes the value passed to it through the `dataRequest` variable in the XMLHttpRequest call and compares that string to each element in the array. If there is a match (even partial), it records that city and then sends the list of matching cities back to the calling page.

7. `typeAhead.css`

   Create an external style sheet that holds your styles for this page and save it as `typeAhead.css` (**Code 22.14**). I used styles similar to those I set up in "Styling Forms" in Chapter 21. Make sure to define a class for `.popUp {…}` and set it to `display: none`.

8. `index.html`

   Set up an HTML file and save it as `index.html` (**Code 22.15**). Steps 9 through 13 apply to this file.

Code 22.14 `typeAhead.css`: Add styles for your forms and type ahead fields, but always include the `.popUp` class.

```
.popUp {
    position: relative;
    font-size: .9em;
    font-family: "Helvetica Neue",
    → Helvetica, Arial, sans-serif;
    background-color: #fff;
    display: none;
    left: 148px;
    padding: 8px;
    width: 200px;
    opacity: .8;
    border: 1px solid black;}
```

Code 22.15 `index.html`: The Web page with a text form field for the visitor and a hidden layer that will eventually display possible matches.

```
<!DOCTYPE html PUBLIC "-//W3C//DTD XHTML 1.0 Strict//EN" "http://www.w3.org/TR/xhtml1/DTD/
→ xhtml1-strict.dtd">
<html xmlns="http://www.w3.org/1999/xhtml">
<head>
<meta http-equiv="Content-Type" content="text/html; charset=utf-8" />
<title>CSS, DHTML &amp; Ajax | Providing Dynamic Type Ahead</title>
<script src="ajaxBasics.js" type="text/javascript"></script>
<script src="typeAhead.js" type="text/javascript"></script>
<link href="typeAhead.css" rel="stylesheet" type="text/css" />
</head>
<body>
<form action="#" method="get" id="myForm">
    <fieldset>
    <legend>Personal Information</legend>
    <label for="cityName">City</label>
    <input type="text" class="formInputText" id="cityName"
    → onkeyup="typeAhead(document.getElementById(this.id));" value="" />
    <div id="results" class="popUp"> </div>
    <input class="formInputButton" type="submit" name="submitButtonName" id="submitButtonName"
    → value="Send" tabindex="9" />
</fieldset></form>
</body></html>
```

DYNAMIC TYPE AHEAD

498

9. `src="ajaxBasics.js"`

Add a call to the `ajaxBasics.js` file created in Chapter 20 (Code 20.6). You will need to add a copy of this file to the directory or change the `src` value to the path where your Ajax basics (`ajaxBasic.js`) file is located.

10. `src="typeAhead.js"`

Add a call to the `typeAhead.js` file you set up in Step 1.

11. `href="typeAhead.css"`

Add a link to the `typeAhead.css` file you set up in Step 7.

12. `<input type="text" class=`
`→ "formInputText" id="cityName"`
`→ onkeyup="typeAhead(document.`
`→ getElementById(this.id));"`
`→ value="" />`

In the form on your page, add an `<input>` element with an ID value of `cityName` and an `onkeyup` event handler that triggers the function `typeAhead()` from Step 2. Pass the function element's ID (`this.id`).

13. `<div id="results"`
`→ class="popUp"> </div>`

Add a layer that will be used to display the type-ahead list as it is generated. Initially it should be hidden.

NAVIGATION

Navigation is what makes the Web run. It can come in many flavors: main menus, submenus, auxiliary menus, image maps, hypertext links, and other schemes that allow visitors to move from page to page. A well-planned navigation scheme lets visitors get to the information they want with minimal fuss. Poorly planned navigation leads to blindness, low sex appeal, and sometimes death. Even worse, poor navigation may upset site visitors enough that they will never return to your site.

Beyond navigating between Web pages, a truly dynamic Web site lets visitors interact with the pages by changing the content after it has loaded. You must provide controls that permit that interaction.

In this chapter, I'll look at some effective ways to create dynamic navigation that gives visitors maximum flexibility and lets you maximize the impact of your content.

Creating Navigation Buttons with CSS Sprites

CSS buttons have become a common technique in most Web developers' arsenal of tricks. Where once we used clunky JavaScript to change the appearance of a graphic when the user rolls over or clicks it, modern Web designers use the CSS :link, :visited,:hover, and :active pseudo-classes to swap out images in the link's background without ever having to program a single line of JavaScript.

However, there is a drawback in the form of a slight (but annoying) delay as the image files swap out. We overcome this delay by bringing all of the images for each state into a single image file.

This technique, referred to as *CSS sprites*, lets you create a single image ile that contains in a grid all four of the rollover-state graphics used for the button. In that file, you place all the individual "sprites" that make up your button, separated by enough space so that they don't start running over each other. You then call this image as the background for an element, and set the background position property (using negative values to move the background up and left) to position the correct sprite (**Figure 23.1**). Because only one image needs to load, the browser needs to make only one server call, which eliminates the file-swap delay.

To add CSS image rollovers to a Web page:

1. buttons_01.png

   Start by creating four different background image states, separated by a small amount of space (**Figure 23.2**). Generally you will want to space the states so that their positions are regularly spaced, making them easy to remember.

Figure 23.1 The button list uses the same image not only to create the graphic background, but all of its states as well.

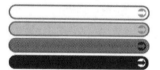

Figure 23.2 buttons_01.png: The image used to create the different rollover states for our navigation button.

Code 23.1 The styles for links in the navigation area use the button_01 graphic to create the multi-state rollover effect.

```
<!DOCTYPE html PUBLIC "-//W3C//DTD XHTML 1.0
→ Strict//EN" "http://www.w3.org/TR/xhtml1/
→ DTD/xhtml1-strict.dtd">
<html xmlns="http://www.w3.org/1999/xhtml">
<head>
<meta http-equiv="Content-Type"
→ content="text/html; charset=utf-8" />
<title>CSS, DHTML &amp; Ajax | Creating
→ Navigation buttons</title>
<script type="text/javascript">
</script>
<style type="text/css" media="screen">
h1 {
    font-size: 1em;
    color: red; }
h2 {
    font-size: .9em;
    color:#999; }
.page { width: 756px; }
#content {
    float: left;
    font-size: 1em;
    font-family: Georgia, 'Times New
    → Roman', times, serif;
    color: #000000;
    margin: 8px;
    width: 300px;
    padding-top: 225px;
    padding-left: 175px;
    background: white url(alice23.gif)
    → no-repeat; }
#navigation { float:left; }
#navigation a {
    text-decoration: none;
    font: bold 12px Arial, Helvetica,
    → sans-serif;
    overflow: hidden;
    display: block;
    background: #fff url(buttons_01.png)
    → -1px -1px no-repeat;
    margin: 4px 2px 0px 2px;
    padding: 4px 8px;
    width: 218px;
    height: 16px; }
#navigation a:link {
    background-position: -1px -1px;
    color: RGB(255,51,51); }
#navigation a:visited {
    background-position: -1px -26px;
    color: RGB(255,102,102); }
#navigation a:hover {
    background-position: -1px -51px;
    color: RGB(255,0,0); }
```

For example, I set the top of each graphic at intervals of 25 pixels.

The images shouldn't use a height much larger then the font size you're using for your text. Save all four button states as a single file. You can use any graphic format supported by browsers (generally GIF, PNG, or JPEG).

2. #navigation a{…}

In your CSS file, set up a style rule for the <a> element as it is presented within the #navigation layer (**Code 23.1**). The rule needs to include:

display: block;

background: #fff url(buttons_01.png)
→ -1px -1px no-repeat;

continues on next page

Code 23.1 *continued*

```
#navigation a:active {
background-position: -1px -76px;
    color: RGB(255,255,255); }
</style>
</head>
<body>
<div class="page">
<div id="navigation">
<a href="index.html" onfocus="if (this.blur)
→ this.blur();">Introduction</a><a href=
→ "ch01.html">Down The Rabbit-Hole</a>
→ <a href="ch02.html">The Pool of Tears</a>
→ <a href="ch03.html">A Caucus-Race and a
→ Long Tale</a><a href="ch04.html">The
→ Rabbit Sends in a Little Bill</a><a href=
→ "ch05.html">Advice from a Caterpillar</a>
→ <a href="ch06.html">Pig and Pepper</a>
→ <a href="ch07.html">A Mad Tea-Party</a>
→ <a href="ch08.html">The Queen's Croquet-
→ Ground</a><a href="ch09.html">The Mock
→ Turtle's Story</a><a href="ch10.html">The
→ Lobster Quadrille</a><a href="ch11.html">
→ Who Stole The Tarts?</a><a href=
→ "ch12.html">Alice's Evidence</a>
</div>
<div id="content">
<h1>ALICE'S ADVENTURES IN WONDERLAND</h1>
→ Lewis Carroll
<h2>THE MILLENNIUM FULCRUM EDITION 3.0</h2>
</div></div>
</body></html>
```

Set the background image to not repeat and position it at the top left of the link area. Then add enough padding to the left side so that the link text isn't on top of the image (generally, the width of the image plus a few pixels). Also set the width and height to create the "mask" around the image.

3. `#navigation a:link {…}`

Now add rules for all of the link states (`:link`, `:visited`, `:hover`, and `:active`), setting the background position property with the correct offset values to load the relevant rollover state. For example, the visited state would use:

`background-position: -1px -26px;`

So only the visited button state is shown (**Figure 23.3**).

You can, of course, include whatever other style changes you want to make. In this example, I'm also changing the text color.

✔ Tips

- The idea (and the last part of the name) for CSS sprites originated in the early days of video games, when memory and speed were at a premium. To overcome system limitations, video game producers would lay out the thousands of small graphics used to create the game into a grid and then display each "sprite" as needed, masking out all but the needed part of the larger image.

- You may notice that when you click on one of these links, there is no annoying border left around it by the browser. For more details, see the sidebar "Getting Rid of Annoying Active Link Borders."

Figure 23.3 Each button state (`:link`, `:visited`, `:hover`, `:active`) is revealed as the background slides up and down within the visible area of the button.

Getting Rid of Annoying Active Link Borders

Internet Explorer 5 introduced (and many other browsers have adapted) what might be one of the most aggravating features possible to Web designers: the active link border. Those are the boxes that appear around a link after it has been clicked. They can interfere with your design, especially if you're using CSS image rollovers or if the links are in a frame, so the border persists even after the linked page has loaded. There is a way to get rid of these, however. Simply place the following code in the links for which you want to turn active link borders off:

`onfocus="if(this.blur)this.blur();"`

This code tells the link to blur itself if it's focused, which gets rid of the border. Keep in mind, though, that by adding this code you are removing a specified browser behavior, which may limit accessibility for some users.

Figure 23.4 The menu headers.

Figure 23.5 When a menu header is rolled over, the rollover effect turns the background red and displays the menu underneath.

Creating Drop-Down Menus

Drop-down menus have been a favorite GUI device for years. The menu header appears as a single word or phrase at the top of the window or screen, and when clicked it reveals a list of further options. In a File menu, for example, you might find Save, Close, and Print.

Now you can achieve the same effect on the Web with DHTML. As with most drop-down menu systems, this Web-based version lets you mouse over a menu header to show the menu immediately underneath it (**Figures 23.4** and **23.5**). You can place anything you want in these menus, not just links, but also forms, images, or other content.

To add drop-down menus:

1. `var objNavMenu = null;`

    Initialize the global variables you'll be using (**Code 23.2**). One variable you'll need to pay special attention to is the number of drop menus (`numDropMenu`), which records the total number of menus on the page. You can also set the colors used for the rollovers.

continues on next page

Code 23.2 The `initDropMenu()` function sets up the global event handlers for the menus; `showDropMen()` is responsible for positioning and displaying the menu; and `hideDropMenu()` will make it vanish when no longer needed.

```
<!DOCTYPE html PUBLIC "-//W3C//DTD XHTML 1.0 Strict//EN" "http://www.w3.org/TR/xhtml1/DTD/xhtml1-
strict.dtd">
<html xmlns="http://www.w3.org/1999/xhtml">
<head>
<meta http-equiv="Content-Type" content="text/html; charset=utf-8" />
<title>CSS, DHTML &amp; Ajax | Drop-down Menu</title>
<script type="text/javascript">
<!-
var objNavMenu = null;
var prevObjNavMenu = null;
var prevObjDropMenu = null;
var numDropMenu = 3;
```

code continues on next page

Because of some slight positioning differences between Internet Explorer and other browsers, we're also going to have to determine whether the code is being run in Internet Explorer.

2. `function initDropMenu ()`

Add the function `initDropMenu()` to your JavaScript. This function sets a global event handler to hide any visible menus whenever the visitor clicks the screen.

The function then uses the variable `numDropMenu` set from Step 1 to cycle through each menu header (`objNavMenu`) and menu (`objDropMenu`) to hide the menus and set how menu headers and menus should behave when moused over, moused out, and clicked. The important event to watch is the one that triggers the initial opening of the menu:

`objNavMenu.onmouseover = showDropMenu;`

If you want to change the behavior so that the menu opens only when the header is clicked, change `onmouseover` to `onclick`.

3. `function menuOut(e) {…}`

Add the function `menuOut()` to your JavaScript.

This function reinstates the global menu-hiding `onclick` event handler when visitors moves their mouse cursor out of a menu header. It also sets the menu header back to its normal style (gray background with black text).

4. `function showDropMenu(e) {…}`

Add the function `showDropMenu()` to your JavaScript.

Code 23.2 *continued*

```
// link styles
var bgLinkColor = '#000';
var bgLinkHover = '#f00'
var bgLinkActive = '#900'
var linkColor = '#fff'
var linkHover = '#fff'
var linkActive = '#fff'
var isIE = null;
if (navigator.appName.indexOf('Microsoft
Internet Explorer') != -1) isIE=1;
function initDropMenu () {
    document.onclick = hideDropMenu;
    for (i=1; i<=numDropMenu; i++) {
        menuName = 'dropMenu' + i;
        navName = 'navMenu' + i;
        objDropMenu =
→ document.getElementById(menuName);
        objNavMenu =
→ document.getElementById(navName);
        objDropMenu.style.visibility =
→ 'hidden';
        objNavMenu.onmouseover = showDropMenu;
        objNavMenu.onmouseout = menuOut;
        objNavMenu.onclick = showDropMenu;
    }
    objNavMenu = null;
    return; }
function showDropMenu(e) {
    menuName = 'drop' +
→ this.id.substring(3,this.id.length);
    objDropMenu =
→ document.getElementById(menuName);
    if (prevObjDropMenu == objDropMenu) {
        hideDropMenu();
        return;
    }
    if (prevObjDropMenu != null)
→ hideDropMenu();
    objNavMenu =
→ document.getElementById(this.id);
    if ((prevObjNavMenu != objNavMenu ) ||
→ (prevObjDropMenu == null)) {
        objNavMenu.style.color = linkActive;
        objNavMenu.style.backgroundColor =
→ bgLinkActive;
    }
    if (objDropMenu) {
        xPos = objNavMenu.offsetParent.
→ offsetLeft + objNavMenu.offsetLeft;
        yPos = objNavMenu.offsetParent.
→ offsetTop + objNavMenu.offsetParent.
→ offsetHeight;
```

code continues on next page

```
Code 23.2 continued

        if (isIE) {
            yPos -= 1;
            xPos -= 6;
        }
        objDropMenu.style.left = xPos + 'px';
        objDropMenu.style.top = yPos + 'px';
        objDropMenu.style.visibility =
        → 'visible';
        prevObjDropMenu = objDropMenu;
        prevObjNavMenu = objNavMenu;
    }
; }
function hideDropMenu() {
    document.onclick = null;
    if (prevObjDropMenu) {
        prevObjDropMenu.style.visibility =
        → 'hidden';
        prevObjDropMenu = null;
        prevObjNavMenu.style.color =
        → linkColor;
        prevObjNavMenu.style.backgroundColor
        → = bgLinkColor;
    }
    objNavMenu = null; }
window.onload=initDropMenu;
// -->
</script>
<style type="text/css" media="screen">
body { url(alice23.gif) no-repeat 0px 8px; }
h1 {
    font:small-caps bold italic 2.5em
    → Georgia, 'Times New Roman', times,
    → serif;
    color: red; }
h2 {
    color:#999; }
.page {
    position: relative;
    top: 190px;
    left: 165px;
    width: 480px; }
#menuBar {
    display: block;
    margin-bottom: 5px;
    position: relative;
    top: 0px;
    left: 0px;
    right: 0px;
    width: 99%;
    overflow: hidden;
    background-color: #000; }
```

code continues on next page

This function is triggered when the visitor clicks a menu header. It first hides the menu currently showing (`prevObjDropMenu`) using the `hideDropMenu()` function you'll add in Step 6. It then sets the style for the menu header option so that it looks selected (white text on a black background), and positions and shows the appropriate menu.

Notice that we use the `isIE` variable from Step 1 to tweak the positioning slightly for Internet Explorer.

5. `function hideDropMenu() {…}`

   Add the function `hideDropMenu()` to your JavaScript.

   This function disables the global `onclick` event and then hides any menus that are showing and sets the menu header style to its normal state (gray background with black text).

6. `window.onload=initDropMenu;`

   In the JavaScript, add an `onload` event handler to trigger the `initDropMenu()` function when the page loads.

7. `body {…}`

   Add styles for the body of your Web page to set the margins and padding. One thing that will greatly equalize the positioning of elements between the different browsers is to set the padding and margins for the body to 0. There will still be some discrepancy, but not nearly as much.

8. `#menuBar {…}`

   Set up a CSS rule for the menu bar, which will hold the menu headers. Beyond using relative positioning, the exact style is up to you.

continues on next page

9. `.menuHeader {...}`

Set up a class to define the appearance of the menu headers. Remember, rather than links (`<a>`) we'll be setting these up using `<div>` tags.

This class will set the initial appearance of the menu headers, which are then changed by the JavaScript depending on the current `:hover` state. Make sure to use relative positioning, but the rest of the styles are up to you.

10. `.menuDrop {...}`

Set up a class to define the drop-down menu's appearance. Make sure to use absolute positioning, set the z-index above all other layers, and set the visibility to `hidden`.

11. `.menuDrop a {...}`

Set up the style for the drop-down menu links that are children of the `.menuDrop` class, setting each of the link pseudo-classes (`:link`, `:visited`, `:hover`, and `:active`).

12. `<div id="menuBar">...</div>`

Set up the menu bar object using a `<div>` element and the `menuBar` ID.

13. `<div id="menuBar">...</div>`

Inside the menu bar object, use `<div>` elements and the `menuHeader` class to add a menu header for each menu. You can add as many menu headers as you want, but make sure that each one has a unique navMenu ID (`navMenu1`, `navMenu2`, `navMenu3`, and so on). Remember to set the variable `numMenus` in Step 1 to the number of menus you create here.

Code 23.2 *continued*

```css
.menuHeader {
    color: #fff;
    font-size: 12px;
    font-family: arial, Helvetica, sans-serif;
    font-weight: bold;
    text-decoration: none;
    white-space: nowrap;
    cursor: pointer;
    padding: 5px;
    margin: 0px;
    padding-right: 15px;
    display: inline;
    position: relative;
    background-color: #000;
    border-right: 1px solid #000000; }
.menuDrop {
    position: absolute;
    visibility: hidden;
    z-index: 1000;
    top: 60px;
    left: 0;
    width: 175px;
    height: auto;
    margin: 0;
    padding: 0;
    color: #999999;
    font-size: 12px;
    font-family: arial, Helvetica, sans-serif;
    background-color: #ffffff;
    background-repeat: repeat;
    border-style: solid;
    border-width: 0 1px 1px;
    border-color: #003365; }
.menuDrop a {
    display: block;
    text-align: left;
    padding: 2px 5px;
    border-top: 1px solid #ccc;
    text-decoration: none; }
.menuDrop a:link {
    color: #f00; }
.menuDrop a:visited {
    color: #f00; }
.menuDrop a:hover {
    color: #fff;
    background-color: #f00; }
.menuDrop a:active {
    color: #ffffff;
    background-color: #c00; }
</style>
</head>
```

code continues on next page

Code 23.2 *continued*

```
<body>
<div id="menuBar">
     <div id="navMenu1"
     → class="menuHeader">Part I</div>
     <div id="navMenu2"
     → class="menuHeader">Part II</div>
     <div id="navMenu3"
     → class="menuHeader">Part III</div></div>
<div id="dropMenu1" class="menuDrop">
<a href="ch01.html">Down The Rabbit-
→ Hole</a><a href="ch02.html">The Pool of
→ Tears</a><a href="ch03.html">A Caucus-
→ Race and a Long Tale</a><a href=
→ "ch04.html">The Rabbit Sends in a
→ Little Bill</a>
</div>
<div id="dropMenu2" class="menuDrop">
<a href="ch05.html" onfocus="if (this.blur)
→ this.blur();">Advice from a Caterpillar</a>
→ <a href="ch06.html">Pig and Pepper</a>
→ <a href="ch07.html">A Mad Tea-Party</a>
</div>
<div id="dropMenu3" class="menuDrop">
<a href="ch08.html">The Queen's Croquet-
→ Ground</a><a href="ch09.html">The Mock
→ Turtle's Story</a><a href="ch10.html">The
→ Lobster Quadrille</a><a href="ch11.html">
→ Who Stole The Tarts?</a><a href=
→ "ch12.html">Alice's Evidence</a>
</div>
<div class="page">
<h1>ALICE'S ADVENTURES IN WONDERLAND</h1>
→ Lewis Carroll
<h2>THE MILLENNIUM FULCRUM EDITION 3.0</h2>
</div>
</body></html>
```

14. `<div id="dropMenu1"`
`→ class="menuDrop">…</div>`

For each menu header you created in Step 14, you should now create the menu to go under it, using `<div>` elements and the `menuDrop` class. These menus are absolutely positioned, so the code can come anywhere in the HTML. However, make sure that each has a unique dropMenu ID (`dropMenu1`, `dropMenu2`, `dropMenu3`, and so on).

✔ Tips

■ This particular menu works much like a standard operating system menu, in that the menu does not pop up until visitors click the menu head, but it then disappears when they click another menu header, one of the options in the menu, or anywhere else on the page.

■ To improve accessibility on your Web site for users who may not be running JavaScript, consider adding accessibility controls to your links. See the sidebar "Using Access Keys to Improve Accessibility" for more details.

CREATING DROP-DOWN MENUS

Using Access Keys to Improve Accessibility

Although most people coming to your Web site will be using their mouse to control what's going on, there are many potential visitors who, for a variety of reasons, may not be able to use a mouse as effectively or at all. To accommodate visitors who are using a keyboard or speech-recognition system to navigate the Web, you can include the `accesskey` attribute for important links:

`<a href="index.html" _accesskey="h">Home</a>`

Whenever visitors press the H key, this link will receive focus, so that they can then press (or speak) Return to access the page.

Creating Collapsible Menus

Anyone who has used a GUI—whether Mac-based, Windows-based, or UNIX-based—has watched menus in a window collapse and expand. Click a folder, and its contents are displayed below the folder, while the other files and directories move down to accommodate the expanded content. In Windows, you click plus and minus signs. On the Mac, you click triangles. You can achieve a similar effect on the Web using the `display` property

In this example (**Figures 23.6** and **23.7**), the menu is placed into a frame to the left of the content, allowing the visitor to quickly move through the pages while maintaining a consistent menu position and open state.

To create a collapsing/expanding menu:

1. `var autoClose=1;`

   In your JavaScript, initialize the variables (**Code 23.3**):

   ◆ `autoClose` controls whether the menu automatically collapses when another menu is opened (`autoClose=1`) or stays open until manually closed (`autoClose=0`).

   ◆ `oldObject` stores the address of the last menu opened.

2. `function toggleClamShellMenu (objectID) {…}`

   Add `toggleClamShellMenu()` to your JavaScript.

   This function uses the `objectID` variable to locate the menu object. It then sets the `display` of that object to `none` if it's already `block`, or `block` if it is already `none`. The effect is that the menu appears and pushes everything after it down.

continues on Page 512

Figure 23.6 The list of menu options is in the left frame, and the content is on the right.

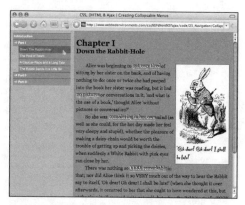

Figure 23.7 The menu for Part I contains links that target the right frame.

Code 23.3 The `toggleClamShellMenu()` function (located in the file menu.html, which is displayed in a frameset) shows or hides submenus.

```
<!DOCTYPE html PUBLIC "-//W3C//DTD XHTML 1.0
→ Transitional//EN" "http://www.w3.org/TR/
→ xhtml1/DTD/xhtml1-transitional.dtd">
<html xmlns="http://www.w3.org/1999/xhtml">
<head>
<meta http-equiv="Content-Type"
→ content="text/html; charset=utf-8" />
<title>CSS, DHTML &amp; Ajax | Creating
→ Collapsable Menus</title>
<script type="text/javascript">
var autoClose=1; var oldObject=null;
function toggleClamShellMenu(objectID) {
    if ((oldObject)&&(autoClose==1))
    → oldObject.style.display='none'
    var object =
    → document.getElementById(objectID);
    if (object.style.display =='block')
    → object.style.display='none';
    else object.style.display='block';
    oldObject = object;
    return; }
</script>
<style type="text/css">
body {
    font-family: "Helvetica Narrow", Arial,
    → Helvetica, Geneva, sans-serif;
    background-color: silver; }
ul {
    margin-top: 0px;
    padding-top: 0px;
    margin-bottom: 0px;
    padding-bottom: 0px; }
#menu1, #menu2, #menu3 {
    display: none; }
.menuHead {
    color: #c00;
    font-size: 14px;
    font-family: Arial, Helvetica, Geneva,
    → sans-serif;
    font-weight: bold;
    text-decoration: none;
    }
.menuOption {
    display: block;
    color: #f00;
    font-size: 12px;
    font-family: Arial, Helvetica,
    → Geneva, sans-serif;
}
.menu { width: 98%; }
```

Code 23.3 *continued*

```
.menu li {
    list-style: none;
    margin-left: -20px;
}
.menu a {
    font-size: .7em;
    display: block;
    text-decoration: none;
    border-top: 1px solid #666;
    border-bottom: 1px solid #666;
    padding: 4px;
    background-color: #999;
    color: #fff;
    margin-left: 2px; }
.menu a:hover {
    font-size: .7em;
    display: block;
    text-decoration: none;
    border-top: 1px solid #666;
    border-bottom: 1px solid #666;
    padding: 4px;
    background-color: #666;
    color: #f99; }
</style>
</head>
<body>
<div class="menu">
<a href="introduction.html" target=
→ "content"><b>Introduction</b></a>
</div>
<div class="menu">
<a class="menuHead" href="#"
onclick="toggleClamShellMenu('menu1')" >&rArr;
→ Part I</a>
<ul id="menu1">
<li><a href="ch01.html"target="content">Down
→ The Rabbit-Hole</a></li><li><a href=
→ "ch02.html"target="content">The Pool of
→ Tears</a></li><li><a href="ch03.html"
→ target="content">A Caucus-Race and a
→ Long Tale</a></li><li><a href="ch04.html"
→ target="content">The Rabbit Sends in a
→ Little Bill</a></li>
</ul></div>
<div class="menu">
<a class="menuHead" href="#" onclick=
→ "toggleClamShellMenu('menu2')">&rArr;
→ Part II</a>
<ul id="menu2">
```

code continues on next page

3. `#menu1, #menu2, #menu3 {…}`

Create a CSS rule for each of your collapsible menus, setting the display property to none (see "Setting How an Element Is Displayed" in Chapter 6). This way, the menus don't appear when the document first loads.

4. `toggleClamShellMenu('menu1')`

Set up links for each menu that will be used to trigger the function you created in Step 2. The function should be passed the ID for the menu that is to be shown.

5. `<ul id="menu1">…</ul>`

Set up a list (`<ul>`) with an ID and each element in your collapsible menu as a list element (`<li>`).

✔ Tips

- You can use any elements in these menus, including graphics, forms, and lists. The content and design is up to you.

- In this example, I chose to use a frame to hold the navigation so that the menu would stay in a fixed position while the visitor is scrolling through it *and* so that the menu wouldn't collapse between pages.

Code 23.3 *continued*

```
<li><a href="ch05.html"target="content">Advice from a Caterpillar</a></li><li><a href=
→ "ch06.html"target="content">Pig and Pepper</a></li><li><a href="ch07.html"target="content">
→ A Mad Tea-Party</a></li>
</ul></div>
<div class="menu">
<a class="menuHead" href="#" onclick="toggleClamShellMenu('menu3')">&rArr; Part III</a>
<ul id="menu3">
<li><a href="ch08.html"target="content">The Queen's Croquet-Ground</a></li><li><a
href="ch09.html"target="content">The Mock Turtle's Story</a></li><li><a
href="ch10.html"target="content">The Lobster Quadrille</a></li><li><a
href="ch11.html"target="content">Who Stole The Tarts?</a></li><li><a
href="ch12.html"target="content">Alice's Evidence</a></li>
</ul></div>
</body></html>
```

Figure 23.8 The tabs are presented in the iframe on the left side of the page.

Figure 23.9 After clicking Part I, its submenu is presented, and the tab and submenu are highlighted.

Creating a Tab Menu

Although drop-down menus and collapsible menus are commonly used to help visitors navigate Web sites, another commonly used metaphor is the tabbed list. Tabbed lists present a set of top-level options, which when clicked reveal the second-level links. This lets you place a large amount of links into a small area, which are easily and consistently available (see the sidebar "Preventing Navigation Noise").

In this example (**Figures 23.8** and **23.9**), a tabbed menu has been set up in an `<iframe>` on the left side of the page, which is used to control the content in the `<iframe>` to its right. As a bonus for this section, I've also added some JavaScript code that will keep the heights of both iframes just a few pixels shorter than the window's height, and the width of the content frame a little shorter than the width of the window.

continues on next page

Preventing Navigation Noise

One of my chief gripes about most Web sites is the overabundance of unorganized links. You've probably seen sites with long lists of links that stretch off the window. These links add visual noise to the design and waste precious screen space without assisting navigation.

Web surfers rarely take the time to read an entire Web page. Instead, they scan for relevant information. But human beings can process only so much information at a time. If a Web page is cluttered, visitors must wade through dozens or hundreds of links to find the one path to the information they desire.

Anything designers can do to aid visitors' abilities to scan a page, such as organizing links in lists and hiding sub-links until they're needed, will improve the Web site's usability. Drop-down, sliding, and collapsible menus are a great way to organize your page to prevent navigation noise.

To set up a tabbed menu:

1. `index.html`

Create a new HTML document with the XHTML Transitional doctype that will be used to hold the menu and content `<iframes>` (**Code 23.4**). Steps 2 through 6 apply to this file.

2. `function initPage() {...}`

Add the `initPage()` function to your JavaScript.

This function determines the width and height of the window and then runs the `resizeObject()` function to set the dimensions of the menu and content iframes.

3. `function resizeObject(newWidth,`
   `→ newHeight, objectName) {...}`

Add the `resizeObject()` function to your JavaScript. This function takes width and height values and applies them to the specified object.

Code 23.4 `index.html`: This page is used to create the interface with a menu and content display. It will resize the iframes to fit the available screen dimensions.

```
<!DOCTYPE html PUBLIC "-//W3C//DTD XHTML 1.0 Transitional//EN"
"http://www.w3.org/TR/xhtml1/DTD/xhtml1-transitional.dtd">
<html xmlns="http://www.w3.org/1999/xhtml">
<head>
<meta http-equiv="Content-Type" content="text/html; charset=utf-8" />
<title>CSS, DHTML &amp; Ajax | Creating a Tabbed Menu</title>
<script type="text/javascript">
function initPage() {
    if (window.innerHeight) var resizeHeight = window.innerHeight - 50;
    if (window.innerHeight) var resizeWidth = window.innerWidth - 300;
    resizeObject(null,resizeHeight,'menuDisplay');
    resizeObject(resizeWidth,resizeHeight,'contentDisplay'); }
function resizeObject(newWidth,newHeight,objectName) {
    var object = document.getElementById(objectName);
    if (newWidth != null) object.style.width = newWidth + 'px';
    if (newHeight != null) object.style.height = newHeight + 'px'; }
window.onload=initPage; window.onresize=initPage;
</script>
```

code continues on next page

Code 23.4 *continued*

```
<style type="text/css" media="screen">
body {
    font-family: Helvetica, Arial, sans-serif;
    font-size: 1em;
    background-color: #fff;
    color: #fff; }
#menuDisplay {
    position: absolute;
    top: 25px;
    left: 10px;
    width: 300px;
    height: 480px;
    overflow: auto;
    background-color: #666; }
#contentDisplay {
    position: absolute;
    top: 25px;
    left: 250px;
    border: 2px solid #999;
    background-color: white; }
</style>
</head>
<body>
<iframe src="menu.html" id="menuDisplay"
→ title="menuDisplay" name="menuDisplay"
→ width="240" height="480" frameborder=
→ "0"></iframe>
<iframe src="introduction.html" id=
→ "contentDisplay" title="contentDisplay"
→ name="contentDisplay" width="756"
→ height="800"></iframe>
</body></html>
```

4. `window.onload=initPage;`
→ `window.onresize=initPage;`

Add **onload** and **onresize** event handlers in the <body> element to trigger the `initPage()` function, which will resize the iframes to fit the window.

5. `#menuDisplay {…}`

Add CSS rules to specify styles for your menu and content iframes. You will need to specify the absolute position for these frames, based on how wide you need the menu to be.

6. `<iframe src="menu.html"`
→ `id="menuDisplay" name="menuDisplay"`
→ `width="240" height="480"`
→ `frameborder="0"></iframe>`

Set up the menu and content iframes, specifying the ID and name, as well as the initial width and height. You will also set the source for both iframes with `menu.html` (Step 7) for **menuDisplay** and the initial page for **contentDisplay**.

7. `menu.html`

Create a new HTML document with the XHTML Transitional doctype that will hold the menu (**Code 23.5**). Steps 8 through 17 apply to this file.

continues on Page 517

Code 23.5 `menu.html`: The menu is made up of two columns, one side with the tabs for top level navigation, and the other side for the second level navigation.

```
<!DOCTYPE html PUBLIC "-//W3C//DTD XHTML 1.0 Transitional//EN"
"http://www.w3.org/TR/xhtml1/DTD/xhtml1-transitional.dtd">
<html xmlns="http://www.w3.org/1999/xhtml">
<head>
<meta http-equiv="Content-Type" content="text/html; charset=utf-8" />
<title>CSS, DHTML &amp; Ajax | Creating a Tabbed Menu</title>
<script type="text/javascript">
var oldObject=null; var oldObjectHi=null;
function openChapter(sectionNum) {
    if (!oldObject) oldObject = document.getElementById('s00Index');
    oldObject.style.display = 'none';
    if (oldObjectHi) oldObjectHi.className = 'sectionDim';
```
code continues on next page

Code 23.5 *continued*

```
        if (sectionNum <= 9) sectionNum = '0' +
    → sectionNum;
        chHi = 's' + sectionNum;
        turnTo = 's' + sectionNum + 'Index';
        objectHi = document.getElementById(chHi);
        object = document.getElementById(turnTo);
        objectHi.className = 'sectionHi';
        object.style.display = 'block';
        oldObject=object;
        oldObjectHi=objectHi; }
</script>
<style type="text/css">
body {
        font-family: Helvetica, Arial, sans-serif;
        font-size: 1em;
        background-color: #fff;
        color: #000; }
.col-A, .col-B{
        float: left;
        display: block; }
.col-A {
        position: relative;
        width: 50px;
        border-right: 2px solid #999;
        left: 2px; }
.col-B {
        width: 175px;
        border-left: 2px solid #666;
        background-color: #999; }
#menuIndex a {
        font-size: .7em;
        display: block;
        text-decoration: none;
        border-top: 1px solid #666;
        border-bottom: 1px solid #666;
        padding: 4px;
        background-color: #999;
        color: #CCFF33;
        margin-left: 2px; }
#menuIndex a:hover {
        font-size: .7em;
        display: block;
        text-decoration: none;
        border-top: 1px solid #666;
        border-bottom: 1px solid #666;
        padding: 4px;
        background-color: #666;
        color: #CCFF33; }
```

Code 23.5 *continued*

```
#menuIndex .col-A a, #menuIndex .col-A
→ a.sectionDim {
        position: relative;
        left: 2px;
        z-index: 100;
        text-align: right;
        border-right: 2px solid #666;
        background-color: #777;
        ; }
#menuIndex .col-A a:hover, #menuIndex .col-A
→ a.sectionDim:hover {
        border-right: 2px solid #f00;
        background-color: #ccc;
        color: #006600; }
#menuIndex .col-A a.sectionHi {
        border-right: 2px solid #999;
        background-color: #999;
        color: #CCFF33; }
.sIndex {
        display: none; }
.sIndex p {
        margin: 0px;
        padding: 0px;
        margin-left: 10px; }
#s00Index {
        display: block;
        padding: 8px; }
</style>
</head>
<body>
<div id="menuIndex">
<div class="col-A">
<a href="#s01Index" onclick="openChapter(1) "
→ id="s01" class="sectionNum">Part I</a>
<a href="#" onclick="openChapter(2)"
→ onfocus="if (this.blur) this.blur();"
→ id="s02" class="sectionNum">Part II</a>
        <a href="#" onclick="openChapter(3)"
        → onfocus="if (this.blur) this.blur();"
        → id="s03" class="sectionNum">Part
        → III</a>
</div>
<div class="col-B">
<div id="s00Index" class="sIndex">
<p>Choose a Part</p>
</div>
```

code continues on next page

8. `var oldObject=null;`

Initialize the variables:

▲ `oldObject` records the most recent menu object.

▲ `oldObjectHi` records the most recent menu-tab object.

9. `function openChapter(sectionNum) {…}`

Add the function `openChapter()` to your JavaScript.

This function takes the number of the menu to be shown and converts it into the right ID. It then checks to see if there is a menu currently selected (`oldObject`), hides it and unhighlights its tab (`oldObjectHi`). Finally, it shows the selected menu (`object`) and highlights its tab (`objectHi`).

10. `.col-A, .col-B{…}`

In your CSS, set up two columns using the float property. These will be used to place the tabs and menus next to each other.

continues on next page

CREATING A TAB MENU

Code 23.5 *continued*

```
<div id="s01Index" class="sIndex">
<a href="ch01.html" target="contentDisplay">Down The Rabbit-Hole</a><a href="ch02.html"
→ target="contentDisplay">The Pool of Tears</a><a href="ch03.html" target="contentDisplay">A
→ Caucus-Race and a Long Tale</a><a href="ch04.html" target="contentDisplay">The Rabbit Sends
→ in a Little Bill</a>
</div>
<div id="s02Index" class="sIndex">
<a href="ch05.html" target="contentDisplay">Advice from a Caterpillar</a><a href="ch06.html"
→ target="contentDisplay">Pig and Pepper</a><a href="ch07.html" target="contentDisplay">A Mad
→ Tea-Party</a>
</div>
<div id="s03Index" class="sIndex">
<a href="ch08.html" target="contentDisplay">The Queen's Croquet-Ground</a><a href="ch09.html"
→ target="contentDisplay">The Mock Turtle's Story</a><a href="ch10.html" target="contentDisplay">
→ The Lobster Quadrille</a><a href="ch11.html" target="contentDisplay">Who Stole The Tarts?</a>
→ <a href="ch12.html" target="contentDisplay">Alice's Evidence</a>
</div></div></div>
</body></html>
```

11. `#menuIndex a {…}`

Set the general style for links in the menu.

12. `#menuIndex .col-A a,`
`→ #menuIndex .col-A a.sectionDim {…}`

Set the style for the menu tabs, which are located in column A, including the various states. Also use these same styles to create a class called `.sectionDim` that will be used to dynamically unhighlight the tab in the `openChapter()` function.

13. `#menuIndex .col-A a.sectionHi {…}`

Set the style for the highlighted state of menu tabs, which will be dynamically assigned in the `openChapter()` function.

14. `.sIndex {…}`

Set a class used to style the sections, setting `display: none` to hide all menus when the page first loads.

15. `#s00Index {…}`

Set the style for the default content to be displayed when the page first loads. In this example, I'm adding a brief instructional message.

16. `onclick="openChapter(1);"`

In the `<body>`, set up the tab controls by adding an `onclick` event handler to an element—in this example a link element. The `onclick` triggers the `openChapter()` function, passing it the number of the menu to be shown.

17. `<div id="s01Index" class=`
`→ "sIndex">…</div>`

Set up the menu objects that will be switched on and off.

✔ Tip

■ The advantage of the tabbed list over the collapsible list is that the top-level controls stay in a fixed position rather than jumping around as the second level links are revealed, although the trade off is that it is less accessible without CSS.

Figure 23.10 The sliding menu tab is visible in the top left corner of the screen.

Figure 23.11 The menu is fully extended and can be used to navigate the site.

Creating Sliding Menus

Are you tired of sites that have the same old sidebar navigation? Are your menus taking more and more valuable screen real estate from the content? Are your pages cluttered with links that visitors need only when they're navigating, not when they're focusing on the content?

If you answered "yes" to any of these questions, I have a simple solution: Let visitors pull out or put away menus as needed.

In this example (**Figures 23.10** and **23.11**), a tab appears on the left side of the screen. When clicked, the menu slides out from the side of the screen and slides back when clicked again.

To set up a sliding menu:

1. `var open = 0;`

Initialize the variables (**Code 23.6**):

▲ open records whether the menu is open or closed.

▲ `slideSpeed` records how many pixels the menu should move in an animation cycle. The larger the number, the faster the menu appears to move.

▲ `object` records the object's address on the screen. This is initially set to `null`.

continues on next page

Code 23.6 The setMenu() function prepares the menu for the slideMenu() function, which animates the slide.

```
<!DOCTYPE html PUBLIC "-//W3C//DTD XHTML 1.0 Strict//EN" "http://www.w3.org/TR/xhtml1/DTD/
→ xhtml1-strict.dtd">
<html xmlns="http://www.w3.org/1999/xhtml">
<head>
<meta http-equiv="Content-Type" content="text/html; charset=utf-8" />
<title>CSS, DHTML &amp; Ajax | Creating a Sliding Menu</title>
<script type="text/javascript">
var open = 0;
var slideSpeed = 5;
var object = null;
```

code continues on next page

2. `function setMenu (objectID) {...}`

Add `setMenu()` to your JavaScript.

This function sets the starting (`cX`) and final (`fX`) points for the sliding menu, based on whether the menu is open or not. `cX` defines the current location of the left edge of the menu and is calculated based on the menu's width minus the width of the tab (`offsetWidth`).

When `cX` is –160, for example, the first 160 pixels of the menu are off the screen to the left. Only the menu tab, which is about another 20 pixels, is visible on the screen, and the menu is closed.

When `cX` is 0, the left edge of the menu is against the left edge of the window, and the menu is open. This function also resets the `open` variable to 0 (closed) if it was open, or 1 (open) if it was closed. The last thing it does is start the `slideMenu()` function.

3. `function slideMenu (cX,fX) {...}`

Add `slideMenu()` to your JavaScript.

This function first checks to see whether the current position (`cX`) is equal to the final position (`fX`). If so, the function stops running. If the positions are not the same, the function subtracts or adds a number of pixels (based on the `slideSpeed` variable set in Step 1) to `cX`, depending on whether the menu is opening or closing.

It also sets the left edge of the menu to this new position. The function then starts over with the new `cX` value. `slideMenu()` continues to loop this way until `cX` increases or decreases to equal `fX`, creating the illusion that the menu is sliding across the screen.

Code 23.6 *continued*

```
function setMenu (objectID) {
    object = document.getElementById
    → (objectID);
    if (open) {
        fX = 15 - (object.offsetWidth);
        cX = 0;
        open = 0;
    }
    else {
        fX = 0;
        cX = 15 - (object.offsetWidth);
        open = 1;
    }
    slideMenu(cX,fX); }
function slideMenu (cX,fX) {
        if ((open==0) && (cX > fX)) {
            cX -= slideSpeed;
            object.style.left = cX + 'px';
            setTimeout('slideMenu(' + cX +
            → ',' + fX + ')', 0);
        }
        else if ((open==1) && (cX < fX)) {
            cX += slideSpeed;
            object.style.left = cX + 'px';
            setTimeout('slideMenu(' + cX +
            → ',' + fX + ')', 0);
        }
    else return; }
</script>
<style type="text/css">
body { url(alice23.gif) no-repeat; }
h1 {
    font:small-caps bold italic 2.5em
    → Georgia, 'Times New Roman', times,
    → serif;
    color: red; }
h2 { color:#999; }
.page {
    position: relative;
    top: 190px;
    left: 165px;
    width: 480px; }
#menu01 {
    position: fixed;
    width: 175px;
    top: 0px;
    left: -160px; }
```

code continues on next page

Code 23.6 *continued*

```
.menuControl {
    width: 15px;
    float: right; }
.menuOptions {
    font-size: 12px;
    font-family: arial, Helvetica,
    → sans-serif;
    width: 158px;
    float: right;
    background-color: #ccc;
    border: 1px solid #999; }
.menuOptions a {
    display: block;
    text-decoration: none;
    padding: 4px 4px;
    color: red;
    border-bottom: 2px solid white; }
</style>
</head>
<body>
<div id="menu01">
<div class="menuControl"
→ onclick="setMenu('menu01')">
        <img src="menuTab.gif" height="100"
        → width="15" alt="Menu" /> </div>
<div class="menuOptions">
<a href="index.html" >Introduction</a>
→ <a href="ch01.html">Down The Rabbit-
→ Hole</a><a href="ch02.html">The Pool of
→ Tears</a><a href="ch03.html">A Caucus-
→ Race and a Long Tale</a><a href=
→ "ch04.html">The Rabbit Sends in a Little
→ Bill</a><a href="ch05.html">Advice from
→ a Caterpillar</a><a href="ch06.html">Pig
→ and Pepper</a><a href="ch07.html">A Mad
→ Tea-Party</a><a href="ch08.html">The
→ Queen's Croquet-Ground</a><a href=
→ "ch09.html">The Mock Turtle's Story</a>
→ <a href="ch10.html">The Lobster Quadrille</a>
→ <a href="ch11.html">Who Stole The
→ Tarts?</a><a href="ch12.html">Alice's
→ Evidence</a>
    </div></div>
<div class="page">
    <h1>ALICE'S ADVENTURES IN WONDERLAND</h1>
Lewis Carroll
    <h2>THE MILLENNIUM FULCRUM EDITION
→ 3.0</h2>
</div>
</body></html>
```

4. #menu01 {…}

Set up a CSS rule for the menu (or for each menu) that will be sliding around your page. You will want to set its position as absolute or fixed (depending on whether you care about earlier versions of Internet Explorer). You'll also want to set its left position so that the menuOptions area is off the screen to the left, but the menuControl (the tab) is peeping out.

5. .menuControl {…} .menuOptions {…}

Add classes to define the menuControl and menuOptions areas of your sliding menu. The width you set for the menuOptions (including any padding and borders) determines the left position you set for the menu (see Step 4).

6. <div class="menuControl" onclick=
→ "setMenu('navigation');">…</div>

In the body of the HTML, create the menu with an event handler used to trigger the sliding. You can put anything you want in the slideout (text, pictures, dynamic content, forms, etc.). I set up a menu of links.

continues on next page

CREATING SLIDING MENUS

✔ Tips

- You can set up as many menus as you want, each in its own `<div>` element and each with a unique ID. Make sure to move the top margin down for each menu so that it doesn't overlap the menu above it. You can use any type of content in the `<div>` elements—graphics, hypertext links, forms, and so on—to create your menus.

- What happens in earlier browsers that do not support CSS or DHTML depends on how you construct the HTML for the menu. In this example, the menu would simply appear above the page content.

- Not all visitors to your Web site will be using JavaScript. For more details on how to handle this, see the sidebar "Navigation for Nondynamic Browsers."

Navigation for Nondynamic Browsers

Almost everyone surfing the Web today uses a browser that supports JavaScript. But a few browsers don't support it, and some people turn JavaScript off in their browsers.

You still need to provide these Web surfers some basic navigation and possibly some content that you otherwise would include dynamically.

Simply use the `<noscript>` tag to hold content that is only to be seen if JavaScript is not available:

`<noscript>`

`Content for non-dynamic browser goes here`

`</noscript>`

The result is that browsers that do not support scripting languages ignore the `<noscript>` tags and display whatever is between them.

Figure 23.12 The links in the remote-control window target the main window.

Creating a Remote Control

Whether you are channel-surfing or Web-surfing, a remote control can make the experience more convenient and comfortable. On the Web, a remote control is a small browser window with links that change the content in the main browser window.

To set up a remote control (**Figure 23.12**), we will open a new browser window (see "Opening a New Browser Window" in Chapter 17) and place in it an HTML file with links that target the main browser window.

To create a remote control:

1. index.html

   Add the following code in the Web page(s) from which viewers will be able to open the remote control (**Code 23.7**). Steps 2 through 5 apply to this file.

continues on next page

Code 23.7 index.html: The openRemote() function can open an external window with a variety of sizes and uses.

```
<!DOCTYPE html PUBLIC "-//W3C//DTD XHTML 1.0
→ Strict//EN" "http://www.w3.org/TR/xhtml1/
→ DTD/xhtml1-strict.dtd">
<html xmlns="http://www.w3.org/1999/xhtml">
<head>
<meta http-equiv="Content-Type"
→ content="text/html; charset=utf-8" />
<title>CSS, DHTML &amp; Ajax | Creating a
→ Remote Control</title>
<script type="text/javascript">
var remote = null;
window.name = "content";
function openRemote(contentURL, windowName,
→ x, y) {
        widthHeight = 'height=' + y + ',width='
        → + x;
        remote = window.open(contentURL,
        → windowName, widthHeight);
        remote.focus(); }
</script>
<style type="text/css" media="screen">
body {
        font-size: 1em;
        font-family: Georgia, 'Times New
        → Roman', times, serif;
        color: #000000;
        margin: 8px;
        background: white url(alice23.gif)
        → no-repeat; }
```

Code 23.7 *continued*

```
h1 {
        font:small-caps bold italic 2.5em
        → Georgia, 'Times New Roman', times,
        → serif;
        color: red; }
h2 {
        color:#999; }
.page {
        position: relative;
        top: 190px;
        left: 165px;
        width: 480px; }
</style>
</head>
<body>
<div class="page">
<h1>ALICE'S ADVENTURES IN WONDERLAND</h1>
Lewis Carroll
<h2>THE MILLENNIUM FULCRUM EDITION 3.0</h2>
<a href="remote.html" onclick=
→ "openRemote(this.href,'remote',200,325);
→ return false;">Open Remote Control
→ </a></div>
</body></html>
```

2. `var remote = null;`

Initialize the variable **remote** to **null** to indicate that the remote is not open.

3. `window.name = "content";`

To target content back to this window, the window has to have a name. In this example, the main window is called **content**.

4. `function openRemote(contentURL,`
`→ windowName, x, y) {…}`

Add **openRemote()** to the JavaScript.

This function first checks to see whether the remote is open. If it is, the window is given focus so that it pops to the top of the screen. If it isn't already open, this function opens a new browser window that is x wide by y tall. This window is called **windowName**. The page to load is **contentURL**.

5. `<a href="remote.html" onclick=`
`→ "openRemote(this.href,'remote',`
`→ 200, 325); return false;">`

The function in Step 4 that opens the remote has to be triggered through an onclick handler on a link. The source file, window name, and dimensions of the new window need to be passed to the function.

6. `remote.html`

Create the file that will be used in the remote control window (**Code 23.8**). Steps 7 through 10 apply to this file.

7. `target="content"`

All links in the control page should target the main window (**content**, in this example).

8. `onload="window.moveTo(100, 100);"`

Add an **onload** event handler in the <body> element to move the new remote window to a specific position on the screen.

continues on Page 526

Code 23.8 `remote.html`: The controls change the content of the main window and also provide a link to close the remote window.

```html
<!DOCTYPE html PUBLIC "-//W3C//DTD XHTML 1.0 Strict//EN" "http://www.w3.org/TR/xhtml1/DTD/
→ xhtml1-strict.dtd">
<html xmlns="http://www.w3.org/1999/xhtml">
<head>
<meta http-equiv="Content-Type" content="text/html; charset=utf-8" />
<title>CSS, DHTML &amp; Ajax | Creating a Remote Control</title>
<style type="text/css" media="screen">
body {
    font-size: 1em;
    font-family: Georgia, 'Times New Roman', times, serif;
    color: #000000;
    margin: 0px; }
.menuOptions {
    width: 100%;
    font-size: 12px;
    font-family: arial, Helvetica, sans-serif;
    background-color: #ccc;
    border: 1px solid #999; }
.menuOptions a {
    display: block;
    text-decoration: none;
    padding: 4px 4px;
    color: red;
    border-bottom: 2px solid white;
    }
.remote {
    text-align: right;
    font-weight: bold;
    color: white;
    background-color: #666;
    padding-right: 8px;
    cursor: pointer; }
</style>
</head>
<body onload="window.moveTo(100,100);" onunload="if (opener) opener.remote = null;">
<div class="menuOptions">
<div class="remote" onclick="self.close;">Alice in Wonderland &times;</div>
<a href="index.html" target="content" onfocus="if (this.blur) this.blur();">Introduction</a>
→ <a href="ch01.html" target="content" >Down The Rabbit-Hole</a><a href="ch02.html" target=
→ "content" >The Pool of Tears</a><a href="ch03.html" target="content" >A Caucus-Race and a Long
→ Tale</a><a href="ch04.html" target="content" >The Rabbit Sends in a Little Bill</a><a href=
→ "ch05.html" target="content" >Advice from a Caterpillar</a><a href="ch06.html" target=
→ "content" >Pig and Pepper</a><a href="ch07.html" target="content" >A Mad Tea-Party</a><a href=
→ "ch08.html" target="content" >The Queen's Croquet-Ground</a><a href="ch09.html" target=
→ "content" >The Mock Turtle's Story</a><a href="ch10.html" target="content" >The Lobster
→ Quadrille</a><a href="ch11.html" target="content" >Who Stole The Tarts?</a><a href=
→ "ch12.html" target="content" >Alice's Evidence</a>
</div>
</body></html>
```

CREATING A REMOTE CONTROL

9. `onunload="if (opener) opener.remote =`
`→ null;"`

Add JavaScript to the `onunload` event handler in the `<body>` element to tell the originating window that the frame has closed by resetting the `remote` variable to `null`.

10. `onclick="self.close;"`

Add a control that allows the visitor to manually close the remote.

✔ Tips

- A remote control can contain anything you can put in an HTML document, but keep in mind that it has to fit into the dimensions you defined in the `openRemote()` function.

- Unlike a standard window, a remote window does not display menus, browser navigation (back and forward arrows), the current URL, or anything other than the basic border around the window. This border (called the *chrome*) does include the standard Close button in the top-right corner, so visitors can close the remote at any time.

- To open the remote, you have to run the `openRemote()` function. You can do this in several ways, such as having it open automatically when the main browser window opens (`onload`), although many browsers will block these "pop-ups." It is a good idea, therefore, to include a link that lets visitors reopen the remote if they close it, or to bring the remote to the front if it disappears behind another window.

CONTROLS

A truly dynamic Web site lets visitors interact with the pages by changing the content after it has loaded. You must provide controls that permit that interaction.

In this chapter, we'll explore how to create a few of the most common dynamic controls, such as page controls, scroll bars, style controls, and photo albums.

Providing Page Controls

Although vertical scrolling is a fact of life on the Web, most users would prefer to not spend their time running up and down the window. However, splitting your content over multiple HTML pages to shorten the height of those scrolls means the user has to wait between page loads.

A better solution is to use a simple DHTML technique to split the content of a single HTML file into multiple page layers, which you can then browse or jump between. All of these page layers are in the same HTML file, but only one is displayed at a time.

Paginating the content of a single Web page involves creating several layers using the ID attribute with DIV elements to create what we'll call "page layers" in this section.

Page layers appear to be distinct pages in the browser window, but they actually are all contained within a single HTML file (**Figure 24.1**). These page layers appear one at a time in the same space, with convenient controls to browse between pages (previous and next) or jump between distinct page numbers **(Figure 24.2)**.

To add pagination controls:

1. `pageControls.js`

   Start a new JavaScript file and save it as `pageControls.js` (**Code 24.1**). Steps 2 through 5 apply to this fie.

2. `var pageCurrent = 1;`

   Initialize two variables:

   ▲ `pageCurrent` holds the page layer that is currently being displayed.

   ▲ `objPage` holds the object node for the current page layer. Set this to `null` for now.

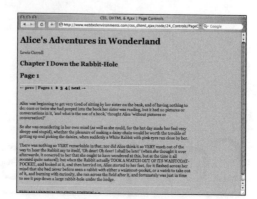

Figure 24.1 When the page first loads, Page 1 is displayed.

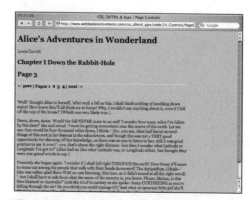

Figure 24.2 The visitor can flip through subsequent pages (without reloading) or jump immediately to a particular page.

3. function writePageControls() {…}

The function writePageControls() writes the pagination controls into each of the page layers, including a jump-to control (which uses the pageJump() function) for each of the page layers and next and previous controls (which use the pageTurn() function).

continues on next page

Code 24.1 pageControls.js: This file includes JavaScript functions used to control pagination.

```
var pageCurrent = 1; var objPage = null;
function writePageControls() {
    document.writeln ('<div class="toolBar">');
    if (pageCurrent!=1) document.writeln ('<a href="#" onclick="pageTurn(\'back\')">&larr; prev</a> | ');
    else document.writeln ('&larr; prev | ');
    document.writeln ('Pages ');
    for (i=1;i<=pageTotal;i++) {
        if (i==pageCurrent) document.write (i)
        else document.write ('<a href="#" onclick="pageJump('+i+')">'+i+'</a>');
        if (i!=pageTotal) document.write('  ');
    }
    if (pageCurrent!=pageTotal) document.writeln (' | <a href="#" onclick="pageTurn(\'next\')">next
    &rarr;</a>');
    else document.writeln (' | next &rarr;');
    document.writeln ('</div>');

    document.writeln (' <br style="clear:both"/>');

    if (pageCurrent==pageTotal) pageCurrent=1;
    else pageCurrent++; }
function pageTurn(direction) {
    if ((direction=='back') && (pageCurrent!=1)) pageCurrent--;
    if ((direction=='next') && (pageCurrent!=pageTotal)) pageCurrent++;
    if (objPage) objPage.style.display = 'none';
    pageName = 'page' + pageCurrent;
    objPage=document.getElementById(pageName);
    objPage.style.display = 'block'; }
function pageJump(pageName) {
    if(!pageName) pageName=1;
    if (objPage) objPage.style.display = 'none';
    pageCurrent = pageName;
    pageName = 'page' + pageCurrent;
    objPage=document.getElementById(pageName);
    objPage.style.display = 'block'; }
```

As an added bonus, these controls will be grayed out, depending on the page layer. So, for example, the control for the previous page and the jump to control for Page 1 will be grayed out (not clickable) on the first page layer.

4. `function pageTurn(direction) {…}`

The `pageTurn()` function uses a variable called `direction` to determine whether to go to the previous (`prev`) or `next` page layer.

5. `function pageJump(pageName) {…}`

The `pageJump()` function takes you directly to the page passed to it through the variable `pageName`.

6. `pageControlStyles.css`

Start a new CSS file and save it as `pageControlStyles.css` (**Code 24.2**). Steps 7 and 8 apply to this file.

7. `.page {…}`

Add the `.page` class to your style sheet, which will be used to control the appearance of each page layer within the Web page. Set the initial display for the `page` class to none, which will hide all of the page layers when the page first loads.

8. `.toolBar {…}`

The `.toolBar` class is used to style the pagination controls.

9. `index.html`

Start a new HTML file, which will contain your page layers, and save it as `index.html` (**Code 24.3**). Steps 10 through 16 apply to this file.

continues on Page 532

Code 24.2 `pageControlStyle.css`: Styles used to set up the pagination controls.

```
a {
     text-decoration: none;
     color: RGB(255,0,0); }
#content {
     display: block;
     width: 600px; }
#footer {
     display: block;
     border-top: 1px solid #fff;
     padding-top: 2px;
     margin-bottom: 8px;
     clear: both; }
.page { display: none; }
.toolBar {
     display: block;
     font-weight: bold;
     border-top: 1px solid #fff;
     padding-top: 2px;
     margin-bottom: 8px;
     clear: both; }
```

Code 24.3 index.html: The Web page where the pagination action all takes place. Although it is a single HTML file, it has been split into four different "pages."

```
<!DOCTYPE html PUBLIC "-//W3C//DTD XHTML 1.0 Strict//EN" "http://www.w3.org/TR/xhtml1/DTD/
→ xhtml1-strict.dtd">
<html xmlns="http://www.w3.org/1999/xhtml">
<head>
<meta http-equiv="Content-Type" content="text/html; charset=utf-8" />
<title>CSS, DHTML &amp; Ajax | Page Controls</title>
<script type="text/javascript">
     var pageTotal=4;
</script>
<script src="pageControls.js" type="text/javascript"></script>
<link rel="stylesheet" href="pageControlStyles.css" type="text/css" media="screen" />
</head>
<body onload="pageJump(1);">
<div id="header">
     <h1>Alice's Adventures in Wonderland</h1>
<span class="authorName">Lewis Carroll</span>
</div>
<div id="content">
<h2>Chapter I <span class="chapterTitle">Down the Rabbit-Hole</span></h2>
<div class="page" id="page1">
<h2>Page 1</h2>
<script type="text/javascript">
writePageControls();</script>
<p>Alice was beginning to get very tired of sitting by her sister on the bank…</p>
</div>
<div class="page" id="page2">
<h2>Page 2 </h2>
<script type="text/javascript">
writePageControls();</script>
<p>In another moment down went Alice after it, never once considering how in the world she was to
→ get out again.</p>
</div>
<div class="page" id="page3">
<h2>Page 3 </h2>
<script type="text/javascript">
writePageControls();</script>
<p>'Well!' thought Alice to herself, 'after such a fall as this, I shall think nothing of tumbling
→ down stairs…</p>
</div>
<div class="page" id="page4">
<h2>Page 4 </h2>
<script type="text/javascript">
writePageControls();</script>
<p>Down, down, down. There was nothing else to do, so Alice soon began talking again…</p>
</div>
<div id="footer">
<p>THE MILLENNIUM FULCRUM EDITION 3.0</p>
</div></div>
</body></html>
```

10. `.var pageTotal=4;`

In the <head> of that document, you will need to specify the number of page layers contained on that page as a JavaScript variable named `pageTotal`.

11. `<script src="pageControls.js"`
`→ type="text/javascript"></script>`

Import your external JavaScript from Step 1.

12. `<link rel="stylesheet"`
`→ href="pageControlStyles.css"`
`→ type="text/css" media="screen" />`

Link to your external style sheet from Step 6.

13. `onload="pageJump(1);"`

In the <body> tag, add an `onload` event handler that will flip to the first page using the `pageJump()` function from Step 5.

14. `<div class="page" id="page1">…</div>`

Finally, add your page content within the body, giving each layer the `.page` class from Step 7 and a unique ID (`page1`, `page2`, `page3`, etc...).

15. `<script type=`
`→ "text/javascript">…</script>`

Before the content but after the page header, add a <script> tag.

16. `writePageControls();`

Within the <script> tag from Step 15, include a function call for the `writePageControls()` from Step 3. This will place the correct pagination controls for each layer.

✔ Tips

- Using a single file with its content split between multiple page layers also makes the job of printing all the content a lot easier than if we had split it across multiple HTML files. It also lets us have a single URL, which provides users a quick and easy way to send the file to friends.

- One little trick I used in the code to avoid having to create graphic arrows, was to use the HTML character entities for the left (←) and right (→) arrow symbols.

Figure 24.3 The controls let the visitor scroll up or down the page, jump to the bottom, and jump back to the top.

Figure 24.4 The header will always stay in a fixed place.

Creating Scroll Bars for a Layer

Without scroll bars, a GUI would be about as useful as a car without a steering wheel. Scroll bars let you place an infinite amount of information in a finite space and move that information around as needed. Because the computer's operating system defines the look and feel of the scroll bars, however, they often limit the design of Web interfaces.

Still, if you can animate a layer (see "Animating an Object" in Chapter 17), then you can scroll the layer up and down (**Figures 24.3** and **24.4**).

continues on next page

To set up scroll bars:

1. `index.html`

Create a frameset file, and save it as `index.html` (**Code 24.4**). Set up two frame columns (**Figure 24.5**).

The first column (named `scrollBar`) is a narrow frame containing the source `scrollBar.html`; the second (named `contentFrame`) contains the file `content.html`.

2. `scrollBar.html`

Create an HTML file, and save it as `scrollBar.html` (**Code 24.5**). This file will contain the scroll bar controls. Steps 3 through 13 apply to this file.

3. `var scrolling = 0;`

Add a JavaScript block to scrollBar.html, and initialize the following variables:

▲ `scrolling` sets whether the layer is currently scrolling.

▲ `yT` records the current top position of the scrolling layer.

▲ `lT` sets the initial position of the top of the layer.

▲ `yI` sets the increment by which the scrolling layer should move. You can change this number as desired. The higher the number, the faster the layer scrolls, but the choppier its movement.

▲ `yH` records the height of the layer.

▲ `object` records the address for the scrolling layer to access its properties.

4. `function startScroll(objectID,`
`→ frameName, direction) {…}`

Add `startScroll()` to the JavaScript.

This function sets `scrolling` to 1 (on), identifies the current location of the top of the layer (yT), the height of the layer (–25, to leave a margin at the bottom), and then triggers the `scroll()` function.

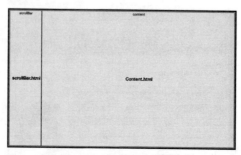

Figure 24.5 The frameset used to hold `scrollBar.html` (left frame) and the pages (right frame).

Code 24.4 `index.html`: This file sets up two frame columns: a narrow column on the left for the scroll bar, and the rest of the space to hold the content.

```
<!DOCTYPE html PUBLIC "-//W3C//DTD XHTML 1.0
→ Frameset//EN" "http://www.w3.org/TR/
→ xhtml1/DTD/xhtml1-frameset.dtd">
<html xmlns="http://www.w3.org/1999/xhtml">
<head>
<meta http-equiv="Content-Type"
→ content="text/html; charset=utf-8" />
<title>CSS, DHTML &amp; Ajax | Creating
→ Scrollbars for a Layer</title>
</head>
<frameset cols="35,*">
    <frame src="scrollBar.html"
    → name="scrollBar" scrolling="no"
    → noresize="noresize" marginwidth="0"
    → marginheight="0" id="scrollBar" />
    <frame src="content.html"
    → name="contentFrame" scrolling="no"
    → noresize="noresize"
    → id="contentFrame" />
</frameset></html>
```

continues on Page 536

Code 24.5 scrollBar.html: This file contains JavaScript for scrolling layers, goes in the scrollBar frame. The scroll() function animates the scrollArea in the content frame, and URT() and URB() take it to the top or bottom.

```
<!DOCTYPE html PUBLIC "-//W3C//DTD XHTML 1.0
→ Strict//EN" "http://www.w3.org/TR/xhtml1/
→ DTD/xhtml1-strict.dtd">
<html xmlns="http://www.w3.org/1999/xhtml">
<head>
<meta http-equiv="Content-Type"
→ content="text/html; charset=utf-8" />
<title>CSS, DHTML &amp; Ajax | Creating
→ Scrollbars for a Layer</title>
<script type="text/javascript">
var scrolling = 0;
var yT = 100;
var lT = 100;
var yI = 15;
var yH = 0;
var object = null;

function startScroll(objectID, frameName,
→ direction) {
    object = top[frameName].document.
    → getElementById(objectID);
    scrolling = 1;
    yT = object.style.top;
    pxLoc = yT.indexOf('px');
    if (pxLoc >= 1) yT =
    → yT.substring(0,pxLoc);
    yH = document.body.clientHeight -
    → object.offsetHeight - 25;
    scroll(direction);
}

function scroll(direction) {
    if (scrolling == 1) {
        if ((direction == 1) && (yT <= lT)) {
            yT = (yT/1) + yI;
            if (yT > lT) yT = lT;
            object.style.top = yT + 'px'; }
        else {
            if ((direction == 0) && (yT >=
            → yH)) {
                yT -= yI;
                if (yT < yH) yT = yH;
                object.style.top = yT + 'px'; }
        }
        yT = object.style.top;
        pxLoc = yT.indexOf('px');
        if (pxLoc >= 1) yT =
        → yT.substring(0,pxLoc);
        code2run = 'scroll('+ direction + ')';
```

Code 24.5 *continued*

```
        setTimeout(code2run,0);
    }
    return false; }
function stopScroll() {
    scrolling = 0;
    return false; }


function URB(objectID, frameName) {
    var object = top[frameName].document.
    → getElementById(objectID);
    yH = document.body.clientHeight -
    → object.offsetHeight - 25;
    object.style.top = yH +'px'; }


function URT(objectID, frameName) {
    var object = top[frameName].document.
    → getElementById(objectID);
    object.style.top = lT + 'px'; }
</script>
<style type="text/css" media="screen">
body {
    background: white url(images/
    → bg_scroll.gif) repeat-y 33px 30px;
    margin-left: 3px; }
a { text-decoration: none; }
</style>
</head><body>
<div onmousedown="startScroll('content',
→ 'contentFrame', 1); return false;"
→ onmouseup="stopScroll();" onmouseover=
→ "window.status='Up'; return true;"> <img
→ id="up" src="images/up_off.gif" height="25"
→ width="25" alt="Up" /> </div>
<div onmousedown="URT('content',
→ 'contentFrame'); return false;"
onmouseover="window.status='Top'; return
→ true;"> <img id="top" src="images/
→ top_off.gif" height="25" width="25"
→ alt="Top" /> </div>
<div onmousedown="URB('content',
→ 'contentFrame'); return false;"
→ onmouseover="window.status='Bottom';
→ return true;" > <img id="bottom"
→ src="images/bottom_off.gif" height="25"
→ width="25" alt="Bottom" /> </div>
<div onmousedown="startScroll('content',
→ 'contentFrame',0); return false;" onmouseup=
→ "stopScroll();" onmouseover="window.status=
→ 'Down'; return true;" > <img id="down"
→ src="images/down_off.gif" height="25"
→ width="25" alt="Down" /></div>
</body></html>
```

5. `function scroll(direction) {…}`

Add `scroll()` to the JavaScript. This function moves the layer up or down incrementally based on the variable yI from Step 3. The direction depends on the `direction` variable: 1 for up, 0 for down. The function will continue to run while `scrolling` is equal to 1.

6. `function stopScroll() {…}`

Add `stopScroll()` to the JavaScript. The function sets the variable `scrolling` to 0 (off), stopping the layer from scrolling.

7. `function URB(objectID, frameName) {…}`

Add `URB()` to the JavaScript. This function scrolls instantly to the bottom of the page (moves the bottom of the layer to the bottom of the window).

8. `function URT(objectID, frameName) {…}`

Add `URT()` to the JavaScript. This function scrolls instantly to the top of the window (moves the top of the layer to the top of the window).

9. `startScroll('content',`
`→ 'contentFrame', 1); return false;`

The controls have to be set up in the HTML in `<div>` tags with event handlers. To add a scroll-up event, trigger `startScroll()` with the `onmousedown` event handler. Pass the function the ID of the object to be scrolled, the name of the frame that contains the object, and a 1 (up).

10. `startScroll('content',`
`→ 'contentFrame', 0);`

Trigger `startScroll()` with the event handler `onmousedown`. Pass the function the ID of the object to be scrolled, the name of the frame that contains the object, and a 0 for down.

11. `stopScroll()`

To stop the layer from scrolling, use the `stopScroll()` function with the event handler `onmouseup`.

Code 24.6 content.html: This file goes into the content frame and contains the scrollArea layer, which is scrolled from the scrollBar frame.

```
<!DOCTYPE html PUBLIC "-//W3C//DTD XHTML 1.0
→ Strict//EN" "http://www.w3.org/TR/xhtml1/
→ DTD/xhtml1-strict.dtd">
<html xmlns="http://www.w3.org/1999/xhtml">
<head>
<meta http-equiv="Content-Type"
→ content="text/html; charset=utf-8" />
<title>CSS, DHTML &amp; Ajax | Creating
→ Scrollbars for a Layer</title>
<link href="default.css" media="screen"
→ rel="stylesheet" type="text/css" />
</head>
<body>
<div id="header">
      <h1>Alice's Adventures in
      → Wonderland</h1>
      <span class="authorName">Lewis
      → Carroll</span>
</div>
<div id="content">
<h2>Chapter I <span class="chapterTitle">
'→ Down the Rabbit-Hole</span></h2>
<div class="dropBox"> <img src=
→ "images/alice02a.gif" alt="The White
→ Rabbit" height="270" width="180" />
      <p>'Oh dear! Oh dear! I shall be
      → late!'</p>
</div>
<div class="copy">
      <p>Alice was beginning to get very
      → tired of sitting by her sister on
      → the bank…</p>
<h2>The End</h2>
</div></div>
</body></html>
```

12. **URT('content', 'contentFrame')**

    To get to the top of the layer, trigger the URT() function, and pass it the ID of the object and the name of the frame that contains the object.

13. **URB('content', 'contentFrame')**

    To get to the bottom of the layer, use the URB() function, and pass it the ID of the object and the name of the frame that contains the object.

14. content.html

    Create an HTML file, and save it as "content.html" (**Code 24.6**). This file will contain the layer that is being scrolled. Steps 15 and 16 apply to this file.

15. **<link href="default.css"**
    → media="screen" rel="stylesheet"
    → type="text/css" />

    Link to an external style sheet to provide the layout for your page.

16. **<div id="content">…</div>**

    Set up the scrollArea layer in a <div> element (see "Setting up an Object" in Chapter 12).

✔ Tips

- I added a simple graphic-toggling function to this example so the controls will appear to light up when clicked.

- You can also place the controls in the same HTML file as the layer (content.html) and then take out the frame reference when you're using getElementById.

- *URT* stands for *ubiquitous return to top,* and *URB* stands for—you guessed it— *ubiquitous return to bottom.* Unlike most return-to-top buttons on most Web pages, these controls are always available.

Adding Style Controls

You may be the designer, but that doesn't mean that everybody is going to like your style. Why not provide your visitors with alternative looks and/or layouts for your Web page? Building on what you learned about disabling style sheets in "Disabling or Enabling a Style Sheet" in Chapter 18, we can do just that.

In this example, four buttons are presented across the top of the page (**Figure 24.6**) The visitor can click one of these at any time, to choose between three alternate styles for the page design (**Figure 24.7**).

To set up style controls for a page:

1. `styleControls.js`

   Save a new external JavaScript file called `styleControls.js` (**Code 24.7**). Steps 2 through 5 apply to this file.

2. `var styleNames = ['style1',`
   `→ 'style2', 'style3'];`

   Initialize the following variables:

   ▲ `styleName[]` is an array with the IDs of the style sheets being used in the HTML.

   ▲ `oldStyle` is used to hold the name of the previous style used so that it can be disabled before enabling the new style.

3. `function initStyles() {…}`

   Add the function `initStyles()`, which is used to loop through the array of style IDs and disable all of the style sheets on the page except for the default style sheet.

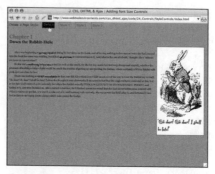

Figure 24.6 The default style for the page.

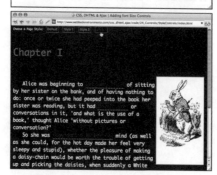

Figure 24.7 The three alternate styles (style1, style2, and style3).

Code 24.7 styleControl.js: The styles are initially set and changed by functions in this file.

```
var styleNames = ['style1', 'style2', 'style3'];
var oldStyle = null;
function initStyles() {
    for (var i = 0; i < styleNames.length;
    → i++) {
        styleObject =
        → document.getElementById
        → (styleNames[i]);
        styleObject.disabled = true;
    }
}
function setStyle(newStyle) {
    if (oldStyle) oldStyle.disabled = true;
    if (newStyle != 'default') {
        var styleObject =
        → document.getElementById(newStyle);
        styleObject.disabled = false;
        oldStyle = styleObject;
    }
    else oldStyle=null; }
window.onload = initStyles;
```

4. function setStyle(newStyle) {…}

Add the function setStyle(), which disables the previous style (if there was one) and then enables the selected newStyle.

5. window.onload = initStyles;

Add a function call for initStyles(). This will cause the function to run as soon as the script loads, which works better than having an onload event handler in the <body> tag.

6. default.css

Create a new external CSS file and save it as default.css (**Code 24.8**). This style sheet will always be applied to the Web page, providing the general styles for the page.

continues on next page

Code 24.8 default.css: The default style sheet that will always be applied to the page.

```
.dropBox {
    float: right;
    padding: 4px;
    margin: 4px;
    background-color: white;
    border: 2px solid #666; }
.dropBox img { display: block; }
h2 {
    padding-bottom: 0px;
    margin-bottom: 0px;
    color: #666; }
h2 .chapterTitle {
    display: block;
    font-size: smaller;
    color: black; }
p a {
    color: #f33;
    text-decoration: none;
    padding-bottom: 0px; }
p a:link {
    color: #f33;
    border-bottom: 2px dotted #fcc; }
#content .copy {
    margin-top: 24px; }
```

Code 24.8 *continued*

```
#content .copy p {
    font-size: smaller;
    line-height: 1.5;
    margin: 0px;
    text-indent: 2em; }
.dropBox p {
    margin: 0px;
    padding: 0px;
    width: 175px;
    font: x-large "Party Let", "Comic Sans
    → MS", Helvetica, Arial, sans-serif; }
.styleControl {
    color: #666;
    font-family: Arial, Helvetica,
    → sans-serif;
    font-weight: bold;
    text-decoration: none;
    margin: 0px 5px 0px 5px;
    border: 1px solid #666;
    padding: 4px; }
.styleControl:hover{
    color: #f00;
    border: 1px solid #666;
    background-color: #300; }
```

7. `style1.css, style2.css, style3.css`

   Create as many alternate style sheets as you want (**Codes 24.9**, **24.10**, and **24.11**). These files can contain any CSS you want to completely restyle the page. In this example, I've kept it simple by changing some styles for the `<body>` element. However, you can completely change the look and layout of your Web site. Remember that any style you add to the `default.css` that you want changed in an alternate style will have to be included to be overridden.

8. `index.html`

   Save a new HTML file as index.html (**Code 24.12**). Steps 9 through 14 apply to this file.

9. `<link href="css/default.css"` → `rel="stylesheet" type="text/css"` → `media="all" />`

   Add a link to the default style sheet (`default.css`), which provides the core styles for the page. These styles can be overridden by the alternate style sheets from Step 7.

Code 24.9 `style1.css`: The first alternate style sheet.

```
body {
    font-size: 1.2em;
    font-family: Georgia, "Times New
    → Roman", times, serif;
    color: #000000;
    background-color: #999;
    margin: 8px; }
```

Code 24.10 `style2.css`: The second alternate style sheet.

```
body {
    font-size: .9em;
    font-family: sans-serif;
    color: #999;
    background-color: #fff;
    margin: 8px; }
```

Code 24.11 `style3.css`: The third alternate style sheet.

```
body {
    font-size: 1.5em;
    font-family: monospace;
    color: #fff;
    background-color: #000;
    margin: 8px; }
h2 .chapterTitle {
    font-size: larger;
    color: black; }
```

Code 24.12 `index.html`: All three alternate style sheets are imported into the page, but they are disabled until needed.

```
<!DOCTYPE html PUBLIC "-//W3C//DTD XHTML 1.0 Strict//EN" "http://www.w3.org/TR/xhtml1/DTD/xhtml1-
strict.dtd">
<html xmlns="http://www.w3.org/1999/xhtml">
<head>
<meta http-equiv="Content-Type" content="text/html; charset=utf-8" />
<title>CSS, DHTML &amp; Ajax | Adding font Size Controls</title>
<link href="css/default.css" rel="stylesheet" type="text/css" media="all" />
<style id="style1" type="text/css" >
@import url(css/style1.css);
</style>
<style id="style2" type="text/css" >
@import url(css/style2.css);
</style>
```

code continues on next page

ADDING STYLE CONTROLS

Code 24.12 *continued*

```
<style id="style3" type="text/css" >
@import url(css/style3.css);
</style>
<script type="text/javascript"
src="styleControls.js"></script>
</head>
<body>
<div id="controls" style="font: bold
→ 10px/10px monospace;">
Choose a Page Style:
<div onclick="setStyle('default')" class=
→ "styleControl" style="font-size: 12px">
→ Default</div>
<div onclick="setStyle('style1')" class=
→ "styleControl" style="font-size: 12px">
→ Style 1</div>
<div onclick="setStyle('style2')" class=
→ "styleControl" style="font-size: 12px">
→ Style 2</div>
<div onclick="setStyle('style3')" class=
→ "styleControl" style="font-size: 12px">
→ Style 3</div> <br style="clear:both" />
</div>
<div id="content">
<h2>Chapter I <span class="chapterTitle">
→ Down the Rabbit-Hole</span> </h2>
<div class="dropBox"> <img src=
→ "alice02a.gif" alt="The White Rabbit"
height="270" width="180" />
<p>'Oh dear! Oh dear! I shall be late!'</p>
</div>
<div class="copy">
<p>Alice was beginning to <a href="#1">get
→ very tired</a> of sitting by her sister
→ on the bank...</p>
</div></div>
</body></html>
```

10. `<style id="style1"`
`→ type="text/css">…</style>`

For each of your alternate styles, set up a `<style>` block with an ID corresponding to one of the IDs you specified in the array from Step 2.

11. `@import url(css/style1.css);`

Within each of the `<style>` tags from Step 10, add `@import` with the `url` pointing to the relevant external CSS file from Step 7.

12. `<script type="text/javascript"`
`→ src="styleControls.js"></script>`

Add a call to your external JavaScript file from Step 1.

13. `<div id="controls" style="font: bold"`
`→ 10px/10px monospace;">...</div>`

Add a control layer to your page, setting the font declaration inline so that the changes in the page style do not make the controls shift around.

14. `<div onclick="setStyle('style1')"`
`→ class="styleControl" style="font-`
`→ size: 12px">Style 1</div>`

Add controls used to enable any of the alternate styles. This uses the function from Step 4, passing it the ID for the style to be used (`setStyle('style1')`).

ADDING STYLE CONTROLS

Putting Together a Photo Album

If you want to show a series of photos (or other content) that would be too large to fit on the screen at full size, then you need to use a photo album. A photo album shows thumbnail photos that, when clicked, reveal the full-size version (**Figures 24.8, 24.9,** and **24.10**). The photo slide is presented in the center of the window, with the page behind grayed out until the visitor clicks the photo slide to close it. They can then choose another photo from the thumbnails to view.

To set up a photo album:

1. slideControls.js

   Create a new external JavaScript file, and save it as slideControls.js (**Code 24.13**). Steps 2 through 6 apply to this file.

2. function findLivePageWidth() {…}

   Add the function findLivePageWidth(), which is described in details in Chapter 13.

3. function initSlides() {…}

   Add the function initSlide(), which identifies the objects on the page you will be changing to create your slide show.

Figure 24.8 The photo album loads showing the thumbnails.

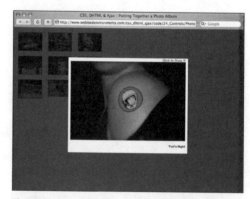

Figure 24.9 Clicking a thumbnail opens the full size version.

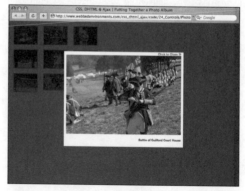

Figure 24.10 You can close and open as many slides as you want.

4. `function showSlide(evt) {…}`

Add the function `showSlide()`.

This function takes the triggering event (`evt`) and then places an image tag into the `#photoSlide` layer with the triggering objects (the thumbnail version of the photo) source as its source (`evt.src`) and the `alt` attribute (`evt.alt`) as its caption. It then places the `#slide` layer, with the photo in it, in the center of the screen and turns it on along with the `#cover` layer. Because the width and height are not defined, the image will appear at its normal size.

5. `function hideSlide() {…}`

Add the function `hideSlide()`, which when triggered, will hide the `#slide` layer and the `#cover` layer.

continues on next page

Code 24.13 `slideControls.js`: The external JavaScript file used to push the larger version of the image onto the page and then hide it when the visitor is finished.

```javascript
function findLivePageWidth() {
    if (window.innerWidth)
        return window.innerWidth;
    if (document.body.clientWidth)
        return document.body.clientWidth;
    return (null); }
function initSlides() {
    objectSlide=document.getElementById('slide');
    objectCover=document.getElementById('cover');
    objectPhotoSlide=document.getElementById('photoSlide'); }
function showSlide(evt) {
    objectPhotoSlide.innerHTML='<img src="' + evt.src +'" id="largePhoto" alt="Large Photo"
    → border="0" />';
    objectPhotoSlide.innerHTML+='<p>' + evt.alt +'</p>';
    objectLargePhoto=document.getElementById('largePhoto');
    livePageWidth = findLivePageWidth();
    newLeft = ((livePageWidth/2)-8) - (200);
    objectSlide.style.left = newLeft + 'px';
    objectSlide.style.display = 'block';
    objectCover.style.display = 'block'; }
function hideSlide() {
    objectSlide.style.display = 'none';
    objectCover.style.display = 'none'; }

window.onload=initSlides;
```

6. `window.onload=initSlides;`

Add a window onload event handler that will trigger the `initSlide()` function from Step 3.

7. `slideStyles.css`

Create a new external CSS file called **slideStyles.css** (**Code 24.14**). Steps 7 through 11 apply to this file.

8. `#slide {…}`

Add the `#slide` ID rule to your CSS. This creates the "slide frame" that the`<img>` element for the large version of the slide will be put into. It will need to be absolutely positioned (`position: absolute`), with a high z-index (`z-index:1000`), and a display setting of none (`display:none`) when the page loads. Other than that, the style is up to you.

9. `#cover {…}`

Add the `#cover` ID rule to your CSS. This will fill the entire browser window, and is used to provide a background for the slide while also disabling all controls on the screen until the slide is closed. It will need to be absolutely positioned (`position:absolute`), filling the entire screen (`width:100%; height:100%`), a z-index lower than the `#slide` layer but higher than the `#photoAlbum` (`z-index:100`), and not displayed when the page first loads (`display:none`). It also helps to make the layer transparent, so that the page underneath is visible but clearly disabled (`opacity: .75`).

10. `#photoAlbum {…}`

Add the `#photoAlbum` ID to your CSS. This layer is used to hold the photo thumbnails, and should have a z-index lower than the other layers (`position:relative; z-index:0`).

Code 24.14 `slideStyles.css`: The styles used to create the thumbnails, cover, and slide for the photo album. The cover is actually just a layer used to darken the page while a slide is being viewed.

```
#slide {
     position: absolute;
z-index: 1000;
display: none;
     top: 100px;
     text-align: right;
     padding: 0px 8px 8px 8px;
     background-color: #fff;
     cursor: pointer;
     font: bold 10px "helvetica neue",
   → Arial, Helvetica, sans-serif; }
#cover {
     position: absolute;
width: 100%;
height: 100%;
z-index: 100;
display: none;
     background-color: #000;
     opacity: .75;
filter:progid:DXImageTransform.
→ Microsoft.BasicImage(opacity=.75);
     top: 0px;
     left: 0px; }
#photoAlbum {
     position: relative;
z-index: 0;
     width: 400px; }
#photoAlbum img {
     width: 20%;
     border: 2px solid red;
     margin: 8px;
     vertical-align: top; }
.slideControl { color: red; }
```

PUTTING TOGETHER A PHOTO ALBUM

Code 24.15 `index.html`: The photo album page with thumbnail images in place.

```
<!DOCTYPE html PUBLIC "-//W3C//DTD XHTML 1.0
→ Strict//EN" "http://www.w3.org/TR/xhtml1/
→ DTD/xhtml1-strict.dtd">
<html xmlns="http://www.w3.org/1999/xhtml">
<head>
<meta http-equiv="Content-Type"
→ content="text/html; charset=utf-8" />
<title>CSS, DHTML &amp; Ajax | Putting
→ Together a Photo Album</title>
<script src="slideControls.js" type=
→ "text/javascript"></script>
<link href="slideStyles.css" rel=
→ "stylesheet" type="text/css"
→ media="screen" />
</head>
<body>
<div id="cover"> </div>
<div id="slide" onclick="hideSlide()">
<span class="slideControl">Click to Close
→ &otimes;</span>
<div id="photoSlide">Loading</div>
</div>
<div id="photoAlbum">
<img src="photos/photo-1.jpg" alt="World's
→ Fair" onclick="showSlide(this);" />
<img src="photos/photo-2.jpg" alt="Video
→ Wall" onclick="showSlide(this);" />
<img src="photos/photo-3.jpg" alt="Dragon"
→ border="0" onclick="showSlide(this)" />
<img src="photos/photo-4.jpg" alt="The
→ answer is 42" border="0" onclick=
→ "showSlide(this)" />
<img src="photos/photo-5.jpg" alt="Manaquin"
→ border="0" onclick="showSlide(this)" />
<img src="photos/photo-6.jpg" alt="Griffen"
→ border="0" onclick="showSlide(this)" />
<img src="photos/photo-7.jpg" alt="Mermaid"
→ border="0" onclick="showSlide(this)" />
<img src="photos/photo-8.jpg" alt="Battle of
→ Guilford Court House" border="0"
onclick="showSlide(this)" />
<img src="photos/photo-9.jpg" alt="Yuri's
→ Night" border="0"
→ onclick="showSlide(this)" />
</div>
</body></html>
```

11. `#photoAlbum img {…}`

    Specify the style for images used within the `#photoAlbum` layer as the thumbnail versions of the photos. For this example, I've set each image to be smaller than the original (`width:20%`). However, the percentage sets the final size of the thumbnail based on the width of the `#photoAlbum` layer rather than the natural size of the original image.

12. `index.html`

    Create a new HTML file and save it as index.html (**Code 24.15**). Steps 12 through 19 apply to this file.

13. `<script src="slideControls.js"`
    `→ type="text/javascript"></script>`

    Add a call to the external JavaScript file `slideControls.js` that you set up starting in Step 1.

14. `<link href="slideStyles.css"`
    `→ rel="stylesheet" type="text/css"`
    `→ media="screen" />`

    Add a link to the external style sheet `slideStyles.css` you set up starting with Step 7.

15. `<div id="cover"> </div>`

    Add your `#cover` layer, which you set the style for in Step 8.

16. `<div id="slide" onclick=`
    `→ "hideSlide();">…</div>`

    Add the `#slide` layer, which you set up in Step 8 with an `onclick` event handler to trigger the `hideSlide()` function from Step 5. In this example, I also added some instructional text to let the visitor know to click the slide to close it.

    continues on next page

17. `<div id="photoSlide">Loading</div>`

Within the #slide layer, add the #photoSlide layer. The function showSlide() from Step 4 will place an image tag within this layer for the triggering photograph.

18. `<div id="photoAlbum">...</div>`

Add the #photoAlbum layer to your HTML. The photo thumbnails will be in this layer.

19. `<img src="photos/photo-1.jpg"`
`→ alt="World's Fair"`
`→ onclick="showSlide(this);" />`

Within the #photoAlbum layer, add the image tags for the photos in your gallery, including the source, an alternative description (used as the caption in the slide), and an onclick event handler to trigger the showSlide() function from Step 4, passing it this event.

✔ Tips

- DHTML slide shows can contain any HTML code you want, not just images.

- Notice that the thumbnails and the full size versions both use the same image file, which speeds the final loading of the image since it will already be cached, although it will delay the initial display.

- If you have a lot of large images and are worried about downloading full size versions for each of the thumbnails, you can create smaller thumbnail versions to use on the page and then simply place the full size versions (using the exact same file name) in a sub-directory, adding the directory name into the source call used to add the <img> tag placed in the showSlide() function in Step 4.

INDEX

Symbols and numbers

. (period), 38, 40
: (colon), 25
; (semicolon), 28
* (asterisk), 52
~ (tilde), 55
| (bar), 55
" (quotation marks), xix, 25, 252
{ } (curly brackets), 28, 36, 38
< > (chevrons), xvi, 50
(number sign), xvii, 42, 43
= (equal sign), 25, 54, 55
+ (plus sign), 51
3D positioning, 209–211
   finding for objects, 334–335
   moving objects using, 365–367

A

abbreviations, browser, xviii
absolute length values, xvi
absolute positioning, 200, 202, 521
accessibility issues, 427, 509
accesskey attribute, 509
:active pseudo-class, 60, 61, 475
active link borders, 504
ActiveX controls, 271–272
addStyleDef() function, 406–407
addStyleDefIE() function, 408–409
adjacent sibling selectors, 48, 51
adjacent siblings, 48
Adobe Flash. See Flash
:after pseudo-element, 71–72
Airgrid, Kevin, 281

Ajax, xiii, 417–449
   acronym for, 419
   advantages of, 425–426
   APIs and design patterns, 449
   components of, 420–421
   disadvantages of, 426–427
   fetching responses in, 439–442
   fetching server data in, 436–438
   filtering data in, 443–446
   function library setup, 447–449
   general overview of, 418–421
   how it works, 422–424
   importing content using, 482–485
   methods used in, 435
   other uses of word, 418
   process flow for, 424–425
   properties used in, 435
   reasons for using, 425–426
   Rich Internet Applications and, 431
   server requests in, 434–435
   user experience and, 424
   Web 2.0 and, 429, 431
Ajax Patterns wiki, 449
ajaxBasics.js file, 447, 449, 484, 488, 493, 499
align property, 212
aligning text
   horizontally, 124–125
   vertically, 126–128
All DOM, 287
Almost Standards mode, 21
altKey property, 346, 347
analogic color scheme, 144
Anderson, Chris, 429
animateObject() function, 380, 381
animateObjectCircle() function, 383

animateSpeed variable, 380, 382
animating objects, 379–383
  in a circle, 382–383
  in a straight line, 379–381
annoyingFlash() function, 377–378
APIs (Application Programming Interfaces),
    420, 421, 449
apparent width/height, 162, 163
Asynchronous JavaScript and XML. *See* Ajax
attribute selectors, 53–55
attributes
  defining selectors based on, 53
  setting styles based on, 54–55
author class, 146
auto value
  mouse pointer appearance, 230
  overflow control, 225
autoClose variable, 510
automatic table layout, 234, 235

B

background property, 148, 154, 156
  frame borders and, 477, 478, 480
  header styling and, 464
background-attachment property, 152
background-color property, 147, 148–149
background-image property, 151–153
background-position property, 153
background-repeat property, 152, 153
backgrounds
  color settings for, 141, 147–149, 156
  headlines with graphic, 463–464
  image settings for, 150–153, 156
  multiple value settings for, 154–158
:before pseudo-element, 71–72
Berners-Lee, Tim, 418
bidi-override value, 138
blinking text, 133, 135
block elements, 167–168
block value, 164, 167–168
block-level tags, 18
<body> tag, 25, 37
  color settings, 146
  margin settings, 173, 203
  positioning and, 203
bolded fonts, 106–107
book support Web site, xiii, xxi
border property, 140, 174–176
border-bottom property, 135

border-collapse property, 238–239
border-color property, 176
border-radius property, 180
borders, 161, 174
  active link, 504
  collapsing in tables, 238–239
  color used for, 142
  creating for frames, 477–480
  finding for objects, 336–340
  form elements and, 472
  Mozilla browsers and, 177–180
  rounding corners of, 177–180
  setting for elements, 161, 174–176, 177
  spacing in tables, 236–237
  styles used for, 477–480
border-spacing property, 236–237
border-style property, 176
border-width property, 176
Bos, Bert, 8
bottom positioning, 207–208
bottom property, 207–208
boxes, 159
  limits of "box" model, 162–163
  properties of, 161
  See also elements
box-shadow property, 123
browser window
  mouse pointer appearance in, 228
  opening/closing new windows from,
      392–395
  positioning on the screen, 396–397
  scrolling Web pages in, 400–402
  sizing and resizing, 398–399
  width/height of, 196, 316–317
browsers
  abbreviations used for, xviii
  detecting type/version of, 308–309
  navigation for nondynamic, 522
  supporting code used in book, xx
browser-safe colors, xvii, 142
browser-safe fonts, 98–100
  Mac system fonts, 99
  Microsoft Core fonts, 100
  Windows system fonts, 100
bullets
  graphics used for, 256–257
  style settings for, 254–255
button event property, 348, 349, 350
button states, 502–504

C

Camino browser, 476
capitalized text, 120
`<caption>` tag, 242
captions, positioning in tables, 242–243
`caption-side` property, 242–243
cascade order, 83–85
Cascading Style Sheets. *See* CSS
centering text, 124, 125
Champeon, Steve, 459
`changePage()` function, 482, 483, 485
`changeStyle()` function, 354–355
`changeWindowSize()` function, 398, 399
`chapterTitle` class, 146
character entities, 95
character sets, 92–93
`charCode` event property, 344
checkboxes, 476
child elements, 41, 135, 161
child selectors, 48, 50
child tags, 48, 81, 160
`chooseCountry()` function, 486, 489
chrome border, 526
circular animation, 382–383
class selectors, 10
  defining, 38–40
  embedded styles and, 28
  external style sheets and, 30
classes
  avoiding overuse of, 457
  changing for objects, 410–411
  defining for tags, 38–40
  pseudo-classes and, 56–66
  See also specific classes
`clear` property, 215, 216–217
`clearField()` function, 476
client-side code, 268
`clientX` event property, 351, 352
`clientY` event property, 351, 352
clip area
  changing, 368–369
  defining, 222–223
  finding, 336–340
`clip` property, 222–223
`closeWindow()` function, 393, 394, 395
Code Browser, xxi
code layout, xix
collapsible menus, 510–512

color, 139
  accessibility issues, 144
  background, 147–149, 156
  browser-safe, xvii, 142
  considerations for choosing, 140–142
  CSS properties with values for, 140
  detecting number of, 312–313
  emotional associations with, 140
  online tools for working with, 144
  schemes for combining, 143–144
  scroll bar, 231–232
  text and foreground, 145–146
`color` property, 145–146
color values, xvii
color wheel, 142–143
columns
  creating layouts with, 460–462
  CSS vs. tables and, 460
comment tags, 28
comments
  adding to CSS, 80
  conditional, 86–88
complimentary color scheme, 143
conditional comments, 86–88
content, 481–499
  changing, 370–371
  form data, 486–489
  importing, 482–485
  overflow, 224
  pop-up layer, 490–494
  styling, 467–468
  type-ahead, 495–499
content generation, 245
  counter lists, 249–251
  defining content, 246–248
  quote styles, 252–253
`content` property, 246–248
content sharing, 426
contextual selectors, 48–52
  adjacent sibling selectors, 48, 51
  child selectors, 48, 50
  descendant selectors, 48, 49–50
  universal selectors, 48, 52
controls, 527–546
  ActiveX, 271–272
  pagination, 528–532
  photo album, 542–546
  remote, 523–526
  scroll bar, 533–537
  style, 538–541

copy
    color for, 142
    styling, 467–468
copy class, 467–468
counter lists, 249–251
counter-increment property, 249, 251
counter-reset property, 249, 250–251
cross-browser DHTML, 272
crosshair cursor value, 230, 388
CSS (Cascading Style Sheets), xii, 6–7
    attribute selectors, 53–55
    cascade order, 83–85
    changing classes in, 410–411
    class selectors, 10, 28, 30, 38–40
    comments added to, 80
    conditional comments in, 86–88
    contextual selectors, 48–52
    disabling/enabling, 412–414
    dynamic, 403
    embedded styles, 26–28
    explanation of, 6–7, 269
    external style sheets, 29–35
    finding property values in, 404–405
    <font> tag vs., 98
    future of, 9
    history of, 8
    HTML selectors, 10, 28, 30, 36–37
    ID selectors, 10, 28, 30, 41–43
    !important declaration, 46–47, 84
    inheritance of styles, 81–82
    inline styles, 24–25
    layers in, 289
    markup languages and, 13–17
    media values and, 73
    naming conventions for, 407
    ownership issues, 22
    property categories, 6
    property value changes, 354–355
    pseudo-classes, 56–66
    pseudo-elements, 67–72
    rules, 10–12
    selector grouping, 44–45
    strategies for using, 89–90
    structuring HTML markup for, 455–459
    switching, 412–414
    tables vs., 460
    value tables for, xviii
    versions of, 8–9
    W3C development of, 4, 7, 8–9
    Web page printing and, 73–79

CSS button, 4
CSS Level 1 (CSS1), 8
CSS Level 2 (CSS2), 8–9
CSS Level 3 (CSS3), 9
CSS Positioning (CSS-P), 8
CSS sprites, 502–504
ctrlKey property, 346, 347
curly quotes, xix
:current pseudo-class, 59
cursive fonts, 94
cursor property, 228, 229–230
cursors
    crosshair, 230, 388
    setting appearance of, 228, 229–230
    types of, 230

D

data filtering, 443–446
dataRequest variable, 487, 498
declaration block, 11
declarations, 11
    changing in objects, 406–407
    !important declaration, 46–47
decorating text, 57, 133–135
default.css style sheet, 89
Degrave.com Color Palette Generator, 144
dependent IDs, 42
descendant selectors, 48, 49–50
descendant tags, 48, 81
design patterns, Ajax, 449
DHTML (Dynamic HTML), xii, 267
    advanced techniques, 375–402
    advantages/disadvantages, 273–275
    Ajax use of, 420
    basic techniques, 353–374
    components of, 268
    cross-browser, 272
    explanation of, 268
    Flash vs., 276–281
    history of, 271–272
    limitations of, 275
    Microsoft-specific, 271–272
    Netscape-specific, 271
    overview of, 268–270
    reasons for using, 273–274
dingbats, 95
direction of text, 136–138
direction property, 136–138
disabling style sheets, 412–414

display
    block settings, 167–168
    changing settings for, 358–360
    inline settings, 165–166
    list settings, 262–263
    removing elements from, 169, 170
    setting for elements, 164–170
display area, 196
`display` property, 164–170, 358, 510
    `block` value, 167–168
    `inline` value, 165–166
    `none` value, 169–170, 356, 360
`<div>` tag, 289, 407, 454, 456–457
doctypes. *See* DTDs
`document.body.clientHeight` object, 318
Document Object Model. *See* DOM
document origin, 197
`document.title` object, 310, 311
Document Type Definitions. *See* DTDs
documents. *See* Web pages
DOM (Document Object Model), 283
    capabilities of, 286
    element properties, 324
    explanation of, 269, 284–286
    history of, 287
    object setup, 288–289
    versions of, 287
    W3C-standard, 286–287
downloadable fonts, 112
drag-and-drop code, 391
draggable objects, 389–391
`dragIt()` function, 389, 390
drop caps, 67, 68–69
drop shadows, 122–123
`dropbox` class, 468
drop-down menus, 505–509
`dropIt()` function, 389, 391
DTDs (Document Type Definitions), 16, 19–21
    choosing, 21
    display modes, 20–21
dynamic CSS, 403
    changing CSS classes, 410–411
    declaration additions/changes, 406–409
    disabling/enabling style sheets, 412–414
    finding style property values, 404–405
    naming conventions, 407, 408
dynamic forms
    type-ahead input fields, 495–499
    updated form data, 486–489

Dynamic HTML. *See* DHTML
dynamic pseudo-classes, 60–62, 469

E

ECMAScript, 270
element origin, 197
element positions, 197
elements, 41, 160
    block placement of, 167–168
    border settings for, 174–180
    box model and, 159, 160, 161, 162–163
    cascade-order values for, 84–85
    changing contents of, 370–371
    clearing floated, 215–217
    clipping of, 222–223
    controlling in frames, 372–374
    determining for events, 322–323
    display settings for, 164–170, 262–263
    DOM access and, 294–295
    first letter styling of, 67–69
    first line styling of, 69–70
    floating in windows, 212–214
    getting by ID or tag name, 294–297
    height settings for, 187, 190, 191–193
    inline placement of, 165–166
    list settings for, 262–263
    margin settings for, 171–173
    non-display of, 169, 170
    opacity settings for, 226–227
    outline settings for, 181–183
    overflow control for, 224–225
    padding settings for, 184–186
    position type settings for, 198–203
    positioning of, 204–208
    properties of DOM, 324
    pseudo-elements and, 67–72
    setting content before/after, 71–72
    stacking order of, 209–211
    style property changes for, 354–355
    visibility settings for, 220–221
    width settings for, 187, 188–189, 191–193
`embed` value, 138
embedded rules, 12, 26–28
`empty-cells` property, 240–241
enabling style sheets, 412–414
equal sign (=), 25, 54, 55
`errorOn()` function, 301
`event.button` property, 348
`event.charCode` property, 344

`event.clientX` property, 351
event handlers, 290–291
  DOM and, 291
  global, 300–301
  key detection, 345
  list of common, 290
  steps for using, 292–293
`event.keyCode` property, 344
`event.screenX` property, 351
`event.type` property, 342
events, 290–291
  binding to objects, 300–301
  detecting type of, 342–343
  identifying objects triggering, 322–323
  key press determination, 344–345
  modifier key detection, 346–347
  mouse button detection, 348–350
  mouse position detection, 352–353
  passing to functions, 298–299
`evt.srcElement.id` object, 322
`evt.target.id` object, 322
expanding menus, 510–512
Extensible Hypertext Markup Language. *See*
  XHTML
Extensible Markup Language (XML), 15, 270,
  419
Extensible Stylesheet Language (XSL), 15
external rules, 12
external style sheets, 29–35
  creating, 30–31
  importing, 34–35
  linking to, 32–33

F

`family-name` property, 97
fantasy fonts, 94–95
feature sensing, 302–303, 308
  browser detection and, 309
`fetchData()` function, 435, 436–438, 447, 448
  dynamic forms and, 486, 489
  filtering data and, 443–446
  importing content using, 482–483
  pop-up layers and, 491
  server responses and, 439–442
  type-ahead fields and, 496
fieldset, 472
`fillScreen()` function, 399

`filterData()` function, 435, 444, 445, 447, 448
  dynamic forms and, 487, 489
  external content and, 482–483
  pop-up layers and, 491, 492
  type-ahead fields and, 496
filtering data responses, 443–446
`findBottom()` function, 330–331
`findBrowserHeight()` function, 317
`findBrowserWidth()` function, 317
`findClipArray()` function, 339
`findClipBottom()` function, 337, 339
`findClipHeight()` function, 337, 339
`findClipLeft()` function, 337, 339
`findClipRight()` function, 337, 339
`findClipTop()` function, 337, 339
`findClipWidth()` function, 337, 339
`findEventType()` function, 342
`findHeight()` function, 325
`findKey()` function, 345
`findLayer()` function, 334, 335, 366, 367
`findLeft()` function, 328–329
`findLivePageHeight()` function, 318–320
`findLivePageWidth()` function, 318–320, 542
`findModifierKey()` function, 346–347
`findMouseButton()` function, 350
`findMouseLocation()` function, 352
`findObjectID()` function, 322–323, 390
`findRight()` function, 330–331
`findStyleValue()` function, 404–405
`findTop()` function, 328–329
`findVisibility()` function, 332–333
`findWidth()` function, 325
Firefox browser, 308, 404
`:first-child` pseudo-class, 63–64
`:first-letter` pseudo-element, 67–69
`:first-line` pseudo-element, 69–70
fixed positioning, 201, 202, 203, 521
fixed table layout, 234, 235
Flash
  advantages of, 276–277
  CSS and, 17
  DHTML vs., 276–281
  disadvantages of, 277–278
  history of, 276
  usability issues, 281
`float` property, 212, 213–214, 460, 462
floating elements, 212–214
  `clear` property and, 215, 216–217
  steps in process of, 213–214

:focus pseudo-class, 60, 61, 62, 475
followMe() function, 387
<font> tag, 98
font families
    explained, 92
    generic, 93–95
    setting, 96–100
font names, 25
font property, 110–111
font-family property, 96–97
fonts, 91–112
    bolded, 106–107
    browser-safe, 98–100
    character entity, 95
    cursive, 94
    dingbat, 95
    downloadable, 112
    fantasy, 94–95
    italicized, 104–105
    mimicking styles of, 112
    monospace, 94
    multiple values for, 110–111
    sans-serif, 94
    serif, 93
    size settings, 101–103
    small caps, 108–109
    symbol, 95
    See also text
font-size property, 102, 128
font-style property, 104
font-variant property, 108
font-weight property, 106
for attribute, 476
foreground color, 145–146
form fields, 384–385
    dynamically updated, 486–489
    type-ahead input, 495–499
formInputButton class, 475
formInputField class, 475
forms
    color for, 142
    dynamic, 486–489
    setting up, 384–385
    styling, 471–476
    visitor input via, 384, 385
frames, 196
    controlling objects between, 372–374
    creating borders for, 477–480
    styling, 477–480

frameset DTDs, 20, 21
fully justified text, 124, 125
functionality sharing, 426
functions
    passing events to, 298
    repeated running of, 376–378
    See also specific functions

G

Garrett, Jesse James, 419
generated content, 245
    counter lists, 249–251
    defining, 246–248
    quote styles, 252–253
generic font families, 93–95
GET method, 442
getElementById() function, 294–295, 324, 332, 353
getElementsByTagName() function, 296–297
global event handlers, 300–301
glyphs, 92
Google Search Ajax API, 449
graphic backgrounds, 463–464
graphic bullets, 256–257
graphic text, 94
grouping selectors, 44–45

H

handheld devices, 76
hanging indents, 258
headers
    color for, 142
    drop-down menu, 505
    styling, 463–464
headlines, 463–464
height, 161
    browser, 196
    finding for objects, 325–326
    maximum/minimum, 191–193
    rendered, 197
    setting for elements, 190
    viewport, 196
height property, 187, 190
hidden value
    overflow control, 224
    visibility settings, 220, 356, 360
hideDropMenu() function, 505, 507
hideSlide() function, 543, 545

hiding
    elements, 220
    empty data cells, 241
    overflow content, 224
horizontal text alignment, 124–125
:hover pseudo-class, 60, 61, 62
    background color and, 149
    form styling and, 475, 476
    table styling and, 469, 470
HTML (Hypertext Markup Language), xiii, 15,
    270
    character entities, 95
    converting to XHTML, 14
    CSS and, 4, 6, 23
    doctypes, 20
    limitations of, 3–4
HTML documents
    embedding styles in, 26–28
    structuring for layout, 455–459
    See also Web pages
HTML selectors, 10
    defining, 36–37
    embedded styles and, 28
    external style sheets and, 30
HTML tags, 4, 6
    adding styles to, 24–25
    categories of, 18
    redefining, 36–37
Hypertext Markup Language. See HTML

I

id attribute, 289, 374
ID selectors, 10
    defining, 42–43
    embedded styles and, 28
    external style sheets and, 30
IE factor, 86
iframes, 420, 513, 514, 515
image maps, 494
image rollovers, 502–504
images
    background, 150–153, 156
    photo album, 542–546
@import rule, 34
!important declaration, 46–47, 84
importing
    external content, 482–485
    style sheets, 34–35

indenting paragraphs, 129–130
inherit value, 81, 82
    border styles and, 176
    display settings and, 165
    element positioning and, 202
    opacity settings and, 227
    visibility settings and, 220
inheritance of styles, 81–82
initAnimate() function, 380
initAnimateCircle() function, 382–383
initDropMenu() function, 505, 506, 507
initPage() function, 300–301, 332–333, 335
initSlide() function, 542, 544
initStyles() function, 538, 539
inline elements, 165–166
inline rules, 12
inline styles, 24–25
inline tags, 18
inline value, 164, 165–166
innerHTML property, 370, 424
<input> tag, 476
interactivity improvements, 426
Internet Explorer
    active link borders in, 504
    adding/changing styles in, 408–409
    box model and, 162–163
    conditional comments used in, 86–88
    dynamically adding new rules in, 408–409
    Mac problems with, 202, 203, 235
    opacity settings in, 226, 227
    outline settings and, 181
    positioning issues in, 202, 203, 208
    scroll bar colors in, 231–232
    style property values in, 404
Internet Explorer All DOM, 287
ISO 8859-1 character set, 93
italicized fonts, 104–105

J

JavaScript
    description of, 269–270
    feature sensing in, 302–303
    naming convention for, 407, 408
    navigation for browsers without, 522
    passing events to functions in, 298–299
JavaScript Style Sheets (JSS), 271
JScript, 270

K

kerning, 114
keyboard keys
    detecting pressing of, 344–345
    improving accessibility using, 509
    modifier key detection, 346–347
keyCode event property, 344

L

labels, 474
:lang() pseudo-class, 65–66
languages
    styles for, 65–66
    text adjustments for, 136–138
Layer DOM, 287
layers
    CSS vs. Netscape, 289
    page, 528–532
    pop-up, 490–494
    scroll bars for, 533–537
    type-ahead, 496–499
layouts, 453–480
    content styling, 467–468
    copy styling, 467–468
    CSS vs. table, 460
    form styling, 471–476
    frame styling, 477–480
    header styling, 463–464
    link styling, 465–466
    multicolumn, 460–462
    structuring pages for, 454–459
    table styling, 469–470
leading, 118–119
left positioning, 204–205
left property, 204–205, 213, 327
left-justified text, 124, 125
legends, 474
length values, xvi, 205, 206, 207, 208
letterforms. *See* fonts
letter spacing, 114–115
letter-spacing property, 114–115
Lie, Hakon Wium, 8
line spacing, 118–119
line-height property, 118–119
:link pseudo-class, 57, 58
<link> tag, 32

linking to style sheets, 32–33
links
    active link borders and, 504
    color for, 142
    pop-up layers and, 490–494
    pseudo-classes for, 57–59
    styles for, 56, 57–59, 465–466
    underlining, 57, 135
list-item value, 164, 262–263
lists, 245
    bullet styles for, 254–255
    colors for, 142
    counters for, 249–251
    displaying elements in, 262–263
    graphic bullets used in, 256–257
    multiple style settings for, 260–261
    wrapped text positioning in, 258–259
list-style property, 260–261
list-style-image property, 256–257
list-style-position property, 258–259
list-style-type property, 254–255
"long tail" approach, 428, 429
looping functions, 376–378
lowercase text, 121

M

Macintosh OS
    browser-safe fonts, 99
    detecting use of, 306
    Internet Explorer problem, 202, 203
    modifier keys on, 347
    screen size, 314
magnifyWindow() function, 398–399
margin property, 171–173
margins, 161, 171
    defining for elements, 171–173
    negative settings for, 173
markup languages, 13–17
    explained, 270
    Flash, 17
    HTML, 14, 15
    origin of, 15
    SVG, 17
    XHTML, 14, 15–17
max-height property, 192
max-width property, 192
menuControl class, 521

`menuDrop` class, 508, 509
`menuHeader` class, 508
`menuOptions` class, 521
`menuOut()` function, 506
menus
    collapsible, 510–512
    drop-down, 505–509
    sliding, 519–522
    tabbed, 513–518
`metaKey` property, 346, 347
Microsoft Core fonts, 100
Microsoft Corporation, 22
Microsoft-specific DHTML, 271–272
`min-height` property, 192
`min-width` property, 192
mini-caps, 108–109
modifier keys, 346–347
monochrome color scheme, 143
monospace fonts, 94
Mosaic browser, xiv
mouse
    button click detection, 348–350
    position detection, 351–352
mouse pointer
    browser defaults and, 228
    creating objects that follow, 386–388
    finding position of, 352
    setting appearance of, 229–230
`moveObject()` function, 301, 373
`moveObjectBy()` function, 364
`moveObjectFrame()` function, 373
`moveObjectTo()` function, 361–362, 384–385
`moveWindowBy()` function, 396, 397
`moveWindowTo()` function, 396, 397
moving objects
    3D positioning and, 365–367
    by designated amounts, 363–364
    from point to point, 361–362
`-moz-border-radius` property, 178
`-moz-outline` property, 182
Mozilla browsers
    opacity settings for, 226–227
    rounding border corners for, 177–180
    style property values in, 404
    window positioning functions in, 397
multicolumn layouts, 460–462

N

`name` attribute, 289, 374
naming conventions, 407, 408
navigation, 501–526
    collapsible menus for, 510–512
    CSS image rollovers for, 502–504
    drop-down menus for, 505–509
    nondynamic browsers and, 522
    preventing noise related to, 513
    remote controls for, 523–526
    sliding menus for, 519–522
    styling links for, 465–466
    tabbed menus for, 513–518
`navigator.platform` object, 306
`navigator.userAgent` object, 308
negative margins, 173
nested tags, 48
Netscape Layer DOM, 287
Netscape layers, 289
Netscape Navigator, xiv, 376, 402, 403
Netscape-specific DHTML, 271
newspaper style text, 124
`newWindow.focus()` function, 394
`newWindow` variable, 392, 394
Nielsen, Jakob, 281
`<nobr>` tag, 131, 132
nodes, 284, 285
nondynamic browsers, 522
none value, 165, 169, 170
normal flow, 197
`<noscript>` tag, 522
`nowrap` value, 131, 132
number sign (#), xvii, 42, 43
`numColors()` function, 313
`numDropMenu` variable, 505, 506

O

objects, 41
    3D position of, 334–335, 365–367
    animating, 379–383
    binding events to, 300–301
    changing contents of, 370–371
    controlling between frames, 372–374
    CSS class changes for, 410–411
    declaration changes in, 406–407
    draggable, 389–391
    event triggers as, 322–323

following the mouse pointer, 386–387
identifying, 41–43
moving, 361–367
position of, 327–331, 334–335
properties of, 324–326
repositioning, 361–362
setting up, 288–289
style property values of, 332–333
visible area of, 336–340, 368–369
width/height of, 325–326
z-index of, 334, 335
objPage variable, 528
objPopUp variable, 491
oblique fonts, 104, 105
offsetLeft property, 327, 328
offsetTop property, 327, 328
oldObject variable, 510, 517
oldObjectHi variable, 517
oldStyle variable, 538
Olsen, George, 22
onclick event handler, 350
onkeydown event handler, 345
onkeypress event handler, 345
onkeyup event handler, 345
onload event handler, 343, 347, 350, 352
onmousedown event handler, 350
onmousemove event handler, 352
onmouseup event handler, 350
onunload event handler, 395
opacity property, 226–227
opacity settings, 226–227
open() method, 438
openChapter() function, 517, 518
openRemote() function, 523, 524, 526
openWindow() function, 393, 394
Opera browser, 308, 397, 404
operating system detection, 306–307
<option> tags, 489
O'Reilly, Tim, 428
orphans, 78
outline property, 140, 181, 182–183
outlines, 181
    Internet Explorer and, 181
    setting for elements, 182–183
overflow control, 224–225
overflow property, 187, 224–225
overlapping text, 173
overlined text, 133

P

padding, 161, 184
    margins distinguished from, 186
    setting for elements, 184–186
page breaks, 77–79
page class, 461–462, 530, 532
page layers, 528–532
pageCurrent variable, 528
pageDim() function, 320
pageJump() function, 529, 530, 532
pageRequest object, 438, 444
pageTotal variable, 532
pageTurn() function, 529, 530
pagination controls, 528–532
Panic Web site, 267
paragraph indentation, 129–130
parent elements, 41, 127, 135
parent tags, 48, 81, 160
passItOn() function, 298–299
percentage values, xvii, 205, 206, 207, 208
photo albums, 542–546
PHP for the World Wide Web: Visual QuickStart Guide (Ullman), 421
PHP scripting language, 421
pickIt() function, 389, 390
picture fonts, 95
pixel-depth values, 313
plus sign (+), 51
poetry kit example, 389–391
point size, 101
popHide() function, 492, 494, 497
popUp() function, 491, 494
pop-up layers, 490–494
pop-up windows
    blocking of, 395
    closing, 394, 395
    modal problems with, 394
    opening, 392–394
position property, 201–202, 204–208
    bottom and right values, 206–208
    position-type values, 201–202
    top and left values, 204–206

positioning
  3D, 209–211
  absolute, 200, 202
  backgrounds, 153, 157
  bottom and right, 206–208, 330–331
  captions in tables, 242–243
  changing for objects, 361–362
  detecting for objects, 327–331
  fixed, 201, 202, 203
  floating elements and, 212–217
  overview of, 196–197
  relative, 200, 202
  setting for elements, 204–208
  stacking order and, 209–211
  static, 198–199, 201
  top and left, 204–206, 327–329
  types of, 198–203
  z-index, 209–211
POST method, 442
<pre> tag, 131, 132
prepData() function, 448–449
printing Web pages, 73–79
  general guidelines for, 74
  preventing widows/orphans, 78
  setting page breaks for, 77–79
  specifying style sheets for, 75–76
progressive enhancement, 458, 459
properties, 6, 11
  changing values of, 354–355
  DOM element, 324
  inheritance of, 81–82
  See also specific properties
pseudo-classes, 56–66
  dynamic, 60–62, 469
  first-child, 63–64
  language, 65–66
  link, 57–59
pseudo-elements, 67–72
  before/after, 71–72
  first letter, 67–69
  first line, 69–70

Q

Quirks mode, 19, 20
quotation marks ("), xix, 25, 252
quotation tag, 252
quote styles, 252–253
quotes property, 252–253

R

radio buttons, 476
readyState values, 444, 446
relative length values, xvi
relative positioning, 127, 200, 202
remote controls, 523–526
rendered width/height, 197
rendering engine, 7
repeating
  backgrounds, 152, 153, 156–157
  functions, 376–378
repositioning objects, 361–362
resizeObject() function, 514
resizing. *See* sizing and resizing
Rich Internet Applications (RIAs), 431
right positioning, 207
right property, 207, 213
right-justified text, 124
rollovers, 502–504
rules (CSS), 10–12
  parts of, 11–12
  placement of, 12
  syntax, 12
rules/borders. *See* borders

S

Safari browser, 308, 309, 404, 476
sans-serif fonts, 94
Scalable Vector Graphics (SVG) format, 17, 94, 270
screen
  color detection, 312–313
  size detection, 314–315, 320
screen.availHeight object, 314, 315
screen.availWidth object, 314, 315
screen.colorDepth object, 312, 313
screen.height object, 314, 315
screen.width object, 314, 315
screenX event property, 351, 352
screenY event property, 351, 352
<script> tag, 532
scroll bars, 533–537
  color settings for, 231–232
  overflow control and, 224–225
  setting up, 534–537
scroll() function, 534–536
scrollbar properties, 140, 231

`scrollbar-3dlight-color` property, 232
`scroll-base-color` property, 232
scrolling
    background options for, 152, 157
    browser window controls for, 400–402
    overflow control and, 224
`scrollPage()` function, 401
`scrollPageTo()` function, 401
search engine optimization, 427, 485
`section.css` style sheet, 90
security issues, 427
`<select>` tag, 489
selectors, 10
    adjacent sibling, 48
    attribute, 53–55
    child, 48
    class, 10, 28, 30, 38–40
    contextual, 48–52
    CSS rules and, 11
    descendant, 48
    grouping, 44–45
    HTML, 10, 28, 30, 36–37
    ID, 10, 28, 30, 41–43
    tags and, 10, 18
    universal, 48
`self.location` object, 310, 311
self-closing tags, 24
serif fonts, 93–94
server files, 421
server requests, 434–435
server-side code, 421
`setCity()` function, 496
`setClass()` function, 410–411
`setClip()` function, 336, 340, 368–369
`setDisplay()` function, 358–359
`setLayer()` function, 366, 367
`setMenu()` function, 519, 520
`setStyle()` function, 412, 539
`setTimeout()` function, 376
`setUpAnnoyingFlash()` function, 377–378
`setVisibility()` function, 357–358
SGML (Standard Generalized Markup
    Language), 15
`shiftKey` property, 346, 347
`showDim()` function, 326
`showDropMenu()` function, 505, 506
`showPosBR()` function, 331
`showPosTL()` function, 328

`showSlide()` function, 543, 546
`showVisibility()` function, 333
siblings, 48
sizing and resizing
    browser window, 398–399
    fonts, 101–103
Slayer Office Color Palette tool, 144
`slideMenu()` function, 519, 520
`slideSpeed` variable, 519
sliding menus, 519–522
small caps, 108–109
smart quotes, xix
SMIL (Synchronized Multimedia Integration
    Language), 270
spacing, text, 114–119
    letter spacing, 114–115
    line spacing, 118–119
    word spacing, 116–117
`<span>` tag, 289, 454
sprites, CSS, 502–504
stacking order, 209–211
Standard Generalized Markup Language
    (SGML), 15
standards, xiv–xv
Standards mode, 19, 21
`startAnimate()` function, 380
`startScroll()` function, 534, 536
static positioning, 198–199, 201
`stopScroll()` function, 536
straight line animation, 379–381
straight quotes, xix
strict DTDs, 20, 21
strikethrough text, 133, 135
style controls, 538–541
style sheets, 6–7
    alternate, 540–541
    cascade order of, 83–85
    comments in, 80
    disabling/enabling, 412–414
    external, 29–35
    finding property values in, 404–405
    media types and, 73, 75–76
    strategies for using, 89–90
    switching, 412–414
    See also CSS
`style.zIndex` property, 334
`<style>` tag, 26, 30, 31, 408, 409, 541
`styleName[ ]` variable, 538

styles
    bullet, 254–255
    changing, 354–355
    content, 467–468
    copy, 467–468
    declarations for, 406–407
    display, 358–360
    embedded, 26–28
    explained, 5
    form, 471–476
    frame, 477–480
    header, 463–464
    inheritance of, 81–82
    inline, 24–25
    link, 56, 57–59, 465–466
    list, 260–261
    quote, 252
    table, 469–470
    visibility, 356–358
subscript text, 126, 128
superscript text, 126, 128
support Web site, xiii, xxi
SVG (Scalable Vector Graphics) format, 17, 94, 270
swapLayer() function, 366, 367
symbol fonts, 95
Synchronized Multimedia Integration Language (SMIL), 270

T

tabbed menus, 513–518
table values, 164
table-layout property, 234–235
tables, 233–243
    border spacing in, 236–237
    collapsing borders in, 238–239
    CSS layouts vs., 460
    empty cells in, 240–241
    layout settings for, 234–235
    positioning captions in, 242–243
    styling, 469–470
tags
    block-level, 18
    case used for, 10
    comment, 28
    defining classes for, 38–40
    HTML, 4, 6, 18
    inline, 18
    nested, 48
    redefining, 36–37
    selectors and, 10
    self-closing, 24
    XHTML, 18
    See also specific tags
<td> tag, 470
tetrad color scheme, 143
text, 113–138
    case settings, 120–121
    color settings, 145–146
    decorations, 57, 133–135
    direction settings, 136–138
    drop caps, 67, 68–69
    drop shadows, 122–123
    first-line styling, 70
    floating, 212–214, 216
    graphic and vector, 94
    horizontally aligning, 124–125
    language adjustments, 136–138
    letter spacing, 114–119
    line spacing, 118–119
    overlapping, 173
    paragraph indentation, 129–130
    superscript/subscript, 126, 128
    underlined, 57, 133, 135
    vertically aligning, 126–128
    white space controls, 131–132
    word spacing, 116–117
    See also fonts
text-align property, 124–125
text-decoration property, 133–135
text-indent property, 129–130
text-shadow property, 122–123, 140
text-transform property, 120–121
<th> tag, 470
three-dimensional (3D) positioning, 209–211
    finding for objects, 334–335
    moving objects using, 365–367
thumbnails, 542, 546
<title> tags, 310, 311
toggleClamShellMenu() function, 510–512
toggleDisplay() function, 359, 360
toggleStyle() function, 412–414
toggleVisibility() function, 357–358, 376
toggleWindow() function, 393, 394
toolbar class, 530
tools and utilities, xx
tooltips, 494

top positioning, 205–206
top property, 205–206, 327
<tr> tag, 470
tracking, 114–115
transitional DTDs, 20, 21, 514, 515
transparent value, 148, 156
triad color scheme, 143
type event property, 342
typeAhead() function, 496, 499
type-ahead input fields, 495–499
    adding to forms, 496–499
    description of, 495
typography. See fonts; text

U

Ullman, Larry, 421
underlined text, 57, 133, 135
unicode-bidi property, 137–138
universal selectors, 48, 52
uppercase text, 120
URB() function, 535, 536, 537
URIs (Uniform Resource Identifiers), 310
URLs (Uniform Resource Locators)
    explanation of, xvii
    finding for Web pages, 310–311
URT() function, 535, 536, 537
UTF-8 character set, 93
utilities and tools, xx

V

values, xvi–xvii, 12
vector text, 94
vertical text alignment, 126–128
vertical-align property, 126–128
viewport, 196
visibility property, 220–221, 332, 356
visibility settings, 220–221
    changing, 356–358
    finding, 332–333
visible area of objects
    changing, 368–369
    finding, 336–340
visible value
    overflow control, 225
    visibility settings, 220
Visibone Webmaster's Color Laboratory, 144
:visited pseudo-class, 57, 58, 62

W

W3C (World Wide Web Consortium), 11
    CSS and, 4, 7, 8–9, 22
    DOM and, 286–287
    goals of, 11
Web 2.0, 428–431
    Ajax and, 429, 431
    core principles of, 428
    design trends related to, 420
    reasons for, 429, 431
Web application delivery
    Ajax model of, 424
    classic model of, 422, 423
Web browsers. See browsers
Web pages
    CSS image rollovers on, 502–504
    determining live area of, 318–320
    dynamically adding new rules to, 408–409
    embedding styles in, 26–28
    finding location/title of, 310–311
    form fields on, 384–385
    global event handlers on, 300–301
    scroll controls on, 400–402
    structuring for layout, 454–459
    styles for printing, 73–79
    width and height of, 197
Web sites
    book support site, xiii, xxi
    determining screen size for, 320
    external style sheets for, 29–35
    style sheet strategies for, 89–90
Web Standards Project, xv, 22
Web user experience, 422–424
Web-interaction model, 422
Wellstyled.com Color Scheme 2 tool, 144
whichLayer() function, 335
white-space property, 131
widows, 78
width, 161
    browser, 196
    finding for objects, 325–326
    maximum/minimum, 191–193
    rendered, 197
    setting for elements, 188–189
    viewport, 196
width property, 187, 188–189, 190
window.innerHeight object, 318
window.innerWidth object, 318

`window.outerHeight` object, 316
`window.outerWidth` object, 316
windows
    floating elements in, 212–214
    opening/closing pop-up, 392–394, 395
    setting position of, 396–397
    width/height of, 196, 316–317
Windows system
    browser-safe fonts, 100
    detecting use of, 307
    screen size, 314
word spacing, 116–117
`word-spacing` property, 116–117
World Wide Web Consortium. *See* W3C
World Wide Web (WWW)
    application delivery on, 422–424
    designing for, xii
    standards for, xiv–xv
    Web 2.0 and, 428–431
    See also Web pages; Web sites
`writeName()` function, 370–371
`writePageControls()` function, 529, 532

X

XHTML (Extensible Hypertext Markup
    Language), xix, 15–17, 270
    converting HTML to, 14
    doctypes, 20, 21
XML (Extensible Markup Language), 15,
    270, 419
XMLHTTP ActiveX object, 420–421
XMLHttpRequest object, 420–421, 434, 437
XSL (Extensible Stylesheet Language), 15

Y

Yahoo! Maps, 449
Yahoo! UI Library, 449

Z

z-index, 209–211, 334, 335